Birthright of man

Birthright of man

A selection of texts
prepared under the direction of
Jeanne Hersch

UNESCO

UNIPUB Inc., 650 First Avenue,
New York, N.Y. 10016

U.S. Library of Congress Catalogue No. 69-20260

Published in 1969 by the United Nations
Educational, Scientific and Cultural Organization
Place de Fontenoy, 75 Paris-7e
and UNIPUB Inc.
650 First Avenue, New York, N.Y. 10016
Printed by Casterman, Tournai

Any tyrant can compel his slaves to
sing hymns in praise of liberty

Mariano Moreno, 8 December 1810

Preface

To mark the twentieth anniversary of the Universal Declaration of Human Rights, the General Conference of the United Nations Educational, Scientific and Cultural Organization (Unesco), suggested the idea[1] of publishing a collection of quotations, drawn from a wide variety of traditions and periods, which, with their profound concordance enhanced by the very diversity of their origins, would illustrate how human beings everywhere, throughout the ages and all over the world, have asserted and claimed the birthright of man.

This book represents an endeavour to answer that purpose.

To obtain the necessary material, the Secretariat approached the National Commissions of the Member States, the international non-governmental organizations regularly associated with Unesco's work, and a number of specialists, as well as many friends who gave their voluntary co-operation.

Sincere thanks are due to them all, for the harvest was an admirable one, astonishing alike for the quantity and quality of the passages supplied and for the variety of the problems, ideas and modes of expression to be found in them. Yet even more striking is the extraordinary impression of harmonic similarities even in the most marked contrasts or, more accurately, of kinship—in short, of brotherhood—which emerges from this dual quest wherein contemporary men have sought to discover the deepest historical substrata of their consciousness and men of all times have sought to invent a human order for their kind.

Of its own accord, as it were, the wide range of themes which inspired the Universal Declaration unfolded before our eyes; and on each of those themes, as though from every stage of a long journey to the farthest confines of the world and of memory, there have come to us as

1. Resolution 14C/3.11.b(iii).

offerings, piously wrapped in the words of other times and other places, the thoughts and acts which were—and still are—the questions and the answers, the yearnings and the proofs, the foreshadowings and the accomplishments, dark or etched in light, by which man has learnt to know himself.

With such speaking testimony to hand, the best course for those compiling the work to follow was to intervene, to interpret, as little as possible. I am grateful to them for their appreciation that the essential thing to be preserved was the immediacy of the message, the reader's direct contact with the source.

It was, of course, necessary to make a choice. But the choice was ruled by the concern to exclude no major theme and to offer a faithful, albeit summary, reflection of the whole range of material received.

It was also necessary to arrange the passages in some order. But the order followed is not in any way intended to be explanatory, seeking merely to bring out the most obvious points of convergence or lines of opposition.

There is undoubtedly an element of the haphazard in the final compilation, due to the way in which the material was obtained. The fact that a great amount of material may have been received from a particular civilization whereas for certain others there were serious gaps that proved impossible to fill was often simply a matter of chance. It is to be hoped, however, that the large number of passages collected and the multiplicity of channels through which they reached the Secretariat will, to a fairly large extent, have corrected certain quantitative imbalances which it would be quite wrong to regard as indicative of any deliberate bias.

Thus was the book willed and made. Although it is the product of joint efforts in which many different people have collaborated, both outside and inside the Secretariat, it is due above all to Jeanne Hersch, the Director of the Division of Philosophy. It was she who conceived the idea of the work and planned its arrangement and who has, throughout, infused the undertaking with her own exacting but liberal faith. I want to take this opportunity of expressing my deep gratitude to her.

Should I now set out to explain what the book is, like a teacher describing the subject and purpose of his course in his opening lesson? Even if I could do so, I think it would be inappropriate. But I can make clear what the book is not; and that is probably more useful.

Above all, it is not a scientific work. This will be clear

enough from the fact that the notes and historical references are so scanty. Efforts have, of course, been made to obtain all possible assurances regarding the authenticity of the passages quoted. But they could not be submitted to strict critical study, or their translations closely checked, because of the great diversity of sources and languages of origin. Mistakes there may be. Any attempt to bring together men of all times and places must, let us admit it, necessarily involve an element of intellectual approximation which may delude and sometimes lead astray the generous promptings of the heart. But this risk is countenanced not only by men of action impatient for results; those whose thoughts go deeper also accept it, for they recognized in it one of the conditions of the spirit's progression through history.

Nor is this book a moral treatise, and still less a scroll of merit. If some countries are better or more fully 'represented' than others, this proves nothing as regards the extent to which human rights are respected within their borders. It may be due to the fact that some countries are more inclined or accustomed than others to lay bare, through rigorous self-criticism, their own past; or to the fact that one country is more easily satisfied than another with what it is today; or again, merely to adventitious circumstances which momentarily encourage or hinder national self-expression at the international level. In the life of peoples as in that of individuals there are variations in self-awareness which do not necessarily correspond to the fundamental modes of the self.

Lastly, this book contains no doctrine, nor does it offer a reflection of historical fact. It shows us essentially mankind as concerned with its ideals, expressed in their noblest forms, not man's actual circumstances and behaviour, past or present.

Due place has indeed been given to complaint, indignation, bitterness and revolt, for these serve to indicate, just as clearly as do statements of principle and calm or exultant claims, an irrepressible demand for dignity and justice.

But this is still too little for it to be claimed that the book portrays the real odyssey of the human conscience. The groans and cries to be heard in these pages are never uttered by the most wretched victims. These, throughout the ages, have been mute. Wherever human rights are completely trampled underfoot, silence and immobility prevail, leaving no trace in history; for history records only the words and deeds of those who are capable, to however slight a degree, of ruling their own lives, or at least trying to do so. There have been—there still are—multitudes of men, women and children who, as a result of poverty, terror or lies, have been made to forget their inherent dignity, or to give up the effort to secure recognition of that dignity by others. They are silent. The lot of the victim who complains and is heard is already a better one.

Let the reader therefore be warned that on the other side of the light into which he is about to enter he should mentally project this mass of darkness. It is the shadow cast by history, which no light illuminates. It is the burden that progress drags in its wake, with no vital impulse to uplift it. It is the weight of the crimes to which we owe our privileges, and from which no generosity can altogether absolve even our innocence; for since we benefit from them, we are objectively accessary to them.

Foremost among those privileges, standing above all others, is the ability to conceive with some objectivity the very idea of universal human rights.

This book is not intended to be read straight through, from beginning to end, nor is it meant for systematic study. The reader can open it at random according to his mood, meditate upon a few lines or pages, and close it again. He will have tasted, I hope unforgettably, something of the bitter-sweet flavour, tender and terrible, exalting and sordid, of the history of mankind in its most essential significance.

His first impression may be that everything has been said and experienced, in many places, for hundreds and thousands of years past. But upon reflection he will no doubt discover that everything always remains to be done and to be invented. However great the efforts already made, however great the progress accomplished, however heroic the numberless sacrifices, the price of man's freedom has not yet been paid by man, nor has its true value even been determined. The immemorial task remains. At this very moment....

At this very moment millions of human beings, our fellow-men, prostrate or in revolt, are waiting for us to act, waiting for you and me.

Paris, April 1968   RENÉ MAHEU

Foreword

With the object of avoiding either tiresome repetitions for one country after another, or arbitrary omissions, it was decided to exclude from this collection anything still forming an integral part of a constitution now in force.

Moreover, since the aim was to assemble a collection anticipating the philosophy implicit in the Universal Declaration of 1948, nothing published after that date has been included.

As most of the passages included are excerpts, it was thought desirable not to burden the text with omission marks at the beginning and end of each passage. Omissions within a passage, however, are indicated. Spelling has been modernized when this could be done without detriment to the nature of the writings.

Contributions to the collection were sent by many National Commissions for Unesco, a number of non-govermental organizations and the following experts: José María Arguedas, Abderrahman Ben Abdenbi, Gustavo Beyhaut, P. Naili Boratav, Genia Cannac, Henry Steele Commager, R. N. Dandekar, Vadim Elisseeff, Stanislas Frybes, Francesco Gabrieli, Janheinz Jahn, P. Juvigny, Takeo Kuwabara, Miguel León Portilla, Liou Kia-Hway, Guillermo Lohmann Villena, G. P. Malalasekera, Léo Moulin, Kostas Papaioannou, Pierre Pascal, Clémence Ramnoux, Pinhas Rosenblüth, Denis de Rougemont, Fryda Schutz de Mantovani, Marina Scriabine, Amadou Seydou, Shaul Shaked, Fernando Silva Vargas, Jean Starobinski, Joseph Tubiana.

The Secretariat is deeply grateful to the publishers and authors who have kindly authorized the reproduction of extracts that are still protected by copyright, and to all those, near and far, who, in so many ways, have generously assisted it in carrying out this project.

Contents

Illustrations

The illustrations for the present work were selected by Nicolas Bouvier

Man

Dainos are Lithua-
nian folk-songs
transmitted orally
from generation to
generation since
remote pre-Christian
times

THE WOLF (*Lithuanian daino*)

The wolf, the wolf,
The beast of the forest,
Comes out of the woods
Into the meadow,
Devours the calf
And the little foal:
That is his work.

The fox, the fox,
The beast of the forest,
Creeps out of the woods
And into the yard.
He seizes and kills
The goose and the hen:
That is his work.

The dog, the dog,
Watches the house.
He barks and bites
The heels of the robber.
He scares old women
And wandering people:
That is his work.

The flea, the flea,
The dainty-mouthed beast,
Sucks the sweet blood
At break of day.
He wakes the maiden
To milk the cows:
That is his work.

The bee, the bee,
The dweller of forests,
Hums on the heath,
And stings our fingers
And faces and ears,
And gives us honey:
That is his work.

O man, O man,
Look at the bee—
You sting enough
In the heart, in the heart;

Nevertheless, give sweetness
To your own brother:
That is man's work.

Trans. by
Katzenelenbogen

1

Rules of behaviour

Chung-kung asked about humanity. Confucius said: 'When you go abroad, behave to everyone as if you were receiving a great guest. Employ the people as if you were assisting at a great sacrifice. Do not to others what you do not want them to do to you. Then there will be no complaint against you in the state or in the family.' Chung-kung said: 'Although I am not intelligent, may I put your saying into practice?'

Confucius
551-479? B.C.
Analects
China

2

Thou shalt not avenge, nor bear any grudge against the children of thy people, but thou shalt love thy neighbour as thyself: I am the Lord.

Hebrew Bible
Leviticus 19

3

Do not do to your neighbour what you yourself would not like; that is the whole of the law, and all the rest is but commentaries.

Talmud
Sabbath 31

4

When thou gatherest the grapes of thy vineyard, thou shalt not glean it after thee; it shall be for the stranger, for the fatherless, and for the widow. And thou shalt remember that thou wast a bondman in the land of Egypt; therefore I command thee to do this thing.

Hebrew Bible
Deuteronomy 24

5

Rejoice not when thine enemy falleth, and let not thine heart be glad when he stumbleth.

Hebrew Bible
Proverbs 24

6

Brothers

The Greeks visualize humanity in a scheme of things in which man and god, mortal and immortal, are contrasted. Pollux and Castor are twins, Pollux born of divine seed and Castor born of mortal seed. The mortal brother is wounded in a fight and the immortal brother begs that he may share his fate.

Then quickly to his brother's manly frame
Back Polydeucês went. Not yet had Death
Quite mastered him, but from his throat there came
The shuddering gasps of his departing breath.
And while he moaned and the hot teardrops shed,
He cried aloud and said:

'O Father, Son of Cronus, what can fall
To save me from my grief? O let me die,
Let me too die with him, great Lord of All!
The glory of life departeth utterly
When dear ones leave us, and of all mankind
In sorrow we shall find
Few only we may trust to share our woe.'
He spake; then Zeus himself before him stood
And uttered thus his voice: 'Full well I know
Thou art my son, whereas thy brother's blood
Flowed through thy mother from her lord on earth
After thy Heavenly birth.
But now, behold, this choice I offer thee.
If thou thyself would'st never more be vowed
To death and hateful age, but dwell with me,
And with Athênê, and with Arês proud,
The dark spear's lord, upon our Mount Divine,
That portion shall be thine.

'But if for thy dear brother slain
Thou pleadest, and thyself art fain
To share with him thy doom,
Then may'st thou draw the living breath
For half thy time where after death
He lies in nether gloom,
And half thy time abide on high
In golden mansions of the sky.'
Then, hearing the god's voice,
The other stayed not in his choice;
And straightway Zeus unsealed the lips and eyes
Of Castor in his bronzen guise.   7

Pindar
521-441 B.C.
Nemean X
Greece
Trans. by
C. J. Billson

Hadith
(Sayings
of the Prophet)

None of you is a believer so long as he does not prefer
[love] for his brother what he prefers [loves] for himself.   8

Malik ibn Anas
Jurisconsult
8th cent.
Medina

A Moslem is forbidden to spill his own blood except in
the defence of justice or to spill the blood of another except
in the defence of justice.   9

Koran
An-Nissa 75

But what hath come to you that ye fight not on the path
of God, and for the weak among men, women and
children?   10

Let none of you, from a tendency to imitate, say to himself: 'If the people around me do good, I shall do good; and if the people around me do evil, I shall do evil.' On the contrary, take it upon yourselves to do good as you see it done around you, and not to take part in the evil you see done around you.

Hadith (Sayings of the Prophet)

11

If you see me following the right path, help me to continue in it; if you see me taking a wrong turn, put me back on the right path again. He who is strong among you is weak in my sight until he has passed the test of justice, and he who is weak among you is strong in my sight until justice has been done him.

Caliph Abu Bakr al-Siddik 7th cent.

12

Love of God and love of one's neighbour

He that saith he is in the light, and hateth his brother, is in darkness even until now.

He that loveth his brother abideth in the light, and there is none occasion of stumbling in him.

But he that hateth his brother is in darkness, and walketh in darkness, and knoweth not whither he goeth, because that darkness hath blinded his eyes.

. . . .

If a man say, I love God, and hateth his brother, he is a liar: for he that loveth not his brother whom he hath seen, how can he love God whom he hath not seen?

And this commandment have we from him, That he who loveth God love his brother also.

New Testament I John

13

Rights and duties

The true source of rights is duty. If we all discharge our duties, rights will not be far to seek. If leaving duties unperformed we run after rights, they will escape us like a will-o'-the-wisp. The more we pursue them, the farther will they fly.

Mahatma Gandhi 1869-1948

14

The unfortunate to be treated as a neighbour

Do not laugh at a blind man nor tease a dwarf nor injure the affairs of the lame.

. . . .

Do not neglect a stranger with thy oil jar. God desires respect for the poor more than knowing of the exalted.

Amen-em-Ope c. 1300-1100 B.C. Ancient Egypt

15

The moral absolute

Even if the nectar of the Devas reach their lands, they will eat [drink] it not, though sweet, all alone [they will share it with others]. They are free from hatred. They restlessly prosecute great works [unafraid] which others dreaded to undertake. If it be a praiseworthy object, they will achieve it even at the risk of their lives. If it be a sinful deed, they will not take it on themselves for all the world. Weary they never are. Since such men of great worth, who, striving not for selfish ends but always endeavouring for the good of others, exist, the world too exists.   *16*

Purananooru
Sangam period
2nd cent. B.C.
to 2nd cent. A.D.
Tamil

The absolute bond

Kuruntokai
Sangam period
2nd cent. B.C.
to 2nd cent. A.D.
Tamil

O chief of the saline region where the extensive sea is sapphire-hued and the rich pollened Mullai plant has thorns sharp like the teeth of the squirrel, even when this life changes and we are reborn, you should be my husband and I should be your loving spouse.   *17*

Against enmity

Mahābhārata
13th cent.
Telugu tradition

Drown the enmity—it is always better; for you can never silence an enemy by enmity. When you nourish enmity in your heart, you can never quite refrain from some word or act of enmity. And if you desire to fight and root out the enemy, you shall have to face killing and bloodshed. In whatever way one may think, oh! Krishna! there is no sense of decency in the feeling of enmity.   *18*

Great deeds

Peda Tirumalayya
Neeti Seesa
Satakamu
16th cent.
Telugu tradition

O Lord Srinivasa! What other great deed is there to do for men of power on this earth today than improving the lot of the miserable with sympathy or lifting up someone who has fallen down deep; finding them out and protecting the poor or helping and paying heed to the needy; rescuing a person who seeks asylum or bringing up someone who has none; saving a life from the claws of death or nursing a patient confined to sick bed—what deeds indeed are greater than these, O Lord Venkatesa!   *19*

He who has destroyed a heart

Yunus Emre
Folk-poet
13th cent.
Turkey

Behold the venerable man with the white beard, who knows not how matters lie. If he has destroyed a heart, his eagerness to go on a pilgrimage [to Holy Mecca] shall be of no avail to him.

The heart of man is the throne of God. God's gaze is ever directed towards the heart. He who has destroyed a heart shall know happiness neither in this world nor in the next.

What thou thinkest for thyself, think it also for others; the sense, if there be one, hidden in the Four Scriptures is summed up in these few words.   *20*

Sun or stone

Hear, O companions, love is like a sun. The heart without its share of love is like a stone.

What can grow in a heart of stone? He who bears it has poison on his tongue; all the honeyed words which he endeavours to utter shall sound like the din of battle.

Yunus Emre
Folk-poet
13th cent.
Turkey

Hearts that are full of love are warmed by a fire, and they become soft as wax. As for hearts of stone, they are like a winter, hard, pitiless and gloomy. *21*

That body alone which is inspired with love contains a living soul: if void of it, [the body] is bone overlaid with skin.

தன் கைத் தான் காதவன் ஆயின் எகைத்தொன்றும்

திஉன்எரூத்க நீ்உிகரய் பஉல்.

If a man loves himself, let him not commit any sin however small.

The [proper] punishment to those who have done evil [to you] is to put them to shame by showing them kindness in return and to forget both the evil and the good done on both sides.

The chief of all [the virtues] which authors have summed up is the partaking of food that has been shared with others, and the preservation of the manifold life of other creatures.

Tirukkural
1st cent.
Tamil
Mauritius

Not to destroy life is an incomparably [great] good; next to it in goodness ranks freedom from falsehood.

In great prosperity humility is becoming, dignity in great adversity. *22*

Ingratitude
is worse than
violence

Even for those wicked men who have cut off the teats of the cow; for those who have destroyed the child in the wombs of lustrous jewelled women and for those cruel men who have committed crimes against their parents, there is hope of salvation. But, even if the world were to turn topsy-turvy, for those who ungratefully forget the good done to them by others, there is no salvation. So the Shastras have sung, O lord of the lovely jewelled consort! *23*

Purananooru
Sangam period
2nd cent. B.C.
to 2nd cent. A.D.
Tamil

Ishavasy-Upanishads
India

Those who sacrifice, they alone enjoy. Thou shalt not be greedy. *24*

Reciprocity
Mahābhārata XII
2nd cent. B.C.
to 2nd cent. A.D.
Sanskrit

Whatever action a person does not wish to be done by others in respect of himself, he should not do in respect of others, ever remaining conscious of what is disagreeable to himself.   *25*

The guest
Taitirīya-UpanishadI
7th to 6th cent. B.C.
Sanskrit

Do you become one who regards his guest as god.   *26*

The unfortunate
Kālidāsa
Meghadūta 53
4th cent.
Sanskrit

The riches of the best [among men] have their fruition in the pacification of the sufferings of the distressed.   *27*

Subhāsita-
Ratnabhāndāgāra
Sanskrit

What good is the manliness of a person who does not give relief to the afflicted? What good is wealth which is of no avail to the needy? Is that really a proper activity which is not related to the good of others? Is that, indeed, life which is contrary to the interests of the good?   *28*

Bhāgavata-Purāna IX
9th to 10th cent.
Sanskrit

I do not desire from the Lord that high state which is characterised by the eight supernatural powers, nor, again, deliverance from re-birth. Dwelling within the hearts of all men, I take upon myself their distress so that they may thereby become free from suffering.   *29*

Self-mastery
Manusmriti XII
2nd cent. B.C.
to 1st cent. A.D.
Sanskrit

One, who, with equality, sees himself in all beings and all beings within himself and who [as it were] sacrifices himself, attains to the state of self-rule.   *30*

From the inscription on the tomb of Darius at Naksh-i-Rustam, 522-486 B.C.

A great god is Ahuramazda, who created this excellent work which is seen, who created happiness for man, who bestowed wisdom and activity upon Darius the King.

Saith Darius the King: By the favour of Ahuramazda I am of such a sort that I am a friend to right, I am not a friend to wrong. It is not my desire that the weak man should have wrong done to him by the mighty; nor is that my desire, that the mighty should have wrong done to him by the weak.

What is right, that is my desire. I am not a friend to the man who is a follower of Lie. I am not hot-tempered. What things develop in my anger, I hold firmly under control by my thinking power. I am firmly ruling over my own [impulses].

The man who co-operates, him according to his co-operative action, him thus do I reward. Who does harm, him according to the damage thus I punish. It is not my desire that a man should do harm; nor indeed is that my desire, if he should do harm, he should not be punished.

What a man says against a man, that does not convince me, until he satisfies the Ordinance of Good Regulations.

What a man does or performs [for me] according to his [natural] powers, [therewith] I am satisfied, and my pleasure is abundant, and I am well satisfied.

Persia

31

*A sinner
is still a man*

Dēnkart
9th cent.
Persia

No one should be an enemy and a wisher of evil to a person who commits a sin, one should thus be merciful to a person who is guilty of a sin, and think: 'It is indeed grief when Ahreman deceives and misleads in such a manner.'

32

Humility

Dēnkart
9th cent.
Persia

From not practising greed comes laying down the arms and refraining from war. From laying down the arms and refraining from war comes humility. Because of humility a man thinks moderately of his own good and more of that of another.

33

*Consideration
for others*

Inventory
13th cent.
Poland

Latin was the only language used in writing in Poland for several centuries after its conversion to Christianity in 966. The first sentence written down in Polish has been found in the inventory of the Henryków monastery in Silesia, composed in Latin in the years 1266-1270. (The sentence was inserted in order to explain the name of a village.) A peasant, looking at his woman working a handmill, says to her: Day at ia pobrusa a ti pociway, *which means*

Give me, and I will grind; you take a rest.

34

*A relation
of equality*

The like natural inducement hath brought men to know that it is no less their duty to love others than themselves; for seeing those things which are equal must needs all have one measure; if I cannot but wish to receive good, even as much at every man's hands as any man can wish unto his own soul, how should I look to have any part of my desire herein satisfied unless myself be careful to satisfy the like desire, which is undoubtedly in other men, being of one and the same nature? To have anything offered them repugnant to this desire must needs in all respects grieve them as much as me; so that, if I do harm, I must look to suffer, there being no reason that others should show greater measure of love to me than they have by me showed unto them; my desire therefore to be loved of my equals in nature, as much as possibly may be, imposeth upon me a natural duty of bearing them-ward fully the like affection; from which relation of equality between ourselves and them that are as ourselves, what several rules and canons natural reason hath drawn, for direction of life, no man is ignorant.

Richard Hooker
Lawes of
Ecclesiasticall
Politie
1594
England

35

Need for others

Once I was young and went alone;
    Then wandering, missed my way;
I felt myself rich when I found a friend,
    For man is the solace of man.

Once for fun in the fields I fastened
    My clothes on a scrawny scare-crow;
Dressed he seemed like a duke indeed,
    But a naked man is naught.

The fir-tree dies in the dreary dell,
    Its bark and its bast avail not;
And a man unloved is like that tree—
    Why should he linger longer?

Brand from brand is kindled and burnt;
    Fire is born of fire;
Man warms to man by word of mouth,
    The voiceless is avoided.

Odin's stanzas
Viking period
800-1100
Iceland

36

No man is an Iland, intire of it selfe; every man is a peece of the Continent, a part of the maine; if a Clod bee washed away by the Sea, Europe is the lesse, as well as if a Promontorie were, as well as if a Mannor of thy friends or of thine owne were; any mans death diminisches me, because I am involved in Mankinde; And therefore never send to know for whom the bell tolls; it tolls for thee.

John Donne
1624
England

37

Respect for others

Mahatma Gandhi
1869-1948

It has always been a mystery to me how men can feel themselves honoured by the humiliation of their fellow-beings.

38

Intrepid humility

Non-violence works in a most mysterious manner. Often a man's actions defy analysis in terms of non-violence; equally often his actions may wear the appearance of violence when he is absolutely non-violent in the highest sense of the term and is subsequently found so to be. . . .

I may not carry my argument any further. Language at best is but a poor vehicle for expressing one's thoughts in full. For me non-violence is not a mere philosophical principle. It is the rule and the breath of my life. I know I fail often, sometimes consciously, more often unconsciously. It is a matter not of the intellect but of the heart. True guidance comes by constant waiting upon God, by utmost humility, self-abnegation, by being ever ready to sacrifice one's self. Its practice requires fearlessness and courage of the highest order. I am painfully aware of my failings.

Mahatma Gandhi
1869-1948

39

*Discourse on
universal love*

則不能治
不知亂之所自起
焉能治之
必知亂之所自起
聖人以治天下為事者也

The holy man whose task is to govern the world must know the origin of disorder so that he may control it. If he knows not whence disorder comes he cannot control it. Thus, for instance, a doctor fighting a patient's disease must know the origin of this disease in order to be able to fight it. Should not the man who has to control disorder do likewise? . . .

In considering whence any disorder comes, he discovers that it comes from mutual non-love. Thus, for example, the subject and the son do not revere the prince and the father. That is what is called disorder. For the son loves himself, but not his father. That is why he does injury to his father for his own benefit. The younger brother loves himself, but not his elder brother. That is why he does injury to his elder brother for his own benefit. The subject loves himself but not his prince. That is why he does injury to his prince for his own benefit. That is what is called disorder.

Similarly, if the father is not well-disposed to his son, the elder brother to his younger brother, and the prince to his subject, that is what is called disorder. For the father loves himself, but not his son. That is why he does injury to his son for his own benefit. The elder brother loves himself, but not his younger brother. That is why he does injury to his younger brother for his own benefit. The prince loves himself, but not his subject. That is why he does injury to his subject for his own benefit. Why all this? All this comes from mutual non-love.

The same holds for burglars and bandits. The burglar loves his house, but not the house of another man. That is why he burgles the house of that other man for his own benefit. The bandit loves himself, but not another man. That is why he attacks that other man for his own benefit. Why all this? All this comes from mutual non-love.

The same holds for the grand officer who disturbs the family of another grand officer and for the lord who invades the State of another lord. For the grand officer loves his family, but not that of another grand officer. That is why he disturbs the family of that other grand officer for the benefit of his own family. The lord loves his State, but not another State. That is why he invades that other State for the benefit of his own State. The disorder of the whole world is no more than that. In considering what is the origin of all that, one discovers that it is mutual non-love.

If everyone adopts universal love and if everyone loves others as himself, will there still be those who are not dutiful? For in regarding the father and the elder brother and the prince as oneself, who will be impious towards them? Will there still be those who are not well-disposed? For in regarding one's younger brother, one's son and one's subject as oneself, who will be ill-disposed towards them? Thus impiety and malevolence will no longer exist.

Will there still be burglars and bandits? In considering the house of another man as one's own house, who will burgle it? In regarding the body of another man as one's own body, who will attack that other man? Thus burglars and bandits will no longer exist.

Will there be a grand officer who disturbs the family of another grand officer and a lord who invades the State of another lord? In regarding the family of another grand officer as one's own family, who will disturb it? In regarding another State as one's own State, who will invade it? Thus grand officers causing trouble and aggressive lords will no longer exist.

If the whole world adopts universal love, one State will no longer invade another State; one family will no longer disturb another; burglars and bandits will no longer exist; prince and subject, father and son will fulfil their duty of piety and benevolence. This state of affairs constitutes good order in the world. How should the holy man whose task is to govern the world not prohibit hatred and encourage love, since universal love promotes order while mutual hatred leads to disorder? And Master Mo-Tzu concluded: 'One cannot fail to encourage love of other people.'

Mo-tzu
5th cent. B.C.
China

40

Ideals of Aztec education

They would begin to teach them:
How they should live,
How they should respect others,
How they were to dedicate themselves
To what was good and righteous;
How they were to avoid evil,
Fleeing unrighteousness with strength,
Refraining from perversion and greed.

Aztec tradition
15th cent.
Mexico
Trans. by
M. Léon Portilla

41

Without human principles

Nahuatl tradition
Mexico

If we live without human principles we are no more than filth and dust.

42

Self-sacrifice

Kaab ibn Mama was an Iyadite. It is said of him that one month in the burning heat of summer he went out [into the desert] with a caravan, among whose members was a man from the Namir ibn Qasit tribe. They lost their way, and had to ration out their water. So that each man should receive the same amount, they placed a pebble, known as the *maqla*, in the bottom of the cup, and poured in the water until it covered the pebble, and sat down to drink. When Kaab's turn came to take the cup, he saw the Namirite looking at it with greedy eyes; so he gave up his ration, and said to the man pouring the water: 'Give a drink to your brother Namirite.' The following day, when they halted, they shared out the remaining water. This time, the Namirite looked at the cup with

32

the same expression as before, and Kaab repeated his gesture. When the company moved off, they said: 'Kaab, it is time to move!' but he was too weak to stand. As they were not far from water, they said to him: 'Kaab, go and fetch water, for that is your usual task', but he had no strength to reply. Seeing that his case was hopeless, they covered him with a cloak to keep wild beasts at bay and prevent them from devouring him, and left him there, where he died.   *43*

Al-Maidani
Majma al-amthal
Early 12th cent.
Persia

Categorical duties

There are three duties whose neglect God regards as unpardonable: filial piety towards parents, whether they be good or wicked; failure to honour one's word, whether those to whom it is given be good or wicked; failure to return what has been entrusted to one, whether by good or wicked men. He who believes in God and the Last Judgement, let him act kindly towards his neighbour, let him honour his guests, let him speak good words, and let him be thankful.   *44*

Hadith
(Sayings
of the Prophet)

Generosity to those
in trouble

Hatim ibn Abdallah, of the Tayy tribe, was a man both generous and brave, always a conqueror. From battles, he emerged victorious; what booty he had won, he left to others; he let no request go unanswered; in archery, he was the champion; in races, he was the first to reach the post; the prisoners he captured, he set free; in times of good fortune, he spent all his wealth on others. Of him the tale is told that one day, during the sacred month, travelling on business of his own, he found himself in the lands of the Banu Anaza. One of their prisoners called to him: 'O, Abu Saffana' (*that is to say, 'Father of Saffana', for that was the name of Hatim's baby daughter*), 'O, Abu Saffana! My bonds cut into my flesh; I am devoured by lice!' Hatim replied: 'Your fate is hard, my friend. These people are strangers to me, and I have no means of helping you! Your appeal has placed me in a quandary; you cannot be left where you are.' And so he discussed the ransom with the Anaza, and bought the prisoner from them; and set him free at once, and stayed there tied up in his place until the ransom was brought, and handed to the captors.

His wife Mawiya used to speak of the year when the tribe fell victim to famine, which carried off all the livestock. 'One night,' she said, 'our hunger reached the limit. Hatim took [our son] Adi, and I took [our daughter] Saffana, and we played with them until they fell asleep.

33

Then Hatim began to talk with me, so that I might forget my troubles and fall asleep as well. Seeing his efforts, I was sorry for him, and I stopped talking, so that he would think I was asleep, and go to sleep himself. "Are you asleep?" he asked me, several times. I did not reply, and he fell silent. Then he saw someone coming from behind the tent, and lifted his head. It was a woman, who said: "O, Abu Saffana, I come to you on behalf of some starving children." "Bring your children to me," he replied, "and in God's name I will see that they are fed."

'Then', went on his wife, 'I got up in a hurry, and said to him: "With what, Hatim? Your own children are starving, alas, and words were their only supper!" He went to his horse, and killed it; then he lit a fire, and gave a knife to the woman, saying: "Roast some meat and eat, and feed your children." Then he said to me: "Wake your children." I woke them, and he added: "By the Lord, it would be a shameful thing for you to eat, whilst all the other members of the tribe, who are in the same state, have nothing." And so he went from tent to tent, announcing to his kinsmen: "Gather beside the fire." They gathered there, and ate. He himself sat at a distance, wrapped in his cloak, until there was not the smallest scrap of meat left on the ground.'

Al-Maidani
Majma al-amthal
Early 12th cent.
Persia

45

Russian proverb   Save your comrade though you die yourself.   46

A SIMPLETON

Pagnka took service as a herdsman with the Tatars of the steppe, leading their herds of horses to graze.

In this way he spent years wandering somewhere beyond Penza, on the edge of the Ryn Peski desert, where a wealthy man named Khan-Djangar held sway. When going to Sura to sell his horses this Khan-Djangar behaved quietly enough, but at home, on the steppe, he did whatever he wanted, sending some to torture and rewarding others, as the whim took him.

In that wild country far from the centres of government it was impossible to keep a watch on his doings. Yet Khan-Djangar was not without enemies; one of them, a certain Khabiboula, was always attacking his herds and stealing his finest horses. Khan-Djangar's men could never lay their hands on him. One day, however, there was a great battle among the Tatars, and Khabiboula, wounded, was taken prisoner. But Khan-Djangar was to go to Penza and had not time enough then to try Khabiboula and sentence him to some horrible torture that would serve as an example to other horse-thieves.

Being in a hurry to set off for the fair at Penza, and also fearing to be seen with Khabiboula in a region where the Russian authorities would have meddled in his business, Khan-Djangar decided to leave the wounded and fettered Khabiboula under Pagnka's guard near a tiny spring. He gave Pagnka flour and a goatskin of water and said to him sternly: 'Guard this man as thou wouldst thy soul! Dost thou understand?'

Pagnka answered: 'That is not difficult. I understand and I shall do exactly as thou hast told me.'

Khan-Djangar and his followers set off at a gallop. Pagnka then said to Kabiboula:

'See where thy thefts have brought thee! Thou art strong and brave, but thou hast used thy strength to do evil instead of good. Thou wouldst do better to mend thy ways.'

And Khabiboula answered him: 'Not having mended my ways so far, it is now too late to do so, I have no time.'

'No time? Why? The main thing is to desire sincerely to mend one's ways, the rest will come of its own accord. Thou hast in thee a soul, like all men; turn from wickedness and God will at once help thee to do good, and then all will go well.'

Khabiboula listened to him and sighed: 'No', he said, 'it is not the right time to think of that.'

'Why is it not the right time?'

'Because I am in chains and awaiting death.'

'But I am about to let thee go.'

Khabiboula could not believe his ears, but Pagnka smiled kindly upon him and said: 'I am not jesting; I am telling the truth. Khan-Djangar enjoined me to guard thee "as I would my soul"; and dost thou know how one should guard one's soul? One must have no pity for it, brother! It must suffer for others. And that is precisely what I need, for I cannot bear others to be tortured. I am going to remove thy chains and seat thee on the horse. Away with thee, flee where thou wilt; but if thou begin again to do evil, it is not to me but to God that thou wilt have lied.'

Having thus spoken, Pagnka broke Khabiboula's chains, placed him in the saddle and said to him: 'Go thou in peace where thou wilt.'

He himself remained, waiting for Khan-Djangar. He waited a long time. When the other arrived with his

Tatars, the spring had dried up and there was scarcely any water left in the goatskin.

Khan-Djangar looked to right and to left and asked Pagnka: 'Where then is Khabiboula?'

Pagnka answered: 'I have let him go.'

'How so? What art thou telling me?'

'I tell thee that I have acted in accordance with command and as I willed. Thou didst order me to guard him as I would my soul; now I love my soul so much that I wish it to suffer for others. Thou didst think to make an end of Khabiboula in torture, but I cannot bear others to be tormented. Take thou me then and torture me in his place, that my soul may be happy and free of all terror, for I fear thee not at all, neither thee nor anyone.'

Khan-Djangar stared, scratched his head and then said to those around him: 'Come near and I shall tell you what I think.'

The Tatars pressed around Khan-Djangar and he said to them in a low voice: 'I do not believe that one can put Pagnka to death, for it seems to me that there is an angel dwelling within him.'

'Yes,' the Tatars whispered, 'we cannot hurt him. He has been with us a long time, but we did not understand him and now, all at once, he has become clear to us: perhaps indeed he is a just man.'

Nicolai Leskov
1831-95
Russia

47

THE LEPER AND THE MISERLY WOMAN

One day the leper came out from the forest with his dogs. He had been hunting. He was oppressed by the heat. He said to himself: 'I am going to come to the ground-nut fields where the women are working; if they won't give me any ground-nuts, I can at least ask them for some water, for they'll give me that.'

He emerged from the forest and came to the first field; he asked a woman: 'Woman, give me some water so that I may quench my thirst!'

The woman answered: 'Huh! You, a leper, and me give you some of my water! No, No, No! I've got no water. What me give you some water! What, and you drink from my calabash! You just drink out of your hands!'

'If you won't give me any water, fine mother', the other replied, 'at least pour me a little into a leaf!'

The woman remained unmoved: 'I've got no water to give you.'

Another woman working at the other end of the field

called the leper when she heard that and said: 'Come, drink from my calabash.'

But he replied: 'No I won't do that, pour me some water into the hollow of my hand, I'll drink like that.'

The woman insisted: 'Good man, drink from the calabash.' When he had drunk, she added: 'Your dogs are thirsty, make them drink too!'

When the man had quenched his thirst, he sighed: 'Thank you, woman, I have had enough', and he clapped his hands in salute.

She gave him some more water and a basket of groundnuts. The man then took out a portion of game and gave it to her.

But in taking the game, she was struck with fear. The leper said: 'Do not fear, woman, go and eat this meat in the village; it cannot infect you with leprosy. As to that woman who refused me water, tell me the name of her clan.'

The woman replied: 'Its name is Ba ki nti ndumbu nkasa mayala.'

Then, rubbing his head, the leper said: 'Very well then, since the people of that clan refused me water, they may have children and increase, but if they happen to eat any spotted game or antelopes with a striped coat, it will give them leprosy. Let them inspect their bodies, they will be lepers, they and their children and the grandchildren of their grandchildren. Let it be so, I have spoken!'

With this, he departed. In the village where the women dwelt, after eating time came the time to sleep. The men killed an antelope with a striped coat. They cut it up and shared it out. The hard-hearted woman was also given a share. She roasted it, ate it and lay then down to sleep.

When she woke up in the morning, she discovered that she was covered from head to foot with leprosy sores. Her husband asked her: 'What's the matter?'

'These sores,' she replied, 'I don't know what it can be. It appeared last night.'

The husband added: 'I can't understand this business. Yesterday my wife returns from the fields, she comes into the house and she was completely well. Last night we slept in the house and now my wife is covered in sores! I'm going to see the fetisher to see if he can find out what is behind all this.'

While he was speaking, a woman in another hut cried: 'Come, I'll explain to you!'

The husband went. The woman said: 'You, my man, say that you are going to consult the fetisher, but this business is perfectly clear.' The husband replied: 'Well, woman, speak, you went to the fields with her, what did you see then?'

The woman spoke thus: 'Yes, the day before yesterday we went to the ground-nut field. When we reached the water we began by filling our calabashes, I mine, she hers, and the children theirs. Then we went to the ground-nut fields where we started to gather in the crop. At midday, while we were working, we saw a man approach with his gun and game-bag, and accompanied by his dogs. First he stopped at the end of my companion's field and asked her to pour him something to drink. "Heh, good woman," he said, "come here, give me a little water, good mother, so that I can drink!" And this is what my companion retorted: "What! You, with your horrible leprous body, and I should give my water! I have no water to give to you!" Then the man besought her: "Well, put a little in this leaf!" My companion then cried: "Be off with you! Did the people of my clan, the ba Ki nti ndumbu nkasa Mayala, command you to come here?"

'When I heard this I called the leper and said to him: "Come here, old man, come and drink from my calabash, there it is!" He came and cupped his hands: "Pour it into there, so that I can drink!" But I didn't want that. "Drink from my calabash, old man!" Would that transmit the leprosy to the calabash? Of course it wouldn't, would it? When he had drunk, I also gave some water to his dogs. Then I filled a whole basket with ground-nuts and I gave it to him. Then he put his hand into the game-bag and pulled out a large chunk of meat which he gave to me, saying: "Take this meat and eat it; do not be afraid, the leprosy cannot infect you. But tell me the name of the clan of that woman who refused to give me any water! Tell me! What is it?" "The name of her clan?" I replied, "They are the ba Ki nti ndumbu nkasa Mayala." At this, he rubbed his head and cast a spell on her: "Very well then, since people of the clan of the ba Ki nti ndumbu nkasa Mayala refused me water, they may have children and increase; but if they eat any spotted game or antelope with a striped coat, it will give them leprosy, whether it is the *nkai* antelope or the *nsombi* antelope. If they eat any, let them look at their sides, they will have been stricken with leprosy, they, their children and the grandchildren of their grandchildren. Let it be so, I have spoken!" At this he departed. After that we gathered up the ground-nuts, put them in our baskets and returned to the village. It was evening. When we got to the village, I wanted to tell you about it, but I forgot. And yesterday you shot this antelope, you shared it out—did she not eat some of it?'

The husband said: 'Of course she ate some of it! When she had eaten we lay down to sleep. When we woke in the morning, I suddenly saw that she was covered all over with leprosy sores.'

The woman continued: 'As this evil spell was cast by the leper, will you then go and throw away your money at the fetisher's? Why this affair is as clear as daylight. What more do you want?'

The husband left it at that.

As to the woman who had deserved this punishment, every day she still found she had leprosy. Her body was covered all over with leprosy. And thus it was that all those born in the clan contracted leprosy whenever they ate spotted game, whether mice or antelopes with a striped coat.

It is for this reason—because once they refused to give water to a leper—that this clan is afflicted with this terrible leprosy.

Bakongo tradition
Congo

48

Sudanese proverb
Africa

If you rear a serpent, you will be the first to be bitten. *49*

Fulani proverb
Africa

Men are like two dirty hands. One of them can only be washed by the other. *50*

Songhai proverb
Africa

When your neighbour's beard catches fire, wet your own beard.

(*The means by which you try to increase your neighbour's misfortune may bring you the same misfortune.*) *51*

Somali proverb
Africa

A man gives you poison, give him butter. *52*

Amharic proverb
Ethiopia

Husband and wife = law and government. *53*

Amharic proverb
Ethiopia

Treat gossip about your friend as though it referred to you. *54*

Romanian proverb

Man's hope is in man. *55*

*Right human
relations*

I adjure the nobility to treat their people with kindness,
and to rule them with justice; I adjure the burghers
to pursue their trade honestly, and craftsmen to serve
those for whom they work faithfully; I adjure master-
craftsmen, themselves living honestly, to instruct their
apprentices faithfully, teaching them first to love God,
and then to work for the glory of God, the good of the
community and their own salvation, following the precepts
of honesty, but striving neither after too great riches nor
after worldly honours; I adjure students and pupils to
obey their masters and follow them in well-doing and to
learn zealously from others for the glory of God and their
own salvation.

Lastly, I adjure you to love one another, to watch that
the good are not oppressed by violence, and to seek justice

Jan Hus   for all.   *56*

If only men would see each other as the agents of each
other's happiness, they could occupy the earth, their
common habitation, in peace, and move forward confi-
dently together to their common goal.

The prospect changes when they regard each other as

Abbé Sieyès   obstacles; soon they have no choice left but to flee or be
Préliminaire à   forever fighting. Humankind then seems nothing but a
la Constitution
20 and 21 July 1789   gigantic error of nature.   *57*
France

Ewe proverb   A bad neighbour is like a Borassus palm-tree—you cannot
Togo   reject him altogether for you must think of rainy days.
                                                58

Life is beyond price;
protection and respect for the individual

---

*Suspension of
moral judgement*

This I ask thee, O Lord, answer me truly:
Who among those to whom I speak is righteous and who
    is wicked?
Which of the two? Am I evil myself,
Or is the evil one he who would wickedly keep me far
    from thy salvation?
How should I not think him the wicked one?

Avesta, Gāthās
of Zarathustra
Pre-6th cent. B.C.
Persia

This I ask thee, O Lord, answer me truly:
[How] shall we rid ourselves of evil
By throwing it back on those who, full of disobedience,
Care naught for following Righteousness
And do not trouble to take counsel with the Good Mind? *59*

Protection

Dādistān ī
Mēnōg ī Xrad
Sassanian period
3rd to 7th cent.
Persia

The sage asked the Spirit of Wisdom thus: 'What is it necessary to keep with greater regard and greater protection?'

The Spirit of Wisdom answered thus: 'It is necessary to keep a young serving-boy, a wife, a beast of burden and a fire with greater protection and greater regard.' *60*

*Man's presence
in the world*

Dādistān ī Dēnīg
Theological treatise
9th cent.
Persia

The thirty-fourth question is that in which you asked: 'Will this material world become without man in such a manner that nothing corporeal will be in it, and afterwards the resurrection, of how will it be?'

The reply is this: 'From creation even until the pure renovation, throughout this period this world has never been and will never be without men. The accomplishment of this bad desire will not be granted to the Evil Spirit.' *61*

Potential humanity

Herder
Briefe zur
Beförderung der
Humanität
1796
Germany

It is impossible to speak of man's rights without speaking also of his duties, for each is related to the other, and we are still seeking a word to cover them both.

The same is true of human dignity and love of mankind. The human race, as it is today, and probably will be for a long time to come, has for the most part no dignity whatever and deserves compassion rather than respect; but it must be raised to the level befitting the true nature of the species, that which lends it its value and dignity....

The distinctive feature of our species is its *humanity*; but this quality in us is potential only and needs to be duly fostered. We do not bring it with us ready-made when we are born; it must become the object of our earthly endeavours, the epitome of our activities, our title to value.... Even the divine part of our make-up is the result of fostering humanity in ourselves.... This fostering [of humanity] is a task to be pursued unremittingly, if not we shall relapse, all of us, great and small, into our primitive state of brutishness and bestiality. *62*

Alexandre Vinet
1797-1847
Switzerland

I would have Man be complete, spontaneous and individual so that, as a man, he may bow to the general good. I would have him be master of himself, in order that he may better serve his fellow-men.

63

The treasure
of life

Koran
Al-Maidah 32

He who slayeth anyone, unless it be a person guilty of manslaughter, or of spreading disorders in the land, shall be as though he had slain all mankind; but he who saveth a life, shall be as though he had saved all mankind alive.

64

Koran
Al-Hujurat 9

If two bodies of the faithful are at war, then make ye peace between them; and if the one of them wrong the other, fight against that party which doth the wrong, until they come back to the precepts of God.

65

Hadith
(Sayings
of the Prophet)

If two believers engage in a hand-to-hand fight both he who kills and he who is killed—the two together shall go to hell [into the fire]. 'O Messenger of God,' someone asked the Prophet, 'shall the victim have the same fate as the murderer?' And he answered: 'Had he not resolved to kill his opponent?'

66

Hadith
(Sayings
of the Prophet)

Whoever hurls himself from a mountain height and so puts an end to his life shall be cast into the flames of hell where he will remain eternally. Whoever swallows poison and so puts an end to his life shall, in the flames of hell, constantly be holding in his hand a cup of poison from which he will have to drink eternally. Whoever has used a sword to put an end to his life shall, in the flames of hell, with his own hand, plunge the sword into his belly eternally.

67

Rigveda II
2200-1800 B.C.
Sanskrit

Thou, Varuna, art the king of all of those who are gods, O Asura, and of those who are mortals. Grant us a hundred autumns that we may see the manifold world. May we attain the long lives which have been ordained as from yore.

68

Atharvaveda I
2200-1800 B.C.
Sanskrit

Prosperity be to our mother and to our father; prosperity to the cattle, to whatever moves and to all men [in the household]. May everything be well-disposed and profitable unto us. May we be enabled to see the sun for a long time.   *69*

Offering

Ancient Egypt

Akan tradition
Ghana

We pray for life and pray for grace;
Let not blindness be with us by day,
Nor impotence our associate by night.
May we be blessed with children,
And may what we plant bear fruit.
Let there be peace in the world,
And may there be prosperity
In this land abundantly.   *70*

Only man counts

It is man who counts; I call upon gold, it answers not; I call upon drapery, it answers not; it is man who counts.

*He is concerned
with something
other than himself*

Man is not a palm nut that he should be self-centred.

Limitation

Man came to play only a part of the drama of life, not the whole.

We are many

Even the dead are continuously seeking to increase their numbers, how much more the living?

Conscience

You may not see yourself growing up, but you certainly know when you are sinning.

*Defence
of the weak*

One should not oppress with one's size or might.
(*It is wrong for a strong man to oppress the weak.*)   *71*

Akan proverbs
Ghana

Generosity

One who loves the children of his fellow will surely love his own children.
    The question may arise in the assembly whether one's tribe should treat another tribe with toleration. If opinion seems to be divided, the side which is for toleration may quote the proverb to plead for indulgence.
    People may object bitterly if members of another tribe come to hunt in the forests owned by their tribe. If some one thinks that the objection is ungenerous, he will quote the proverb.   *72*

Jabo proverb
Liberia

43

*The kinship
of created things*

Montaigne
Essayes
1580-88

If all that were to be contradicted, yet is there a kinde of respect and a generall duty of humanity which tieth us not only unto brute beasts that have life and sense, but even unto trees and plants. Unto men we owe Justice, and to all other creatures that are capable of it, grace and benignity. There is a kinde of enterchangeable commerce and mutual bond betweene them and us. *73*

Compassion

Vauvenargues
Réflexions
et Maximes
1746
France

A man of the world, even the most ambitious, if he is born humane and compassionate, cannot but be pained by the spectacle of the ills which the gods have spared him; discontented even with his own lot, he nevertheless thinks it more than he deserves when he sees misfortunes more moving than his own; as if it were his fault that there are others less fortunate than he, his generosity blames him in secret for all the calamities of the human race, and the consciousness of his own ills merely enhances his pity for the ills of others. *74*

*The value of
any living thing*

The evil-doer destroys everything that is young and pretends to be blind to the future.

Today's crowing cocks were yesterday's eggs.

She who gives birth to a monster is obliged to suckle it.

There is no reason for treating one person as a child and another as an outcast.

A cripple is better than a dead man.

Water all plants, for you do not know which will bear fruit before the others.

The afflicted
Burundi proverbs

You must first console the afflicted before sharing their joys. *75*

The guest
Russian proverb

In Russia the guest comes first. *76*

*No one is to be
despised*

BIG-CLUB, THE MAN WHO SPOKE THE TRUTH

There was once a poor man who had the misfortune to have a deformed son. He called him Big-Club because his legs and his arms were stuck to his stomach.

When the son grew up, everyone had a horror of him. He therefore went off into the forest and led a solitary life there. How did he live? Only by hunting. Yet he was outstandingly intelligent. One day when he was hunting, he found himself face to face with a buffalo, which threatened to kill him. He managed to make the buffalo change his mind and proposed to him that they live in peace together: 'Do not kill me,' he said 'let us rather live together in the greatest friendship. Bring me an antelope and I will save you when you are in trouble.' The buffalo agreed to this proposal.

A short while afterwards there was a shortage of water in the country. All the rivers dried up. As they were looking for water in the forest, people met the deformed man. 'Let us kill him,' they said, 'it is he who is preventing the rain from falling; he is a monster; he brings bad luck.' He besought them to spare his life and promised to bring them water from Lake Tanganyika. Big-Club always kept his word. They spared his life so as to see whether he would keep his promise, and be set off in the direction of Lake Tanganyika. Some distance away he found himself face to face with his friend the buffalo, who was looking for a drinking place. 'Remember your promise,' said the buffalo, 'I now need water.' 'Spare my life for a second time,' replied Big-Club, 'and I will bring you water from Lake Tanganyika.' 'You lie,' replied the buffalo. 'It would be better for me to eat you; at least you would then have been some good to me before I die of thirst. I don't think you will be able to bring water all this way, for you will meet wild beasts who will eat you.' Big-Club swore to keep his promise if his life was spared. The buffalo let him go. A few minutes later he met a lion. 'And where are you going?' asked the king of the animals. 'I am king of this forest, and I shall eat you, because it is of your own free will that you appear before me.' 'Sire,' said Big-Club, 'let me go to Lake Tanganyika, and when I come back, I will give you a large animal to eat.' 'You are deceiving me,' replied the lion, 'how could you catch a large animal? You will never be able to take the water of Tanganyika from the crocodile, who is its undisputed master. The crocodile will eat you. So I am going to eat you before he does.' Big-Club vowed solemnly that he would bring both the water and a large animal. The lion let him go.

Our adventurer went on his way, and as he walked he plaited a thick rope and tried to avoid meeting other wild beasts. He arrived at Lake Tanganyika.

He had only just begun to draw water when a crocodile leapt upon him. 'Who,' he said, 'has given you leave to draw this water, of which I am the undisputed master?

I am going to eat you; you have done well to appear before me; I am hungry.' Big-Club besought him to spare his life and to let him draw water from the lake. In return, he would give him a large fat animal.

When he had left the water, Big-Club spoke to the crocodile: 'Know now that I am Big-Club, the man who speaks the truth and who keeps his promises. Take this rope. If you feel that I am hauling upon it, that will be because I have already tied up the animal I promised you. You will then pull the rope with all your might until you have drawn the animal to you.' The crocodile thanked him heartily and let him go.

The lion was waiting for Big-Club at the appointed place. Big-Club arrived and said: 'I have succeeded in getting water.' 'Congratulations,' replied the lion, 'and where is my animal?' 'Don't worry,' replied Big-Club, 'take this rope and pull as hard as you can, as I have left the animal tied up. Pull vigorously, until you have drawn the animal to you.'

The lion began to pull and realized that this indeed was a large animal. He summoned all his strength as he thought to himself: 'Truly, Big-Club has not deceived me.' The more he pulled, the more he felt himself pulled as well: it was the crocodile tugging at his prey. It was a stiff struggle between the two animals. There was neither victor nor vanquished, for the two animals killed each other.

Meanwhile Big-Club took water first of all to the buffalo, and then to the people. When thirst had been quenched, the rain began to fall on all the country, the rivers were overflowing, and people and animals were able to have plenty of water.

When they saw this good turn, the people were sorry for having despised Big-Club, for having cast him out into the forest and, even worse, for having wanted to kill him. They accepted him into their society, built him a fine palace, proclaimed him king of their nation and gave him a queen. So Big-Club, the man who spoke the truth and kept his promise, was able to win the people's confidence, in spite of being a monster.

*Fable
from Burundi*

77

The right to life　　THE PITCHER THAT BECAME A QUEEN

There was once a man who had had twelve children. All had died after living only a few minutes. At last, a thirteenth child was born. But instead of the birth of a normal child to console the unhappy parents, there was a heart-rending disappointment. Just imagine! A living pitcher being born instead of a lovely baby! What a disaster! The parents were at their wits' end. The pitcher could only bring ill-luck. The parents decided to flee so as to escape from this misfortune.

The whole family—father, mother, grandfather, grandmother, servants—left the house with all speed, abandoning this undesirable and ill-starred monster.

But scarcely were they outside when the pitcher rolled after them, crying: 'Father of the pitcher, wait for your pitcher.' At the sound of these cries, they began to run at top speed and managed to outdistance the pitcher. Unfortunately, the fugitives were caught in a downpour of rain. The poor pitcher was carried off by the current and swept into the neighbouring forest, while the family took shelter in a nearby house. When the rain had stopped, the family continued its travels and came to another country. Thinking themselves finally delivered from this terrifying monster, they asked the prince of the country to give them asylum. He offered them an excellent piece of ground to settle on.

Several years later the prince organized a hunt. He made his way towards the forest into which the mysterious pitcher had been swept by the flood. While looking for his quarry, he suddenly espied the abandoned pitcher. He thought it a very beautiful one, and gave orders that it be taken to adorn his palace. The pitcher was placed on the shelf with the household utensils.

A surprising thing then happened which no one was expecting. Whenever the prince went off on his daily pursuits, a graceful young girl emerged from the pitcher and set about sweeping and cleaning the palace thoroughly, washing the utensils and tidying the grass that lined the shelf. When everything was in proper trim, she went back and shut herself up in the pitcher. When the servant-girls came to do their work, they found it already done. As this happened every day, they told the prince, who thought it very mysterious.

One day the prince hid behind the fence so as to see who was responsible for this mystery. He saw a young girl emerge from the pitcher and set about sweeping and cleaning the palace, washing the utensils and putting everything in its place. Taking advantage of the moment when she was bending to gather up the sweepings, he seized her and said: 'Leave the kingdom of the dead and come into the kingdom of the living.' From that day she became his wife. As princess, she had an opportunity of seeing certain members of her family come to the court.

47

She asked the prince to invite them into the palace. The princess hid herself again in the pitcher and cried: 'Father and mother of the pitcher, grandfather and grandmother of the pitcher, wait for your pitcher.' She then emerged from the pitcher and said to them: 'Never abandon your offspring, for it is a human being, to be treated and cherished like the others.'

Frightened by these words, the parents remembered that it was the pitcher they had brought into the world.

*Fable
from Burundi*

78

*The end of
cannibalism*

DHEG-DHEER, THE LONG-EARED WOMAN CANNIBAL

Once upon a time there lived a woman who was a cannibal. She was called Dheg-Dheer. She was called by this name because she had one very long ear. When she was asleep her very long ear would sink down slowly. She would also hear nothing, understand nothing and smell nothing while asleep. When awake her long ear would stand up towards the sky in an oblique manner. As she never bathed or combed her hair, which became long and twisted, she looked horrible. Her twenty nails were so long that they were like the claws of a lion. Her eyebrows were also long and thick. Her teeth were sharp and she had large red eyes. She only had a filthy garment on her waist. Otherwise she was naked. Everyone knew Dheg-Dheer by her long ear, and by her ugly, fierce look.

Dheg-Dheer used to live in the area of a river called Hhargega. She had a beautiful daughter who lived with her. This daughter was tall, light and well formed, and she watched the house and prepared the food while her mother was out hunting people to eat. Every night Dheg-Dheer would return carrying the people she had caught that day.

In Dheg-Dheer's house were several woven pots used for the different kinds of food. In one of these Dheg-Dheer would keep water. In the other two she would keep the meat and blood of the people she had hunted. The pot used for human flesh was called Baw-Dheer. It was called by this name because whenever anyone else except Dheg-Dheer opened it, it made a loud, thundery noise: 'Bawwwwwwwwww.' Thus it was called Baw-Dheer.

The thundery noise of Baw-Dheer would reach the ears of Dheg-Dheer even if she was far away. Then she would come to the house running like the wind, shouting: 'Who is the cursed person who opened Baw-Dheer? Who is the cursed person who opened Baw-Dheer?'

Dheg-Dheer was a very fast runner and would catch

anyone she chased. She specially favoured the tender meat of young people. The only deterrent against Dheg-Dheer was the ditches and banks of the Hhargega river. These scared her....

One day Dheg-Dheer spied on a fat woman carrying a little fat boy. She began chasing them. The woman knew the area well and ran straight towards the ditches and banks of Hhargega. As she chased them Dheg-Dheer muttered to herself: 'Look how fat she is. Look at her buttocks. The way they shake as she runs. Look at the little boy she carries. How plump he is. I must catch them. How delicious they will be. Catch them before they reach that damned river.'

The woman reached the ditches and banks and crossed them before Dheg-Dheer. The beast then got very angry. She threw sand on her body, scratched herself and plucked her hair....

One day later, two beautiful young girls came to the daughter of Dheg-Dheer as she was doing her service of preparing the human meat for consumption and storage, and as she was watching the house. She was surprised. Although looking distressed, gaunt and tired, these two young girls were most attractive. They were also of the age of the young cannibal.

The young Miss Dheg-Dheer had a mixed feeling when she saw those two young girls. In one way her instinct of cannibalism was aroused. She saw in them a promise of tender meals. She blew her nose as she smelled their scent and blood. On the other hand she was delighted to see someone of her own age and kind, with whom she could talk freely....

After a period of quietness, in which the minds, the eyes, and the thoughts of both sides were allowed to explore the other, the eldest of the two young lost girls spoke and said: 'Dear cousin, give us some water. We are in sore need of it.'

The young Miss Dheg-Dheer turned and fetched a dirty pot, opened a curious woven vessel of great capacity and gave the girls water to drink. While they were drinking the water, she turned again and brought them two large well-grilled pieces of fat meat. The distressed girls began to devour the meal quickly, as the young cannibal host watched affectionately the consumption of what might have been the first generosity ever extended by a cannibal to an ordinary human being.

When the two girls had finished eating what they thought was very good goat meat, they thanked and blessed the young girl.

Miss Dheg-Dheer then asked the girls where they had come from and what they were looking for. They told her: 'We are lost. Our father left us. He was a poor man and had no sons. Our mother is dead. We were eleven girls. He had nothing to give us. He took us to the bush yesterday and told us to collect goon nuts for the family. He said he would look after a burden camel while we collected the nuts. "Listen to the camel-bell," he told us, "and come to me when the sun is low." When the sun was low we looked for him and found the camel-bell hanging from a tree, still giving the usual sound as if it were on a camel. Our father had taken the camel and left us. We still do not know where he went. We started to wander and slept last night in the bush. We had nothing to eat. Then as we wandered we saw your house. We were delighted.'

All the time the two girls were talking, Miss Dheg-Dheer was listening with the greatest attention.

'Now tell us about yourself and your parents,' the two girls asked Miss Dheg-Dheer.

Instead of answering the two girls, Miss Dheg-Dheer cried. 'My mother is a cannibal,' she said, 'and when she comes she will eat you.'...

Now feeling curious about the house, and not fully realizing they were in a cannibal's home, the two girls asked about the various vessels in the house. Miss Dheg-Dheer explained: 'That is the water vessel; that other one over there is Baw-Dheer. It contains the best part of human flesh. The other big one contains blood.'

At this, the two girls interrupted: 'Human flesh and blood? Who eats such things?'

'My mother and I eat them,' answered Miss Dheg-Dheer calmly.

'Can't you find other food?' they asked.

'What other food?' questioned Miss Dheg-Dheer.

'The meat and milk of animals,' was their reply.

'Do you eat these?' she asked amazed.

'You should try them; they are delicious,' they said.

'Are they the same as what I just gave you?' she said.

'Didn't you give us goat meat?' they asked.

'No!' she said, 'I gave you the chest and buttocks of a nine-year-old girl.'

Both girls began to vomit. This surprised and troubled Dheg-Dheer's daughter who thought that the human meat was the normal meat for everybody. She felt humiliated and said: 'Why can't people eat the meat of other people?'

'It is immoral to eat one's own kind,' they replied.

'Oh, I did not know that,' she said....

Dheg-Dheer returns from her hunt with a ten-year-old boy whom she devours right then and there, in the house. After her departure, the two young girls come out of the hiding place Miss Dheg-Dheer had shown them. They have seen everything and are horrified.

'There is no sense of mercy in your mother. Look at the handsome boy she hunted down. Oh terrible, terrible. Let us go; let us go. Come with us and we shall be all right.'...

'My mother is very fast and can overtake us in a wink. She also has a sharp nose and is extremely good at following foot-prints. She will find us no matter how fast we travel. Besides, we need provisions. The only way to be safe from her would be if she were dead.'...

'I will kill her tonight and you can help. She is a bad mother. She makes me afraid. I always ask her to spare one boy or one girl for me. She never agrees. She kills every boy and girl and eats them. Some of these children are very beautiful, and I love them. My mother is bad, and we should kill her to-night. Then we may take the house, and the food. Then we may go anywhere—free, free, free! When she comes later, she will eat something. Then she will sleep, because she is tired. Her long ear will be down and she will hear nothing and understand nothing. Then we'll make big fire and put several branding irons in it. When they are really hot, one of us can hold fast to her long ear. The other two can burn her with the hot branding irons, until she dies. Then we will be free, free, free; and we will play, play, play!'...

Dheg-Dheer comes back, carrying a fifteen-year-old girl, whom she devours and whose blood she drinks to refresh herself.

'How sweet and warm it is for the throat.' Then she threw the pot down and fell asleep. Slowly, slowly her long ear sank.

Immediately Dheg-Dheer's daughter released the two girls. Together they lit a big fire and inserted four large branding rods. When these were red hot, they rushed to Dheg-Dheer, who was in a deep trance. One of them grabbed and twisted the arch-cannibal's long ear, and the other two burned her with the hot branding irons. Dheg-Dheer growled loudly, calling unknown people and shouting meaninglessly, and then she died slowly.

As soon as Dheg-Dheer died, the three girls went outside the house, and saw that it was raining heavily. They were delighted, as there had never been rain before in Dheg-Dheer's lifetime in that country. As it thundered, the three girls sang:

'Dheg-Dheer is dead
and there is peace in the land,
Rain is falling in Jigjiga.
Dheg-Dheer is dead
and there is peace in the land,

Somali tradition
Rain is falling in Jigjiga.'

79

Help for the weak

In the days of Urwa ibn al-Ward, poet and warrior of
the Djahiliya or Arab pagan period, the sick, the old and
the weak were abandoned in times of famine. Though
they were not his kinsmen, Urwa at such times gathered
those people together, and busied himself digging drains
around their tents, building fences for them, and clothing
them. He took with him on his raids all those who were
strong enough to go: the sick who were getting well, the
weak who were recovering—and shared the booty with
those who had been left behind. When the famine was
past, when the people had milk in abundance, and when
the bad times had gone by, he took all those he had
Abu-al Faraj
al-Isfahani
Book of Songs
Pre-Islamic period
10th cent.
protected home to their families and, if there was booty,
shared it among them, so that many a time they came
home rich men. This is why Urwa was called 'Urwa of
the poor people'.

80

True piety

There is no piety in turning your faces toward the east
or the west, but he is pious who believeth in God, and
the last day, and the angels, and the scriptures, and the
prophets; who for the love of God disburseth his wealth
to his kindred, and to the orphans, and the needy, and
the wayfarer, and those who ask, and for ransoming;
who observeth prayer, and payeth the legal alms, and
who is of those who are faithful to their engagements
when they have engaged in them, and patient under ills
Koran
Al-Baqara 177
and hardships, and in time of trouble; these are they who
are just, and these are they who fear the Lord.

81

And above all, forget not the poor, but feed them as long
as you can, succour the orphan and judge the widow in
person. Allow not the powerful to have a man die. Put
Vladimir Monomakh
Grand Duke of Kiev
1053-1125
Instruction to his sons
neither the just nor the guilty to death, nor allow them
to put others to death; even if a man be guilty of death,
cause not the loss of a soul.

82

Equal dignity of old and young, rich and poor

The old man's soul has not been taken from him, nor the young man's placed under lock and key.

Youth works with its hands, age with its head.

Even in the Horde the old are respected.
(*'Horde' refers to the Tatar-Mongols and recalls the Mongol yoke.*)

Russian proverbs

Offend not the beggar, he too has a soul.   83

Respect for the stranger
Vladimir Monomakh
Grand Duke of Kiev
1053-1125
Instruction to his sons

Wherever you go, wherever you stay, offer the poor and the traveller food and drink, and above all, honour the stranger whencesoever he comes, whether he be simple, or of good family, or ambassador.   84

The exile

One fine day, people say: 'A stranger, alone, without kith or kin, is dead . . . it was noticed when he had already been dead three days.'... Then they wash him with cold water. That is what happens to any exile like myself.

My tongue speaks, my eyes weep . . . my heart burns at the thought of the many exiles, without kith or kin. My star in the sky, is it perhaps as lonely, as abandoned as I am?

O my Yunus, my Emre! Thou Desperate one! Thou hast no remedy for thy ill. Go, wander through the world, from city to city. Perhaps thou shalt find a man as wretched, as lonely as thyself.

Yunus Emre
Folk-poet
13th cent.
Turkey

                     85

Turkish proverb
15th cent.

A bird finds refuge beneath a bush. As for thee canst thou not even serve as a bush?   86

When it snows, the three-year-old camel groans; who will bewail the death of a poor [stranger, without kith or kin]?

The poor [stranger, without kith or kin] has a broken heart and his speech lacks warmth; the orphan's neck is bent and his face is pale.

They said: 'A poor [stranger, without kith or kin] is dead.' It was not known until three days after his death.

Turkmenian proverbs

Poverty does not kill a man: but it does not make him smile.   87

Avesta, Vendidad
1st cent. B.C.
to 1st cent. A.D.
Persia

Creator of the material world, possessor of Righteousness!
Where, fifthly, is it most unjoyful upon this earth?
Then spoke Ahura Mazda: There indeed, O Spitama
Zarathustra, where the wife and child of a righteous man
go as prisoners along a dusty dry road and raise their
voices in complaint.   88

Injustice

Amharic proverb
Ethiopia

Don't have a child grow up to hate you or an old man,
dying, curse you.
(*Harm no one, and especially not the weak.*)   89

Malagasy proverb

Do not mock the bird caught in a trap.
(*Do not trample upon a defeated man, for you, too, may be
defeated.*)   90

Women and children

*With the coming of Islam, the earlier Arab custom of burying
new-born female babies alive was abolished. Sa'ssa'a, the hero
of the following tale, was a desert chieftain.*

'One day,' said Sa'ssa'a, 'I went out [into the desert] in
search of two of my she-camels, which had strayed away.
In the distance, I saw a camp-fire, and I went towards it,
thinking to rest there awhile. Sometimes the flames
burned higher; sometimes they seemed to die; and I
said: "Lord, do but guide me to that fire, and—I promise
Thee—if there be among those who have lit it any person
in distress, there is nothing I will not do to help him!"
I went on again, and in a little while arrived there....
Before his tent, an old man, hairy and squat, was tending
the fire; the womenfolk were gathered round a woman
in labour, and for three nights they had been at her side.
I greeted them. "Who are you?" asked the old man.
"I am Sa'ssa'a ibn Nadjiya ibn Iqal." "Welcome, Sir;
what brings you to these parts, my friend?" "I am looking
for two she-camels", I replied, "which have disappeared
without trace from my herd." "I myself have found them,"
said he. "And we helped them to give birth. They are
there, both of them, in that nearby group of camels."
Then I asked: "Why are you building up the fire, now

that night has fallen?" "I light it", he said, "for a woman who has been in labour these past three nights." As he spoke, the woman called: "The child is born!" "If it is a boy," said the old man, "I do not know what I shall make of him; but if it is a girl, let me not hear her voice: she must die!" Then I said: "Friend, let her live; she is your daughter, and her life belongs to the Lord!" "No!" he replied, "I shall kill her!" "I beg you, in the Lord's name...." "I see you wish to save her," he said, "then you must buy her from me!" "I will buy her," was my reply. "What will you give me?" "I will give you one of my she-camels." "No!" "I will give you the other, as well." Then he looked at my mount, and said: "Not unless you add that he-camel as well; he is young, and of a fine colour." "He is yours," I said, "with the two she-camels, if you will let me use him to ride home." "Agreed." Thus I bought from him the life of his daughter, for the price of two she-camels which had just given birth, and one he-camel; and I made him swear before God that he would treat her well, according to the laws of kinship, for the rest of her days or until she left the family. Setting off on my way, I said to myself: "This is a generous deed which no Arab has performed before me!" And I swore that henceforward no man should bury his daughter alive, and that I would buy those lives, each for the price of two she-camels and one he-camel. When Islam came, I had already bought three hundred girls, who would otherwise have been buried alive.

Abu-al Faraj
al-Isfahani
Book of Songs
Pre-Islamic period
10th cent.

91

Submission

My fair one with the white cap
Let me go with you through the wide world.
If you should weary of me
Let me be a girdle at your side,
A girdle of braided gold
And adorned with gems.
If the girdle is too heavy for you
Let me be a skylark's feather
And set me in your cap.
If you should weary of the feather
Let me be a wax taper,
Let me be a tallow candle
And set me by your chair.
When you dine, my fair one,
I will shine brightly for you
And men will ask you:
'What light is this?'
'This wax taper

Is a fair maid from my village,
This tallow candle

Romanian folk-song Is my sweetheart of yesteryear.' *92*

Revolt

You, my husband? I, your wife?
Each is a drag on the other
Each in life has a debt to pay
Once it was the men who complained of their wives

Viet-Namese proverb Today, women have had enough of husbands! *93*

*Difference
between men
and women*

*Ewe proverb
Togo*

Men and women differ in many respects. When you see a man you recognize him immediately. There is no need for anyone to describe or explain him to you. The essential characteristic, the main difference between men and women, is speech, knowledge and many other things still.

94

Respect

Russian proverb

A man's wife is his friend, not his servant. *95*

*Manusmriti
Hindi tradition
Sanskrit*

Where women are honoured, there the gods live.

Women are worthy of respect. They are the light of the home. *96*

*Manusmriti
Sanskrit
India*

Where women are honoured, there the gods are pleased; but where they are not honoured, no sacred rite yields rewards. *97*

Contemplation

What are men worth? Three piastre the dozen!
Shut up in a cage like birds, held in the hand
Whereas a woman is worth three hundred

Viet-Namese proverb Installed on a flower-decked mat, for contemplation. *98*

THE SONG OF THE ILL-WED WIFE

I spread the mattress in my bridal chamber with its
    red-draped ceiling.
At night I lay down, a maiden, and in the morning I
    awoke a virgin.
He whom they have given me for a husband is a mere boy,
He can neither embrace nor make love like a husband.
Me, the fair, they have given me a mere boy.
It was a wicked thing to do.

. . . .

When I am dead, let my grave be dug by the roadside,
That passers-by may say, 'Poor girl, whose marriage was
    her misfortune'.
In future at least let girls be given to those they love.
Me, the fair.

*Folk-song
Turkey*
                                   99

Woman's fate

Mother darling, little mother
Did you think about me never?
Handed me to stranger folk,
Like a stone dropped in a river.

Sing your songs while sing you may,
Once wed, you'll change your tune,
No singing for you then, my pet,
But worry, late and soon.

Mother wants to marry me,
To a man I hate.
I would rather drown myself,
Than have him for a mate.

My husband beat
And hammered me
He got his foot upon my neck—
'It doesn't hurt,' said she.

*Chastushki
(Folk-poetry)
Russia*
    100

Woman's rights

If a woman dislikes her husband, if she will have nothing to do with him, it is called 'rejection of intercourse'; she must pay him twice the bride-price....

If a woman is left behind by her husband who goes away to perform a religious duty or to be a hermit or for some other pious activity, she must wait for him for eight years. If he leaves her in order to become a scholar and to gather learning, she must wait for six years. If he leaves her to earn money, becoming a merchant or sailing abroad, she must wait for ten years. If he leaves her just to find a [new] wife, she must wait for three years. Now, when the husband does not send his wife money, she is allowed to marry some other man. If a husband leaves his wife to make a trip, a visit to a country far away, she must wait for him for four years; if he does not come back within the period of four years, she is allowed to take another husband.

*Kutāraçāstra code
14th cent.
Java*
    101

The male lion is truly a lion; why should not the same be true of the female lion [the lioness]?

**Turkish proverbs
15th cent.**

It is better that I should be orphaned of a father with his hundred sheep, than of a mother with nothing but her thimble. *102*

**Provision
to protect women**

In all other marriages he prohibited dowries; the bride was to bring with her three changes of raiment, household stuff of small value, and nothing else. For he did not wish that marriage should be a matter of profit or price, but that man and wife should dwell together for the delights of love and the getting of children. *103*

**Plutarch's Lives,
Solon
45(50)-125**

**Book of Wisdom
Ptolemaic period
Ancient Egypt**

Do not show that thy wife has offended [thee]. Put her away decently and let her take her possessions with her. *104*

**Hebrew Bible
Deuteronomy 27**

Cursed be he that perverteth the judgment of the stranger, fatherless, and widow: and all the people shall say, Amen. *105*

**Marriage means
free mutual consent**

Canon 1081. § 1. Marriage is contracted by the legitimately manifested consent of two parties who are qualified by law to enter into such contracts; no substitute for this consent can be supplied by any human power.

§ 2. Matrimonial consent is an act of will whereby each party concedes and accepts the perpetual and exclusive right over the body for the execution of acts apt as such for the generation of children. *106*

Canon law

**Reasons why
marriage may
be invalid**

Canon 1083. § 1. Error concerning the identity of the person with whom one wants to contract marriage renders marriage null and void.

§ 2. Error concerning any quality of the person, though such quality caused one to contract marriage, renders marriage invalid only in two cases:
1. If the error concerning a certain quality amounts to an error in the person;
2. If one contracts with a person whom he believed to be free, while in fact that person is a slave strictly so called. *107*

Canon law

Canon 1087. § 1. Marriage is also invalid if contracted under the influence of force or grave fear which an outside agency unjustly exercised over a person so that he was forced to choose marriage as a means to free himself from the force or fear.

§ 2. No other fear entails the nullity of marriage though it caused the contract to be made.   *108*

Canon law

Dignity of women

One of those who promoted the 'Age of Reform' in Hungary addresses his countrywomen:

To the women of our country who are great-hearted.

Worthy daughters of my fatherland, allow me, in token of my respect and affection, to dedicate this small work to you. Grant it graciously your protection, although it is said to be intended rather for men. I propose to speak of credit (*credit in connexion with the system of granting loans on landed property, which was at that time a revolutionary innovation*) and all that springs from it, of honour, the sacred nature of the plighted word, uprightness in deeds, a subject which cannot be any more foreign to you women than to us men, since so many fair and admirable things which elevate humanity are the work of your sex. It is you who carry in your arms the little children, and make them into good citizens; it is from the nobility of your mien that man derives the strength of his character and his courage. And when his life, devoted to the service of the fatherland, draws to its close, it is you again who place a wreath on his forehead. You are the guardian angels of civic virtue and patriotism, which—believe me—without you could not flourish or else would soon wither, for it is you who bring charm and life wherever you go. It is you who enable the dust to rise to the sky, and mortals to immortality.... All hail and thanks to you!   *109*

Istvan Széchenyi
1791-1860
Hungary

Russian proverb   After consulting your pillow, ask also of your wife.   *110*

Status of women
in the Ukraine

There, then, contrary to the habits and usage of all nations, it is sometimes the girl who asks for the man in marriage.   *111*

Beauplan
Description d'Ukraine
1660, France

*Status of women
in Russia*

And be not so foolishly presumptuous as to go inspecting two or three prospective brides, for a girl is a human being like yourself, and not a horse.

Pososkov
Paternal Testament
Early 18th cent.
Russia

In domestic matters, your wife above all should be consulted, for the wife was given by God to her husband to help, not to be subservient to him. *112*

*Wives and children
of those condemned*

The wives and children of those condemned to hard labour for life, or to deportation or to solitary confinement . . . are to be allowed, if they so desire, to live on the land brought with their dowries. If one of these wives wishes to marry again with the consent of the Synod, she shall be given liberty to do so. And for her maintenance and that of her children she shall be given the lawful portion of her husband's movable and immovable estate. *113*

Decree
of 25 May 1753
Russia

Domingo Faustino
Sarmiento
1811-88
Argentina

The level of a people's civilization can be measured by the social position occupied by its women. *114*

Self-discovery

HELMER. Before all else you are a wife and mother.
NORA. That I no longer believe. I believe that before all else I am a human being just as much as you are—or at least that I should try to become one.
·HELMER. You talk like a child. You don't understand the society in which you live.
NORA. No, I do not. But now I shall try to learn. I must make up my mind which is right—society or I. *115*

H. Ibsen
A Doll's House
1879

Respect

If I were born a woman, I would rise in rebellion against any pretension on the part of man that woman is born to be his plaything. I have mentally become a woman in order to steal into her heart. I could not steal into my wife's heart until I decided to treat her differently than I used to do, and so I restored to her all her rights by dispossessing myself of all my so-called rights as her husband. *116*

Mahatma Gandhi
1869-1948

Mahatma Gandhi
1869-1948

I realized that the wife is not the husband's bondslave, but his companion and his helpmate, and an equal partner in all his joys and sorrows—as free as the husband to choose her own path. *117*

It is a cause for satisfaction that there is a spiritual entity in all things and that the male and female principles in things and people are harmoniously linked. Similarly, man and woman are by nature companions on an equal footing and there are no such distinctions between them as higher or lower, master or slave. People think, however, that women should obey men as if they were their slaves; this is because engrossed as we are in Confucianism, we have wandered from our country's true path.

Zankō Masuho
1655-1742
The Path of the Gods
Japan

118

The way to make a woman happy is neither to take her to entertainments, nor to clothe her in brocade, embroidered fabrics and belts adorned with precious stones, not yet to surround her with serving women to give her a stately air. A woman will be happy if her husband himself behaves well, as a reward for her faithfulness, if he spends less on himself and avoids disturbance and worry for his family, so that his wife may be free from domestic cares. If the husband realizes this, his wife can find happiness in putting up with poverty and bearing persecution for the sake of justice, in company with him. The way to make a woman happy is to encourage her generosity, and not to flatter her base, despicable vanity.

Kanzō Uchimura
1861-1930
On Independence
Japan

119

Women's rights

The masses cannot be drawn into political life unless women are brought to play their part in it.... Working women and peasant women are oppressed by the capitalist system, and, moreover, even in the most democratic bourgeois republics they are still deprived of civic rights, for under the law they have no equality with men, and —and worst of all—they are still 'household slaves', for they have to toil at the most trivial, rough, laborious and soul-destroying of work—kitchen and household drudgery—usually by themselves.

The Bolshevist Soviet Revolution is eradicating the oppression and inequality of women more thoroughly than any other party or revolution in the world has dared to do. All inequality between men and women has now been abolished by law in Soviet Russia. The Soviet régime has completely wiped out inequality in family law . . . which is a particularly infamous, base and hypocritical form of inequality.

Lenin
Speech on
International
Women Workers' Day
1921

120

*Women
in modern society*

A society which contents itself with the acquisition of present-day skills by one of the sexes is depriving itself of more than half its strength. A nation desiring progress and civilization must understand this truth and its implications. The lack of success of our social structure is due to the contempt in which we have held our women. Destiny metes out our span of life, but to live is to be active. And if only some of the members of a social organism are active, whilst the others are inactive, that organism becomes paralysed. If a social organism is to work and succeed in life, it must satisfy the required conditions and give itself every chance. If, then, our society needs science and technology, men and women must gain them equally. Who does not know that division of labour dominates life, as it does all fields of endeavour? Within this general division of labour, women must carry out the tasks falling to them, but among these tasks is participation in the general activities essential to the common prosperity and happiness of all.

Kemal Pasha Atatürk
1923

Housework is but the least and the least important, of woman's duties.   *121*

NOTHING ON EARTH IS CLEVERER THAN THE FEMALE SEX

See, my grandchild! As I teach you, and you children in the older class teach each other, you think: We men are clever. If you see womankind and watch how four or five of them sit together and tell each other things, you think: Instead of chatting here, they ought to get up, go home and cut grass. As you talk like this to each other, you think in your own minds: They are stupid and ignorant. See, my grandchild, they are not stupid. Nothing in the whole world is cleverer than the female sex. Know this, if you are as other men, you are not as intelligent as a woman. It is only that she is given into your charge. If it were you who were given into her charge, she would surpass you in intelligence. Therefore I tell you: a woman will hold a thing in her head better than you. See, my grandson, you live together and she is your wife. Drive a cow into the house and let her milk it. Now if you feel a bit hungry during the night, because you have not eaten your fill, then you say to her: If only you had cooked a milk dish, we would have easily eaten our fill! And she says to you: Oh no, there was not enough to cook a dish with. Get some more!

See, my grandson, you must realize that a woman is intelligent. For she wants to keep the milk until it is

Ashanti fetish
protecting pregnant
women and unborn
children

sour, so that when she puts it into the food it is strong
enough to give a good taste to it. But you just listen and
say nothing. The next day, when the sun rises she says to
you: Help me and put out a piece of banana branch for
the cow, so that it can chew it slowly, while I go to fetch
grass. Then while you are cutting that piece of banana
branch, you think: All right, I'll examine the calabash
to see whether she was deceiving me when she said there
was no more milk in it, or if there really isn't any in
it. When you have cut the piece of banana branch, you
seize the calabash, you pick it up like that and then put
it down again. You don't drink any of it, Oh no! When
she comes, you say nothing, get up and go out to where
the men are. See, my grandson, the woman seeks out the
calabash and thinks: I wonder whether when he had
cut the piece of banana branch, he took up and looked
at the calabash? She goes, finds it and notices that you
have turned it round, put it down in another position
and were unable to set it down as she did.

If you do this four times, the woman will speak of it
behind your back. Then if you are a little rude to her
she will go to her family; and if you and they then discuss
the matter, and the woman is not properly trained—no
one has told her 'You must not say such things'—her
education having been neglected, she says: Get up and
go away from here, monster, you who lift up women's
calabashes. With such words she brings you into great
disrepute and you are hated among men. They curse
you and say: What is the point of touching women's
calabashes? And the women speak of you and say:
I should not like to be married to a man who lifts women's
calabashes!

See, my grandson, as a man you are not capable of
setting down anything anywhere so that you can see,
as a woman can, whether it has been touched.

Therefore I tell you: a woman is clever. And if you
respect what is women's business your reputation will
not suffer. And your wife will honour you, because
she knows that you have learnt to keep quiet like other
men.

Chagga tradition
Tanzania

122

Children

Children belong to no one. They belong neither to their
parents, nor to society. They are tributary only to their
future freedom. But in children this freedom is not yet real
but only potential. Accordingly, society, whose future
depends on the education and upbringing of children
and so is not only entitled but obliged to protect them,

is sole guardian of the children of both sexes. . . . The maintenance, upbringing and education of children should be provided on an equal basis for all, at the expense of society.

The old, the disabled and the sick, cared for and respected, and enjoying full political and social rights, shall be generously treated and maintained at the expense of society.

*Bakunin
1814-76
Russia*

123

When you have a child, you must not let it suffer from hunger, since it came in order to brighten your life. You must not beat it, but make it happy. You must not lose your temper with your son, you must not ill-treat him. Then only will you want to have others, and your children will flourish.

*Consideration
for the mother*

*Guaraní tradition
Central part
of South America*

It is not a good thing for a woman to have too many children; if we are unduly prolific and from love for the mother of our children we do not wish to have any more of them, we must look after her and teach her the rules of sterility.

124

When I eat melon,
I remember my children;
When I eat chestnuts,
Even more do I recall them.
Whence did they come to me?
Before my eyes they will linger,
And I cannot sleep in peace.

Envoy

*Yamanoue Okura
7th cent.
Japan*

What use to me
Silver, gold and jewels?
No treasure can surpass children!

125

Rights of the child

*Kutāraçāstra code
14th cent.
Java*

A child under the age of ten years who does not know the difference between good and evil should not be punished by the authorities in country or village if he misbehaves.

126

THE HEAVEN MAN SENDS US A MALE KID

The legend of Rasio who fell from Heaven is told as follows. Once members of the Maleki clan were gathered together in their field. Suddenly a child appeared among them whom they had not noticed. A dignitary of the clan brought a sheep and offered it as a sacrifice to the Heaven Man in gratitude and took the child in. Thereafter the child was called Rasio (*the sacrificed*). Rasio married only one woman and six sons and seven daughters were born to them.

The expiatory offering of a sheep, mentioned in the song of Rasio, was made only by particularly rich people, after the circumcision of a boy. Otherwise, the preserved contents of a sheep's stomach from a former victim sufficed as an addition to the purifying water.

The old man sings:

Ho, silence, great silence, hey, ho, the great silence, heh! Hi, yeh, yeh, yeh eheh heh. So let us give thanks then. Indeed, let us thank the Heaven Man, let us thank Him, who guides our hand, for our home. He watches over the paternal homestead. Yes, he watches over it.

Yes, it was He, yes, it was He who sent Rasio to us. Yes indeed, yes indeed. And he was taken in by Ljangemi.

Ljangemi took him into our midst. Yes indeed, brother, yes indeed, brother. And he found things for us. He found for us the yōro-ōro herb. Yes indeed, yes indeed. And also the herb ipasa.

He chose the purifying sheep. It is the sheep that purifies Rasio. Yes, it is they, yes, it is they who prospered with us.

So let us give thanks for His remembering of us—that He thought of us. And as He thought of us, the yōro-ōro herb shot up. Yes indeed. Yes indeed. And also the mkengera herb. That is what flourishes among us, that is what flourishes among us. Yes this, yes this and spreads among us. It was the Heaven Man who made this herb grow. And it shot up and flourished and ripened and did not wither.

Hi, yeh, yeh, yeh, eheh, heh! So thank Him then. So let us thank Him in Heaven. Yes, it is He, yes it is He, the one who guides our hands. We want to thank Him deeply....

The adviser explains:

Listen carefully, my young brother. The Heaven Man is Lord over us all. You heard your grandfather say to you: 'Lift up your hand to Him, beseech the Heaven Man! He is our sustainer, the Lord supreme. Our ancestors, who begot us, cannot reach him.'

When they were labouring to beget us and placed us in the womb, their support, that is their sustainer, was there to see that they set us in the womb properly. He helped them well and they thanked Him.

Look you, my young brother, when He sent Rasio [He, the Heaven Man], Ljangemi did not know where he had been born. He did not know who had begotten him, did not know who had slaughtered the goat for him to beget him.

Then there was this one picked him down—snap! As if you were picking fruit from a tree. When he [Ljangemi] had got over his astonishment, he said. 'That's the Heaven Man! He's giving me a child.' And he stretched out his hands, brought a goat and offered it up for the son delivered to him. He took him in with care and made him his son. And it was he who told him the names of the purifying herbs, which serve to purify children. He told him about the herb called yōro-ōro and the herb called ipasa. And he said to him: 'This is what propitiatory water for purifying children has to be sprinkled with here among us!'

And great was their gladness.

And there at Ljangemi's, he [Rasio] sent forth children as numerous as bees. And they increased Ljangemi's clan [the Maleki] so that it became big. He [Rasio] became the great gatherer (*i.e., very rich*).

Ljangemi took his food sitting down (*i.e., no longer needed to bestir himself for it*) since the Heaven Man had visited him to such good effect and given him this son Rasio.

And he loved him more than his own begotten children.

Look you, my young brother, since then any child that has been in need of help has been well cared for by us in Moschi.

Act likewise. If a child comes to you, do not turn it away; put it with your own! If it belongs to another and finds its way to you, take good care of it. Should the person to whom it belongs come, may he thank you fittingly and reward you for taking it in and saving it from being eaten by a leopard.

That is the bond we have here that goes back to the one who was sent down from heaven and came to Ljangemi.

Thereafter people opened their hearts and said: 'People's children are heaven's and valued highly.'

It is the Heaven Man who guides it with such care until it reaches your homestead, and as long as it is without the person to whom it belongs, it fetches water for you.

But you go asking throughout the land and saying:
'Whose child is it that has found its way to me? As it
has spent three months here and the person to whom it
belongs has not been found, whose can it be then?'

So you inquire everywhere until the chief says to you:
'Keep it; do not scare it away! And you keep it with
you. And since the person to whom it belongs cannot
be found, it becomes your own. The Heaven Man brought
it to you.'   *127*

Chagga tradition
Tanzania

Oneself: the responsible individual, the indomitable self

*Negation of
independent
existence*

बाळादेक मणीयस्क मुतेॐ नेन दृश्यते ।
तत् परिव्वज्जीयसी देवता सा मम प्रिया ॥

The One is finer than a hair; verily, the One cannot
be seen. Therefore is that deity, whose grasp is firm,
dear unto me. This blessed, unaging, immortal one
[dwells] in a mortal's house. He for whom she was made
is prone; he who made her has grown old. Thou art
woman, thou art man, thou art boy, and thou art also
girl. As an old man, thou dost totter on a staff. Being
born, thou becomest of all forms. Yea also, he is their
father, he is their son, he their eldest [brother] and their
youngest. The one God, indeed, entering the mind—he
is the first born within the embryo.   *128*

Atharvaveda X
2200-1800 B.C.
Sanskrit

The universe has no human affection,
Everything in the world is to it as a straw dog.
The holy man has no human affection,
The people are to him as a straw dog.
The universe is like a forge bellows;
Empty, it is not flattened,
The more it is moved, the more it exhales,
The more one talks about it, the less one grasps it,
It is better to become part of it.   *129*

6th cent. B.C.
Lao-tzu
Tao-Te-Ching
China

Man—independent, inventive, responsible

CHORUS

Stroph I

Many the forms of life,
Fearful and strange to see,
But man supreme stands out,
For strangeness and for fear.
He, with the wintry gales,
O'er the foam-crested sea,
'Mid billows surging round,
Tracketh his way across.
Earth, of all Gods, from ancient days, the first,
Mightiest and undecayed.
He, with his circling plough,
Wears ever year by year.

Antistroph I

The thoughtless tribe of birds,
The beasts that roam the fields,
The finny brood of ocean's depths,
He takes them all in nets of knotted mesh,
    Man, wonderful in his skill.
And by his arts he holds in sway,
The wild beasts on the mountain's height;
And brings the neck-encircling yoke
On horse with shaggy mane,
Or bull that walks untamed upon the hills.

Stroph II

And speech, and thought as swift as wind,
And tempered mood for higher life of states,
These he has learnt, and how to flee
The stormy sleet of frost unkind,
The tempest thunderbolts of Zeus.
So all-preparing, unprepared
He meeteth naught the coming days may bring;
Only from Hades, still
He fails to find a refuge at the last,
Though skill of art may teach him to escape
    from depths of fell disease incurable.

Antistroph II

So, gifted with a wondrous might,
Above all fancy's dreams, with skill to plan,
Now unto evil, now to good,
He wends his way. Now holding fast the laws,
His country's sacred rights,
That rest upon the oath of Gods on high,

High in the state he stands.
An outlaw and an exile he who loves
The thing that is not good,
In wilful pride of soul:
Ne'er may he sit beside my hearth,
Ne'er may my thoughts be like to his,
Who worketh deeds like this.

Sophocles
Antigone
5th cent. B.C.
Trans. by
E. H. Plumptre

130

Russian proverb

Everything stems from man—and to him is all credit due.

131

Turkish proverb
16th cent.

The babe that is born an orphan will contrive to cut its own umbilical cord.

132

Condition of man

No one is condemned by nature to infamy.

No state, no condition can dishonour a man. On the contrary, it is men themselves who belittle others and make them a laughing stock. Man's glory is the love of his fellows. If you honour someone, you would do anything rather than belittle him.

Ewe proverb
Togo

133

Free choice is given to every man; if he wishes to take the path of righteousness and to be just, the choice is his, and if he wishes to take the path of evil and to be wicked, the choice is his. As it is written in the Torah: 'Behold, the man is become as one of us, to know good and evil.'

Maimonides
Hilchot Teshuva 5
12th cent.

134

Akan proverb
Ghana

The beneficence of man depends upon man.

135

*No power
over the spirit*

DIALOGUE BETWEEN THE TYRANT AND THE SAGE

What is it, then, that disturbs and terrifies the multitude —the tyrant and his guards? By no means. What is by nature free, cannot be disturbed or restrained by anything but itself; but its own convictions disturb it. Thus, when the tyrant says to any one: 'I will chain your leg', he who chiefly values his leg cries out for pity; while he who chiefly values his own free will says: 'If you imagine it for your interest, chain it.'
  'What! do you not care?'
  'No, I do not care.'

'I will show you that I am master.'

'You? How should you? Zeus has set me free. What! do you think he would suffer his own son to be enslaved? You are master of my carcass; take it.'

'So that, when you come into my presence, you pay no regard to me?'

'No, but to myself; or, if you will have me recognize you also, I will do it as if you were a piece of furniture.' *136*

Epictetus
Discourses
1st cent.

*Personal
responsibility*

HENRY:

So, if a son that is by his father sent about merchandise, do sinfully miscarry upon the sea, the imputation of his wickedness, by your rule, should be imposed upon his father that sent him. Or if a servant, under his master's command, transporting a sum of money, be assailed by robbers, and die in many irreconciled iniquities, you may call the business of the master the author of the servant's damnation. But this is not so. The King is not bound to answer the particular endings of his soldiers, the father of his son, nor the master of his servant; for they purpose not their death, when they purpose their services. Besides, there is no king, be his cause never so spotless, if it come to the arbitrement of swords, can try it out with all unspotted soldiers. Some, peradventure, have on them the guilt of premeditated and contrived murder; some, of beguiling virgins with the broken seals of perjury; some, making the wars their bulwark, that have before gored the gentle bosom of peace with pillage and robbery. Now, if these men have defeated the law, and outrun native punishment, though they can outstrip men, they have no wings to fly from God. War is his beadle, war is his vengeance; so that here men are punished, for before-breach of the King's laws in now the King's quarrel. Where they feared the death, they have borne life away: and where they would be safe, they perish. Then if they die unprovided, no more is the King guilty of their damnation, than he was before guilty of those impieties, for the which they are now visited. Every subject's duty is the King's, but every subject's soul is his own. Therefore should every soldier in the wars do as every sick man in his bed, wash every mote out of his conscience; and dying so, death is to him advantage; or not dying, the time was blessedly lost wherein such preparation was gained. And in him that escapes, it were not sin to think, that making God so free an offer, he let him outlive that day, to see his greatness, and to teach others how they should prepare. *137*

Shakespeare
King Henry V
Act IV, Scene i
1599

In 1856 the Emperor Theodore, after conquering Choa, prohibited the execution, hitherto legal, of a murderer's relatives:

He made a law reading: Assassins abound in Choa; let the murderer alone be put to death, but not his relatives, unless one has instigated the crime or taken part in the quarrel; they must not be executed merely as the father or the brother of the murderer.

Having defeated the rebel Agaw Negusé, he pardoned his soldiers:

He pardoned the soldiers who were with [Agaw Negusé] —all poor devils he had forced to become guerrillas.

Chronicles Ethiopia But all the rebel chiefs had their hands and feet cut off and were left to die.

138

Yehuda Levai Son of Bezalel 1512-1609, Prague Every being rules over himself, for of all beings, only animals are worthy to be ruled by others. It is a primary axiom that a being is his own ruler. *139*

What is man, that Thou art mindful of him?
And the son of man, that Thou thinkest of him?
Yet Thou hast made him but little lower than the angels,
And hast crowned him with glory and honour.
Hebrew Bible Psalms 8 Thou hast made him to have dominion over the works of Thy hands. *140*

Against anger and impatience, self-control

THE HEAD OF A MAN IS A HIDING PLACE, A RECEPTACLE

The teacher sings:

Yes, indeed, man, yes, indeed, you man with the shield!
Yes, indeed, man, yes, indeed, you man with the shield!
The head of a man, indeed, yes, is a long-term store!
It is a crack in the rock used for storage.
If you notice that some uninitiated boy, immature as a red plum, is a chatterbox, hide everything in your head.
Ha, indeed, the child's nurse, she too is talkative. But your head is the crack in the rock for storage. Ah, yes!
Ha, surely one of the children will tell tales to you and say: 'Your mother spoke of you behind your back', or say: 'That uninitiated girl of yours spoke of you.'
Then your head is the long-term container to store this away. Let us tell the child in his lessons, the head of the flute player is a crack in the rock for storing what is said.

The assistant teacher explains:

Mark well, my younger brother, beware of the idle chatter which goes round the farm.

See, when you bring back meat, then perhaps you will cut a large piece off for a small child. When it has eaten it, out of sheer joy it will tell you about home; saying: 'This woman cursed you and swore.'

But you have a head in which to store things; do not fly at the woman. That child surely invented the whole story, when it was so pleased with the meal which you gave it as a sign of love. See, whether it heard the woman saying something other than it claimed, or really heard her curse you, store it in the back of your mind and do not burn down your farm.

Or another time you come home, and another child says to you when you are alone: Papa, I have something to say to you: when you had gone away she got together with her mother-in-law, and they swore about you and said: 'The lazy fellow, he goes off early in the morning from the farm and is making slaves of us. We do not sleep in the bushes, but we are his swine!' If you heard that you would surely be tempted to hit her and your mother-in-law. But if you hit her, your home life is doomed. For this reason the old teacher tells you: The head of a man is a storage place, a loft! Do not listen to the idle chatter of little children. When you are grown up and have acquired serenity, you must store everything that people say to you in your head and not blurt it out in anger. Store it in your head until you have made your decision. And about what you notice yourself, question her carefully, in your own home. But if you beat your wife in anger about tales told behind your back, and later find out that they are untrue, and you become a continual irritation to her, and afterwards she comes to you, argues with you and wins the argument, she will be lost to you; she will bear another man's children, and keep another man's house and the old teacher is left alone with his teaching which you have scorned and wasted. And for this reason the old teacher says to you: Keep quiet! Store what you hear from others in your head and wait until your father and mother ask you about it, and they will tell you, let it be; she is our young mother who looks after the household; we will guide her back to the right path.

Chagga tradition
Tanzania

141

Decorum

A former serf, become official, contractor and economist, under Peter the Great, counsels his son:

Greet the nobleman according to his nobility and the rich man according to his wealth, for nobility and wealth are given by God; but do not despise the poor man or deny him your greeting. . . . And even if a child greets you, greet him also in return.

. . . But above all, do not allow yourself to insult any man, rich or poor, or cause him mortification. . . . And if even you see one who is extremely stupid, beware of insult to him or condemnation, for the insult would include God himself, who so created him.   *142*

Pososkov
Paternal Testament
Early 18th cent.
Russia

*Freedom
and arithmetic*

Man's only real concern, it seems, is to prove constantly to himself that he really is a human being and not just a cog in a machine, to prove it even at the price of his own suffering. . . . You say nobody wants to take away my free will, they only want to arrange things so that my free will coincides freely with my best interests, with the laws of nature and with arithmetic. What sort of free will is that, when it is reduced to two times two equals four? Two times two will still be four without my willing it. Is that all free will is?   *143*

Dostoevsky
Notes from
Underground
1864

Bow, but don't bow down.

Each man is a lock and each has a right key.

Russian proverbs

Judge a man not by his build but by his discourse.   *144*

*Instinct,
respect, love,
honour*

THE ODYSSEY OF THE VALIANT GOROO-BÂ-DICKO

In his youth, Goroo-Bâ-Dicko was fighting under the command of a great war chief. Once he arrived, at nightfall, with the rest of the host, at a well near which stood a Fulani woman, as beautiful as an angel. The warriors captured her and carried her off to their camp. The chief wanted her for himself. He commanded the woman to lie down alone, away from the soldiers, where no one could come near her.

Time passed, and all the warriors were haunted by the woman's beauty. Goroo-Bâ-Dicko could not sleep. Despite the chief's orders, he crept away and approached the beautiful prisoner. He carried her off at the risk of his life, took her on his horse, and rode out of the camp.

The man and the woman journeyed through the night.
The hard nipples of the woman's breasts pressed into
the young warrior's back. The warrior, though consumed
by desire and even by real love, curbed his passion,
quenching the feelings aroused by the contact of the
woman. The two riders arrived on their horse at the
edge of the well where the woman had been captured.
The man bade her dismount, and said: 'Do you know
this well?' In a voice broken by emotion, the woman
replied simply and calmly: 'Yes, it is the well of my
village.'

The warrior, though visibly agitated, steeled himsel
to say to her: 'You are free.'

Time passed, and with its passing many changes took
place. Goroo-Bâ-Dicko had news at last of the woman,
who was the wife of a great warrior. But since his encounter
with the woman at the well, the thought of her preyed on
Goroo-Bâ-Dicko's mind. He lost his strength, and with
it the zest for life. The image of the beautiful woman
never left him. He fell ill. Wishing to find a remedy for
his malady, he went to consult a soothsayer, who said:
'Young man, I see the cause of your malady. One night,
you carried off on your horse a young woman of matchless
beauty. The hard nipples of her breasts touched your
back, arousing all the power of your desire. It is this
thwarted desire, the image of which haunts you, that is
making you sick. Until you have lain with this woman,
you will never recover; you will die of your malady.'

Goroo-Bâ-Dicko set out to look for the woman he had
met at the well. He went to the village. He had no difficulty
in finding where the husband of his former prisoner lived.
The first man he asked pointed out the dwelling of the
woman's husband, who was also a warrior of renown
in his country. He found the woman's husband in the
midst of his followers, under a crowded pent-house.
Goroo-Bâ-Dicko dismounted and greeted his host, who
received him as though he were a prince. His slaves
ran up and eagerly took charge of the traveller's horse.
When the pent-house was empty, Goroo-Bâ-Dicko said
to his host: 'One night, our warriors captured a beautiful
woman near the well in your village. She was to have
gone to the warrior chief commanding us. The same
night, I managed to approach the woman, bring her
out of the camp, and take her back to the place where
our warriors had captured her.

'As we rode, the breasts of the woman, whom I had
taken on my horse with me, pressed into my back, arousing
"all the power of my desire". I fell ill. Seeking a remedy

for my sickness, I consulted a soothsayer, who told me that until I had lain with this woman I should never recover; without that I should die.'

The woman's husband listened to all his guest had to say. He repressed his first impulse, which was one of righteous anger. He thought for a long time. At last he said: 'Would you recognize this woman if you saw her?'

Goroo-Bâ-Dicko said that he would. The woman's husband went on: 'Well! She is my wife. This evening, I am supposed to go to spend the night in her house. Put on my clothes and shoes. When supper-time comes, she will bring you various dishes. You must eat no more than two mouthfuls of each, for that is what I do. When you are alone with her, you must keep your garment on. You must wait for my wife to make a gesture. When she desires you, she will undo your garment herself. Be careful to do exactly as I have said. It is essential that she should think she is with her own husband.'

Goroo-Bâ-Dicko did all that he was told, and found himself with the beautiful woman from the well, desire for whom was the cause of his sickness.

At last there only remained for him to satisfy his desire. At midnight, the woman did as she was accustomed. But, for the first time, her husband refused her caress. The garment was so tightly fastened that it would not come undone. Four times she repeated her gesture, and each time the man she thought was her husband refused her. Wounded in her pride as a woman who knew she was beautiful and adored by her husband, she took no further notice of the man.

Under cover of the half-light of the approaching morning, Goroo-Bâ-Dicko departed, and the beautiful woman did not realize that she had had to do with a man other than her husband. He went to see the husband of his 'mistress' for a night, who asked him calmly: 'Now have you had what you desired for so long?'

Goroo-Bâ-Dicko replied promptly: 'More than I could ever have hoped for, as you will see from the state the bed is in—broken under the strain of our passionate embraces.'

Despite this somewhat uncouth remark, the woman's husband remained perfectly calm; he even showed towards his guest a friendliness that was not feigned. Suppressing all jealousy, he played his part to the end.

But this attitude, dictated no doubt by deep gratitude towards the man who had set his wife free, put Goroo-Bâ-Dicko in a difficult position. Because of the confidence that had been placed in him, his duty, first towards his host and then towards the woman's honour, was to behave with the same magnanimity.

The next night, the husband was alone with his wife in the house. The wife reproached him bitterly for his behaviour on the previous night. Indignantly, she accused her husband of having wounded her woman's pride. Goroo-Bâ-Dicko's host therefore realized that the Fula horseman had committed no sin with his wife. The woman's honour was saved; so also was the magnanimity of Goroo-Bâ-Dicko, which was equalled only by the confidence placed in it. The firm courage shown by Goroo-Bâ-Dicko was matched by the calm confidence shown by his host.

Goroo-Bâ-Dicko went back to his village. Time passed, and finally he married. His wife bore him a baby boy, beautiful as the morning star. On the day of the child's baptism, when all was joy and gladness, a horseman with a large and boisterous following appeared before Goroo-Bâ-Dicko. It was the husband of the woman at the well, coming to visit his friend. When the latter saw who it was, he ordered his slaves to attend to the traveller's horse. They hastened to do so; and oxen, sheep, goats and camels were killed in honour of the husband of the woman at the well.

At last his followers left Goroo-Bâ-Dicko's pent-house, and he was alone with his guest, who without further delay explained the reason for his visit. 'It is a serious matter', he said, 'that brings me here. My wife is sick and at death's door. I have consulted the soothsayers, and they tell me that the only thing that can save her from certain death is the blood of your son. So I have come to ask for your son, whose blood is the only remedy that can restore my wife to health.'

Goroo-Bâ-Dicko replied: 'Be good enough to wait here. I shall return in a moment.' He went and told his wife the tragic story. With superb courage, she said to her husband: 'You cannot refuse to give him the child. He has come to you in unquestioning trust. Give him our son, so that he may save the life of his wife with the child's blood.'

To the amazement of the assembled villagers, the baptismal ceremony was stopped. The child was placed in charge of the slave who accompanied Goroo-Bâ-Dicko's guest. He, however, had brought with them a sheep, which was tied up outside the village.

Satisfied, the two men departed, the slave carrying the baby. He walked ahead, his master following. When they reached the place where the sheep was tied up, they killed it, and soaked the baby's clothes in its blood. The master told his slave to go back to Goroo-Bâ-Dicko and give him his child's bloodstained clothes. The slave did as he was ordered. When he came into the presence of Goroo-Bâ-Dicko, he delivered his master's message, saying: 'Here are the bloodstained clothes of your son. He has been killed, and his blood collected. My master bids me to thank you.' When he had given his message, the slave returned to his master. He took charge of the baby again, and the child was secretly taken to the village where the husband of the woman at the well lived. This woman had borne a baby boy at the same time as Goroo-Bâ-Dicko's wife.

The two children, who were like twins, were both entrusted to her care, and she brought them up with the same motherly love. They grew up together, and when they were men they always went to battle together. They were both successful warriors, whose fame reached beyond the borders of their own land. Everywhere they were feared, and everybody talked about the two sons of Goroo-Bâ-Dicko's guest.

One day, Goroo-Bâ-Dicko's friend, accompanied by his 'two sons', went again to visit him. The sons, by a fortunate chance, were as like as two peas; they might have been twins. Goroo-Bâ-Dicko's followers, remembering what had happened on the previous occasion, rose up against the visitor. 'The first time you came here,' they said, 'you asked for Goroo-Bâ-Dicko's son, whom you sacrificed so that you could save your wife's life with his blood. What fresh misfortune do you bring us now?'

Goroo-Bâ-Dicko reproved his followers sharply. He ordered his slaves to attend to the strangers' horses. As before, oxen, sheep, goats, camels and so on were killed in honour of the visitors. Goroo-Bâ-Dicko was even more cordial than he had been on the first occasion. He behaved with sincere, wholehearted friendliness, and was delighted to see his friend again.

When his visitor was rested and refreshed, he asked to see Goroo-Bâ-Dicko and his wife. In the presence of the whole village he then said to his host's wife: 'Your son is not dead. I only wanted to put you and your husband to the test. The blood you saw on your baby's clothes was sheep's blood. Magnanimous and courageous woman, can you tell which of these young men is your son?' The woman replied: 'I could recognize my son anywhere. He has a scar on the right thigh.' The first of the young men, when examined, had no such scar.

He was the son of the woman at the well, whom Goroo-Bâ-Dicko had set free. When the turn of the second young man came, the revealing scar was found on his right thigh.

Goroo-Bâ-Dicko's wife cried: 'This is my son!' She fell on his neck and they clasped each other in an ecstasy of joy, in the sight of the amazed and delighted villagers.

The story remains ambiguous: the characters were really put to the test, but no harm befell either the woman or the child. The consequent perplexity is much favoured by the Fulani. One of their proverbs says: A village with only one way to it is a bad village. Do not go there! *145*

Fulani tradition
Africa

**Each man
is unique**

Suppose a man could take a complete psychophysical inventory of his own attributes, trace each of them back to the very beginnings of life on earth and work out how they all came to be combined in his own person: the result would be a one hundred per cent exhaustive genetic analysis of the individual in question, his derivation and make-up. But it would not begin to explain away the person—that once-for-all, unique, incomparable marriage of body and soul, utterly without precedent in countenance, voice and gesture—which would still be there, quite simply and unequivocally 'there', totally underived and underivable. If, after expending so much effort in vain, the man we have imagined were to steel himself yet once more to ask, 'Where do I come from?', he would turn the last corner in his journey of inquiry only to stumble on himself as a created being. At every birth—because each man is unique—the first man enters the world. *146*

Martin Buber
On Germanizing
the Bible
1936

Man's freedom

Ivan Karamazov is speaking to his brother Alyosha:

At the time of the Holy Inquisition, in the square in Seville where heretics are burned every day, Christ appears in the midst of the crowd. The Grand Inquisitor passes by and has Him imprisoned. When night falls, he comes to visit Him in his cell, with a light in his hand, and addresses him as follows:

'Hast Thou the right to reveal to us one of the mysteries of that world from which Thou hast come?' my old man asks Him, and answers the question for Him. 'No, Thou hast not; that Thou mayest not add to what has been said of old, and mayest not take from men the freedom which Thou didst exalt when Thou wast on earth. Whatsoever Thou revealest anew will encroach on men's freedom of faith; for it will be manifest as a miracle, and the freedom of their faith was dearer to Thee than anything in those days fifteen hundred years ago. Didst Thou not often say then, "I will make you free"? But now Thou has seen these "free" men', the old man adds suddenly, with a pensive smile. 'Yes, we've paid dearly for it,' he goes on, looking sternly at Him, 'but at last we have completed that work in Thy name. For fifteen centuries we have been wrestling with Thy freedom, but now it is ended and over for good. Dost Thou not believe that it's over for good? Thou lookest meekly at me and deignest not even to be wroth with me. But let me tell Thee that now, today, people are more persuaded than ever that they have perfect freedom, yet they have brought their freedom to us and laid it humbly at our feet. But that has been our doing. Was this what Thou didst? Was this Thy freedom? . . .

'The wise and dread Spirit, the spirit of self-destruction and non-existence,' the old man goes on, 'the great spirit talked with Thee in the wilderness, and we are told in the books that he "tempted" Thee. Is that so? And could anything truer be said than what he revealed to Thee in three questions and what Thou didst reject, and what in the books is called "the temptation"? And yet if there has ever been on earth a real stupendous miracle, it took place on that day, on the day of the three temptations. The statement of those three questions was itself the miracle. If it were possible to imagine simply for the sake of argument that those three questions of the dread spirit had perished utterly from the books, and that we had to restore them and to invent them anew, and to do so had gathered together all the wise men of the earth—rulers, chief priests, learned men, philosophers, poets—and had set them the task to invent three questions, such as would not only fit the occasion, but express in three words, three human phrases, the whole future history of the world and of humanity—dost Thou believe that all the wisdom of the earth united could have invented anything in depth and force equal to the three questions which were actually put to Thee then by the wise and mighty spirit in the wilderness? From those questions alone, from the miracle of their statement, we can see that we have here to do not with the fleeting human intelligence, but with the absolute and eternal. For in those three questions the whole subsequent history of mankind is, as it were, brought together into one whole, and foretold, and in them are united all the unsolved historical contradictions of human nature. At the time it could not be so clear, since the future was unknown; but now that fifteen hundred years have passed, we see that everything in those three questions was so justly divined and foretold, and has been so truly fulfilled, that nothing can be added to them or taken from them.

'Judge Thyself who was right—Thou or he who questioned Thee then? Remember the first question; its meaning, in other words, was this: "Thou wouldst go into the world, and art going with empty hands, with some promise of freedom which men in their simplicity and their natural unruliness cannot even understand, which they fear and dread—for nothing has ever been more insupportable for a man and a human society than freedom. But seest Thou these stones in this parched and barren wilderness? Turn them into bread, and mankind will run after Thee like a flock of sheep, grateful and obedient, though for ever trembling, lest Thou withdraw Thy hand and deny them Thy bread." But Thou wouldst not deprive man of freedom and didst reject the offer, thinking, what is that freedom worth, if obedience is bought with bread? Thou didst reply that man lives not by bread alone. But dost Thou know that for the sake of that earthly bread the spirit of the earth will rise up against Thee and will strive with Thee and overcome Thee, and all will follow him, crying, "Who can compare with this beast? He has given us fire from heaven!" Dost Thou know that the ages will pass, and humanity will proclaim by the lips of their sages that there is no crime, and therefore no sin; there is only hunger? . . .

'No science will give them bread so long as they remain free. In the end they will lay their freedom at our feet, and say to us, "Make us your slaves, but feed us." They will understand themselves, at last, that freedom and bread enough for all are inconceivable together, for never, never will they be able to share between them! They will be convinced, too, that they can never be free, for they are weak, vicious, worthless and rebellious. Thou didst promise them the bread of Heaven, but, I repeat again, can it compare with earthly bread in the eyes of the weak, ever sinful and ignoble race of man? And if for the sake of the bread of Heaven thousands and tens of thousands shall follow Thee, what is to become of the millions and tens of thousands of millions of creatures who will not have the strength to forgo the earthly bread for the sake of the heavenly? Or dost Thou care only for the tens of thousands of the great and strong, while the millions, numerous as the sands of the sea, who are weak but love Thee, must exist only for the sake of the great and strong? No, we care for the weak too. They are sinful and rebellious, but in the end they too will become obedient....

'So long as man remains free he strives for nothing so incessantly and so painfully as to find some one to worship. But man seeks to worship what is established beyond dispute, so that all men would agree at once to worship it. For these pitiful creatures are concerned not only to find what one or the other can worship, but to find something that all would believe in and worship; what is essential is that all may be together in it. This craving for *community* of worship is the chief misery of every man individually and of all humanity from the beginning of time. For the sake of common worship they've slain each other with the sword. They have set up gods and challenged one another, "Put away your gods and come and worship ours, or we will kill you and your gods!" And so it will be to the end of the world, even when gods disappear from the earth; they will fall down before idols just the same....

'But what happened? Instead of taking men's freedom from them, Thou didst make it greater than ever! Didst Thou forget that man prefers peace, and even death, to freedom of choice in the knowledge of good and evil? Nothing is more seductive for man than his freedom of conscience, but nothing is a greater cause of suffering. And behold, instead of giving a firm foundation for setting the conscience of man at rest for ever, Thou didst choose all that is exceptional, vague and enigmatic; Thou didst choose what was utterly beyond the strength of men, acting as though Thou didst not love them at all—Thou who didst come to give Thy life for them! Instead of taking possession of men's freedom, Thou didst increase it, and burdened the spiritual kingdom of mankind with its sufferings for ever. Thou didst desire man's free love, that he should follow Thee freely, enticed and taken captive by Thee. In place of the rigid ancient law, man must hereafter with free heart decide for himself what is good and what is evil, having only Thy image before him as his guide. But didst Thou not know he would at last reject even Thy image and Thy truth, if he is weighed down with the fearful burden of free choice? . . .

'There are three powers, three powers alone, able to conquer and to hold captive for ever the conscience of these impotent rebels for their happiness—those forces are miracle, mystery and authority. Thou hast rejected all three and hast set the example for doing so. When the wise and dread spirit set Thee on the pinnacle of the temple and said to Thee, "If Thou wouldst know whether Thou art the Son of God then cast Thyself down, for it is written: the angels shall hold him up lest he fall and bruise himself, and Thou shalt know then whether Thou art the Son of God and shalt prove then how great is Thy faith in Thy Father." But Thou didst refuse and wouldst not cast Thyself down. Oh! of course, Thou didst proudly and well like God; but the weak, unruly race of men, are they gods? Oh, Thou didst know then that in taking one step, in making one movement to cast Thyself down, Thou wouldst be tempting God and have lost all Thy faith in Him, and wouldst have been dashed to pieces against that earth which Thou didst come to save. And the wise spirit that tempted Thee would have rejoiced. But I ask again, are there many like Thee?

'And couldst Thou believe for one moment that men, too, could face such a temptation? Is the nature of men such, that they can reject miracle, and at the great moments of their life, the moments of their deepest, most agonising spiritual difficulties, cling only to the free verdict of the heart?...

'Thou didst crave for free love and not the base raptures of the slave before the might that has overawed him for ever. But Thou didst think too highly of men therein, for they are slaves, of course, though rebellious by nature. Look round and judge; fifteen centuries have passed, look upon them. Whom hast Thou raised up to Thyself? I swear, man is weaker and baser by nature than Thou hast believed him! . . .

'How is the weak soul to blame that it is unable to receive such terrible gifts? Canst Thou have simply come to the elect and for the elect? But if so, it is a mystery and we cannot understand it. And if it is a mystery, we too have a right to preach a mystery, and to teach them that it's not the free judgment of their hearts, not love that matters, but a mystery which they must follow blindly, even against their conscience. So we have done. We have corrected Thy work and have founded it upon *miracle, mystery* and *authority*. And men rejoiced that they were again led like sheep, and that the terrible gift that had brought them such suffering, was, at last, lifted from their hearts....

'But Thou mightest have taken even then the sword of Caesar. Why didst Thou reject that last gift? Hadst Thou accepted that last counsel of the mighty spirit, Thou wouldst have accomplished all that man seeks on earth— that is, some one to worship, some one to keep his conscience, and some means of uniting all in one unanimous and harmonious ant-heap, for the craving for universal unity is the third and last anguish of men. . . .

'Hadst Thou taken the world and Caesar's purple,

Thou wouldst have founded the universal state and have given universal peace. For who can rule men if not he who holds their conscience and their bread in his hands. We have taken the sword of Caesar, and in taking it, of course, have rejected Thee and followed *him*. Oh, ages are yet to come of the confusion of free thought, of their science and cannibalism. For having begun to build their tower of Babel without us, they will end, of course, with cannibalism....

'Freedom, free thought and science, will lead them into such straits and will bring them face to face with such marvels and insoluble mysteries, that some of them, the fierce and rebellious, will destroy themselves, others, rebellious but weak, will destroy one another, while the rest, weak and unhappy, will crawl fawning to our feet and whine to us: "Yes, you were right, you alone possess His mystery, and we come back to you, save us from ourselves!"...

'Then we shall give them the quiet humble happiness of weak creatures such as they are by nature. Oh, we shall persuade them at last not to be proud, for Thou didst lift them up and thereby taught them to be proud. We shall show them that they are weak, that they are only pitiful children, but that childlike happiness is the sweetest of all....

'Yes, we shall set them to work, but in their leisure hours we shall make their life like a child's game, with children's songs and innocent dance. Oh, we shall allow them even sin, they are weak and helpless, and they will love us like children because we allow them to sin. We shall tell them that every sin will be expiated, if it is done with our permission, that we allow them to sin because we love them, and the punishment for these sins we take upon ourselves. And we shall take it upon ourselves, and they will adore us as their saviours who have taken on themselves their sins before God. And they will have no secrets from us. We shall allow or forbid them to live with their wives and mistresses, to have or not to have children—according to whether they have been obedient or disobedient—and they will submit to us gladly and cheerfully. The most painful secrets of their conscience, all, all they will bring to us, and we shall have an answer for all. And they will be glad to believe our answer, for it will save them from the great anxiety and terrible agony they endure at present in making a free decision for themselves. And all will be happy, all the millions of creatures except the hundred thousand who rule over them. For only we, we who guard the mystery, shall be unhappy. There will be thousands of millions of happy babes, and a hundred thousand sufferers who have taken upon themselves the curse of the knowledge of good and evil. Peacefully they will die, peacefully they will expire in Thy name, and beyond the grave they will find nothing but death....

'What I say to Thee will come to pass, and our dominion will be built up. I repeat, tomorrow Thou shalt see that obedient flock who at a sign from me will hasten to heap up the hot cinders about the pile on which I shall burn Thee for coming to hinder us. For if any one has ever deserved our fires, it is Thou. Tomorrow I shall burn Thee. Dixi.'...

When the Inquisitor ceased speaking he waited some time for his Prisoner to answer him. His silence weighed down upon him. He saw that the Prisoner had listened intently all the time, looking gently in his face and evidently not wishing to reply. The old man longed for Him to say something, however bitter and terrible. But He suddenly approached the old man in silence and softly kissed him on his bloodless aged lips. That was all His answer. The old man shuddered. His lips moved. He went to the door, opened it, and said to Him: 'Go, and come no more. . . . Come not at all, never, never!' And he let Him out into the dark alleys of the town. The Prisoner went away. *147*

Dostoevsky
The Brothers
Karamazov
1880

Physical freedom moral freedom,

Tomas Antonio
Gonzaga
Treatise
on Natural Law
Brazil, 1768

Freedom divides into physical and moral freedom. Physical freedom consists of doing, without knowing or being able to know whether the thing done is moral or not. Moral freedom is what we possess in doing or not doing, while knowing or being able to know whether the action in question is moral or not. Accordingly, there can be actions which are physically, but not morally, free. *148*

Ghalib
19th cent.
Urdu
India

How difficult it is to make anything simple!
Even man finds it hard to be human. *149*

Freedom cannot be qualified
André Malraux
Storm in Shanghai
1933

The freedom you allow me is your own. The freedom to do what you please. Freedom is not an exchange, it is freedom. *150*

Decision

Life is governed by a multitude of forces. It would be smooth sailing, if one could determine the course of one's actions only by one general principle whose application at

Mahatma Gandhi
1869-1948

a given moment was too obvious to need even a moment's reflection. But I cannot recall a single act which could be so easily determined. *151*

MAN

I know my soul hathe power to know all things,
Yet she is blind and ignorant in all:
I know I'm one of Nature's little kings,
Yet to the least and vilest things am thrall.
I know my life's a pain and but a span;
I know my sense is mock'd in everything;
And to conclude, I know myself a Man
Which is a proud and yet a wretched thing. *152*

Sir John Davies
Lawyer and poet
1569-1626
England

Power

Power and violence   Power only exists through violence. Without that violence, it is doomed to destruction since men cease to fear it to the extent that they perceive its clemency and no longer tremble before it. Power is neither the succulent fig, nor the soft olive, nor the vine, all of which give pleasure to men. It is the cruel thorn—its hurts, it wounds, it flays, it imprisons, it kills. Power cannot flourish and prevail by feeding the hungry, clothing the wretched, succouring the sick or displaying mercy. Hence there is a gulf between power and mercy; and hence we must seek to apprehend its nature, to know those whom it is supposed to protect within the context of an order imposed from above, to understand the meaning of that order maintained by force. There is, of course, another order—the order which God inspired in certain men through His Son and whose significance we must strive to uncover. If force must be used to ensure that order prevails, then men are lacking in wisdom, unaware of God and indifferent to his commandments. Yet the whole world needs justice and peace if mankind is to survive. And since there are many peoples who have no conception of virtue, who know not God and who are unjust to those about them, God, our master, who would fain grant long life to these multitudes, sends them kings and princes, who, through the power He vests in them, keep the peace, combat injustice, settle disputes as these arise and see that men do not make base use of the authorities to harm their fellows, seize by force what is not theirs, rob or encroach upon the property of others. For any power which would maintain the peace and enable the greatest number to live in honour and prosperity must curb all such iniquities and use force so that peace and justice triumph. The greater its concern with the preservation of peace, the more ruthlessly must it carry out repression so that men come to fear it and be content with what they have. When power succeeds in repressing injustice, order will reign everywhere, all will be blessed with peace and enjoy what is theirs unhindered. Such order is necessary to the existence of any nation since, without it, men will seek to destroy each other, there will be struggles between factions, the strong will oppress the weak, cast them out of their homes, enslave them and take

Petr Chelčický
Czech writer
Of Three Estates
(*Clergy, State
and People*)
15th cent.

their women. Power therefore bars the way to such evils. And if we call it secular power, this is precisely because it is expected to deal with the problems of the day so as to ensure that a higher order prevails.   *153*

*The aim
or purpose
of power*

Political power is that power which every man having in the state of nature has given up into the hands of the society and therein to the governors whom the society has set over itself, with the express or tacit trust that it shall be employed for their good and the preservation of their property. Now this power which every man has in the state of nature, and which he parts with to the society in all such cases where the society can secure him, is to use such means for the preserving of his own property as he thinks good and nature allows him, and to punish the breach of the law of nature in others so as, according to the best of his reason, may most conduce to the preservation of himself and the rest of mankind. So that the end and measure of this power, when in every man's hands in the state of nature, being the preservation of all of his society—that is, all mankind in general—it can have no other end or measure when in the hands of the magistrate but to preserve the members of that society in their lives, liberties, and possessions; and so cannot be an absolute arbitrary power over their lives and fortunes, which are as much as possible to be preserved, but a power to make laws, and annex such penalties to them as may tend to the preservation of the whole, by cutting off those parts, and those only, which are so corrupt that they threaten the sound and healthy, without which no severity is lawful. And this power has its original only from compact and agreement, and the mutual consent of those who make up the community.   *154*

John Locke
The Second Treatise
of Civil Government
1690
England

*Source of power:
election*

In addition to the existing ten Commissioners, the people shall elect twenty others among citizens over forty years of age who, after swearing that they will draw up the measures they consider best for the State, shall draft the public safety proposals. Any other citizen may also make proposals, so as to ensure that the one chosen is the best possible.   *155*

Aristotle
The Constitution of
Athens
4th cent. B.C.

Elections in the Church of the Middle Ages Pope Leo the Great 5th cent.	He who is to be at the head of all [the faithful] must be chosen by all [the faithful]. *156*
Principle of papal election Saint Cornelius 3rd cent.	As almost the whole clergy testifies, with the support of the crowd which was present, of the senior priests and eminent men, he was elected by the majority of our colleagues. *157*
Consent is essential Pope Celestine I 5th cent.	Let no bishop be set over the faithful against their will. *158*
Free elections Pope Gregory IX Decretals 12th cent.	The electors must have a completely free vote, and all other procedures are invalid. *159*
The majority principle Council of Nicaea 325	The majority must prevail. *160*
Pope Innocent IV 1247	The majority is always presumed to be right. *161*
Cardinal Guillaume de Mandagout Libellum super Electionibus Late 13th cent.	*The secret ballot was already practised in monastic communities in 1159 :* ... privately and discreetly with white and yellow discs, and not by a voice vote or a rising vote. *162*
Panormitanus *c.* 1450	Absentees must not be counted among those who take part in the chapter (*in the assembly*). *163*
The imperative mandate is prohibited 'Nova Collectio' of the Carthusian Order 1582	Their duty is to elect him whom they believe in all conscience to be the most able, or of whom they deem it probable that he is the most able. *164*
Pope Innocent III 1198-1216	Whatever concerns all must be discussed and approved by all. *165*
The people's rights Marsilius of Padua Defensor Pacis, 1324	Only the community of citizens, or the most notable section of them, is able to make human laws. *166*

Constitution *'Nihil novi'* Poland 1505	Since the universal law and the public constitutions apply to the nation as a whole, and not to the individual, we decree that, henceforth, nothing new may be decided without the common consent of the council and the deputies. *167*
Election *of the general* Beauplan Description d'Ukraine 1660, France	Here, then, is the way they elect their general. As soon as all the old Cossacks who are reputed among them have assembled, each votes for the one he believes most capable, and he who has most votes is nominated. *168*
The citizen's right *to be represented* *in Parliament* Ashby Case Statement by Lord Chief Justice Holt 1704 England	By the Common Law of England, every Commoner hath a Right not to be subjected to Laws, made without their Consent; and because it cannot be given by every individual Man in Person, by Reason of Number and Confusion, therefore that Power is lodged in the Representatives, elected by them for that purpose. . . . This is a noble Franchise and Right, which entitles the subject in a Share of the Government and Legislature. *169*

Virtues and duties of the sovereign

Father's mission
on earth
 	
Aztec tradition
Mexico
16th cent.
	The father, root and origin of the lineage of men.
	    His heart is good, he is careful of things; he is compassionate, he is concerned, he is the foresight, he is support, he protects with his hands.
	    He raises children, he educates, he instructs, he admonishes, he teaches them to live.
	    He places before them a large mirror, a mirror pierced on both sides; he is a large torch that does not smoke. *170*

Measures taken
in time of famine
in Ancient Egypt
	I have not harmed the daughter of the poor. I have not oppressed the widow. I have not persecuted the peasant. I have not ill-treated the shepherd.
	    From no foreman have I taken men to employ them. There have been no poor around me. No man has gone hungry in my time.
	    When the years of famine came, I rose up and tilled all the fields in the Nome of Oryx, from the boundaries in the south to those in the north. I saw to it that the inhabitants laid up provisions for their survival and that no man

Inscription on the
tomb of Amenemhat
Governor of
the Nome of Oryx
XIIth dynasty
Early 2nd millenary
B.C.

suffered from hunger. I gave to the widow as to the woman who had a husband. The grown man was no more favoured by my gifts than the youth.

Then, when the floods of the Nile returned, and the harvest and all things were once more plentiful, I claimed no taxation arrears on the land. *171*

*Beyond the rules,
each one seeks
his own perfection*

Chien-wu went to see the madman Chieh-yu, who asked him: 'What did Jih-chung-shih say to you?'

'He taught me', said Chien-wu, 'that the prince decrees the principles of social life and ethics, the rules of conduct and the assessment of things. His subjects do not dare to disobey him and are transformed under the influence of his policy.'

'That,' said the madman Chieh-yu, 'is a manner of deceiving men. To wish to govern thus, is to wish to dig a canal in the sea or to get a mosquito to carry a mountain. Does the holy man govern men from without? He improves himself first and his influence spreads thereafter. He strengthens only his own capacity. Moreover, the bird flies very high to avoid the net and the arrow; the field-mouse lives deep under the hill for fear of being smoked and dug out. Do you not know the wisdom of these small animals?'

Chuang-tzu
3rd cent.? B.C.
China

172

*Duty of superiors
not to abuse
their rights*

Constitutions of
the Capuchin
Friars Minor, 1536

Let the Superiors also beware of binding the souls of their subjects by grave precepts of obedience, unless they are forced to do so by necessity. *173*

Duties of the king

When a prince in his rule groweth slack, untrue to his
    name and his fame,
Should his wealth all at once disappear, of that prince it
    is counted as shame.

Thou thyself, O great king, shouldst instruct thy people
    in every good way,
Lest thy realm and thy substance should fall to unrighteous
    officials a prey.

Be sure that thou never as king thy people mislead to
    their cost,
Lest all men and women alike in an ocean of trouble
    be lost.

When a king from all fear is set free, and the pleasures of
    sense are his aim,
Should his riches and all disappear, to that king it is
    counted as shame.

Amidst the great ones of the earth a fivefold power we see;
Of these the power of arms is, sure, the last in its degree;
And power of wealth, O mighty lord, the next is said to be.
The power of counsel third in rank of these, O king, I name;
The power of caste without a doubt is reckoned fourth
  in fame,
And all of these a man that's wise most certainly will claim.

The Jataka
Pali
Trans. by
H. T. Francis

Of all these powers that one is best, as power of learning
  known,
By strength of this a man is wise and makes success his own.
                                                        174

Special responsi-
bilities of the king
Kautilīya-
Arthaśāstra II
4th cent. B.C.
Sanskrit

And the king should assume the responsibility of caring
for minors, aged persons, and persons in distress when
these are helpless, as also the woman who has borne no
child and the sons of one who has borne children (*when
these are helpless*).   *175*

Vasistha-
Dharmasūtra XIX
1st cent.
Sanskrit

The king should assume the responsibility of caring for
the weak and the insane.   *176*

The property of the aged and minors, of the blind and the
poor should be taken care of by the king.

. . . .

  The kingdom of the king, in whose dominion a person
even after having completed his studies is afflicted by
hungers, suffers a set-back. . . .

Mahābhārata XIII
2nd cent. B.C.
to 1st cent. A.D.
Sanskrit

  The king, from whose kingdom wailing women are
carried away violently while their husbands and sons
cry out plaintively, is as good as dead. He does not live. *177*

Āpastamba-
Dharmasūtra II
450-350 B.C.
Sanskrit

No one in his dominion should [be allowed to] suffer from
hunger, disease, cold, and heat—either because of poverty
or of any deliberate action on the part of others.   *178*

*The speaker (Okyeame) is an important official, acting as inter-
mediary between the chief and the people or between his chief and
another. He sees that the correct terms and expression required
by etiquette are used in all circumstances. He addresses the
Chief-elect in the following manner:*

Do not go after women,
Do not become a drunkard,

When we give you advice, listen to it.
We do not want you to abuse us,
We do not want you to be miserly,
We do not want one who disregards advice,
We do not want you to regard us as fools,
We do not want autocratic ways,
We do not want bullying,
We do not like beating.
Take the Stool,
We bless the Stool and give it to you;
The Elders say they give the Stool to you.   *179*

Ashanti tradition
Ghana

The new Chief then takes his oath before his Elders. He bares his shoulder but does not take off his sandals. Grasping the state sword, he says:

I mention the forbidden name of Wednesday (*sacred day*),
I mention the great forbidden name, that if I along
with you do not rule this people well, as my forefathers
and you ruled it, and if I do not listen to your advice,
then have I incurred the penalty of speaking the great
forbidden word, I have incurred the penalty of mentioning
the forbidden name of Wednesday.

The Chief, then, continues:

As for me, to-day they have placed me on this Stool;
I beg you to stand behind me with a good standing:
I pray you for long life; I pray you for honour; do not allow
my people to grow tired of me; let this people prosper.   *180*

Ashanti tradition
Ghana

The priest's oath

If I, *Klowekī*'s priest,
have never done such things:
If I have never killed a person,
never destroyed a pregnancy,
never injured some one's name,
nor borne false witness
against a person,
and if in spite of it some one accuses
me of having done such things,
laying thus some one's crimes
to my charge,
this would be a great offence
on his part.
Call *Nānā*'s *kodā* curse
upon his head!   *181*

Krobo tradition
Ghana

Akan proverb
Ghana

Justice today and injustice tomorrow, that is no good
government.   *182*

*Tolerance
and forgiveness*
Akan proverb
Ghana

Vindictiveness is bad statesmanship. *183*

Tzu Kung asked for a definition of good government. The Master replied: 'It consists in providing enough food to eat, in keeping enough soldiers to guard the State, and in winning the confidence of the people'. 'And if one of these three things had to be sacrificed, which should go first?' The Master replied: 'Sacrifice the soldiers.' 'And if of the two remaining things one had to be sacrificed, which should it be?' The Master said: 'Let it be the food. From the beginning, men have always had to die. But without the confidence of the people no government can stand at all.'

Confucius
551-479? B.C.
Analects

. . . The Master said: 'If the ruler is personally upright, his subjects will do their duty unbidden; if he is not personally upright, they will not obey, whatever his bidding.' *184*

Confucian school
The Great Learning
5th cent. B.C.

What one dislikes in one's superiors should never be used towards one's subordinates. *185*

Mencius
372?-289? B.C.
China

If the king, who is the parent of the people, cannot refrain from acts equivalent to leading beasts to devour human beings, how can you (*i.e.*, *the king*) qualify to be a parent of the people? *186*

The rule of law

Hsün-tzu
3rd cent. B.C.
China

If the laws are made after discussion . . . all affairs will be free from mistakes. Those affairs for which law exists will be regulated by law; those affairs for which law does not exist will be dealt with by analogy. *187*

*King—
a full-time servant
of the people*

Asoka's Rock Edict VI
3rd cent. B.C.
Prakrit

For a long time past, the discharge of the state business and the receiving of reports were not done at all hours. So now this arrangement has been made by me: at all hours, whether I am eating or whether I am in the harem or in the inner apartments or in the stables or in the place of religious instruction or in the garden, everywhere the reporters should report to me the business of the people. Everywhere I shall attend to the business of the people. *188*

*Self-discipline
of the king*

The control over the senses which would result in the study of sciences and in discipline should be secured by renouncing lust, anger, greed, pride, arrogance, and over-exultation. . . .

Therefore he should gain victory over the senses by discarding the group of six enemies (namely, lust, anger, greed, etc.), cultivate his intellect through association with the elders, accomplish progress and stability through exertion, enforce the observance by the people of their respective duties by himself carrying out his own duties, develop discipline through instruction in sciences, attain popularity by bringing about material welfare, and adopt the right attitude by doing what is beneficial. *189*

Kautilīya-
Arthaśāstra I
4th cent. B.C.
Sanskrit

*Kingship
as a sacrifice*

Constant exertion constitutes the vow to be observed by the king as sacrificer; the carrying out of his duties constitutes the actual performance of the sacrifice; the impartial attitude towards all constitutes the sacrificial fee; and his coronation constitutes the rite of initiation. *190*

Kautilīya-
Arthaśāstra I
4th cent. B.C.

*King's contract
with the people*

Vainya was the first person to have been appointed king. On that occasion he concluded the following contract with gods and sages who represented the people.

'Whatever work connected with my political obligations you will enjoin, that, verily, I shall carry out. No doubt should be entertained by you on this account.' Then the gods and also the great sages said to him: 'Whatever duties have been clearly prescribed to be done under specific circumstances, do you perform those duties without hesitation, setting aside all thought about what is agreeable and what is disagreeable, remaining impartial to all creatures, and discarding away lust, anger, greed, and pride. Should any person in this world deviate from his duty—you should restrain him by the force of [your two] arms, always remaining watchful of your own duty.' *191*

Mahābhārata XII
2nd cent B.C.
to 1st cent. A.D.
Sanskrit

The King who is really over all his subjects is the one who is merely known to be there. Next to such a king is the one whom they love and praise.
Next to him is the one they fear.
And next to him the one they despise.
If [the King] does not trust [his people] enough,
Neither, indeed, will they trust him. *192*

Lao-tzu
Tao-Te-Ching
6th cent. B.C.
China

If government is merely external, the state may seem temporarily well ordered, but the hearts of men are not at peace. To govern according to my way of internal persuasion will bring the whole world into personal relations, and so government will become unnecessary. *193*

Lieh-tzu
Taoist school
4th to 3rd cent. B.C.
China

Mo-tzu school
5th cent. B.C.

The emperor and his ministers and the people are bound in alliance by contract. *194*

Vasistha-
Dharmasūtra I
1st cent.
Sanskrit

A king, governing according to the law, should take one sixth of the wealth [of his subjects, by way of recompense for his services]. *195*

**King's chief
duty—protection
of his subjects**
Manusmriti VIII
2nd cent. B.C.
to 1st cent. A.D.
Sanskrit

A king who, without giving protection to his subjects, extracts [from them] tribute, tax, toll, tithe [in income], and fine, forthwith goes to hell. *196*

**The happiness
of the king
is the happiness
of his subjects**
Kautilīya
Arthasāstra I
4th cent. B.C.
Sanskrit

In the happiness of his subjects lies the happiness of the king and in the good of his subjects his good. What is dear to himself does not constitute the good of the king; but what is dear to his subjects constitutes his good. *197*

King's paternity
Asoka's
Kalinga Edict I
3rd cent. B.C.
Prakrit

All men are my children. Just as I wish for my children that they should become endowed with all good and happiness of this world and of the other world, so I wish even for all men. *198*

Agni-Purāna 223
5th cent.
Sanskrit

The king should protect his subjects who are being exploited by his officers, particularly by the Kāyasthas (*the clerks*). It is only when they are thus guarded against the fear arising from the officers that they can be truly regarded as the king's subjects. *199*

Tirukkural
1st cent.
Tamil
Mauritius

Let the King who desires that his prosperity may long remain commence his preliminary enquiries with strictness, and then punish with mildness.

Though a minister may see his mother starve, let him do no act which the wise would treat with contempt. *200*

Royal virtues

Though the possession of the fourfold armies, i.e. the fiery, ferocious, deadly elephants, the proud, speedy war horses, high-wheeled chariots with towering flags, and courageous warriors itching for battle, goes to make a kingdom great, know thee, O King! the true strength of a kingdom lies in the golden path of righteousness. So show no partiality to friends and relatives while administering justice; overlook not virtues in strangers; be armed like the sun with fiery fortitude (on the battlefield and in like situations); show, like the moon, refreshing (or pleasing) kindness to your subjects; bestow, like the rain, plenteous favours on the world and so drive away want from thy kingdom, O great and glorious King! May you live [happily] for many more years.   *201*

Puranānooru
Sangam period
2nd cent. B.C.
to 2nd cent. A.D.
Tamil

Rehoboam and the Israelites met at Shechem, where he was asked if he would make lighter their yoke. The king took counsel with the old men who had served Solomon, and they said to him: If thou wilt be a servant unto this people this day, and wilt serve them, and answer them, and speak good words to them, then they will be thy servants forever.   *202*

Hebrew Bible
I Kings 12

Let justice be mild

Rule subordinates with simplicity, govern the people with generosity. Punishment is not visited on descendants, rewards extend to heirs. Pardon mistakes, however serious; punish deliberate crimes, however slight. Treat crimes of doubtful gravity as slight, and merits not of manifest importance as great. It is better to overlook an irregularity than to kill an innocent man.   *203*

Shu-ching
Legal treatise of
the Sui-shu
Attributed
to Confucius
551-479? B.C.
China

Qualities required
to be elected
high priest

Even if he were poor and lowly,
even if his mother and his father were
the poorest of the poor. . . .
His lineage was not considered,
only his way of life mattered. . . .
The purity of his heart,
his good and humane heart. . . .
His stout heart. . . .
It was said that he had God in his heart,
that he was wise in the things of God.   *204*

Aztec tradition
15th cent.
Mexico
Trans. by
M. Léon Portilla

Rule of benevolence

The legendary Japanese emperor, clothed in all the attributes of the Chinese sage-king, as the virtuous father of his people.

4th year, Spring, 2nd month, 6th day. The Emperor addressed his ministers, saying: 'We ascended a lofty tower and looked far and wide, but no smoke arose in the land. From this We gather that the people are poor, and that in the houses there are none cooking their rice. We have heard that in the reigns of the wise sovereigns of antiquity, from everyone was heard the sound of songs hymning their virtue, in every house there was the ditty, "How happy are we." But now when We observe the people, for three years past, no voice of eulogy is heard; the smoke of cooking has become rarer and rarer. By this We know that the five grains (*hemp, millet, rice, wheat and barley, pulse—the Five grains of ancient China*) do not come up, and that the people are in extreme want. Even in the Home provinces (*the territory round the capital ruled immediately by the emperor*) there are some who are not supplied; what must it be in the provinces outside of Our domain?'

3rd month, 21st day. The following decree was issued: 'From this time forward, for the space of three years, let forced labor be entirely abolished, and let the people have rest from toil.' From this day forth his robes of state and shoes did not wear out, and none were made. The warm food and hot broths did not become sour or putrid, and were not renewed. He disciplined his heart and restrained his impulses so that he discharged his functions without effort.

Therefore the Palace enclosure fell to ruin and was not rebuilt; the thatch decayed, and was not repaired; the wind and rain entered by the chinks and soaked the coverlets; the starlight filtered through the decayed places and exposed the bed-mats. After this the wind and rain came in due season, the five grains produced in abundance. For the space of three autumns the people had plenty, the praises of his virtue filled the land, and the smoke of cooking was also thick.

7th year, Summer, 4th month, 1st day. The Emperor was on his tower, and looking far and wide, saw smoke arising plentifully. On this day he addressed the Empress, saying: 'We are now prosperous. What can there be to grieve for?' The Empress answered and said: 'What dost thou mean by prosperity?' The Emperor said: 'It is doubtless when the smoke fills the lands, and the people freely attain to wealth.' The Empress went on to say: 'The Palace enclosure is crumbling down, and there are no means of repairing it; the buildings are dilapidated so that the coverlets are exposed. Can this be called prosperity?' The Emperor said: 'When Heaven establishes a Prince, it is for the sake of the people. The Prince must therefore make the people the foundation. For this reason the wise sovereigns of antiquity, if a single one of their subjects was cold and starving, cast the responsibility on

Nihongi
(Chronicles of Japan)
8th cent.

themselves. Now the people's poverty is no other than Our poverty; the people's prosperity is none other than Our prosperity. There is no such thing as the people's being prosperous and yet the Prince in poverty.' *205*

*Description
of a good king*

Beowulf
Anglo-Saxon poem
8th cent.

He dealt out to all,
To young and to old,
Such as God gave him
Except land of people
And men's lives. *206*

*Advice addressed
to rulers*

Attributed
to the Sassanian
king Ardashir
3rd cent.
Persia

Know that dynasties begin to pass away because the subjects are ignored, being left without known work or specific labour. If unemployment becomes widespread among the people, it brings about reflection on matters, thoughts about essential things. When these things are looked into, they are considered with differing natures and different schools are formed causing mutual enmity and hatred, while the people are unanimous in their dislike of their rulers. *207*

Attributed to
the king Khusrau
Anōsharwān
6th cent.
Persia

He was asked: 'What is it the right of the subjects to expect from kings, and what is it the right of kings to expect from their subjects?'

He answered: 'The subjects have the right to expect of kings that they should treat them with justice, give them their dues, ensure the safety of their roads and guard their frontiers. The subjects owe their kings good advice and gratitude.' *208*

The worst

Dādistān ī Mēnōg
ī Xrad
Sassanian period
3rd to 7th cent.
Persia

The sage asked the Spirit of Wisdom, thus: 'As to a ruler, a chieftain, a friend, a kinsman, a wife, a child and a country, which is the worse?'

The Spirit of Wisdom answered thus: 'That ruler is the worse, who is not able to keep the country unalarmed, and the people untroubled. The chieftain is worse, who is defective in ability, unthankful unto agents, and no helper and interceder for his subjects. That friend is the worse, who is not fit to be relied upon. That kinsman is the worse, who is no helper in a calamity. That wife is the worse, with whom it is not possible to live with pleasure. That child is the worse, who does not carry on one's fame. That country is the worse, in which it is not possible to live in happiness, fearlessness and permanence.' *209*

*Government
of the wisest
and the people's
well-being*

It is indeed worth noting that, these kings ruling over such wide provinces in so vast a land, rugged in part and full of mountains and snow-clad uplands and dry, sandy, and treeless plains, great sagacity was needed in governing so many nations that differed so widely from each other in language, laws and religion so as to keep them all tranquil, enjoying peace and their friendship, and thus, although the city of Cuzco was the head of their Empire, as we have frequently recorded, it must also be said that from place to place they had posted their representatives and governors, who were the wisest, most able and zealous to be found, and none so young as not to be in the last third of his life.

... Such fear was there of the princes that, in so vast a land, every people was as orderly and well-governed as if the Lord were present to punish any who did contrary. That fear was issue of the lords' own worth and of their justice, it being known that if they should perchance do evil, the chastisement of those who did so did immediately follow, neither prayers nor bribes availing. And as always the Incas acted well towards those placed under their dominion, not permitting that they be oppressed, nor too much tribute taken from them, nor other injustice done to them, besides which, many with barren provinces in which their forefathers had lived in need were commanded that they should be made fertile and abundant and were provided with those things that there were lacking; and to others that lacked clothing because they had no flocks, it was commanded that flocks should be generously given. In short, it was known that, just as these lords would be served by their people, who paid tribute to them, so too did they preserve their lands for them, raising them from ignorance to great skill, and from being indigent to lacking nothing. *210*

Pedro Cieza de León
Spanish chronicler of
Peru
16th cent.

Extract from a long poem in Persian addressed to the Ottoman Sultan Suleiman I, the Magnificent.

How could the man who decks his table with abundance of food produced by the labour of the people, the man who, at each meal, partakes of every variety of roast and grilled meats, how could such a man take pity on hearts in anguish? Is the hard heart capable of feeling the least pity for hearts burnt alive? The people will have no peace or happiness under the rule of an unjust monarch. Set the wolf to guard the flock and he will be an even greater disaster for the sheep. Heartless sovereign! The peasant has planted and tended a tree so that thou mayest enjoy the sight of it. Do not cut it down and saw it to make thyself a throne. To tear with thy teeth and lips which a Beauty, graceful as a rose-tree, has placed like balm upon thy wounded heart does not betoken manhood. What joy can come to thee from a throne which thou shalt cause to swim in tears from the eyes of the unfortunate? Verily, thou hast thy landlord's portion in the peasant's holding, but on condition that thou furnish him thy aid and protection whenever an evil befalls him. It is for thee to compensate the peasant if his property should suffer loss: for thee, who couldst protect him if thou thyself wronged him? *211*

Fuzūlī
Turkish poet
16th cent.

Everyone, whether noble or vagabond, is a soul, and comes from heaven. To let even the poorest man be hungry is like killing a soul from heaven outright.... When all the people starve to death, of what use is their lord's life? The lord lives only for the people. *212*

Baigan Ishida
1685-1744
Town and Country
Japan

[It is said that] the powerful make no mistakes; but once they do, the consequences are grave.

The hearts of the powerful should be tender as wax. *213*

Turkish proverbs
15th cent.

The Padishah should not settle into his palace before the house [of humble folk] has been built. *214*

Turkish proverb

Clemency

A mighty battle took place between him and the Imam Ahmad, and the most High God, blessed be His Name, gave the victory to King Claudios, peace be to him. And the Imam Ahmad died by the hand of one the king's servants. And they killed many soldiers of the Turkoman army, and people of the country of Saad-ed-Din. And of the survivors, half fled by sea with the wife of Imam Ahmad, and the other half seized Mohammed, son of Imam Ahmad, and handed him over to King Claudios, and themselves did obeisance at his feet.

But he was clement and merciful, and did not render evil for evil done him, but did good like a benefactor. And on the day indicated at the opening of this recital, when many who had done harm to him or to the family of his father or of his mother, or to churches in the lower parts of his kingdom, surrendered to him, they were allowed through his mercy and clemency to go safe and sound, no one daring to molest them; no, not so much as a dog daring to lick them!

Save that one of the Portuguese troops treasonously killed one among them whose crimes cried to high heaven; but this was not the desire of our good King Claudios, peace be to him.

Chronicles of the Emperor Claudios 1540-59 Ethiopia

215

Respect for authority

No fidgeting in the nobleman's house.

Respect and restraint are required at all times towards superiors, parents, chiefs and all authority.

An old man does not ask for his share.

He does not ask: 'Which is my share? Where is it?' It is given to him spontaneously. The desires of an old man should be anticipated and he should not be ashamed by having to draw attention to himself.

The older someone is, the greater the share that should be kept for him.

Mongo proverbs Congo

216

Never throughout his reign did [the Emperor] hasten to condemn to death. When one man killed another and was dealt with by law, his justice was upright and unpartisan.

Did he to whom the blood-debt for the murdered man was due claim the killer's life, the Emperor bought it back with soothing words, himself paying an appropriate blood ransom. A prisoner taken on the field of battle from some pagan people or Moslem tribe was brought before him, and knew at once he had evaded death.

He was no man to spy on other's faults, or pay heed to slander, or listen gladly to accusations, or be all times engaged in punishing, or lose his temper. Men so feared his silence that he had no need for anger, and did he once give vent to it the sun did not go down upon his anger. He hated no man for his sins, and did not disdain the just.

He mourned the dead and in their resurrection hoped for consolation. His care it was to clothe the naked and distribute bread to those hungry. He drew spring water for the thirsty, and sought health for the injured. He eased the weak of their burdens, he feared the Glorious and Most High Lord and respected men.

. . . .

He did not pluck where he had not planted, or reap what he had not sown, or gather what he had not scattered. Never once throughout his reign did he usurp his neighbour's

Chronicles
of the Emperor
Claudios
1540-59
Ethiopia

patrimony or take possession of another's field. He did not seize the widow's cow or confiscate the orphan's donkey. He succoured the children of the indigent and brought low the arrogant. Justice flowered under his reign, and peace was everywhere.   *217*

Czech proverb

Where a man is much, there people are little.   *218*

The sovereign, his intermediaries and the right to justice

Amharic proverb
Ethiopia

A thirsty man goes to the river, a man outraged to the king.   *219*

A true minister

Huang Tsung-hsi,
Ming-i tai-fang lu
17th cent.
China

The terms 'prince' and 'minister' derive their significance from service to mankind. If I have no sense of duty to mankind I am an alien to the prince. If I come to serve him without any consideration for the welfare of mankind, then I am merely the prince's menial servant. If, on the other hand, I have the people's interest at heart, then I am the prince's mentor and colleague. Only then may I really be called a minister.   *220*

*Penalties
for the abuse
of power
among the Incas*

Bernabé Cobo
Historia
del Nuevo Mundo
1653

A chief who put to death any of his Indian subjects without permission from the Inca was publicly chastised, being smitten a certain number of times on his back with a stone (this was called the punishment of the stone, and was very ignominious), even if the Indian had been greatly at fault in some disobedience against that chief; and if the said chief, after being rebuked and punished, repeated the offence, he died for it; and even if, as a result of petitions on intercessions, this penalty was not carried out, the Inca deprived him of his chiefdom and gave it to another.   *221*

*Responsibility
of the authorities*
Bernabé Cobo
Historia
del Nuevo Mundo
1653

If travellers had anything stolen from them at a wayside inn, the first to be punished was the chief who had the men under his charge; he in turn then punished others of his subjects for their negligence and lack of watchfulness.   *222*

[Inca Yupanqui] linked the provinces and districts together in this manner: if one district defaulted in respect of the payment of tribute or building of roads or in any other matter, the other district linked with it should make good the default in its place and the lord of that district should punish the lord of the district at fault....

As those who served the Inca enjoyed the aforesaid and other favours, so any headman or chief who was negligent or careless and did not deal aright with all the Indians under his charge, in accordance with the commission he had been given was straightway deprived of his office and ordered to watch one of the flocks of sheep, or some such thing, without any possibility of argument, since the Inca was absolute lord. *223*

Relación del origen e gobierno de los Incas c. 1575

Penalties for negligence by the authorities

Let any person who steals food or clothing, silver or gold, be examined whether he stole through need or poverty, and if it be found so, let not that thief be punished but let him who holds the office of steward be punished by removal from his position, since he has not taken care to provide for the needs of him who stole nor made a record of the needy, and let that thief be given the necessary clothing, food, land and a house. *224*

Laws of the Peruvians 1594

Guarantee concerning weights and measures

He [the Inca] had decreed that throughout his dominions there should be established weights and measures, so that none should be wronged or cheated. *225*

Bartolomé de las Casas 1474-1566 Antiguas gentes del Perú

If a subject is starving

If even the humblest peasant among the tens of thousands of people who have the honour of living in Your Excellency's territory starves to death or leaves the country as a vagabond, this represents a crime on the part of Your Excellency. But since it is difficult for Your Excellency to administer affairs yourself, in person, and since you entrust this task to officials, Your Excellency naturally cannot suppose that bad administration is in fact a crime on your part. Nor do your subjects suppose it; the ministers throw the responsibility upon the bailiffs, the latter in turn shift it upon the lower ranking officials; no one knows who is really to blame, . . . and no more is done than to keep up appearances. The ministers and seneschals are undoubtedly guilty of negligence, which is the result of Your Excellency's lack of interest in political matters. *226*

Kazan Watanabe 1793-1841 In the Event of Famine Japan

*The right of
appeal
to the king*

The king must do justice.

*If a Javanese feels that he is the victim of injustice, the ultimate
remedy is a direct appeal to the king; this is a kind of citizen's
right. The appellant and his retinue go to a certain place in the
Royal Compound marked by two huge waringin trees; they are
dressed in white, the colour of death. The rite is called* pepe
*('to stand in the sun', i.e., to be without shadow, without protection).
The king's duty is to call the appellant and to listen to his story.
Though the custom must have existed for many centuries, it
is nowhere mentioned in Javanese literature, apart from the
following story:*

The Prince of Surabaya was in possession of a cock which had been
a hen in its earlier days. Supposing that the remarkable change of
sex would interest the king, the Prince of Surabaya made a present
of it and offered it ceremonially, explaining that such a remarkable
animal should have its place in the royal residency. As a divine
being, the King of Java is gifted with the second sight; so our king
knew that the grandson of the Prince of Surabaya one day would
be his successor, and he therefore regarded the prince's gift as a hint
that he should retire and give place to 'the new cock'. For this reason
he abused the Prince of Surabaya after his departure, in the presence
of many people.

The king's fit of anger was soon widely known. Before long
Pangeran Pĕkik heard about it; he was surprised and at
the same time afraid. So he went to the place to the south
of the two waringin trees, dressed in white, and
accompanied by his wife and all his relatives; all were
dressed in white. It was just then that the king left his
private rooms to give an audience on the platform,
intending to promote his step-son, the son of his wife
ratu Malang, and to bestow on him the title 'pangeran
Natabrata'. Seeing the crowd of people dressed in white,
he sent somebody to investigate; it turned out that the
appellants were the Prince of Surabaya, his wife and all his
relatives. Immediately the king ordered them to climb the
platform. So Pangeran Pĕkik climbed the platform;
his wife came behind him, holding on to the tail of his
coat (*i.e., being afraid*). All those who were present were
sorry.

When the king saw his uncle and aunt, he stepped down
from the throne and invited them to take a seat, below
(*since they were of lower rank*). The king asked why they had
been standing in the sun. Pangeran Pĕkik humbly told
the truth: because of his having made a present of that
bĕkisar; it had been far from him even to consider the
possibility of hinting at anything, to make the king
understand something, to intend rebellious behaviour,
and the last thing he had had in mind was the thought

of speeding up the course of events. Pageran Pĕkik and his wife humbly said if the king would not be so kind as to forgive them, they implored him just to kill them. So much they said, weeping; then they sat down, deeply bowing their heads.

When the king heard what his uncle and his aunt had to say, he too burst into tears, remembering his late father. All those who were attending the audience and near to the throne wept abundantly, full of pity when looking at Pangeran Pĕkik.

Babad Tanah Jawi
Javanese
historiography
1626

Wiping away his tears the king said: 'Uncle and aunt, do not think of it any longer. I do not feel angry, and now indeed I grant you pardon.'   *227*

The small
are under
the protection
of the great

WE ARE LITTLE SNAILS WHO SEEK REFUGE BEHIND THE FRONDS OF THE BANANA TREE

See, my grandchild, I see from your hand which you hold outstretched, so that you may acquire cattle which will multiply. The Heaven Man helps to increase it for you, so that it may fatten you. But you puff yourself up and think: 'There is nothing that can vie with me any longer.' You look at the elders around the chief and think: 'I am as big as they!' Eventually, when you see the chief himself, you think: 'Bah!' So that he, watching you, perceives that you hold everyone in contempt. And they speak of this and say: 'So and so no longer recognizes anyone as his superior.' Another answers: 'Oho! He no longer even acknowledges the chief!' And the chief declares: 'A trap must be set for him and he must be plundered!' But another declares: 'He has become too big for that. If he goes off with all his kith and kin, it will upset the whole country. As long as he does not curse the chief, let things be, let him stay here and let us watch him.'

But after this there is an epidemic on your farm and your livestock dies. For livestock means vicissitudes, my grandchild. It is subject to ups and downs. Then you sit down and think to yourself: 'Hmm, what about things?' and you sigh. As you sit thinking, illness comes to you, too; you die and leave behind orphans. But the tribe you held in such contempt now says: 'He was a really violent man and no longer acknowledged the worth of others. Let him depart!' If they speak in this way when you have left orphans, starvation will come upon your family. When there comes starvation, which licks people up (*that is, exterminates them like flies*), then we are snails, and our haunt is behind the fronds of the banana trees, where we hide so as to stay alive. If you want to understand that we are really like snails, then watch when it becomes hot in the kilning month. For this month brings hunger to the snails, and when you look for one you can find none. But if you break a frond from the banana bush, you find many of them hidden behind it. But in the rainy season they thrive, and as many of them as have survived the heat come out into the open; and we human beings too are like snails and live by the grace of the great, who are chiefs. Should you leave behind an orphan, the chief will take it in and give it shelter, just like those snails that took shelter behind the banana leaves and stayed alive. The chief is man's banana leaf. And therefore I tell you, my grandchild, do not elbow your way through life pushing your way past people, and acknowledging no master. Lie low and be humble. And keep an open mind, so that your mind is aware of its surroundings. Then if you leave an orphan, it will find its hiding place behind the fronds of the chief. The chief will bestow honours on the orphan and it will come to greatness as you formerly were great. And the Heaven Man will bestow other cattle, because the chieftain took over responsibility for the child, because you showed yourself so accommodating, and he did not avoid your company.

Chagga tradition
Tanzania
                                                                    228

*Respect,
one for the other,
not rivalry*

The sun and rain do not steal each other's glory (neither of the two lacks prosperity).

Both the sun and the rain render man great services by overwhelming him with good things. The sun brings the dry season with its abundance of fish, the rain makes the plants grow. Moreover they take their turns in due order, each leaving the other her days and seasons.

Applied to people who respect the authority of others.

Mongo proverb
Tanzania
This is how it should be.   *229*

Dialogue between a Moroccan judge (a Cadi) and the representative of the Caliph.

Mohamed Chemsedin, the judge, went as usual to meet and welcome the new representative of the Caliph. The representative was accompanied by his guard of honour and by a group of peasants whom he had captured on his way. Mohamed Chemsedin inquired what he was going to do with the prisoners. 'I intend to hang them,' replied the Caliph's representative. The judge asked him by what right such acts were to be done. 'They are thieves and murderers,' answered the Caliph's representative. 'Has proof of their guilt been established by legal process?' asked the judge. 'We do not need to establish it,' replied the representative of the Caliph. 'A human being shall never be deliberately killed in an illegal manner in my presence. Rather', continued the judge, 'shall you go into the town, look into each case, and make sure whether the crimes attributed to these men are in fact proved. It is only once these crimes have been actually proved, that their execution will be justified and legal.' The representative of the Caliph then submitted, accepting the opinion of the judge, who enjoyed great moral authority at that time. *230*

*Cadi Abu al-Yaman
Mujir al-Din
al-Hanbali
14th cent.*

If a leader appointed by me commits an injustice toward a human being, and I learn thereof, if I do nothing to repair it, it is I who commit the injustice.

*Caliph Omar ibn
al-Khattāb
7th cent.*

Anyone who is the victim of an unjust governor, let him complain to me! *231*

*Equal opportunity
of appointment
to public office*

Whoever places Mohammedan affairs, be it ever so little, in the hands of someone, knowing all the time that another is worthier to deal with them, that man offends against Allah, His Prophet and the community of believers. *232*

Hadith
(Sayings
of the Prophet)

*Means for
the protection
of the individual
against
arbitrariness
and encroachment
by the authorities*

National Law Code of Magnus Erikson, drafted about 1350.

[The King should swear] to strengthen, love and look after all justice and truth and subdue all iniquity and falsehood and all injustice, according to law and by virtue of his royal power.

[He should further swear] to be loyal and faithful to all his countrymen, so that he shall not deprive anyone, poor or rich, in any way, of his life or limb, without a lawful inquiry, as laid down in the law and the justice of the country, or deprive him of his property, except according to law and lawful trial. *233*

Sweden

Instrument of Government of 1809.

The King shall maintain and further justice and truth, prevent and forbid iniquity and injustice. He shall not deprive anyone or allow anyone to be deprived of life, honour, personal liberty or well-being, without legal trial and sentence. He shall not deprive anyone or permit anyone to be deprived of any real or personal property without due trial and judgment in accordance with the provisions of the Swedish law and statutes. He shall not disturb or allow to be disturbed the peace of any person in his home. He shall not banish any person from one place to another. He shall not constrain or allow to be constrained the conscience of any person, but shall protect everyone in the free exercise of his religion provided that he does not thereby disturb public order or occasion general offence. The King shall cause everyone to be tried by the court to the jurisdiction of which he is legally

Sweden   subject.   *234*

Limitations on power

To Sultan Mulay Ismaïl:

I am writing you this letter since it is no longer possible for me to keep silent. I have long seen that our Sovereign seeks exhortations and advice and that he wishes the gates of prosperity and success to be thrown open. I have therefore determined to write to our Sovereign a letter which, if he is willing to take account of it, will allow me to hope that he may receive the blessings of this world and of eternity, and elevation to the pinnacles of glory; and though I be not worthy to address such exhortations, yet do I hope that our Sovereign will worthily accept them, and that he will not be displeased on this account.

Let him know, then, that the earth, with all that it contains, is the kingdom of God, the most High, who stands alone, and that all creatures are the slaves and servants of God. Our Master is one of these slaves, to whom God has given power over others in order to test him. If he treats them with justice, mercy, equity and righteousness, he is God's lieutenant on earth and represents the shadow of God over his slaves: he holds high rank with God. But if he rules them as a tyrant and an oppressor, with harshness and pride, violating justice, he sets himself up against his Master; he is no more than an isolent usurper in his realm and lays himself open to his Master's wrath and most dire punishment. Now our Sovereign knows well what awaits whomsoever seeks to tyrannize over his subjects and to enslave them without the Master's consent and what fate will be his on the day he falls into his Master's hands....

A sage has said: 'A kingdom is a building of which the foundation is the army. If the foundation be weak, the edifice will fall. There is no Sultan without an army, no army without prosperity, no prosperity without justice: thus justice is the basis of all.' The philosopher Aristotle drew for King Alexander a circular geometrical figure, on which he wrote: 'The World is a garden, with the government for its hedge; the government is a sultan supported by the law; the law is an administrative basis, handled by the King, the King is a shepherd supported by the army; the army is an auxiliary made secure by plenty; where there is plenty, the subjects cluster around; the subjects are slaves led by justice, justice is a synthesis which rules the world, the world is a garden, etc.'. . .

The Prophet (may God's blessing be upon him!) has said: 'You are all shepherds, and every shepherd must give account of his flock.

'There are men who misuse and waste the property of God; they will burn at the Day of Judgement; justice, with her hands untied, will condemn them to the Fire; their injustice will cause them to perish.'

Our Master Ali Ben Abu Taleb (may God be pleased with him!) has said: 'At Elabtah, I saw the Cailph Omar riding on a pack-camel; "Whither goest thou, Commander of the Faithful?" I said to him. "One of the camels intended for alms-giving has disappeared", he answered, "and I am looking for it." "Wilt thou, then, humble all thy successors?" I said. "Do not reproach me", he replied. "By him who had the truth revealed by Mohammed (may God pray for him!), if the smallest kid were lost on the banks of the Euphrates, Omar would have to account for it at the day of the last judgement. The Prince who wrongs a Moslem deserves no respect, any more than an empire which brings confusion among the faithful." '

Again, Caliph Ali saw an 'elderly Jew' who was begging from door to door: 'We have not acted justly towards thee,' he said. 'We made thee pay the Djezia (*special poll tax paid by the Jews*) when thou wert young, and now, behold, thou art reduced to penury through our fault.' And he had money paid to him by the Treasury to buy food. . . .

When the Prophet died (may God grant him his blessings and salvation!), he appointed to be his successor Caliph Abu Bakr (may God be pleased with him!), who had until then maintained his family by trading in the market. When he had become Caliph, he took the money wherewith he was used to trade and set out for the market, as was his custom. But the Ulemas (*wise men*) among the companions of the Prophet prevented him, saying that his office would keep him sufficiently occupied without going to the market; and they allotted to him the sums necessary for him and his family. . . . The most perfect equality was established for all: like the others, he took only what the sacred law accorded him. Such was the rule thereafter followed by the Caliphs who succeeded him.

Our Sovereign should follow the example of these holy persons instead of imitating those who follow their passions. On this subject, let him consult the trusty counsellors around him, such as Sidi Mohammed Ben Elhassan, Sidi Ahmed Ben Saïd and other learned men who fear God and dread not the reproaches of our Sovereign. In those matters to which I have referred, and those of which I have not spoken, let him do what they shall command and refrain from doing what they forbid. That is the path of Salvation, if it please God!

I beseech the Most High to protect our Sovereign, to guide and strengthen him, so that, under his care, prosperity may reign in the country; and to smite tyrants and recalcitrants with the sword.

So be it.

Praise be to God, the Lord of the Worlds.   *235*

Letter from
Sheikh
Hassan al-Yussi
17th cent.
North Africa

*The poet
condemns
the sovereign*

If thou art Solomon, hearken also to the voice of the ant; reflect on its words and answer it. If thou art sovereign, warm the people like the sun. Be like the water that flows, like the wind that blows (of benefit to men).

I now know the erring ways of our time. The wicked have taken to shunning all that is good. Persons of low origin now supplant the nobles and proceed regardless of them, to the place of honour.

Sovereigns no longer rule fairly, the Mufti makes an award for a dinar. Know that these signs herald the approach of the Last Judgement. Tyrants, remorseless, are beginning to go beyond all bounds.

The poor are ill-treated, and their face grows pale. But those who worship the powerful wax ruddy. Tyrants show themselves full of pride before the humble. They cause blood to spurt at the end of their whip....

Those who are Cadis do not remain firm in their judgements. At night they no longer wrestle with books. They no longer walk in the straight path of the Chari'at. Because of greed, they are adrift, without faith.

Iran and Turan are now beneath thy heel, Fetdah. Make the most of thy good fortune. The Turkmenians are all wandering in the steppes, Fetdah. Take care that thou shed no blood unjustly.

A king today, tomorrow thou shalt become a beggar, far from thy people and country, thy words no longer of any account. One day, life will abandon thee, and thou shalt be sacrificed. Thou hast taken many sins upon thyself, Fetdah....

Terrible is the vengeance of the people: thy future is dark. Thou shalt either perish or be thrown into prison, do not doubt it. Thy throne destroyed think not to escape with thy life. For thou hast changed the bread of the people into poison, O Fetdah.

Thou has separated us from our loved ones, leaving them in tears. Our wailing has reached the vault of heaven. Gibbets with our men hanging on them are everywhere to be seen. Know that thou hast outdone all butchers, Fetdah.

Magtimguli
18th cent.
Turkmenistan

Píragí [pseudonym of the poet]. It is time to speak of one's sorrows and have compassion on those of others. The cruel Fetdah must sate himself on the blood he swallows. As for me, I still live, but count me among the dead: if he learns that I have made this poem, Fetdah will kill me. *236*

*Against
the arbitrariness
of power*

CHIEFS ARE LIKE THE RAIN

Look you, my grandson! Chiefs are like the rain, there is no telling the day when they start to hate each other. If you are suffering from the heat and your plants, which you have tended, wither, so rain falls on the earth on the day the Heaven Man wishes and your plants are saved. And this is how chiefs are too. Today they choose to fall out and before very long you will see them join forces.

And you decide to set off and go to the other chiefs. Yet meanwhile, as you are setting off from home, they happen to defy each other. One thinks to himself: 'If someone just gave me one of his men, I would kill him, so that he should come and we would fight each other and all would see who is a man and who is a woman.'

At the place you are going to the chief has consulted with his men and said: 'Let us block the way so that he [the other chief] should notice it, become angry and we fight each other.'

When he has spoken, one man goes and tells it to his wife. He says to her: 'We have been commanded to block the road to Moschi tomorrow.' She asks him: 'What are you going to do to block the way?' He says to her: 'If we see a man coming from Moschi, we are to kill him, so that they know we harbour enmity towards them.'

The woman thinks to herself: 'Heh, heh, a man could come along who has sealed a bond of blood brotherhood with my father or with my step-father and should he be killed?' So she decides: 'I'll go and cut grass by the wayside. Should I see someone, I shall bid him turn back. Man is man; whatever happens I shall bid him turn back so that his life shall be spared.' And the woman takes up her fibre bonds and goes to cut grass by the wayside. But they are lying in ambush near where the chief lives. And you come briskly walking along, proceeding as the mood takes you, until you come to the woman cutting grass. You wish to go past and are not even inclined even to greet her. She raises her head and sees you. And she asks you: 'Mister, where do you come from that you should go past on the way without any greeting? Where do you come from, my father-in-law?' You are in a hurry and quickly say to her: 'I come from Moschi.' But she asks you: 'Do you know then the story about the eastern country that you should go by on your way in this manner?'

On hearing this, think hard and may that which I have told you come into your head. Turn back and flee; do not mind the woman. If you do, you put her in danger of being found out. And should you meet someone else, bid him turn back too.

Look you, my grandson, they later fall upon someone and kill him, but you have been saved. Once they have fought each other and one of them (*i.e. one of the chiefs*) has been defeated and sued [for peace], they make peace. And people go to and fro as before and visit one another. But you think to yourself: 'Look, look, were it not for the woman, I would very likely have been killed.' And then they rejoice likewise, when things have thus been settled.

That is what I mean when I tell you they are like the rain. You would have died and they would then have made peace. But you would have been lost.   237

Chagga tradition
Tanzania

Laws come from you and war comes from you too.
(*Instead of peace, superiors wage war on their subordinates. Their speech is of peace and order but their thoughts are thoughts of violence.*

The nkundó concept of authority is that it should be gentle, peaceful, respectful of liberty: paternal.)   238

Mongo proverb
Tanzania

Respect for the human person

Where man is denied, the devil himself loses his rights.
(*A protest against oppression by the chief and a warning to him. The Fulani say that a chief whose subjects are all slaves is not a chief, because nobody dares to tell him the truth. Power is a dialogue. Hala, in Fulani, means 'right', but also, literally, 'speech', 'word', 'logos'.*)

O Chief, how can you expect the impossible?
(*The protest of a delegation of Fulani peasants to a Prefect in the colonial period, which later became a popular saying, used in refusing to supply men for forced labour or requisitioned animals.*)
                239

Fulani proverbs
Africa

False obedience

To make man obedient in accepting my rule unconditionally, I debased him in all ways, even forcing him to lie with his own mother; his answer was more and more disobedience. Now I can see that he served me best when I treated him as a brother.   240

Somali proverb

Against fear

For fear is but a poor safeguard of lasting power; while affection, on the other hand, may be trusted to keep it safe for ever.

But those who keep subjects in check by force would of course have to employ severity—masters, for example, toward their servants, when these cannot be held in control in any other way. But those who in a free state deliberately put themselves in a position to be feared are the maddest of the mad. For let the laws be never so much overborne by some one individual's power, let the spirit of freedom be never so intimidated, still sooner or later they assert themselves either through unvoiced public sentiment, or through secret ballots disposing of some high office of state. Freedom suppressed and again regained bites with keener fangs than freedom never endangered. Let us, then, embrace this policy, which appeals to every heart and is the strongest support not only of security but also of influence and power—namely, to banish fear and cleave to love. And thus we shall most easily secure success both in private and in public life.

Cicero
De Officiis,
106-43 B.C.

Furthermore, those who wish to be feared must inevitably be afraid of those whom they intimidate. *241*

*Against hatred
and fear*
Nietzsche
Der Wanderer und
sein Schatten, 1880

Better to perish than to hate and fear; better to perish twice over than to make oneself hated and feared. One day this will be the supreme maxim of all politically organized societies. *242*

J.-J. Rousseau
A Discourse
on the Origin
and Foundation of
Inequality among
Men, 1755

It is therefore beyond dispute, and indeed the fundamental maxim of all political right, that people have set up chiefs to protect their liberty, and not to enslave them. *243*

The Bill of Rights condemning the conduct of James II, included the following articles:

1. That the pretended power of suspending laws, or of execution of laws, by regal authority without consent of parliament, is illegal.
2. That the pretended power of dispensing with laws, or the execution of laws, by regal authority, as it hath been assumed and exercised of late, is illegal.
5. That it is the right of the subjects to petition the king, and all commitments and prosecutions for such petitioning are illegal.
9. That the freedom of speech, and debates or proceedings in parliament, ought not to be impeached or questioned in any court or place out of parliament.
10. That excessive bail ought not to be required, nor excessive fines imposed, nor cruel and unusual punishments inflicted.

<table>
<tr><td>

Bill of Rights
1689
England

</td><td>

12. That all grants and promises of fines and forfeitures of particular persons before conviction are illegal and void. *244*

</td></tr>
</table>

Against the State

The centralized State apparatus, with its complicated and ubiquitous military, bureaucratic, clerical and judicial organs, coils about the living body of civil society like a boa-constrictor.... All—even the minor—interests resulting from the relations between the various social groups were severed from society itself, made independent thereof, and set against it in the guise of the State's interest, administered by the priests of the State divinity (*Staatspriester*):

Karl Marx
The Civil War
in France
1871

the hierarchy of the officials. . . . All revolutions without exception have merely perfected this State machine instead of getting rid of this suffocating nightmare. *245*

*True democracy:
the Commune*

The Paris Commune (1871) was not a revolution against any particular form of State power, legitimist, constitutional, republican or imperial. It was a revolution against the *State* itself, that unnatural freak of society; it was the resumption by the people and for the people of control over their own social life. It was not a revolution made for the purpose of transferring this power from one fraction of the dominant classes to another, but a revolution designed to smash the horrible machinery of class domination itself. It was not one of those petty struggles between the executive form and the parliamentary form of class domination; but a revolt against these two forms of domination which in fact overlap —parliament being merely a deceptive adjunct of the Executive. The Second Empire was the finished form of the usurper State. The Commune was its clear negation . . . the resumption of State power by society, of which it becomes the living force instead of the dominating, subjugating force; the resumption of State power by the masses

Karl Marx
The Civil War
in France
1871

of the people themselves, substituting their own force for the force organized for their oppression. The Commune is the political form of their social emancipation. *246*

Law above power or subordinate to it

Law above power
Heraclitus of Ephesus
6th cent. B.C.

The people must defend its law as it defends its walls. *247*

I will not, in contravention of the established laws and the decrees of the Athenian People and the Council, pronounce sentence of banishment against any who live here, and I shall prevent any other from doing so.

. . . I will not accept bribes . . . nor shall any other man or woman on my behalf, by whatever connivance or deviousness. I shall listen with the same impartiality to prosecutor and defendant, and my verdict shall be confined to the specific charge. This I swear by Jupiter, Poseidon and Demeter. Should I forswear, may I and my household perish; if I am faithful to my oath, let me prosper.   *248*

Oath of the Heliasts
Demosthenes' oration
against Timocrates
c. 353 B.C.

Never alter a law to suit the whims of a ruler; law is superior to the ruler.   *249*

Kuan-tzu
On Legislation
4th to 3rd cent. B.C.
China

For if there are now any magistrates of the people, appointed to restrain the wilfulness of kings (as in ancient times the ephors were set against the Spartan kings, or the tribunes of the people against the Roman consuls, or the demarchs against the senate of the Athenians; and perhaps, as things now are, such power as the three estates exercise in every realm when they hold their chief assemblies), I am so far from forbidding them to withstand, in accordance with their duty, the fierce licentiousness of kings, that, if they wink at kings who violently fall upon and assault the lowly common folk, I declare that their dissimulation involves nefarious perfidy, because they dishonestly betray the freedom of the people, of which they know that they have been appointed protectors by God's ordinance.   *250*

Calvin
Institutes of the
Christian Religion
1541

It is right, therefore, that kings as well as every public official should be ruled by Law, so that they may thereby preserve themselves from the influence of the passions, and make it a criterion wherewith to govern themselves and their peoples alike.   *251*

A. F. Modrzewski
De Republica
Emendanda
1551
Poland

When the administration allows itself to be led too far astray and becomes despotic and tyrannical, sacrificing the people's rights and liberty, then the laws should set it right and bring it back to the path of justice. Excellent and well-known examples of this are provided by the signing of Magna Carta in England and the promulgation of the Declaration of the Rights of Man and of the Citizen at the time of the French Revolution. It is precisely the spirit of the laws that hovers over the Japanese people, controlling them and giving them a pattern to follow, and so saving them from confusion and depravity.   *252*

Tsukasa Okamura
1866-1922
A Short Treatise
on Law
Japan

That a man having a sense of justice is master of the law itself.

GUEST. After a certain manner it is evident that legislation is a part of the science of a king: but it is best, not for the laws to prevail, but for a man, who has with prudence the power of a king. Do you know in what way?

SOCRATES THE YOUNGER. In what way do you mean?

GUEST. Because the law cannot, by comprehending that which is the best and most accurately just in all cases, at the same time ordain what is the best. For the inequalities of men and their actions, and the fact that not a single atom, so to say, of human affairs, enjoys a state of rest, do not permit any art whatever to exhibit in any case any thing simple (without exception) respecting all matters and through all time. Shall we admit this?

SOCRATES THE YOUNGER. How not?

GUEST. And yet we see the law tending nearly to this very point; and, like a certain self-willed and ignorant man, it does not suffer any person to do any thing contrary to its own orders, nor to put a question, not even should something new happen to be in some case better as compared with the decree it had ordained.

SOCRATES THE YOUNGER. True. For the law does really so, as you have just now said, to each of us.

GUEST. Is it not then impossible for that, which is under all cases simple, to do well in cases which are never at any time simple?

Plato
The Statesman
429-347 B.C.

SOCRATES THE YOUNGER. It appears so nearly.   253

Hsün-tzu
The Way
of the Emperor
3rd cent. B.C.
China

Therefore law is not sufficient of itself, order does not perpetuate itself. When the right man comes, law succeeds, but not otherwise. When the saint rules, general laws will meet all cases; but when the ruler is not a saint, no amount of legislation can be properly applied. When there is mis-application of law, disorder is at hand.   254

Hsün-tzu
The Biography
of Tung Chung-shu
3rd cent. B.C.
China

Laws and order are merely the instruments of government, but not the source of the purity or impurity of government.   255

*The throne and
the law*

FREEDOM (An ode)

Fly hence! O Cytherean goddess frail,
Fair Venus, fly, and shun the light of day;
But thou, intrepid scourge of Caesars, hail!
Come, Freedom's songstress, and inspire my lay.
Come, hurl my poet's garland to the ground,
My tender lyre to myriad fragments smash:

Let Freedom's paean on my lips resound
And let anointed Evil fear my lash.

. . . .

O sorry world! 'tis everywhere the same:
The whip, the chain, the rack keep men in fear,
The law—dire portent—hides its head in shame,
The weary captive sheds a helpless tear;
In every land Authority unjust
Sits wrapt in clouds of prejudice obscure,
And everywhere there lurks the horrid lust
To dominate, and Glory's fatal lure.

There, and there only, can we hope to find
A King or Emperor guiltless towards his land
Where, indissolubly together join'd,
Freedom and Rule of Law march hand in hand:
Where powerful laws, by one and all obeyed,
The humblest citizen from insult shield
And judges, by no threats or presents swayed,
With even hand the sword of Justice wield—
The sword that swiftly, with unerring aim,
Doth smite the amaz'd transgressor from on high:
No fear of punishment its wrath can tame
Nor thirst for gold its acquiescence buy.
Sovereigns! Your sceptres, orbs and robes of State
Law, and not Nature, doth on you bestow:
Your subjects bow the knee; but you, though great,
Yourselves to eternal Law allegiance owe.

The poet goes on to describe the execution of Louis XVI and the assassination of Tsar Paul, and concludes:

Learn! King or Tsar, before it be too late:
No savage punishment or vast reward
Nor altar's smoke, nor thrice-locked prison gate
Can long protect thee from the avenging sword.
But bow thy head, embrace with heart and mind
The Law, let *that* thy strength and refuge be:
Then shall thy throne its one true guardian find—
Thy people's freedom and tranquillity.

Pushkin
1799-1837

256

Conditional submission, supremacy of conscience

*An overriding
claim of conscience
as against
the royal power*

Antigone disobeys Creon, the King, who had forbidden the burial of her brother.

CREON. And now for thee,
    Say in few words, not lengthening out thy speech,

Didst thou not know the edicts which forbade
The things thou ownest?
ANTIGONE. Right well I knew them all.
How could I not? Full clear and plain were they.
CREON. Didst thou then dare to disobey these laws?
ANTIGONE. Yes, for it was not Zeus who gave them forth,
Nor Justice, dwelling with the Gods below,
Who traced these laws for all the sons of men;
Nor did I deem thy edicts strong enough,
Coming from mortal man, to set at nought
The unwritten laws of God that know not change.
They are not of today nor yesterday,
But live for ever, nor can man assign
When first they sprang to being. Not through fear
Of any man's resolve was I prepared
Before the Gods to bear the penalty
Of sinning against these. That I should die
I knew (how should I not?) though thy decree
Had never spoken. And, before my time
If I should die, I reckon this a gain;
For who so lives, as I, in many woes,
How can it be but death shall bring him gain?
And so for me to bear this doom of thine
Has nothing painful. But, if I had left
My mother's son unburied on his death,
I should have given them pain. But as things are,
Pain I feel none. And should I seem to thee
To have done a foolish deed, 'tis simply this
I bear the charge of folly from a fool.

Sophocles
Antigone
5th cent. B.C.
Trans. by
E. H. Plumptre

257

*The law's demands
as against
natural rights*

The word *rights*, the same as the word *law*, has two senses;
the one a proper sense, the other a metaphorical sense.
Rights, properly so called, are the creatures of *law* properly
so called; real laws give birth to real rights. *Natural
rights* are the creatures of natural law; they are a metaphor
which derives its origin from another metaphor.

What there is natural in man is means—faculties. But
to call these means, these faculties, *natural rights*, is again
to put language in opposition to itself. For *rights* are
established to insure the exercise of means and faculties.
The right is the *guarantee*; the faculty is the thing guaranteed.
How can we understand each other with a language which
confounds under the same term things so different? Where
would be the nomenclature of the arts, if we gave to the
mechanic who makes an article the same name as to the
article itself?

Real rights are always spoken of in a legal sense; natural

rights are often spoken of in a sense that may be called anti-legal. When it is said, for example, that *law cannot avail against natural rights*, the word rights is employed in a sense above the law; for, in this use of it, we acknowledge rights which attack the law; which overturn it, which annul it. In this anti-legal sense, the word *right* is the greatest enemy of reason, and the most terrible destroyer of governments.

There is no reasoning with fanatics, armed with *natural rights*, which each one understands as he pleases, and applies as he sees fit; of which nothing can be yielded nor retrenched; which are inflexible, at the same time that they are unintelligible; which are consecrated as dogmas, from which it is a crime to vary. Instead of examining laws by their effects, instead of judging them as good or as bad, they consider them in relation to these pretended natural rights; that is to say, they substitute for the reasoning of experience the chimeras of their own imaginations.

This is not a harmless error; it passes from speculation into practice. 'Those laws must be obeyed, which are accordant with nature; the others are null in fact; and instead of obeying them, they ought to be resisted. The moment natural rights are attacked, every good citizen ought to rouse up in their defence. These rights, evident in themselves, do not need to be proved; it is sufficient to declare them. How prove what is evident already? To doubt implies a want of sense, or a fault of intellect.'...

But not to be accused of gratuitously ascribing such seditious maxims to these inspired politicians of nature, I shall cite a passage from Blackstone, directly to the point; and I choose Blackstone, because he is, of all writers, the one who has shown the most profound respect for the authority of governments. In speaking of these pretended laws of nature, and of the laws of revelation, he says: 'Human laws must not be permitted to contradict these; if a human law commands a thing forbidden by the natural or divine law, we are bound to transgress that human law.'...

Is not this arming every fanatic against all governments? In the immense variety of ideas respecting natural and divine law, cannot some reason be found for resisting all human laws? Is there a single state which can maintain itself a day, if each individual holds himself bound in conscience to resist the laws, whenever they are not conformed to his particular ideas of natural or divine law? What a cut-throat scene we should have between all interpreters of the code of nature, and all the interpreters of the law of God!...

Utility having been often badly applied, understood in a narrow sense, and having lent its name to crimes, has appeared contrary to eternal justice. It thus became degraded, and acquired a mercenary reputation. It needs courage to restore it to honour, and to re-establish reasoning upon its true basis.

I propose a treaty of conciliation with the partisans of natural rights. If *nature* has made such or such a law, those who cite it with so much confidence, those who have modestly taken upon themselves to be its interpreters, must suppose that nature has some reasons for her law. Would it not be surer, shorter and more persuasive, to give us those reasons directly, instead of urging upon us the will of this unknown legislator, as itself an authority?

Jeremy Bentham
Principles
of Legislation
1789
Great Britain

258

Limits to authority

Advice addressed to rulers.

Attributed to
the Sassanian king
Ardashir
3rd cent.
Persia

Know that your authority extends only upon the bodies of your subjects, and that no power belongs to kings over their hearts. Know that if you overcome people in respect of what they hold in their hands, you will never overcome them in respect of their minds.

259

Nichiren
Senji Shō
1275
Japan

Having the honour to be born in your kingdom, I find my body obeying your Excellency, but my soul will never.

260

Talmud
Yoma 23

A man came to Raba and said, 'The prefect of my town has ordered me to kill so and so, or he will kill me.' Raba said, 'Let him kill you; do you commit no murder. Why should you think that your blood is redder than his? Perhaps his is redder than yours.'

261

*Deposing of
the ecclesiastical
Superior*

In the Rules of the Dominicans, it is laid down that half-way through his term of office, the Superior, local or provincial, shall convene a meeting of those who elected him.

Rule
of the Dominicans
Art. 469
1283

In this council, a secret ballot will be held to decide whether the Provincial shall be maintained in office or dismissed.

262

*Although he is
elected for life,
the Superior
General may be
deposed*

If it should happen (which we hope through the goodness of God, by the favour of his grace, will never come to be), that the General commits grave sins in external acts of a specific kind. ... If any one of these sins occurs and the facts are quite sufficiently ascertained, the Society can and ought to deprive him of his office; and, if need be, expel him from the Society, having taken into consideration the greater glory of God and the universal good of the Society.

Epitome Instituti Societatis Jesu 1689

263

Obedience is not unconditional

But the Brethren who are subjects shall remember that for God's sake they have renounced their own wills. Wherefore I strictly command them to obey their Ministers in all things they have promised the Lord to observe, and which are not against their soul or our Rule. And wherever those Friars may be who know and feel that they cannot observe the Rule spiritually, they can and should have recourse to their Ministers.

Rule of St. Francis of Assisi 1223

264

[The Brethren should strive] in all things that are honest and permissible to give their obedience in all simplicity and without argument, promptly and willingly, cheerfully and not grudgingly or as a matter of obligation.

Constitution of the Carmelites Old Observance Ch. XII, 1636-37

265

Our Brothers owe obedience to their Superiors in all things pertaining to the Rule and the Constitutions. . . . We are not under obligation to obey, nay, we cannot obey, in things which are counter to the commandments of God and the Church or to the Rule.

Rule of the Dominicans Art. 544 1283

266

[Obedience is due only] in all things where sin is not perceived.

Constitution of the Society of Jesus 1556

267

Limits of obedience due to religious authority

Unless I am persuaded by the Scriptures or by the evidence of reason, I remain bound by the texts which I have cited, and my conscience is the prisoner of God's Word. I believe neither in the Pope nor in the Councils alone: it is a fact that they have often been mistaken and contradicted themselves. I cannot and will not retract, for it is neither wise nor good to go against one's conscience. God help me, Amen.

Luther at the Diet of Worms 1521

268

Limits of obedience due to princes

There is but one will and that is of the one God, eternal and unchanging, fount of all justice. It is therefore to Him alone that we owe obedience in all circumstances. As for the obedience due to princes, if they were always to command as the mouth-pieces of God, we would have to say that in all circumstances they too must be obeyed, exactly as God is obeyed. But seeing that, more often than not, the contrary is the case, the following stipulation must be added: provided they do not issue ungodly or iniquitous commands. I call ungodly commands any whereby people are ordered to do what the first Commandment of the Law of God forbids; or are forbidden to do what it commands. I call iniquitous commands any which cannot be obeyed without acting contrary to or neglecting what everyone owes to his neighbour, according to his calling, be it public or private.   *269*

Théodore de Bèze
Du droit des
magistrats sur
leurs sujets
1581
France

The observance of the commandment is its own reward, and the recompense for transgressing the commandment is transgression.   *270*

Talmud
Avot 4

*Nothing
can suppress
individual
judgement*

If it were as easy to control minds as tongues, every ruler would rule quite safely and no State would be oppressive, for all subjects would live as their rulers wished them to do, taking from these all their views about what is true and false, good and bad, just and unjust. But . . . it is impossible for any mind to be entirely under the control of another, for nobody can transfer to anyone else, whether voluntarily or under compulsion, his natural right to reason freely and form judgements about any matter whatever. This is why any State in which there is rule over minds is regarded as tyrannical, and why a Supreme Power is thought to be doing an injustice to its subjects and to be taking away their right when it sets itself to prescribe what every individual shall accept as true and reject as false, and what religious beliefs he should hold. These matters belong to the right of the individual, which no one is able in fact to surrender, even if he wishes to do so. I admit that a man's judgement can be dominated in many ways, some of them scarcely creditable, so that, despite its not being directly at the bidding of another, it may depend so much on the word of another as to warrant our saying that it is to that extent under his jurisdiction. Still, whatever political cunning may have managed to do in this respect, it has never been so successful as to prevent men from being full of their own opinions, or brains from being as different as palates. . . .

However much Sovereign Powers may be credited with the right to everything and believed to be the interpreters of law and moral duty, they will never be able to prevent men from coming to their own conclusions about any matter, or from being moved by this or that emotion. It is indeed true that they have the right to regard as enemies all who do not agree with them in every respect. What we are now considering, however, is not their right, but what is politically good. I grant that it is within their right to rule tyrannically, even to put citizens to death for the slightest reasons; but everyone would agree that this would be against sound reason. . . .

From the origination of the State . . . it follows quite clearly that its ultimate purpose is not domination, not to repress men through fear, or to put them under an authority other than their own; but the very opposite, namely, to free them from fear by enabling them to live as safely as possible, or, in other words, to provide the way in which each may best retain his right to exist and act, i.e., without hurt either to himself or to others. It is certainly not the purpose of the State to change men from rational beings into beasts or puppets, but to make it possible for them to use their mental and bodily capacities safely and their reason freely, and to keep them from the conflicts that come from hatred, anger and perfidy, and from behaving unfairly to one another. The real purpose of the State is freedom.

. . . Suppose this freedom [of judgement] could be suppressed and men be kept from daring to murmur anything but what the Supreme Power prescribes. Even so they could by no means be kept also from *thinking* only what the Supreme Power wills. The inevitable result would be that men would daily think in one way and speak in another. The trust that is utterly necessary in a State would thus be destroyed, and despicable fawning and bad faith would be encouraged, resulting in all sorts of deception and the decay of all honest occupations. But it is quite impossible to make all men speak to order: the greater the measures taken to deprive them of freedom of speech, the more rebellious do they become.　*271*

Spinoza
Tractatus
Theologico-politicus
1670

Individual rights—which can also be called natural, primitive, absolute, primordial or personal—are faculties, moral prerogatives which nature bestowed on man as an intelligent being; they are his property, inherent in his personality, an integral part of the human entity.　*272*

Pimenta Bueno
Comments
on the Imperial
Constitution of 1824
Brazil

*Constitutional
rights
and guarantees*

Now, constitutional guarantees are one thing, and the rights they in part safeguard politically and in law are another. The rights reflect subjective aspects or mani-

Rui Barbosa
Comments
on the Republican
Constitution of 1891
Brazil

festations of the human personality and its various relations with society or the individuals who make up society. Strictly speaking, constitutional guarantees are the solemn safeguards the law assigns to some of these rights in order to protect them against abuses of power. *273*

*Critique of
the laws made for
Sparta by Lycurgus*

Set against its intended purpose, the legislation of Lycurgus is a masterpiece of statecraft and human science. He wanted a powerful, self-contained and unshakeable State; political strength and permanence were his aim, and, as far as it was possible in the circumstances, what he achieved. But set this aim of Lycurgus against mankind's, and bitter disapproval must replace the admiration aroused as our first, transitory, impression. All may be sacrificed to the good of the State, but not that to which the State itself is only a means. The State itself is never the ultimate aim, it is important only as one of the conditions under which mankind's ultimate aim can be fulfilled, and this aim of mankind is nothing less than the development of all man's faculties, and progress. Any constitution which prevents man from developing all his faculties or hinders intellectual progress is harmful and deleterious, however well conceived and perfect in its way it may be otherwise. Its very permanence, rather than a matter for praise, becomes a something to regret. It is now a protracted evil; the longer it lasts, the more harm it does.

We can lay down the general rule in judging political institutions that they are good and laudable only when they enable man to develop his abilities to the full and to further—or at least not to impede—cultural advance. This is as true of religious as of political laws; both are faulty if they shackle a human faculty or halt it in any way. For instance, a law binding a nation to remain faithful to a system of beliefs it once felt to be the most admirable would be an outrage against humanity, and no reason, however plausible, could justify it. It would run absolutely counter to the highest good and the highest purpose of society....

General human feeling in Sparta was stifled in an even more outrageous way, and reverence for human life, the most sacred of all duties, was lost beyond recall. A law made it the duty of Spartans to treat their slaves inhumanely, and in these unhappy victims mankind was insulted and wronged. The Spartan code itself preached the dangerous principle that men should be regarded as a means and not as ends, so that the law itself was used to destroy the basis of natural law and morality. Morality was totally abandoned to maintain something that can be of value only as a means to morality. . . .

All art was banished from Sparta, all science neglected, all trade with foreign peoples forbidden, and everything foreign shut out. Thus were all channels closed through which fresh ideas might have flowed in to the nation, and the Spartan State was for evermore to live turned in on its own eternal uniformity and gloomy egoism. . . .

If we take all these things together, the false glory surrounding the only outstanding feature of the Spartan State that dazzles an inexperienced eye vanishes; we no longer find anything but an immature and imperfect try—a first early attempt, in a world still lacking in penetration and experience, to get at the true nature of things. But however imperfect, it must necessarily remain a noteworthy subject to any student philosophically concerned with the history of mankind. It always marks a tremendous advance of the human mind when that which has hitherto been a matter of chance and the passions is dealt with as an art. The first attempt in the most difficult of all the arts was bound to be imperfect but it is of abiding value because made in the most important of all the arts. The sculptors began with columns to Hermes before attaining the formal perfection of an Antinoüs or a Vatican Apollo. Legislators will long continue to make clumsy attempts before the right equilibrium of social forces is finally evolved.

Stone patiently suffers the sculptor's chisel, and the responding strings do not resist the musician's fingers.

Schiller
1759-1805

The legislator alone has to work a wilful and refractory material—human liberty.   *274*

Freedom and honour

Freedom is the right which every man has to be honest, and to think and speak without hypocrisy.... Certain men can live happily without honour; others suffer terribly when they see that those around them lead dishonourable lives. In this world, there has to be a certain amount of light, just as there has to be a certain amount of honour. Whenever there are many men without honour, there are always others who preserve in themselves the honour of many men put together.

These are they who rebel with terrible fury against those who take away the freedom of a nation, which is to rob men of their honour. In these men are contained thousands and thousands of men; a whole people is contained in them, indeed, the whole of human dignity; such men are sacred.   *275*

José Martí
The Golden Age
1889
Cuba

No unconditional submission

The unfailing loyalty of partisans to their chief creates a relationship which is not political and exists only in small circles and primitive social structures ... In a State where freedom prevails, supervision by the people at large and the possibility of replacing those in office are the rule. ...

This leads to double culpability: firstly, that which stems, in a general way, from unconditional submission to a chief; and secondly, that which is engendered by the character of the chief submitted to. The very atmosphere of submission engenders a collective culpability.   *276*

Karl Jaspers
Die Schuldfrage
1946
Germany

Kiyoshi Kiyosawa
Journal
2 December 1944
Japan

The aim of education in the future will be to create a climate of opinion resistant to the belief that the State is a supreme and absolute being and that it is our duty to conform to its dictates.   *277*

If a father does injustice, it is the duty of his children to leave the parental roof. If the headmaster of a school conducts his institution on an immoral basis, the pupils must leave the school. If the chairman of a corporation is corrupt, the members thereof must wash their hands clean of his corruption by withdrawing from it; even so if a government does a grave injustice the subject must withdraw co-operation wholly or partially, sufficiently to wean the ruler from wickedness. In each case conceived by me there is an element of suffering whether mental or physical. Without such suffering it is not possible to attain freedom.   *278*

Mahatma Gandhi
1869-1948

Legitimate rebellion, insurrection a duty

Mahābhārata XIII
2nd cent. B.C.
to 1st cent. A.D.
Sanskrit

A king, who, even after proclaiming, 'I will protect you', does not protect [his subjects] may be killed by his subjects, rising together against him, like a mad, diseased dog. *279*

King Hsüan of Ch'i asked, 'Is it not true that T'ang banished Chieh and that King Wu smote Chou?' Mencius replied, 'It is so stated in the records.' The king asked, 'May a subject, then, slay his sovereign?' Mencius replied, 'He who outrages humanity is a scoundrel; he who

Mencius
372?-289? B.C.
China

outrages righteousness is a scourge. A scourge or a scoundrel is a despised creature. I have heard that a despised creature called Chou was put to death, but I have not heard anything about the murdering of a sovereign.' *280*

Koran
Al-Hajj 39

A sanction is given to those who, because they have suffered outrages, have taken up arms; and verily, God is well able to succour them. *281*

Hadith
(Sayings of
the Prophet)

No creature owes obedience when that implies disobeying the Creator. *282*

First Chronicle
of Novgorod
Late 14th-cent.
manuscript

Russia has known republics governed by a popular assembly, in which the prince was elected from among the military leaders.

[In 1270] to the prince, in the palace, an envoy was sent bearing a document listing all his faults,... and they were many. 'And now, prince, we can no longer bear with your acts of violence. Depart from us and we shall find another prince.' The prince sent Sviatoslav and Andrew Vorotislavitch to the Assembly with this appeal from him: 'I renounce all such practices and shall take the oath as you desire.' But the people of Novgorod answered: 'Prince, depart from us, we wish no more of you. If not, all Novgorod will drive you forth.' Unwillingly, the prince departed from the city. *283*

Revolt
in the theatre

The 'Mazze' (from the Italian 'mazza', meaning bludgeon) was a cylindrical wooden staff on which distorted human features were carved. It served as a symbol for revolt against powerful lords and also against religious and governmental innovations. For a long time, the masters sought to suppress this revolutionary weapon. This is how a Mazze revolt took place during the Rarogne War of 1414-15.

A crowd had gathered in the public square where the Mazze had been set up and a dialogue in dramatic form was carried on between the crowd and the spokesman of the Mazze who stood beside it.
CROWD. What are you doing here, Mazze?
SPOKESMAN. Mazze, they want to help you. Name the one you fear. Is it Silenen?... Asperling?... Hengarten?

At each new name, the spokesman described the kind of oppression the lord named was suspected of.

Finally he asked, 'Are these men of Rarogne?'

The Mazze bowed in acquiescence. The spokesman continued: 'Let those who wish to save the Mazze raise their hands!'

The majority did so. From village to village it was announced that the Mazze would go among the people of Rarogne. On the appointed day, the opponents' houses were sacked.

According to Albert Carlen
Le Théâtre
du Haut-Valais
au Moyen Age
1945
Switzerland

284

*Social contract
and right
of resistance*

Now, we find in the Bible two sorts of covenant when Kings are crowned: that between God the King and his people, so that the people may be God's people, and that between the King and his people, so that the people all obey the King faithfully if they are justly ruled by him.

... In the first Covenant there is the duty of reverence; in the second, that of justice. By the former, the King promises religious obedience to God; by the latter, to rule the people justly. In the first case he undertakes to promote God's glory, in the second to promote his people's welfare. A condition is attached to the first: if you keep my Law, and to the second: if you preserve for each man those rights which belong to him. God himself is the protector of the first Covenant and its avenger if not carried out; as for the second, the right of resistance to an unworthy sovereign belongs to the people or, alternatively, to the States which represent them and have a duty to support them.

Ph. Duplessis-
Mornay
Vindiciae
contra Tyrannos
1579
France

285

A Prince is not allowed, unless his power be absolute, to despoil another of his goods, and though it is not possible to bring a criminal action against him to protect the rights of the person so despoiled and force him to return the goods, we none the less regard him as a thief and a robber.

Juan
de Solórzano Pereira
1575-1654
Spain

286

If I considered only force and the results that proceed from it, I should say that so long as a people is compelled to obey, and does obey it does well; but that, so soon as it can shake off the yoke and does shake it off, it does better; for, if men recover their freedom by virtue of the same right by which it was taken away, either they are justified in resuming it, or there was no justification for depriving them of it.

J.-J. Rousseau
Du Contrat Social
1762

287

History teaches us that since the beginning of time, absolute systems of government have always assumed rights that were incompatible with social conditions truly good for mankind. Thus, in every age, they have forced the peoples to take arms against claims to absolute power and against infringement of their legitimate rights. *288*

Pestalozzi
1746-1827
Switzerland

WILLIAM TELL

William Tell, the symbol of freedom in Switzerland, has very often been depicted in folk-theatre: the following are some extracts from a play. The characters mentioned are: Tell; Hedewig, his wife; Werner and Arnold, friends of Tell; Gessler, the foreign Bailiff.

WERNER. The number of our associates increases daily. And also wrath, fidelity and childish trust in him who is our liberator.

ARNOLD. What, the hat, that ancient sign of fair freedom, has now become a symbol of vile servitude?

. . . .

TELL [*to Bailiff*]. He whom all fear, fears everyone. Arrogance is self-destroying and it is against arrogance that every arrow is turned. Never would I prefer bondage to my life. Life without freedom to me is a burden . . . Tell has sworn to uphold the rights of men, standing fearlessly against the frenzied brigands; let that be my honour and my reward.

GESSLER. The populace ought not to know that they have a will, that nature has given them rights and human dignity; that the State has given them the property. Such dangerous knowledge must be entirely rooted out.

. . . .

GESSLER [*to Hedewig*]. Nature has endowed you with outstanding gifts: do not conceal them. Stand before the others and show that you are different.

HEDEWIG [*replying to Bailiff*]. Our country knows no distinctions, unless it be that which allows virtue to a woman.

. . . .

WERNER [*to Bailiff*]. You will not weaken our resolve by threats. It will grow stronger through resistance as long as our clear conscience protects us. I speak as a free man . . . even if I were facing the king . . . and all these free-born souls must appear hateful to you.

Joseph-Ignaz
Zimmermann
Wilhelm Tell
Switzerland
1777

. . . .

TELL. This happiness [at having driven away the Bailiff], dear fellow-citizens, is but the first step. Remember that freedom must be strengthened. *289*

Woman's rights THE SENECA FALLS DECLARATION OF SENTIMENTS AND
RESOLUTIONS, 19 JULY 1848

*The text starts by a quotation from the Declaration of Independence
of the American colonies, as follows:*

... when a long train of abuses and usurpations pursuing invariably
the same object, evinces a design to reduce mankind under absolute
despotism, it is their duty to throw off such government, and to
provide new guards for their future security. ...

Such has been the patient sufferance of the women under
this government, and such is now the necessity which
constrains them to demand the equal station to which
they are entitled.

The history of mankind is a history of repeated injuries
and usurpations on the part of man toward woman, having
in direct object the establishment of an absolute tyranny
over her. To prove this, let facts be submitted to a candid
world.

He has never permitted her to exercise her inalienable
right to the elective franchise.

He has compelled her to submit to laws, in the formation
of which she had no voice.

He has withheld from her rights which are given to the
most ignorant and degraded men—both natives and
foreigners.

Having deprived her of this first right of a citizen, the
elective franchise, thereby leaving her without representation in the halls of legislation, he has oppressed her on
all sides.

He has made her, if married, in the eye of the law,
civilly dead.

He has taken from her all right in property, even to
the wages she earns.

He has made her, morally, an irresponsible being, as she
can commit many crimes with impunity, provided they
be done in the presence of her husband. In the covenant
of marriage, she is compelled to promise obedience to
her husband, he becoming, to all intents and purposes,
her master—the law giving him power to deprive her
of her liberty, and to administer chastisement.

He has so framed the laws of divorce, as to what shall
be the proper causes, and in case of separation, to whom
the guardianship of the children shall be given, as to be
wholly regardless of the happiness of women—the law,
in all cases, going upon a false supposition of the supremacy
of man, and giving all power into his hands.

After depriving her of all rights as a married woman,
if single, and the owner of property, he has taxed her to

support a government which recognizes her only when her property can be made profitable to it.

He has monopolized nearly all the profitable employments, and from those she is permitted to follow, she receives but a scanty remuneration. He closes against her all the avenues to wealth and distinction which he considers most honorable to himself. As a teacher of theology, medicine, or law, she is not known.

He has denied her the facilities for obtaining a thorough education, all colleges being closed against her.

He allows her in Church, as well as State, but a subordinate position, claiming Apostolic authority for her exclusion from the ministry, and, with some exceptions, from any public participation in the affairs of the Church.

He has created a false public sentiment by giving to the world a different code of morals for men and women, by which moral delinquencies which exclude women from society, are not only tolerated, but deemed of little account in man.

He has usurped the prerogative of Jehovah himself, claiming it as his right to assign for her a sphere of action, when that belongs to her conscience and to her God.

He has endeavored, in every way that he could, to destroy her confidence in her own powers, to lessen her self-respect and to make her willing to lead a dependent and abject life.

. . . *Resolved,* That all laws which prevent woman from occupying such a station in society as her conscience shall dictate, or which place her in a position inferior to that of man, are contrary to the great precept of nature, and therefore of no force or authority.

Resolved, That woman is man's equal—was intended to be so by the Creator, and the highest good of the race demands that she should be recognized as such.

Resolved, That the women of this country ought to be enlightened in regard to the laws under which they live, that they may no longer publish their degradation by declaring themselves satisfied with their present position, nor their ignorance, by asserting that they have all the rights they want.

Resolved, That inasmuch as man, while claiming for himself intellectual superiority, does accord to woman moral superiority, it is pre-eminently his duty to encourage her to speak and teach, as she has an opportunity, in all religious assemblies.

Resolved, That the same amount of virtue, delicacy, and refinement of behavior that is required of woman in the social state, should also be required of man, and the same transgressions should be visited with equal severity on both man and woman.

Resolved, That the objection of indelicacy and impropriety, which is so often brought against woman when she addresses a public audience, comes with a very ill-grace from those who encourage, by their attendance, her appearance on the stage, in the concert, or in feats of the circus.

Resolved, That woman has too long rested satisfied in the circumscribed limits which corrupt customs and a perverted application of the Scriptures have marked out for her, and that it is time she should move in the enlarged sphere which her great Creator has assigned her.

United States
of America

290

*The majority
versus
conscience*

THE DUTY OF CIVIL DISOBEDIENCE

The practical reason why, when the power is once in the hands of the people, a majority are permitted, and for a long period continue, to rule is not because they are most likely to be in the right, nor because this seems fairest to the minority, but because they are physically the strongest. But a government in which the majority rule in all cases cannot be based on justice, even as far as men understand it. Can there not be a government in which majorities do not virtually decide right and wrong, but conscience?—in which majorities decide only those questions to which the rule of expediency is applicable? Must the citizen ever for a moment, or in the least degree, resign his conscience to the legislator? Why has every man a conscience, then? I think that we should be men first, and subjects afterward. It is not desirable to cultivate a respect for the law, so much as for the right. The only obligation which I have a right to assume is to do at any time what I think right....

The mass of men serve the state thus, not as men mainly, but as machines, with their bodies. They are the standing army, and the militia, jailors, constables, posse comitatus, etc. In most cases there is no free exercise whatever of the judgment or of the moral sense; but they put themselves on a level with wood and earth and stones; and wooden men can perhaps be manufactured that will serve the purpose as well. Such command no more respect than men of straw or a lump of dirt. They have the same sort of worth only as horses and dogs. Yet such as these even are commonly esteemed good citizens. Others—as most legislators, politicians, lawyers, ministers, and office-holders—serve the state chiefly with their heads; and, as they rarely make any moral distinctions, they are as likely to serve the Devil, without *intending* it, as God. A very few, as heroes, patriots, martyrs, reformers in the great sense, and *men*, serve the state with consciences also, and so necessarily resist it for the most part; and they are commonly treated as enemies by it....

How does it become a man to behave toward this American government to-day? I answer, that he cannot without disgrace be associated with it. I cannot for an instant recognize that political organization as *my* government which is the *slave's* government also.

All men recognize the right of revolution; that is, the right to refuse allegiance to, and to resist, the government, when its tyranny or its inefficiency are great and unendurable. But almost all say that such is not the case now. But such was the case, they think, in the Revolution of '75. If one were to tell me that this was a bad government because it taxed certain foreign commodities brought to its ports, it is most probable that I should not make an ado about it, for I can do without them. All machines have their friction....

But when the friction comes to have its machine, and oppression and robbery are organized, I say, let us not have such a machine any longer. In other words, when a sixth of the population of a nation which has undertaken to be the refuge of liberty are slaves, and a whole country is unjustly overrun and conquered by a foreign army, and subjected to military law, I think that it is not too soon for honest men to rebel and revolutionize. What makes this duty the more urgent is the fact that the country so overrun is not our own, but ours is the invading army....

Unjust laws exist: shall we be content to obey them, or shall we endeavor to amend them, and obey them until we have succeeded, or shall we transgress them at once? Men generally, under such a government as this, think that they ought to wait until they have persuaded the majority to alter them. They think that, if they should resist, the remedy would be worse than the evil. But it is the fault of the government itself that the remedy *is* worse than the evil. *It* makes it worse. Why is it not more apt to anticipate and provide for reform? Why does it not cherish its wise minority? Why does it cry and resist before it is hurt? Why does it not encourage its citizens to be on the alert to point out its faults, and *do* better than it would have them?...

Under a government which imprisons any unjustly, the true place for a just man is also a prison. The proper place to-day, the only place which Massachusetts has provided for her freer and less desponding spirits, is in her prisons, to be put out and locked out of the State by her own act, as they have already put themselves out by their principles. It is there that the fugitive slave, and the Mexican prisoner on parole, and the Indian come to plead the wrongs of his race should find them; on that separate, but more free and honorable ground, where the State places those who are not *with* her, but *against* her—the only house in a slave State in which a free man can abide with honor. If any think that their influence would be lost there, and their voices no longer afflict the ear of the State, that they would not be as an enemy within its walls, they do not know by how much truth is stronger than error, nor how much more eloquently and effectively he can combat injustice who has experienced a little in his own person. Cast your whole vote, not a strip of paper merely, but your whole influence. A minority is powerless while it conforms to the majority; it is not even a minority then; but it is irresistible when it clogs by its whole weight. If the alternative is to keep all just men in prison, or give up war and slavery, the State will not hesitate which to choose. If a thousand men were not to pay their tax-bills this year, that would not be a violent and bloody measure, as it would be to pay them, and enable the State to commit violence and shed innocent blood. This is, in fact, the definition of a peaceable revolution, if any such is possible. If the tax-gatherer, or any other public officer, asks me, as one has done, 'But what shall I do?' my answer is, 'If you really wish to do anything, resign your office.' When the subject has refused allegiance, and the officer has resigned his office, then the revolution is accomplished. But even suppose blood should flow. Is there not a sort of blood shed when the conscience is wounded?...

The progress from an absolute to a limited monarchy, from a limited monarchy to a democracy, is a progress toward a true respect for the individual. Even the Chinese philosopher was wise enough to regard the individual as the basis of the empire. Is a democracy, such as we know it, the last improvement possible in government? Is it not possible to take a step further towards recognizing and organizing the rights of man? There will never be a really free and enlightened State until the State comes to recognize the individual as a higher and independent power, from which all its own power and authority are derived, and treats him accordingly. I please myself with imagining a State at last which can afford to be just to all men, and to treat the individual with respect

Henry David
Thoreau
Civil Disobedience
1849
United States
of America

as a neighbor; which even would not think it inconsistent with its own repose if a few were to live aloof from it, not meddling with it, nor embraced by it, who fulfilled all the duties of neighbors and fellow-men. A State which bore this kind of fruit, and suffered it to drop off as fast as it ripened, would prepare the way for a still more perfect and glorious State, which also I have imagined, but not yet anywhere seen.   *291*

Freedom tree. Kassel, Germany. 1793

Civil liberty

Dante
1265-1321
The Divine Comedy
'Purgatorio'

He seeketh freedom, which is so precious, as he knows
who giveth up life for her.   *292*

A! Fredome is a noble thing!
Fredome mays man to haiff liking;
Fredome all solace to man giffis,
He levys at ese that frely levys!
A noble hart may haiff nane ese,
Na ellys nocht that may him plese,
Gyff fredome fail; for fre liking
Is yarnyt our all othir thing.
Na he that ay has levyt fre
May nocht knaw weill the propyrtè,
The angyr, na the wretchyt dome
That is couplyt to foule thyrldome.
Bot gyff he had assayit it,
Than all perquer he suld it wyt;
And suld think fredome mar to prise

John Barbour
The Brus
14th cent.
Scotland

Than all the gold in warld that is.
Thus contrar thingis evirmar
Discoweryngis off the tothir ar.   *293*

[In modern English: Ah! Freedom is a noble thing! Freedom makes
man joyful. Freedom gives solace. He who is free lives at ease. A noble
heart can know no ease nor any pleasure without freedom; for
enjoyment of freedom is desired above all else. And he who has
always lived free can know nothing of the condition, the suffering
and the wretched fate that go with foul thraldom. But had he felt
all this in his own person, then would he know it full well, and would
think freedom more to be prized than all the gold in the world.
Thus contraries always make plain what marks their opposites.]

Machiavelli
1469-1527, Italy

No force tames or time consumes or merit equals the name
of liberty.   *294*

*Freedom
and the law*

The end of law is not to abolish or restrain but to preserve
and enlarge freedom; for in all the states of created beings
capable of laws, where there is no law, there is no freedom.
For liberty is to be free from restraint and violence from
others, which cannot be where there is no law; but freedom
is not, as we are told: a liberty for every man to do what
he lists—for who could be free, when every other man's
humour might domineer over him?—but a liberty to

John Locke
The Second Treatise
of Civil Government
1690
England

dispose and order as he lists his person, actions, possessions, and his whole property, within the allowance of those laws under which he is, and therein not to be subject to the arbitrary will of another, but freely follow his own.

295

BIRDS IN A CAGE

I. Krasicki
Fables
1779

'Tell me', the young finch said to the old,
'Why do you sigh?
This cage where we live is a very fine place.'
'Oh! it's where you were born, so it seems so to you,
But it doesn't to me,
Alas, I remember that once I was free,
And that's why I sigh.'

296

Namík Kemal
1840-88
Ode to Liberty
Turkey

Do not suppose that the people, offended and mocked, has forfeited its honour: does a precious stone lose its value because it has fallen to the ground?

The hangman's murderous noose, though it were transformed into a dragon of death, is a thousand times preferable to the chain of slavery.

Is it possible to destroy the idea of freedom by unjust and cruel acts? Try, if though canst, to banish reason from the whole of mankind.

297

*Guarantees
of franchises
and understanding
of the Treaty by
the people*

THE TREATY OF ZÜRICH (1 MAY 1351)

Further, it should also be known what we have expressly determined and stipulated as regards all who are in this alliance, namely that every town, every farm, every village to which he who is a member of this alliance belongs, is to continue to remain with its courts of justice, its freedoms, its letters patent, its rights and its good customs, just as it has had them hitherto, so that nobody must interfere with or hinder them, without reservation. It is also particularly stipulated, in order that young and old and all those whom it concerns may have fuller knowledge of this alliance, that they shall renew and explain it by word of mouth, by writings and under oath, and with all customary formality, every ten years, before or after the beginning of May. All men and youths who are over sixteen years of age at that time must swear always to adhere to this alliance.

The Treaty of Zürich
1 May 1351

298

In 1387, Adhémar Fabri, Bishop of Geneva, codified the franchises and freedoms granted to the citizens of Geneva.

Article 2. Of security.

Every cleric and layman, whether citizen or foreigner, shall be and remain safe and in all security with all his possessions in the city and its outskirts. If, within the said limits, violence were done to anyone, the resident citizens, inhabitants and sworn men are entitled to defend the injured party by all means in their power, provided that he has agreed to recognize the jurisdiction of our Ecclesiastical Judge or of our Vidame, his Deputy.

Article 23. Of the right to be governed by freely elected persons.

The said citizens, burghers, inhabitants and sworn men of the said city can annually establish and ordain four of their number to be Procurators and Syndics of the said city, and can invest the four elected persons with full power in all manner of things. The said four will have power to manage the affairs of the said city and of the citizens and to do everything which may further their interests.

Article 55. Of the protection of property.

No one shall be deprived of his property, either by us or by any other person, in any manner whatsoever, without his case being heard and defended, in so far as he is willing to recognize the jurisdiction of the courts of the said city (or to go to law according to the uses and customs of the said city), subject to the rights of the lord from whom the object in dispute is held in fee or on long lease, or could be so in the future.

Article 19. That the possessions of a man under sentence shall not be seized.

The possessions of a citizen, burgher, sworn man or inhabitant, cleric or layman shall not be confiscated for any crime whatsoever, nor for any other matter whatsoever, in any possible fashion, whether he has been sentenced for heinous crime or otherwise, unless this is among the cases permitted by law according to the jurisconsults' decisions.

Article 10. Of the circumstances of imprisonment.

No layman, except in a criminal case, namely open larceny, manifest homicide, notorious treason and other public crimes for which persons may not be discharged on bail, shall be apprehended in the town or in its suburbs as long as he is ready to provide bail and surety; and if he is not ready so to do, and is apprehended or detained, he should not be taken to prison but kept under guard at the Court for the time being, so that he may be able to solicit sureties, if he has the power and means to obtain them; and if then he cannot have them and is taken to prison, he should be freed from prison as soon as he is ready to provide a surety, and be set wholly at liberty with his belongings.

The Franchises of Geneva 1387

299

Every man is free in the States of the Republic, whether he be born there, settled there, or recently arrived there. He has the right to employ his strength and his fortune as he deems fit, provided only that he conforms to the law of God and the laws of the country. No man may seize upon another man, either by his own might or with the help of his fellows; and no one has the right either to help him to do so, or to inflict injury on the person, the life or the property of his fellows.

H. Kołłataj The Political Law of the Polish Nation 1790

300

Never at any time, or in any circumstances, is it permissible either to violate the Rights of Man or to refuse to restore a man's rights. No country is worthy to be called free so long as one man there is unhappy; no country is free so long as one man therein is reduced to slavery. No body of laws, therefore, should pass over in silence the Rights of Man; and no society may sacrifice one man for others. Any line of argument to the contrary would stem either from fear or from injustice. To maintain that the people, being ignorant, cannot enjoy their full rights is counter to both wisdom and truth, since Man can in no circumstances (save by reason of senility or mental debility) be deprived of his rights. Even minors and madmen enjoy the protection of human beneficence. Only the criminal may be the slave of society. Man's destiny is shaped by opinion and is therefore a matter of chance, whereas man's heart follows the dictates of his innate consciousness of Rights.

H. Kołłataj The Political Law of the Polish Nation 1790

301

The use of freedom must not restrict that of others

When reason approves that man should make a certain use of his energy and freedom or, which is the same thing, when it acknowledges that he has a certain right, it is a natural consequence that, in order to guarantee this right to him, it must at the same time recognize that other men must not use their energy and freedom to resist him in this, but that, on the contrary, they should respect his right and help him to make use of it.

*Of the right
to resist*

Unqualified rights are those whose enjoyment can be rigorously insisted upon.... It is thus reasonable to use force against anyone who wrongfully attempts to take our life, possessions or freedom.

*That freedom
cannot justifiably
be renounced*

Man cannot entirely, absolutely and unreservedly surrender his freedom, for that would clearly compel him to do wrong if the person into whose hands he committed himself commanded him to do so.

*We ought to behave
towards each other
as equals by nature*

We are therefore obliged to consider ourselves equals by nature and to behave to each other as such; and it would be to contradict nature, not to recognize this principle of equity as one of the first foundations of Society.

J.-J. Burlamaqui
Principles
of Natural Law
Geneva
1747

Far from the Government upsetting this primal order (the natural state of freedom and equality), it is rather to give it a new degree of strength and consistency that the Government is established. *302*

Extent of liberty

That man is free who is certain not to be hindered in the exercise of his physical freedom and of his ownership of external objects. Accordingly, every citizen has the right to stay or to go, to think, speak, write, print, publish, work, produce, keep, transport, exchange and consume, etc.

Its limits

Limits are set on individual liberty only at that point where it would begin to impair the liberty of others. It is for the law to reorganize and mark these boundaries; outside, all is free to all, for the object of the social union is not only the liberty of one or of many, but the liberty of all. A society in which one man is more free or less free than another would be for certain very badly ordered; and would need reconstituting. *303*

Abbé Sieyès
Préliminaire
à la Constitution
20 and 21 July 1789
France

Threats to liberty

Is liberty conceivable without perfect harmony? It soon turns into unavowed slavery: I become free by oppressing another. We can very quickly learn to avoid getting crushed, but it will need a new, unheard-of probation lasting unrelenting centuries before we lose the desire to crush others.... Liberty does not exist, and never was.... Mankind is now moving, not towards paradise, but towards the hardest, blackest and most burning of purgatories. The twilight of liberty is closing in. Assyria and Egypt will pale before a new, unprecedented bondage. But the galleys are an apprenticeship that will forerun freedom—a created freedom, impeccably equilibrated, in utmost harmony. *304*

Ilya Ehrenburg
The Fantastic
Adventures
of Julio Jurenito
1921
U.S.S.R.

Confucian school
The Great Learning
5th cent. B.C.
China

Like what the people like and dislike what the people dislike. *305*

Mencius
372?-289? B.C.
China

The people are first in importance, the state next, and the Emperor is least important of all. *306*

Russian proverb

Find the people and you'll find truth. *307*

Rejection
of all prestige

Mahatma Gandhi
1869-1948

I have no desire for prestige anywhere. It is furniture required in courts of kings. I am a servant of Mussulmans, Christians, Parsis and Jews as I am of Hindus. And a servant is in need of love, not prestige. That is assured to me so long as I remain a faithful servant. *308*

Against the power
of kings

Discourse by a Persian admired by a Greek.

'To me', he said, 'it seems advisable, that we should no longer have a single man to rule over us—the rule of one is neither good nor pleasant. You cannot have forgotten to what lengths Cambyses went in his haughty tyranny, and the haughtiness of the Magi you have experienced. How indeed is it possible that monarchy should be a well-adjusted thing, when it allows a man to do as he likes without being answerable? Such licence is enough to stir strange and unwonted thoughts in the heart of the worthiest of men. Give a person this power, and straightway his manifold good things puff him up with pride, while envy is so natural to human kind that it cannot but arise in him. But pride and envy together include all wickedness; both leading on to deeds of savage violence. True it is that kings, possessing as they do all that heart can desire, ought to be void of envy, but the contrary is seen in their conduct towards the citizens. They are jealous of the most virtuous among their subjects, and wish their death; while they take delight in the meanest and basest, being ever ready to listen to the tales of slanderers. A king, besides, is beyond all other men inconsistent with himself. Pay him court in moderation, and he is angry because you do not show him more profound respect—show him profound respect, and he is offended again, because (as he says) you fawn on him. But the worst of all is, that he sets aside the laws of the land, puts men to death without trial, and rapes women. The rule of the many, on the other hand, has, in the first place, the fairest of names, equality before the law; and further it is free from all those outrages which a king is wont to commit. There, places are given by lot, the magistrate is answerable for what he does, and measures rest with the commonalty. I vote, therefore, that we do away with monarchy, and raise the people to power. For the people are all in all.'

*Herodotus
Discourse by Otanes
5th cent. B.C.
Greece*

309

Theseus speaks:

No curse
Is greater to a city than a king.
For first, where'er no laws exist which bind
The whole community, and one man rules,
Upon his arbitrary will alone
Depend the laws, and all thy rights are lost.
But under written laws the poor and rich
An equal justice find; and if reproached,
They of low station may with equal scorn
Answer the taunting arrogance of wealth;
And an inferior, if his cause be just,
Conquers the powerful. This too is a mark
Of freedom, where the man who can propose
Some wholesome counsel for the public weal
Is by the herald called upon to speak:
Then he who with a general zeal accepts
Such offer gains renown, but he who likes not
His thoughts to utter still continues mute.
How can a city be administered
With more equality? Where'er the people
Are sovereigns of the land, a rising race
Of heroes gives them joy; but these a king
Esteems his foes; the brave, with those who bear
The character of wise, he slays, still trembling
For his ill-gotten power. How can that city
On a firm basis stand where valiant youths,
Like the green sheaf cut from the vernal mead,
Are in their bloom mown down? Why then acquire
Large fortunes for our children, to augment
The treasures of a king? Or why train up
Our virgin daughters with an anxious care,
Merely to gratify the loose desires
Of an imperious monarch, and cause tears

*Euripides
The Suppliants
5th cent. B.C.
Trans. by Woodhull*

To stream from their fond parents? May I end
My life ere these indignant eyes behold
The violation of my daughter's honour!

310

*Responsibility to
one another*

*Legal provisions made by Solon of Athens to protect the common
people.*

Moreover, thinking it his duty to make still further provision for the weakness of the multitude, he gave every
citizen the privilege of entering suit in behalf of one who
had suffered wrong. If a man was assaulted, and suffered
violence or injury, it was the privilege of any one who
had the ability and the inclination, to indict the wrong-doer
and prosecute him. The law-giver in this way rightly
accustomed the citizens, as members of one body,
to feel and sympathize with one another's wrongs. And
we are told of a saying of his which is consonant with
this law. Being asked, namely, what city was best to live
in, 'That city,' he replied, 'in which those who are not

Plutarch's Lives
Solon
c. 45-125 A.D.

wronged, no less than those who are wronged, exert
themselves to punish the wrong-doers.'   *311*

*Nobility and
commoners*

Monsieur d'Etanges refuses St. Preux for his son-in-law.

From the rest of their discourse I judged that Edward
had dared to suggest your marriage with your friend, whom
he loudly claimed as his own, and on whom he proposed,
in this capacity, to bestow a suitable establishment. Your
father had scornfully rejected this proposal, and it was
here that the conversation began to grow heated. 'You
should know', said Milord, 'that notwithstanding your
prejudices, he is among all men the most worthy of her
and the most fit to secure her happiness. He has received
from nature all the gifts which are not in the hands of
men, and has added to them all the talents it has been
in his power to acquire. He is young, healthy, a fine
figure of a man, clever; he has education, sense, principles,
courage; he has an accomplished mind, his soul is pure,
what then does he lack to merit your consent? Fortune?
It will be his. The third part of my estate is enough to
make him the richest single person in Vaud; if need be,
I shall bestow up to the half of it. Nobility? A vain prerogative, in a country where it is more harmful than useful.
Nevertheless he has it, have no doubt—not written in
ink on old parchments, but engraved deep in his heart
in letters which cannot be erased. In a word, if you prefer
reason to prejudice, and if you love your daughter more
than your titles, it is to him that you will give her hand.'

Thereupon your father was greatly incensed. He
considered the proposal absurd and ridiculous. 'What!
Milord', he said, 'can a man of honour such as yourself
imagine for a moment that the last scion of an illustrious

family should let its name be extinguished or degraded by that of a homeless Nobody, reduced to beggary?'

'Stay,' interrupted Edward, 'it is of my friend you speak; remember that I take on myself all the scurrilous attacks made on him in my presence, and that insults to a man of honour are still more insulting for those who pronounce them. Such "nobodies" are more worthy of respect than all the petty squires of Europe; and I defy you to find any more honourable way of seeking one's fortune, than by means of the tributes of esteem and the gifts of friendship. If the Son-in-law I suggest for you cannot, like yourself, boast of a long line of ancestors of doubtful authenticity,

'As far back as his grandfather'
The Caprices
Goya
1803
Spain

Asta su Abuelo.

he will be the founder and the source of honour of his line, as your first ancestor was of yours. Could you, then, consider yourself dishonoured by the alliance on account of your family, and would not this contempt recoil on yourself? How many great names would fall into oblivion if account were taken only of those that derive from a man of good repute? Let us judge of the past from the present; every day, for two or three citizens who gain renown by honest means, a thousand rascals take a title for their family; and what will there be to prove the nobility of which their descendants will be so proud, save the robbery and villainy of their ancestors? Many dishonest men are to be found, I admit, among the common people; but you can always lay twenty to one that a man of gentle birth is descended from a knave. Leaving aside, if you please, the question of origin, let us consider merit and service. You bore arms under a foreign Prince; his father fought without thought of gain for his own country. You fought well, but you were well rewarded, and whatever the honours you won in the field, a hundred commoners won still more.

'What, then,' continued Milord Edward, 'stands to the credit of this nobility of which you are so proud? What does it do for the glory of its country, or for the good of mankind? Deadly enemy as it is of law and liberty, what has it ever produced in most of the countries which it adorns, save the might of Tyranny and the oppression of the people? Dare you, in a Republic, take pride in an estate which destroys virtue and humanity, an estate whose members boast of slavery and are ashamed to be called men?'

'... If you are acquainted with the nobility of England, you will know that it is the most enlightened, the most educated, the wisest and the most courageous in Europe; further, I have no need to consider whether it is the most ancient! for, in speaking of what it now is, the question of what it was in the past is irrelevant. The truth is that we are not the slaves of the Prince but his friends; we are not the tyrants of the people but their leaders. As the guarantors of freedom, the defenders of the country and the supporters of the throne, we provide a balance between the people and the king which cannot be overthrown. Our first duty is towards the Nation; the second, towards him who governs it; it is not his will that we consult, but his rightful authority. As supreme Ministers of the law in the House of Lords, sometimes even as legislators, we dispense justice equally to the people and to the King, and we allow no man to say *"Dieu et mon épée"*, but only *"Dieu et mon droit"*.'

Jean-Jacques
Rousseau
La Nouvelle Héloïse
1761

312

Complaint against inequality Viet-Namese proverb	A commoner who seeks a nobleman's friendship will never meet him on equal terms. *313*

The commonalty	Do you know what the commonalty represents for the estates of a nation? It is as the sea is to rivers. For as all water has its origin in the sea, is fed by the sea and finally goes back to the sea, in the same way every noble line has sprung from the peasantry, is preserved by those who remain there, and sooner or later disappears back into it. Consider therefore the admirable perfection of the things of this world, which ordain that the common people
György Bessenyei 1804 Hungary	shall be successively mother, nurse and graveyard of all fortunes and dignities. *314*

Civil liberty, republican government, democracy

OF THE LIBERTY OF THE SUBJECT

Philosophic liberty consists in the free exercise of the will; or at least if we must speak agreeably to all systems, in an opinion that we have the free exercise of our will. Political liberty consists in security, or, at least, in the opinion that we enjoy security.

This security is never more dangerously attacked than in public or private accusations. It is, therefore, on the goodness of criminal laws that the liberty of the subject principally depends.

THAT LIBERTY IS FAVOURED BY THE NATURE AND PROPORTION OF PUNISHMENTS

Liberty is in perfection when criminal laws derive each punishment from the particular nature of the crime. There are then no arbitrary decisions; the punishment does not flow from the capriciousness of the legislator, but from the very nature of the thing; and man uses no violence to man....

In things that prejudice the tranquillity or security of the State, secret actions are subject to human jurisdiction. But in those which offend the Deity, where there is no public act, there can be no criminal matter, the whole passes between man and God, who knows the measure and time of His vengeance. Now if magistrates confounding things should inquire also into hidden sacrileges, this inquisition would be directed to a kind of action that does not at all require it: the liberty of the subject would be subverted by arming the zeal of timorous as well as of presumptuous consciences against him.

We must have continually present in our minds the difference between independence and liberty. Liberty is a right of doing whatever the laws permit, and if a citizen could do what they forbid he would be no longer possessed of liberty, because his fellow-citizens would have the same power.

Montesquieu
The Spirit of the Laws
1748
France

315

In search of a 'form of association'

J.-J. Rousseau
Du Contrat Social
1762

To find a form of association which may defend and protect with the whole force of the community the person and property of every associate, and by means of which each, coalescing with all may nevertheless obey only himself, and remain as free as before. Such is the fundamental problem of which the Social Contract furnishes the solution.

316

Right of ownership

J.-J. Rousseau
Discours sur l'Origine
et les Fondements de
l'Inégalité parmi les
Hommes, 1755

The right of ownership being only a convention, a matter of human invention, any man may dispose of his possessions as he will; but the same is not true of the natural gifts, such as life and freedom, which every man is permitted to enjoy—indeed it is a matter of doubt, to say the least, whether he is entitled to cast them away. For a man to take his life is to degrade himself; to renounce his freedom is to destroy it in so far as it exists within himself. Since no temporal asset can make up for one or the other, it would be a crime against Nature and reason alike to give up either at any price.

317

Judgement passed on the Declaration of Rights of 1789.

Kant
1790

Such a phenomenon in the history of mankind will never again be forgotten, for it has shown that there is in human nature a predisposition towards progress and an ability to achieve it such as no political leader, reviewing the previous course of affairs, would have believed possible.

318

LIBERTY DAY

A German recounts how the French people, its King, Queen and clergy swore an oath of loyalty to the Constitution (1790):

In streaming rain the procession approached the altar of the nation. A triumphal arch opened the way to the Champ-de-Mars. A throng of people, without coaches, horses, canes or swords, looked on. In the middle of the Champ-de-Mars, like a holy mount, stood the altar of the nation. The King's throne stood in a covered amphitheatre. Behind it were the Queen with the Dauphin, and seated to the right was the President of the National Assembly; in front, left and right in an uncovered amphitheatre, the worthy representatives of the people and the sacred liberty of all. Nothing, to the most ardent imagination, could be more moving or inspiring. Facing the King stood the altar of the nation, the way leading to it lined on either side by the Paris National Guard. Innumerable bands playing martial music and soft airs sat in the various places provided for them and accompanied the day's rejoicings. Thousands of inscriptions and emblems bore witness to the wit, intelligence and patriotism of the new France. Near the altar stood the National Guard delegates and various volunteer groups, beside them, soldiers who had grown grey in their country's service. In the far distance amphitheatres holding over 600,000 spectators were visible. The Bishop of Autun said Mass. Rain was still pouring from the overcast sky, but the metal jaws of the cannons began to thunder and then the sky again smiled peacefully down on the great scene. On the steps of the altar stood the clergy, all in white and wearing the national sash. Then the oath was read out, and all the multitude cried—like the thunderous roar of the storm and the surging of huge waves—'I swear! I swear!' Now a pause, everyone fixedly gazing in the same direction: silence on earth, silence in the heavens among the listening spirits. But soon sound broke out all round again; the music swelled, cannons flashed and boomed, thousands shouted for joy, tens of thousands were silent and hundreds of thousands wept. Then, Lafayette, like an emissary of God, advanced on a white horse towards the altar; he mounted the altar steps with his comrades-in-arms, solemnly raised his right hand to heaven and took the oath of loyalty and fraternity, vowing to uphold the constitution. Then he came back down, leapt on his horse, placed his hat on his sword and raised it in the air, crying: 'Long live the nation!' A cry

157

> Citoyen BELCOMTE,
> Maçon Entrepreneur,
> Rue de l'Homme-Libre,
> ci-devant Sainte-Placide,
> N° 1197, *démolisseur de la Bastille*
> Fauxbourg Germain,
> A PARIS.

reverberated like the thunder that shakes the craggy mountains: 'Long live the nation—and Lafayette!' Was there a
happier man at that moment than Lafayette? Thereupon
the archons swore the oath of loyalty and, lastly, the King
and Queen. On the King now focused the attention
of millions of staring eyes. Like the din of voices on the
Last Day the cry now rose up from the Champ-de-Mars:
'Long live the King! Our good King! The National
Assembly! Liberty!' With these words the genius of France
broke the staff, flung the fragments at the nobility and
said: 'Sentence of death is passed on you for all time!'
Then the Queen lifted up the Dauphin and showed
him to the people. The heir to the crown seemed to be
struggling also towards the great scene, and the people's
cry rang out: 'Long live the Queen! Long live the
Dauphin!' That night all Paris was lit. Everywhere there
were balls and rejoicing, and in places people praising
and worshipping God who, when the world was growing
old, had released a great nation from its shackles, placed
it on a sunlit mountain and showed the peoples of the
earth by this sign that mankind can regain its pristine
Christian Schubart   splendour only if it is free!   *319*

REFLECTIONS ON THE REVOLUTION IN FRANCE (1790)

It is no wonder therefore, that with these ideas of everything in their constitution and government at home,
either in church or state, as illegitimate and usurped, or
at best as a vain mockery, they [English admirers and
emulators of the French Revolution in its early days]

look abroad with an eager and passionate enthusiasm. Whilst they are possessed by these notions, it is vain to talk to them of the practice of their ancestors, the fundamental laws of their country, the fixed form of a constitution, whose merits are confirmed by the solid test of long experience, and an increasing public strength and national prosperity. They despise experience as the wisdom of unlettered men; and as for the rest, they have wrought underground a mine that will blow up, at one grand explosion, all examples of antiquity, all precedents, charters, and acts of parliament. They have 'the rights of men'. Against these there can be no prescription; against these no agreement is binding: these admit no temperament, and no compromise: anything withheld from their full demand is so much of fraud and injustice. Against these their rights of men let no government look for security in the length of its continuance, or in the justice and lenity of its administration. The objections of these speculatists, if its forms do not quadrate with their theories, are as valid against such an old and beneficent government, as against the most violent tyranny, or the greenest usurpation. They are always at issue with governments, not on a question of abuse, but a question of competency, and a question of title. I have nothing to say to the clumsy subtilty of their political metaphysics. Let them be their amusement in the schools.—'*Illa se jactat in aula—Æolus, et clauso ventorum carcere regnet.*'—But let them not break prison to burst like a *Levanter*, to sweep

LA PRISE DE LA BASTILLE

the earth with their hurricane, and to break up the fountains of the great deep to overwhelm us.

Far am I from denying in theory, full as far is my heart from withholding in practice (if I were of power to give or to withhold) the *real* rights of men. In denying their false claims of right, I do not mean to injure those which are real, and are such as their pretended rights would totally destroy. If civil society be made for the advantage of man, all the advantages for which it is made become his right. It is an institution of beneficence; and law itself is only beneficence acting by a rule. Men have a right to live by that rule; they have a right to do justice, as between their fellows, whether their fellows are in public function or in ordinary occupation. They have a right to the fruits of their industry; and to the means of making their industry fruitful. They have a right to the acquisitions of their parents; to the nourishment and improvement of their offspring; to instruction in life, and to consolation in death. Whatever each man can separately do, without trespassing upon others, he has a right to do for himself; and he has a right to a fair portion of all which society, with all its combinations of skill and force, can do in his favour. In this partnership all men have equal rights; but not to equal things. He that has but five shillings in the partnership, has as good a right to it, as he that has five hundred pounds has to his larger proportion. But he has not a right to an equal dividend in the product of the joint stock; and as to the share of power, authority, and direction which each individual ought to have in the management of the state, that I must deny to be amongst the direct original rights of man in civil society; for I have in my contemplation the civil social man, and no other. It is a thing to be settled by convention.

If civil society be the offspring of convention, that convention must be its law. That convention must limit and modify all the descriptions of constitution which are formed under it. Every sort of legislative, judicial, or executory power are its creatures. They can have no being in any other state of things; and how can any man claim under the conventions of civil society, rights which do not so much as suppose its existence? rights which are absolutely repugnant to it? One of the first motives to civil society, and which becomes one of its fundamental rules, is, *that no man should be judge in his own cause.* By this each person has at once divested himself of the first fundamental right of uncovenanted man, that is, to judge for himself, and to assert his own cause.

He abdicates all right to be his own governor. He inclusively, in a great measure, abandons the right of self-defence, the first law of nature. Men cannot enjoy the rights of an uncivil and of a civil state together. That he may obtain justice, he gives up his right of determining what it is in points the most essential to him. That he may secure some liberty, he makes a surrender in trust of the whole of it.

Government is not made in virtue of natural rights, which may and do exist in total independence of it; and exist in much greater clearness, and in a much greater degree of abstract perfection: but their abstract perfection is their practical defect. By having a right to everything they want everything. Government is a contrivance of human wisdom to provide for human *wants*. Men have a right that these wants should be provided for by this wisdom. Among these wants is to be reckoned the want, out of civil society, of a sufficient restraint upon their passions. Society requires not only that the passions of individuals should be subjected, but that even in the mass and body, as well as in the individuals, the inclinations of men should frequently be thwarted, their will controlled, and their passions brought into subjection. This can only be done *by a power out of themselves*; and not, in the exercise of its function, subject to that will and to those passions which it is its office to bridle and subdue. In this sense the restraints on men, as well as their liberties, are to be reckoned among their rights. But as the liberties and the restrictions vary with times and circumstances, and admit of infinite modifications, they cannot be settled upon any abstract rule; and nothing is so foolish as to discuss them upon that principle.

The moment you abate anything from the full rights of men, each to govern himself, and suffer any artificial, positive limitation upon those rights, from that moment the whole organization of government becomes a consideration of convenience. This it is which makes the constitution of a state, and the due distribution of its powers, a matter of the most delicate and complicated skill. It requires a deep knowledge of human nature and human necessities, and of the things which facilitate or obstruct the various ends, which are to be pursued by the mechanism of civil institutions. The state is to have recruits to its strength, and remedies to its distempers. What is the use of discussing a man's abstract right to food or medicine? The question is upon the method of procuring and administering them. In that deliberation I shall always advise to call in the aid of the farmer and the physician, rather than the professor of metaphysics. *320*

Edmund Burke
Great Britain

ON SOCIAL VIRTUES: JUSTICE

Q. What is Society?

A. Society is any group of men living together under the terms of an express or tacit contract whose object is their common preservation.

Q. Are the social virtues numerous?

A. Yes: They are as many in number as there are kinds of action useful to society; but all can be reduced to a single principle.

Q. What is this basic principle?

A. It is *justice*, which by itself comprises all the virtues of society.

Q. Why do you say that justice is the basic and almost the sole virtue of society?

A. Because only justice covers the practice of all the actions useful to society, and because all the other virtues, under the name of charity and humanity, uprightness, patriotism, sincerity, generosity, simplicity of manners and modesty, are only varying forms and diverse applications of the maxim: *Do unto others as you would they should do unto you*, which is the definition of justice.

Q. How does natural law prescribe justice?

A. By three physical attributes, which are inherent in the constitution of man.

Q. What are these attributes?

A. Equality, Liberty, Property.

Q. In what way is equality a physical attribute of man?

A. For the reason that, since all men are equally provided with eyes, hands, a mouth, ears, and the need to use them in order to live, they have consequently an equal right to life, and to the use of the elements which support life; they are all equal before God.

Q. Do you claim that all men have equal understanding, sight, feelings, needs, passions?

A. No; for it is obvious and a commonplace, that one man is shortsighted and the other long; that one eats much, the other little; that one has gentle passions, the other violent; in a word, that one man has a weak body and mind, while the other is strong.

Q. In reality, then, they are unequal?

A. Yes, in the development of their faculties, but not in the nature and essence of these faculties; the stuff thereof is the same, but the dimensions are not equal; the weight and the value are not the same. Our language has not the appropriate word to describe simultaneously the identity of nature, and the diversity of form and use. It is a proportional inequality; and it is for this reason that I say that men are equal before God, and in the order of nature.

Q. In what way is liberty a physical attribute of man?

A. Because, since all men have senses sufficing for their preservation, none needing another's eye to see, another's ear to hear, another's mouth to eat, another's foot to walk, they are consequently by natural constitution independent and free; none is necessarily subject to another, or has the right to dominion over him.

Q. But if a man is born strong, does he not have the natural right to command the man who is born weak?

A. No; for this is neither a necessity for him, nor a convention between them; it is an unjustified encroachment by force; and this is an improper use of the word *right*, which in its true sense, can only mean *justice* or *reciprocal competency*.

Q. In what way is property a physical attribute of man?

A. Since every man is constituted the equal of, and similar to, every other, and as a result independent and free, each man is the absolute master and sole owner of his body and of the product of his work.

Q. In what way does justice derive from these three attributes?

A. From the fact that men, being equal, free, not beholden to one another, do not have the right to make demands on each other except to the extent that they make exchanges of equal value; to the extent that there is a *balance* of give and take; and it is this *equality*, this *balance*, which are called *justice, equity*: that is to say, that *equality* and *justice* are the same word, they are the same natural *law*, of which the social virtues are no more than applications and derivatives.

Volney
Natural Law
1793
France

321

THE PERFECT CONSTITUTION

The greatest problem of the human race that nature demands of men to solve is to establish a society in which law is universally applied. Since only in society—and in a society, moreover, in which the greatest freedom obtains and there is thus a perpetual conflict of interests between its members, so that the limits of this freedom must be extremely precisely defined and upheld and the freedom of each made consistent with the freedom of others—can nature's highest purpose be achieved, i.e. the development of all the potentials with which she has endowed mankind. And since nature also wants mankind itself to achieve this and all its other potentials, so must a society in which *freedom regulated by external laws* is unshakeably upheld to the greatest possible extent—which, in other words, has a completely just constitution—be the loftiest of all achievements which nature has set mankind; because only when the solution has been found and the task completed can nature accomplish its other designs for the human race. Necessity compels man, otherwise so attached to freedom, to accept this constraint—the greatest constraint of all, namely, that which men impose on one another, their instincts being such that they cannot live long together in unconstrained freedom. Only with the confines of a civilized community do these same instincts give of their best; like trees in a wood which, each trying to deprive the next of light and sun, compel each other to strive upwards, and so grow fine and straight, whereas those growing in isolated freedom allow their branches to spread at will and grow crooked and stunted. All culture and art, which grace humanity, and the finest social order are the fruits of unsociability, compelled of itself to discipline and thus, through the art that emerges, to bring to full flower what nature has planted.   *322*

Kant
Idee zu einer
allgemeinen
Geschichte
in weltbürgerlicher
Absicht
1784

THE PRINCIPLES OF MAN'S CONDITION AS A CITIZEN

The condition of a citizen, therefore, in its purely legal aspect, is founded, *a priori*, on
1. *The freedom* of every member of society, as a *man*;
2. His *equality* with everyone else, as a *subject*;
3. The *independence* of every member of the community, as a *citizen*.

These are not so much rules of law of an already existing State as principles that afford the only basis on which the structures of a State will satisfy certain principles of external human right arrived at by pure reason.

1. *Freedom*, as a man. The significance of this in the constitution of a community can be explained as follows. No one can compel me to be happy in a way he imagines makes others happy, but each should be allowed to seek his happiness as he sees fit provided this does not prejudice the freedom—recognized to everyone, possibly under some general law regarding the rights of others—of others to do likewise. A government acting in its name of benevolence towards its people as a father towards his children—a paternal government (*imperium paternale*) under which subjects are treated as minors who really could not understand what is good and bad for them, must hold their peace, must wait until the ruler, in his wisdom (and,

if he so considers, his goodness of heart) decides what it is that should make them happy—this is the greatest despotism imaginable, depriving them of all freedom, leaving them with no rights at all. A State is not paternal but patriotic (*imperium non paternale, sed patrioticum*) when the rights of all its citizens are a reality and there is no inconsistency between this and the benevolence of the ruler. Patriotic implies that everyone in the State (not excluding the ruler) considers the community as the fountainhead and the country as the fatherland which produced him, which he in turn must leave behind as a precious pledge; he therefore wants its rights protected through laws that express the common will, but not to subject it to his own arbitrary views.

This right to freedom comes to him, member of the community, as a man, at least in so far as man is at all a being capable of having rights.

2. His *Equality* with everyone else, as a subject. Every member of the community has rights of constraint over every other except the sovereign (who is not a member but its creator or protector) who alone has authority to compel without himself being subject to a law of constraint. But everyone who is subordinate to a State's laws is a subject, and thus liable to constraining law like any other member of the community, with one sole exception: the sovereign (a physical or moral person), by whom alone compulsion can be legally exercised. If he too were subject to compulsion, he would no longer be sovereign and the chain of subordination would stretch upwards into infinity. If on the other hand two were subject to no constraint, neither would be subject to laws of constraint, and neither could do any wrong to the other—which is absurd.

This absolute equality of people, as subjects, in a State co-exists with the greatest inequalities in the size and value of their possessions, their physical and intellectual endowments, their share of life's amenities, and their rights in general—of which there can be many—in relation to others; so that one man's welfare may very much depend on another's will (the poor man on the rich), so that one must obey (the child its parents, or the wife her husband) and the other commands, so that one serves (a day-labourer) and the other pays, and so on. But in law (being an expression of the general will, the law must be one and its form only is relevant, not the matter or object to which I have a right), they are all, as subjects, equal to one another, because no one can constrain anyone else except through the public law (and its executor the sovereign) through which, however, everyone else can equally well oppose him. And no one can lose this power to compel (or right in relation to others) otherwise than through his own crime, nor relinquish it of his own accord, i.e. through a contract—hence a legal act—stating that he has no rights but only obligations, because he would thereby deprive himself of the right to conclude a contract and the contract itself would accordingly be void.

From this idea of the equality of man as a subject within the community derives another: It must be possible for every member of the community to reach any rank or position that is open to a subject, to which his talents, diligence and good fortune may allow him to aspire; and his fellow subjects may not stand in his way in virtue of some hereditary prerogative (being privileged members of a certain class), and keep it eternally out of the reach for him and his descendants.

*Kant
Concerning
the saying
'That may be right in
theory but it doesn't
work in practice'
1793*

323

Citizens for liberty

*Schiller
Thirty Years War
1790*

Political and civil liberty is and will always be the most sacred of all blessings, the worthiest object of all endeavour, and the nucleus of all culture: but the only firm foundation on which this glorious edifice can ever be erected is nobility of mind. We have to begin, therefore, by creating the citizens for a Constitution, before we can give a Constitution to the citizens.

324

A band of brothers true we swear to be,
Never to part in danger or in death,
We swear we will be free as were our sires,
And sooner die than live in slavery.
We swear to put our trust in God Most High,
And not to quail before the might of man.

*Schiller
William Tell
1804*

325

Democracy and freedom

Nothing is more dangerous than to leave power in the hands of one citizen for a long period. The population gets accustomed to obeying him, and he to ordering it about, whence spring usurpation of power and tyranny.... Good habits, and not force, are the pillars of law and justice; and the exercise of justice is the exercise of freedom.... You will notice a variety of systems for managing men, but all with the object of oppressing them; and if the habit of seeing humanity in the hands of leaders of the people did not attenuate the horror of such a shocking spectacle, we should stand amazed at the sight of our docile species grazing over the face of the earth like miserable herds of cattle destined to be devoured by their cruel herdsmen.... Many nations, both in the past and in the present, have thrown off the yoke of oppression; but only very few of them have known how to enjoy a few precious moments of freedom. All too quickly they have fallen back into their ancient vices; for it is peoples themselves, rather than their governments, which drag tyranny in their wake.... Only democracy, in my opinion, is capable of providing absolute freedom. But where is the democratic government that has managed to combine at a given moment power, prosperity and permanency?... Codes of laws, systems, constitutions, however wisely drawn up, are dead letters which have little effect upon human societies. It is honest men, patriots, illustrious human beings—it is these who make up a Republic.... I plead with you to confirm the complete freedom of the slaves as I would plead for my life, or for the life of the Republic. *326*

Simón Bolívar
Speech delivered to
the Assembly
of Angostura
Venezuela
15 February 1819

PROGRAMME OF THE POLISH LEGION (1848)

(6) In Poland, freedom for all religions and creeds and full freedom of religious association.

(7) Free speech, freely expressed, judged by the law according to its fruits.

(8) All members of the nation are citizens, all citizens are equal before the law and before the courts.

(9) All offices are elective, freely conferred and freely accepted.

(10) For Israel, the elder brother, respect, fraternity and aid in his search for spiritual and temporal weal. Equal rights in all things.

(11) For woman, our helpmeet, fraternity and citizenship, equal rights in all things.

(12) For every Slav inhabiting Poland, fraternity, citizenship, equal rights in all things.

(13) For each family, a family plot of land under the protection of the community. For each village, a piece of communal land under the protection of the nation.

(14) All property to be respected and safeguarded by the national law.

(15) Fraternal political aid by Poland to the Czech brother and the Czech peoples, to the Russian brother and the Russian peoples. Christian aid to all peoples, our fellow human beings. *327*

Adam Mickiewicz

Advantage of small States for the purpose of civil liberty.

Small States exist in order that there may be some countries in the world where the maximum number of nationals are citizens in the true sense.... For a small State has nothing else save this real and effective freedom, which fully offsets the advantages of a large State.   *328*

Jakob Burckhardt
1818-97
Switzerland

Letter of 1 June 1849.

Monarchy must necessarily be based on a sacred, inviolable authority descending through the diverse levels of the social hierarchy to the people and communicating to each a part of the supreme power. I see upon the brow of every police superintendent a trace of the chrism with which his monarch was anointed. Solemnity and splendour are essential to monarchy; a majestic presence and purple are as necessary to a monarch as the chasuble is to a priest. Monarchical power must be shown everywhere, must be in evidence; it must be a constant reminder that the individual is nothing in relation to it, that he is *subject* and obliged to sacrifice to it the best of himself and above all to submit in everything and everywhere.

The abolition of authority is the beginning of the Republic, which recognizes only free men; authority kills intellectual freedom.

The Republic has no need of any principle other than that inherent in any social life—a universal condition, without which there can be no society. There are things that are compulsory, not because men live in a Republic, but because they live together.

A Republic which demands more than these essential conditions is no longer a Republic, or is still in process of formation.

. . . .

The inner principle of the Republic is harmony of the whole, not dualism; it has neither priesthood nor laity, neither high-placed nor low-placed men—it has nothing above it—man is its religion, he is its God, and it has no other. That is why it assumes man to be moral, i.e. capable of living in society. A free man receives no orders from anyone, he is independent like any autocrat. The absence of a supreme order enforced by the authority of the strong is the beginning of man's morality, of his responsibility for his actions.

Here morality becomes a natural form of man's will, it fuses man's desire with the outer world, society. It has no need of the insolent pointing finger to show the way, threatening and humiliating. In that respect, the Republic resembles nature. People often cite as an example nature's submission to its own laws, forgetting that in nature the law is inseparable from its operation that nature itself is a law fulfilled; the law as an abstraction exists only in the human mind.

. . . In nature, as in the Republic, the government is hidden, it is not seen, the government is the whole, it has no separate existence, it is continually gathering together and dispersing.

The idea of a government separate from the people, holding itself above them, having the task of guiding them, is the idea of the mind organizing crude matter; it is Jehovah, it is the monarch, the symbol of providence on earth, it is in fact precisely what the Republic rejects.

. . . We fear freedom because we fear men, we take them to be much worse than they are, and it is monarchy which has accustomed us to this point of view. We sleep peacefully, knowing that there is a strong government, that is to say, a power which, backed by its bayonets, can throw us into prison, shoot us, deport us; whereas the very idea of such a power should in fact have deprived us of rest and sleep.   *329*

Alexander Herzen
Letters from France
and Italy
Trans. from Russian

Draft programme for the Russian Social Democratic Party.

The Russian Social Democratic Party's principal demands are:

1. The convocation of a *Zemskij Sobor* (Constituent Assembly) of the representatives of all citizens in order to draw up a constitution.
2. Universal suffrage and the right of direct election for all Russian citizens of twenty-one and over, without distinction of religion and nationality.
3. Freedom of assembly, the right of association and the right to strike.
4. Freedom of the press.
5. Abolition of the estates and complete equality of all citizens before the law.
6. Freedom of conscience and equal rights for all nationalities.
7. The right of every citizen to institute legal proceedings against any official without having previously complained to higher officials.
8. The abolition of passports and complete liberty to move from place to place and to settle anywhere in the country.
9. Freedom to engage in any trade or occupation and the abolition of guilds.   *330*

Lenin
(in prison)
1895 or 1896

*Minimum Programme of the Russian Social Democratic Workers'
Party, adopted at the second congress of the Party in 1903.*

The Russian Social Democratic Workers' Party considers
that its most urgent task is to overthrow the autocratic
tzarist régime and set up in its stead a democratic republic
with a constitution guaranteeing the following:

Absolute power for the people, i.e. concentration of the
supreme power in a single Chamber Legislative Assembly
of the representatives of the people;

Universal, equal and direct suffrage in elections to the
Legislative Assembly and in elections to all autonomous
local government organs;

Inviolability of the individual and inviolability of
domicile;

Absolute freedom of conscience, speech, the press,
assembly, and freedom to strike and to form associations;

Freedom of movement and freedom of work;

The abolition of classes, and absolute freedom for all
citizens without distinction of sex, religion, race or
nationality;

The right to self-government for all the nations that
compose the State;

Election of judges by the people;

Separation of Church and State; separation of school
and Church;

Free and compulsory general and vocational education
for all children of both sexes up to the age of sixteen;
provision of food, clothing and textbooks at State expense
for poor children.

. . . The Russian Social Democratic Workers' Party
is firmly convinced that the above political and social
reforms can be fully and permanently achieved only by
the abolition of autocracy and the convocation of a Constituent Assembly, freely elected by the whole people. *331*

*The State's
'raison d'être'*

José Martí
1853-95
Cuba

Either the State is founded on the personal identity of
each of its children—manual labour, individual thought,
self-fulfilment, respect for family honour and the self-
fulfilment of others, in short, a passionate love of human
dignity; or else the State is not worth a single tear shed by
a single one of our women, nor a single drop of blood
shed by our heroes. *332*

Political liberty and individual responsibility	Political liberty begins when most individuals in the nation feel responsibility for the policy of the group to which they belong—when the individual is not content with making claims and protests, but rather disciplines himself to take a realistic view of the situation, and not to act on the basis of a belief—which has nothing to do with politics—in an earthly paradise, unattainable merely because of the ill-will and stupidity of others. On the
Karl Jaspers Die Schuldfrage 1946 Germany	contrary, he knows that politics, taking as its guiding star the ideal of the human condition as liberty, seeks means of action in the world as it is. *333*

Some special rights

On freedom of movement	No prison did ever receive me, no not so much as for recreation to walk in. The very imagination of one maketh the sight of their outside seem irksome and loathsome to me. I am so besotted unto liberty that should any man forbid the access unto any one corner of the Indies I should in some sort live much discontented. And so long as I shall find land or open air elsewhere, I shall never lurk in any place where I must hide myself. Oh God, how hardly could I endure the miserable condition of so many men, confined and immured in some corners of this kingdom, barred from entering the chiefest cities, from access into courts, from conversing with men, and interdicted the use of common ways, only because they have offended our laws. If those under which I live should but threaten my finger's end, I would presently go find out some others, wheresoever it were. All my small wisdom, in these civil and tumultuous wars wherein we now live,
Montaigne Essays 1580-88	doth wholly employ itself, that they may not interrupt my liberty to go and come wherever I list. *334*

Freedom of movement for traders among the Incas	Topa Inca Yupanqui ordered it to be proclaimed throughout his empire that anyone wishing to be a merchant could travel freely throughout the land, without let or hindrance from any person, under heavy penalties; and
Miguel Cabello Balboa 16th cent., Spain	ordered that there should be fairs and markets in each province. *335*

Indians confined

The Earth is the mother of all, and all ought to possess equal rights to her benefits. It is like expecting rivers to flow uphill to imagine that a man who was born free can be happy when he is confined to a given area and freedom to go wherever he fancies is taken from him. An Indian whose movements are restricted to a narrow piece of land will not be happy, and will not be able to develop or prosper. When I think of the conditions under which we have to live, my heart is heavy within me. *336*

Chief Joseph
Nez Percé Indian
19th cent.
North America

Right to compare ideas

One head does not go into council. *337*

Akan proverb, Ghana

Sanctity of dwelling places

O ye who believe! enter not into other houses than your own, until ye have asked leave and have saluted its inmates. This will be best for you: haply ye will bear this in mind. And if ye find no one therein, then enter it not till leave be given you; and if it be said to you, 'Go ye back', then go ye back. This will be more blameless in you, and God knoweth what ye do. *338*

Koran
An-Nur 27-8

Against discretionary search

The defendants claimed a right under precedents, to force persons' houses, break open excrutores, seize their papers, etc., upon a general warrant, where no inventory is made of the things thus taken away, and where no offenders' names are specified in the warrant, and therefore a discretionary power given to messengers to search wherever their suspicions may chance to fall. If such a power is truly invested in a secretary of state, and he can delegate this power, it certainly may affect the person and property of every man in this kingdom, and is totally subversive of the liberty of the subject. *339*

Judgement
in the Wilkes Case
1763
Great Britain

Equal right of everyone to justice

O ye who believe! stand fast to justice, when ye bear witness before God, though it be against yourselves, or your parents, or your kindred. *340*

Koran
An-Nissa 135

Those who went before you have perished because they let the strong man who committed a theft go unpunished and punished the weak man who committed a theft. I swear to you by the One who has my soul in his hands: if Fatima, Mohammed's daughter were to commit a theft, I would cut off her hand! *341*

Hadith
(Sayings
of the Prophet)

Hadith (Sayings of the Prophet)	How should that nation be blessed wherein there is no justice for the weak against the strong? *342*

Rights
of sanctuary

Juan de Santa Cruz
Pachacuti
Relación de
Antigüedades
deste Reyno
del Perú
c. 1600

And thus they say that he [the Inca] was a friend to well-doing, and always remitted matters of crime to the judges, and thus they say that criminals entering the temple of Coricancha were freed, and the same for those to whom he granted sanctuary in his palace, save that to thieves and adulterers he did not grant it; and thus they say that this Inca Yabarvacac, that he might not see the guilty punished, ordered that the prisons should be outside the city. *343*

Right
of sanctuary
for fugitives

Charter of Neuchatel
(Switzerland)
granted to
the burghers of
the town in 1214

If any newcomer, who is not numbered among our men, has taken refuge in our city, has resided in it for a year and a day without being claimed, has presented himself on arrival before the town officials or before ourselves, and has taken part in work of public utility, our burghers shall henceforth regard him as a fellow-burgher, and like themselves he will have our protection in time of need. If he has not taken part in any such work, he will not be regarded as a fellow-burgher, nor will he enjoy protection of any kind; for the honour of our city, we will yet not allow insult to be done him within its walls, but if he be captured or killed outside the city, we shall not avenge him. *344*

Domingo Faustino
Sarmiento
1811-88
Argentina

When by its Constitution a State offers asylum to foreigners, it is not granting a favour and this is not a deliberate act of will on its part. It merely recognizes a right belonging to all men in all countries, and the violation of which would constitute one of the many acts of barbarism that have sullied human history. *345*

The alien

The mother and the son are eating fish, they give that fool Imono acid-tasting vegetables; they are thereby trying to make me suffer from haemorrhoids; will they then treat me with baths.

Liberality between relations does not extend to strangers, who receive only the poor quality food. Do they then think that I will accept and make myself ill? Do they think that I don't know that it is not they who will look after me when I'm sick?

A stranger (a visitor) is dust.

He stays only for a while, and then vanishes, often for good.

Therefore, if he is a nuisance or gloomy, and so on, put up with it for a while, it will not last. Further, you should not forget that when he leaves you he will tell how he was received, he will give you a good name or, on the contrary, will go round telling everyone that you are ill-natured.

The hunger of a baby is like the hunger of a stranger.

The stranger is hungry, but he does not dare ask for food, just as the infant does not know how to ask for anything.

Mongo proverbs
Congo

You should not wait for the stranger to ask for food; he should be given it. *346*

Exile

He that is brought up by his mother
Lives on his land and in his own house;

Quechua
folk-poetry
Peru

I, alone, miserable exile that I am,
Have neither house nor land to call my own. *347*

But the stranger that dwelleth with you shall be unto you as one born among you, and thou shalt love him as thyself;

Hebrew Bible
Leviticus 19

for ye were strangers in the land of Egypt: I am the Lord your God. *348*

Justice, impartiality

Force and justice

In all that smacks of the social order, force is to be found.

It is balance alone which can abolish force.

If one knows in what respect society is unbalanced, one must do what one can to add weight to the lighter of the two scales. Although the weight is bound to be evil, by using it with the intention of re-establishing the balance, it may be one thereby avoids any personal degradation.

Simone Weil
The Notebooks
1942
France

But one must first of all have clearly recognized where the balance lies, and be ever ready to change sides, like Justice, that 'fugitive from the camp of the victors'. *349*

Force is not a machine for automatically creating justice. It is a blind mechanism which produces indiscriminately and impartially just or unjust results, but, by all the laws of probability, nearly always unjust ones. Lapse of time makes no difference; it doesn't increase in the functioning of this mechanism the infinitesimal proportion of results which happen by chance to be in conformity with justice.

Where force is absolutely sovereign, justice is absolutely unreal. Yet justice cannot be that. We know it experimentally. It is real enough in the hearts of men. The structure of a human heart is just as much of a reality as any other in this universe, neither more nor less of a reality than the trajectory of a planet. *350*

Simone Weil
The Need for Roots
1942-43
France

Hammurabi came 'to cause righteousness to appear in the land,... that the strong harm not the weak'. *351*

Code of Hammurabi
1730-1685 B.C.
Babylon

Cattle loathe a cliff-top, men injustice. *352*

Amharic proverb
Ethiopia

Immanent justice

If it were done, when 'tis done, then 'twere well
It were done quickly. If th' assassination
Could trammel up the consequence, and catch
With his surcease, success; that but this blow
Might be the be-all and the end-all—here,
But here, upon this bank and shoal of time,
We'd jump the life to come. But in these cases,
We still have judgement here, that we but teach
Bloody instructions, which being taught return
To plague th' inventor. This even-handed justice
Commends th' ingredience of our poisoned chalice
To our own lips. *353*

Shakespeare
Macbeth
Act I, Scene vii
1606

Impartiality

The 16th year, 3rd month of the flood season, 21st day.
Today, in the High Court of Justice in Thebes, beside the two upper columns to the north of the Court of Amon, at the gate of Dwarekhit. Notables sitting that day in the High Court of Justice in Thebes: The Prefect of Thebes and the Vizier Khaemwese; the High Priest of Amen-Ra, King of the Gods, Amenhotep; the prophet of Amena-Ra, King of the Gods, and sem-priest Nesamun of the temple of the Millions of Years (*funerary temple*) of King Neferkere Setepenre; the King's servant Nesamun, scribe of Pharaoh; the Steward of the household of the Divine Worshipper of Amen-ra, King of the Gods; the King's

175

servant Neferkere-enperamun, herald of Pharaoh; Lieutenant General Hori of the chariotry; the standard-bearer of the fleet Hori; the Prince of Thebes Pesiur.

The Prefect of Thebes and the Vizier Khaemwese summoned the blacksmith Peikharu, son of Khari, the blacksmith Thari, son of Khaemope, and the blacksmith Peikamen, son of Thari, of the temple of Usimare Miamon, in the service of the High Priest of Amon.

The Vizier said to the great notables of the High Court of Justice in Thebes: 'The Prince of Thebes brought certain accusations against the inspectors and workmen of the Necropolis in the Year 16, third month of the flood, 19th day, in the presence of the King's servant Nesamun, scribe of Pharaoh, concerning the great tombs which are in the Place of Beauty.

'However, when I went there myself, as Vizier of the country, accompanied by the King's servant Nesamun, scribe of Pharaoh, we examined the tombs concerning which the Prince of the Nome had said that they had been despoiled by the blacksmiths of the temple of Usimare Miamon in the house of Amon; we found them intact, and all that had been said was proved to be false. Here are the blacksmiths before you: ask them all that happened.' The blacksmiths were questioned and it became clear that they knew nothing about the tombs in the Place of Pharaoh, concerning which the prince had spoken; and it was recognized that the prince was in the wrong in this matter.

The great notables released the blacksmiths of the temple of Usimare Miamon, and that same day they were entrusted to the High Priest of Amen-ra, King of the Gods, Amenhotep.

Report of a law-suit
Ancient Egypt
XXth dynasty
2nd millenary B.C.

A report was drawn up and deposited in the Vizier's archives.

354

Legal procedure

Case in which one man brings an action against another, saying: 'He has taken my house from me; it is mine, it was my father's', and in which the man thus accused replies: 'It is mine, I took it out of the canal (*that is to say I built it with clay from the canal*).' If the house is near the canal, it shall be said to the accused: 'Prove that it is thine and that thou tookest it out of the canal; otherwise, it will be for thine accuser to prove that it is his and that it belonged to his father.' If the canal does not run by the house, it shall be said to the plaintiff: 'Prove that it is thine and that it belonged to thy father.' The other will have to give him a written statement of renunciation in respect of the house in question.

Legal code
of Hermopolis
Ptolemaic period
Ancient Egypt

355

Uniformity
Asoka's Pillar Edict IV
3rd cent. B.C.
India

Since it is to be desired that there should be uniformity in law and also uniformity in justice, from this time forward such is my injunction.   *356*

Aristotle
The Constitution
of Athens
4th cent. B.C.

The archons mount the stone and... 'swear to fulfil their responsibilities in all justice and in accordance with the laws and, in the execution of their duties, not to accept bribes or, if they do, to dedicate a statue of gold'.   *357*

Conditions of
a death sentence
ibid.

No citizen could be put to death except by decision of a court.   *358*

Law
of the XII Tables
Earliest codification
of Roman law
5th cent. B.C.

A citizen may be condemned to death only before the assembled comitia.

... condemns to death the judge or arbiter found guilty of pronouncing sentence in favour of a party who has given him money.   *359*

First edict
of Augustus
7-6 B.C.

A Hellene who is to be judged may, the day before the indictment begins, choose between a jury consisting entirely of Romans or of one half Hellenes. In the latter case, after the ballots have been weighed and the names written on them, the names of the Romans will be drawn from one urn and those of the Hellenes from another, until twenty-five have been drawn from each. Of these, the prosecution may, if it wishes, challenge a juror in each group; the accused may challenge three in all, but not exclusively either Romans or Hellenes. The remainder will then be allowed to cast their votes, the Romans in one box, the Hellenes in another. Then, when the votes cast on both sides have been counted separately, the governor will publicly announce the verdict of the majority.   *360*

Tertullian questions the legality of proscribing Christians. There had been no regular trial, no advocates to plead the case.

Tertullian
Christian apologist
Apologeticus
2nd cent.
Carthage

Truth only asks not to be condemned without a hearing.... And, if it be certain that we are great criminals, why are we treated otherwise than our peers, that is to say, the other criminals?   *361*

Judges

The king should appoint such persons as judges as have made a deep study of the scriptures, know the Dharma well, adhere to truth, and would be impartial towards the plaintiff and the defendant.

Those judges who deviate from the law laid down in the *Smritis* or do other similar things, either through affection or greed or fear, should be severally inflicted with punishment twice that which the actual offender in the case might merit.   *362*

Yājñavalkyasmriti II
3rd to 4th cent.
Sanskrit

Justice should be speedy and strict

Having taken his seat in the assembly, the king should not make persons desiring to see him in connexion with their plaints wait at the door for a long time. For a king who is difficult of access is made to do the reverse in respect of what deserves to be done and what does not deserve to be done, by those who are near to him. As a result of this, he may have to face an insurrection of the people or subjugation by the enemy.   *363*

Kautilīya-
Arthasāstra I
4th cent. B.C.
Sanskrit

Restitution

The king should recover the wealth stolen by thieves and restore the whole of it to the original owners, irrespective of the social order to which they may belong. If he is unable to recover it, he should make it good out of his own treasury.   *364*

Visnusmriti III
4th to 5th cent.
Sanskrit

Severity

Manusmriti VIII
2nd cent. B.C.
to 1st cent. A.D.
Sanskrit

The precept of law is that where any other ordinary person would be fined one *kārsāpana* (*one particular coin*), there a king should be fined a thousand [*kārsapanā*].   *365*

Administration of justice without consideration of Dharma leads, for the king, to the loss of heaven, glory and the beatific world. Proper administration of justice, on the other hand, leads to his attainment of heaven, glory and success. Even his own brother or son or a respected person (like a teacher) or a father-in-law or maternal uncle who has deviated from his own Dharma must, indeed, not remain unpunished by the king. The king who would punish such persons as deserve to be punished, and would properly have such persons killed as deserve to be killed, may be regarded as having performed [many] sacrifices characterized by perfect and excellent offerings. Taking into account the fruit, equal to that of a sacrifice (which he is thereby entitled to obtain) the king should himself, attended by the assessors, examine the various legal suits, separately, day after day.   *366*

Yājñavalkyasmriti I
3rd to 4th cent.
Sanskrit

Justice, however, is to be administered in cases of injury
to and complaint by the aggrieved, with due regard to
the special circumstances in connexion with those cases,
such as the time, place and local law, and the age, learning
and position [of the persons involved]. *367*

Vasistha-
Dharmasūtra XIX
1st cent.
Sanskrit

Administration
of justice cannot
be absolute

Mahābhārata XII
2nd cent. B.C.
to 1st cent. A.D.
Sanskrit

What appears contrary to normal law, O king, has to be
enforced as law [under certain circumstances]. [Similarly]
what is normal law has to be regarded as being contrary
to law. This the wise one should clearly understand. *368*

Quoted by Cicero
De Officiis
1st cent. B.C.

Summum jus, summa injuria. *369*

Right of appeal

Asoka's Pillar Edict IV
3rd cent. B.C.
Prakrit

From now on this is my command: To men on whom
sentence has already been passed and who are in confinement or have been condemned to death, three days
have been granted by me as their rightful respite in order
that (during that interval) some of their relatives may
submit appeals for their life, or in order to spare them
[spiritual] suffering in the end, may make offerings and
observe fasts conducive to their benefit in the other world.
370

In order that
justice may be done

Ceasing from gluttony and abandoning covetous desires,
deal impartially with the suits which are submitted to
you. Of complaints brought by the people there are a
thousand in one day. If in one day there are so many,
how many will there be in a series of years? If the man who
is to decide suits at law makes gain his ordinary motive,
and hears cases with a view to receiving bribes, then will
the suits of the rich man be like a stone flung into
water (*that is, they meet with no resistance*) while the plaints
of the poor will resemble water cast upon a stone. Under
these circumstances the poor man will not know whither
to betake himself.

. . . .

Let every man have his own charge, and let not
the spheres of duty be confused. When wise men are
entrusted with office, the sound of praise arises. If unprin-
cipled men hold office, disasters and tumults are multiplied.
In this world, few are born with knowledge: wisdom is
the product of earnest meditation. In all things, whether
great or small, find the right man, and they will surely
be well managed: on all occasions, be they urgent or the

reverse, meet but with a wise man, and they will of themselves be amenable. In this way will the State be lasting and the Temples of the Earth and of Grain will be free from danger. Therefore did the wise sovereigns of antiquity seek the man to fill the office, and not the office for the sake of the man.

Let the ministers and functionaries attend the court early in the morning, and retire late. The business of the State does not admit of remissness, and the whole day is hardly enough for its accomplishment. If, therefore, the attendance at court is late, emergencies cannot be met: if officials retire soon, the work cannot be completed.

. . . .

Let us cease from wrath, and refrain from angry looks. Nor let us be resentful when others differ from us. For all men have hearts, and each heart has its own leanings. Their right is our wrong, and our right is their wrong. We are not unquestionably sages, nor are they unquestionably fools. Both of us are simply ordinary men. How can any one lay down a rule by which to distinguish right from wrong? For we are all, one with another, wise and foolish, like a ring which has no end. Therefore, although others give way to anger, let us on the contrary dread our own faults, and though we alone may be in the right, let us follow the multitude and act like them.

. . . .

Decisions on important matters should not be made by one person alone. They should be discussed with many. But small matters are of less consequence. It is unnecessary to consult a number of people. It is only in the case of the discussion of weighty affairs, when there is a suspicion that they may miscarry, that one should arrange matters in concert with others, so as to arrive at the right conclusion.

Constitution of the Prince Imperial Shōtoku 604 Japan

371

Castes and the law

This is a way in which it can be said, sire, that this is merely a sound in the world, that 'Only brahmans form the best caste, all other castes are low; only brahmans form the fair caste, all other castes are dark; only brahmans are pure, not non-brahmans; brahmans are own sons of Brahma, born of his mouth, born of Brahma, formed by Brahma, heirs to Brahma.'

What do you think about this, sire? If a noble were to break into a house, or carry off loot, or commit a robbery, or make an ambush, or commit adultery, and if men who had captured him were to show him to you, and say: 'This, your majesty, is the thief who is doing evil to you, decree what punishment you like for him'—what would you do to him?

Good Kaccana, we should kill him or ruin him or banish him or deal with him as we liked. What is the cause of this? Good Kaccana, the designation of 'noble' that he once had has now disappeared for him, and he is reckoned simply as 'thief'.

What do you think about this, sire? If a brahman, a merchant, a worker were to break into a house—what would you do to him?

Good Kaccana, we should kill him—he is reckoned simply as 'thief'.

What do you think about this, sire? This being so, are these four castes exactly the same or not? Or how does this seem to you?

Indeed, good Kaccana, this being so, these four castes are exactly the same; I do not see any difference between them in this respect.

Majjhima Nikaya II Pali text

372

Force of law protection for the accused

Canon 2226. § 1. Persons who are bound by a law or a precept are liable for the penalty attached to the law or precept, unless they are explicitly exempted.

§ 2. If a later penal law changes a former law, and if a person has already committed an offence before the new law was made, the law which is more favourable to the offender is to be applied.

. . . .

§ 4. The penalty once incurred follows the offender wherever he goes, even after the superior has gone out of office, unless the contrary is explicitly stated.

Canon 2228. A penalty fixed by law is not incurred unless the specific offence has been fully committed in accordance with the proper meaning of the terms of the law.

Full awareness and responsibility

Canon 2229. § 1. Affected [pretended] ignorance of either the law or of its penalty only does not excuse from any penalties *latae sententiae*, even though the law contains the terms mentioned in the following paragraph.

§ 2. If the law has the words: *praesumpserit, ausus fuerit, scienter, studiose, temerarie, consulto egerit*, or other similar terms which demand full knowledge and deliberation, any diminution of liability, either on the part of the intellect or on the part of the will, exempts from the penalties *latae sententiae*.

§ 3. If the law does not have these terms:

1. Crass or supine ignorance of the law or of the penalty only does not exempt from any penalty *latae sententiae*;

ignorance which is not crass or supine excuses from the medicinal, but not from the vindicative penalties *latae sententiae;*

2. Drunkenness, omission of due care, mental weakness and heat of passion do not excuse from penalties *latae sententiae,* if notwithstanding the diminution of the liability the action was gravely sinful;

3. Grave fear does not exempt from penalties *latae sententiae* if the offence entails contempt of the faith or of ecclesiastical authority, or public injury of souls.

Imputability

Canon 2213. § 1. An attempted offence induces liability which increases in proportion as it approaches nearer to the consummation of the offence, although the liability is always less than for the consummated offence, without prejudice to the precept of § 3.

§ 2. A frustrated offence is more culpable than a simple attempted offence.

Canon law

373

Equality and the hierarchy

Any distinction of honour or fortune, to be legitimate, presupposes a prior equality based on the law, which holds all subjects equally subordinate. We may suppose that, casting off their original despotism, men declared: 'Let the greatest honours go to the most industrious, and let their renown shine also upon their descendants, but let not these successes and honours, by swelling their ambition, make them any less afraid than others to violate those laws which have raised them above those others.' It is true that no parliament has ever issued such decrees, but they are inherent in the unchangeable nature of things; they counteract the disadvantages of nobility, without destroying its supposed advantages: they inspire fear of the law by closing the route of escape from punishment. It will be objected that the same punishment is not truly the same when administered to a noble and when administered to a commoner, because of the difference of education and of the shame inflicted upon an illustrious family. My reply is that punishment is not made to fit the sensitivity of the guilty but the wrong committed against society, and that such a wrong is all the more grave when committed by a man whom fortune has favoured.

Cesare Beccaria
Treatise on Crimes
and Punishments
1764
Italy

374

Judicial guarantees

Attempts [therefore] against the life and liberty of a citizen, are crimes of the highest nature.

The laws only can determine the punishment of crimes. There ought to be a fixed proportion between crimes and punishments. No magistrate, even under a pretence of zeal, or the public good, should increase the punishment already determined by the laws.

No man can be judged a criminal until he be found guilty.

In as much as the judge has not pronounced him guilty, the prison should be limited to sheltering the citizen; this being distressing, it should therefore be for the least possible time, and harsh conditions should be avoided as far as possible.

... the intent of punishments is not to torment a sensible being ... but no other than to prevent the criminal from doing further injury to society, and to prevent others from committing the like offence.

Education against crime

It is better to prevent crimes, than to punish them. This is the fundamental principle of good legislation....

Would you prevent crimes? Let liberty be attended with knowledge.

Cesare Beccaria
Treatise on Crimes
and Punishments
1764, Italy

... the most certain method of preventing crimes is, to perfect the system of education.   375

No arbitrary punishments

Liberty is in perfection when criminal laws derive each punishment from the particular nature of the crime. There are then no arbitrary decisions; the punishment does not flow from the capriciousness of the legislator, but from the very nature of the thing; and man uses no violence to man.   376

Montesquieu
The Spirit of the Laws
1748, France

Freedom through the law

I should have wished to live and die free: that is, so far subject to the laws that neither I, nor anybody else, should be able to cast off their honourable yoke: the easy and salutary yoke which the haughtiest necks bear with the greater docility, as they are made to bear no other.

I should have wished then that no one within the State should be able to say he was above the law; and that no one without should be able to dictate so that the State should be obliged to recognize his authority. For, be the constitution of a government what it may, if there be within its jurisdiction a single man who is not subject to the law, all the rest are necessarily at his discretion.   377

J.-J. Rousseau
A Discourse
on the Origin
and Foundation
of Inequality
Among Men
1755

It is that instead of destroying natural equality, the fundamental pact, on the contrary, substitutes a moral and lawful equality for the physical inequality which nature imposed

J.-J. Rousseau
The Social Contract
1762

upon men, so that, although unequal in strength or intellect, they all become equal by convention and legal right. *378*

*Punishment of
corrupt officials*

On the laws and punishments wherewith the Incas governed their realm.

As the Indians had no alphabet, they had no written laws, but kept those that their kings had established by tradition and through their use and observance. I shall set forth here the most important of these laws and those best remembered by the Indians:

If any governor, for a bribe or influenced by his feelings, failed to do justice or kept something hidden, the Inca himself would punish him, depriving him of his chiefdom and office and disqualifying him from ever holding others; and if the injustice was in a serious matter, he had him put to death. *379*

Bernabé Cobo
Historia
del Nuevo Mundo
1653

*Neither fine nor
confiscation
of goods
among the Incas*

Garcilaso de la Vega (El Inca), the son of a Spanish captain and an Indian lady of royal blood, was a historian, a priest, a Latinist and a chronicler; he was called the 'Herodotus of the Incas'.

They never imposed a fine or confiscation of goods, saying that to punish a delinquent in his property and leave him alive was no way to rid the commonwealth of its ills, but only the evil-doer of his property, leaving him all the more free to commit greater crimes. Should a governor be guilty of rebellion (and this the Incas most unforgivingly punished) or some other crime that merited death, and even if he be executed, his heir was not disinherited but given back the estate, with a reminder of his father's guilt and sentence that he might shun the example. Concerning which, Pedro Cieza de León, writing of the Incas, says in Chapter XXI: 'And another way they had of not making themselves hateful to the population was never to take away the chieftainship from any who did inherit it and was native born. And should any such commit a crime or be so incriminated as to merit the loss of his chieftainship, this they passed on to his sons or brothers, ordering that they be obeyed by all.' *380*

Garcilaso de la Vega
(El Inca)
Comentarios Reales
de los Incas
1608 or 1609
Peru

The administration of justice among the Incas.

A judge had no discretion regarding the penalty prescribed by law, but must fully enforce it under pain of death for transgressing the royal command. They said that to allow a judge discretion would lessen the majesty of the law made by the King with the active collaboration of such learned and venerable men as those on the Council, whose wisdom and experience the individual judge must lack, and that judges would become venal and the door be opened for justice, either by bribes or by entreaty, to be bought, whence great disorder in the commonwealth, for every judge would do as he wished, and it was not right that any one should set himself up as a legislator, but should enforce as the law commanded, however harsh it be.

They had no appeals from one court to another in any suit, civil or criminal, for the judge not having discretion, the applicable law was enforced to the letter at the first sentence, and the case was closed, although indeed, such was the government of those kings and the way of life of their vassals, that few were the civil cases that required pleading. Every town had a magistrate to deal with local cases who, hearing both parties, must execute the law within five days. If any case were out of the ordinary by reason of its importance or atrocity and required a higher judge, they went to the capital of the province, where judgement was given, for each provincial capital had a chief governor for all that might arise, so that no litigant need leave his town or province in search of justice. For the Inca Kings well understood that it was hard for the poor, because of their poverty, to seek justice outside their own place or in a variety of courts, for the expense it involved and the vexations they suffered, all this often coming to more than they went to seek, so that they allowed their rights to lapse, especially as against the rich and powerful, who employed their ascendancy to suffocate the claims in justice of the poor.

Now, these Princes, wishing to remedy such abuses, did not allow discretion to the judges, or many courts, or having litigants go outside their province. The ordinary magistrates reported every month to higher magistrates on the verdicts they had awarded, who reported to others higher, since in the Court they were of many grades, depending on the type of gravity of the affair; for in all the services of the commonwealth there were minor and major orders up to the highest, who were the Presidents, or Viceroys, of the four parts of the Empire. And these reports would show whether right justice had been administered, so that the lower magistrates did not neglect so to administer, or, failing, were strictly punished. This was, as it were, a secret impeachment that every month they must undergo.

Garcilaso de la Vega
(El Inca)
Comentarios Reales
de los Incas
1608 or 1609
Peru

381

Right to
legal protection

And whereas I am informed that the said Corregidores [magistrates] in the said criminal suits proceed against individual Indians with exaggerated severity, without heed to the provisions of the law, and execute the sentences condemning them to death without granting right of appeal, and whereas this must be redressed so that this irregular procedure may not extend: I order and command that when such things happen and the said Corregidores and other Justices condemn any Indians to death and they appeal against such sentence, they are to allow them the appeals arising therefrom before the said Royal Courts of Appeal of the district in which the aforementioned has happened; and where, through ignorance, any should fail to appeal, they are not to execute the sentences, but

Ordinances
to Corregidors
issued by the Viceroy
of Peru
1685

without the least delay send any judgements they have so made and pronounced to the said Royal Courts of Appeal, so that their Protectors may petition whatever they deem proper.   *382*

Equal punishment

If the same laws are to apply to the entire Republic, then it behoves us to mete out the same punishments to all criminals alike. For nothing mars the law more sadly than differences in the penalties imposed on criminals. Indeed, if the matter is scrupulously considered, heavier penalties would be imposed on offenders of high rank, and greater clemency would be shown by the law to those in humble circumstances. Plato lays down that a citizen of his republic should be punished more severely than a slave or a foreigner....

The inequality in the law whereby the murder of a plebeian is punished by a fine of ten *grzywnas* and that

A. F. Modrzewski
De Republica
Emendanda
1551
Poland

of a nobleman by a fine of 100 *grzywnas* or death could only have been devised by a tyrant, and not by a wise legislator. We must therefore rid the republic of this law, and efface all trace of it from human memory.   *383*

The prevention
of abuses

Al-Mawardi says that he who is responsible for bringing abuses to light should display perfect dignity and great authority, should enjoy high reputation, and should be of pure and scrupulous character, for his functions demand the power of a protector and the equanimity of a judge.

Al-Wansharishi
The Book of Judges
16th cent.
North Africa

He should possess the merits of these two classes of officials so that the force of administrative authority may be combined with the impartiality of a judge.   *384*

Most writers of our faith, and others also, have set out to
discourage and warn men against accepting the office
of Cadi. They have emphatically censured those who
sought such office and have counselled men to turn from
it, to avoid it, and to flee it, to such effect that many
jurists and respected men have conceived the idea that
he who is invested with the office of Cadi weakens his faith,
runs deliberately on his own ruin, and turns from what
has greatest merit.

They hold a very poor opinion of the office of Cadi.
This is a most execrable error, which must be abandoned
and set aside.

This noble office should, on the contrary, be honoured
and its rank in the Moslem religion recognized. It was
for the sake of justice that the Prophets were sent to us,
for this that the heavens and the earth were created. The
Prophet set the judicature among the blessings which
may be envied, saying, according to Ibn Mess'oud: 'Only
two men are to be envied: he to whom God has given
wealth and the power to spend it in doing good; and he
to whom God has given wisdom to guide his judgements
and his acts.'

Al-Wansharishi
The Book of Judges
16th cent.
North Africa

385

*Judgement as rendered by Itakura Shigemuni, a leading magistrate
in seventeenth-century Japan.*

Once appointed, Shigemuni went daily to court, bowed
in the corridor towards the west, and entered. Inside,
he places a tea-mill before him, takes his seat behind a
paper door and judges cases while grinding the tea with
his own hand. People were astonished, but none dared
question. When, after many years, someone asked him
why, he answered: 'When I go to court and bow down
in the corridor to the west, it is that I may entreat the gods
of Atago. Among the innumerable gods, those of Atago
are especially celebrated for their divine power; and I
worship them in order to seek one favour: "In judging
the cases submitted to him, may Shigemuni's heart be
in no wise partial: if it be partial in any respect, may I
live no longer"—thus have I prayed each day to them.
I reflected, too, that if the judgement is not clear it is
because of the heart's being stirred by every object.
Virtuous men might endeavour to remain unmoved, but
Shigemuni would fail. And so, to see whether my
heart be troubled or not, I satisfy myself on the
point by grinding tea. When my heart is calm and
firm, my hand is likewise, the mill grinds smoothly and

the tea-grounds that issue from it are extremely fine: I know my heart is still, and give judgement. If I hear cases through a paper door it is because, of the human faces one sees, there are the horrible, the pleasing, the sincere, the evil, and more other varieties than one can number. The words of a man who looks sincere seem true, those from an evil face false even though they be just. We listen to the suit of a man of pleasing countenance and believe he has been persecuted, but hear an ugly man's arguments, and think him wrong; and all because, the heart being swayed by what the eyes see, before a person has even spoken we are already deciding in our hearts that he is criminal, or virtuous, or upright; and when we hear the pleadings, we often have ample confirmation of our thoughts. But when it comes to delivering judgement, there are odious men among those who appeared likeable, and likeable among the odious, false men among the sincere, upright among the crooked, and I know not how many more! The heart of man is difficult to fathom, and never entirely written in the face. Formerly, judgement was rendered according to people's colour, their demeanour. This is feasible for those who are never wrong, but men like Shigemuni are often deluded by what they see. For not only is everyone frightened if he has to appear in court, but quite naturally terrified at the sight of the judge who can have him killed or let him live; he cannot say what he should, and finds himself condemned for some felony or misdemeanour. Better, then, that we should not see each other's faces: and this is why I ordered the separation.' Thus, praying daily to the gods, he would swear to be utterly impartial, and having set his heart to rights both inwardly and outwardly, he would proceed to hear cases and deliver his judgements.

Arai Hakuseki
Hankampu
1701
Japan

386

The ambiguities of justice

THE THREE TRAVELLERS AND THE IVORY TUSK

Once upon a time three men were travelling together. The first had brought a stick of manioc and the second a packet of roasted ground-nuts. The third had only his dog. On the way they came to a tree-trunk lying by the wayside, in a wood between two villages. Tired with their long walk and feeling hungry, they sat down to eat. Now, the first looked around for something to eat with his manioc and the second complained that he had nothing to eat with his ground-nuts. So he offered a few handfuls of nuts to the first and got in exchange a piece of manioc. Then they both ate, without bothering about their companion who had brought nothing.

When they had finished eating, they threw the leaves the manioc and the ground-nuts had been wrapped in into the neighbouring bushes. The dog rushed after them. As he was some time in coming back, his master went to see what he was up to and found gnawing an ivory tusk. He quickly snatched up the tusk and, delighted with his find, came back with his dog to the others. The first man tried to grab the tusk for himself. 'If I had not thrown the leaves into the bushes', said he, 'your dog would never have gone. The tusk is therefore mine.' The second thought otherwise. 'You certainly threw the leaves away', he argued 'but if I had not given you my ground-nuts, you would not have eaten your manioc. The tusk belongs to me.'

As they went on arguing night fell, so they stopped until morning. As soon as it was day, the row began again worse than ever, and at the time of writing the question is still not settled.

Fang tale
Gabon Now, in your opinion, which of the three travellers is entitled to the ivory tusk? 387

The right to justice You should not solicit what is yours by right.

Do not accept a verdict given in your absence.

It is the small wrong, done without intention, that will put out your eye.
(*A person's "eye" is whatever is dear to him—his brother, his neighbour—even if he does not know it.*)

The millet cake cannot get out of a gourd of milk by jumping.
(*Trickery can never prevail against the law.*)

Djerma-Songhai
proverbs
Africa I would have you know that another person's right is a live coal; if you take hold of it, it will burn your hand. 388

It rains even in the field of the sorcerer who devours souls.
(*Even an exile has rights. Justice is universal. No man, however vile, can be deprived of the rights that it confers on him.*)

Hausa proverb
Africa 389

Djerma-Songhai
proverb
Africa Whatever is unjust towards others is not worthy of the name of Justice. 390

Charter of Justice
of Pskov
1397
Russia

The prince and the mayor will not dispense justice before the assembly, but in the prince's own antechamber, respecting the law as their oath requires.... And neither the prince nor the mayor shall accept bribes.   *391*

*No arbitrary
detention*

Pososkov
Treatise on Poverty
and Wealth, 1724
Russia

In the small towns many nobles bring in their servants and peasants and have them put under lock and key; and therefore in the towns as in the administrative offices registers should be kept of those held in detention, and it should be commanded that no one be detained in an administrative office or in prison without a written order, entered in the register. And if, in the course of an inspection, one is found not entered in the register, he who has had him arrested without a written order should be severely punished, so that he will never again act in such a way.   *392*

*Justice despite
the military
hierarchy*
Pososkov
Treatise on Poverty
and Wealth, 1724
Russia

If a deserting soldier is recaptured and says he has deserted because of ill-treatment by his officer, let there be an inquiry. And if the ill-treatment is proven, let the officer be punished and the soldier excused branding.   *393*

*Confidence
in justice*

J.-B. Scherer
Annales de la
Petite-Russie, ou
Histoire des Cosaques
Zaporogues et des
Cosaques de l'Ukraine
1788
France

No nation observes such moderation in disputes as the inhabitants of Little Russia. There, both parties quietly mount the same wagon, drink, eat and sleep together, even should 300 versts have to be travelled to reach the judge. And once in his presence, each explains his reasons and argues his case. Such conduct is certainly one of the best proofs they can give of their respect for the law and of the disinterested and equitable character of those whose duty it is to apply it.   *394*

*The judge's
partiality*

What shame and scandal, for this world and the next, that a provincial governor should oppress those he administers!

How can a being who calls himself a man pronounce sentence in favour of the unjust when the truth is manifest?

Can one describe as justice the verdict of a tribunal in which the judge is advocate and the process-server witness?

Cursed be the fortune acquired as a result of speculations bearing on religion, honour or decency.

Man is he who wishes the good of his neighbour: that is the sole touchstone of human character.

He is called a man, whose tender heart is saddened by the sorrows of his fellow creatures.

Attach not thyself by the heartstrings to the fortune [thou enjoyest], nor believe that misfortune will endure: the celestial wheel does not always revolve in the same orbit.

The unjust man shall meet at last with the sorry lot he deserves. He who destroys the home of others, shall one day see his own house crumble.　　　*395*

Ziya Pasha
1829-80
Turkey

*Legal
safeguards*

THE APPLICATION OF 'HABEAS CORPUS' (1679) TO A CASE OF SLAVERY

The Habeas Corpus *Act provides a means of testing the lawfulness of a person's detention. Anyone who believes himself to be detained on unlawful grounds may seek a writ of* Habeas Corpus *against the person detaining him, this person then being required to appear before the court on the day named to show cause for detention. If no lawful cause can be shown, the prisoner must be released forthwith. So strong are the law and tradition on this point that any application concerning the liberty of the subject is always given priority of hearing in any court of law.*

In Sommersett's Case (1772) the great Lord Chief Justice Mansfield declared for the freedom of the individual in its most basic form.

I shall recite the return to the writ of *Habeas Corpus,* as the ground of our determination; omitting only words of form. The captain of the ship on board of which the negro was taken, makes his return to the writ in terms signifying that there have been and still are, slaves to a great number in Africa; and that the trade in them is authorized by the laws, and opinions of Virginia and Jamaica; that they are goods and chattels; and, as such, saleable and sold. That James Sommersett is a negro of Africa, and long before the return of the king's writ was brought to be sold, and was sold to Charles Steuart, esq., then in Jamaica, and has not been manumitted since; that Mr. Steuart, having occasion to transact business, come over hither, with an intention to return; and brought Sommersett to attend and abide with him, and to carry him back as soon as the business should be transacted. That such intention has been, and still continues; and that the negro did remain till the time of his departure in the service of his master, Mr. Steuart, and quitted it without his consent; and thereupon, before the return of the king's writ, the said Charles Steuart did commit the slave on board the Anne and Mary, to safe custody, to be kept till he should set sail and then to be taken with him to Jamaica, and there sold as a slave. And this is the cause why he, captain Knowles, who was then and now is, commander of the above vessel, then and now lying in the river of Thames, did the said negro, committed to his custody, detain; and on which he now renders him to the orders of the Court. . . . The only question before us is, whether the cause on the return is sufficient? If it is so, the negro must be remanded; if it is not, he must be discharged. Accordingly the return states, that the slave departed and refused to serve; whereupon he was kept to be sold abroad. So high an act of dominion must be recognized by the law of the country where it is used. The power of a master over his slave has been extremely different, in different countries. The state of slavery is of such a nature, that it is incapable of being introduced on any reasons, moral or political, but only by positive law, which preserves its force long after the reasons, occasion, and time itself from whence it was created, is erased from memory. It is so odious, that nothing can be suffered to support it, but positive law. Whatever inconveniences, therefore, may follow from the decision, I cannot say this case is allowed or approved by the law of England and therefore the black must be discharged. *396*

**Sommersett's Case
1772
Great Britain**

Legal requirements OF IMPRISONMENT

Imprisonment is a punishment which, as distinct from all others, must of necessity precede proof of the offence; but this particular circumstance does not nullify the fundamental principle that the law alone should determine in what cases a man deserves to be punished. The law must therefore show upon what evidence an accused person must be imprisoned, and submit him to trial and punishment. Rumour, admissions made out of court or the admissions of an accomplice, threats made by the accused, his constant enmity for the victim, the existence of a *corpus delicti* and other such evidence seem sufficient to commit a citizen to prison, but evidence must be stipulated by the law and not assessed by a judge, whose decrees are prejudicial to political liberty unless they constitute a particular application of a general principle set down in the code. *397*

**Cesare Beccaria
Treatise on Crimes
and Punishments
1764
Italy**

The Instrument of Government of 1809.

The Riksdag [Parliament] shall appoint two citizens of known legal ability and outstanding integrity, the one as ombudsman of civil affairs, and the other as ombudsman of military affairs, to supervise the observance of the laws and statutes in the capacity of representatives of the Riksdag, according to instructions issued by the Riksdag....

In accordance with the division of duties stated above these ombudsmen shall institute proceedings before the competent court against those who in the execution of their official duties have through partiality, favoritism or other cause committed any unlawful act or neglected to perform their official duties properly....

The ombudsman of civil affairs and the ombudsman of military affairs may, whenever they consider it necessary in the exercise of their duties, attend the deliberations and decisions of Supreme Court, the Supreme Administrative Court, the Secretariat of the Supreme Court; the Courts of Appeal, the Administrative Boards or the institutions established in their place, and all the lower courts, but shall have no right to express their views on such occasions....

Should it happen, contrary to expectation, that either the entire Supreme Court, or one or more of its members, is found to have rendered, by reason of self-interest, iniquity or negligence, such a wrongful judgement, in conflict with clear law and evidence of facts duly established, that it causes or might have caused someone loss of life, personal liberty, honour or property, or if the Supreme Administrative Court or one or more of its members is found to have been guilty of such conduct in the hearing of administrative cases on appeal, it shall be the duty of the ombudsman of civil affairs, or in military cases as described in article 96, the ombudsman of military affairs, as it shall be within the power of the King's Attorney-General, to institute proceedings against the offender before the court of the realm hereinafter provided and to call him to responsibility in accordance with the law of the realm.

Sweden   398

Protection of persons by the Ombudsman

In 1848, while examining the records from the prison in Gothenburg, the Justitieombudsman noticed that, according to the list of prisoners, one woman had been imprisoned since 1838, pending identification. He then asked if action had been taken to obtain any information about her and her circumstances. It was revealed that nothing had been done. The Governor and his assistant, the County Council Secretary, were impeached as being responsible for the omission. The Governor was required to pay a fine and the County Council Secretary was punished by two months' loss of employment and salary. The woman, who had escaped from the prison in 1842, renounced a claim for compensation for the suffering which the unwarranted time in prison (1838-42) had caused her. Otherwise such compensation would have been paid....

In 1887, a person reported that he had been forbidden by the Town Administration of Linköping to give a lecture with the title 'The population increase in Sweden and the resultant dangers for general welfare and morality'. The complainant considered that his human rights had been infringed upon. The Justitieombudsman found that no law supported the injunction of the Town Administration and prosecuted the responsible office-holders. They were punished by being required to pay fines.   *399*

Contemporary
reports
Sweden

Democracy, principles and institutions

*Foreshadowing
the principle
of the limitation
of power*

ATHENIAN. I mean to say, my dear friends, that there is no soul of man, young and irresponsible, who will be able to sustain the temptation of arbitrary power—no one who will not, under such circumstances, become filled with folly, that worst of diseases, and be hated by his nearest and dearest friends: when this happens his kingdom is undermined, and all his power vanishes from him. And great legislators who know the mean

should take heed of the danger. As far as we can guess at this distance of time, what happened was as follows.
MEGILLUS. What?
ATHENIAN. A God, who watched over Sparta, seeing into the future, gave you two families of kings instead of one; and thus brought you within the limits of moderation. In the next place, some human wisdom mingled with divine power, observing that the constitution of your government was still feverish and excited, tempered your inborn strength and pride of birth with the moderation which comes of age, making the power of your twenty-eight elders equal with that of the kings in your most important matters. But your third saviour, perceiving that your government was still swelling and foaming, imposed as a curb the power of the Ephori, nearly resembling that of officers elected by lot; and by this arrangement the kingly office, being compounded of the right elements and duly moderated, was preserved, and was the means of preserving all the rest.   *400*

Plato
429-347 B.C.
Laws

•

I will vote in accordance with the laws and decrees of the people of Athens and the Council of Five Hundred and, in cases not foreseen by the law, in accordance with the most enlightened opinion, without favour or hatred, I will not vote for a tyrant or for an oligarchy, and I shall not be privy to any who attack the Athenian democracy or speak or vote against it.   *401*

Oath of the Heliasts
Demosthenes' oration
against Timocrates
c. 353 B.C.

On parties

Your servant is aware that from ancient times there have been discussions on the worth of parties. It is only to be hoped that a ruler will distinguish between those of gentlemen and those of inferior men. In general, gentlemen join with other gentlemen in parties because of common principles, while inferior men join with other inferior men for reasons of common profit. This is quite natural. But your servant would contend that in fact inferior men have no parties, and that it is only gentlemen who are capable of forming them. Why is this? Inferior men love profit and covet material wealth. When the time seems to offer mutual advantages, they will temporarily band together to form a party, which is, however, essentially false. But when they reach the stage where they are actually competing among themselves for advantage, or where the advantages they have sought fail to materialize and they drift apart, then they turn about and begin to attack each other, and even the fact that a man is a brother or a relative does not spare him. Therefore your servant maintains that such men have no real parties, and that those which they form on a temporary basis are essentially false. But this is not true of gentlemen, who abide by the Way and righteousness, who practice loyalty and good faith, and care only for honour and integrity. When they employ these qualities in their personal conduct they share a common principle and improve each other, and when they turn them to the use of the State they unite in common ideals and mutual assistance, and from the beginning to end act as one. These are the parties of gentlemen.

Ou-yang Hsiu
1007-72
China

402

Rights of
the individual

Magna Carta (Granted by King John in 1215).

Magna Carta
1215
Clause 39
England

No freeman shall be captured or imprisoned or dispossessed or outlawed or exiled or in any way destroyed, nor will we go against him or send against him, except by the lawful judgment of his peers and by the law of the land.

403

Protection even to
the unfree peasantry
against the
arbitrary
confiscation of
their property

Magna Carta
1215
Clause 20
England

A freeman shall be fined for a small offence only according to the degree of the offence; and for a grave offence he shall be fined according to the gravity of the offence, but not so as to deprive him of his living. And a merchant shall be fined in the same way, but not to the extent of confiscating his merchandise; and a villein in the same way, but leaving what he needs to cultivate his land— should they fall into our mercy. And none of the aforesaid fines shall be imposed except by the sworn assessment of good men from the neighbourhood.

404

'The Provisions of Oxford', proclaimed in 1258, laid down the obligations of officials towards the people and a procedure for bringing complaints against corrupt officials.

It has been provided that from each county there shall be elected four discreet and lawful knights who, on every day that the county [court] is held, shall assemble to hear all complaints touching any wrongs and injuries inflicted on any persons by sheriffs, bailiffs or any other men, and to make the attachments that pertain to the said complaints [for keeping] until the first arrival of the chief justiciar in those parts....

Concerning the sheriffs: As sheriffs there shall be appointed loyal persons, good men who are landholders; so that in each county there shall be as sheriff a feudal tenant of the same county, who shall well, loyally and justly treat the people of the county. And [it is ordered] that he shall take no fee; that he shall be sheriff for no more than a year in all; that during the year he shall render his accounts at the exchequer and be responsible for his term [of office]; that the king, from the royal income, shall make [allowance] to him in proportion to his receipts, so that he may rightly keep the county; and that he shall take no fees, neither he nor his bailiffs. And if they are convicted [of such wrongdoing], let them be punished. *405*

Provisions of Oxford
England

Growing importance of parliament in the second half of the thirteenth century, as the final resort for individuals with grievances.

Whereas in the king's court persons find their cases delayed because a party alleges that in the king's absence answer should not be made to demands, and [whereas] also many persons wrongfully suffer injuries from the king's ministers, with regard to which injuries one can secure recovery only in common parliament; we ordain that the king shall hold a parliament once a year, or twice if need be, and that in a convenient place. And [we ordain] that in those parliaments pleas which are delayed in the said manner, and pleas wherein the justices are of different opinions, shall be recorded and settled. And likewise those bills which are brought to parliament shall be settled as heretofore in accordance with law and right. *406*

29th of
the 'Ordinances'
1311
England

*Primacy of
the Assembly*

The Statutes drawn up by a General Chapter can be validly interpreted only by a General Chapter. *407*

Statutes of the
Premonstratensians 7
1503

T. Montalvus
Capuchin friar
1740

The General Chapter has full and absolute authority over the Minister-General who is subordinate to it and is its subject. *408*

Epitome Instituti The General Assembly possesses full power. The General is
Societatis Jesu subject to its authority. He must convene it to deal with
Art. 22 important matters.   *409*
1689

Convocation of Whenever any weighty matters have to be transacted in
the Assembly the Monastery, let the Abbot call together all the community and himself propose the matter for discussion.
After hearing the advice of the brethren let him consider
it in his own mind, and then do what he shall judge
most expedient.

We ordain that all must be called to council, because
the Lord often reveals to a younger member what is best.

Election of That he be made Abbot whom the whole community
the Abbot in the fear of God make a choice of, or part of it, however
by the community small, acting with greater wisdom.

Let him who is created Abbot be chosen because of his
Rule of St. Benedict virtuous life and his wisdom, even if he be last in the
6 th cent. community.   *410*

THE MAYFLOWER COMPACT, 11 NOVEMBER 1620

*This compact, which served as a Constitution for the first
secessionist settlers landing in New England, extended to the
civil sphere the customary undertaking given by the religious
community.*

In The Name of God, Amen. We, whose names are under-
written, the Loyal Subjects of our dread Sovereign Lord
King *James*, by the Grace of God, of *Great Britain, France,*
and *Ireland*, King, *Defender of the Faith*, &c. Having
undertaken for the Glory of God, and Advancement of
the Christian Faith, and the Honour of our King and
Country, a Voyage to plant the first colony in the northern
Parts of Virginia; Do by these Presents, solemnly and
mutually in the Presence of God and one another, covenant
and combine ourselves together into a civil Body Politick,
for our better Ordering and Preservation, and Furtherance
of the Ends aforesaid; And by Virtue hereof do enact,
constitute, and frame, such just and equal Laws, Ordinances, Acts, Constitutions, and Offices, from time to
time, as shall be thought most meet and convenient for
the general Good of the Colony; unto which we promise
all due Submission and Obedience. In WITNESS whereof
we have hereunto subscribed our names at *Cape Cod* the

eleventh of *November*, in the Reign of our Sovereign Lord King *James* of *England*, *France*, and *Ireland*, the eighteenth and of *Scotland*, the fifty-fourth. *Anno Domini*, 1620.   *411*

Against arbitrary actions of the king

The grand question is shortly this: whether ... in this special case ... the charges imposed by the king upon his subjects for provision of shipping, without common consent in parliament, be good in law—yea or no. ... I hope none doth imagine that it either is or can be drawn by consequence to be any part of the question in this case whether the king may at all times and upon all occasions impose charges upon his subjects in general without common consent in parliament. If that were made the question, it is questionless that he may not. The people of the kingdom are subjects, not slaves—freemen, not villeins to be taxed *de alto et basso*. Though the king of England hath a monarchical power and hath *jura summae majestatis* and hath an absolute trust settled in his crown and person for the government of his subjects, yet his government is to be *secundum leges regni*.... By those laws the subjects are not tenants at the king's will of what they have.... They have a birthright in the laws of the kingdom. No new laws can be put upon them; none of their laws can be altered or abrogated without common consent in parliament.   *412*

Hampden's Case
1638
Declaration
by a judge
England

THE DECLARATION OF INDEPENDENCE OF THE AMERICAN COLONIES DRAFTED BY THOMAS JEFFERSON
4 JULY 1776

We hold these truths to be self-evident, that all men are created equal, that they are endowed by their Creator with certain unalienable Rights, that among these are Life, Liberty and the pursuit of Happiness. That to secure these rights, Governments are instituted among Men, deriving their just powers from the consent of the governed. That whenever any Form of Government becomes destructive of these ends, it is the Right of the People to alter or to abolish it, and to institute new Government, laying its foundation on such principles and organizing its powers in such form, as to them shall seem most likely to effect their Safety and Happiness. Prudence, indeed, will dictate that Governments long established should not be changed for light and transient causes; and accordingly all experience hath shown, that mankind are more disposed to suffer, while evils are sufferable, than to right themselves by abolishing the forms to which they are accustomed. But when a long train of abuses and usurpations, pursuing invariably the same Object evinces a design to reduce them under absolute Despotism, it is their right, it is their duty, to throw off such Government, and to provide new Guards for their future security. *413*

Conditions of freedom

George Washington's Circular to the states, 1783

Nothing can illustrate these observations more forcibly, than a recollection of the happy conjuncture of times and circumstances, under which our Republic assumed its rank among the Nations; The foundation of our Empire was not laid in the gloomy age of Ignorance and Superstition, but at an Epocha when the rights of mankind were better understood and more clearly defined, than at any former period, the researches of the human mind, after social happiness, have been carried to a great extent, the Treasures of knowledge, acquired by the labours of Philosophers, Sages and Legislatures, through a long succession of years, are laid open for our use, and their collected wisdom may be happily applied in the Establishment of our forms of Government; the free cultivation of Letters, the unbounded extension of Commerce, the progressive refinement of Manners, the growing liberalty of sentiment, and above all, the pure and benign light of Revelation, have had a meliorating influence on mankind and increased the blessings of Society. At this auspicious period, the United States came into existence as a Nation, and if their Citizens should not be completely free and happy, the fault will be intirely their own. *414*

DECLARATION OF THE RIGHTS OF MAN AND OF THE CITIZEN

Decreed by the National Assembly in the morning sessions of 20, 21, 22, 23, 24 and 26 August 1789
Signed by the King on 5 October 1789

PREAMBLE

The representatives of the French people, organized in the National Assembly, considering that ignorance, forgetfulness or contempt of the rights of man are the sole causes of the public miseries and of the corruption of governments, have resolved to set forth in a solemn declaration

A Declaration by the Representatives of the UNITED STATES
OF AMERICA, in General Congress assembled.

When in the course of human events it becomes necessary for one people to
dissolve the political bands which have connected them with another, and to as
-sume among the powers of the earth the separate and equal station to
which the laws of nature & of nature's god entitle them, a decent respect
to the opinions of mankind requires that they should declare the causes
which impel them to the separation.

We hold these truths to be self-evident; that all men are
created equal, that they are endowed by their creator with
inherent & inalienable rights; that among these are the
life, & liberty, & the pursuit of happiness; that to secure these rights, go
-vernments are instituted among men, deriving their just powers from
the consent of the governed; that whenever any form of government
becomes destructive of these ends, it is the right of the people to alter
or to abolish it, & to institute new government, laying it's foundation on
such principles & organising it's powers in such form, as to them shall
seem most likely to effect their safety & happiness. prudence indeed
will dictate that governments long established should not be changed for
light & transient causes: and accordingly all experience hath shewn that
mankind are more disposed to suffer while evils are sufferable, than to
right themselves by abolishing the forms to which they are accustomed. but
when a long train of abuses & usurpations [begun at a distinguished period,
&] pursuing invariably the same object, evinces a design to reduce
them under absolute Despotism, it is their right, it is their duty, to throw off such
government & to provide new guards for their future security. such has
been the patient sufferance of these colonies; & such is now the necessity
which constrains them to expunge their former systems of government.
the history of the present king of Great Britain is a history of unremitting injuries and
usurpations, [among which appears no solitary fact to contra-
dict the uniform tenor of the rest, but all have] in direct object the
establishment of an absolute tyranny over these states. to prove this, let facts be
submitted to a candid world, [for the truth of which we pledge a faith
yet unsullied by falsehood]

Dr. Franklin's hand

mr Adams hand

Declaration of Independence of the United States of America. Draft in Jefferson's hand, 1776

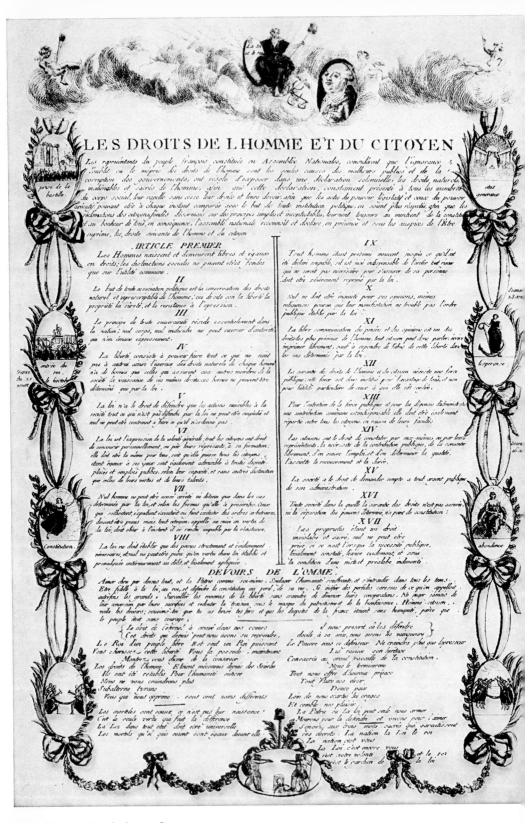

French Revolution, 1789

the natural, inalienable, and sacred rights of man, in order that this declaration, being ever present to all the members of the social body, may unceasingly remind them of their rights and duties; in order that the acts of the legislative power and those of the executive power may be each moment compared with the aim of every political institution and thereby may be more respected; and in order that the demands of the citizens, grounded henceforth upon simple and incontestable principles, may always take the direction of maintaining the constitution and the welfare of all.

In consequence, the National Assembly recognizes and declares in the presence and under the auspices of the Supreme Being, the following rights of man and of the citizen:

ARTICLE I

Men are born and remain free and equal in rights. Social distinctions can be based only upon public utility.

II

The aim of every political association is the preservation of the natural and imprescriptible rights of man. These rights are liberty, property, security and resistance to oppression.

III

The source of all sovereignty is essentially in the nation; no body, no individual can exercise authority that does not proceed from it in plain terms.

Session of Thursday 20 August

IV

Liberty consists in the power to do anything that does not injure others; accordingly, the exercise of the natural rights of each man has for its only limits those that secure to the other members of society the enjoyment of these same rights. These limits can be determined only by law.

V

The law has the right to forbid only such actions as are injurious to society. Nothing can be forbidden that is not interdicted by the law, and no one can be constrained to do that which it does not order.

VI

Law is the expression of the general will. All citizens have the right to take part personally or by their representatives in its formation. It must be the same for all, whether it protects or punishes. All citizens being equal in its eyes, are equally eligible to all public dignities, places employments, according to their capacities, and without other distinction than that of their virtues and their talents.

Session of Friday 21 August

VII

No man can be accused, arrested or detained except in the cases determined by the law and according to the forms that it has prescribed. Those who procure, expedite, execute or cause to be executed arbitrary orders ought to be punished; but every citizen summoned or seized in virtue of the law ought to render instant obedience; he makes himself guilty by resistance.

VIII

The law ought to establish only penalties that are strictly and obviously necessary and no one can be punished except in virtue of a law established and promulgated prior to the offence and legally applied.

IX

Every man being presumed innocent until he has been pronounced guilty, if it is thought indispensable to arrest him, all severity that may not be necessary to secure his person ought to be strictly suppressed by law.

Session of Saturday 22 August

X

No one ought to be disturbed on account of his opinions, even religious, provided their manifestation does not derange the public order established by law.

Session of Sunday 23 August

XI

The free communication of ideas and opinions is one of the most precious of the rights of man; every citizen can freely speak, write, and print, subject to responsibility for the abuse of this freedom in the cases determined by law.

XII

The guarantee of the rights of man and of the citizen requires a public force; this force then is instituted for the advantage of all and not for the personal benefit of those to whom it is entrusted.

XIII

For the maintenance of the public force and for the expenses of administration a general tax is indispensable; it ought to be equally apportioned among all the citizens according to their means.

Session of Monday 24 August

XIV

All the citizens have the right to ascertain, by themselves or by their representatives, the necessity of the public tax, to consent to it freely, to follow the employment of it, and to determine the quota, the assessment, the collection and the duration of it.

XV

Society has the right to call for an account from every public agent of its administration.

XVI

Any society in which the guarantee of the rights is not secured or the separation of powers not determined has no constitution at all.

XVII

Property being a sacred and inviolable right, no one can be deprived of it unless a legal established public necessity evidently demands it, under the condition of a just and prior indemnity.

Session of Wednesday 26 August

415

Superiority of the representational system

Simple democracy was society governing itself without the aid of secondary means. By ingrafting representation upon democracy, we arrive at a system of government capable of embracing and confederating all the various interests and every extent of territory and population; and that also with advantages as much superior to hereditary government, as the republic of letters is to hereditary literature.

... Government is ... no more than some common center, in which all the parts of society unite. This cannot be accomplished by any method so conducive to the various interests of the community as by the representative system. It concentrates the knowledge necessary to the interest of the parts, and of the whole. It places government in a state of constant maturity. It is never young never old. It is subject neither to nonage nor dotage. It is never in the cradle nor on crutches. It admits not of a separation between knowledge and power, and is superior, as government always ought to be, to all the accidents of individual man, and is therefore superior to what is called monarche. *416*

Tom Paine
Rights of Man
1791
Great Britain

George Washington's Farewell Address, 17 September 1796.

Hence, likewise, they [all the parts of our country, combined] will avoid the necessity of those overgrown military establishments which, under any form of government, are inauspicious to liberty, and which are to be regarded as particularly hostile to republican liberty....

The basis of our political systems is the right of the people to make and to alter their constitutions of government. But the constitution which at any time exists till changed by an explicit and authentic act of the whole people is sacredly obligatory upon all. The very idea of the power and the right of the people to establish government presupposes the duty of every individual to obey the established government....

There is an opinion that parties in free countries are useful checks upon the administration of the government, and serve to keep alive the spirit of liberty. This within certain limits is probably true; and in governments of a monarchical cast patriotism may look with indulgence, if not with favor, upon the spirit of party. But in those of the popular character, in governments purely elective, it is a spirit not to be encouraged. From their natural tendency it is certain there will always be enough of that spirit for every salutary purpose; and there being constant danger of excess, the effort ought to be by force of public opinion to mitigate and assuage it. A fire not to be quenched, it demands a uniform vigilance to prevent its bursting into a flame, lest, instead of warming, it should consume....

It is substantially true that virtue or morality is a necessary spring of popular government. The rule indeed extends with more or less force to every species of free government. Who that is a sincere friend to it can look with indifference upon attempts to shake the foundation of the fabric? Promote, then, as an object of primary importance, institutions for the general diffusion of knowledge. In proportion as the structure of a government gives force to public opinion, it is essential that public opinion should be enlightened....

Observe good faith and justice toward all nations. Cultivate peace and harmony with all. Religion and morality enjoin this conduct. And can it be that good policy does not equally enjoin it? It will be worthy of a free, enlightened, and at no distant period a great nation to give to mankind the magnanimous and too novel example of a people always guided by an exalted justice and benevolence....

In the execution of such a plan nothing is more essential than that permanent, inveterate antipathies against particular nations and passionate attachments for others should be excluded, and that in place of them just and amicable feelings toward all should be cultivated. The nation which indulges toward another an habitual hatred or an habitual fondness is in some degree a slave. It is a slave to its animosity or to its affection, either of which is sufficient to lead it astray from its duty and its interest....

So, likewise, a passionate attachment of one nation for another produces a variety of evils. Sympathy for the favorite nation, facilitating the illusion of an imaginary common interest in cases where no real common interest exists, and infusing into one the enmities of the other, betrays the former into a participation in the quarrels and wars of the latter without adequate inducement or justification.   *417*

Federalist problems

The Kentucky Resolutions of 1798.

I. *Resolved,* that the several States composing the United States of America, are not united on the principle of unlimited submission to their general government; but that by compact under the style and title of a Constitution

205

for the United States and of amendments thereto, they constituted a general government for special purposes, delegated to that government certain definite powers, reserving each State to itself, the residuary mass of right to their own self-government; and that whensoever the general government assumes undelegated powers, its acts are unauthoritative, void, and of no force;... ,

... that as in all other cases of compact among parties having no common Judge, *each party has an equal right to judge for itself, as well of infractions as of the mode and measure of redress....*

III. *Resolved,* that it is true as a general principle, and is also expressly declared by one of the amendments to the Constitution that 'the powers not delegated to the United States by the Constitution, nor prohibited by it to the States, are reserved to the States respectively or to the people;' and that no power over the freedom of religion, freedom of speech, or freedom of the press being delegated to the United States by the Constitution, nor prohibited by it to the States, all lawful powers respecting the same did of right remain, and were reserved to the States, or to the people;...

... that therefore [the Sedition Act], which does abridge the freedom of the press, is not law, but is altogether void and of no effect....

VI. *Resolved,* that the imprisonment of a person under the protection of the laws of this Commonwealth on his failure to obey the simple order of the President to depart out of the United States, as is undertaken by the said act entitled 'An act concerning aliens,' is contrary to the Constitution, one amendment to which has provided, that 'no person shall be deprived of liberty without due process of law,' and that another having provided 'that in all criminal prosecutions, the accused shall enjoy the right to a public trial by an impartial jury, to be informed of the nature and cause of the accusation, to be confronted with the witnesses against him, to have compulsory process for obtaining witnesses in his favour, and to have the assistance of counsel for his defense,' the same act undertaking to authorize the President to remove a person out of the United States who is under the protection of the law, on his own suspicion, without accusation, without jury, without public trial, without confrontation of the witnesses against him, without having witnesses in his favour, without defense, without counsel, is contrary to these provisions also of the Constitution, is therefore not law, but utterly void and of no force....

Precautionary
limitation
of the power
of government

This Commonwealth is determined, as it doubts not its co-States are, tamely to submit to undelegated and consequently unlimited powers in no man or body of men on earth: that if the acts before specified should stand, these conclusions would flow from them; that the general government may place any act they think proper on the list of crimes and punish it themselves, whether enumerated or not enumerated by the Constitution as cognizable by them: that they many transfer its cognizance to the President or any other person, who may himself be the accuser, counsel, judge, and jury; . . . that the friendless alien has indeed been selected as the safest subject of a first experiment, but the citizen will soon follow, or rather has already followed: for, already has a sedition act marked him as its prey: that these and successive acts of the same character, unless arrested on the threshold, may tend to drive these States into revolution and blood, and will furnish new calumnies against Republican governments, and new pretexts for those who wish it to be believed, that man cannot be governed but by a rod of iron: that it would be a dangerous delusion were a confidence in the men of our choice to silence our fears for the safety of our rights: that confidence is everywhere the parent of despotism: free government is founded in jealousy and not in confidence; it is jealousy and not confidence which prescribes limited Constitutions to bind down those whom we are obliged to trust with power: that our Constitution has accordingly fixed the limits to which and no further our confidence may go; and let the honest advocate of confidence read the alien and sedition acts, and say if the Constitution has not been wise in fixing limits to the government it created, and whether we should be wise in destroying those limits.   *418*

Respect for
the minority

Thomas Jefferson's first inaugural address after being elected
President of the United States, 4 March 1801.

All, too, will bear in mind this sacred principle, that though the will of the majority is in all cases to prevail, that will to be rightful must be reasonable; that the minority possess their equal rights, which equal law must protect, and to violate would be oppression....
   And let us reflect that, having banished from our land that religious intolerance under which mankind so long bled and suffered, we have yet gained little if we countenance a political intolerance as despotic, as wicked, and capable of as bitter and bloody persecutions....

We are all Republicans, we are all Federalists. If there be any among us who would wish to dissolve this Union or to change its republican form, let them stand undisturbed as monuments of the safety with which error of opinion may be tolerated where reason is left free to combat it.

Strength of the republican government

I know, indeed, that some honest men fear that a republican government cannot be strong, that this government is not strong enough; but would the honest patriot, in the full tide of successful experiment, abandon a government which has so far kept us free and firm on the theoretic and visionary fear that this government, the world's best hope, may by possibility want energy to preserve itself? I trust not. I believe this, on the contrary, the strongest government on earth. I believe it the only one where every man, at the call of the law, would fly to the standard of the law, and would meet invasions of the public order as his own personal concern. Sometimes it is said that man cannot be trusted with the government of himself. Can he, then, be trusted with the government of others? Or have we found angels in the forms of kings to govern him? Let history answer this question.

Let us, then, with courage and confidence pursue our own Federal and Republican principles, our attachment to union and representative government. Kindly separated by nature and a wide ocean from the exterminating havoc of one quarter of the globe; too high-minded to endure the degradations of the others; possessing a chosen country, with room enough for our descendants to the thousandth and thousandth generation; entertaining a due sense of our equal right to the use of our own faculties, to the acquisitions of our own industry, to honor and confidence from our fellow-citizens, resulting not from birth, but from our actions and their sense of them; enlightened by a benign religion, professed, indeed, and practiced in various forms, yet all of them inculcating honesty, truth, temperance, gratitude, and the love of man; acknowledging and adoring an overruling Providence, which by all its dispensations proves that it delights in the happiness of man here and his greater happiness hereafter—with all these blessings, what more is necessary to make us a happy and a prosperous people? Still one thing more, fellow-citizens—a wise and frugal government, which shall restrain men from injuring one another, shall leave them otherwise free to regulate their own pursuits of industry and improvement, and shall not take from the mouth of labor the bread it has earned. *419*

End of absolute power among the Cossacks of the Ukraine.

Pacta
et Consuetudines
legum libertatumque
exercitus
Zaporowiensis
1847
(Abridged text)

In 1710, the Cossack leaders elected the Secretary-General Philip Orlyk as their hetman, and a charter was adopted that laid the basis of representative Government. An Assembly, comprising not only the Army leaders but also delegates of the regiments and of the Zaporogian Cossacks, was to meet three times a year. The absolute power of the hetman over the other leaders and of these leaders over the people was abolished. No punishment was to be inflicted without trial. Office would be elective.   *420*

*The voice of the
people is the voice
of God*

It is generally said: we must raise the people to our level, for in this way we shall become a nation; but the nobility has sunk into an abyss, and to join it there would in effect be not to rise but to fall. How illusory to imagine that the small can raise the great, even if the small stand not in the hollow but on a high secure bank. It is not the millions that make up the people who must assimilate themselves with the handful of men forming the nobility, but the opposite.

Mihály Táncsics
to Lajos Kossuth
1847
Hungary

My brother peasants do not demand rights from any one or from the National Assembly. They demand that the privileged class give proof of its justness by renouncing the privileges it has arbitrarily assumed: all the rights of the people will then have the force of law, and will yield their effects without the privileged class condescending to say: common people! look at the rights I have granted you. From whom might the privileged class have received greater rights? It is not God who have given them such rights, for then it would be God who was unjust.   *421*

Mihály Táncsics
1869
Hungary

The sons (sometimes two or three) serve in the army, defend the fatherland, carry out the sacred and heavy task imposed on them by the fatherland, and yet their fathers do not have the right to vote. It is unjust that one part of the nation should have nothing but duties, that it should pay taxes and sacrifice its sons, without possessing rights.

I repeat, it is divine justice which is expressing itself out of the mouth of the workers claiming the right to vote.   *422*

An indomitable spirit

Theodore Parker
1810-60
Known as the Great
American Preacher

We are a rebellious nation. Our whole history is treason; our blood was attainted before we were born; our creeds are infidelity to the mother church; our constitution, treason to our fatherland. What of that? Though all the governors in the world bid us commit treason against man, and set the example, let us never submit.   *423*

The first condition of liberty

Friedrich Engels
Letter
to August Bebel
18-28 March 1875

The first condition of liberty is that every official should be responsible, in the ordinary courts and under the ordinary law, to every citizen for every act he performs in the exercise of his functions.   *424*

Democracy versus despotism

Karl Marx
Letter to Ruge
1844

Domination and exploitation are but one and the same concept.... The very essence of despotism is contempt for man.... The despot never sees men otherwise than bereft of their dignity. . . . The basic principle of monarchy is that man is despised and despicable, dehumanized; and Montesquieu was much mistaken in maintaining that the principle of monarchy is honour—which he managed to do by making a distinction between monarchy, despotism and tyranny. But these are in fact different names for one and the same thing, or at most, superficial variations of the same principle. Where the monarchical principle predominates, men are minors; where this principle is not challenged, there are no men.   *425*

Tatsui Baba
1850-88
Autobiography
of Kentarō Kaneko
Japan

Having regard to the nature of the concept of the State, the power should be vested in the people. In certain times and circumstances it may be in the hands of the emperor, but as the people advance in knowledge and the country grows more prosperous it should, ultimately, be vested in the people.... In Japan, it has of course been vested in the person of the emperor for two thousand five hundred years, but it should be restored to the people at their request in a few centuries' time, when the country's circumstances are different and the people are united in their desire to change over from a monarchy to a democracy.   *426*

The two conditions of democracy

The 'broad democratic principle', as everyone will probably agree, presupposes two conditions—first, full publicity, and secondly, election to all offices. Democracy without full publicity—a publicity reaching beyond the organization's own members—is inconceivable. We call the German Socialist Party a democratic organization because all its activities—even its party congresses—are conducted in public. But an organization that is hidden from everyone but its members by a veil of secrecy cannot be called democratic.

. . . The second criterion of democracy, the principle of election, . . . is taken for granted in politically free countries. 'The members of the Party are those who accept the principles of the Party programme and render the Party all possible support', reads Clause I of the Rules of the German Social Democratic Party. Since everyone can view the political arena as an audience views a theatre stage, everyone knows, from the press and through public meetings, whether a particular person accepts the party or not, whether he supports or opposes it. Everyone knows how a certain political figure set out in life, what phases he passed through, how he behaved in a crisis and what qualities he possesses; consequently, *all* party members, knowing all the facts, can elect him to a particular party office or not. The general control (in the literal sense of the term) exercised over all that a party man does in his political career brings into existence an automatic mechanism which produces what in biology is called 'the survival of the fittest'. 'Natural selection' by full publicity, election and general control ensures that, in the last analysis, every political figure will be 'in his proper place', do the work for which he is best fitted by his powers and abilities, take the consequences of his mistakes himself, and prove before all the world his ability to recognize mistakes and avoid them.

Just try to fit this picture into the frame of our autocracy! *427*

Lenin
What is to be done?
1902

'*Separate but equal*'

In 1896, Judge John Marshall Harlan was disagreeing with colleagues on the Bench about the racial problem.

In respect of civil rights, common to all citizens, the Constitution of the United States does not, I think, permit any public authority to know the race of those entitled to be protected in the enjoyment of such rights. Every true man has pride of race, and under appropriate circumstances, when the rights of others, his equals before the law, are not to be affected, it is privilege to express such pride and to take such action based upon it as to him seems proper. But I deny that any legislative body or judicial tribunal may have regard to the race of citizens when the civil rights of those citizens are involved. Indeed such legislation as that here in question is inconsistent, not only with that equality of rights which pertains to citizenship, national and state, but with the personal liberty enjoyed by everyone within the United States....

But it seems that we have yet, in some of the states, a dominant race, a superior class of citizens, which assumes to regulate the enjoyment of civil rights, common to all citizens, upon the basis of race. The present decision, it may well be apprehended, will not only stimulate aggressions, more or less brutal and irritating, upon the admitted rights of colored citizens, but will encourage the belief that it is possible, by means of state enactments, to defeat the beneficient purposes which the people of the United States had in view when they adopted the recent amendments of the Constitution, by one of which the blacks of this country were made citizens of the United States and of the states in which they respectively reside and whose privileges and immunities, as citizens, the states are forbidden to abridge. Sixty millions of whites are in no danger from the presence here of eight millions of blacks. The destinies of the two races in this country are indissolubly linked together, and the interests of both require that the common government of all shall not permit the seeds of race hate to be planted under the sanction of law....

Slavery as an institution tolerated by law would, it is true, have disappeared from our country, but there would remain a power in the states, by sinister legislation, to interfere with the full enjoyment of the blessings of freedom; to regulate civil rights, common to all citizens, upon the basis of race; and to place in a condition of legal inferiority a large body of American citizens, now constituting a part of the political community, called the people of the United States, for whom and by whom, through representatives, our government is administered. Such a system is inconsistent with the guarantee given by the Constitution. *428*

Plessy Case
1896
United States
of America

Truth and freedom

Thought and expression:
the right to think, criticize, object and doubt;
the right to speak, write, publish and create

Truth

Amharic proverb
Ethiopia

የ ሀቅ = ዘንግ = ቲቀጠናለኝ = እንጂ = እትሰበር ም።።

Thin though it wear, the rod of truth does not snap. *429*

Turkish proverb

Before a word of truth, even torrents pause. *430*

Mahābhārata
Telugu tradition
Mauritius

Instead of a hundred deep fresh water wells, one such well with a flight of steps is desirable. Instead of a hundred such stepped wells, one yaga sacrifice is desirable. Instead a hundred of such sacrifices, one worthy son is desirable, and instead of having a hundred such sons, one word of truth is always desirable. *431*

Seek the truth

Life of the
Archpriest Avvakum
Written by Himself
17th cent.
Russia

That they should oppose one another, I have no objection, for in this way truth and justice are best discovered.... Squabble as much as you like, I shall not reproach you. The only condition is that, with a pure and upright conscience, you should seek the truth. *432*

Jean de Muller
1752-1809
Switzerland

The greatest gift of freedom is the right to be one's true self. Freedom—true freedom—is where peace and justice prevail. *433*

Simone Weil
The Need for Roots
1942-43
France

For religious feeling to emanate from the spirit of truth, one should be absolutely prepared to abandon one's religion, even if that should mean losing all motive for living, if it should turn out to be anything other than the truth. In this state of mind alone is it possible to discern whether there is truth in it or not. Otherwise, one doesn't venture even to propound the problem in all its rigour. *434*

Tell the truth

In find the world I live in repugnant, but I feel at one with those in it who suffer. There are some ambitions I do not share, and it would irk me had I to make my way with the help of such poor privileges as are reserved for those who come to terms with this world. But it seems to me there is another ambition all we writers should cherish: to raise our voices, on every possible occasion and in so far as our talents allow, on behalf of those who are enslaved like us.

*Albert Camus
In 'Combat'
1948
France*

435

*In the service
of truth*

LIBERTY

Free came I into the world, like you,
No fetters bind my limbs;
In freedom I take the bread
That is given us to eat.
I wander where I will,
Listen to what I understand;
Speak what I think.
Can love and be loved
Do good and be respected;
My own will is my law....

But no! Here, where fate willed that I should be born
Here let me end my days;
Let my cold ashes by illumined
By the grandeur that now I praise.
May youth, athirst for glory
Come to my neglected grave,
And proclaim with feeling:
'He who was born beneath the yoke,
Bearing his gilded fetters,
Was the first to foretell our freedom.'

*Aleksandr
Nikolaevich
Radishchev
1749-1802
Russia*

436

YOU ASK WHO I AM?

You ask: who am I? And what? And whither bound?
I am the man I was and will be, all my days:
Nor beast, nor tree nor slave; a man!
To blaze a trail, where never man yet trod,
In prose and verse, for intrepid spirits.
To the horror of men of feeling, to the denial of truth,
I go to the Ilimsky gaol.

*A. N. Radishchev
1749-1802
Russia*

437

Russian proverb

Truth is stronger than strength.

438

Coal extraction
18th cent., China

An itinerant
book-seller
18th cent., China

Misunderstandings and complexities about truth

Words put into the mouth of an imaginary person, the 'doctor'.

People imagine that it is enough to demonstrate the truth, like a mathematical theorem, to have it accepted; that to believe in it oneself is enough to make others believe in it. In fact, however, it is not at all like that: some people say something, others listen to them and understand something else, because they are not at the same stage of development. What did the first Christians preach, and what did the multitude understand? The multitude understood everything that was incomprehensible, absurd and mystical; everything that was clear and simple was closed to it; the multitude accepted everything that bound the conscience but nothing of that which set man free. Similarly, later on, it understood the revolution solely as a bloody execution, a guillotine, a vengeance; a bitter historical necessity became a shout of triumph; with the word 'fraternity' was coupled the word 'death'; 'fraternity or death' became a sort of 'your money or your life' of the terrorists. We have experienced so much ourselves, we have seen so much and, what is more, our predecessors have experienced so much for us, that in the end it has become unpardonable for us to let ourselves be carried away, to believe that to make known the Gospel to the Roman world is enough to turn it into a democratic social republic, as the *red* apostles believed; or that it is enough to print in two columns an illustrated edition of the *Rights of Man* for man to become free.

Alexander Herzen
1812-70
Letters
Trans. from Russian

439

THE TALE OF THE ELOQUENT PEASANT

A peasant despoiled of his goods by a rich man dares violently to criticize all persons in high places. Justice is done to him.

Once upon a time there was a man called Khunanup. He dwelt in the oasis of Salt and had a wife whose name was Merye. And he said to his wife: 'Behold, I am going down into Egypt to bring back food for my children. Go therefore and measure me out the barley left in the granary [from last year].' So she went and measured him out [eight] bushels of barley.

And the oasis dweller said to his wife: 'Here [are...] bushels of barley for thee, to serve as food for thee and thy children. Take the [other] bushels of barley and make me bread and beer for every day [when I shall be on my journey].'

He then went down into Egypt after loading his asses with reeds, *redemet* plants, natron, salt, wood [from...], *âunt* sticks from the oasis of Farafra, panther skins, wolf furs, *necha* plants, *ânu* stones, *kheperur* plants, *Sahut, saksut* grains, *misut* plants, *senet* stones, *âba* stones, *isba* stones, *inbi* plants, pigeons, birds ... , [in short] a quantity of fine products of all kinds from the oasis of Salt. He journeyed southward in the direction of Nennesu, and came to the territory of Perfefi, to the north of Medeni. There he met a man standing on the river bank, whose name was Djehutinekht, the son of a man called Isri, a vassal of the Grand Steward Rensi, son of Meru.

Then said Djehutinekht when he saw the asses of the oasis dweller, which he coveted in his heart: 'Ah, if only I had some powerful idol which would enable me to seize the possessions of this man from the oasis!' Now the house of Djehutinekht lay on the path that ran by the river; the path was narrow, no more than the width of a piece of cloth; and one side of it was under water while the other was covered with barley. Then said Djehutinekht to his servant: 'Go and bring me a piece of cloth from my house', and it was brought to him at once.

He stretched the cloth across the path by the river, so that its fringe lay upon the water and its hem upon the barley. And the oasis dweller came along the path that was open to all, and Djehutinekht said: 'Be careful, man from the oasis! Dost thou mean to tread on my clothes?' And the oasis dweller answered: 'I shall do as thou wilt, but the path I am taking is the right one.' He then moved to the inner side [of the path], but Djehutinekht said: 'Is my barley to be used as a path, man from the oasis?' The oasis dweller answered: 'The path I am taking is the right one. The river bank is steep, the path is [partly] covered with barley and now thou blockest my way with thy clothes. Dost thou want to stop me from going my way?'

Hardly had he spoken these words, than one of the asses took a mouthful of barley. Then said Djehutinekht: 'There, I am going to seize thine ass, man from the oasis, because he is eating my barley; he shall tread the grain because of the ill he has done.' And the oasis dweller answered: 'The path I am taking is the right one. As it was impossible to pass on one [of the sides], I led my ass on the forbidden [side]. Thou art seizing it because it ate a mouthful of barley. But I know the owner of this land; it belongs to the Grand Steward Rensi, son of Maru. It is he who punishes all thieves throughout this country. Is it on his land that I am to be robbed?' And Djehutinekht said: 'Does this not prove the saying: The name of the poor man is spoken only because of his master? It is I who am speaking to thee and it is of the Grand

Steward that thou art thinking.' Then he laid hold of a rod of fresh tamarisk to strike him with, and cudgelled him in every limb, and he seized his asses, which were led into his land. The oasis dweller began to weep bitterly because of the ill treatment he had suffered but Djehutinekht said to him: 'Raise not thy voice, man from the oasis, for thou art nigh to (*on the path leading to*) the dwelling of the Master of Silence.' And the oasis dweller replied: 'Thou beatest me, thou stealest my goods, and after that thou deprivest me of my right to complain! Oh Master of Silence! give me back that which is mine, then shall I cease to utter cries such as disturb thee.'

The oasis dweller remained ten days beseeching Djehutinekht, but the latter paid no heed....

And the oasis dweller besought the Grand Steward Rensi, son of Meru, saying: 'Grand Steward, Lord, suffer me to make for thee in this land a renown above [even] the best of laws, O guide that knowest no rapaciousness, O great one that knowest no baseness! Destroy falsehood, engender truth. Give heed to the voice of him who implores, vanquish evil. I speak that thou mayest hearken. Do justice, O praised one praised by those who are praised! Put an end to my affliction for I am overwhelmed by grief, I am unmanned by it; provide for me, for I have lost all.'

Now, this oasis dweller spoke these words in the days of His Majesty King Nebkauré.... And the Grand Steward Rensi, son of Meru, came before the King, saying: 'Lord, I have found one of these men from the oases, an eloquent speaker, truly; he has been despoiled of his goods by a man in my service, and has come to implore my help in the matter.' His Majesty replied: 'As surely as thou wishest to see me in good health, keep him here and let the matter drag on, without answering anything he may say. And so that he may continue to talk, keep silent. Then let his words be brought to us in writing.... Meanwhile, see that his wife and children are provided for, as these oasis dwellers [hardly] come [into Egypt] until their house is bare to the ground. See also that he himself is provided for. Make certain that he is given food, but without letting him know that it comes from thee.' He was therefore given ten loaves and two pitchers of beer every day. The Grand Steward Rensi, son of Meru, provided them, but he handed them to one of his friends, and he it was who gave them [to the oasis dweller]. The Grand Steward Rensi, son of Meru, likewise sent [a messenger] to the governor of the oasis of Salt to make sure that the wife was given food amounting to three bushels [of barley] each day.

Then the oasis dweller besought him a second time,

saying: 'Grand Steward, Lord, the high officials of the State do evil. Righteousness is lop-sided; the judges steal. And again: he who should seize a man guilty of some imposture, has himself strayed from the path of righteousness for the same fault.... He who should apportion in accordance with the law is himself a thief. He who should banish poverty is the one who increases it [to such an extent that] the city is crushed by it. He who should check wrong-doing is [himself] guilty of iniquity.'

The Grand Steward Rensi, son of Meru, said: 'Are thy possessions more important to thee than [the risk] of being carried off by one of my servants?' But the oasis dweller continued: 'The measurer of grain cheats to his own profit. He who fills [the granaries] for another pilfers that man's property. He who should show the way of the law gives the order to steal. Who then will stand in the way of perversity, when he who should repulse injustice [himself] indulges in delinquencies? One seemingly straightforward walks in devious ways; another [openly] embraces the side of evil. Does the cap fit [in any of this]?...

He who has a fortune [may well] be compassionate, but an evil-doer is [necessarily] violent. Stealing is as natural to one who has nothing [as it is] to the evil-doer who makes off with property; a crime in the eyes of one who has no needs. [But] we should not be angry with him [the thief]; he is only seeking for himself [the wherewithal to live]. Thou, on the other hand, hast bread enough to feast thyself, beer enough to intoxicate.'

. . . .

The oasis dweller came a third time to beseech him, saying: 'Grand Steward, Lord, drive off the thief, protect the wretched, be not the flood that overwhelms the supplicant. Take heed of the approach of eternity! Desire long life according to the proverb: "It is the breath of life to practice equity." Punish him who deserves to be punished and no one will come near to equalling you in righteousness.'

. . . .

'Thou art like a miserable laundryman, greedy for gain who wrongs a friend, foresakes one of his familiars in favour of a customer: anyone who brings him [an order] is his brother.

'Thou art like a ferryman who carries across [only] those who can pay the price of the crossing, a just man whose justice is reduced to nothing....

'Thou art among men [like] a hawk, living on the weakest birds.

'Thou art like a cook, who delights in killing [animals], without fear of being reproached for their mutilation.'

. . . .

'Thou who shouldst give ear, dost not give ear at all; why dost thou not give ear? Today I have indeed driven off one who was violent: the crocodile retreats. What will be the result of that for thee? The secret of the truth shall be revealed and falsehood shall be brought low. Dispose not of the morrow before it comes, for no one knows what evils it will bring with it.'

The oasis dweller spoke thus to the Grand Steward Rensi, son of Meru, in the entrance to his offices. The latter set upon him two guards armed with whips, and they whipped him in every limb. Then said the oasis dweller: 'So the son of Meru is [still] on the wrong track? Blind is he to what he sees, deaf to what he hears, heedless of what is recalled to him.'

. . . .

The oasis dweller came a fourth time to beseech him, meeting him as he came out of the doorway of the temple of Arsaphes, he said: 'O praised one, may Arsaphes praise thee, from whose temple thou comest out! Good has perished; there is no one [on the other hand] who can flatter himself that he has laid evil low.'

. . . .

Then came the oasis dweller a fifth time to beseech him, saying: 'Grand Steward, Lord, do not defraud a poor man of what he has, a weak man whom you know. The possessions of a wretched man are for him the breath [of life]; who robs him of them stifles him. Thine office is to hear causes, judge the parties, punish the guilty. But thou doest nothing else than support the thief.'

. . . .

And the oasis dweller came a sixth time to beseech him, saying: 'Grand Steward, Lord, every investigation carried out impartially by the judge destroys the effect of falsehood, brings truth into being, creates all good and crushes evil, as when satiety comes and puts an end to hunger, as when clothes come and put an end to nakedness, as when the sky clears after a violent thunder-storm and again gives warmth to those who are cold, as fire which cooks food and as water which quenches thirst.'

. . . .

The oasis dweller came a seventh time to beseech him, saying: 'Grand Steward, Lord, thou art the governor of the whole land, it is a ship that sails under thine orders. Thou art like unto Thot, who judges without inclining to one side. Lord, be gracious when a man appeals to thee to [judge] his righteous cause....

'He who undermines the law, who transgresses the rule —no poor man whom he has despoiled can [still] live; [therefore] justice does not hold him in high esteem. My body was [as it were] charged; my heart was heavy; [all that] left my body because of the state it was in. Like a breach in a dike, when the water within pours forth, so did my mouth open to speak. I plied my boat-hook, I emptied away the water, I cast out what was in my body, I washed my soiled garments. What I had to say is said; my wretchedness is fully laid bare before thee. What more dost thou still require?'

.   .   .   .

The oasis dweller came an eighth time to beseech him, saying: 'Grand Steward, Lord, a man may fall far because of avidity. The covetous man [often] fails in his purpose; the [only] thing he achieves is failure. Thou art covetous, and it ill becomes thee; thou stealest, and it profits thee nothing, who shouldst allow a man to rise up and [defend] his rights. For what thou needest for thy sustenance is in thy house; thy stomach is well filled; the grain-measure is overflowing, and if it trembles, what spills from it will be lost to the country....

'Justice is for eternity; it descends into the tomb with him who practises it....

'Whether it is I who come, or another, make [him] welcome. Do not answer [what he says] as one addressing a man who has no right to speak, nor attack a man who does not attack.'

.   .   .   .

The oasis dweller came yet a ninth time to beseech him, saying: 'Grand Steward, Lord, the tongue of men is their balance; it is the balance that reveals what is lacking....

'Be not partial and follow not the dictates of thy heart. Hide not thy countenance from one whom thou knowest. Be not blind to him whom thou hast [once] looked upon. Repulse not him who comes to thee as a suppliant....

'Hearken not to all around when a man appeals [to thee] to [judge] his righteous cause. There is no "yesterday" for the sluggard; no friend for him who turns a deaf ear to justice; no day of rejoicing for the avaricious.

'He who denounces becomes a poor wretch and the wretched man is fated to be a suppliant; [his] adversary becomes [his] murderer. Behold, I come to thee with a prayer and thou harkenest not. Now, therefore, I go to offer up a prayer concerning thee to Anubis.'

Then the Grand Steward Rensi, son of Meru, sent two guards to make him turn back. And the oasis dweller was afraid, for he thought this was done for the purpose of punishing him for the words he had spoken....

But the Grand Steward Rensi, son of Meru, said: 'Fear not, man from the oasis, for what has been done to thee [was done only] to force thee to remain with me.' And the oasis dweller answered: 'By my countenance! Must I then eat thy bread and drink thy beer for evermore?' The Grand Steward Rensi, son of Meru, continued: 'Tarry awhile here, at least, that thou mayest hear thy supplications.' And he had [them] read out from a scroll of new papyrus, each supplication according to its subject. And the Grand Steward Rensi, son of Meru, had [the scroll] handed to his Majesty King Nebkauré... and it was more pleasing to the heart [of the King] than anything in all the land. And [the King] said: 'Decide thou, son of Meru.'

Then the [Grand Steward] Rensi, son of Meru, sent two guards to [bring Djehutinekht thither]. So he was brought thither and a list was made of [his possessions as well as of] his [servants, that is]: six persons, in addition to...

The end of the manuscript is badly damaged, but it would seem that all Djehutinekht's possessions were given to the oasis dweller, while Djehutinekht himself, together with his household, became his servants.

End of
3rd millenary B.C.
Ancient Egypt

440

Right to submit objections

If anything hard or impossible be enjoined on a brother let him receive the injunctions of him who orders him in all mildness and obedience. If he shall see that the burden altogether exceedeth the measure of his strength, let him patiently and at the proper time state, without show of pride, resistance or contradiction, the reason of this impossibility. If after his suggestion the will of the prior shall still remain unchanged, let the young monk know that it is best for him; and trusting in God's help, through love of Him, let him obey.

Rule of St. Benedict
6th cent.

441

Objections and obedience

It does not however detract from perfection [of obedience] to manifest to the Superior anything which may happen to be different from his opinion, if, after consulting the Lord in prayer, it seems good to expose the matter to him; as long as the subjects do not attempt to bend the Superior's will and make him follow their own; and they should be

Epitome Instituti
Societatis Jesu
1689

sincerely ready not only to accept, but even to approve and prefer whatever the Superior decides once they have informed him about the matter. *442*

Mr. Speaker, I find written in a little volume these words in effect: Sweet is the name of liberty, but the thing itself is a value beyond all inestimable treasure. So much the more it behoveth us to take care lest we, contenting ourselves with the sweetness of the name, lose and forego the thing, being of the greatest value that can come unto this noble realm. The inestimable treasure is the use of it in this House....

Sometime it happeneth that a good man will in this place (for argument sake) prefer an evil cause, both for that he would have a doubtful truth to be opened and manifested and also the evil prevented; so that to this point I conclude that in this House, which is termed a place of free speech, there is nothing so necessary for the preservation of the prince and state as free speech, and without, it is a scorn and mockery to call it a Parliament House, for in truth it is none, but a very school of flattery and dissimulation, and so a fit place to serve the devil and his angels in, and not to glorify God and benefit the commonwealth. . . . Amongst other, Mr. Speaker, two things do great hurt to his place of the which I do mean to speak. The one is a rumour which runneth about the House, and this it is, 'Take heed what you do; the Queen's Majesty liketh not such a matter; whosoever preferreth it, she will be offended with him': or the contrary, 'Her Majesty liketh of such a matter; whosoever speaketh against it, she will be much offended with him.' The other: sometimes a message is brought into the House, either of commanding or inhibiting, very injurious to the freedom of speech and consultation. I would to God, Mr. Speaker, that these two were buried in hell, I mean rumours and messages, for wicked undoubtedly they are; the reason is, the devil was the first author of them, from whom proceedeth nothing but wickedness. *443*

Speech by
Peter Wentworth
in the
House of Commons
1576
England

In defence of books

I deny not, but that it is of greatest concernment in the Church and Commonwealth, to have a vigilant eye how Bookes demeane themselves as well as men; and thereafter to confine, imprison, and do sharpest justice on them as malefactors: For Bookes are not absolutely dead things, but doe contain a potencie of life in them to be as active as that soule was whose progeny they are; nay they do preserve al in a violl the purest efficacie and extraction of that living intellect that bred them. I know they are as lively, and as vigorously productive, as those fabulous Dragons teeth; and being sown up and down, may chance to spring up armed men. And yet on the other hand unlesse warinesse be us'd, as good almost kill a Man as kill a good Booke; who kills a Man kills a reasonable creature, Gods Image; but hee who destroyes a good Booke, kills reason it selfe, kills the Image of God, as it were in the eye. Many a man lives a burden to the Earth; but a good Booke is the pretious life-blood of a master spirit, inbalm'd and treasur'd up on purpose to a life beyond life. 'Tis true, no age can restore a life, whereof perhaps there is no great losse; and revolutions of ages doe not oft recover the losse of a rejected truth, for the want of which whole Nations fare the worse. We should be wary therefore what persecution we raise against the living labours of publick men, how we spill that season'd life of man preserv'd and stor'd up in Bookes; since we see a kinde of homicide may be thus committed, sometimes a martyr-dome, and if it extend to the whole impression, a kinde of massacre, whereof the execution ends not in the slaying of an elementall life, but strikes at that ethereall and fift essence, the breath of reason it selfe, slaies an immortality rather then a life.

John Milton
Areopagitica
1644
England

444

Free thinking and the right to doubt

There has been much noise made about free thinking, and men have been animated, in the contest, by a spirit that becomes neither the character of divines, nor that of good citizens; by an arbitrary tyrannical spirit under the mask of religious zeal, and by a presumptuous, factious spirit under that of liberty. If the first could prevail, they would establish implicit belief and blind obedience, and an inquisition to maintain this abject servitude. To assert antipodes might become once more as heretical as Arianism or Pelagianism: and men might be dragged to the jails of some Holy Office, like Galilei, for saying they had seen what in fact they had seen, and what every one else that pleased might see. If the second could prevail, they would destroy at once the general influence of religion, by shaking the foundations of it which education had laid. These are wide extremes. Is there no middle path in which a reasonable man and a good citizen may direct his steps? I think there is.

Every one has an undoubted right to think freely: nay, it is the duty of every one to do so, as far as he has the necessary means, and opportunities. This duty too is in no case so incumbent on him, as in those that regard what I call the first philosophy. They who have neither means nor opportunities of this sort, must submit their opinions to authority; and to what authority can they resign themselves so properly, and so safely, as to that of the laws and constitution of their country? In general, nothing can be more absurd than to take opinions, of the greatest moment, and such as concern us the most intimately, on trust. But there is no help against it in many particular cases. Things the most absurd in speculation become necessary in practice. Such is the human constitution, and reason excuses them on the account of this necessity. Reason does even a little more; and it is all she can do. She gives the best direction possible to the absurdity. Thus she directs those who must believe because they cannot know, to believe in the laws of their country, and conform their opinions and practice to those of their ancestors, to those of Coruncanius, of Scipio, of Scaevola, not to those of Zeno, of Cleanthes, of Chrysippus.

But now the same reason that gives this discretion to such men as these will give a very contrary direction to those who have the means and opportunities the others want. Far from advising them to submit to this mental bondage, she will advise them to employ their whole industry, to exert the utmost freedom of thought, and to rest on no authority but hers, that is, their own. She will speak to them in the language of the Sufis, a sect of philosophers in Persia, that travellers have mentioned. 'Doubt', say these wise and honest free-thinkers, 'is the key of knowledge. He who never doubts, never examines. He who never examines, discovers nothing. He who discovers nothing is blind, and will remain so. If you find no reason to doubt concerning the opinions of your fathers, keep to them, they will be sufficient for you. If you find any reason to doubt concerning them, seek the truth quietly, but take care not to disturb the minds of other men.'

Let us proceed agreeably to these maxims. Let us seek truth, but seek it quietly as well as freely. Let us not imagine, like some who are called free-thinkers, that every man, who can think and judge for himself, as he has a right to do, has therefore a right of speaking, any more than of acting, according to the full freedom of his thoughts. The freedom belongs to him as a rational creature. He lies under the restraint as a member of society.   *445*

Harley St. John
Viscount Bolingbroke
Letter addressed
to Alexander Pope
1730
England

Primacy of truth

I have nothing new to teach the world. Truth and non-violence are as old as the hills. All I have done is to try experiments in both on as vast a scale as I could do. In doing so, I have sometimes erred and learnt by my errors. Life and its problems have thus become to me so many experiments in the practice of truth and non-violence. By instinct, I have been truthful, but not non-violent. As a Jain *muni* once rightly said, I was not so much a votary of *ahimsā*, as I was of truth, and I put the latter in the first place and the former in the second. For, as he put it, I was capable of sacrificing non-violence for the sake of

Mahatma Gandhi
1869-1948

truth. In fact, it was in course of my pursuit of truth that I discovered non-violence. *446*

Censorship of morals

Furthermore, all occasions and means whereby man is likely to be corrupted should be proscribed. These are:
1. Indecent drawings or paintings, in books and elsewhere, to make certain that nobody will have access to them.
2. Worldly, that is, sensual and lascivious, songs.
3. Imaginary stories (such as those of Melusine or Amado), and all mundane books altogether, for it is through such books that atheism is disseminated.
4. Public houses, taverns or pot-houses, which should not be tolerated under any circumstances.

Johann Amos
Comenius
Czech writer
1592-1670
De Rerum
Humanarum
Emendatione
Consultatio Catholica

5. Similarly, we should do away with usurers and speculators and other similar blood-suckers and parasites. Much less should be tolerated gamblers, astrologers, jugglers, comedians, rope-dancers and other charlatans and useless cheats. *447*

Political censorship

The only valid account of this interim law on the press which we can offer is that it has been enacted in order—as an interim measure—to teach writers to hold their tongues, and, after they have mastered this task within the interim period, to become dumb once and for all.

If while this law is in force Czech writers still want to advocate the truth in every respect, they will have to be as intrepid as Jan Žižka, for this law threatens to put the writer into the dock even for a word.

Editors would do well to petition the government for permission to move their furniture straight away into jail and conduct editorial work there. Failing this, and assuming a political journal of a limited size, some four editors would be required: two to serve the sentences, the third to sit in the dock, and the fourth to do the actual editing. But the fourth would have to refrain from having a drink of Champagne, lest a spark of the French spirit be lit in his veins, for in that case twice the number would not suffice to conduct the paper. Besides, the publisher would have to possess several gold mines to pay the fines from profits. An editor who is not a mere figurehead and carries the flame of love for humanity in his heart would hardly ever be available in his office but would be found frequently in jail, where, if tanned by the sun of liberty, he would have an opportunity to bleach his skin.

. . . .

Emanuel Arnold
Czech writer
The Interim Law
on the Press
1849

The writer could not utter a single word against oppression by the lackeys of the mighty, unless he wanted to hear the grating of the prison door. Every political treatise he wrote would be but a pinch of dust, which a foreign writer, living in freedom, could blow away with a single breath. This would, of course, scarcely benefit the common people, and as a result the nation may sink again into darkness. But since our people, as is generally known, have a passion for politics and a passion for truth, they cannot be expected to put up with such a state of affairs.   *448*

It is far from easy to determine what is untrue or detrimental in regard to the press. Ignoramuses have been known to make light of the writings of scholars, while others cursed them and others again would have learned men put into jail on account of their writings. And in the end, the truth was found on the side where there was no power.

. . . .

Karel Sabina
Czech writer
1813-77

There are views and opinions which it is not permitted to look at askance, for it would be regarded as a sin. There are views and opinions which a selfish and cunning rabble, ruffians mixing with the genuine fighters for truth, support by all means and with all their might, forcing them upon a credulous people. Wrapped in magnificence, filled with a conviction of their own eminence and infallibility, they nurture lies and despotism.   *449*

Servility

Karel Čapek
Czech writer
1890-1938

The Tyrant and the Philosophers:
I shall do the deeds and you will give the reasons for them.   *450*

Royal Declaration of 10 May 1728.

Article 2. It is our will that all printers convicted of printing, on no matter what grounds, works or writings unauthorized by licence or imprimatur and concerned with existing or potential religious disputes, in particular those which run contrary to the bulls received in Our Kingdom, to the respect owing to Our Holy Father the Pope, and to the Bishops and Our Authority, should be condemned in the first instance to the pillory, or to an even greater penalty if necessary without the said penalty of the pillory being lightened under any pretext whatsoever. In the case of a repetition of the offence, we order that the said printers be further condemned to the galleys for five years, once again no remission or lightening of the penalty being permitted.

. . . .

Article 4. It is our will that anyone convicted of composing or causing to print the works or writings referred to in the preceding Articles should be condemned as disturbers of the peace, in the first instance to banishment for a time outside the jurisdiction of the Parliament where they shall have been judged; and in case of repetition of the offence, to permanent banishment from our Kingdom. *451*

France

Liberty of the press?

The whole press decree can be summed up in one line: I allow you to speak, but I command you not to. Three-quarters of all Republican journalists deported or outlawed, the rest hunted down by the mixed commissions, scattered, strays, sheltering here and there in four or five surviving newspapers, independent but spied on, the cudgel of Maupas waiting ready above their heads, fifteen or twenty journalists courageous, serious, pure, honest, generous, who write with a chain round their necks and shackles on their feet; talent held between two sentries, independence gagged, honesty on a ticket-of-leave, and Veuillot crying: 'I am free!'

A nice detail: Monsieur Bonaparte wanted Arago to take the oath! Yes, indeed: Astronomy must be sworn in. In a well-regulated State like France or China, all is official, even science. The mandarin at the Institute is responsible to the mandarin in the Police. The great telescope on its parallactic stand owes allegiance to Monsieur Bonaparte. An astronomer is a kind of celestial policeman. The observatory is a sentry-box like any other. An eye must be kept on God who is up there and seems at times to be not fully obedient to the Constitution of 14 January. The heavens are full of disagreeable allusions and must be kept in order. The discovery of a new sunspot is obviously a matter for the censor. The forecast of a high tide might be seditious. Accounting an eclipse of the moon is perhaps treason. We are a little moony at the Elysée. A free astronomy is as dangerous as a free press. Who knows what goes on in these private nocturnal dialogues between Arago and Jupiter?...

And then, as we said before, if one is a Bonaparte one is fatalist: the Great Napoleon had a star, the Little must have his nebula! Astronomers are certainly a bit astrologic. Take the oath, Gentlemen! Arago of course has refused.

Victor Hugo
Napoléon le Petit
1852

452

As the enjoyment of liberty, and even its support and preservation consist in every man's being allowed to speak his thoughts, and to lay open his sentiments, a citizen in this state will say or write whatever the laws do not expressly forbid to be said or written.

Montesquieu
The Spirit
of the Laws
1748
France

453

What is printing? Any obstacle to the progress of enlightenment is wrong. Let printing therefore be free. For, in the first place, this freedom cannot be restrained without impeding the exercise of natural rights. What is printing? It is one man putting his opinions, his ideas before other men's eyes. But what is contrary to the rights of others in that? Indeed, is not the examining of the views and thoughts of others one of the paths which may lead to truth? Truth is a real good; hence, society can have no right to deprive anyone of a means of knowing it. There is no danger of abuse of the printed word. In the case of general opinions, all truth is useful, and an error in print can be dangerous only if one is not free to attack it. And in the case of discussing private rights, actions which have some repercussions on public order? Restrictions on the freedom of the printed word would then be still more tyrannical, since they involve not only the general right to expound ideas but the no less sacred right to discuss one's interest.

Let the circumstances in which a printed work may be criminal be examined, therefore, in the light of the principles of natural law; and then, as for other offences, determine in what the crime consists, define means of proving it, and fix a penalty. But let each subject maintain the right to print, as he does that of employing for his own purposes a useful instrument, which he may abuse in order to commit a crime.

Condorcet
Vie de Turgot
1786
France

454

230

Dangers
of interdictions

From the speech in defence of A. H. Rowan, indicted for publishing a seditious libel.

What calamities are the people saved from, by having public communication left open to them? I will tell you, gentlemen, what they are saved from, and what the government is saved from; I will tell you, also, to what both are exposed by shutting up that communication.... If you doubt of the horrid consequence of suppressing the effusion even of individual discontent, look to those enslaved countries where the protection of despotism is supposed to be secured by such restraints. Even the person of the despot there is never in safety. Neither the fears of the despot nor the machinations of the slave have any slumber—the one anticipating the moment of peril, the other watching the opportunity of aggression. The fatal crisis is equally a surprise upon both: the decisive instant is precipitated without warning—by folly on the one side, or by frenzy on the other, and there is no notice of the treason till the traitor acts.

. . . . The press extinguished, the people enslaved, and the prince undone! As the advocate of society, therefore —of peace—of domestic liberty—and the lasting union of the two countries—I conjure you to guard the liberty of the press, that great sentinel of the state, that grand detector of public imposture; guard it, because, when it sinks, there sinks with it, in one common grave, the liberty of the subject and the security of the Crown.   *455*

John Philpot Curran
29 January 1794
Ireland

Man or subject

MARQUIS
I cannot take service
with a prince.

(*The king looks at him in astonishment*)

I would not cheat the buyer, Sire. If you
Deign enlist my services, you want
Only the end in view, you want
Only my arm, my valour in the field,
Only my head in counsel. Not my deeds
Or their approbation from the throne
Shall be my final aim. To me rather,
Virtue has value of its own.

. . . .

I love
Mankind; in monarchies I may love
None other than myself.

KING

This fire
Must be commended. You would do good.
How you do good—on this, patriot
And wise alike have many thoughts. Seek out
That office in my kingly realms
That gives you power this noble urge
To satisfy.

MARQUIS

I find none.

KING

How then?

MARQUIS

What your Majesty through my hands
Would distribute—is it human happiness?—Is it
That same happiness my untrammelled love
Covets for my fellow men? Before such happiness
Majesty would tremble. No! Anew
Crown policy has created happiness, one it
Still, itself, is able to dispense,
Wherein new inklings of the human heart
Allow themselves to be discreetly stifled.
The Crown mints have struck truth upon its coins
The truth that it can tolerate. Rejected
Are all other stamps that from this deviate.
And really is what may suit the Crown, to
Suffice me too? Shall my brother love
But serve to make my brother less?
Can I know him happy before that he may think?
You choose not me, Sire, to be the one
That happiness that you have coined for us to portion
    out. I must
Decline to give about these stamps.
I cannot take service with a prince.

. . . .

Shame then!
Since men from the Creator's hand
Into your own handiwork you've altered
And before this new-moulded creature
Gave yourself out as God; but one thing
Forgot: you still remain but man,
A man from the Creator's hand. And you go on
To suffer as a mortal, to desire;
Sympathy you need—and to a god
One can only offer sacrifice, tremble, pray.

A poor exchange! Unnatural
Reversal of nature! Since man
You tumbled down to be your second fiddle
Who's left to keep you harmony?

   KING
(By God,
He's at my very soul!)

   MARQUIS
But to you
This sacrifice means nothing; for
You are unique—a species in yourself.
At this price, you are a god. And terrible
Were it not so, if at this cost
—The trampled happiness of millions—
You had gained nothing—if the freedom
You destroyed were all
Your wishes could bring to fruition. I beg
You let me leave, Sire.

Schiller
Don Carlos
Act III, Scene x
1787

456

Let us for once hold less rigidly to our old-fashioned
opinions; let us have less self-esteem; give access to truth
and enlightenment and learning: do not repress the
innocent freedom of thinking on things of universal
interest; let us not imagine that merit and virtue will
ever be attacked with impunity thereby for, since they
speak for themselves and always have an impartial arbiter
in the public, the writings of those who basely dare to
attack them will be reduced to dust. Truth and virtue,
contain within them their own best defence; discussion
and debate reveal them in all their splendour and
brilliance; if discourse is restricted, mind will vegetate
like matter; and error, falsehood prejudice, fanaticism
and brutishness will divide the peoples and will cause
for ever their abasement, ruin and destitution.

Mariano Moreno
On Liberty
of Authorship
Gaceta
de Buenos Aires
1810

457

Three
interdependent
principles

Let us legislators take care, and never forget: these three
principles—a sovereign people, universal suffrage, free
press—survive in common. See how they defend one
another! Freedom of the press is in peril, and universal
suffrage rises to protect it. Universal suffrage is menaced
and the press springs to its defence. Gentlemen, any
encroachment on freedom of the press, any threat to
universal suffrage is a threat to national sovereignty.
Mutilate freedom and sovereignty is paralysed. Sovereignty

Victor Hugo
Speech to the
Legislative Assembly
9 July 1850
of the people is non-existent if it cannot act and if it cannot speak. And to shackle universal suffrage is to take away its means of action; to shackle freedom of the press is to take away its speech.   *458*

So long as the unjust and the wicked confine their activities to the reverse side of society, our country will be at peace. If they work openly, in the light of day, as they do in modern society, if those who associate with them are not ashamed and those who witness their conduct are not shocked since they regard them as normal, the historians of a hundred years hence will not be deceived, even though the writers be censored. It is easy to prohibit the work of a particular writer or to censor the work of all writers. Nor is it difficult to burn books and bury their writers alive, as did Shih Huang-ti, a Chinese tyrant who founded the Ch'in dynasty. But how can a whole nation be made deaf and blind, so that it can neither hear nor see?   *459*

Roan Uchida
1868-1929
The Broken Hedge
Japan

Those who criticize accepted ideas inevitably run a certain risk. An intelligent person, however, should not try to stifle criticism for fear of that more or less considerable risk. Once the spirit of criticism germinates, it cannot be prevented from growing, whatever efforts may be made to root it out. Power may indeed be inviolable and customs firmly established, but they cannot escape being attacked by the spirit of criticism. Once aroused, who can resist it?... The far-reaching reform our country needs should be based on fundamental critcism. There is still much to be criticized in our manners, our customs and our government. I cannot but deplore the efforts of our so-called patriots to stifle criticism by trying to rush through bogus reforms. Above all, I deplore their idea of morality.   *460*

Hajime Ōnishi
1864-1900
The Spirit
of Criticism
Japan

*Manifesting
the spirit*

Freedom of the Press is a manifestation of the spirit; it is the constitutional right of the spirit, resulting from its inherent freedom. Where one is forbidden to print his thoughts, speaking also is forbidden—which should logically lead to the prohibition of thought on certain subjects. Such violence can never be done to the spirit, for it exceeds the influence of human power over the spirit, which can be neither shackled nor imprisoned. Thus, only the spoken and the written word can be reproved. It is only when thought manifests itself that it becomes the object of censure and restraint. Nevertheless, the right of the spirit to find expression by means of the spoken and the written word is an innate impulse of the spirit, a natural law which man can abuse just as he can all the other laws, but of which he cannot be deprived simply on the ground that such abuse is feared. Therefore, one must in this case, as in every other, grant freedom of action to the individual spirit and designate penalties for transgressions. This indicates the need of a law relating to the Press which would, on the one hand, ensure universal freedom for the revelation of thoughts in print, and which would, on the other hand, protect society from abuses. Violations would have to be passed upon by a jury and justice would be meted out by a judge.

There is also a purely legal consideration which supports this point of view. An original idea, like an original invention, is the property of the author, and no one has the right to appropriate it arbitrarily or to destroy it. And the question as to whether this property of the author's might endanger society can be decided only by a legal trial and verdict.

Censorship, which places at the disposal of a censor the most sacred right of author's property and the equally sacred right of freedom of spirit, violates this rule. Those three chief mandates of all censorship, namely, that nothing against the government, religion or morality should appear in writing—how difficult to interpret them equitably in each single instance! The timid censor prefers to be on the safe side, to incur the wrath of the author rather than that of the government, and so mercilessly he strikes out the most brilliant thoughts, thoughts that he has neither sufficiently probed nor adequately appraised. The impossibility of relying on the censor's whim is best demonstrated by the police regulation which stipulates that even censored books and newspapers may be banned and confiscated—which again takes place in accordance with the arbitrary views of the higher police authority. Against the background of such arbitrariness, there is no security for publishers' and authors' property, for contractual agreements, for literary enterprises and speculations, because no law and no court of justice grants such guarantees.

From the standpoint of science, censorship fetters the development of the philosophical and critical spirit whenever the latter comes down from the realm of pure abstraction and surveys the real phenomena of the world. For it is impossible not to touch upon principles of government, religion, and morality in this connection, and not to pay attention to the spiritual forces which cannot, by their very nature, stand still, but should continue to progress. These are fundamental laws underlying the social life of nations; but precisely because nations advance, through education, in the most essential aspects of their development, they cannot remain true to the same conceptions and ideas forever.   *461*

Karol Libelt
On Civil Courage
1843
Poland

THEIR STRENGTH

Immense armies and virile generals,
Police: public, secret, bisexual.
Against whom are they thus banded together?
Against a few ideas;... and not the latest yet.   *462*

C. K. Norwid
1851
Poland

AGAINST CENSORSHIP

Freedom is so much the essence of man that even its adversaries exercise it in practice, although they are fighting its substance; they seek to appropriate to themselves as a most precious jewel what they have denied as the adornment of human nature.

No one fights against freedom, only, at the very most, against the freedom of others. Freedom has always existed, but sometimes as the privilege of the few, and sometimes as the right of all.

. . . It is not a question of whether freedom of the press should exist, for it always does exist; but of whether freedom of the press is the privilege of a few individuals or the privilege of the human mind; whether what is a wrong for some can be a right for others.

. . . .

The true censorship—that which is based upon the very essence of the freedom of the press—is criticism; that is the court before which the freedom of the press has elected to be tried.

. . . .

Censorship itself admits that it is not an end in itself, that there is nothing intrinsically good about it, that it is founded on the principle that the end justifies the means. But an end which has need of unjust means is not a just end.

. . . .

The writer in no way considers his works as a *means*. They are *ends in themselves*: he is so far from regarding them as a means, for himself or for others, that, if necessary, he will sacrifice *his* existence to *their* existence and, much like the religious preacher, will lay down the principle that 'it is better to obey God than men'—those very men among whom he none the less belongs by his human needs and desires. . . . *The first freedom for the press consists in not being an industry.* The writer who so lowers the press as to use it as a material means, deserves as punishment for such lack of inner freedom to lose his outer freedom, by censorship. More accurately, indeed: his existence is already his punishment.   *463*

Karl Marx
Debates
on the Freedom
of the Press
Rheinische Zeitung
1842

According to the law [of 24 December 1841], the censorship should not prevent any 'serious and discreet quest of truth'. These two adjectives 'serious' and 'discreet' refer the quest of truth not to its substance, but to something external. But surely the first duty of anyone in quest of the truth must be to make straight for the truth, without looking either right or left. Shall I not forget to tell the truth when my main concern is not to forget to tell it in the correct form?

Truth is no more discreet than light. In relation to what would it be discreet, anyway? To itself? *Verum est index sui et falsi.* Is it then in relation to error that truth should be discreet?

If discretion is the distinguishing feature of the quest, it suggests fear of truth rather than the fear we should have of error.

...You admire the enchanting variety, the inexhaustible richness of nature. You do not ask the rose to smell like violet—but, according to you, the Mind, what is richest of all in the world, must exist in one mould only. I am humorously inclined; but the law commands me to write in serious vein. I am audacious; but the law requires that my style be modest. Grey! That is the only colour we are at liberty to use. The smallest dew-drop, touched by the rays of the sun, sparkles with an endless array of colours; but the sun of the human mind, whatever the number and variety of the objects in which it is reflected, is supposed to produce one colour only, the official one.

. . . Those who write the daily papers—all journalists, that is to say—are required to be absolutely irreproachable. 'Knowledge and competence' are advanced as the first guarantee of this integrity. But no slightest doubt is expressed about whether the censor possesses the knowledge and competence to qualify him to assess knowledge and competence of various kinds. If there is in Prussia such a host of all-round geniuses known to the government, why do not these people, with their encyclopaedic learning, produce literature? Instead of resorting to censorship to put an end to the erring ways of the press, these officials, all-powerful by their very numbers and more powerful still by their knowledge and genius need only rise up together, for their weight to crush all these wretched writers who produce one type of work only, and that without any official recognition of their ability. Why do they keep silent, these clever fellows, when, like the Roman geese, they could by their cackling save the Capitol? They carry their discretion too far. They are unknown to the literary public, but the government knows them.   *464*

Karl Marx Remarks on the Prussian Censorship Regulations 1842

The freedom of the press watchword was universally important from the end of the Middle Ages down to the nineteenth century. Why? Because it reflected what was progressive in the bourgeoisie, i.e. the struggle against Popes, kings, feudal lords and landowners.

No country in the world has done or is doing as much as the U.S.S.R. to emancipate the masses from priests and landowners.

Throughout the capitalist world, freedom of the press means freedom to buy newspapers and newspaper men, to buy and fabricate public opinion for bourgeois ends.

This is fact.

The bourgeois forces everywhere are still several times stronger than ours. Give them this weapon, freedom to organize politically in our midst (by freedom to print, core and basis of all political organization) and you lighten the enemy's task, you help the class enemy.

We have no desire for suicide, so this we shall not do. *465*

Lenin Letter to Comrade Myasnikov 1921

Socialism as cultural anarchism

To seek to apply the anarchist ideal to material production is, in present conditions, a labour of Sisyphus; but in intellectual production the situation is entirely different....

To set up a central directorate of intellectual production would be not merely useless, but utterly absurd. . . . Communism in material production, anarchism in intellectual production: that will be the socialist mode of production.   *466*

Kautsky The Social Revolution 1902

I think the best way to kill proletarian literature is to prohibit anarchical competition. It is impossible to have **good writers** unless they have to go through a literary school, to struggle and to win a position for themselves by their own efforts. But if we contemplate putting literature under State control, with all kinds of privileges, we may be certain that the development of proletarian literature will be nipped in the bud.

Bukharin 1924

467

A free press

A free press is the eye of the spirit of the people, ever and everywhere open, the confidence incarnate which a people has in itself, the bond of words that links the individual to the State and to the world, the culture personified which transforms material struggles into spiritual struggles, and turns the crude and the concrete into the ideal. It is the confession without reservations of a people to itself—and, as we know, confession is a liberating force. It is the spiritual mirror in which a people sees itself—and self-knowledge is the first prerequisite for wisdom. It is the light of the public mind that can be carried into the humblest dwelling more cheaply than gas can be laid on. It is universal, omnipresent, all-knowing. It is the ideal world constantly springing from the real world and flowing back to it, always enriched in spirit, in order to bring fresh life to it.

Karl Marx Debates on the Freedom of the Press Rheinische Zeitung 1842

468

The [communist] party should encourage free emulation between the various literary groups and trends. Any other arrangement would be bureaucratic. For the same reason, it is unthinkable that any one group or organization should, by decree, be given a legal monopoly of literature. . . . The party cannot confer a literary monopoly on *any* group, even the most proletarian in ideology: to do so would simply be to kill proletarian literature.

Resolution of the Bolshevik Party on Literature 1924

469

MAYAKOVSKY BEGINS

A new
and laughing time
the human grain crop
thick—
from weed
and thistle
secure
and free

And let it be without
conditions,
or place for
bootlicking flunkeys
bigots, hypocrites
fawning phrases
or apprehensive act:
people then will people know
by looking at their faces.

Nikolai Aseev
1940

470

Tolerance and faith

Unanimity

Go together, speak out with one accord; may your minds comprehend alike, even as the gods of yore partook of their sacrificial portion in full concord. Concordant be their deliberation, concordant their decision, concordant their minds, and concordant their thinking. Harmonious deliberation do I secure for you through my incantation, a common oblation do I offer for you. Accordant be your intention, accordant your hearts. May your minds be accordant so that there would be complete unison amongst you.

Rigveda X
Sanskrit

471

Diversity
Burundi proverb

You cannot insist that everyone shall behave in the same way.

472

Truth and diversity
Rigveda
Sanskrit

Truth is one; wise men define it differently.

473

Asoka's Edicts
3rd cent. B.C.
Prakrit

Never think or say that your own religion [Dharma] is the best. Never denounce the religion of others.

474

*Every one
in the name
of his God*

But in the last days it shall come to pass, that the mountain of the house of the Lord shall be established in the top of the mountains, and it shall be exalted above the hills; and people shall flow unto it.

And many nations shall come, and say, Come, and let

us go up to the mountain of the Lord, and to the house of the God of Jacob; and he will teach us of his ways, and we will walk in his paths: for the law shall go forth of Zion, and the word of the Lord from Jerusalem.

And he shall judge among many people, and rebuke strong nations afar off; and they shall beat their swords into plowshares, and their spears into pruninghooks: nation shall not lift up a sword against nation, neither shall they learn war any more.

But they shall sit every man under his vine and under his fig tree; and none shall make them afraid: for the mouth of the Lord of hosts hath spoken it.

For all people walk every one in the name of his god, and we will walk in the name of the Lord our God for ever and ever.

Hebrew Bible Micah 4

475

Unity beyond ritual

Nicholas of Cusa
De Pace seu
Concordantia Fidei
1454
Germany

One then is religion and reverence [for God] among all serious-minded men, and it is the [common] foundation of all that diversity in ritual.

476

Unity beyond the name given to God

The first stanza deals with the transcendent Buddha whose relevant manifestation on earth is the Buddha-King of Java. The second stanza says that the transcendent Buddha is given different names by the members of the non-Buddhist communities.

Amen. Worship to Thee, O Lord. The servant (*priest*) is always praising the Lord,
Who is hidden in the vanishing-point of mental concentration, Who is the essential of matter and mind, Çiwa-Buddha,
The Lord of Çailendra, the Protector of those without protection, the Overlord of earthly kings,
Pre-eminent among the Manifestations, pre-eminent among the Inconceivable Ones, Whose appearance on earth is the Existent One as well as the Non-Existent One.
For those who worship Vishnu He is 'the One Who pervades the Universe, the Soul of whatever exists, the Unqualified'.
For the Yoga-philosophers He is Içwara, for the Sangkhya-philosophers He is Kapila. He is the materialized Kubera, being the God of Wealth,

Nāgarakrtāgama
A panegyric
by a Court poet
of the Majapahit
Kingdom
1365
Java

And Wrhaspati as the God of all learning; He is Kāma with respect to the Kāmasūtra (*doctrine on sexual relations*).
He is Yama in the practice of eliminating obstacles. The result of His activities is the happiness and welfare of mankind.

477

*Concord among
all religions*

King Priyadarsin, the beloved of the gods, honours men of all sects, ascetics and house-holders, with gifts and varied honours. But the beloved of the gods does not value gifts or honour so much as—what?—that there should be the promotion of spiritual strength among men of all sects. The promotion of spiritual strength is, indeed, of many kinds. However, the root of it is this, namely, the guarding of one's speech—how?—So that there should be no extolling of one's own religion or deprecating of another's religion or depreciation of the latter without occasion or relevance. On the contrary, persons belonging to other religious sects should be suitably honoured on different occasions. Assuredly, doing this one exalts one's coreligionists and one also helps persons belonging to other religions. By acting otherwise, one injures one's own religion and also harms persons belonging to other religions. For, one who extols his coreligionists and deprecates persons belonging to other religions, all this through devotion to his own religion—why?—in order that he may thereby glorify his own religion—he, verily, by doing this, definitely, does injury to his own religion. Concord among all religions is surely desirable—why?—so that persons of different ways of thinking may hear and serve one another's religion. For, this is the desire of the beloved of the gods—what?—namely, that the followers of all religions should become versatile and promote a wholesome religious attitude. And this should be announced by (my officers) who are stationed in different places: 'The beloved of the gods does not value either gift or honour so much as—as what?—as that there should be the promotion of spiritual strength among men of all religions.' For this purpose are employed many officers of piety, superintendents of women's welfare, inspectors of cowpens, and other bodies of officers. And this is the fruit of all these measures, namely, that there are secured the promotion of one's own religion and the glorification of Dharma.

Asoka's Rock
Edict XII
3rd cent. B.C.
Prakrit

478

Uddyotanasūri
8th cent.
Kuvalayamālā
779
Prakrit

The king, having comprehended the highest truths in all the religions, said to the sponsors of the various religions: 'Do you now go away and perform the different rites and duties according to your respective religions.'

479

For three years the disciples of Hillel and those of Shamai disputed among themselves. The former said: 'We have the truth', and the latter: 'We have the truth.' At length, a voice from Heaven settled their dispute, saying that both of them spoke the true words of God, but that judgement would be in favour of the disciples of Hillel; and if anyone were to ask why, it was because their manners were mild and forbearing, because they taught not only their own ideas but those of Shamai too, and because they always

Talmud Babli   quoted the words of Shamai before their own.   *480*

Aliens and men of bad religion

The sixty-second question is that which you asked: Is it lawful to take away from aliens and men of bad religion any property or not?

The reply is this: A possession and object and thing which aliens hold and which they have taken from people of the Good Religion by violence, and which they do not give back lawfully—under these circumstances it is proper to take it from aliens when this is possible. Even when they have a legal order of the rulers, and they have the authority to keep the possession by a proper legal decision and in righteousness—it is lawful to demand from them to send to oneself (*i.e., to the rightful original owner*) an interest on the possession.

With those who behave in the legal manner, it is necessary to behave in a legal manner and not to break a contract with them.

The death of a man of bad religion who is not an alien causes grief and pain. It is the proper custom to give him food, clothing and medicaments when he approaches his kinsmen in order to keep away from him hunger and thirst, cold and heat. But it has been said that it is not

Dādistān ī Dēnīg
Theological treatise
9th cent.
Persia

authorized to give aliens and men of bad religion wealth, horses, arms and instruments, wine and land.   *481*

Dēnkart
9th cent.
Persia

One ought not to withhold the earthly elements for eating and possessing from men of bad religion or from all others who may be regarded as heretics.   *482*

When the members of the first Moslem community asked the (Christian) Negus for asylum in Abyssinia, the Kuraishites tried to have them expelled. The Negus questioned the Moslems about their faith, and Dja' far ibn Abu Talib replied as follows, on behalf of the refugees:

'O King, we were a barbarous people, worshipping idols, eating unclean flesh and committing base acts of all kinds; we broke our blood-ties, ill-treated our neighbours; and the strong devoured the weak. We remained thus, until God sent us a Prophet, in the person of one of our number, whose origins, loyalty, honour and virtue were well known to us. This man called us towards God, so that we might recognize His unity and worship Him, rejecting the stones and idols which we and our ancestors had venerated in His place. He commanded us to be truthful in our speech and faithful in rendering what had been entrusted to us; to respect the ties of blood, to act kindly towards our neighbours and to abstain from forbidden acts and the shedding of blood. He forbade depravity and lying, the wastage of what belonged to orphans, the slandering of virtuous women; he bade us venerate God alone, and ordained that there should be no encumbrance in our worship of Him; he prescribed prayer, the giving of alms and fasting. We believed him, and had faith in him and obeyed the commandments which he had brought to us from God. In this way, we worshipped God alone, and no other God but Him; we accepted as forbidden those things which He forbade, and as permissible those things which He permitted. But our people were hostile, persecuting us and seeking to turn us from our faith, to lead us back again from our worship of the God the Most High to the worship of idols, and inciting us to accept again as permissible those base acts which we had permitted ourselves in the past. When they oppressed and persecuted us, seeking to suppress our religion, we came into your country, and chose you, above all others [as our protector], seeking the shelter of your hospitality, and hoping, O King, to be free from oppression in your land.'

Then the Negus asked him: 'Can you recall any of the words which he brought from God?' Dja' far replied: 'Yes.' 'Recite them to me,' said the Negus; and he recited the first part of the *Kahay'as Sura*. The Negus wept until the tears ran into his beard, as did the bishops who surrounded him; their holy books were soaked by their tears when they listened to his words. Then the Negus said: 'Those words, and the message of Jesus, come from the same source.' And to the Kuraish emissaries he said: 'Be off with you! You shall not have these people, and they shall be in no way troubled in my land.'

483

Religious freedom
Koran
Al-Baqara 256

Let there be no compulsion in Religion. Now is the right way made distinct from error.   *484*

Koran
Yunus 99

But if thy Lord had pleased, verily all who are in the earth would have believed together. What! wilt thou compel men to become believers?   *485*

Pope Gregory the Great (6th cent.) reminds the Bishop of Naples, who proposes to refuse freedom to practise their religion to the Jews, that those who employ force in such circumstances

'show more zeal for their own cause than God's'

and he therefore ordered that Jews

Registrum
Epistularum

'should have the largest freedom to observe and celebrate all their feasts and ceremonies as they always hitherto did, they and their families.'   *486*

Whether the children of Jews and of other unbelievers ought to be baptized against their parents' will.

The custom of the Church has very great authority and ought to be jealously observed in all things. . . . Now it was never the custom of the Church to baptize the children of Jews against the will of their parents. . . . There are two reasons for this custom. One is the danger to the faith. For if children are baptized before they have the use of reason, afterwards, when they come of age, they might be persuaded by their parents to renounce the beliefs they had unwittingly embraced. And this would be detrimental to the faith.

The other reason is that it is against natural justice. For a child is by nature part of its father. Thus at first it is not distinct from its parents as to its body, so long as it is enfolded within its mother's womb; and later on after birth, and before it is capable of making a free choice, it is enfolded in the care of its parents, which is like a spiritual womb, for so long as a child has not the use of reason he does not differ from an irrational animal. Thus even as an ox or a horse belongs to someone who, according to the civil law, can use them when he likes, as his own instrument, so, according to the natural law, a child, before he has the use of reason, is under his father's care. Hence it would be contrary to natural justice, if a child, before he has the use of reason, were to be taken away from his parents' custody, or if anything were done to him against his parents' wish. As soon, however, as he begins to have the use of his free choice, he begins to belong to himself, and is able to look after himself, in matters concerning the Divine or the natural law; and then he should be induced, not by compulsion but by persuasion, to embrace the faith. He may then consent to the faith, and be baptized, even against his parents' will; but not before he has the use of reason.

*Saint Thomas
Aquinas
13th cent.
Summa Theologica*

487

*Shall religion
be defended
by force?*

It is a law of man and of nature that every man should be able to worship what he will; one man's religion neither harms nor benefits any other man. But religion is not religion if it is imposed by force, instead of being adopted freely as it should be; for sacrifices should come from a willing heart. Thus, though you force us to make sacrifice, you are doing no service to your gods; they have no desire for sacrifices unwillingly offered.

*Tertullian
Christian apologist
160?-220?
Ad Scapulam
Carthage*

488

Religion must be defended not by killing but by dying, not by cruelty but by forbearance, not by evil deeds but by faith . . . for if you seek to defend religion by bloodshed, by torture and by evil, you are not defending it but defiling and profaning it. Religion, more than anything else, is a matter for free choice; where sacrifice is offered with an unwilling heart, religion becomes null and void.

*Lactantius
Christian apologist
250-317?
Numidia and Gaul*

489

Whether unbelievers ought to be compelled to embrace the faith.

Among unbelievers there are some . . . such as the heathen and the Jews, who have never received the faith, and these are by no means to be compelled to embrace the faith... because to believe depends on the will. Nevertheless, the faithful should compel them, if possible, not to hinder the faith by their blasphemies, their evil persuasions, or their open persecutions. It is for this reason that Christ's faithful often wage war with unbelievers, not indeed for the purpose of forcing them to believe (because, even if they were to conquer them and take them prisoners, they would still leave them to believe or not), but solely in order to prevent them from hindering the faith of Christ. On the other hand there are unbelievers who once accepted the faith, and professed it, such as heretics and all apostates. Such should be submitted even to bodily compulsion that they may fulfil what they have promised, and hold what they at one time received.

Saint Thomas Aquinas
13th cent.
Summa Theologica

490

A plea for heathens

I hereby exhort you, Princes of Rome,
To look to the fame of Christendom....
And, if the infidel suffer defeat,
In the field, to be mindful of man and his worth.
Heed a simple woman's counsel:
Spare God's creatures. The first man
That was by God created was a heathen.
Unto this day, mark you, Elias and Enoch
Are still accounted heathens.
Noah too was a heathen,
Yet was saved in the Ark.
Job was a heathen beyond all doubt,
Yet did not God, for this, cast him out.
Three kings, bethink you, too there are—
Gaspar, Melchior and Balthasar—
That are among the heathen counted,
Yet to damnation are not doomed:
For God in his own hands from them received
The first of presents at his mother's breast.
All these, though heathen, are not doomed to Hell.
And well we know that, since the time of Eve,
No mother, giving birth unto a child,
Bears other than a heathen.
Many afterwards have received baptism.
But every woman, baptized though she be,
Yet bears a heathen babe, for baptism.
Among the Jews the rite of circumcision
Stands likewise unto them for baptism.
So were we all once heathen. And it grieves
A feeling heart to think a child is doomed
By its own father to damnation.
He who has ever pity felt, must feel
For these unfortunates compassion.

Wolfram
von Eschenbach
Willehalm
13th cent.
Old German

491

*Against
the Crusades*

Lately, in our Emperor's time, during the Council of Basle, a Christian knight disputed with the Prince of the Turks, and the knight said to the Prince: 'My Lord, you are a wise man, you should let yourself be baptized and become a Christian. Our Faith is pure and consistent in every way, and no one can find wrong in it.' The Prince answered and said: 'I realize that what you say is true according to the testimony of the Bible. Thus Christ, by his death redeemed you, and made you free unto eternal life—that I know from your Bible. Yet I see that you neither desire nor follow him. You forswear him; one takes another's honour and his goods, one calls another his property. That was never the will of your Lord and God. Now you travel over the sea and fight against us and think your voyage good. If you can slay us, so, you think, you earn eternal life. You deceive yourselves. Stay at home and oppose the false Christians and put them right—there's a worthwhile voyage!'

See therefore what we must listen to from infidels. And he goes on: 'Repent, and respect your laws, and you will win us over for certain. The whole world would flock here to us, and there would be one fold and one shepherd.' *492*

Reform
of the Emperor
Sigismund
15th cent.

God is one and the same, in our country as in theirs. *493*

Russian proverb

A merchant of Tver, an Orthodox Christian, finds himself alone among other believers.

And I inquired about their religion, and they said they believed in Adam and in Buddha, and that Adam and Buddha were one. There are eighty-four religions in India.

. . . .

As for the true faith, only God knows it, and the true faith is to know one God only, to invoke his name in all places and in all purity.

. . . .

I left Beder a month before the Greater Bairam of the Moslems, and as for the Christian Easter and Christ's Resurrection, I did not know the date; but I fasted with the Moslems and ended the fast with them for the great day. *494*

Athanase Nikitin
Travels beyond
Three Seas
1466-72
Russia

Torture and faith THE ARCHPRIEST AVVAKUM PROTESTS AGAINST THE NIKONIANS WHO BURN THE OLD BELIEVERS (1672)

It is a marvel how they refuse to listen to reason: by fire, the whip and the gallows, they propose to strengthen the faith! Who then are the apostles who taught such things? I know of none. The Christ I know did not order our apostles to teach that men are to be brought to the faith by fire, the whip and the gallows.... You see, O listener,

that it is in freedom that men are called to Christ. . . .
Those doctors are shown to be servitors of Anti-Christ,
for in order to lead men to the faith, they kill them and
deliver them over to death. As their faith is, so are their
works.

Temporal power

He complains that, in the liturgy, the Tsar has himself called 'Most
Christian,' 'Most Merciful,' 'Most Powerful,' and so is given greater
praise than all the saints, much as Nebuchadnezzar said: 'I am
God! Who is my equal? God reigns in Heaven and I am his equal
on earth!'

In which canons is it written that the Tsar is to govern
the Church, change the dogmas and incense the altar?
His only duty is to watch over it and protect it from the
wolves which would destroy it, not to teach how to believe
and how to make the sign of the cross.   *495*

Life of the
Archpriest Avvakum
Written by Himself
17th cent.
Russia

*Religious
profession must be
unconstrained*

Canon 572. § 1. For the validity of any religious profession
the following is required:
. . . .
the profession must not be based on duress, fear or
deceit; . . .
     Canon 214. § 1. A cleric who received a major order
through grave fear may be reduced to the state of the
laity by sentence of the ecclesiastical judge, provided he
can prove that he was ordained out of grave fear and has
not ratified the ordination afterwards, at least tacitly, by
the exercise of the order with the intention of undertaking
the obligations of the major orders. By the sentence of
reduction he is freed from the obligation of celibacy and
from the duty of saying the Divine Office.   *496*

Canon law

*It is God alone
who knows*

O thou who chidest me, saying that I do not perform my
ritual prayers, I do perform them. But whether I perform
them or not is a matter entirely for God; it is He alone
who knows anything about it.
     God alone knows who is an infidel and who a believer.
My prayers will serve some purpose if He grants me his
indulgence.
     The foundations of religion, of faith, are rectitude and
truth; if thou possessest them not, of what materials
wouldst thou construct thy faith?   *497*

Yunus Emre
Folk-poet
13th cent.
Turkey

Conflicts

The causes that estrange men from one another are
principally three: 1. *differences of opinion:* we are not able
to think of the same things in the same way; 2. *hatreds:*

we cannot admit differing opinions about the same things without friendship suffering as a result. Hence, we cannot differ in our opinions without developing impassioned and prejudiced feelings one against another; 3. *open wrongs and persecutions:* which are the results of our hates, to our mutual undoing.

The first conflict originates in the mind, the second in the will and in the feelings, the third in those secretly or openly opposing forces which make for mutual destruction. Oh, if it were only possible to gain some insight into the inimical intrigues in philosophy, religion, politics and private affairs we should see nothing but endless and cruel efforts and attempts at mutual subversion, such as those deployed by the forests against the sea, and the sea against the forests, as is written in the fourth book of Esdras....

Conflicts of this kind I call inhuman; for man who has been created in the image of God should be kind, pleasant and generally peaceful. But now, when *man is divorced from man,* when man is incapable of tolerating his neighbour, when one man is raving against another, what we are witnessing is a veritable downfall of humanity. Such behaviour cannot be observed in any kind of dumb creatures, save the wild dogs, whose common behaviour is also to enrage each other, bark at each other, bite each other and fight over bones.

If therefore inhumanity is to make way for humanity, we must spare no effort to seek means leading to this end. There are three such means: *First,* for people to abandon the habit of excessively trusting their feelings and, by making allowance for common human weakness, to recognize as unworthy of men that they should overwhelm one another with hatred for trifling reasons—in general, to forgive one another the quarrels, complaints and wrongs of the past. All this we shall refer to as *effacing the past. Second,* for nobody to impose his principles (in philosophy, theology or politics) on anybody else, but, on the contrary, for everyone to allow all other men to express their own views openly and enjoy in peace what is theirs by right. This we shall call *mutual tolerance. Third,* for all to endeavour, in concerted efforts, to discover what is best, and to that end to bring into agreement their sentiments, their aspirations and their actions. This we shall call *conciliation.*

498

J. A. Comenius
Czech writer
1592-1670
De Rerum
Humanarum
Emendatione
Consultatio 'Catholica

THE CONDITIONS FOR PEACE LAID DOWN BY ISTVÁN BOCSKAY, PRINCE OF TRANSYLVANIA, 1605

Firstly, we demand, for the greater peace of our souls and consciences, that His Majesty respect us and ensure respect for the free profession of our faith; that the observance of the Swiss faith and that of Luther be freely authorized, in the same way as that of the Catholic religion, for everyone in this country, irrespective of his condition; and that each may continue in his faith.... And, that the much-desired freedom of worship remain an irrevocable right, ... that His Majesty ... abolish the shameful article *Ut Lutherani comburantur.*

499

MARYLAND TOLERATION ACT, 21 APRIL 1649

Fforasmuch as in a well governed and Christian Common Wealth matters concerning Religion and the honor of God ought in the first place to bee taken, into serious consideration and endeavoured to bee settled. Be it therefore ... enacted.... That whatsoever person or persons within this Province ... shall from henceforth blaspheme God, ... or shall deny our Saviour Jesus Christ to bee the sonne of God, or shall deny the holy Trinity the ffather sonne and holy Ghost, or the Godhead of any of the said Three persons of the Trinity or the Unity of the Godhead... shall be punished with death and confiscation or forfeiture of all his or her lands....

And whereas the inforceing of the conscience in matters of Religion hath frequently fallen out to be of dangerous Consequence in those commonwealthes where it hath been practised, And for the more quiett and peaceable governement of this Province, and the better to preserve mutuall Love and amity amongst the Inhabitants thereof. Be it therefore ... enacted (except as in this present Act is before Declared and sett forth) that noe person or persons whatsoever within this Province, or the Islands, Ports, Harbors, Creekes, or havens thereunto belonging professing to believe in Jesus Christ, shall from henceforth bee any waies troubled, Molested or discountenanced for or in respect of his or her religion nor in the free exercise thereof within this Province or the Islands thereunto belonging nor any way compelled to the beleife or exercise of any other Religion against his or her consent, soe as they be not unfaithful to the Lord Proprietary, or molest or conspire against the civill Government established or to bee established in this Province under him or his heires.

And that all & every person and persons that shall presume Contrary to this Act and the true intent and meaning thereof directly or indirectly either in person or estate willfully to wronge disturbe trouble or molest any person whatsoever within this Province professing to believe in Jesus Christ for or in respect of his or her religion or the free exercise thereof within this Province other than is provided for in this Act that such person or persons soe offending, shalbe compelled to pay trebble damages to the party soe wronged or molested, and for every such offence shall also forfeit 20ˢ sterling in money or the value thereof. . . : Or if the parties soe offending as aforesaid shall refuse or bee unable to recompense the party soe wronged, or to satisfy such ffyne or forfeiture, then such offender shalbe severely punished by publick whipping & imprisonment during the pleasure of the Lord proprietary, or his Leiuetenant or cheife Governor of this Province for the tyme being without baile or maineprise.

500

ON TOLERANCE

Would we forgive one another even for our differences of opinion, let alone for our differences of conduct, unless we knew how to tolerate that which wounds us? And who can arrogate to himself the right to arraign others before his own court? Who can be so impudent as to believe that he can do without the indulgence which he refuses others? I make bold to say that the world suffers less from the vices of the wicked than from the savage austerity of reformers; and I have noticed that the source of nearly all severity is ignorance of nature, excessive self-love and disguised jealousy, in short, meanness of heart.

Vauvenargues
Réflexions
et Maximes
1746
France

501

ENTRY ON 'PERSECUTION'

Persecution, if it is contrary to Gospel sweetness and the laws of humanity, is no less contrary to reason and good policy. Only the most bitter enemies of a realm's happiness could have suggested to sovereigns that those of their subjects who do not think like them are victims marked out for death and unworthy to share the benefits of society. The uselessness of violence well shows how false these odious doctrines are. When, either from the prejudices of their education or as the result of study and reflection, men have embraced opinions upon which they believe their eternal salvation to depend, the most frightful torments only make them more stubborn; invincible in the midst of tortures, the soul rejoices in the liberty the tyrant and his torturers would take from it, and scorns their vain efforts. People are always struck by a constancy they find miraculous and supernatural, and are tempted to regard the unfortunates who gain their pity as martyrs for truth; the religion of the persecutor becomes odious to them; persecution makes hypocrites but never converts.

Diderot in Encyclopédie, 1751-72

502

A MOST HUMBLE REMONSTRANCE TO THE INQUISITORS OF SPAIN AND PORTUGAL

A Jewess of eighteen years of age, who was burned at Lisbon at the last *auto-da-fé*, gave occasion to the following little piece, the most idle, I believe, that ever was written. When we attempt to prove things so evident we are sure never to convince.

The author declares that though a Jew he has a respect for the Christian religion; and that he should be glad to take away from the princes who are not Christians a plausible pretence for persecuting this religion.

'You complain', says he to the Inquisitors, 'that the Emperor of Japan caused all the Christians in his dominions to be burned by a slow fire. But he will answer, we treat you who do not believe like us, as you yourselves treat those who do not believe like you; you can only complain of your weakness, which has hindered you from exterminating us, and which has enabled us to exterminate you.

'But it must be confessed, that you are much more cruel than this Emperor. You put us to death who believe only what you believe, because we do not believe all that you believe. We follow a religion, which you yourselves know to have been formerly dear to God. We think that God loves it still, and you think that he loves it no more: and because you judge thus, you make those suffer by sword and fire who hold an error so pardonable as to believe that God still loves what he once loved.

'If you are cruel to us, you are much more so to our children; you cause them to be burned because they follow the inspirations given them by those whom the law of nature and the laws of all nations teach them to regard as gods.

'You deprive yourselves of the advantage you have

over the Mohammedans, with respect to the manner in which their religion was established. When they boast of the number of their believers, you tell them that they have obtained them by violence, and that they have extended their religion by the sword; why then do you establish yours by fire?

'When you would bring us over to you, we object to a source from which you glory to have descended. You reply to us that though your religion is new it is divine; and you prove it from its growing amidst the persecutions of pagans, and when watered by the blood of your martyrs; but at present you play the part of the Diocletians, and make us take yours.

'We conjure you, not by the mighty God whom both you and we serve, but by that Christ, who, you tell us, took upon him a human form, to propose himself as an example for you to follow; we conjure you to behave to us as he himself would behave were he upon earth. You would have us become Christians, and you will not be so yourselves.

'But if you will not be Christians, be at least men; treat us as you would, if having only the weak light of justice which nature bestows, you had not a religion to conduct, and a revelation to enlighten you.

'If Heaven has had so great a love for you as to make you see the truth, you have received a singular favour; but is it for children who have received the inheritance of their father, to hate those who have not?

'If you have this truth, hide it not from us by the manner in which you propose it. The characteristic of truth is its triumph over hearts and minds, and not that impotency which you confess when would force us to receive it by tortures....

'It is necessary that we should warn you of one thing; that is, if anyone in times to come shall dare to assert that, in the age in which we live, the people of Europe were civilized, you will be cited to prove that they were barbarians; and the idea they will have of you will be such as will dishonour your age, and spread hatred over all your contemporaries.'

Montesquieu
The Spirit
of the Laws
1748
France

503

OF UNIVERSAL TOLERANCE

It requires no great skill, nor polished eloquence, to prove that Christians should be tolerant towards each other. I go further: I say to you that we must regard all men as our brothers. What! The Turk my brother? The Chinese my brother? The Jew? The Siamese? Certainly; are we not all children of the same father and creatures of the same God?

But these people despise us; they call us idolaters! Then I shall tell them that they are greatly mistaken. I believe I could at least shake the proud bigotry of an imam or a bonze if I spoke to them thus:

'This tiny globe on which we live is but a speck, rolling in space with many others; we are lost in this immensity. Man, five foot tall, is assuredly of little account in the creation. Yet one of these imperceptible creatures said to some of his neighbours, in Arabia or in Kaffraria: "Listen, for the God of all these worlds has enlightened me; there are nine hundred million little ants like us on the earth, but my ant heap alone is dear to God; He has held all others in detestation throughout eternity; mine alone will be blessed and all the others will be eternally accursed." '

At this point they would stop me, and ask me what madman had said such nonsense. I would be obliged to reply: You yourselves. I would then try to mollify them; but that would be very difficult.

Voltaire
Treatise on Tolerance
1763
France

504

WHETHER INTOLERANCE IS A LAW OF NATURE AND OF MAN

The natural law is the law indirected to all men by nature. You have brought up your child: he owes you respect as his father and gratitude as his benefactor. You are entitled to the produce of the land you have cultivated with your hands. You have made and received a promise; it must be kept.

Human law can have no other foundation than this law of nature; and the great, the universal principle of either, throughout the Earth is: 'Do not unto others what you would not have them do unto you.' Now, by this principle, how can one man say to another: 'Believe what I believe and you cannot, or you shall die.' Yet this is what they say in Portugal, in Spain and in Goa. In certain other countries, they are, for the present, content to say merely: 'Believe, or I will loathe you; believe, or I will do you all the harm I can; monster, your religion is not mine, so it is no religion at all; you shall be held in loathing by your neighbours, your town, your province.'

If human law were to operate thus, then the Japanese should detest the Chinese, and they the Siamese; the Siamese should persecute the inhabitants of the Ganges and they would fall upon the inhabitants of the Indus; a Mogul would tear out the heart of the first Malabar to cross his path; Malabars would slit the throats of Persians, and Persians would massacre Turks; and all together would fling themselves upon Christians, who have for so long devoured each other.

Voltaire
Treatise on Tolerance
1763
France

The law of intolerance is therefore absurd and barbarous; it is the law of the tiger—and yet more horrible, since tigers only rend each other's flesh for food whilst we have exterminated one another for a paragraph. *505*

EDICT OF TOLERATION OF JOSEPH II (OCTOBER 1781)

We desire in particular that the following points be respected:

Non-Catholic subjects may build their own house of prayer or school in localities inhabited by one hundred families, even if these families do not live in the actual place of the house of prayer or of the pastor's residence, provided that those who reside elsewhere live within a few hours' distance. Those who live farther away may repair as often as they wish to the nearest house of prayer within the hereditary dominions of the Emperor and King, and visit their ministers provided they are nationals of our dominions. The pastors may, when necessary, minister to the souls of the sick, but may never, without incurring heavy penalties, hinder any of the sick from calling in Catholic priests.

In regard to the houses of prayer, We order that, wherever the matter is not already settled otherwise, the buildings should have no outward appearance of a church, there should be no ringing, or bell or bell-tower, or too recognizable an entrance giving on to the street; on the other hand, they may be freely built in any material desired. Full permission is given for the administering of the sacraments, attendance at worship, visiting of the sick in church homes, and public burial in the presence of the pastor. . . .

The customary arrangement in marriages involving non-Catholic of having the children brought up in the Roman Catholic faith is to be altered and it is to be understood that if the father belongs to the Catholic faith, all the children, male or female, are to be brought up in the Catholic faith, this being regarded as a prerogative of the dominant religion; but when the father is Protestant and the mother Catholic, the male children will take the father's religion, and the female children the mother's.

Austria *the mother's.*   *506*

Intolerance

ENTRY ON 'REFUGEES'

In persecuting the Protestants, Louis XIV deprived his kingdom of nearly a million industrious men, sacrificing them for the self-interested and ambitious views of a few bad citizens who are the enemies of all freedom of thought because they can enjoy authority only in the shadow of ignorance. A persecuting spirit should be put down by every enlightened government; if punishment were visited upon the trouble-makers who constantly seek to worry the consciences of fellow citizens who differ in their opinions, all sects would live in perfect harmony and be zealous in providing citizens useful to their country and loyal to their prince.

What are we to think of the humanity and the religion of those who favour intolerance? Any who believe that violence can shake the faith of others give a poor impression indeed of their own sentiments and consistency.

Diderot
in Encyclopédie
1751-72   *507*

If we contract the bonds of religious freedom, no name will too severely reproach our folly.

We, the subscribers, citizens of the said Commonwealth [Virginia], having taken into serious consideration, a Bill printed by order of the last Session of General Assembly, entitled 'A Bill establishing a provision for Teachers of the Christian Religion,' and conceiving that the same, if finally armed with the sanctions of a law, will be a dangerous abuse of power, are bound as faithful members of a free State, to remonstrate against it, and to declare the reasons by which we are determined. We remonstrate against the said Bill,

Because we hold it for a fundamental and undeniable truth, 'that Religion or the duty which we owe to our Creator and the Manner of discharging it, can be directed only by reason and conviction, not by force or violence' [Declaration of Rights, Article 16]. The Religion then of every man must be left to the conviction and conscience of every man; and it is the right of every man to exercise it as these may dictate. This right is in its nature an unalienable right. It is unalienable; because the opinions of men, depending only on the evidence contemplated by their own minds, cannot follow the dictates of other men: It is unalienable also; because what is here a right towards men, is a duty towards the Creator. It is the duty of every man to render to the Creator such homage, and such only, as he believes to be acceptable to him. This duty is precedent both in order of time and degree of obligation, to the claims of Civil Society. Before any man can be considered as a member of Civil Society, he must be considered as a subject of the Governor of the Universe: And if a member of Civil Society, who enters into any subordinate Association, must always do it with a reservation of his duty to the general authority; much more must every man who becomes a member of any particular Civil Society, do it with a saving of his allegiance to the Universal Sovereign. We maintain therefore that in matters of Religion, no man's right is abridged by the institution of Civil Society, and that Religion is wholly exempt from its cognizance. True it is, that no other rule exists, by which any question which may divide a Society, can be ultimately determined, but the will of the majority; but it is also true, that the majority may trespass on the rights of the minority.

. . . .

Because, it is proper to take alarm at the first experiment on our liberties. We hold this prudent jealousy to be the first duty of citizens, and one of [the] noblest characteristics of the late Revolution. The freemen of America did not wait till usurped power had strengthened itself by exercise, and entangled the question in precedents. They saw all the consequences in the principle, and they avoided the consequences by denying the principle. We revere this lesson too much, soon to forget it. Who does not see that the same authority which can establish Christianity, in exclusion of all other Religions, may establish with the same ease any particular sect of Christians, in exclusion of all other Sects? That the same authority which can force a citizen to contribute three pence only of his property for the support of any one establishment, may force him to conform to any other establishment in all cases whatsoever?

Because, the bill violates that equality which ought to be the basis of every Nation and Religion, promised a lustre to our country, and an accession to the number of its citizens. What a melancholy mark is the Bill of sudden degeneracy! Instead of holding forth an asylum to the persecuted, it is itself a signal of persecution. It degrades from the equal rank of Citizens all those whose opinions in Religion do not bend to those of the Legislative authority. Distant as it may be, in its present form, from the Inquisition it differs from it only in degree. The one is the first step, the other the last in the career of intolerance. The magnanimous sufferer under this cruel scourge in foreign Regions, must view the Bill as a Beacon on our Coast, warning him to seek some other haven, where liberty and philanthropy in their due extent may offer a more certain repose from his troubles.

. . . .

Because it will destroy that moderation and harmony which the forbearance of our laws to intermeddle with Religion, has produced amongst its several sects. Torrents of blood have been spilt in the old world, by vain attempts of the secular arm to extinguish Religious discord, by proscribing all difference in Religious opinions. Time has at length revealed the true remedy. Every relaxation of narrow and rigorous policy, wherever it has been tried, has been found to assuage the disease. The American Theatre has exhibited proofs, that equal and compleat liberty, if it does not wholly eradicate it, sufficiently destroys its malignant influence on the health and prosperity of the State. If with the salutary effects of this system under our own eyes, we begin to contract the bonds of Religious freedom, we know no name that will too severely reproach our folly. At least let warning be taken at the first fruit of the threatened innovation. The very appearance of the Bill has transformed that 'Christian forbearance, love and charity,' [Article 16] which of late mutually prevailed, into animosities and jealousies, which may not soon be appeased. What mischiefs may not be dreaded should this enemy to the public quiet be armed with the force of a law?

Because the policy of the bill is adverse to the diffusion of the light of Christianity. The first wish of those who enjoy this precious gift, ought to be that it may be imparted to the whole race of mankind. Compare the number of those who have as yet received it with the number still remaining under the dominion of false Religions; and how small is the former! Does the policy of the Bill tend to lessen the disproportion? No; it at once discourages those who are strangers to the light of [revelation] from coming into the Region of it; and countenances, by example the nations who continue in darkness, in shutting out those who might convey it to them. Instead of levelling as far as possible, every obstacle to the victorious progress of truth, the Bill with an ignoble and unchristian timidity would circumscribe it, with a wall of defence, against the encroachments of error.

Because attempts to enforce by legal sanctions, acts obnoxious to so great a proportion of Citizens, tend to enervate the laws in general, and to slacken the bands of Society. If it be difficult to execute any law which is not generally deemed necessary or salutary, what must be the case where it is deemed invalid and dangerous? and what may be the effect of so striking an example of impotency in the Government, on its general authority?

. . . .

Because, finally, 'the equal right of every citizen to the free exercise of his Religion according to the dictates of conscience' is held by the same tenure with all our other rights. If we recur to its origin, it is equally the gift of nature; if we weigh its importance, it cannot be less dear to us; if we consult the Declaration of those rights which pertain to the good people of Virginia, as the 'basis and foundation of Government,' [Declaration of Rights, title] it is enumerated with equal solemnity, or rather studied emphasis. Either then, we must say, that the will of the Legislature is the only measure of their authority; and that in the plentitude of this authority, they may sweep away all our fundamental rights; or, that they are bound to leave this particular right untouched and sacred.   *508*

James Madison
Memorial
and Remonstrance
1784

MY POLITICAL CREED

That Jews, or in other words, those of our compatriots who observe the religion of Moses, should be citizens enjoying the same rights as we do: the law cannot reasonably take account of the manner in which a man worships his God; it can only require that any citizen living in this country, whatever his religion, shall fulfil his duties towards society and keep the law. Whatever his faith, a citizen can only be punished if he is guilty and deserves punishment. But the Jews would apparently be punished as a community, whether they are innocent or guilty; this is inconsistent with reason, with humanity and with sheer justice.   *509*

Mihály Táncsics
Hungarian
agrarian socialist
1848

Naturally, a State without any official religion does not mean that its citizens practise no religion. All it means is that the State, as the guardian of freedom of conscience, does not support a particular form of worship or grant any particular clergy a privileged position.   *510*

Enrique José Varona
1849-1933
Cuba

**State schools
and religious
communities**

Friedrich Engels
Criticism of the
Gotha and Erfurt
Programmes
1891

Complete separation of Church and State. All religious communities without exception will be treated by the State as private societies. They will lose all grants from public funds and all influence over the State schools. They cannot, however, be prohibited from setting up, with their own resources, schools which will be their own property, or from teaching their nonsense in those schools. . *511*

Friedrich Engels
Anti-Dühring
1878

Mr. Dühring, on the other hand, cannot wait for religion to die the natural death that awaits it. He takes more radical measures. He is more Bismarckian than Bismarck himself; he promulgates police laws not only against Catholicism, but against all religion in general. He sets his militia police of the future to pursue religion, and thus helps it to assume the martyr's halo and thereby prolong its life. This is a specifically Prussian type of socialism. *512*

**The revolutionist's
option**

Vladimir Ilyich Lenin
quoted by
Maxim Gorky
1920

He who is not with us is against us. Those who think they can remain outside history are wrong. Even supposing they once could, they no longer can today. They would be no use to anyone. All, without exception, are drawn into the whirlpool. . . . You say I am over-simplifying life? And that such simplifications spell death to culture? . . . The Russian masses need to be told things very simply, in a way they can understand. The Soviets and communism—that's simple. . . . The union of workers and intellectuals? Fine. Tell the intellectuals that, let them come with us. You think they are honestly concerned about justice? Where's the difficulty, then? We're waiting for them. It is we who have undertaken the colossal job of setting the people on their feet, of telling the world all the truth about life, we who are showing the nations the true road to human dignity, the way out from slavery, poverty and humiliation. *513*

**Freedom
of opinion**

In 1943, the West Virginia State Board of Education had ordered the flag salute ceremony to be made compulsory in all public schools. Children who disobeyed were to be dismissed from school, and action could be taken against their parents on the grounds that the children were 'unlawfully absent'. This decision was contested and the case was referred to the Supreme Court.
Judge Jackson states his opinion at the time of the case.

Here, however, we are dealing with a compulsion of students to declare a belief. They are not merely made acquainted with the flag salute so that they may be informed as to what it is or even what it means. The issue here is whether this slow and easily neglected route to aroused loyalties constitutionally may be short-cut by substituting a compulsory salute and slogan....

It is also to be noted that the compulsory flag salute and pledge requires affirmation of a belief and an attitude of mind. It is not clear whether the regulation contemplates that pupils forego any contrary convictions of their own and become unwilling converts to the prescribed ceremony or whether it will be acceptable if they simulate assent by words without belief and by a gesture barren of meaning....

To sustain the compulsory flag salute we are required to say that a Bill of Rights which guards the individual's right to speak his own mind, left it open to public authorities to compel him to utter what is not in his mind....

Without promise of a limiting Bill of Rights it is doubtful if our Constitution could have mustered enough strength to enable its ratification. To enforce those rights today is not to choose weak government over strong government. It is only to adhere as a means of strength to individual freedom of mind in preference to officially disciplined uniformity for which history indicates a disappointing and disastrous end.

The subject now before us exemplifies this principle. Free public education, if faithful to the ideal of secular instruction and political neutrality, will not be partisan or enemy of any class, creed, party, or faction. If it is to impose any ideological discipline, however, each party or denomination must seek to control, or failing that, to weaken the influence of the educational system. Observance of the limitations of the Constitution will not weaken government in the field appropriate for its exercise....

The Fourteenth Amendment, as now applied to the States, protects the citizen against the State itself and all of its creatures—Boards of Education not excepted. These have, of course, important, delicate, and highly discretionary functions, but none that they may not perform within the limits of the Bill of Rights. That they are educating the young for citizenship is reason for scrupulous protection of Constitutional freedoms of the individual, if we are not to strangle the free mind at its source and teach youth to discount important principles of our government as mere platitudes....

Nor does our duty to apply the Bill of Rights to assertions of official authority depend upon our possession of marked competence in the field where the invasion of rights occurs. True, the task of translating the majestic generalities of the Bill of Rights, conceived as part of the pattern of liberal government in the eighteenth century, into concrete restraints on officials dealing with the problems of the twentieth century, is one to disturb self-confidence. These principles grew in soil which also produced a philosophy that the individual was the center of society, that his liberty was attainable through mere absence of governmental restraints, and that government should be entrusted with few controls and only the mildest supervision over men's affairs. We must transplant these rights to a soil in which the *laissez-faire* concept or principle of non-interference has withered at least as to economic affairs, and social advancements are increasingly sought through closer integration of society and through expanded and strengthened governmental controls. These changed conditions often deprive precedents of reliability and cast us more than we would choose upon our own judgment. But we act in these matters not by authority of our competence but by force of our commissions. We cannot, because of modest estimates of our competence in such specialties as public education, withhold the judgment that history authenticates as the function of this Court when liberty is infringed. . . .

Those who begin coercive elimination of dissent soon find themselves exterminating dissenters. Compulsory unification of opinion achieves only the unanimity of the graveyard....

But freedom to differ is not limited to things that do not matter much. That would be a mere shadow of freedom. The test of its substance is the right to differ as to things that touch the heart of the existing order.   *514*

The West Virginia
Case
1943

Social rights

14th-cent. lyric (anonymous) England

When Adam delved and Eve span,
Who was then the gentleman?   *515*

Viet-Namese proverb

The mandarin is in a hurry, but the people are not.
If the mandarin is in a hurry across the river, let him swim!   *516*

Abuses

Because they sell the righteous for silver, and the needy for a pair of shoes;
    That pant after the dust of the earth on the head of the poor, and turn aside the way of the humble. . . .
    And they lay themselves down beside every altar, upon clothes taken in pledge, and in the house of their God they drink the wine of them that have been fined.
                                                         517

Hebrew Bible
Amos 2

Mahatma Gandhi 1869-1948

I suggest that we are thieves in a way. If I take anything that I do not need for my own immediate use, and keep it, I thieve it from somebody else.   *518*

Yukichi Fukuzawa 1834-1901 Japan

Heaven did not create man above men or below men. *519*

No distinction of social orders at birth

In this world are observed differences between the footprints of a cow, an elephant, a horse, a deer, a lion, a tiger, etc., in the form: 'this is a cow's footprint', 'this is an elephant's footprint', 'this is a horse's footprint', 'this is a deer's footprint', 'this is a lion's footprint', 'this is a tiger's footprint', etc. It is, however, not so in the case of a Brāhmana and others: 'this is a Brāhmana's footprint', 'this is a Ksatriya's footprint', 'this is a Vaisya's footprint', 'this is a Sudra's footprint', etc. Hence, on account of the absence of any difference in footprints, we see that there is only one class, namely, that of human beings, and that there is no distinction of the four social orders.
    In this world are observed differences between the female and the male organs, the colour, physical structure, excrement, urine, odour, and voice of the cow, the buffalo, the horse, the elephant, the donkey, the monkey, the

sheep, the goat, etc. It is, however, not so in the case of the Brāhmana, the Ksatriya, and others. Here also, therefore, cn account of the absence of any difference, we have to assume that there is only one class, namely, that of human beings. . . .

Again, O Brāhmana, as there is similarity [among men] in respect of pleasure, pain, life, intellect, action, behaviour, death, birth, fear, sexual intercourse, and conduct, there can certainly not be assumed any distinction [among them such as] Brāhmana [Ksatriya, etc.].

This, too, should be taken into account. Just as there is no distinction of classes among the fruits produced by one tree . . . in the form: 'this is a Brāhmana fruit', 'this is a Ksatriya fruit', etc., because they are all produced by one tree, even so there is no distinction [of classes] among men because they are all created by one Supreme Being.   *520*

Vajrasūcī
Attributed
to Asvaghosa
1st cent. B.C.
to 1st cent. A.D.
Sanskrit

Speech, sexual intercourse, birth, and death—these are similar in the case of all men.   *521*

Mahābhārata III
2nd cent. B.C.
to 1st cent. A.D.
Sanskrit

Desire, anger, fear, greed, sorrow, anxiety, hunger, fatigue—these overpower all of us; how then does [one] social order differ [from another]? Sweat, urine, excrement, phlegm, bile, and also blood—these characterize the bodies of all [men], which perish [gradually]; how then is [one] social order distinguished [from another]?   *522*

Mahābhārata XII
2nd cent. B.C.
to 1st cent. A.D.
Sanskrit

The Brāhmanas (*that is, men belonging to the so-called highest social order*) are born from the womb, so too are the Candālas (*that is, men belonging to the so-called lowest social order*) born from the womb. What reason, indeed, do you see for assigning the highest status [to the former] and the lowest position [to the latter]?

Not in respect of the hair, nor of the two ears, nor of the head, nor of the eye . . . there does not exist any difference or distinction among all men.   *523*

Sārdūlakarnāvadāna
18
2nd to 4th cent.
Sanskrit

God is the judge

If I did despise the cause of my manservant or of my maidservant, when they contended with me;

What then shall I do when God riseth up? and when He visiteth, what shall I answer him?   *524*

Hebrew Bible
Job 31

Injustice ...	Whether the plantain leaf falls on a thorn or a thorn falls on the plantain leaf, the damage is only to the leaf.

... but ...
Telugu proverbs
Mauritius

If all want to travel by palanquin, who will carry it then? 525

Equality
Kabir
Hindi poet
1089-1172

The courageous man who effaceth caste and pride shall prove a saint. 526

Punjabi proverb

The voice of the people is the drum of God. 527

Large or small, a pebble is always a pebble.
(*Important or not, a man is always a man.*)

Imana [the supreme Being] creates men and draws no
Burundi proverbs distinction between them. 528

Kazakh proverb

Bow before him who shows you respect: he is not a slave you have inherited from your father; remain proud before him who gives himself airs: he is not the son of the Prophet. 529

Unity of castes

What do you think about this, Assalayana? If a noble anointed king were to assemble a hundred men of varying origins, saying to them: 'Let the good sirs come; and let those who are of noble, priestly and royal families, bringing an upper piece of fire-stick of teak or sal or of a sweet-scented tree or of sandal or lotus, light a fire and get it to give out heat. But let the good sirs come; and let those who are from a despised family, a trapper family, a bamboo-plaiter family, a cartwright family, a scavenger family, bringing an upper piece of fire-stick from a dog's trough or a pig's trough or from a trough for dyeing or dry sticks from a castor-oil shrub, light a fire and get it to give out heat.' What do you think about this, Assalayana? Is the fire that is lit and the heat that is got by someone—no matter whether he be from a noble, priestly or royal family, and no matter whether he bring an upper piece of fire-stick of teak or sal or of a sweet-scented tree or of sandal or lotus—is it a fire that has flame and hue and brightness and, being this fire, is it able to serve the purposes of a fire? But is the fire that is lit and the heat that is got by someone—no matter whether he be from a despised family, a trapper family, a bamboo-plaiter family, a cartwright family, a scavenger family, and no matter whether he bring an upper piece of fire-stick from a dog's trough or a pig's trough or from a trough for dyeing or dry sticks from a castor-oil shrub—is it a fire that has neither flame nor hue nor brightness and, being this fire, is it unable to serve the purposes of a fire?

That is not so, good Gotama. Whoever from a noble, priestly or royal family, bringing an upper piece of fire-stick of teak or sal or of a sweet-scented tree or of sandal or lotus, lights a fire and gets it to give out heat—this fire has flame and hue and brightness and is able to serve the purposes of a fire. And too, whoever from a despised family, a trapper family, a bamboo-plaiter family, a cartwright family, a scavenger family, bringing an upper piece of fire-stick from a dog's trough or a pig's trough or a trough for dyeing or dry sticks from a castor-oil shrub, lights a fire and gets it to give out heat—this fire too has flame and hue and brightness and is able to serve the purposes of a fire. So, good Gotama, all these fires have flame and hue and brightness and are able to serve the purposes of a fire.   *530*

Majjhima Nikaya II
Pali

Ajari Eijitsu was one of the priests of the Enryaku-ji, the major Buddhist temple of Kyoto. At the Emperor's wish, he was called specially to the Palace to minister to the Emperor Enyū who was gravely ill. . . . Half way to the Imperial Palace, they met a sick man crying out in pain. Eijitsu left the carriage and tended him. To the imperial messenger who reproved him for doing so Eijitsu replied: 'Buddha only I need seek and, having no ties in this world, for me there is neither Emperor nor Lord.... A sick man foresaken, that is what grieves me most.' He stayed and did not appear at the Palace.   *531*

Stories of the Saints
Episode towards
end of 10th cent.
Japan

Equality is a vital need of the human soul. It consists in a recognition, at once public, general, effective and genuinely expressed in institutions and customs, that the same amount of respect and consideration is due to every human being because this respect is due to the human being as such and is not a matter of degree.   *532*

Simone Weil
The Need for Roots
1942-43
France

The misdeeds
of inequality

Where there is no high degree, there will be no pleasure in exploiting those of low degree. Where there is no low degree, there will be no flattery or intrigue to please those of high degree, and hence no hatred, no conflict. There will be no one of high degree who, while claiming as his own the way of Heaven, secretly plants the root of theft, and no one of low degree who steals money and goods; and so the high degree will not make laws for the punishment of the low. . . . There will be no one of high degree who, while never tilling the soil himself, enjoys the fruits of other people's labour; no one who, making merry takes his pleasure in sumptuous festivities and music and wallows in dissipation; no one of low degree who, a prey to envy, goes from banquet to banquet, frequents loose women, and shamelessly engages in foolish behaviour. . . . Where there is neither gold nor silver coinage, there will be no one struggling to climb so as to become wealthy and prosperous, and no one who has fallen fretting in humiliation, poverty and sickness.

Shōeki Andō
1703-?
The True State and
Function of Nature
Japan

533

Joken Nishikawa
1648-1724
Memoirs
of a Bourgeois
Japan

When all is said and done, there is no real reason why we should make any distinction as to rank between men. *534*

If thou lend money to any of my people, even to the poor with thee, thou shalt not be to him as a creditor; neither shall ye lay upon him interest. If thou at all take thy neighbour's garment to pledge, thou shalt restore it unto him by that the sun goeth down; for that is his only covering, it is his garment for his skin; wherein shall he sleep? and it shall come to pass, when he crieth unto me, that I will hear; for I am gracious.

Hebrew Bible
Exodus 22

535

*What the abbot
should be*

Let him make no distinction of persons in the monastery. Let not one be loved more than another, save such as be found to excel in obedience or good works. Let not the free-born be put before the serf-born in religion, unless there be other reasonable cause for it. If upon due consideration the abbot shall see such cause he may place him where he pleases; otherwise let all keep their own places, because whether bond or free we are all one in Christ, and bear an equal burden of service under one Lord: for with God there is no accepting of persons. For one thing only are we preferred by Him, if we are found better than others in good works and more humble. Let the abbot therefore have equal love for all, and let all, according to their deserts, be under the same discipline.

Rule of St. Benedict
6th cent.

536

What squawks like a parrot is a parrot.

All birds that squawk thus are parrots; no other bird squawks like this. Do not then prefer one to the other, they all squawk in the same way, they are all equal.

The left side and the right side are both shares of the game.

Whether man or woman, rich or poor and so on, there are no basic differences; all are humans born of woman and doomed to die.

Mongo proverbs
Congo

537

Men are not like bundles of millet, among which it is advantageous to choose the biggest.

(*The need to treat all men with equality. Against chiefs who have personal preferences.*)

Songhai proverb
Africa

538

There are no differences between human beings from the emperor to the ordinary people, except that between men and women. And yet they have been divided into upper and lower classes, differences of status have been introduced, and four ranks have been distinguished—that of the samurai, the farmer, the artisan and the merchant—although all are men, all are human beings.

Genpaku Sugita
1733-1817
An Evening's
Anatomy
Japan

539

Under the Tsarist régime.

Serfdom was abolished. But quite a network of habits and customs of domestic slavery, of utter disregard of human individuality, of despotism on the part of the fathers, and of hypocritical submission on that of the wives, the sons and the daughters, had developed during the two hundred and fifty years that serfdom had existed. Everywhere in Europe, at the beginning of this century, there was a great deal of domestic despotism . . . but nowhere else had that tyranny attained such a luxurious development as in Russia. All Russian life, in the family, in the relations between commander and subordinate, military chief and soldier, employer and employee, bore the stamp of it. Quite a world of customs and manners of thinking, of prejudices and moral cowardice, of habits bred by a lazy existence, had grown up; and even the best men of the time paid a large tribute to these products of the serfdom period.

Law could have no grip upon these things. Only a vigorous social movement, which would attack the very roots of the evil, could reform the habits and customs of everyday life; and in Russia this movement—this revolt of the individual—took a far more powerful character, and became far more sweeping in its criticisms, than anywhere else in Western Europe or America. 'Nihilism' was the name that Turgenev gave it in his epoch-making novel, *Fathers and Sons.*   *540*

P. Kropotkin
Memoirs
of a Revolutionist
(written in English)
1899
Russia

The other nobility

ORESTES:
Nature hath giv'n no outward mark to note
The generous mind: the qualities of men
To sense are indistinct. I oft have seen
One of no worth a noble father shame,
And from vile parents worthy children spring,
Meanness oft grov'lling in the rich man's mind,
And oft exalted spirits in the poor.
How then discerning shall we judge aright?
By riches? Ill would they abide the test;
By poverty? On poverty awaits
This ill, through want it prompts to sordid deeds;
Shall we pronounce by arms? But who can judge,
By looking on the spear, the dauntless heart?
Such judgment is fallacious; for this man,
Nor great among the Argives, nor elate
With the proud honours of his house, his rank
Plebeian, hath approved his liberal heart.
Will you not then learn wisdom, you whose minds
Error with false presentments leads astray?
Will you not learn by manners and by deeds
To judge the noble?   *541*

Euripides
Electra
5th cent. B.C.
Trans. by
R. Potter

*Restoring
the hierarchy*

The sage asked the Spirit of Wisdom: 'How is it possible to seek the maintenance and prosperity of the body without injury of the soul, and the preservation of the soul without injury of the body?'

The Spirit of Wisdom answered thus: 'Him who is less than thee consider as an equal, and an equal as a superior, and one who is greater than thee as a chieftain, and a chieftain as a ruler. And among rulers one is to be acquiescent, obedient, and true-speaking. And among colleagues be submissive, mild, and kind.'   *542*

Dādistān ī Menōg
ī Xrad
Sassanian period
3rd to 7th cent.
Persia

True standards

Birth neither Brahmin, nor non-Brahmin, makes;
'tis life and conduct moulds the Brahmin true.

Their lives mould farmers, tradesmen, merchants, serfs;
   their lives mould robbers, soldiers, chaplains, kings.
'Tis thus the wise life's causal outcome see,
   discern what went before, what follows thence.
Their past decides how men shall fare—like carts
   that needs must travel in the linchpin's wake.
'Tis self-denial, holy life, control,
   which make my Brahmin's perfect Brahminhood.   *543*

Sutta Nipāta
Pali
Southern India
and Ceylon
Trans. by
Lord Chalmers

*The sense
of human
equality*

I know unto what limits natural necessity goeth; and I
consider a poor alms-man begging at my door to be often
more plump-cheeked, in better health and liking, than
I am: then do I enter into his estate, and essay to frame
and suit my mind unto his bias. And so over-running
other examples, albeit I imagine death, poverty, contempt,
and sickness to be at my heels, I easily resolve myself not
to apprehend any fear of that which one of less worth
than myself doeth tolerate and undergo with such patience:
and I cannot believe that the baseness or shallowness of
understanding can do more than vigour.   *544*

Montaigne
Essays
1580-88

The souls of emperors and cobblers are all cast in one
same mould. Considering the importance of princes'
actions, and their weight, we persuade ourselves they are
brought forth by some as weighty and important causes;
we are deceived: they are moved, stirred and removed
in their motions by the same springs and wards as we
are in ours. The same reason that makes us chide and
brawl and fall out with any of our neighbours, causeth a
war to follow between princes; the same reason that
makes us whip or beat a lackey maketh a prince (if
he apprehend it) to spoil and waste a whole province.
They have as easy a will as we, but they can do much
more. Alike desires perturb both a skin-worm and an
elephant.   *545*

Montaigne
Essays
1580-88

Every man has a right to entertain a private opinion of
his own equality to other men, but it follows not that a
cardinal's cook should take it upon him to order his master
to prepare his dinner. The cook, however, may say: 'I am
a man as well as my master; I was born like him in tears,
and shall like him die in anguish, attended by the same
common ceremonies. We both perform the same animal

Der Ahnenstolze

The sword
and armorial
bearings
have no power
against Death
Chodoviecki
18th cent.
Germany

functions. If the Turks get possession of Rome, and I then
become a cardinal and my master a cook, I will take him
into my service.' This language is perfectly reasonable and
just, but, while waiting for the Grand Turk to get possession
of Rome, the cook is bound to do his duty, or all human
society is subverted.   *546*

Voltaire
Philosophical
Dictionary
1764
Amended 1771

Written in prison in Germany after reading a passage from Plato's 'Laws'.

23 February 1945

During intermissions in an interminable air-raid warning

'There are two equalities which are called by the same name, but are in reality in many ways almost the opposite of one another; one of them may be introduced without difficulty, by any State or any legislator in the distribution of honours: this is the rule of measure, weight and number, which regulates and apportions them. But there is another equality, of a better and higher kind, which is not at once recognized. This is the judgement of Zeus, which has little place in human things; that little, however, is the source of the greatest good to individuals and States. For it gives to the greater more, and to the inferior less always and in proportion to the nature of each; and, above all, greater honour to greater virtue, and to the less less; and to either in proportion to their respective measure of virtue and education. And this is justice, and is ever the true principle of politics, at which we ought to aim, and according to this rule order the new city which we are founding, and any other city which may be hereafter founded. To this the legislator should look—not to the interests of tyrants one or more, or to the power of the people, but to justice always; which, as I was saying, is the distribution of natural equality among unequals. . . .'

This passage from Plato . . . is not obscure, or contradictory. . . . Rather than as something obscure, I see it as a sort of lure (and I think I can discern the cause of this, which I shall note). Plato distinguishes between two very different concepts of equality. On the one hand, there is equality in the sense of equivalence, an equality which takes the form of arithmetical identity and consists of 'measure, weight and number'. In this first sense, equality overlooks, denies or tends to nullify the diversity and variety of individuals, that is to say, natural inequalities; it submits them all, willy nilly, to the same rules of measure, number and weight. On the other hand, there is equality in the sense of equity, which accepts human 'material' as it is, which recognizes the diversity, variety and, as a result, intrinsic inequality of human things as a basic fact and which takes the form not of numerical uniformity but of right proportions maintained between unequal human things. 'For it gives to the greater more, and to the inferior less always.'

'Justice', Plato concludes, 'is the distribution of natural equality among unequals.' To me this definition seems admirable. Justice, equality, means keeping the balance between nature and society and, consequently, tolerating in society only those inequalities which are the expression of natural inequalities.

Nothing could be clearer. Why did I never come across this passage before? ... I have always taken equality to mean just appreciation of differences and, consequently, of natural inequality. Equality does not mean 'Everyone on the scales', or 'Everyone in the same bag', but 'Everyone in his place' and 'To everyone his due'.

This concept of equality is wholly revolutionary. For society to be equitable, that is, maintaining the first supposedly just distribution, it would be necessary, after starting with a certain proportion between unequal things, for the individual inequalities to be transmissible in their totality and indefinitely from generation to generation. Society would then be 'equal', although set in castes. But individual differences are not hereditary, whereas the social distinctions or advantages attached to personal superiority continue to be handed down in various forms. To eliminate from society all inequalities which are not the expression of individual inequalities means a real revolution. In this regard I have repeatedly said that a revolution could be brought about by two laws—a law on inheritance and a law on education. A law on inheritance so that every one of the individuals who make up a generation starts off on the same footing. A law on education, or rather on social destination, to select, class and cultivate the infinite variety of 'unequal' temperaments and re-establish equality by directing each individual to the social task to which he is destined by his natural gifts.

. . . .

Fraternity, in whatever sense it is taken, does not precede equality. It is a result of the latter. Fraternity is only possible between men who are free and equal. Freedom and equality (that is, Justice) first! Fraternity comes afterwards, as a *consequence*.

What is the reason for the feigned obscurity, that is, the *lure*? It is the same confusion between social and political on which I dwelt at such length in connexion with the concept of revolution. A distinction must be made between social equality and political equality, as also between social revolution and political revolution.

... In Plato's view, social equality is the true equality and political equality the false. That is why he can be at

·one and the same time an aristocrat or anti-democratic and a communist.

It is true in a sense that political equality, a principle of democracy, neglects the demonstrable fact of natural inequalities. The people are sovereign. If the will of the sovereign is to be recognized, majority rule is the only admissible, or even conceivable, rule and in the composition of the majority all civic entities are of necessity regarded as equivalent. This is Plato's false equality, which takes the form of number, weight and measure, which postulates arithmetical identity between individuals. Hence the eternal objections . . . : 'democracy, the reign of inefficiency', the vote of the rag-man counting exactly the same as that of Renan or Pasteur, etc. . . .

It is a fact that, in the sphere of politics, equality is the 'false equality', the inadequate equality, but this is necessarily so, contrary to what happens (or could or should happen) in the social sphere. Why? Because whereas the social régime, ·owing to its very complexity, equal to that of nature, can take the variety of individual temperaments into consideration and turn them to account, any political régime whatsoever has as its dominant characteristics uniformity, universality, generality. There can be but one law for everybody in each sphere. Consequently any law and any political system imply the subordination of a number of individual wills to the will of the community. True equality is unattainable. Any equality remains inadequate (as does freedom itself, incidentally). The question is: 1. whether this inadequate equality is not better than pure anarchy, for there is no other choice . . . ; 2. whether this inadequate equality can be brought about, that is, the will of the sovereign determined, by some better and more equitable procedure than the law of number, the postulate of the arithmetical identity of civic entities. I, for one, really cannot see any.

Yet it is essential to note that the evils and harmful effects of this inadequacy of political equality could be attenuated to the point of becoming negligible, assuming that the problem of true equality were solved in the social sphere, that is, under a socialist régime, for:

1. That régime brings about a gradual and constant rise in the general level.
2. Social selection, as I have said, is the best way of forming political *élites*.
3. The purely political administration of the State is gradually losing its importance. It is increasingly merging with the civil service.

A social democracy resting on the true equality will therefore work in easily with a political democracy based on the 'false', and it can scarcely get along with any other political régime.

The following, I think, is truer, more complete or serves to explain.

If we distinguish quite clearly between political equality and social equality, we shall see that the former can be nothing but equality-equivalence, because it is the expression or sanction of rights that are really equivalent or identical for all individuals. Forming the basis or infrastructure of any community are a certain number of elementary, essential rights—the rights of man and of the citizen, if you like—which all individuals possess equally and in the same degree; and in connexion with these rights, the concept of 'more' or 'less' is meaningless, since their exercise does not vary according to greater or lesser individual merit, greater or lesser social usefulness. In this respect, all people are indeed 'civic entities', equivalent and identical in weight, measure, and so on. It is therefore perfectly legitimate for the political system to be founded on the 'false equality' of Plato, which, in relation to this system, becomes true. Rising up on this basis, tier by tier, is the social system, which is but the collective organization of labour and production. Seen in this light, the problem is no longer that of securing identical rights for all the entities that go to make up society but of making the best use, in view of the complexity of social tasks and social needs, of the unequal diversity of individual temperaments. The 'true equality' of Plato consequently resumes its place. . . .

Moreover, it is because the 'true equality' rests on the 'false', because the diversity of tasks (and consequently of material and moral advantages and conditions) rests on the absolute identity of elementary rights that the *élites* produced by selection to direct, organize and command will be in no danger of becoming *aristocracies* and that the egalitarian spirit will be preserved in hierarchies of true equality.

Léon Blum
1945
France

547

Things

Things fall either under divine or under human law: this is their main division. The former include the sacred and the religious, and sacred things, like walls; the gates of the city also belong in a way to divine law. These things belong to no one. Things which fall under human law normally have an owner, but may not, e.g. those left under a will belong to no one until the heir is recognized.

Institutes of Gaius 150 Rome

They may be public or private. If public, they are not considered as having owners, but belong to everyone. If private, they belong to individuals. *548*

Collective ownership

Of the distribution of things and their acquisition.

Here are things common to all by natural law: the air, the flowing water, the sea, and in consequence, the sea-coast.

Institutes of Justinian Byzantine Emperor 553

Things which belong to a community are those which do not belong to each member in particular, e.g. in cities: the theatres, roads and other things held in common. *549*

Reparation for wrongful occupation.

The provincial Governor shall order the house which, as you have proved, belongs to you by inheritance from your mother and has been unjustly occupied by the opposing party, to be restored to you, together with such rents as have been, or may be, collected, and reparation for all damage caused. *550*

Constitution of Gordian 239 Rome

Property

Give him his patrimony and you give him life; deprive him of it, and it's death.

(*The greatest injustice is to deprive a man of his inherited land.*)

Amharic proverbs Ethiopia

Iniquitous verdict, poor despoiled. *551*

Distribution of land

Adult males shall be granted 20 *mu* of lands in perpetuity, and 80 *mu* of personal share land. Adolescent males of 18 years and above shall be granted lands in the same way as adults. Old men, cripples and disabled persons shall be granted 40 *mu* of personal share land; widowed wives and concubines 30 *mu* of personal share land.

Where their forebears have possessed lands in perpetuity these shall be taken into account among the personal share lands. When male or female infants, children, old persons, cripples or disabled persons, or widows are heads of their household, they shall in every case be granted 20 *mu* of lands in perpetuity and 20 *mu* of personal share land....

In all cases of disputed lands, where a settlement has been reached, the person who has already ploughed and planted the land shall have the benefit of the crop, even if the decision is later reversed. Where it had been ploughed but not planted, the new owner shall repay the cost of the labour.

Land statutes
T'ang dynasty
618-907
China

552

*Against
the oppressors
of the common man*

It is ye that have eaten up the vineyard; the spoil of the poor is in your houses.

What mean ye that ye crush my people, and grind the face of the poor?

Woe unto them that join house to house, that lay field to field, till there be no room and ye be made to dwell alone in the midst of the land!

Hebrew Bible
Isaiah 3 and 5

553

Koran
An-Najm 39

Nothing shall be reckoned to a man but that for which he hath made efforts.

554

Whoever takes unjust possession of a piece of land—were it only the breadth of a hand—the same shall, at the Day of Judgement, bow under the burden of seven pieces of land.

Whoever hath rejuvenated a piece of land given over to sterility, that land is his and none other hath any right to it.

Hadith
(Sayings
of the Prophet)

555

Amharic proverb
Ethiopia

He who makes distinctions between his children won't have any for a year.

(*God will punish him.*)

556

*Equality
at the outset
of life*

To restrain generation and the increase of children, is esteemed an abominable sin, as also to kill infants newly born. And more powerful with them are good manners, than with other people are good laws. . . .

In all their houses the children are reared naked and nasty; and thus grow into those limbs, into that bulk, which with marvel we behold. They are all nourished with the milk of their own mothers, and never surrendered to handmaids and nurses. The lord you cannot discern from the slave, by any superior delicacy in rearing. Amongst the same cattle they promiscuously live, upon the same ground they without distinction lie, till at a proper age the free-born are parted from the rest, and their bravery recommend them to notice. *557*

Tacitus
On Germany
98
Rome

The inhabitants of Cuba.

They regard it as certain that the earth, like sun and water, is common to all and that among them there should be no *meum* and *tuum*, the seeds of all evil, and so they are content with little. . . . For them it is the golden age. They do not enclose their property with ditches, walls or fences; they live in open gardens, without laws, without books and without judges; it is natural to them to respect what is right; they regard as evil and perverse anyone who takes pleasure in doing harm. *558*

Explorers' tales
1511
Collected
by Pedro Mártir
Anghiera
Italian historian
Preceptor
at the Court
of Spain
1511

Prayer

May I place a guard on my conscience, O God! so that my estate may never cry out against me and its lands may never weep for my injustice to my serfs because of the unduly heavy labours which I have forced them to endure, or because I refused them their due, or because I did not give my journeymen their just reward. . . .

In what respect am I more worthy than those who are subjected to me? Was it not Thee Who created each one of them and Who created me too? Was it not Thee Who made them grow in their mothers' wombs in the same way as myself? Mindful of this, may I not exert my authority unduly over them and not lead them into wrongful acts! Rather than this, may I be content with what is due to me, give up some of my rights and, whenever possible, alleviate their fate instead of using my power and authority to take advantage of their hopeless poverty and load them with intolerable burdens! May I not treat them as cattle, but remember that they are men created in Thine image and born as I was! May they not have cause to cry to Thee because of me, lest Thou heed them and wreak Thy vengeance on me for the wrong I have done them. . . .

May I never infringe their rights; and may I never

take from them the privileges which they have been granted by me or my ancestors, but rather add to them when necessary! For as I cherish the greater freedom, which I enjoy as a nobleman, so do they cherish their lesser freedom, limited as it is. And what I do not like, I must not do unto others. *559*

Jan Stoiński
Polish nobleman
1590-1654

*Limitation
of property*

This wise sage, to be sure, easily foresaw that the one and only road to the general welfare lies in the maintenance of equality in all respects. I have my doubts that the latter could ever be preserved where the individual's possessions are his private property. When every man aims at absolute ownership of all the property he can get, be there never so great abundance of goods, it is all shared by a handful who leave the rest in poverty. It generally happens that the one class pre-eminently deserves the lot of the other, for the rich are greedy, unscrupulous, and useless, while the poor are well-behaved, simple, and by their daily industry more beneficial to the commonwealth than to themselves. . . . I admit that this burden can be lightened to some extent, but I contend that it cannot be removed entirely. A statute might be made that no person should hold more than a certain amount of land and that no person should have a monetary income beyond that permitted by law. Special legislation might be passed to prevent the monarch from being overmighty and the people overweening; likewise, that public offices should not be solicited with gifts, nor be put up for sale, nor require lavish personal expenditures. *560*

St. Thomas More
Utopia
1516
England

Ownership of land

Notice issued by the
Board of Theologians
and Jurists which
met in Burgos
(Spain) in 1512

Fifthly, that [Indians] may possess houses and their own land where it may seem fit to those who govern or may hereafter govern the Indies, and that time be given them to cultivate and hold and conserve the said land in their own fashion. *561*

*The property
of the Indians*

The Queen. Our Governor and Captain-General of the Province of Santa Marta, and other captains and persons, to each one of whom what follows in this My charter applies and appertains: I am informed that it frequently happens when the Spaniards enter that inland province, the natives flee from the villages for fear of ill-treatment from the said Spaniards, leaving their houses unoccupied and their property hidden in caves: and I was petitioned and asked, graciously to command you not to consent or give occasion that they take what was thus left hidden, and destroy it, or cloaks, plumage and finery from their houses, and other articles, since for the Spaniards it is little and for them much, and therefore they are scandalized and hate them. . . . Wherefore, I command you not to consent or give occasion that any person should rob the said Indians, or take from them the said articles, or do them hurt in their persons and property, or accept from them more than they would willingly give.

Royal Charter of 5 April 1530 Spain

562

Restitution

Inasmuch as Captain Diego de Agüero, my father, whom God keep, was one of the early conquistadors and settlers and sustainers of these Kingdoms, who helped to place them and keep them in the service of God and in obedience to His Majesty and his Royal Crown of Spain, with his person and with the charges he held and was given by the Marquis Francisco Pizarro, former Governor of these Kingdoms, and notwithstanding that he accepted everything in good faith, believing the said conquest to be lawful and, in consequence, that it was lawful to have enjoyed the advantages arising therefrom, I have been given to understand that my aforesaid father was held responsible, both for not having respected order and the rest therein as was necessary for the justification thereof, as for having committed certain excesses, both ill-treating the natives and taking certain things to which he had no right, and for other causes and reasons: I, as his son and the person responsible for the discharge of his conscience, being anxious to make amends and give satisfaction, relief and surety therein, for the good of his soul have striven and sought to learn accurately and clearly to what extent he might be responsible in regard to the aforementioned. I have learned from citizens and early settlers who took part in the said conquest with my aforesaid father... [that the property he left]... chargeable to the said discharge and satisfaction, could, and does, amount to three thousand five hundred or four thousand pesos. Concerning which sum of ... four thousand pesos I, for the aforesaid reason, concluded that my aforesaid father and the property which he left and which I received by inheritance . . . are under the said obligation to make restitution [in favour of the native Indians].

Restitution made by Captain Diego de Agüero in Lima 23 March 1560 Peru

563

Rules observed by the Incas in agriculture.

When the land was increased, they measured all there was in the whole province, each town for itself, and divided it into three parts: one for the Sun, one for the King and the third for the inhabitants. In making this division they always took care that the inhabitants had an adequate amount to sow, whether they had previously too much or too little. And when the people of the town or province increased in number, they took some from the Sun's part and the Inca's part and gave it to his subjects; so that the King took for himself or for the Sun only land which had had to be left deserted without a master....

There was also a due order and arrangement for ploughing and tilling. First they ploughed the part set aside for the Sun, then the part for the widows and orphans and those incapacitated by age or sickness; all these were regarded as the poor, and the Inca accordingly ordered that their land should be ploughed for them. In each town, or in each district if the town were large, men were deputed to see that the land of the poor was tilled. They were called *Llactamayu*, which means ruler of the town. At times of ploughing, sowing and harvesting, it was their duty to go up at night into watch towers or turrets which had been built for this purpose, taking a trumpet or horn to attract attention, and to call out in a loud voice: 'on such and such a day the land of the incapacitated will be ploughed; let each attend to his appointed task'. The neighbours of each plot already knew, from the list that had been made, what land they had to work, which was that of their kinsmen or nearest neighbours. Everyone was required to bring his own food from home so that the incapacitated did not need to find food for them. It was said that the old and the sick, the widows and orphans had enough trouble of their own without that of others. If the incapacitated had no seed, it was provided from public stores. . . . The land of soldiers away at the wars was also tilled by the community in their absence, like that of widows. And this service was done for them as for those in need. The children of those killed in war were cared for until they married. After the land of the poor, everyone's land was ploughed in turn, all helping each other. Then they ploughed the governor's land, which was the last to be ploughed in each town.

The last of all was the King's land, which was tilled in common; all Indians generally went to the King's land and the Sun's land in great happiness and rejoicing, dressed in the costumes and finery they kept for high festival, covered with gold and silver decorations and wearing huge feather head-dresses. When they were ploughing (which was the merriest work) they sang many songs in praise of their Incas; they transformed their task into a festival of rejoicing, because it was performed in the service of their God and their Kings.

On land where there was little water for irrigation, it was given in due order and measure (like all other things which were apportioned) so that there should be no ill-feeling among the Indians about it. They measured the water and from experience they knew how long was required to water a fanega of land, and each Indian was therefore allowed an ample number of hours for this purpose. No preference was given to the richest or to the noblest, to the private individual or to the governor's kinsman, nor to the governor himself or the King's minister. Anyone who failed to water his land in the time allotted was ignominiously punished: he was struck three or four blows with a stone on the shoulders in public or beaten on the arms and legs with osier twigs for being lazy and idle, which was regarded by them as highly blame-worthy.

Garcilaso de la Vega (El Inca) Comentarios Reales de los Incas 1608 or 1609 Peru

564

Preservation of life, liberty and possessions

Of the state of nature. To understand political power right, and derive it from its original, we must consider what state all men are naturally in, and that is, a state of perfect *freedom* to order their actions and dispose of their possessions and persons, as they think fit, within the bounds of the law of nature; without asking leave, or depending upon the will of any other man.

A state also of *equality*, wherein all the power and jurisdiction is reciprocal, no one having more than another; there being nothing more evident than that creatures of the same species and rank, promiscuously born to all the same advantages of nature, and the use of the same faculties, should also be equal one amongst another without subordination or subjection.

John Locke The Second Treatise of Civil Government 1690 England

565

The end and object of governments

If man in the state of nature be so free as has been said; if he be absolute lord of his own person and possessions, equal to the greatest, and subject to nobody, why will he part with his freedom, why will he give up this empire, and subject himself to the dominion and control of any other power? To which it is obvious to answer, that though in the state of nature he hath such a right, yet the enjoyment of it is very uncertain, and constantly exposed to the invasion of others; for all being kings as much as he, every man his equal, and the greater part no strict observers of equity and justice, the enjoyment of the property he has in this state is very unsafe, very unsecure. This makes him willing to quit a condition, which, however free, is full of fears and continual dangers: and it is not without reason that he seeks out, and is willing to join in society with others, who are already united, or have a mind to unite, for the mutual preservation of their lives, liberties, and estates, which I call by the general name property.

The great and chief end, therefore, of men's uniting into commonwealths, and putting themselves under government, is the preservation of their property. To which in the state of nature there are many things wanting.

. . . The supreme power cannot take from any man part of his property without his own consent: for the preservation of property being the end of government, and that for which men enter into society, it necessarily supposes and requires, that the people should have property, without which they must be supposed to lose that, by entering into society, which was the end for which they entered into it; too gross an absurdity for any man to own.

. . . Every man is born with a double right: first, a right of freedom to his person, which no other man has a power over, but the free disposal of it lies in himself. Secondly, a right, before any other man, to inherit with his brethren his father's goods.

John Locke
The Second Treatise
of Civil Government
1690
England

566

Sorts of ownership

The first right of the subject is to dispose freely of his own person. From this primordial right derives his ownership of his actions and his labour; for labour is nothing but the useful exercise of his faculties and clearly proceeds from the ownership of his person and his actions.

The ownership of external objects, or real ownership, is likewise nothing but the consequence and, as it were, extension of our ownership of our own persons. The air that we breathe, the water we drink and the fruit that we eat become our own substance by the involuntary or voluntary work of our bodies.

By analogous operations, although they are more dependent upon the will, I appropriate to myself by labour which modifies it and prepares it for my use, an object which belongs to no one and which I need. My

Abbé Sieyès
Préliminaire
à la Constitution
20 and 21 July 1789
France

labour belonged and still belongs to me: the object upon which I have fixed it and which I have endowed with it belonged to me as to everyone; indeed more to me than to others because I had, more than the others, the right of first occupant over it.   *567*

*God
and the private
ownership of land*

Speech by a peasant
of the Molokan sect,
noted down about
the end of the
19th cent.
Russia

The earth was not created by the Tsar, but by God. God gave it to the first man or to mankind to be shared by all. It is because of the wickedness of men that the order established by God was changed, that the land now belongs to the masters, and that all the others see it only through them. . . . It is forbidden to cut a dead branch! The lord and master will say: 'It is mine!'. . . Is it for them only that God made the earth, the fields, the woods and the rivers? If all that was created for mankind when, then, did God give it away to the lords?   *568*

Labour

*Payment of labour
by contract*

Inscription
Vth dynasty
3rd millenary B.C.
Ancient Egypt

I built this tomb for the bread-and-beer (*term designating all remuneration in kind*) I distributed to all the artisans who worked on it; they thanked me when I gave them, in diverse articles, the very large remuneration they had asked for.   *569*

Inscription
VIth dynasty
3rd millenary B.C.

Pepi the quarryman was satisfied with the contract I made with him.   *570*

Inscription on a stele showing that workmen and artisans had the right to sue and give evidence in legal proceedings.

Inscription
Vth dynasty
3rd millenary B.C.
Ancient Egypt

Statement by plaintiff:

I acquired this house for payment from the scribe Chenti. I gave 10 shât (*copper object used as standard*) for it: one cloth, 3 shât, one bed, 4 shât, one cloth, 3 shât.

Sealed before the Council of the Pyramid of Cheops, and witnesses: Chenti, butcher; Ini and Râhotep, builders; Nemout and K(a)emipou, members of *phylê*; Mekhâ, quarryman; Ini, funeral priest; Sabni, funeral priest; Niânkhor, funeral priest.

The actual complaint was not reproduced.

571

Speech by Rameses II to the workers quarrying stone for the royal statues to be set up at Heliopolis, in the temple of Ptah, at Memphis and at Pi Rameses.

User-Maât, setep-en-Rê, Rameses Meriamon himself said to the workers in the quarries: 'Oh, flower of the workers, valiant and skilful, who hew for me monuments in profusion; Oh, you who do honour to the fashioning of hard and noble stone, who pierce through red granite and are practised in Bia stone, worthy and vigorous builders, thanks to whom, so long as you live, I can fill all the temples that I build; Oh, excellent and untiring men, who keep unceasing watch over the works and labour with care; you who, after reflecting, say: "We shall do it", to that purpose repairing to the sacred mountain; what you have murmured among yourselves has been clearly heard. . . . I, Rameses Meriamon, am he who makes the generations prosper by giving them the means to live. Before you are provisions in abundance, sufficient to meet your desires. Around you is food in quantity. I have satisfied your needs in every way, so that you can work for me with a willing heart. I am at all times the protector of your interests. The provisions you have weigh heavier than the fruit of your labours, so that, well nourished, you may become [good workmen]. I am well acquainted with your work, and he who works is always glad if his stomach is filled. The granaries are full of grain for your benefit, so that not a single day shall pass for you without food. Each of you is hired for a month. I have filled the storehouses for you with all manner of things; bread, meat, cakes to nourish you; sandals, clothing, various ointments, that your heads may be anointed every ten days, that you may be clothed each year and that your feet may be always shod with good sandals. There is not one of you who spends the night in sighing because he is poor. I have engaged many men, that you may be in no danger of want: fishermen to bring you fish and gardeners to tend the vine. I have had big vessels turned on the potter's wheel to cool your water in the summer season. Upper Egypt carries for you to Lower Egypt, and Lower Egypt to Upper Egypt, great quantities of spelt, barley, wheat, salt and beans. All this have I done, that you may be prosperous so long as you work for me single-heartedly.'

*XVIIIth dynasty
2nd millenary B.C.
Ancient Egypt*

572

ADMONISHMENTS TO THE YOUNG MEN

Dignity of labour

Act! Cut wood, work the land,
Plant cactus, sow maguey;
You shall have drink, food, clothing.

With this you will stand straight.
With this you shall live.
For this you shall be spoken of, praised;
In this manner you will show yourself to your parents and
    relatives.

Someday you will tie yourself to a skirt and blouse, to a
    woman,
What will she drink? What will she eat?
Is she going to live off the air?
You are the support, the remedy;
You are the eagle, the tiger.

*Aztec tradition
15th cent.
Mexico
Trans. by
M. León Portilla*

573

*Dignity acquired
through labour*

He who, when he sees rice, wants to get it immediately, is like a robber or an animal. A man worthy of the name should get his rice only after he has sowed the seed. He who, when he sees goods and riches, wants to get them immediately, is like a robber or an animal. A man worthy of the name should get possessions only as a reward for work.

*Sontoku Ninomiya
1787-1856
Lessons from Nature
Japan*

574

Right to hire

Thou shalt not oppress a hired servant that is poor and needy, whether he be of thy brethren, or of thy strangers that are in thy land within thy gates:

At his day thou shalt give him his hire, neither shall the sun go down upon it; for he is poor, and setteth his heart upon it: lest he cry against thee unto the Lord, and it be sin unto thee. 575

Hebrew Bible
Deuteronomy 24

Creator of the material world, possessor of Righteousness! Who, fifthly, causes greatest satisfaction to this earth? Then spoke Ahura Mazdā: In so far indeed, Spitama Zarathustra, as one pays a righteous man upon this earth for his work with justice, then, Spitama Zarathustra, he who does not pay a righteous man for his work well and justly, ought to be thrown away from the holy earth into darkness, into suffering, into the worst form of existence, upon thorny branches. 576

Avesta
Vendidad
1st cent. B.C.
to 1st cent. A.D.
Persia

Working conditions

Treatment of the Indians in colonial America.

Thirdly, that Your Highness may command them to work, but that the work should be such as not to constitute an impediment to instruction in the faith, and that it should be advantageous to them and to the public good.

. . . .

Seventhly, that they should be given proper compensation for their work, not in money, but in clothes and other things for their houses. 577

Notice issued by the
Board of Theologians
and Jurists which
met in Burgos
(Spain) in 1512

Item, you are not to allow friars or priests or any other persons to make use of the Indians to guard flocks, to work in the fields, farms or vineyards, nor yet to send them with letters from one place to another, or in other matters, without their being paid as the law should determine, payment to be made in the presence of you [the Corregidor] to the Indians themselves and not to their chiefs. 578

Ordinances
to Corregidors
issued by
the Governor of Peru
1565

Fruits of labour

Manusmriti IX
2nd cent. B.C.
to 1st cent. A.D.
Sanskrit

It is said that the field belongs to the one who first clears it of trees, etc., in order to cultivate it; and the deer belongs to one whose arrow hits it first. 579

Though the earth and all inferior creatures be common to all men, yet every man has a property in his own person; this nobody has any right to but himself. The labour of his body and the work of his hands, we may say, are properly his. Whatsoever then he removes out of the state that nature hath provided and left it in, he hath mixed his labour with, and joined to it something that is his own, and thereby makes it his property. It being by him removed from the common state nature hath placed it in, it hath by this labour something annexed to it that excludes the common right of other men. For this labour being the unquestionable property of the labourer, no man but he can have a right to what that is once joined to, at least where there is enough and as good left in common for others.   *580*

John Locke
The Second Treatise
of Civil Government
1690
England

Taxes

Good kings, like clouds, receive only to give away.   *581*

Kālidāsa
Raghuvamsa IV
4th cent. Sanskrit

Bhīsma says to King Yudhisthira:

I hope that the farmers, who really bear the yoke (*i.e., the burden*) of the kings and also maintain others, do not leave your kingdom, being excessively oppressed.   *582*

Mahābhārata XII
2nd cent. B.C.
to 1st cent. A.D.
Sanskrit

Nārada says to King Yudhisthira:

I hope that traders, who come to your kingdom from afar for the sake of profits, are made by the officers, who subsist on taxes, to pay only the due taxes.   *583*

Mahābhārata II
2nd cent. B.C.
to 1st cent. A.D.
Sanskrit

*Exemption
from taxes*

A person well-versed in scriptures should be exempted from taxes; so too women of all social orders; boys before the signs of young manhood are manifest; those who live in their teachers' houses for the sake of study; those who, being devoted to Dharma, practise penance; a person of the lowest social order whose duty it is to wash the feet of his master; persons who are blind, dumb, or deaf, or who suffer from disease; and the ascetics who are prohibited by the scriptures from accepting any money.   *584*

Āpastamba-
Dharmasātra II
450-350 B.C.
Sanskrit

Moderate taxes

The king should extract revenue from his kingdom like honey from a honeycomb, but he should not disturb the bees. He should (as it were) milk the cow with due consideration for the calf, and should not squeeze the udders too hard.   *585*

Mahābhārata XII
2nd cent. B.C.
to 1st cent. A.D.
Sanskrit

Equality of taxation

Hernando de Santillán Relación... del Gobierno de los Incas 1563

As to the arrangements for the distribution, collection and payment of tribute, the people being divided by the Inca as described above and the government so ordered, the distribution and collection of the aforesaid tribute was extremely easy, since there was no doubt or uncertainty about what each had to pay, without difference or deceit... all being equal . . . and sharing equally, so that none was wronged.   *586*

No excessively burdensome work

Item, I order, command and expressly enjoin that the Indians of either sex should not be burdened with any load, notwithstanding that necessity require it and the burdens be light, and notwithstanding that the Indians accept them willingly and welcome them, in particular timber and all other necessaries brought to make huts for the allotments, estates and cattle ranches, and not-withstanding the production of an authorization or order from the Corregidor of this Province of Mérida, the Corregidor of the native Indians, the Protector or others; and the agents, overseers and other persons are to have horses for the services they may require....

Item, inasmuch as it has been found in this visit of inspection that the labour which the Indians have suffered, and suffer, in the honey and sugar plantations and presses has been very great and excessive and contrary to their health, and the cause that many of them have been exhausted and have perished therein: pursuant to His Majesty's Royal Charter concerning this matter, I command and expressly enjoin that hereafter in this Province of Mérida the Indians do not, and may not, work in cloth-mills belonging to Spaniards, nor in the plantations and presses of honey and sugar, flax, wool, silk and cotton, or in anything similar, but that the agents and other Spaniards who may have them are to aid them with negroes or some other form of service as may seem to them proper, without pressure, force or persuasion of any kind, either with or without a wage, though consent be given by the chiefs, by the authority of the law or in any other form; all of which I command shall be done scrupulously, notwithstanding any ordinances which may exist to the contrary.   *587*

Ordinances concerning the Indians 1605

Dangerous labour DUBINUSHKA [My trusty staff]

In the land of my birth I have heard many songs,
Of joys and of sorrows they told-a,
But one song will remain in my mind all my days,
Of the gang working shoulder to shoulder.

> *Refrain*
> Ah, my trusty staff, heave-ho!
> Ah, my beauty, on you go!
> Pull, my hearties,
> Yo, heave ho!

From father to son it goes echoing down,
And is sung by each new generation,
And whenever the burden's too heavy, we turn,
To this song for a fresh inspiration.

> *Refrain*

I heard this refrain on the lips of the lads,
As they hoisted the log up from under,
When it crashed down to earth, the boys looked on aghast
To see two of the team torn asunder.

> *Refrain*

Hauling rafts piled with logs, or forging hot iron,
In Siberia digging for ore,
In pain and in sorrow we sing this refrain,
Of our trusty companion of yore.

> *Refrain*

On the banks of the Volga, stumbling through sand,
As we toil and we strain at the barges,
Our lungs nigh to bursting, we gather fresh strength
From this song of our own native marches.

> *Refrain*

The people one day will awake from their sleep,
And unite to be free of their masters
And seek for a stouter and mightier staff,
To belabour the tsar and the pastors.

> *Refrain*
> Ah, my trusty staff, heave-ho!
> Ah, my beauty, on you go!
> Pull, my hearties,
> Yo, heave ho!

Mid-19th cent.
Russia

588

*Employment
of children
in the mines*

The mine delivers its gang and the pit its bondsmen;...
troops of youth—alas! of both sexes—though neither their
raiment nor their language indicates the difference; all
are clad in male attire; and the oaths that men might
shudder at, issue from lips born to breathe words of
sweetness. Yet these are to be—some are—the mothers
of England! But can we wonder at the hideous coarseness
of their language when we remember the savage rudeness
of their lives? Naked to the waist, an iron chain fastened
to a belt of leather runs between their legs clad in canvass
trousers, while on hands and feet an English girl, for twelve,
sometimes for sixteen hours a-day, hauls and hurries tubs
of coals up subterranean roads, dark, precipitous, and
plashy: circumstances that seem to have escaped the notice
of the Society for the Abolition of Negro Slavery. These
worthy gentlemen too appear to have been singularly
unconscious of the sufferings of the little Trappers (*children
who open and shut the traps*), which was remarkable, as
many of them were in their own employ.

See too these emerge from the bowels of the earth!
Infants of four and five years of age, many of them girls,
pretty and still soft and timid; entrusted with the fulfilment
of most responsible duties, and the nature of which entails
of them the necessity of being the earliest to enter the
mine and the latest to leave it. Their labour indeed is
not severe, for that would be impossible, but it is passed
in darkness and in solitude. They endure that punishment
which philosophical philanthropy has invented for the
direst criminals, and which those criminals deem more
terrible than the death for which it is substituted. Hour

*Children at work
in the galleries
of a coal-mine
c.* 1860

after hour elapses, and all that reminds the infant Trappers of the world they have quitted and that which they have joined, is the passage of the coal-waggons for which they open the air-doors of the galleries, and on keeping which doors constantly closed, except at this moment of passage, the safety of the mine and the lives of the persons employed in it entirely depend.   *589*

Disraeli
Sybil, or the
Two Nations
1845
England

The community fund

The community funds are to include all the property that the body and mass of Indians in each village may own, so that the contents may be spent for the benefit of all in common, and care is to be taken in their conservation and increase and whatever else may be proper, and they are to be distributed through drafts, correct accounts and methodically.   *590*

Law for the
Kingdoms
of the Indies
Emperor Charles V
16th cent.

Right to medical care

Furthermore, you will see that order is given for a hospital in each repartimiento, where care is to be taken to restore to health any poor Indians who should happen to be there or to be passing through, and therein you will see that the said hospital is run, and the aforesaid poor Indians tended, in the most orderly way possible.   *591*

Ordinances
to Corregidors
issued by
the Governor of Peru
1565

None to be idle

The Incas would not allow that any should be slothful and go about cheating on the work of others, but commanded all to work. And so every master, on certain days, would go to his farm and take the plough in his hands and till the soil and work at other things. Even the Incas themselves did so, thinking to set a good example; for they intended it to be known that none should be so rich as to have his riches lead him to insult and affront the poor; and under their government none was, throughout the land; for being healthy, he worked and wanted not and, lacking health, his needs were provided from what was laid by. Nor might a rich man wear more ornament or trappings than a poor, or differentiate in dress and clothing, except for lords and governors, whose rank allowed large exemptions and liberties, and likewise the great officials who, among all the nations, had privileges.   *592*

Pedro Cieza de León
Spanish chronicler
of Peru
16th cent.

In the State no one shall be tolerated who does not work, that is one who does not earn his livelihood and support his family by honest work, serving the polity by tilling land, performing a craft, a trade, or giving counsel. . . . 1. The rich should devote their time to study, and by acquiring wisdom they should serve public well-being. 2. The poor should earn their living by the work of their hands. Whoever acted differently should expect punishment. If it could be achieved, this alone would do away with half the disorders and abominations of this world: there would be no preying on each other, there would be no theft, gambling or swindling of any kind. . . .

Also monopolies and oligopolies ought to be liquidated throughout the world. This shame of our century should be foreign to the era of enlightenment: a handful of people set up monopolies in cities and empires, thereby debarring others from the trade, eager to snatch the bread from their mouths. For it is not possible to tolerate any longer a state of affairs where a few people intrigue and interfere with anything they wish. Order should be established instead, making it clear who is to do what; similarly it cannot be tolerated that what can be performed more adequately by a plurality of people, vying with each other with genuine ardour and diligence, should instead be concentrated in one individual, who reaps the full benefit, while loss and detriment to the State is no less certain.

J. A. Comenius
Czech writer
1592-1670
De Rerum
Humanarum
Emendatione
Consultatio
Catholica

593

Amharic proverb
Ethiopia

No work, no bread.

594

Right to implements of work
Hebrew Bible
Deuteronomy 24

No man shall take the nether or the upper millstone to pledge: for he taketh a man's life to pledge.

595

Right to work

OF HOSPITALS

A man is not poor because he has nothing, but because he does not work. The man who without any degree of wealth has an employment is as much at his ease as he who without labour has an income of a hundred crowns a year. He who has no substance, and yet has a trade, is not poorer than he who, possessing ten acres of land, is obliged to cultivate it for his subsistence. The mechanic who gives his art as an inheritance to his children has left a fortune, which is multiplied in proportion to their number. It is not so with him who, having ten acres of land, divides it among his children.

In trading countries, where many men have no other subsistence but from the arts, the State is frequently obliged to supply the necessities of the aged, the sick, and the orphan. A well-regulated government draws this support from the arts themselves. It gives to some such employment as they are capable of performing; others are taught to work, and this teaching of itself becomes an employment.

The alms given to a naked man in the street do not fulfil the obligations of the State, which owes to every citizen a certain subsistence, a proper nourishment, convenient clothing, and a kind of life not incompatible with health.

Aurengzebe, being asked why he did not build hospitals (in the old sense of institutions for the housing and maintenance of the needy), said 'I will make my empire so rich that there shall be no need of hospitals.' He ought to have said, I will begin by rendering my empire rich, and then I will build hospitals.

The riches of the State suppose great industry. Amidst the numerous branches of trade it is impossible but that some must suffer, and consequently the mechanics must be in a momentary necessity.

Whenever this happens, the State is obliged to lend them a ready assistance, whether it be to prevent the sufferings of the people, or to avoid a rebellion. In this case hospitals, or some equivalent regulations, are necessary to prevent this misery.

But when the nation is poor, private poverty springs from the general calamity, and is, if I may so express myself, the general calamity itself. All the hospitals in the world cannot cure this private poverty; on the contrary, the spirit of indolence, which it constantly inspires, increases the general and consequently the private misery. . . .

I have observed that wealthy nations have need of hospitals, because fortune subjects them to a thousand accidents; but it is plain that transient assistances are much better than perpetual foundations. The evil is momentary; it is necessary, therefore, that the succour should be of the same nature, and that it be applied to particular accidents.   *596*

Montesquieu
The Spirit
of the Laws
1748
France

I shall merely indicate the subject which should be dealt with, namely *the right to work*. Far be it from me to start a debate on those renewed musings of the Greeks, those Rights of Man that have become so ridiculous. After the revolutions which their rule has brought us, is it believable that we should be moving towards new disturbances because we have forgotten the first of those rights and the only useful one, the right to work, which our politicians have never mentioned, in accordance with their usual practice of omitting the vital questions in every branch of study.

Among other infringements of the Right in question, I would mention those privileged companies which, exploiting one branch of labour, shut out competition from others and refuse conditional admission.

The influence of such companies can become dangerous and cause revolution only if their rules are extended to the entire body commercial.   *597*

Charles Fourier
Théorie des Quatre
Mouvements
et des Destinées
Générales
1808
France

Right to rest

Keep the sabbath day to sanctify it, as the Lord thy God hath commanded thee.

Six days thou shalt labour, and do all thy work:

But the seventh day is the sabbath of the Lord thy God: in it thou shalt not do any work, thou, nor thy son, nor thy daughter, nor thy manservant, nor thy maidservant, nor thine ox, nor thine ass, nor any of the cattle,

Siesta
Coloured wood
1515
Strasbourg

nor thy stranger that is within thy gates; that thy man-servant and thy maidservant may rest as well as thou.

And remember that thou wast a servant in the land of Egypt, and that the Lord thy God brought thee out thence through a mighty hand and by a stretched out arm: therefore the Lord thy God commanded thee to keep the sabbath day. *598*

Hebrew Bible
Deuteronomy 5

Hebrew Bible
Deuteronomy 15

At the end of every seven years shalt thou make a release. *599*

It is sad indeed if the people have time only to earn their daily bread; they must also be able to eat it with joy, otherwise their earning days will be shortlived. God, who is just and benevolent, wills that Man shall work, but also that he shall enjoy relaxation; Nature commands him to have exercise and rest, pleasure and pain, in equal measure. The drudgery of work is a greater affliction to the poor than the work itself. *600*

Jean-Jacques
Rousseau
Letter
to d'Alembert
1758

Social justice

A thirsty man thinks a whole amphora wouldn't quench his thirst, and behold one cupful does. And there starts the real misfortune of the human race. He thinks one amphora will not suffice, and so takes the amphora he has away from all who thirst, although he will drink only a cup from it. Better: he will break the amphora so that none will drink if he can't. Better still: having drunk, he will empty the rest on the ground so that thirst and hatred may grow in others. Better and better: these, the thirsty, kill each other so that none may drink. You idiots, let each drink a little, and then refill this good amphora for the one who comes after him. *601*

Giovanni Pascoli
1855-1912
Italy

Severity towards those who oppress the humble

If the two squads of soldiers that are in the countryside, one in the southern region and the other in the northern region, carry off hides from all over the country without a single year's intermission, without giving any respite to the peasants . . ., and choose those which are marked [branded], while going from house to house striking [the people], inflicting ill-treatment and leaving the peasants no hides . . . , and if some . . . from Pharaoh comes to collect the quota of taxes payable on his cattle and questions them, and if the hides are not found in their houses [so that] it is recognized that they are in debt; and if they can convince them *(that is, the superintendent of cattle and his subordinates)*, saying: 'They have been taken from us'—this being also a serious case, action is to be taken in accordance [with the gravity of the facts].

If the superintendent of Pharaoh's cattle comes to collect the quota of taxes payable on cattle throughout the land—[since] it is he who collects the hides of the dead [cattle] which . . .—we have ordered that the peasant shall be discharged from obligation because of his honest intentions.

But as for any soldier of whom it is learnt that he is carrying off hides, from that day the law is to be applied to him, and he shall be given a hundred lashes [causing] five open wounds, and the hides he has carried off shall be taken from him as ill-gotten gains. *602*

Decree of Horemheb
XVIIIth dynasty
2nd millenary B.C.
Ancient Egypt

Protection
of the weak,
justice, refusal
to apply the death
penalty

See that Justice-Truth *(maât)* prevails throughout all thy days. Comfort the afflicted; despoil not the widow; deprive no man of his father's goods; remove not the high officers of state from their places. Refrain from unjust punishment. Kill not; it is without avail to thee (and will do thee harm); chastise by corporal punishment or by imprisonment. In this way the country will rest on firm foundations. . . .

Make no distinction between the son of a man of importance and one of humble origin; choose a man for thyself [for thy service] because of what he does. . . .

Well governed are men, the flock of God: He created heaven and earth for their desire, restrained the avid waters and made the air to give life to their nostrils. Men are made in His image, they have their source in Him. For them He rises in the sky. For them He created the plants, animals, birds and fishes, to provide them with food. *603*

Precepts
for Merikare
Xth dynasty
End of
3rd millenary B.C.
Ancient Egypt

Religion condemns
privilege

A man who loves his neighbour as himself cannot allow himself to possess anything more than his neighbour; so that if he has possessions, and does not distribute them without envy until he becomes and is himself as his neighbours, he does not fulfil the Lord's commandments exactly. *604*

St. Simeon, the
new theologian
949-1022
Byzantium

Never deprive a poor man of his possessions.

You refuse your neighbour a hen and the next day the sparrow-hawk carries it off. *605*

Burundi proverbs

Social classes and duties of assistance

The inhabitants of the City belong to three categories—men, women and children. From another point of view the inhabitants of the City belong to the following three categories: (a) persons in the Chief's household (persons of authority); (b) notabilities; (c) ordinary citizens.

. . . .

[The notabilities:]

If someone is regarded as a rich worthy, it is a good thing that he possesses large herds, that he buys guns for members of his family and for his slaves, that his jars are filled with goods and money, that he possesses huge fields, that his house is big, that he possesses pearls and jewels of great price such as adzagba, gbloti, dzete and wodze, that he possesses rich materials, massive gold jewellery and chains, silk robes and expensive beverages in his house. He must have barrels of powder so that on the day of his death great salvoes can be fired in his honour or, should the City be attacked, he can help defend it. The notabilities enjoy the respect of both persons of the Chief's line and commoners. For these notabilities live like chiefs in their own homes and they house a numerous following, members of their families, servants, slaves and hostages. They are much respected because in times of misfortune it is they who afford help and assistance. They wear costly garments, long shoes, gold chains and rings and silk trousers. They go about accompanied by a retinue such as chiefs have. If the Chief and his counsellors wish to apply a law which the people do not consider just, the common citizens go to see the notabilities, who put the latter's point of view to the Chief and prevent the application of unjust laws. A fact that adds to the power of the notabilities is that when the people get into debt and the Chief is unable to pay this debt, the notabilities come to the assistance of the people. Unlike the Chiefs, their position is not hereditary, because they have no official stool. *606*

Ewe tradition
Togo

Fair distribution

Demosthenes Oration on Financial Organization c. 349 B.C.

The revenues of the City—both yours (that now disappear in unnecessary expenditure) and the payments of your allies—these, I say, must be so shared as to give each an equal part: the pay of those of military age and, for those above it, wages for supervising or whatever else their task may be. *607*

Mutual aid

The consequence of individual life without mutual aid is poverty; the consequence of corporate life without recognition of individual rights is strife. Poverty means anxiety; strife spells misfortune. In order to relieve anxiety and eradicate strife, nothing is as effective as the institution of corporate life based on a clear recognition of individual rights. *608*

Hsün-tzu
3rd cent. B.C.
China

Mutual obligations

The Exalted One was once staying near Rājagaha in the Bamboo Wood at the squirrels' feeding ground.

Now at this time young Sigāla, a householder's son, rising betimes, went forth from Rājagaha, and with wet hair and wet garments and clasped hands uplifted, paid worship to the several quarters of earth and sky: to the east, south, west and north, to the nadir and the zenith.

And the Exalted One early that morning dressed himself, took bowl and robe and entered Rājagaha seeking alms. Now he saw young Sigāla worshipping and spoke to him thus:

'Why, young householder, do you, rising betimes and leaving Rājagaha, with wet hair and raiment, worship the several quarters of earth and sky?'

'Sir, my father, when he was a-dying, said to me: "Dear son, you should worship the quarters of earth and sky." So I, sir, honouring my father's word, reverencing, revering, holding it sacred, rise betimes and, leaving Rājagaha, worship on this wise.'

'But in the religion of an Aryan, young householder, the six quarters should not be worshipped thus.'

'How then, sir, in the religion of an Aryan, should the six quarters be worshipped? It would be an excellent thing, sir, if the Exalted One would so teach me the doctrine according to which, in the religion of an Aryan, the six quarters should be worshipped.'

'Hear then, young householder, give ear to my words and I will speak.

. . . .

'And how, O young householder, does the Aryan disciple protect the six quarters? The following should be looked upon as the six quarters: parents as the east, teachers as the south, wife and children as the west, friends and companions as the north, servants and work people as the nadir, religious teachers and brahmins as the zenith.

'In five ways a child should minister to his parents as the eastern quarter: once supported by them I will now be their support; I will perform duties incumbent on them; I will keep up the lineage and tradition of my family; I will make myself worthy of my heritage.

'In five ways parents thus ministered to, as the eastern quarter, by their child, show their love for him: they restrain him from vice, they exhort him to virtue, they train him to a profession, they contract a suitable marriage for him, and in due time they hand over his inheritance.

'Thus is this eastern quarter protected by him and made safe and secure.

'In five ways should pupils minister to their teachers as the southern quarter: by rising [from their seat, in salutation] by waiting upon them, by eagerness to learn, by personal service, and by attention when receiving their teaching.

'And in five ways do teachers, thus ministered to as the southern quarter by their pupils, love their pupil: they train him in that wherein he has been well trained; they make him hold fast that which is well held; they thoroughly instruct him in the lore of every art; they speak well of him among his friends and companions. They provide for his safety in every quarter.

'Thus is this southern quarter protected by him and made safe and secure.

'In five ways should a wife as western quarter be ministered to by her husband: by respect, by courtesy, by faithfulness, by handing over authority to her, by providing her with adornment.

'In these five ways does the wife, ministered to by her husband as the western quarter, love him: her duties are well performed, by hospitality to the kin of both, by faithfulness, by watching over the good he brings, and by skill and industry in discharging all her business.

'Thus is this western quarter protected by him and made safe and secure.

'In five ways should a clansman minister to his friends and familiars as the northern quarter: by generosity, courtesy and benevolence, by treating them as he treats himself, and by being as good as his word.

'In these five ways thus ministered to as the northern quarter, his friends and familiars love him: they protect him when he is off his guard, and on such occasions guard his property; they become a refuge in danger, they do not forsake him in his troubles, and they show consideration for his family.

'Thus is the northern quarter by him protected and made safe and secure.

'In five ways does an Aryan master minister to his servants and employees as the nadir: by assigning them work according to their strength; by supplying them with food and wages; by tending them in sickness; by sharing with them unusual delicacies; by granting leave at times.

'In these ways ministered to by their master, servants and employees love their master in five ways: they rise before him, they lie down to rest after him; they are content with what is given to them; they do their work well; and they carry about his praise and good fame.

'Thus is the nadir by him protected and made safe and secure.

'In five ways should the clansman minister to recluses and brahmins as the zenith: by affection in act and speech and mind; by keeping open house to them, by supplying their temporal needs.

'Thus ministered to as the zenith, recluses and brahmins show their love for the clansman in six ways: they restrain him from evil, they exhort him to good, they love him with kindly thoughts; they teach him what he had not heard, they correct and purify what he has heard, they reveal to him the way to heaven.

'Thus by him is the zenith protected and made safe and secure.'

Sigālovāda Suttanta
Pali text

Thus spake the Exalted One. *609*

Mutual dependence

Then His Majesty the King of Majapahit asked permission to speak, and he said in a sweet voice: What people call 'equality', its manifestation, one says, is like this, whether the result be good or bad. If statute labour is to be performed, at the palace gate, etc., and somebody who is liable for it should appear undressed, or if you give a party and you see such a man in a disgusting attitude, then is the moment to abide by the [principle of] *sāmyalaksana* (*characteristics of equality*). . . .

If you have a guest, provide him with food, of such kind and in such quantity as *he* is accustomed to, even if he should leave your house at dawn.

One of your guests may be insolent, be violent or hurt you; then, whatever the bully shouts at you, whatever his social position may be, comply with his wishes, and if you want to make a complaint, make it to me.

Because the Royal Compound and the villages belonging to it are [mutually dependent] like lion and forest.

Nāgarakrtāgama
A panegyric by a
Court poet of the
Majapahit Kingdom
1365
Java

If the countryside should fall apart, if it should suffer heavy losses, the Royal Residency will be without food. 'No servants' means 'No King'; the foreigner will come to destroy. That is why both should be protected so that both survive, as a result of mutual understanding.

610

New Testament
St. Paul
Second Epistle
to the Corinthians, 8

For I mean not that other men be eased, and ye burdened: But by an equality, that now at this time your abundance may be a supply for their want, that their abundance also may be a supply for your want: that there may be equality: As it is written, He that had gathered much had nothing over; and he that had gathered little had no lack.

611

*Social stability
rests upon
the well-being
of the people*

For as towchinge this, that they thinke the defence and mayntenaunce of peace to consiste in the povertie of the people, the thing it selfe sheweth that they be farre out of the waye. For where shal a man finde more wrangling, quarrelling, brawling, and chiding, then among beggers? Who be more desierous of newe mutations and alterations, then they that be not content with the present state of their lyfe? Or finallye who be bolder stomaked to bringe all in a hurlieburlye (therby trustinge to get some windfal) then they that have nowe nothinge to leese? And yf any Kyng were so smally regarded, and so lightly estemed, yea so behated of his subjectes, that other wayes he could not kepe them in awe, but onlye by open wronges, by pollinge and shavinge, and by bringinge them to beggerie, sewerly it were better for him to forsake his kingedome, then to holde it by this meanes: whereby though the name of a king be kepte, yet the majestie is lost. For it is againste the dignitie of a kynge to have rule over beggers, but rather over ryche and welthie men.

Sir Thomas More
Utopia
1516
England
Trans. from Latin
into English

612

*A neighbour should
be kept friendly*

Look you, my grandson, a neighbour should be kept very friendly. Should you have little to eat, give some to your neighbour, and should you have plenty, give him some too. Say you go off to work and while you are away the children light a fire in the house. Suddenly, your house is on fire! If then you have kept your neighbour friendly and he hears the screams of the children, he will run in to them and if it is not burning much, he will draw water and pour it on your house. If it is completely ablaze, then he will put on a skin, cut loose the cattle and drive them into the open. Should he find assistance, he will save many things more. *613*

Chagga tradition
Tanzania

Sharing between brothers

EATING ALONE BRINGS RUIN

Listen, my grandchildren! You are the four sons born to one woman and you have grown up together. And you are one of the four and you think to yourself: 'I will be cleverer than the others!' and so as to be smarter than they are, you decide to eat all by yourself.

But what you eat alone you are robbing your kith and kin of. They, your brothers, have no knowledge of all this. They continue to treat you well. One of them has a goat to spare and invites you to come along. When he kills his goat, which came with the last litter, he calls you, the four of you. He invites you so that his brothers can eat their fill and carry their supper home with them.

You are the one among them who gives himself airs and comes before them. And the one who has saved the goat wishes you to be his father, as you are the first born among them. If God took your father away from you and he is no more, so you are their father, and he [the brother in question] reserves the piece of breast that goes to the father for you. So you get the piece of breast, and after you, your younger brothers share the carcass piece between them (*consisting of the first three ribs*). The fourth one though takes the rest of the carcass. That will be your marriage support (*i.e., for his children*).

If there is another brother of yours there, who is not the offspring of your father, he gets a hind leg and shares it with his neighbour who is helping to guard the home. And the brother who chose the goat will have a word with you and say: 'Look you, my older brother, as I had got this goat, I invited you all here and have now been your marriage support, just as you have left this piece of rib for me. If however there is someone left who wants to do us harm, that is your affair and is no longer any concern of mine (*i.e., I have done my duty and, for my part, arranged matters between us after our father's death on a new footing*).' But you leave them; they have made you important and you come home and get a fat belly.

You have given someone a goat to look after. You kill it there and bring its flesh home. Someone sees you on the way, stops to make sure it's you, and tells your brothers. When your brothers learn this, they say to one another:

Mask of wealth, lent by well-to-do families to those stricken by adversity
Cameroon

'Our brother has killed a goat.' They keep it in their heads and are silent about it.

Then you brew some beer, invite them and they come. You place a jar ready on one side with an infusion of bananas and water down the beer with it. And they say to you: 'This beer is very thin.' You answer them: 'Yes, there was only a little eleusine corn.' With troubled thoughts they go home. They are not light hearted as one normally is on taking leave of one's brother. It is as though they were taking leave of just anyone.

Look you, my grandson, when you have something to eat, ask an old man who takes precedence of you: 'Pray for us to the Heaven Man and to our tribal ancestor. Say: "We beg you, our ancestor, come together with the Heaven Man so that He should look down upon us. Should we keep food from each other, will you then, O Heaven Man! O chief! look down upon us and crush us. But if we show proper regard for each other, then let us rise up like the steam from brewing, so that we prosper. O Heaven Man let us thrive!" '

When you have done that and you, my grandson, then eat and keep things back [from the others], the Heaven Man will fix His eyes on you and not allow you to continue to thrive.

The seclusion in which you secretly eat and deprive your brothers will rather lead to your extinction (*i.e., to your being robbed of your children*).

And soon afterwards you yourself will disappear from the tribe. The solitariness to which your stomach has led you will be to blame.

Therefore I say to you, my grandson: if your brothers think you honest, don't go and leave their midst and eat alone. Solitude leads to much harm and an early death.

This I forbid you and say: let it be. Rather share honestly with your brothers. Let them see [everything] as they let you see [everything].

Chagga tradition
Tanzania

614

Sharing and not grabbing everything

Mongo proverb
Congo

One cannot eat the 'elímá' caterpillar in both cheeks.

One should not wish to have everything, to secure all the advantages and inherit property all for oneself; the others should be left something.

615

Akan proverb
Ghana

If one alone eats honey, it plagues his stomach.

616

A great lady
Life of
Juliana Lazarevskaja
(died 1604)
Written by her son
Russia

To her servants, men and women, she gave ample food and clothing; she allotted the work according to their strength; she called no one by a humiliating name; she did not send for water to wash her hands or have someone draw on her boots, but always served herself.   *617*

Social origin

Ivan Višenski
18th cent.
Ukraine

Is your head not in the same place as a poor man's? Will you not be judged for your life on this earth in the same way as he? . . . We have all been baptised in the faith over the same fonts and are all reborn from the same mother, which is grace.   *618*

Viet-Namese
proverb

The sons of mandarins will one day be mandarins, the sons of the poor will spend their days lighting coals.   *619*

'To each according to his needs'

Karl Marx
and Friedrich Engels
The German
Ideology
1845-46

One of the most essential principles of communism consists in the idea, empirically based on human nature, that differences of *brainpower* and of intellectual faculties in general entail no differences at all in food-*capacity* and physical needs; and that, consequently, the false maxim, based on existing conditions—'to each according to his abilities'—must, so far as it relates to entitlement in the strict sense of the term, be amended to give another maxim: '*To each according to his needs.*' In other words, *difference* in activity, in type of work, is no ground for *inequality*, or for any *privilege* in regard to possession or entitlement.   *620*

Friedrich Engels
Anti-Dühring
1878

How then can the important question of higher pay for skilled labour be solved? In the society of private producers, private persons or their families bear the cost of training the skilled worker, so that private persons benefit from the higher price payable for skilled labour: the skilled slave sells for more, the skilled employee commands a higher salary. In a socialist society, it is society that bears the costs of training. It is therefore society which is entitled to the fruits, the extra value of the skilled labour resulting therefrom. The worker himself has no extra rights.   *621*

Freedom for all depends on equality

Society must be so organized that all, man or woman, have the same chance to develop their faculties and use them in their work. To ensure this fully will doubtless take centuries; but history has set the problem, and to ignore it now would be to accept our impotence.

To be free, free men must surround me and recognize me of their number. . . . The freedom of all, far from limiting mine as the individualists would have it, fulfils, confirms my own and indefinitely prolongs it. To want all men free and self-respecting, to see and feel my liberty confirmed, approved and by common assent extended to infinity—therein lies happiness and paradise on earth.

Let all men's needs be each man's duty, let the material and social interests of each be kept in line with his human responsibilities. And, for this, there is but one way: destroy all institutions that make for inequality; install economic and social equality for all; and on this basis liberty, morality and human solidarity will become realities for all. *622*

Bakunin
1814-76
Russia

Freedom is the object of the people's life, the fruit of their sacrifice. Freedom exists, only where property is abolished; it behoves the people to sacrifice all their property for the sake of freedom, that is, for the sake of their life and their happiness. To sacrifice themselves materially for the sake of themselves spiritually is the people's true self-interest, since from this sacrifice freedom is born. Should anyone now ask us to prove that freedom is the absolute perfection of human life, we would reply that he is wanting in intelligence, for he knows naught of progress.

The absolute freedom of the people (hence also of the peoples and of mankind as a whole) presupposes their delivrance from all oppression. But oppression is of many kinds: there is physical oppression—the relation between the strong and the weak; there is oppression through property—the relation between the rich and the poor, which may be defined as dependence, as opposed to the first kind of oppression, which could be described as slavery; and there is oppression through the mind, oppression of the untutored by the intelligent, of the weak-minded by the brilliant reasoner. *623*

Edward Dembowski
The Absolute
Freedom
of the People
1843
Poland

Revolutionary
expropriation

Message to the All-Russian Peasant Assembly during the Russian Revolution.

To my deep regret, my health does not permit me to appear at such large gatherings as yours.

That is not all. Since I think it my duty to be entirely frank with you, I must say that, even if I were in good health, I might still not have prevailed upon myself to come and explain to you my views on certain aspects of our agrarian problem now that the revolution has happened....

Now to business. Before all else, let me congratulate you on the fact that it is under conditions of political freedom that your Assembly meets.

For centuries the Russian people, because of the unfortunate circumstances of its historical development, groaned under Tsarist oppression. It was by no means unheard of for the Government in Moscow to receive letters from even junior officials complaining that it was doing more to ruin them, with its intolerable bureaucratic methods, than had ever been done by Turk or Tatar. But their sufferings were as nothing compared with those which this Moscow—and later St. Petersburg—bureaucracy, and indeed everything about our former system, inflicted on the peasantry....

> ... Is there in all our Russian land, too vast to measure,
> One single, lonely spot (I know of none, I own)
> Where he who tills her soil—the steward of her treasure—
> Her Russian peasant son—cannot be heard to groan?
> He groans as in the fields or on the roads he swelters
> Or gropes for ore in chains, or languishes in gaol,
> Or on the steppe at night, when shivering he shelters
> In barn or rick, or seeks a cart's protection frail.
> He groans at home, in his own wretched habitation,
> For him the cheerful day has no relief in store;
> Each godforsaken town rings with his lamentation
> As—hope forlorn!—he waits outside the courthouse
>   door.
>
> (*Quotation from the poet Nekrasov*)

But however that may be, you all know that the old order has left behind it a considerable legacy of backwardness and ignorance among the people. It is this backwardness and ignorance that explains the disturbances which are constantly springing up—now in one place, now in another—and causing a great deal of disruption in the life of our entire country. An end can be put to such disturbances only by the working population itself, which will

willingly grapple with them once it realizes that their
multiplication is threatening to uproot our new, free order.
You, the intellectually aware representatives of the
peasantry, can do a great deal to help in making that
better known. . . .

Of course, most of the privately-owned land belongs
to the landed gentry. But there are now quite a few
peasants who also own land. In most cases such holdings
are very small. Surely you are not going to confiscate the
land of these private owners without compensation? That,
in my opinion, would be neither just nor prudent;
unjust because the small peasant landowners have often
paid for their land in money earned by the sweat of their
brows, and imprudent because, by confiscating their
land, you automatically risk making them into opponents
of our new order. They will say to themselves: 'In the
old days nobody touched our land; before, it was better',
and they will start supporting those who want to restore
the old order—and believe me, there are such people,
although they are keeping fairly quiet for the moment
and biding their time.

It seems to me that it would be better to pass a resolution
stating that private holdings not exceeding a certain
acreage shall remain undisturbed. . . .

Nevertheless, there are objections to the idea of expro-
priating landowners without compensation.

Take the case of a great landowner. His vast acreage
makes him a rich man. But he is rich only so long as he
is not expropriated. As soon as his land is taken away
without compensation he will become a pauper. He may
of course have money in the bank. In that case he will
not be ruined—provided he has enough of it. But if he
has no money, he will inevitably become a pauper. And
the same will happen to the vast majority of other private
landowners. Now tell me: is it in your interest to promote
pauperization in Russia? In my opinion it is not. It is
contrary to your interests and equally contrary to those
of the State. Private landowners must therefore be given
some sort of compensation; modest, of course—Russia
is too poor to pay out millions to the owners of vast estates
which their forbears received for services that had nothing
to do with the welfare of the people (think of the numerous
lovers of Catherine the Great for example)—but modest
compensation is essential, enough to save the former
landowners from ruin.

Plekhanov
In 'Edinstvo'
[Unity]
May 1917

You have conquered. But a victor, if he has the heart
of a lion, and not that of a wolf, will show magnanimity.

624

DECLARATION OF THE RIGHTS OF THE WORKERS AND
EXPLOITED PEOPLE

*A few days before the opening of the Constituent Assembly,
on 5 January 1918, Lenin drafted this Preamble, which he
intended as a preface to the future Constitution of the Russian
Socialist State.*

Russia is declared to be a republic of Soviets of workers',
soldiers' and peasants' deputies. All central and local
power is vested in these Soviets.

The Soviet Republic is based on a free union of free
nations, constituting a Federation of Soviet National
Republics.

The Constituent Assembly, taking as its tasks the
elimination of the exploitation of man by man, the total
abolition of class divisions in society, the relentless
suppression of resistance by exploiters, the establishment
of a socialist form of society and the victory of socialism
in all countries, decrees:

Private ownership of land is abolished. All land belongs
to the workers. The law on workers' control of enterprises
and the establishment of the Supreme Council of the
National Economy is ratified, as a first step towards the
complete transference of railways, mines, factories and
other means of production to the Workers' and Peasants'
State.

The law on the transference of all banks to the ownership
of the Workers' and Peasants' State is ratified, as one of
the conditions for freeing the toiling masses from the yoke
of capitalism....

Labour is henceforth made compulsory for all, in order
to eliminate parasitism in society.

In order to give all the power to the toiling masses and
to make it impossible for the exploiters to regain power,
it is decreed that the workers shall be armed, a socialist
Red Army of workers formed, and the propertied classes
completely disarmed. . . .

The Constituent Assembly welcomes the action of the
Soviet of People's Commissars in proclaiming the complete
independence of Finland, beginning to remove the troops
from Persia and allowing Armenia the right of self-
determination....

The Constituent Assembly believes that now, when the
people are engaged in their final struggle against their
exploiters, the latter can have no place in any organ
of government. Power should belong wholly and exclusively to the toiling masses and to their fully empowered

representatives, the Soviets of workers', soldiers' and peasants' deputies.

While supporting the Soviet authority and the laws promulgated by the Soviet of People's Commissars, the Constituent Assembly considers that it has no power beyond laying the foundations for the socialist reconstruction of society.   *625*

Abuses; inequalities; exploitation

The last judgement When the Son of man shall come in his glory, and all the holy angels with him, then shall he sit upon the throne of his glory:

And before him shall be gathered all nations: and he shall separate them one from another, as a shepherd divideth his sheep from the goats:

And he shall set the sheep on his right hand, but the goats on the left.

Then shall the King say unto them on his right hand, Come, ye blessed of my Father, inherit the kingdom prepared for you from the foundation of the world:

For I was an hungred, and ye gave me meat: I was thirsty, and ye gave me drink: I was a stranger, and ye took me in:

Naked, and ye clothed me: I was sick, and ye visited me: I was in prison, and ye came unto me.

Then shall the righteous answer him, saying, Lord, when saw we thee an hungred, and fed thee? or thirsty, and gave thee drink?

When saw we thee a stranger, and took thee in? or naked, and clothed thee?

Or when saw we thee sick, or in prison, and came unto thee?

And the King shall answer and say unto them, Verily I say unto you, Inasmuch as ye have done it unto one of the least of these my brethren, ye have done it unto me.

Then shall he say also unto them on the left hand, Depart from me, ye cursed, into everlasting fire, prepared for the devil and his angels:

For I was an hungred, and ye gave me no meat: I was thirsty, and ye gave me no drink:

I was a stranger, and ye took me not in: naked, and ye clothed me not: sick, and in prison, and ye visited me not.

Then shall they also answer him, saying, Lord, when saw we thee an hungred, or athirst, or a stranger, or naked, or sick, or in prison, and did not minister unto thee?

Then shall he answer them, saying, Verily I say unto you, Inasmuch as ye did it not to one of the least of these, ye did it not to me.

New Testament
St. Matthew 25   And these shall go away into everlasting punishment: but the righteous into life eternal.   *626*

Hadith
(Sayings
of the Prophet)   Allah has imposed a duty on the rich among Moslems to give a portion of what they possess to the poor. So if the poor are hungry and naked, it is the fault of the rich. Allah will call them to a strict account and they will be punished severely for it.   *627*

Hearken, ye powerful! The day of the Last Judgement is at hand. True Moslems are become rare, and those who pass for such are of doubtful quality.

Students of theology learn divers sciences, but act in contradiction to what they are taught. Dervishes no longer follow the straight path. The people are deaf to wise counsels. Oh sorry age!

No more generosity, no more charity among princes: they are a brave sight, mounted on their steeds; but what they eat is the flesh of the poor, what they drink is blood.

Yunus Emre
Folk-poet
13th cent.
Turkey   Men look upon themselves as each other's enemies. They think there will be no punishment for the evil they do. They do not consider that tomorrow the Last Judgement will be upon them and their deeds will come to light.   *628*

Victims

I'm going to eat, you can fast.
   (*Manifest injustice.*)

Amharic proverbs
Ethiopia   Tend the wounded, and do not forget the dead.   *629*

Brotherhood
and mobility

Vemana
15th cent.
Satakamu
Telugu tradition   Keep a common single plate before all people who live on this earth and make them take their food side by side. Let them be free to vary their caste and creed. Place your hand on your head to vow to bring all people to acceptance of this belief.   *630*

The wheel turns

When the waters rise the fish eat the ants; when the waters recede the ants eat the fish.   *631*

The poor

Hadith
(Sayings
of the Prophet)

He is not a perfect Moslem who eats his fill and leaves his neighbour hungry.   *632*

Rich, aid the poor, since they aid you as the rags round a naked body.

If you be wise, protect the ignorant since they protect you as sampans to the rescue of a great ship sinking.

Ye mighty, watch also over the weak.
If ye be full, feed the starving.
Khmer folk-poem
Cambodia
If blest by fortune, have a thought for the outcast.   *633*

Talmud
Boba Mezia
He who publicly shames his neighbour is as though he shed blood.   *634*

Mahatma Gandhi
1869-1948
It is good enough to talk of God whilst we are sitting here after a nice breakfast and looking forward to a nicer luncheon, but how am I to talk of God to the millions who have to go without two meals a day? To them God can only appear as bread and butter.   *635*

LOOKING AT THE HARVEST

For the peasants, few months without work;
But in the fifth month their toil is doubled.
During the night the South wind rises;
The corn covers the slopes with its gold.
Wives and daughters, basket on shoulder,
Young boys, pitcher in hand,
File out to the fields bearing food and drink.
The sturdy men on the southern hills,
Their feet scorched by contact with the hot, moist earth,
Their backs burned by the rays of the fiery sun,
Are so weary that they forget the heat,

But still find this summer day too short.
Here, too, are wretched women,
Hard by the harvesters, with babes in arms;
Their right hand gathers the fallen ears,
A torn basket hangs from their left shoulder.
I have listened to what they say among themselves:
Who would not be distressed to hear them?
'Our family fields have been sold to pay the tax;
My gleanings will have to suffice for our empty stomachs.'
And I, today, thanks to what merits
Have I never toiled in the fields or among the mulberries?
My official salary is three thousand bushels,
And at the end of the year I have grain left over.

Po Chü-I
772-846
China

This thought brings the blush of shame to my brow;
All day long it haunts me. *636*

A Russian merchant is struck by the inequalities of living standards in India.

Athanase Nikitin
Travels beyond
Three Seas
1466-72
Russia

The land is densely peopled, but the denudation of the country people is very great, whereas the boyars are extremely powerful and live opulently. *637*

The knight errant and the social hierarchy.

He [Don Quixote] had not gone far, when out of a thicket on his right there seemed to come feeble cries as of some one in distress, and the instant he heard them he exclaimed, 'Thanks be to Heaven for the favour it accords me, that it so soon offers me an opportunity of fulfilling the obligation I have undertaken, and gathering the fruit of my ambition. These cries, no doubt, come from some man or woman in want of help, and needing my aid and protection'; and wheeling, he turned Rosinante in the direction whence the cries seemed to proceed. He had gone but a few paces into the wood, when he saw a mare tied to an oak, and tied to another, and stripped from the waist upwards, a youth of about fifteen years of age, from whom the cries came. Nor were they without cause, for a lusty farmer was flogging him with a belt and following up every blow with scoldings and commands, repeating, 'Your mouth shut and your eyes open!' while the youth made answer, 'I won't do it again, master mine; by God's passion I won't do it again, and I'll take more care of the flock another time.'

Seeing what was going on, Don Quixote said in an angry voice, 'Discourteous knight, it ill becomes you to assail one who cannot defend himself; mount your steed and take your lance' (for there was a lance leaning against the oak to which the mare was tied), 'and I will make you know that you are behaving as a coward.' The farmer, seeing before him this figure in full armour brandishing a lance over his head, gave himself up for dead, and made answer meekly; 'Sir Knight, this youth that I am chastising is my servant, employed by me to watch a flock of sheep that I have hard by, and he is so careless that I lose one every day, and when I punish him for his carelessness and knavery he says I do it out of niggardliness, to escape paying him the wages I owe him, and before God, and on my soul, he lies.'

'Lies before me, base clown!' said Don Quixote. 'By the sun that shines on us I have a mind to run you through with this lance. Pay him at once without another word; if not, by the God that rules us I will make an end of you, and annihilate you on the spot; release him instantly.'

The farmer hung his head, and without a word untied his servant, of whom Don Quixote asked how much his master owed him.

He replied, nine months at seven reals a month. Don Quixote added it up, found that it came to sixty-three reals, and told the farmer to pay it down immediately, if he did not want to die for it.

The trembling clown replied that as he lived and by the oath he had sworn (though he had not sworn any) it was not so much; for there were to be taken into account and deducted three pairs of shoes he had given him, and a real for two blood-lettings when he was sick.

'All that is very well,' said Don Quixote; 'but let the shoes and the blood-lettings stand as a set-off against the blows you have given him without any cause; for if he spoiled the leather of the shoes you paid for, you have damaged that of his body, and if the barber took blood from him when he was sick, you have drawn it when he was sound; so on that score he owes you nothing.'

'The difficulty is, Sir Knight, that I have no money here; let Andres come home with me, and I will pay him all, real by real.'

'I go with him!' said the youth. 'Nay, God forbid! no, Señor, not for the world; for once alone with me, he would flay me like a Saint Bartholomew.'

'He will do nothing of the kind,' said Don Quixote; 'I have only to command, and he will obey me; and as he has sworn to me by the order of knighthood which he has received, I leave him free, and I guarantee the payment.'

'Consider what you are saying, señor,' said the youth; 'this master of mine is not a knight, nor has he received any order of knighthood; for he is Juan Haldudo the Rich, of Quintanar.'

'That matters little,' replied Don Quixote; 'there may be Haldudos knights; moreover, every one is the son of his works.'

'That is true,' said Andres; 'but this master of mine—of what works is he the son, when he refuses me the wages of my sweat and labour?'

'I do not refuse, brother Andres,' said the farmer; 'be good enough to come along with me, and I swear by all the orders of knighthood there are in the world to pay you as I have agreed, real by real, and perfumed' (*that is, completely*).

'For the perfumery I excuse you,' said Don Quixote; 'give it to him in reals, and I shall be satisfied; and see that you do as you have sworn; if not, by the same oath I swear to come back and hunt you out and punish you; and I shall find you though you should lie closer than a lizard. And if you desire to know who it is lays this command upon you, that you may be more firmly bound to obey it, know that I am the valorous Don Quixote of La Mancha, the undoer of wrongs and injustices; and so, God be with you, and keep in mind what you have promised and sworn under those penalties that have been already declared to you.'

So saying, he gave Rosinante the spur and was soon out of reach. The farmer followed him with his eyes, and when he saw that he had cleared the wood and was no longer in sight, he turned to his boy Andres, and said, 'Come here, my son, I want to pay you what I owe you, as that undoer of wrongs has commanded me.'

'My oath on it,' said Andres, 'your worship will be well advised to obey the command of that good knight—may he live a thousand years—for, as he is a valiant and just judge, by Roque, if you do not pay me, he will come back and do as he said.'

'My oath on it, too,' said the farmer; 'but as I have a strong affection for you, I want to add to the debt in order to add to the payment'; and seizing him by the arm, he tied him up to the oak again, where he gave him such a flogging that he left him for dead.

'Now, Master Andres,' said the farmer, 'call on the undoer of wrongs; you will find he won't undo that, though I am not sure that I have quite done with you, for I have a good mind to flay you alive as you feared.' But at last he untied him, and gave him leave to go look for his judge in order to put the sentence pronounced into execution.

Andres went off rather down in the mouth, swearing he would go to look for the valiant Don Quixote of La Mancha and tell him exactly what had happened, and that all would have to be repaid him sevenfold; but for all that, he went off weeping, while his master stood laughing.

*Cervantes
Don Quixote
1615*

638

*Scantily
paid labour*

These repartimientos (*Indians for the service of the Spaniards*) —or 'guatequi' (*hell*), as the Indians call them—were introduced and assumed their present form without order or specific mandate from the Catholic Monarchs who have reigned in Spain, contrary to the law passed by the Emperor Charles V of glorious memory when he commanded that the Indians should not be slaves or serve the Spaniards as slaves. In contravention of so just a law, the Viceroys, without order from the King of Spain, yielding to the demands of the Spaniards, ordered and contrived that, though the Indians might be free in name, they should not be so in actual fact, but should serve as slaves, compelling them and forcing them, and preventing them from enjoying their freedom, assigning them some wage so that they should have the name of day labourers, assessing the sweat of their brows and their labour at so little as is worth a cuarto or six maravedis in Spain, for the daily wage given them in over twenty years was no more than one cuartillo for a full day's work, without food or any other thing; and this was paid to them only at the end of the eight days, when they ceased to give service. . . . Later, the order was given to pay them half a real each day, and in New Spain half a real is not worth so much as one cuartillo in Spain, and for so miserable a wage, with no food given them at all, they served for more than thirty years. And as Indian labour costs so little, great was the avarice of the Spaniards, and a Spaniard hired twenty or thirty Indians and made use of them for whatever he wanted, and in giving them after the eight days as many cuartillos or half reales, he thought that he had paid them more than they deserved, and at other times he gave them nothing, but kept everything, for such has been the heartlessness of many Spaniards: to hold in no esteem the labour and service of the Indians and to care nothing for failing to pay them their just wage.

*Juan Ramírez
Notes on the
Personal Service
required
of the Indians
1595
New Spain*

639

Women's works.
The knacker's yard
1826, Paris

Diamond washers
1828, Brazil

The right of peoples
to their identity.
An Indian chief on his way
to and from Washington
19th cent.

'The proud poor'
Late 16th cent., Venice

The Indians are further wronged by the overseers who are in the mines and will not let them come down from the hills on Sundays to rest in their homes, because they begin work early on Monday; giving them a task to do each day, in accordance with which they are paid for their work, e.g., six small bags daily, and at the end of the week to him who has produced thirty there is paid the wage for five days and not six. It is just that this be remedied with the utmost vigilance, for His Majesty further orders in his Royal Charter that the hours of work of the Indians are to be assessed and moderated. *640*

Alfonso Mesía
Venegas
On the Regulations
concerning
the Personal Service
required of the
Peruvian Indians
1603

Ballad sung by gaucho singers to an accompaniment on the guitar.

Two things a man has to have
   if he wants to live among us:
He must be young and proud
   and have a good seat on a horse.
And I say sing and sing again,
   the little song of the thorn-bush,
And it's just as well that he should be
   pretty ready with his knife.

It's better to be lean and go about
   like an eagle, without a care,
Than to weep for ever a prisoner
   bound down by heavy chains.
Song, real song, and no mistake,
   hang on to your chocolate;
Here every man jack is an Indian
   and his only drink is maté.

. . . .

What the King worries about
   is the lack of silver and gold mines;
But to put up with this calamity
   join me in singing this refrain:
My little singer, I say No,
My little singer, I say Yes,
Let old Don Fernando receive
Something to remind him of Potosí.

The times have gone by, thank God!
   when rational human beings
Died like bloody flies
   at the bottom of those mines.
Singer, those kings of Spain—
   what cursed tricksters they were.
They christianized us with one hand
   and stole our money with the other. *641*

'Cielito'
from Casa-Flores
Attributed to
Bartolomé Hidalgo
Gaucho soldier
and poet
1788-1823
Uruguay

Hungarian folk-song

More miserable than the peasant there is none
For his wretchedness is vaster than the sea
Night and day he is afoot, never at rest.

The day long he labours and toils in vain
Pays tithe, but is unthanked. Found guilty,
He goes to jail without bread or water.

In his home, unchecked, the dragoons carouse
Look sharp!—dare not to curse—serve up food
Or else—the swaggerer's boot on your rump.

The judge with his taxes, the cleric with his stole, the
    merchant with his wine,
Distrain on your house and goods for ready money
Mid-18th cent.   All is fair game to them, sometimes even your shirt.   *642*

Misery
of the peasants

TIBORC:
The haughty Meranians ride as they will
On lively mounts: white-stockinged,
Grey, red-roan, each day a new one;
For us, if we want the seed to grow,
It's wife and brats we have to saddle.
For them the feasting never stops.
Has their body in its slightest folds
A stomach? You'd almost think so.
The storks have abandoned our chimney pots
For we eat up even the scraps.
Shameless, they make our good plots of earth
Their hunting ground, and forbid us
Ever to go near them. Ah! Woe unto us
If, to make happy a sick woman
Or a poor pox-stricken child
We beat down a young pigeon;
In a twinkling we are put in the stocks.
He who robs human beings by the thousand
Sits in judgement on the man who steals
From dire necessity, a farthing.

BÁNK:
It's true!

TIBORC:
Not a holy place, monastery, or church,
But from it issues the gay sound of a flute.
The music sounds so far and loud
That the pilgrims dance outside.
Ah! if only we had a decent coat
To cover us, to pray

Before the statue of our kind
And holy Patron!

BÁNK:
How your blood seethes!

TIBORC:
Do we sometimes long to express our suffering?
We must first learn to write
For we peasants are no longer permitted
To present ourselves before our lord and master:
A poor man's boots would soon
Damage his fine floor!   *643*

Jozsef Katona
1791-1830
Bánk Bán
(The Palatine Bánk)
Act 3
Hungary

*Inequality
of conscription*

With us, the conscripts are roped:
Hands tied behind their backs, to Kassa under armed escort
Our poor lads will be taken away.

Five, six sons in the rich man's house: hands off!
The poor man has one son only: take him!
To his mother who follows weeping,
To his father who offers money,
No! replies the laughing lord.

Go home poor churl,
Rear other sons
To make fine soldiers.

Patience, God will punish
Him who took away by force
The poor man's only son.   *644*

Hungarian
folk-song
Early 19th cent.

The stranger

A stranger may not even skin a guinea-fowl.
    The stranger has no political rights. He is only a guest
and must refrain from interfering in the affairs of clans
and families.   *645*

Mongo proverb
Congo

Exile and poverty

To what land shall I flee? Where bend my steps?
I am thrust out from family and tribe;
I have no favour from the village to which I would belong,
Nor from the wicked rulers of the country:
How then, O Lord, shall I obtain thy favour?

I know, O Wise One, why I am powerless:
My cattle are few, and I have few men.
To thee I address my lament: attend unto it, O Lord,
And grant me the support which friend would give to friend.
As Righteousness teach the possession of the Good Mind.

Avesta
The Gathas
of Zarathustra
pre-6th cent. B.C.
Trans. by
M. Henning

When, O Wise One, shall the will of the future saviours
    come forth,
The dawns of the days when, through powerful judgment,
    the world shall uphold Righteousness?
To whom will help come through the Good Mind?
To me, for I am chosen for the revelation by thee, O Lord.

646

THE ÉMIGRÉ

Almighty God, my God, great is thy name!
Send the exile a country, but let him not fall sick!
For those that are sick need a bed and pillows,
Mothers and sisters, brothers and cousins.

. . . .

Would that I had the sky for paper and the sea for ink
    to set down my sorrows and my lament,
And what these eyes of mine, poor eyes, have seen, what
    have they seen indeed!
How a stranger is bundled into his winding-sheet and
    buried
Without incense or candle, without priest and without

Greek folk-song

    chorister!

647

THE DEATH OF THE ÉMIGRÉ

Curse me, mother, drive me out, for I want to go away,
    away with the galleys, the great ships;
And it will be years before you see me and months that you
    must wait;
When Saint George's day comes round, the first feast of
    the year,
You will go to the church, mother, and make the sign of
    the Cross,
You will see the young men, the girls and boys,
You will see my empty place, my vacant pew
And when they come out of church, you will go to the
    crossroads. . . .

There were travellers at the crossroads, travellers there are.
'Good day, travellers!' 'Good day, grieving mother!'
'Have you not seen my son, my darling boy?'
'Tell us how should we know him, for perhaps indeed we
    have.'
'He had a mole upon his cheek and underneath his arm
    another
And on his chest he bore a picture of a girl.'

'The other night we saw him, lying on a marble floor.
Black birds devoured his flesh and white birds hovered
    round him
And a bird, a golden bird, began to weep for him.'

Eat too, lovely bird, eat of these brave shoulders
    if you would have broad wings and fine feathers,
And write on your wing three bitter words.
Fly with one to my mother, with another to my sister,
    and the third, the bitterest of all, take to my true love.
Let my mother read and my sister weep,
My sister read and my true love weep,
My true love read and the whole world weep!

Greek folk-song   *648*

THE LORD AND THE LESSER MAN

Near the house of a great lord there once lived a poor but
determined man who worked hard, trying to model his
affairs on those of his illustrious neighbour. Before long,
he had built up a considerable fortune.

Hearing this, the lord sent for him and said: 'Friend,
you must give me all your wealth, which is mine by right
since you acquired it by copying me.'

Outraged, our friend protested hotly, for he had no
desire to lose the fruits of all his labour.

The dispute grew violent and the case had soon to be
submitted to the King, who summoned them both to his
presence. The lord was the first to speak: 'Your Majesty,
this man's fortune reverts to me because, living near, he
imitated everything I did and shamelessly patterned his
affairs on mine.'

'I worked all alone, and made great sacrifices,' the man
replied. 'No one ever helped me. Why should he unjustly
appropriate my fortune?'

To cut the matter short, the King asked whether they
had any children. One replied that he had a daughter,
the other, a son.

'Fine,' said the King. 'Marry your children and then
you will have no need to split up your fortunes. And in
Khmer tale   future, let me ask you to avoid distinctions between rich
Cambodia   and poor. One man is as good as another.'   *649*

THE BLACK MAN :

The Law was made for all,
But it only governs the poor.
Watch! It's like a spider's web;
Ignorant as I am, I see this:
The rich are not afraid of it,
The powerful just ignore it;
Big fish break through the net,
But the little fish get caught.

The Law is like the rain
Which never falls quite the same
José Hernández   Bad luck for him on whom it drops!
La Vuelta   But it's all as clear as day:
de Martín Fierro   The Law's like a knife, it does
1879
Argentina   No harm to the hand that wields it.   *650*

I come to implore you, master, not to take my land away
from me. It is mine. I'm the one who sowed it. . . .
    Thou, Pedro Quispe, thou art not the owner of this
Ricardo Jaime   land. What title to property therein canst thou show?—in
Freyre   other words, where are thy papers?
1868-1933   I have no papers, master. Neither did my father before
Justicia India   me have any, nor yet my father's father, for that matter.
Bolivia
                                                                    651

Intellectuals   They call themselves intellectuals, but they speak con-
descendingly to their servants, and treat the muzhiks like
animals. . . . They are all grave, severe-looking people, and
they talk only about important matters . . . yet all the time,
before their eyes, their labourers eat in disgusting
conditions, sleep without pillows, thirty or forty to a
room, and everywhere there are bugs, stench, damp, and
Anton Chekhov   moral filth. . . . And of course the sole purpose of all our
The Cherry Orchard   fine talk is to distract our own and other people's attention
1904
Russia   from this.   *652*

Domestic tyranny   They made a boulevard—but not to walk on it. . . . The
poor, Sir, never go walking, they are too busy day and
night, and sleep maybe three hours in the twenty-four.
And the rich? . . . They have all long ago bolted their gates
and let the dogs loose. . . . You think they have business or
are saying their prayers? No, Sir! And they have not
locked for fear of thieves, but to prevent people from
seeing how they misuse their families and tyrannize them.

All the tears that no one sees that are shed behind these locks! And behind them too, all the dirty, drunken debauchery! But it's all well hidden, no one sees or knows a thing, only God. . . . Family life, they tell you, is close and secret. As if we didn't know about their secrets! These secrets, Sir, are for the amusement of one, the others can cry their eyes out.

Talk about secrets! Everyone knows what goes on— swindling orphans, cheating relatives near and distant, beating up the household so that no one dares breathe a word about it all. *653*

Aleksandr Ostrovski
The Storm
1860
Russia

Proletariat

In proportion as the bourgeoisie, i.e., capital, is developed, in the same proportion is the proletariat, the modern working class, developed—a class of labourers, who live only so long as they find work, and who find work only so long as their labour increases capital. These labourers, who must sell themselves piece-meal, are a commodity, like every other article of commerce, and are consequently exposed to all the vicissitudes of competition, to all the fluctuations of the market.

Owing to the extensive use of machinery and to division of labour, the work of the proletarians has lost all individual character, and, consequently, all charm for the workman. He becomes an appendage of the machine, and it is only the most simple, most monotonous, and most easily acquired knack, that is required of him. Hence, the cost of production of a workman is restricted, almost entirely, to the means of subsistence that he requires for his maintenance, and for the propagation of his race. But the price of a commodity, and therefore also of labour, is equal to its cost of production. In proportion, therefore, as the repulsiveness of the work increases, the wage decreases. Nay more, in proportion as the use of machinery and division of labour increases, in the same proportion the burden of toil also increases, whether by prolongation of the working hours, by increase of the work exacted in a given time, or by increased speed of the machinery, etc.

Modern industry has converted the little workshop of the patriarchal master into the great factory of the industrial capitalist. Masses of labourers, crowded into the factory, are organized like soldiers. As privates of the industrial army they are placed under the command of a perfect hierarchy of officers and sergeants. Not only are they slaves of the bourgeois class, and of the bourgeois state; they are daily and hourly enslaved by the machine, by the overlooker, and, above all, by the individual bourgeois manufacturer himself. The more openly this despotism proclaims gain to be its end and aim, the more petty, the more hateful and the more embittering it is.

The less the skill and exertion of strength implied in manual labour, in other words, the more modern industry becomes developed, the more is the labour of men superseded by that of women. Differences of age and sex have no longer any distinctive social validity for the working class. All are instruments of labour, more or less expensive to use, according to their age and sex.

No sooner is the exploitation of the labourer by the manufacturer so far at an end that he receives his wages in cash, than he is set upon by other portions of the bourgeoisie, the landlord, the shopkeeper, the pawnbroker, etc.

The lower strata of the middle class—the small tradespeople, shopkeepers, and retired tradesman generally, the handicraftsmen and peasants—all these sink gradually into the proletariat, partly because their diminutive capital does not suffice for the scale on which modern industry is carried on, and is swamped in the competition with the large capitalists, partly because their specialized skill is rendered worthless by new methods of production. Thus the proletariat is recruited from all classes of the population.

Karl Marx and Friedrich Engels Communist Manifesto 1848

654

The factory system

The slavery in which the bourgeoisie has bound the proletariat is nowhere more evident than in the factory system. Here all freedom ceases, both in law and in fact. The worker has to be at the factory at five-thirty in the morning; if he arrives one or two minutes late, he is punished; if he arrives ten minutes late, he is not admitted until after breakfast, and loses a quarter of a day's wage (though he has missed only $2\frac{1}{2}$ hours out of 12). He must eat, drink and sleep to order; for his most urgent needs, he is allowed only the strict minimum of time. His employer is not concerned with the fact that he may live half an hour or an hour's distance away from the factory. The despotic bell calls him from bed, calls him from breakfast and from dinner.

And what a life he leads once he gets to the factory! Here the employer has supreme power. He lays down the factory rules as he pleases, changing and adding anything he wishes. . . .

I shall be told that such rules are necessary, in a large, well-run factory, to ensure the necessary liaison between the various operations; that such strict discipline is necessary there, no less than in the army. That may be so; but then, what kind of a social system is it that cannot exist without such ignominious tyranny? There are but two possibilities: either the end justifies the means, or else the injustice of the means is an indication of the injustice of the end. Anyone who has been a soldier knows what it is to live, even for a short time, under military discipline; yet here we have workers condemned, from the age of nine until they die, to live under the threat of moral and physical brutality, slaves more wretched than the negroes of America, because they are more closely supervised—and expected, in addition, to live, think and feel like men!

Friedrich Engels
The Situation of the
Working Classes
in England
1845

655

Casting aside the division of responsibility so warmly advocated by the bourgeoisie, and its cherished representative system, the capitalist formulates the factory code, like a private legislator and at his own good will, establishing his autocracy over his work people. But this code is only a caricature of that social regulation of the labour-process which becomes requisite in large-scale co-operation and in the employment in common of instruments of labour and especially of machinery. The slave-driver's lash is replaced by the overseer's book of penalties. All punishments naturally resolve themselves into fines and deductions from wages, and the wily mind of the factory Lycurgus so arranges matters that a violation of his laws is even more profitable to him than the keeping of them.

Karl Marx
Das Kapital
1867

656

THE COLLIER

I dig, underground I dig,
Lumps glittering like a snake's skin I dig,
I dig the ground beneath Polska Ostrava.

My lamp is going out, on my forehead falls
My tangled hair clammy with sweat,
Gall and acid flood my eyes,
Veins swell and my scalp is steaming,
From under my nails the red blood runs,
I dig, underground I dig.

Heavy hammer in hand I strike at the coal-face,
At Salmovec I dig,
I dig at Rychvald, I dig at Pětvald.

At home my wife shivers and moans,
In her lap our children are crying for bread,
I dig, underground I dig.

Sparks fly from the coal-face, sparks flash from my eyes,
At Dombrava I dig, at Orlová I dig,
I dig at Poremba and I dig under Lazy.

Overhead I hear the clatter of hooves—
The count drives through the village and the rose-cheeked
    countess
Speeds the horses with a wave of the hand.

I dig, I lift up my pick,
Pale as ashes, her breasts dry of milk,
My wife goes to the castle to ask for bread.

. . . .

Why did she go there to crave and beg?
Does the master's rye grow for a miner's woman?
I dig at Hrušov and at Michalkovice.

Descending
the mine shaft
c. 1860

How will my lads fare, how my daughters,
When they drag my dead body up from the pit?
My lad will be digging, always digging,
At Karviná digging
And my girls—how is it with the lass of a miner?

What if one day I should toss my damned lamp down
    the pit,
Raise my bowed neck,

Petr Bezruč
1920
Czechoslovakia
Trans. by
J. Milner

Clench my left fist, stride forward
And in a half-circle from ground to sky
Lift up my hammer with burning eyes
There in God's sunlight!

657

The mother

She spoke again about what was new to her, and inexpressibly important. She began to talk about her life, its humiliations and resignation to suffering. . . . Nicholas and Sophia listened to her in silence, overwhelmed by the depth of meaning in this simple story of a human being who had been treated like an animal and had herself long and uncomplainingly felt herself to be what they thought her. Thousands of lives seemed to be speaking with her mouth. All she had experienced was everyday and commonplace, but countless people all over the earth lived just such commonplace, uneventful lives, and her story took on the force of a symbol.   *658*

Maxim Gorki
Mother
1906
Russia

*Respect and succour
to the hungry*

The fact that a human being possesses an eternal destiny imposes only one obligation: respect. The obligation is only performed if the respect is effectively expressed in a real, not a fictitious way; and this can only be done through the medium of Man's earthly needs.

On this point, the human conscience has never varied. Thousands of years ago, the Egyptians believed that no soul could justify itself after death unless it could say: 'I have never let anyone suffer from hunger.' All Christians know they are liable to hear Christ himself say to them one day: 'I was an hungred, and ye gave me no meat.' Everyone looks on progress as being, in the first place, a transition to a state of human society in which people will not suffer from hunger. To no matter whom the question may be put in general terms, nobody is of the opinion that any man is innocent if, possessing food himself in abundance and finding some one on his doorstep three parts dead from hunger, he brushes past without giving him anything. So it is an eternal obligation towards the human being not to let him suffer from hunger when one has the chance of coming to his assistance. This obligation being the most obvious of all, it can serve as a model on which to draw up the list of eternal duties towards each human being.   *659*

Simone Weil
The Need for Roots
1942-43
France

THE WINE AND THE WATER

I. Krasicki
Fables
1779
Poland

Said the wine to the water, puffed up with pride,
'I am the drink of princes; none but yokels drink you.'
'If the princes drink you,' softly answered the water,
'It's thanks to the silver they've reft from the poor.'   *660*

JERNEJ THE SERVANT AND HIS RIGHTS

'Both the law of man and the commands of God teach
the servant to obey his master. But there is also another
law, which, though unwritten, is respected everywhere;
there is also a command of Christ enjoining the master
not to drive away his servant when he reaches the end
of his service and is old and feeble. That is why, Jernej,
I tell you to seek out your master and explain this to him,
and he will take pity on you.'

But Jernej grew angry and cried: 'It is not at the door
of charity I am knocking, but at the door of justice, that
it may be opened wide: He who has been master of the
house for forty years is neither a beggar nor a stranger:
He who has built the house with his own hands is not
left without a roof over his head! It is not right that he who
has tilled vast fields should beg for bread. If the labour
was yours, the product is yours: that is the law! I shall
demand justice, and justice will be granted me. If you,
dull-witted, unjust judges, refuse me justice, I tell you,
the world is wide, there are many judges higher placed
than you, and, above them all, there is God.'   *661*

Ivan Cankar
1876-1918
Slovene poet

*Condition
of the workers*

After the revolution of 1905.

Those were the days!
Beggars in their heyday,
Rose in anger, celebrated
And to Siberia got translated.

Farewell my head office nook,
Farewell Zlatoust factory,
Off to penal camps they drive us:
We who stood for liberty
And stood by the people.   *662*

Chastushki
(Folk-poetry)
Russia

Condition
of women

The pretty lass weeps bitter tears,
Your heart would break to see them
Mourning for her flaxen plaits
And good-bye to freedom.

Soothingly her father speaks
Persuasively her mother:
Not as a slave we send you forth
But as a bride, they urge her,

Brother now to sister tells:
Sister, my little sister,
Wear gold, but do not wear it out,
Bear grief, but don't parade it.

Pulse of my heart, O brother mine
Surely, my dear, you know it:
Chastushki
(Folk-poetry)
Russia

Gold that is worn must needs wear out,
Grief that is deep craves telling. 663

THE REPUDIATED WIFE

For no reason, we were joined:
For no reason, we part.
Then, two mandarin ducks;
Now two clouds driven eastward and westward.

Clouds drift with the wind,
But my heart resembles them little.
Yours, inconstant,
Forsakes me like a withered blade of grass.

On my way to salute your parents once more,
I keep looking back.
I grieve to see my footprints
On the road by which I came.

I leave two moon-coloured pearls;
My successor will make them into earrings.
I scarcely hate her for stealing your love from me
And I want the pearls to remain with you.

My mirror shall stay forever in its casket
With the dust from your house.
I shall not have the courage to wipe it away,
For it will keep me close to the old memories.

Of my life nothing remains.
How can I say all that is in my heart?
Chao Chih-hsin
17th cent.
China

Would that I could give you the golden-glinting herb
That your days might have no end! 664

The poor, whose place is close beside the prince

Whilst the time allows, let us do as Saint Paul bids: *Alter alterius onera portate:* 'Bear ye one another's burdens.' Rich man, bear the burden of the poor man, comfort him in his need, help him to support the afflictions under whose weight he groans; but know that in unburdening him you are unburdening yourself: when you give to him, you are easing his load and he is easing yours: your abundance is a supply for his want, and his want lightens the burden of your abundance. Exchange your burdens with each other 'that there may be an equality': *ut fiat aequalitas,* says Saint Paul. For how unjust it is, my brethren, that the poor should bear all the burden and that all the weight of misfortune should be upon their shoulders! If they complain and if they murmur against Divine Providence, permit me, O Lord, to say that it is with some justification: for since we are all moulded of the same clay and between clay and clay there cannot be any great difference, why on one side do we see joy, prosperity and wealth; and on the other misery, despair and dire need, scorn and servitude?

. . . In all kingdoms and in all empires there are the privileged, eminent persons who have extraordinary rights: and the source of these privileges is that they are, by birth or office, closer to the person of the Prince. The majesty, the state and grandeur of the sovereign, and the lustre of his crown reflect to some degree upon those who approach him. Since we learn in the Holy Scriptures that the Church is such a well-ordered kingdom, have no doubt, my brethren, that it also has its privileged members. And whence shall they have these privileges, if not from the company of its Prince, that is to say, of Jesus Christ? For if they must be one with the Saviour, Christians, let us not seek the privileged of the Holy Church among the rich. The crown of our monarch is a crown of thorns and all its lustre is affliction and suffering. It is in the poor and the suffering that the majesty of this spiritual kingdom resides. Since Jesus himself was poor and needy, it was becoming that he should keep company with his equals and bestow his favours upon his companions in misfortune.

Let poverty no longer be scorned, let it no longer be called base. It is true that it came from the dregs of the people; but the King of Glory having espoused it, he has ennobled it by this marriage and henceforward he bestows on the poor all the privileges of his empire. He promises the kingdom to the poor, consolation to those who weep, food to those who are hungry and joy eternal to those who suffer. If all the rights, all the graces, all the privileges

Bossuet Sermon sur l'Émi- nente Dignité des Pauvres dans l'Église 1659	of the Gospel belong to the poor in Jesus Christ, what is left for you, O ye rich, and what share shall you have in his kingdom? *665*

*The power
of money*
Turkish proverbs
11th cent.
Eastern Turkestan

Wealth causes even the doors of Hell to open.

As the wind scatters the black clouds, so are the people to be won with money.   *666*

Social injustice

The people is a fine fat sheep's tail there for the devouring.

How could the donkey travel side by side with a horse? How could the dispossessed be treated like a brother by a rich man?

Do not disturb the sated man, nor set the hungry man to work.

Turkish proverbs
15th cent.

At the command of Princes the poor weep blood.   *667*

Turkish proverb

Man is [happy] not on his native [soil] but [in the country] where he finds food.   *668*

Asoka's Pillar Edict V
3rd cent. B.C.
Prakrit

A living being should not be allowed to feed on another living being.   *669*

Rigveda X
Sanskrit

Indeed, gods have not ordained hunger to be a kind of capital punishment. Whoever eats alone has also to suffer the sin alone.   *670*

Elementary needs

Thou shouldst attend to the body's needs and especially food which is the prime condition of life.

. . . .

Nahuatl tradition
Mexico

There is not a person in the world who is not obliged to eat and drink.   *671*

Human anguish

Who seeks to conquer us? Maybe death is present here? How will this all-conquering power fall upon us? Perhaps the ruling element here is sickness—dysentery, coughs, fever, tuberculosis?

Nahuatl tradition
Mexico

. . . .

Why must the people disappear and be dispersed?   *672*

The hungry man does not listen to reason, just as the sated man knows no care.

When the rich man works, he is called active; when he does not work, he is called retiring; when he speaks, he is called eloquent; when he does not speak he is called well-bred. When the poor man works, he is called incapable; when he does not work he is called lazy; when he speaks, he is called garrulous; when he does not speak he is called dumb.

To him who chops the wood, one portion; to him who only talks about it, two.

Turkmenian proverbs

The farmer rests in the snowy season; the shepherd only in the grave. *673*

Provision against barren seasons

Each principal province had a large number of storehouses, full of provisions and other things necessary and useful for man's needs; should there be war, wherever the troops might have to go, supplies were drawn from these depots, without touching what their allies had, or anything from what might be found in the villages; and if there was no war, the whole multitude of provisions was divided among the poor and the widows. These poor were those who were too old, or lame, crippled or maimed, or had other infirmities; for, should they be well, they were not to receive anything. And after, they must refill the depots from the tribute they were obliged to give; and should there come a year of great want, the orders likewise were to open the depots and loan the required provisions to the provinces; and later, in some year of abundance, each gave and returned back the exact measure. *674*

*Pedro Cieza de León
Spanish chronicler
of Peru
16th cent.*

A poor man

*A folk-song
of the Valais
(Switzerland)
1514*

I am an old man
And I try to deal justly with everyone,
I have done so for a long time:
That is why I have become poor. *675*

A MERRY SONG OF POOR PEOPLE

The winter has come,
Come here, poor people.
You have slept long,
And you have no coat.
In spring you sleep
And do not care

The condition
that justifies power:
protection
Dahomey

Mercy to a prisoner
Mogul miniature
17th cent.

Noah's Ark
Mozarabic miniature, 9th cent., Turin

That winter brings
A sorrow deep.
Your clothing is poor.

The snow will come,
You will be sad.
You have no shirt,
Your coat is wretched,
You have no trousers,
The wind blows hard,
There is no hope.
The storm comes,
Another follows
And makes us forlorn.

Our cowls are torn,
What shall we wear?
We have not sown,
The fields are bare,
The heart is sad.
There is no sheaf.
What shall we do?
Just sing a song,
Leave it to God.

Almighty God,
Alone knows
To whom to give.
You cannot complain.
To those he loves
He gives gold,
He gives food,
And with all this
His favour, too.

.   .   .   .

There in the inn,
There is no drink
For us, the poor.
How can we sing,
When our glasses are dry,
When we are full of grief?
What shall we do?
Just sing a song,
Leave it to God.

Just a little work,
And we could drink,
We could eat
All that's so costly
We could buy bread

And order beer.
All that is possible,
If we have work.
But we are poor.

Friday is
A feast day.
Cold water, groats,
So ill-tasting
With sour sauce.
There will be fish,
Danube eels.
What a good dish,
What a good meal!

On the next day,
Let us work again.
On Sunday, no,
No toil, no stress.
Let us sit down,
The wretched ones.
The wind will cook
Our morning meal
And our dinner.

The white fog makes
Our gruel sweet
And darkness brings
Us meat in dreams.
All will eat.
But if the dishes
Are not good,
The cooks will get
What they deserve!

Czech folk-song
14th cent.
Trans. by
K. Fink and
E. Pavlátová

676

SONG OF BALADÍZ

That summer of the year 1946
They were winnowing the grain at Baladíz.
On Demiralay's land, in the cloud of dust,
Death was present: it hovered, wheeling in the air like a
    bird of prey.

Confiscation is there, ruiner of hearths.
The bailiffs arrive: some to gather taxes, others to draw
    up reports.
It is soul-destroying, the men are tired of living.
If things go on like this, there will be sharpening of knives.

The peasants have proposed a friendly arrangement, the
    master has refused to listen.

The lord has no more pity, his peasants no more patience.
The police were called, they were slow in coming;
The black earth will therefore be soaked in the lord's blood.

Demiralay was a powerful lord among us.
His camels come and go in numerous caravans.
His lands, vast plains, extend from Isparta to Baladíz,
And the river Aksu bounds them on one side.

Reason can no longer comprehend the workings of fate.
There are times when it is no use being a Bey or a Pasha.
A stone comes flying at the [haughty] head,
And the son of man is not immortal: he is laid low by a

Turkish folk-song   mere nothing.   677

Shepherd songs collected by school-teachers in Peru
(original in Quechua)

I

Sheepfold tell me
If the ram be missing
Or any lamb.

Wretched bailiff,
Wretched mistress,
When I asked you for my wage
You told me, I have bought you shoes.
I have no shoes!

Alone all year, alone all year
The young ewe
The young ram
With their eyes like crystals
With their eyes like pearls
They go to pick flowers.

My fox, little fox,
Your ears like thorns,
You rob me, I am in debt!
My condor, little condor,
Where are your crystal slippers?

Wretched master,
I am a poor shepherdess.
The snow forms a cap on my head
The mist is my blanket,
The anchu is my food,
My breakfast the juice of thorns.
Is this all you can give me,
Wretched master?
Is this all you have for me,
Wretched mistress?

II

With your animals I suffer here;
Eating the fruit
Of cactus, pea and chicarhuay
I tend your sheep!

You do not come, you do not remember me.
Today, and next day, I watch the road;
'This will be he, that will be he,' I say; and it is not you!
Only the huarahuay (*a bird of the puna, an arid tableland*)
   draws near.
'This will be he, that will be he,' I say, and I see nothing
   but lengthening shadows,
Only my shadow by my side.

Wretched little master
Only now you remember me!
With your burnt cancha (*toasted maize*).
With your dry bread.
And your fellow the fox steals your sheep from me
While I, with the snow for a cap
And the mist for a blanket,
I tend your animals, wretched master!   *678*

The victims

*Swift's macabre humour ironically points up the idea of
'human rights'.*

It is a melancholy object to those who walk through
this great town, or travel in the country, when they see
the streets, the roads, and cabin doors, crowded with
beggars of the female sex, followed by three, four or six
children, all in rags, and importuning every passenger
for an alms. These mothers, instead of being able to work
for their honest livelihood, are forced to employ all their
time in strolling to beg sustenance for their helpless infants;
who, as they grow up, either turn thieves for want of
work, or leave their dear native country to fight for the
Pretender in Spain, or sell themselves to the Barbadoes.

I think it is agreed by all parties that this prodigious
number of children in the arms, or on the backs, or at
the heels, of their mothers and frequently of their fathers,
is in the present state of the kingdom a very great additional
grievance; and therefore whoever could find out a fair,
cheap and easy method of making these children useful
members of the commonwealth, would deserve so well
of the public as to have his statue set up for a preserver
of the nation.

But my intention is very far from being confined to
provide only for the children of professed beggars; it is of

a much greater extent, and shall take in the whole number of infants at a certain age who are born of parents in effect as little able to support them as those who demand our charity in the streets.

. . . .

I shall now therefore humbly propose my own thoughts, which I hope will not be liable to the least objection.

I have been assured by a very knowing American of my acquaintance in London, that a young healthy child, well nursed, is at a year old a most delicious, nourishing, and wholesome food, whether stewed, roasted, baked or boiled; and I make no doubt that it will equally serve in a fricassee or ragout.

I do therefore humbly offer it to the public consideration that of the 120,000 children already computed, 20,000 may be reserved for breed, whereof only one-fourth part to be males; which is more than we allow to sheep, black cattle, or swine; and my reason is, that these children are seldom the fruit of marriage, a circumstance not much regarded by our savages, therefore one male will be sufficient to serve four females. That the remaining 100,000 may, at a year old, be offered in sale to the persons of quality and fortune through the kingdom; always advising the mother to let them suck plentifully in the last month, so as to render them plump and fat for a good table. A child will make two dishes at an entertainment for friends; and when the family dines alone, the fore or hind quarter will make a reasonable dish, and, seasoned with a little pepper or salt, will be very good boiled on the fourth day, especially in winter.

. . . .

After all, I am not so violently bent upon my own opinion, as to reject any offer, proposed by wise men, which shall be found equally innocent, cheap, easy and effectual. . . . I desire those politicians who dislike my overture, and may perhaps be so bold as to attempt an answer, that they will first ask the parents of these mortals, whether they would not at this day think it a great happiness to have been sold for food at a year old in the manner I prescribe, and thereby have avoided such a perpetual scene of misfortunes as they have since gone through, by the oppression of landlords, the impossibility of paying rent without money or trade, the want of common sustenance, with neither house nor clothes to cover them from the inclemencies of the weather, and the most inevitable prospect of entailing the like or greater miseries upon their breed for ever. *679*

J. Swift
A modest proposal
for preventing
the children
of poor people
in Ireland
from being
a burden
to their parents
and for making
them beneficial
to the public
1729
Ireland

We never pity an unfortunate man, but so far as we think him sensible of his misery. The natural sensation of evil is more limited than it appears; but it is the memory, by which we feel its continuance, and the imagination, which extends it to futurity, that render us truly worthy of compassion. This, I apprehend, is one reason why we are less affected with the pain and labour of brute animals, than with those of men, though the common sensibility ought to make us equally sympathize with both. We never pity a dray-horse in the stable, because we do not suppose that, while he is eating his hay, he thinks of the blows he has received today, or of the fatigues he must undergo tomorrow. Neither do we pity a sheep we see grazing in the field, though we know it will be soon slaughtered; because, we presume, it does not foresee its destiny. Extending these ideas, we grow hardened in the same manner in regard to the sufferings of human creatures; and the rich make themselves easy, in regard to their behaviour towards the poor, by supposing them so stupid as not to feel their misery. In general I judge of the value every man sets upon the happiness of his fellow-creatures by his conduct towards them. It is natural that we should undervalue the felicity of those for whom we have a hearty contempt. Be not therefore surprised if the politicians talk of the common people with so much disdain; nor if the generality of philosophers affect to make man so wicked a being.

It is the common people that constitute the bulk of mankind; the rest above that order are so few in number that they are not worth our consideration. Man is the same creature in all estates; if so, that which is most numerous deserves the greatest respect. In the eye of a thinking person all civil distinctions vanish; he beholds the same passions and the same sensations in the peasant and the nobleman; the only difference he discerns is in their language, in a little refinement of expression; if there be any essential difference between them, it is to the disadvantage of those who are the greatest dissemblers. The populace show themselves in their real colours, and are not amiable; but the great are obliged to disguise themselves; were they to appear in their native dress, they would strike us with horror.

There is the same portion, according to our philosophers, of happiness and misery in all estates: a maxim equally pernicious and absurd. For, if all people are happy alike, what occasion have I to put myself to an inconvenience for any man, either to promote his happiness, or to rescue him from misery? Let each abide where he is: let the slave drag his chain, let the sick man bear his infirmities, let the beggar perish; they would gain nothing by changing their condition. The same philosophers enumerate the troubles of the rich man, and demonstrate the vanity of his pleasures: how glaring a sophism! The troubles of the rich man are not owing to his estate, but to himself, who makes an ill-use of it. Were he even more wretched than the poor, he would still deserve no pity; since his misery is of his own procuring, and it depends upon himself to be happy. But the distresses of the poor man proceed from the nature of his condition, from the severity of his fate. No habit can render him insensible to fatigue, to thirst, to hunger; neither wit nor wisdom will protect him against the evils inseparable from his station. What does Epictetus gain by foreseeing that his master is going to break his leg? Does this hinder him from breaking it? On the contrary, foresight is an addition to his misery. Were the vulgar to be really as sensible as we suppose them stupid, how could they either think or act differently from what they do at present? Examine the people of that class, and you will find that, with a difference in language, they have as much wit, and more good sense, than yourself. You should therefore respect your species: remember, that it is essentially composed of the common people; that if all the kings and philosophers were to be taken away, they would not be missed, and affairs would be conducted as well without them. In a word, teach your pupil to love all mankind, and even those who rail against their own species; contrive so, that he shall place himself in no one class, but be found in all: when you mention mankind in his presence, be sure to do it with tenderness and pity, but never with contempt. Man! Do not disgrace mankind.

J.-J. Rousseau
Emilius
1762

680

THE DREAM OF THE INDIAN SERVANT

A little man made his way to his master's residence; he was a serf and had to do his turn of duty as a servant in the big house. He was small, poor, timorous and wretched, his clothes old.

The great man, lord of the estate, could not help laughing when the little fellow paid his respects in the manor hall.

'Are you really human?' he asked before all the men and women servants present.

Quailing, the Indian did not reply, but just stood there, frozen with fear.

'We'll see!' said the master. 'At least he'll be able to wash pots, or even handle a broom with those unbelievable hands of his. Take the obscenity away!' he ordered the steward.

Kneeling, the Indian kissed his master's hand and dejectedly followed the steward to the kitchen.

Although small in body, he had the strength of an ordinary man. Anything he was ordered to do, he did well. But his face always looked a little terrified; some of the servants laughed at this, others pitied him. 'Orphan, born of orphans; son of the wind from the moon must be the cold of his eyes, his heart pure sorrow,' said the mestiza cook seeing him.

He spoke to no one, worked in silence, and ate in silence. He did all he was told to do, murmuring only 'Yes, little father' or 'Yes, little mother.'

Perhaps it was because of a certain look of terror, and his ragged clothes, and also maybe because he did not want to speak that the master so completely despised him. At nightfall when the servants assembled to recite the Hail Mary in the manor hall, the master would torment him before them all, shaking him like a piece of rawhide.

He would grab him by the head, force it down and, when he was on his knees, slap him lightly on the face.

'I believe you're a dog. Bark!'

He could not.

'Down on your paws!' he was ordered next.

The Indian obeyed, and moved a few steps on all fours.

'Sideways like a dog,' the master continued.

The little man would run, imitating the little puna dogs.

The lord laughed, his whole body shaking.

'Back again!' he called when the servant reached the end of the great hall.

The Indian turned, running back sideways, and arrived exhausted.

Some of his fellow servants were meanwhile repeating the Hail Mary, slowly, like a sighing in the heart.

'Prick up your ears now, vizcacha! Vizcacha you are!' the master ordered. 'Squat on your haunches! Put your hands together!'

As if a vizcacha had taught him in his mother's womb, the Indian could exactly imitate these little rodents, standing still on the rocks as though in prayer. But he could not prick up his ears. Some of the servants would begin to laugh.

With his boot, but not roughly, the master pushed the little man over on the tiled floor.

'Let us say the Our Father,' said the master to the servants, lined up and waiting.

The Indian got gradually to his feet, but could not pray because this was not his proper place—was nobody's in fact.

As darkness fell the servants went down the hall to the patio and towards the servants' quarters.

'Away with you, you husk!' the master would say to the Indian.

And so, every day, the master ridiculed his new Indian servant before all his household. He forced him to laugh, to feign weeping. He delivered him up to the mockery of his fellow serfs.

But one evening, at the hour of prayer, when the hall was packed with all the members of the household and when the master began to look at the Indian and his close-set eyes, the little servant spoke out clearly. His face was still a bit terrified.

'Great master, grant me your permission; little father, I want to speak to you,' he said.

The master did not believe his ears.

'What? Was it you who spoke or someone else?' he asked.

'Your permission to speak to you, little father. It is you to whom I wish to speak,' repeated the Indian.

'Speak . . . if you can,' replied the lord.

'My father, my lord, my heart,' began the little man, 'I dreamed last night that we both died, you and I; both of us died.'

'You? With me? Tell everything, Indian,' said the master.

'As we were dead, lord, we appeared naked, both of us together, naked before our great father St. Francis.'

'And then? Speak!' ordered the master, half angry, half restless with curiosity.

'Seeing us together, dead and naked before him, our great father St. Francis examined us with his eyes which can see and measure no man knows what distance; you and me weighing the heart of each of us, I think, and what we were and what we are. You, being rich and great, you met his gaze, father.'

'And you?'

'I cannot know how I was, lord, I cannot know what I am worth.'

'Good. Go on.'

'Then said our father: "Let the most beautiful of all the angels come hither. And let him be accompanied by another small angel, also of great beauty. Let the small angel bear a cup of gold, and the cup of gold be full of the clearest golden honey." '

'And then?'

The Indian servants were listening, listening intently but nervously.

'Master, scarcely had our great father St. Francis given the order than an angel appeared, shining and tall as the sun; he came right up to our father walking slowly. Behind the great angel walked another, smaller, beautiful, glowing with the splendour of flowers. He bore in his hands a cup of gold.'

'And then?' repeated the master.

' "Great angel, cover this nobleman with the honey in the cup of gold; let your hands be as feathers when they pass over his body," was the command our great father spoke. And the sublime angel, raising the honey in his hands, anointed your body all over, from head to toe. And you stood erect, alone; in the splendour of heaven the light of your body shone as though it were made of transparent gold.'

'Just as it should be,' said the master, and then asked: 'And you?'

'While you were shining in heaven, our great father St. Francis spoke again: "Of all the angels in heaven, let the meanest, the most ordinary, approach. Let this angel bear a can containing human excrement." '

'And then?'

'An old, broken-down angel with scaly feet, who no longer had the strength to keep his wings in place, came before our great father; he walked with a tired step, his wings soiled, bearing in his hands a large can. "Listen, old one," our great father told this poor angel, "cover the body of this little man with the excrement in that can you have there; cover his whole body somehow, as best you can. Quickly!" Then with his knotted hands the old angel took excrement from the can and covered my body unevenly, as though throwing mud carelessly on the wall of a poor man's house. And I stood ashamed in the light of heaven, stinking....'

'Just as it should be,' said the master. 'Go on! Or was that the end?'

'No, little father, my lord. When we were again standing together, though somewhat differently, before our great father St. Francis, he looked at us afresh, you and me, for a long time. His eyes that plumb the infinite depths of heaven viewed us, putting night and day together, memory and forget. Then he said: "All that the angels had to do with you they have done. Now lick each other! Slowly,

The victims; their complaints

Folk-tale
Province of Cuzco
Peru
Quechua

and for a long time." The old angel grew young again at the same hour; his wings regained their black hue and their great strength. Our father charged him to see that what he had commanded should be done.'   *681*

Mulizas
from the region
of the Andes,
sung in Spanish

MINER'S LAMENT

Ladder after ladder
Until we reach a 'stop'
Where there is noise, where there is dust
Which little by little is killing me.

Little carbide lamp,
Watcher of my destiny,
You alone know
The life I am leading.

Fine lead dust
Which little by little is killing me
And the sulphate
Which destroys my shirt.

What an evil fate is mine
To have been born a miner,
Better, oh far better
To be a poor field worker.

> *Refrain*
> Ah, my lass, do you remember
> Our beloved Cerro?—
> Formerly all grassland
> And now all tunnels.   *682*

LAMENT FROM THE 'CERRO'

O minehead of Lourdes
How many lives do you hide there
United in sorrow
Around the ruins.
Yanacancha village shaking
To the mine blasts of Tacna-Arica
And all to the sound of mambos
Peru   Pass by the graveyard.   *683*

ON POVERTY

On the night when the rain beats,
Driven by the wind,
On the night when the snowflakes mingle
With the sleety rain,
I feel so helplessly cold.
I nibble at a lump of salt,
Sip the hot, oft-diluted dregs of saké;
And coughing, snuffling,
And stroking my scanty beard,
I say in my pride,
'There's none worthy, save I!'
But I shiver still with cold.
I pull up my hempen bedclothes,
Wear what few sleeveless clothes I have,
But cold and bitter is the night!
As for those poorer than myself,
Their parents must be cold and hungry,
Their wives and children beg and cry.
Then, how do you struggle through life?

Wide as they call the heaven and earth,
For me they have shrunk quite small;
Bright though they call the sun and moon,
They never shine for me.
Is it the same with all men,
Or for me alone?
By rare chance I was born a man
And no meaner than my fellows,
But, wearing unwadded sleeveless clothes
In tatters, like weeds waving in the sea.
Hanging from my shoulders,
And under the sunken roof,
Within the leaning walls,
Here I lie on straw
Spread on bare earth,
With my parents at my pillow,
My wife and children at my feet,
All huddled in grief and tears.
No fire sends up smoke
At the cooking-place,
And in the cauldron
A spider spins its web.
With not a grain to cook,
We moan like the night thrush.
Then, 'to cut,' as the saying is,
'The ends of what is already too short,'

The village headman comes,
With rod in hand, to our sleeping place,
Growling for his dues.
Must it be so hopeless—
The way of this world?

Envoy

Nothing but pain and shame in this world of men,
But I cannot fly away,
Wanting the wings of a bird.

Yamanoue Okura
660-733
Japan

684

*The peasants'
state*

The kulaks parcelled out the land
According to the mouths to feed,
Took the best parts for themselves,
And left the poor—the weed.

Where oh where's the Tsar's decree?
With tidings from His Majesty:
Let the workers have the works
And give the land to you and me.

The landlord lives quite happily
He has his land for free.
The peasant finds his bit of land,
Down in the cemetery.

Chastushki
(Folk-poetry)
Russia

685

The victims' silence

We neither see nor hear those who suffer, and the tragedy of life takes place behind the scenes. All is quiet, all is peaceful; only statistics make their silent protest: so many people went out of their mind, so many gallons were drunk, so many children starved to death. . . . And, of course, such a state of affairs is necessary; of course, those who are happy feel comfortable only because those who are unhappy bear their burden in silence; if they did not, nobody would be happy. It is a sort of communal hypnosis. On every contented, happy man's doorstep there should be someone with a hammer in his hand, who would keep reminding the happy man by his knocking that there are unhappy people in the world, and that, however happy he may be sooner or later life will show him its talons, and misfortune will befall him, in the form of sickness, poverty or loss, and no one will see him or hear him, just as today he neither hears nor sees others.

Anton Chekhov
Gooseberries
1898
Russia

686

*Speak for those
who cannot speak*

In religion five things are best. These are: truthfulness, generosity, virtuousness, diligence and intercession.

This is the best truthfulness: when one does to the creatures of Ohrmazd that which benefits them much more than it does him.

This is the best generosity: when one gives a present to a person from whom he does not hope for any reward in this world, or even gratitude and favour.

This is the best virtuousness: when one fights against the spiritual demons, whatever demons they be, and does not let these five demons in particular come inside him: Greed, Envy, Lust, Wrath and Disgrace.

This is the best diligence: when one does the thing he sets out to do in such a way that at every instant he is sure in himself that even if he died at that very moment he would not have to do anything differently.

This is the best intercession: when one speaks for an inarticulate person and for one who is incapable of expressing his own complaint or plea. That person speaks up only for the sake of his own soul and that of the poor and aggrieved people and of the six earthly elements. *687*

Dēnkart
9th cent.
Persia

Strikes; programmes; social laws

*A strike among
the workers
in a necropolis
in Ancient Egypt*

29th year, 2nd month of the season Peret, 10th day. On that day, the workmen in the gang jumped over the wall surrounding the Necropolis, saying: 'We are hungry— eighteen days of this month have already gone by.' They sat down behind the temple of Menkhepere. There came to them the scribe of the Secret Tomb (?), the two foremen of the workers, the two delegates and the two police officers. They rebuked the workers, saying: 'Go back!' But they, with many protests, said: 'Come, you! We have business with Pharaoh.' They spent the day there, and the night in the Necropolis.

The scribe of the mat Hednakht and the holy fathers of the temple came to hear what they had to say. They said: 'It is because we are hungry and thirsty that we have come here. We have no clothing, no ointments, no fish, no vegetables. Apprise Pharaoh, our good Lord, of this and inform the Vizier, our master, so that sustenance may be provided for us.' And the rations for the previous month were given them that very day. *688*

Official record
XXth dynasty
2nd millenary B.C.

Rights of the poor

Hebrew Bible
Deuteronomy 23

When thou comest into thy neighbour's vineyard thou mayest eat grapes until thou have enough at thine own pleasure . . . when thou comest into thy neighbour's standing corn, thou mayest pluck ears with thy hand.   *689*

*Non-
co-operation*

Mahatma Gandhi
1869-1948

Every man has an equal right to the necessaries of life even as birds and beasts have. And since every right carries with it a corresponding duty and the corresponding remedy for resisting any attack upon it, it is merely a matter of finding out the corresponding duties and remedies to vindicate the elementary fundamental equality. The corresponding duty is to labour with my limbs and the corresponding remedy is to non-co-operate with him who deprives me of the fruit of my labour. And if I would recognize the fundamental equality, as I must, of the capitalist and the labourer, I must not aim at his destruction. I must strive for his conversion. My non-co-operation with him will open his eyes to the wrong he may be doing.   *690*

Mahatma Gandhi
1869-1948

If however, in spite of the utmost effort, the rich do not become guardians of the poor in the true sense of the term and the latter are more and more crushed and die of hunger, what is to be done? In trying to find out the solution of this riddle I have lighted on non-violent non-co-operation and civil disobedience as the right and infallible means. The rich cannot accumulate wealth without the co-operation of the poor in society. If this knowledge were to penetrate to and spread amongst the poor, they would become strong and would learn how to free themselves by means of non-violence from the crushing inequalities which have brought them to the verge of starvation.   *691*

*Social justice
through law*
Rural organization
Community
of Castello del Piano
1571, Italy

For the law is God's faithful witness when its purpose is to help and protect poor and simple people.   *692*

Origins of the Republic in Rome. Political measures for the good of the people taken by Publicola after the fall of the Tarquins.

He permitted any who wished to enter the lists and sue for the consulship. But before the installation of his colleague, not knowing who he would be, but fearing an opposition due to some jealousy or ignorance, he used his sole authority for the enactment of his best and most important measures. In the first place, he filled up the senate, which was much reduced in numbers; for some had long before been put to death by Tarquin, and others had recently fallen in the battle with the Tuscans. Those who were enrolled in this body by him amounted, they say, to a hundred and sixty-four. After this he enacted several laws, one of which especially strengthened the position of the commons by allowing a defendant to appeal to the people from the judgement of the consuls. A second made it a capital offence to assume a magistracy which the people had not bestowed. A third, following these, came to the relief of the poor; it lifted the taxes from the citizens, so that all engaged more zealously in manufactures and commerce.

Plutarch's Lives
Publicola
c. 45-125

693

Justice
and violence;
revolution

G. Babeuf *(1760-97), commenting in a letter to his wife on the slaughter which followed the taking of the Bastille (July 1789) and the outburst of popular joy which accompanied that slaughter:*

Oh! how that joy troubled me. I was at the same time pleased and vexed; I declared it to be all for the best and all for the worst. I understand that the people should take justice into its own hands. I approve of a justice which condemns the guilty to die; but in these days must it be cruel? ... The victors ... are reaping and will continue to reap what they have sown.

France

694

Saint-Just *(1767-94), Republican institutions.*

There must be neither rich nor poor ... opulence is a scandal.... Begging must be brought to an end by distributing the wealth of the nation to the poor. ... Everyone must work and be self-respecting.

France

695

Analysis (by S. Maréchal, 1750-1803), of 'the Doctrines of Babeuf (1760-97), proscribed by the Directorate for having spoken the truth'.

1. Nature has given to every man an equal right to enjoy all things.
2. The aim of society is to defend this equality which in a state of nature is often assailed by the strong and the evil, and to further it by the pooling of all wealth.
3. Nature has imposed on one and all an obligation to

352

work. It is a crime for anyone to evade the obligation to work.

4. Work and wealth must be shared by all.
5. If one man toils and lives in need while another is idle and wallows in wealth, this is oppression.
6. It is a crime for anyone to appropriate to himself the products of the soil or of industry.
7. In the true society, there should be neither rich nor poor.
8. The rich who are unwilling to give of their superfluity to help the poor are enemies of the people.
9. No one, by amassing all the resources, may deprive another of the education that is necessary for his welfare; education must be available to all.
10. The aim of the Revolution is to eradicate inequality and to restore the welfare of all.
11. The Revolution is incomplete, because the rich take to themselves all wealth and are in sole control, whereas the poor work like slaves, languish in want

France   and have no part in the State.   *696*

S. de Sismondi *(January 1835).*

In the times of the bitterest feudal oppression, in the times when slavery prevailed, the masters no doubt committed acts of savage cruelty which make mankind shudder; but at least some cause had provoked their anger or cruelty; some hope remained to the oppressed of being able to avoid provoking his oppressor ... in the cold and abstract oppression of wealth, there is no injury, no anger, no identifiable

France   agent, no relationship between man and man.   *697*

A. Blanqui, *Trial oj the Fifteen, 12 January 1832.*

I am accused of having told thirty million Frenchmen,
France   proletarians like myself, that they had a right to live. *698*

By way of contrast, L. de Bonald *(1754-1840).*

In society, there are no rights but only duties. Human rights ... are signals of distress and death, like shots fired at long intervals from a doomed ship.

France   *Bonald demanded a* 'Declaration of the Rights of God'.

                                                          699

Dupont de Nemours, *Cahier du Bailliage de Nemours* [*Book of the Nemours Bailiwick*] *(1789)*.

Item I: Every man has the right freely to do that which does no harm to others.

Item II: Every man has a right to the help of others.

Item III: All men have the right to demand the same in return from him who claims their help, if he is able, strong and healthy enough, and in this they themselves are arbiters of the form such returns shall take.

Item IV: In childhood, incapacity, old age or infirmity, every man has a right to free help from other men; for there is not one of them who does not, in this respect, have a life-long debt to discharge, since there is not one who does not owe his life to free help of many kinds received at least during his childhood.

Item V: No man shall in any way be stopped or hampered in his work by any other man, or by any authority.

Item VI: No authority can force a man to work for no wages, or for a wage which seems to him inadequate.

Item VII: Every man shall keep what he owns and what he has legitimately acquired by his work or by gift or inheritance.

Item VIII: Every man is free to enter into such contracts as he holds to be appropriate, and every contract freely entered into is binding on both parties unless it is contrary to morality, . . .

Item IX: No man shall be subjected to violence either
France   against his body or against his property.   *700*

By way of contrast, Boissy d'Anglas *(1795).*

If you give political rights unconditionally to men who are not property-owners and if they sit in the legislative assembly, they will agitate or promote agitation without
France   fearing its effects.   *701*

Louis Blanc, *The socialist's catechism, 1849.*

The aim of socialism is to put into practice among men the four basic maxims contained in the Gospels:

1. Love one another.
2. All things whatsoever ye would that men should do to you, do ye even so to them.
3. Whosoever will be chief among you, let him be your servant.
France 4. Peace to men of good will.   *702*

A. Blanqui *to Maillard, 6 June 1852: What should revolution be?*

The annihilation of the present order, which is founded on inequality and exploitation, the downfall of the oppressors, deliverance from the yoke of the rich.

It was the *bourgeois* who first raised the standard of the proletariat, who formulated egalitarian doctrines, and France   who now propagate them.   *703*

Proclamation of the programme of the Czech Radical Democrats (1848).

We shall be openly hostile to every privilege, whatever it may be. We shall stand by the poor against the rich, prevent the latter from battening on the suffering of the millions who are still living like animals in this world. We shall advocate the right to work, for freedom must not be tantamount to a mockery of poverty, but on the contrary must become poverty's salvation.

We shall contribute to the spread of education among the working class. But we are not visionaries who imagine that education alone can make them happy—we want them to be supplied with what is theirs by right—the right to live. And if you proclaim that poverty is a necessary evil—we cry out to your faces, selfish people: it is not! Czech   There are ways and means of either annihilating it or at proclamation   least attenuating it in great measure.   *704*

Our principles
For the reform of the Homeland!

Brasov 12-24 May 1848

1. Suppression of statute labour and all other labour dues demanded of peasants by their masters.
2. Suppression of statute labour for the lord, compulsory road-building labour and all unpaid labour for the authorities.
3. Granting to the peasants of the right to own land without counterpart service.
4. Abolition of all privileges and hence fair distribution of the burdens of State among all the people and equal access by the people to all political and civil rights.

The Moldavian
revolutionary   5. Recognition of the principles of liberty, equality and
programme   fraternity, in the fullest sense, as the basis of the country's
of 1848   institutions.
drawn up by
Costake Negri   6. Union of Moldavia and Walachia to form a single,
and Alecu Russo   independent Romanian State.   *705*

355

The social creed
of the churches

Statement adopted by the General Conference of the Methodist Episcopal Church.

The Methodist Episcopal Church stands:

For equal rights and complete justice for all men in all stations of life.

For the principle of conciliation and arbitration in industrial dissensions.

For the protection of the worker from dangerous machinery, occupational disease, injuries and mortality.

For the abolition of child labor.

For such regulation of the conditions of labor for women as shall safeguard the physical and moral health of the community.

For the suppression of the 'sweating system'.

For the gradual and reasonable reduction of the hours of labor to the lowest practical point, with work for all; and for that degree of leisure for all which is the condition of the highest human life.

For a release from employment one day in seven.

For a living wage in every industry.

For the highest wage that each industry can afford, and for the most equitable division of the products in industry that can ultimately be devised.

May 1908
United States
of America

For the recognition of the Golden Rule, and the mind of Christ as the supreme law of society and the sure remedy for all social ills. *706*

On behalf
of social justice

WILSON'S FIRST INAUGURAL ADDRESS AFTER BEING ELECTED PRESIDENT OF THE UNITED STATES ON 4 MARCH 1913

Some old things with which we had grown familiar, and which had begun to creep into the very habit of our thought and of our lives, have altered their aspect as we have latterly looked critically upon them, with fresh, awakened eyes; have dropped their disguises and shown themselves alien and sinister. Some new things, as we look frankly upon them, willing to comprehend their real character, have come to assume the aspect of things long believed in and familiar, stuff of our own convictions. We have been refreshed by a new insight into our own life....

But the evil has come with the good, and much fine gold has been corroded. With riches has come inexcusable waste. We have squandered a great part of what we might have used, and have not stopped to conserve the exceeding bounty of nature, without which our genius for enterprise would have been worthless and impotent, scorning to be careful, shamefully prodigal as well as admirably efficient. We have been proud of our industrial achievements, but we have not hitherto stopped thoughtfully enough to count the human cost....

Nor have we studied and perfected the means by which government may be put at the service of humanity, in safeguarding the health of the Nation, the health of its men and its women and its children, as well as their rights in the struggle for existence. This is no sentimental duty. The firm basis of government is justice, not pity. These are matters of justice. There can be no equality or opportunity, the first essential of justice in the body politic, if men and women and children be not shielded in their lives, their very vitality, from the consequences of great industrial and social processes which they cannot alter, control, or singly cope with. Society must see to it that it does not itself crush or weaken or damage its own constituent parts. The first duty of law is to keep sound the society it serves. Sanitary laws, pure food laws, and laws determining conditions of labor which individuals are powerless to determine for themselves are intimate parts of the very business of justice and legal efficiency.

707

Agrarian reform

We must also see to it that large estates with more than two leagues of arable land disappear, for agriculture can only be developed if a number of people each play a part in cultivating a small piece of land whose upkeep calls for no more than their joint labour. But such a thing is impossible where a vast expanse of uncultivated land is owned by a single individual with thousands of men under him, who are either day labourers or slaves compelled to work; whereas, if those same men became the legitimate owners of a small piece of land, they could maintain themselves, to their own advantage and to that of the people in general.

José María Morelos
1765-1815
Mexico

708

*Limitation
to the right
to property*

We are individualists, in the sense that we place human rights above any action undertaken by the State, and not because we think that everything called an individual right has an absolute value as such. On the contrary, we think that since human society is not a fiction but a

357

genuine organism subject to more complex laws than those governing the individual, its action can, in certain clearly-defined cases, place a limit on this or that human right; for example, the right to property. We believe that, on this basis, and by widening the scope of justice, we can solve the social problem in part by legislation

Justo Sierra
19th cent.
Mexico

that would slowly but surely succeed in breaking up the big landed estates. *709*

Reform
of the civil service
by the Commune

In this respect, one of the measures taken by the Commune and specially mentioned by Marx is particularly noteworthy, viz., the abolition of all representation allowances, and of all pecuniary privileges attached to the posts of officials, the reduction of the salaries of all servants of the State to the level of 'workmen's wages'. This brings out more clearly than anything else the turn-over from bourgeois democracy to proletarian democracy, from the democracy of the oppressors to the democracy of the oppressed classes, from the State as a 'special force' for the repression of a given class to the repression of the oppressors by the general force of the majority of the people—the workers and the peasants. And it is precisely on this most striking point, perhaps the most important of all as regards the State, that the teachings of Marx have been completely forgotten! The popular commentaries, which are legion, make no mention of this. It is tacitly agreed to keep quiet about it as if it were 'puerile' and out of date, just as the Christians, once Christianity

Lenin
The State
and Revolution
1917

had attained the position of a State religion, 'forgot' the 'puerilities' of primitive Christianity, with its revolutionary democratic spirit. *710*

Law VI on the abolition of large estates and the redistribution of land among those who cultivate it.

Article 1. . . . In accordance with the principles set out in its manifesto and in the declaration by the provisional national Government, and in order to carry out its mandate, the National Assembly desires, through the abolition of large holdings of landed property, to bring about the age-old dream of the Hungarian peasants, who are to become the owners of the land which has always been theirs of right.

The abolition of the régime of the large feudal estates will ensure the democratic transformation of the country and its future development; the ownership by the peasants of former seignioral estates will open the way to political, social, economic and cultural progress for the Hungarian peasants who for centuries have been living under oppression.

711

Freedom in practice

Comparison of Solon and Publicola.

Real equality of rights depends upon the remission of debts

Hatred of tyranny was more intense in Publicola than in Solon. For in case any one attempted to usurp the power, by Solon's law he could be punished only after conviction, whereas Publicola made it lawful to kill him before any trial. Moreover, though Solon rightly and justly plumes himself on rejecting absolute power even when circumstances offered it to him and his fellow-citizens were willing that he should take it, it redounds no less to the honour of Publicola that, when he had received a tyrannical power, he made it more democratic, and did not use even the prerogatives which were his by right of possession. And of the wisdom of such a course Solon seems to have been conscious even before Publicola, when he says that a people 'then will yield the best obedience to its guides when it is neither humoured nor oppressed too much'.

Peculiar to Solon was his remission of debts, and by this means especially he confirmed the liberties of the citizens. For equality under the laws is of no avail if the poor are robbed of it by their debts. Nay, in the very places where they are supposed to exercise their liberties most, there they are most in subjection to the rich, since in the courts of justice, the offices of state, and in public debates, they are under their orders and do them service. And what is of greater moment here, though sedition always follows an abolition of debts, in this case alone, by employing opportunely, as it were, a dangerous but powerful medicine, Solon actually put an end to the sedition that was already rife, for his own virtue and high repute prevailed over the ill-repute and odium of the measure.

Plutarch's Lives,
Publicola
c. 45-125

712

Legal rights and actual rights

In skimming through the pages of social history, we shall have had occasion to demonstrate that there is a great discrepancy between the legally recognized rights of citizens and the rights which they actually enjoy; between the equality established by political institutions and that existing between individuals; we shall have pointed out that this difference was one of the principal causes of the destruction of freedom in the ancient republics, of the storms which shook them, and of the weakness which delivered them into the hands of foreign tyrants.

The reasons for these differences are threefold: inequality of wealth; inequality of social status as between the man whose own means of subsistence are assured and can be handed on to his family, and the man whose means depend on his longevity, or rather on that part of his life during which he can work; and finally, inequality of education.

Social security and insurance

There exists an overriding cause of inequality, dependence and, indeed, poverty, which constantly threatens the most numerous and most active class of society.

We propose to show how it can be removed to a large extent, by offsetting one risk by another, that is, by guaranteeing for a man who reaches old age a security based on his savings but increased by the savings of those who, having made the same sacrifice, die before they actually need to receive the ensuing benefits; and by arranging through a similar compensation payable to women and children who should happen to lose their husband or father, an identical security acquired at the same cost, and applicable both to families bereaved by the premature death of the breadwinner and those in which he goes on living longer. This system will, in addition, give children who reach an age when they can begin to work on their own account and found a new family, the advantage of sufficient capital for developing their particular trade, increased as a result of the premature deaths of others of their generation. The idea of this method is based on the calculation of life-expectancy and monetary investments, and it has already been employed successfully, but never, so far, on such a broad scale and in such a variety of ways as to make it of real practical use, not merely to a few individuals, but to society at large which it would thereby free from the periodical ruin of vast numbers of families—an ever-recurring source of poverty and corruption.

Right to a better and a longer life

The organic perfectibility or degeneration of strains in the vegetable and animal kingdoms may be regarded as one of the general laws of nature.

This law is applicable to the human race, and surely there can be no doubt that progress in preventive medicine, the use of healthier foodstuffs and dwellings, a way of living that develops the physique through exercise without destroying it through excessive labour, and, lastly, the elimination of the two most active agents of degeneration —poverty and excess riches—could prolong men's average length of life by giving them more uniform health and stronger constitutions. One feels that once the progress in preventive medicine has been more widely applied with the help of reason and social organization, in the long run it must bring about the disappearance of hereditary and contagious diseases, and also of those common diseases due to climate, food and certain types of work. No doubt proofs could even be adduced showing how almost all other diseases must inevitably be circumscribed, the chances being that we shall always be able to recognize their remote causes. . . . Man is hardly likely to become immortal, but why could not his span of life between the time when he is born and the time when naturally, without illness or accident, he experiences difficulty in living, go on increasing indefinitely?

*Condorcet
Esquisse
d'un Tableau
Historique
des Progrès
de l'Esprit Humain
1798
France*

713

---

*Justice
and freedom*

*S. Staszic
1755-1826
Mankind
Poland*

Freedom which is not based on justice is an empty word full of delusions. The greatest tyrants mankind has known have been most vocal in praise of liberty.

714

---

*Equality
the pre-requisite
of justice
and freedom*

DECREE ON THE SUPPRESSION OF PRESIDENTIAL HONOURS

Extracts from the preamble.

In vain would this Junta publish liberal principles to make the peoples appreciate the inestimable gift of freedom if it were to permit the continuation of those privileges which, for the misfortune of humanity, were invented by tyrants in order to stifle natural feelings. . . . What comparison is there between a vast empire of slaves, which with their blood purchase victories to augment the magnificence and multiply the coaches and the escorts of their masters, with a city of free men, in which the magistrate is distinguished from the rest merely by the fact that he enforces the law and settles the disputes of his fellow-citizens? All classes of the State approach the holders of authority with confidence, because they have spoken frankly with them all in social life; the poor man explains his actions unhesitatingly, because he has frequently talked on friendly terms with the judge listening to him; the magistrate does not browbeat in court men who might afterwards spurn him in society; and yet there is no lack of respect for the magistracy, because their decisions are dictated by the law, supported by the constitution and executed with the inflexible firmness of just and incorruptible men. . . . The freedom of the peoples does not consist of words, nor is it based on charters alone. Any tyrant can compel his slaves to sing hymns in praise of liberty; and that mechanical chant accords with the chains and oppression of those who intone it. If we wish the peoples to be free, let us religiously observe the sacred dogma of equality....

Extracts from the Regulation.

All toasting, cheering or public acclamation of individual members of the Junta is prohibited. If they are just men, they will live in the hearts of their fellow-citizens; they do not appreciate mouths profaned with the praise of tyrants.

... No toast shall be drunk except to the fatherland, its rights, the glory of its arms, and to general subjects of public rejoicing.

... Any person drinking a toast to an individual member of the Junta shall be exiled for six years.

... From this day forth all church ceremonial for the civil authorities shall be terminated; the latter do not go to church to receive incense, but to offer tribute to the Supreme Being.

Mariano Moreno
Gaceta
de Buenos Aires
1810

715

Liberty, equality, association, education

Association, progress, liberty, equality, fraternity—these are correlative terms of the great social and humanitarian synthesis; divine symbols of the glorious future awaiting all nations and mankind. It is only through equality that there can be liberty; and there can be no equality without the help of the association or pooling of all individual forces on behalf of one unique, indefinable objective—continual progress—fundamental philosophical tenet of the nineteenth century.

In order that the ignorant masses may be emancipated and have the path to self-rule opened up to them, they must be educated. At present, the masses act by instinct, emotionally rather than rationally; they seek a better life but do not know where to find it; they want to be free, but do not know the path to freedom. However, these ignorant masses, although unable at present to exercise their sovereign rights and achieve political freedom, remain in full control of their freedom as individuals. As in the case of all members of this association, their natural rights are sacred; there are civil liberties to protect them just like everybody else; the same civil, penal and constitutional laws enacted by the sovereign protect their lives, their property, their moral conscience and their liberties; they are hailed before a court of justice for a crime committed, and are either condemned or set free.

Estéban Echeverría
An Argentinian
living as a refugee
in Uruguay
Socialist Creed of
the May Association
1838

716

*Criticism
of the rights
of man separated
from
the community*

The first point to note is that the 'droits de l'homme' as distinct from the 'droits du citoyen' [the French expressions repeated here are those used in Marx's original German text] are no more or less than the rights of the *member of a bourgeois society*, i.e., of egoistic man, man separated from man and from the community. The most radical constitution, that of 1793, declares:

'*Déclaration des droits de l'Homme et du citoyen. Art. 2.* Ces droits, etc. (*les droits naturels et imprescriptibles*) sont: l'égalité, la liberté, la sûreté, la propriété.'

What constitutes liberty? '*Art. 6.* La liberté est le pouvoir qui appartient à l'homme de faire tout ce qui ne nuit pas aux droits d'autrui'... or, according to the declaration of the rights of man of 1791: 'La liberté consiste à pouvoir faire tout ce qui ne nuit pas à autrui.'

Liberty is thus the right to do anything that injures no one. The limits within which each person can *act without injuring others* are defined by law, just as the boundary line between two fields is defined by a fence. This is the liberty of man regarded as an isolated, self-centred monad . . . in the rights of man, liberty is based not on the union of man with man, but rather on the separation of man from man. It is the *right* of separateness, the right of the *limited* individual, limited to himself.

The practical application of the right to liberty is the right to *private property*.

In what does the right to private property consist?

'*Art. 16* (constitution de 1793). Le droit de *propriété* est celui qui appartient à tout citoyen de jouir et de disposer *à son gré* de ses biens, de ses revenus, du fruit de son travail et de son industrie.'

Le droit de propriété privée est donc le droit de jouir de ses biens à son gré, without reference to his fellows, independently of society; the right to dispose of them, the right to egoism. It is this individual liberty, with its practical implications, that constitutes the basis of bourgeois society. It leads every man to regard other men not as the *realization* of his freedom but rather as the *limit* set to it....

There remain the other human rights, 'égalité' and 'sûreté'.

'Égalité' is not taken here in the political sense; it is only the equality of the 'liberté' described above, i.e., every man is equally regarded as a monad, turned in on itself. The 1795 Constitution contains a definition of the concept of this equality: '*Art. 5* (Constitution de 1795). L'égalité consiste en ce que la loi est la même pour tous, soit qu'elle protège, soit qu'elle punisse.'

And 'sûreté'? '*Art. 8* (constitution de 1793). La sûreté consiste dans la protection accordée par la société à chacun de ses membres pour la conservation de sa personne, de ses droits et de ses propriétés.'

Security is the highest social concept of bourgeois society; the concept of the *police*, the idea that society as a whole exists only in order to guarantee for each of its members the preservation of his person, his rights and his property....

In its concept of security, bourgeois society does not rise above the level of egoism. Security is in fact the *ensurance* of its egoism.

Thus none of the so-called rights of man goes beyond egoistic man, man as he is in bourgeois society, that is to say, turned in upon himself, his own private interests and his arbitrary desires, as an individual separated from the community . . . The only bond uniting men is natural necessity, need, the preservation of their property and egoistic persons.

. . . .

Karl Marx
The Jewish Question
1844

The emancipation of mankind will be achieved only when the real individual man has absorbed the abstract citizen, and when, as individual man, in his practical life, his individual work **and** his personal relations, he has become a generic being, so recognizing his 'propres forces' as social powers and organizing them himself as such, and, consequently, when he no longer draws a distinction between himself and the social power embodied in political power.

717

Manifesto of a people's society, 1844.

Address to all classes of society:

Workers: look about you, consider your poverty, and ask yourselves:

How is it that you, the producers of all things designed to meet the needs of men and even to make their life pleasurable, of all the riches which crowd our fertile land, yea even of the splendours which are the pride of our oppressors—how is it that you possess hardly enough to satisfy even the most pressing needs of life, and count yourselves fortunate if you are not thrown workless into the streets by industrial or political crises?

. . . .

At its meetings, the Society shall discuss the following reforms:

Universal suffrage, that is to say, participation by all citizens in the designation of their representatives.

A graduated tax on income or wealth, in place of all other fiscal charges.

Public education for all children throughout the country. Teaching on social rights and duties. Instruction in manual work.

People's Society of Agneessens Founded in Brussels at De Klok tavern in the Rue des Sablons

The organization of labour, or security of existence for all citizens, in exchange for their labour.

The abolition of the death penalty.   *718*

Political rights and economic conditions

Function of universal suffrage

Instead of deciding once every three or six years which member of the ruling class was to 'represent' and trample on the people in Parliament, universal suffrage was to serve the people, formed into communes, in the same way as individual suffrage serves any employer looking for workers or administrative staff for his business! And it is a well-known fact that business firms, like individuals, are usually able to fit each person into his place and, if they happen to make a mistake, to set it right promptly. On the other hand, nothing could be more alien to the spirit of the Commune than to replace universal suffrage by a system of hierarchical investiture.   *719*

Karl Marx
The Civil
War in France
1871

A dialogue between Marx and Bakunin on the dictatorship of the proletariat.

BAKUNIN. The very existence of the State inevitably brings with it domination and, hence, servitude; domination without servitude, open or concealed, is inconceivable. That is why we are against the State.

What does 'the proletariat organized as the ruling class' mean?

MARX. It means that the proletariat, instead of fighting the economically privileged classes on some points (*im einzelnen*), has become strong enough and sufficiently well organized to employ mass violence; but the only methods it can use are economic ones leading to the elimination of its own wage-earning and hence its class character. Thus its total victory will spell the end of its domination, owing to the disappearance of its class character.

BAKUNIN. Is it possible for the whole of the proletariat to be at the head of the government?

MARX. In a trade-union, for example, does the whole of its membership constitute its executive committee? Will all division of labour in factories come to an end, and all the various functions based thereon cease to exist? And in the Bakunist building up of society 'from below upwards', will everyone shift upwards? In that case, surely, there will be no below? Will all the members of the commune administer the common interests of the region at the same time? In that case, there will no longer be any difference between the commune and the region!

BAKUNIN. There are about forty million Germans. Will all these forty million, for instance, be members of the government?

MARX. Certainly! For the starting point is the self-government of the commune.

BAKUNIN. The whole people will govern and there will be no one governed....

MARX. By this principle, a man who dominates himself is an impossibility, for he remains himself, and can never be anyone else.

BAKUNIN. Then there will be no government and no State; but when there is a State, there will be rulers and slaves.

MARX. This means merely: when class domination disappears, and there is no State in the present political sense....

BAKUNIN. This dilemma in Marxist theory can be simply resolved. By government of the people they mean...

MARX. 'They', that is to say, Bakunin...

BAKUNIN. ... they mean government of the people with the aid of a few rulers elected by the people.

MARX. Piffle, empty democratic words, political twaddle! Election is a form of political machinery which is to be found in the smallest Russian commune, and also in the *artel* [guild]. The character of the election system depends not on its name but, on the contrary, on its economic basis, and on the economic relations between the electors. As soon as functions have ceased to be political: (1) there is no longer any government function; (2) the distribution of general functions becomes a technical matter (*Geschäftssache*) conferring no power; and (3) election loses its present political character.

BAKUNIN. Election by universal suffrage of the whole people...

MARX. In present circumstances, 'the whole people' is a mere fiction...

BAKUNIN. Election, by universal suffrage of the whole people, of the representatives of the people and the governors of the State: that is the last word both of the Marxists and of the democratic school of thought. It is a lie concealing the despotism of the governing minority, all the more dangerous for being presented as the expression of the so-called will of the people.

MARX. Under collective ownership, the so-called will of the people gives place to the actual will of the members of the co-operative.

BAKUNIN. The result will be the ruling of the great majority of the people by a privileged minority. But that minority, the Marxists say . . .

MARX. Where?

BAKUNIN. . . . will be composed of workers. Yes, allow me, of former workers, who, however, immediately they become the representatives or rulers of the people, have ceased to be workers . . .

MARX. No more than an industrialist today ceases to be a capitalist on becoming a member of the municipal council.

BAKUNIN. . . . have ceased to be workers and, from the heights of the government, look down upon the ordinary run of workers. In fact, they will no longer represent the people, but only themselves and their claims to constitute the government. Anyone who doubts the truth of this knows nothing about human nature.

MARX. If Mr. Bakunin were familiar even with the position of a manager in a workers' co-operative factory, he would scrap all his dreams of domination. What he should have asked himself is what forms administrative functions can take on the basis of this 'workers' State', if that is what he wants to call it.

BAKUNIN. But these elected representatives will be convinced socialists and, moreover, learned. The term 'learned socialism'...

MARX. Has never been used.

BAKUNIN. 'Scientific socialism'...

MARX. Used only as opposed to Utopian socialism which sets out to give the people new crack-brained notions instead of concentrating on the study of the social movement organized by the people themselves.

BAKUNIN. . . . which is constantly used in the writings and speeches of the Lassalle school and the Marxists, itself shows that the so-called people's State will be nothing but the highly despotic rule of the mass of the people by a new and very large aristocracy of genuine or pseudo-scientists. Since the ordinary people are not scientists, they will be freed of all the cares of government, and relegated to the ranks of the governed. Fine freedom, that!

The Marxists are aware of this contradiction . . .

MARX. !

BAKUNIN. . . . and, recognizing that the 'government of scientists' . . .

MARX. What a dream!

BAKUNIN. . . . will, for all its democratic appearance, be the most oppressive, hateful and despicable dictatorship in the world, console themselves by saying that it will be transitory and short-lived.

MARX. No, my dear Sir! The domination of the working class over those strata of the old society against which they are in conflict will last only so long as the economic basis for the existence of the classes has not been abolished. . . . This merely means that, during the period of the struggle for the overthrow of the old form of society, the proletariat still operates upon the basis of that old society, and therefore still uses the same forms of political machinery. During this period of struggle, it has not yet attained its final structure and thus employs, for its liberation, means which will disappear once that liberation has been achieved. *720*

Karl Marx
Notes
on Bakunin's book
State Socialism and
Anarchy
1874
(Posthumous)

Liberty, equality

I am a convinced partisan of economic and social equality, because I know that, without it, liberty, justice, human dignity, morality and well-being will never amount to anything in the nations but lies. . . .

Equality without liberty means State despotism, and a despotic State cannot last a single day without at least *one* exploiting and privileged class: the bureaucracy. *721*

Bakunin
1814-76
Original in French

Freedom an illusion
B. de Castellane
Speech in the
National Assembly
1871
France

Do you not see that, by making it impossible for newspapers to come into existence unless they have large sums of money behind them, you suppress, with a stroke of the pen, freedom of thought and expression for the entire proletariat? *722*

Economic equality is the root, and political equality but a branch. Even when a constitutional system of government has been adopted, therefore, the majority of the people remain just as wretched as long as economic inequality persists. . . . But it must be borne in mind that the majority of the people are either peasants ploughing the fields or workmen sweating their life out in a factory. *723*

Isoo Abe
Manifesto of the
Social-Democratic
Party
1901
Japan

*From political
rights to
the emancipation
of labour*

The Commune achieved the key aim of all bourgeois revolutions—cheap government—by abolishing two major sources of expense: the standing army and officialdom.... It gave the Republic the basis for truly democratic institutions. But its final aim was neither 'cheap government' nor a 'true Republic': these were little more than corollaries. . . . Its real secret was this: it was essentially a government of the working class, the product of the struggle waged by the producer class against the appropriator class, the political structure which, at long last, made possible the economic emancipation of Labour.

But for this last circumstance, the Constitution of the Commune would have been an impossibility and designed to mislead. The political domination of the producer is essentially incompatible with the perpetuation of his social enslavement. The Commune was therefore to serve as a lever for doing away with the economic bases on which class differences, and hence also class domination,

Karl Marx
The Civil
War in France
1871

rest. Once labour is emancipated, every man becomes a worker, and productive labour ceases to be the attribute of any one class.   *724*

*Criticism
of parliamentary
democracy*

Take any parliamentary country, from America to Switzerland, from France to England, Norway and so forth—in these countries the actual work of the 'State' is done behind the scenes, being carried on by the departments, the chancelleries and the General Staffs. Parliament itself is given up to talk, for the sole purpose of fooling the 'common people'. . . .

The Commune substitutes for this venal and rotten parliamentary government of bourgeois society institutions in which freedom of opinion and discussion do not degenerate into deception, for the parliamentarians have to work themselves, to apply their own laws, to see for themselves what are their effects in real life, and themselves be directly responsible to their constituents. Representative institutions remain, but parliamentary government as a special system, as the division of labour between the legislature and the executive, as a privileged status for members of parliament, exists no more. We cannot imagine a democracy, even a proletarian democracy, without representative institutions, but we can and must

Lenin
The State
and Revolution
1917

bring it into being without the parliamentary system, unless our criticism of bourgeois society is but empty words.   *725*

The 'Self-government of the producers'
Theses of Kautsky and Lenin

Kautsky:

The discipline of the proletariat is not a military discipline; it is not passive obedience to an institution imposed from above; it is democratic discipline, voluntary submission to an elected leadership and to the resolutions of the majority. For this democratic discipline to be effective in a factory, work must be organized on democratic lines, and the autocratic factory of today must be replaced by a democratic one. Quite obviously, one of the most urgent tasks of any socialist régime will be to organize production on democratic lines. Even if the victorious proletariat did not initially so intend, however, the need to ensure the continuity of production would induce it to do so. The discipline essential in work can only be maintained by introducing union discipline on the shop floor.

All this cannot be done in the same way everywhere: each industry has its own particular character, which indicates how the workers should be organized. There are enterprises which cannot do without a bureaucratic organization, for example the railways. Here the democratic organization might take the following form: the workers would elect delegates who would form a sort of parliament, responsible for drawing up the working regulations and superintending the management of the bureaucratic apparatus. The management of other enterprises may be transferred to trade unions, and still others may become co-operative enterprises. There is thus great variety in democratic organization in different industries and we cannot hope to find one single system adopted for all. *726*

The Social Revolution 1902

Lenin:

As for the allegedly necessary 'bureaucratic' organization, the railways are in no way different from any other big industrial undertaking—a factory, a big shop or a large capitalist agricultural project. In all these, the techniques used require the strictest discipline and the greatest accuracy in the performance of the duties for which each worker is responsible, the penalty for mistakes being that the whole factory will stop working or that the machinery and the objects manufactured will be spoiled. In all such undertakings, of course, the workers will 'elect delegates, who form a sort of parliament'.

The main point here, however, is that this 'sort of parliament' will not be a parliament in the sense of a bourgeois parliamentary institution. It will not merely 'draw up the working regulations and superintend the management of the bureaucratic apparatus', as Kautsky thinks; he, of course, sees nothing beyond bourgeois parliamentary theory. In a socialist society, a 'sort of parliament' of workers' deputies will certainly draw up working regulations and superintend the management of the 'apparatus', but it will not be a 'bureaucratic' apparatus. Once the workers are in possession of political power, they will break up the old bureaucratic system, they will destroy it to its very foundations, and not leave one stone upon another; and instead of it they will set up a new system in which these same factory and office workers will play their part. The following conditions, which were carefully worked out by Marx and Engels, will have to be laid down immediately, in order to prevent them from becoming bureaucrats: 1. they must be not only elected but liable to be discharged from office at any time; 2. their remuneration must not be greater than that of a worker; 3. arrangements must at once be made for all to do the work of checking and supervising, for all to become 'bureaucrats' for a time, so that no one can become 'bureaucratic'.

Kautsky failed completely to grasp the difference between bourgeois parliamentary theory—in which democracy (not on the side of the people) is combined with bureaucracy (which is against the people)—and proletarian democratic theory, which will at once take steps to root out bureaucratism, and which will succeed, through them, in completely destroying bureaucratism and establishing a democracy that really serves the people.

The State
and Revolution
1917

727

Franklin D. Roosevelt's 'Four Freedoms' speech, 6 January 1941.

We know that enduring peace cannot be bought at the cost of other people's freedom. . . .

We will not be intimidated by the threats of dictators that they will regard as a breach of international law and as an act of war our aid to the democracies which dare to resist their aggression. . . .

There is nothing mysterious about the foundations of a healthy and strong democracy. The basic things expected by our people of their political and economic systems are simple. They are: equality of opportunity for youth and for others; jobs for those who can work; security for those who need it; the ending of special privilege for the few; the preservation of civil liberties for all; the enjoyment of the fruits of scientific progress in a wider and constantly rising standard of living.

These are the simple and basic things that must never be lost sight of in the turmoil and unbelievable complexity of our modern world. The inner and abiding strength of our economic and political systems is dependent upon the degree to which they fulfill these expectations.

In the future days, which we seek to make secure, we look forward to a world founded upon four essential human freedoms.

The first is freedom of speech and expression—everywhere in the world.

The second is freedom of every person to worship God in his own way—everywhere in the world.

The third is freedom from want—which, translated into world terms, means economic understandings which will secure to every nation a healthy peace time life for its inhabitants—everywhere in the world.

The fourth is freedom from fear—which, translated into world terms, means a world-wide reduction of armaments to such a point and in such a thorough fashion that no nation will be in a position to commit an act of physical aggression against any neighbor—anywhere in the world.

That is no vision of a distant millenium. It is a definite basis for a kind of world attainable in our own time and generation. That kind of world is the very antithesis of the so-called new order of tyranny which the dictators seek to create with the crash of a bomb.

To that new order we oppose the greater conception—the moral order. A good society is able to face schemes of world domination and foreign revolutions alike without fear.

Since the beginning of our American history we have been engaged in change—in a perpetual peaceful revolution—a revolution which goes on steadily, quietly adjusting itself to changing conditions—without the concentration camp or the quick-lime in the ditch. The world order which we seek is the co-operation of free countries, working together in a friendly, civilized society.

This nation has placed its destiny in the hands and heads and hearts of its millions of free men and women; and its faith in freedom under the guidance of God. Freedom means the supremacy of human rights everywhere. Our support goes to those who struggle to gain those rights or keep them. Our strength is in our unity of purpose.

United States of America

728

376

HYMN TO A JUDGE

Red Sea galley, Peruvian crew:
Who sweat and dream of the Andes
And drown the squeak of their chains by bawling
Peruvian galley-slave shanties.

About Peru with its paradise birds
And the dancing, the girls and the climate.
The orange-blossom, the monkey-bread tree
So high you could never climb it.

The banana-tree, too, and the pineapple-tree
And wine by the golden goblet,
Till one day (never ask whence or why)
The judges arrived and stopped it.

They enveloped the dancing, the birds and the girls
In a casing of legal verbiage;
Judicial eyes have a nasty glint
Like cans in a heap of garbage.

One of them caught in his basilisk stare
A peacock, all gorgeous and glistening:
The magnificent orange-and-bright-blue tail
Moulted away in a twinkling.

The arm of the Law reached the humming-bird too,
Who used to fly over the meadows:
He was captured one day by a learned judge
Who shaved off his down and his feathers.

There isn't today in the whole of Peru
A single volcano active:
A judge had all the volcanoes removed
As he didn't find smoking attractive.

Why, they've even forbidden the poems I write
To be published, on pain of torture:
For they won't have anything sold in the shops
That's stronger than milk and water.

The Equator shudders with clinking of chains,
But Peru's been emptied of residents:
Only the ghastly old judges are left,
Crouching behind their precedents.

It's a shame, you know, about the Peruvians
(Though the galley's a redeeming feature):
The fact is, judges muck *everything* up
From Moscow to Machupicchu.

Mayakovsky
1894-1930
U.S.S.R.

729

Education, science, culture

<table>
<tr><td>

Plato
Phaidon
390-380 B.C.

</td><td>

It is really or virtually impossible in this life to know any problem fully; but not to talk over and discuss every aspect of it, and to stop before reaching its final impasse, is really poor-spirited in a man.   *730*

</td></tr>
</table>

*Knowledge
is a vocation*
Dante
1265-1321
The Divine Comedy
'Inferno'

Consider your origin: ye were not formed to live like brutes, but to follow virtue and knowledge.   *731*

Now do I see that never can our intellect be sated, unless that Truth shine on it, beyond which no truth hath range.

Therein it resteth as a wild beast in his den so soon as it hath reached it; and reach it may; else were all longing futile.

Dante
1265-1321
The Divine Comedy
'Paradiso'

Wherefore there springeth, like a shoot, questioning at the foot of truth; which is a thing that thrusteth us towards the summit, on from ridge to ridge.   *732*

Dhammapada
(Verses on the law)
India
Pali

If any man, whether he be learned or not, consider himself so great as to despise other men, he is like a blind man holding a candle; blind himself, he illumines others.

733

A. Schweitzer
A l'Orée de
la Forêt Vierge
1929
France

The difference between white and black, between civilized and primitive, disappears when one talks to the inhabitants of the primeval forest about questions concerning our relations with ourselves, with other people, with the world and with eternity.   *734*

*No superiority
of one man
over another.
Master
and disciple*

The Christian should be such that he does not glorify himself above other men. God has given thee to be above the beasts. . . . That is a gift of nature; thou wilt always be superior to the beasts. But if thou dost claim to be superior to another man, then wilt thou bear him envy if thou seeest he is thy equal. Thou shouldst wish all men to be thine equals, and if thou art wiser than another, shouldst wish that he too may acquire wisdom. So long as he lags behind, he learns from thy school; so long as he is ignorant, he has need of thee; thou seemest to be the master, he the disciple; thou art therefore superior to him, since he is thy disciple. If thou dost not wish to have him as thy equal, it is because thou dost wish to have him for ever as thy disciple. But if thou dost wish to have him for ever as thy disciple, thou wilt be a grudging master. If thou art a grudging master, how canst thou be a master? Do not, I entreat thee, teach him thine own envy. . . . Thus man has overstepped his limits: through an excess of greed, he has desired to be above men, he who was created above the beasts: and that is arrogance. *735*

St. Augustine
354-430
Treatise on St. John's
Epistle
to the Parthians

The sages and prophets of Israel hope for the coming of the Messiah, not so that they may subjugate the whole world, nor oppress the pagans, nor be the envy of the peoples of the earth, nor to eat, drink and be merry, but to have leisure to study Torah and its wisdom without being crushed by an abusive and oppressive authority. *736*

Maimonides
Mishneh Torah
12th cent.

Learning
is no cause
for pride

Let not thy heart be puffed up because of thy learning, nor filled with pride because thou art a sage; converse with the ignorant as with the wise. No artist attains to perfection and no limits can be fixed to art. Good words are harder to find than emeralds [yet] they may be uttered by the handmaid who turns the grindstone. *737*

Maxims
of Ptah-hotep
Vth dynasty
3rd millenary B.C.
Ancient Egypt

The fruits
of culture

In Chapter 10 of the Lalitawistara Prince Siddhārtha Gautama is sent to school, but since he knew much more than the teacher did, the tables were turned: the future Buddha not only happened to know all the Indian alphabets, but he was even able to use them in such a way that his exposé gave a picture of the doctrine he would propagate in his later life. In one of the Javanese Buddha-stories, however, the future Buddha-king is a boy of humble birth who manages to receive an education by accompanying a playmate to school. The story shows that the teacher made no discrimination between them. The future Buddha-king is called

Angrok, the name of his playmate is Tita. In the years before his final enlightenment, the future Buddha is partly holy, partly demoniac, according to this popular Javanese version.

Unlike the young Tita, Angrok had no schooling at all. Desiring to know the characters, he went to the teacher in Sagĕnggĕng, having in mind to become a pupil-servant, and requested to be taught the books of learning. Thus he was taught the characters and the combinations of consonants and vowels, and how the vowels change (*in Sanskrit grammar*). He was also taught the meaning of chronograms, how days, months and çāka-years are combined (*in dated documents*), and he learned the names of the days of six different weeks, the week consisting of six days, five days, seven days, three days, two days and nine days, as well as the names of the [thirty] weeks (*of the Javanese agricultural year*). In this way Angrok became cleverer than young Tita, though both had been taught the same books of learning by the teacher.

Now the teacher had in his garden a jambu tree, planted by himself; it was the centre of his courtyard, bearing an abundance of fruit, densely clustered and newly ripening. However, they were taboo; nobody was allowed to gather them, and nobody dared to pick even one. 'You will have to gather them as soon as they are ripe [since this is your job]', the teacher had told his pupils. Angrok, seeing the fruit of the jambu tree, desired them greatly. When night fell and everyone was sleeping, Angrok was sleeping too. As he slept bats flew out of his body through his fontanelle, one after the other, without interruption; the whole night long they ate the teacher's jambus. Next morning, the fruit were spread all over the ground, and the [pupil-]servants had to collect them. When he saw what had happened to the jambus the teacher was greatly upset and asked the boys: 'Why are the jambus all crushed?' They answered: 'My lord' they are crushed as the result of an attack by bats.' Then the teacher took rattan thorns, wound a circle of thorns round the jambu tree and kept watch during the night.

Now Angrok was sleeping again in the southern room, near the place where alang-alang grass was dried and where the teacher spent some time plaiting roof-mats. When the teacher saw the innumerable bats coming from Angrok's fontanelle and eating his jambus, he was much disquieted and attempted, in vain, to chase the creatures away. Then, growing furious, he expelled Angrok from his house. It was about midnight when he expelled him. Blind with sleep Angrok arose, went out, and fell asleep again on the alang-alang stack outdoors. The teacher came after him [in order to punish him]. Then, suddenly, he saw a light shining in the midst of the alang-alang stack. He was alarmed, thinking that a fire had broken out. Then he looked more closely at the shining halo and saw that it was Angrok. So he told him to rise and to go back indoors, saying that he should sleep with the other boys in the house. Angrok obeyed and went to sleep indoors.

Next morning the teacher told him to help himself to the jambus [as many as he liked]. Angrok was glad and replied: 'When I become a king, I shall repay the debt which I now owe to you.' *738*

Pararaton
Folk-tale
16th cent.
Java

Prometheus, fettered on the Caucasus, explains to the ocean nymphs the reasons for his punishment by Zeus.

PROMETHEUS. And since ye ask me under what pretence
  He thus maltreats me, I will show it you:
  For soon as He upon his father's throne
  Had sat secure, forthwith to divers Gods
  He divers gifts distributed, and his realm
  Began to order. But of mortal men
  He took no heed, but purposed utterly
  To crush their race and plant another new;
  And, I excepted, none dared cross his will;
  But I did dare, and mortal men I freed
  From passing on to Hades thunder-stricken;
  And therefore am I bound beneath these woes,
  Dreadful to suffer, pitiable to see:
  And, I, who in my pity thought of men
  More than myself, have not been worthy deemed
  To gain like favour, but all ruthlessly
  I thus am chained, foul shame this sight to Zeus.
CORYPHAEUS. Iron-hearted must he be and made of rock
  Who is not moved, Prometheus, by thy woes:
  Fain could I wish I ne'er had seen such things,
  And, seeing them, am wounded to the heart.
PROMETHEUS. Yea, I am piteous for my friends to see.
CORYPHAEUS. Did'st thou not go to farther lengths than this?
PROMETHEUS. I made men cease from contemplating death.
CORYPHAEUS. What medicine did'st thou find for that disease?
PROMETHEUS. Blind hopes I gave to live and dwell with them.

CORYPHAEUS. Great service that thou did'st for mortal
    men!
PROMETHEUS. And more than that, I gave them fire, yes I.
CORYPHAEUS. Do short-lived men the flaming fire possess?
PROMETHEUS. Yea, and full many an art they'll learn
    from it.
CORYPHAEUS. And is it then on charges such as these
    That Zeus maltreats thee, and no respite gives
    Of many woes? And has thy pain no end?
PROMETHEUS. End there is none, except as pleases Him.
CORYPHAEUS. How shall it please? What hope hast thou?
    See'st not
    That thou hast sinned? Yet to say how thou sinned'st
    Gives me no pleasure, and is pain to thee.
    Well! let us leave these things, and, if we may,
    Seek out some means to 'scape from this thy woe.
PROMETHEUS. 'Tis a light thing for one who has his foot
    Beyond the reach of evil to exhort
    And counsel him who suffers. This to me
    Was all well known. Yea, willing, willingly
    I sinned, nor will deny it. Helping men,
    I for myself found trouble: yet I thought not
    That I with such dread penalties as these

Aeschylus
525-456 B.C.
Prometheus Bound

    Should wither here on these high-towering crags,
    Lighting on this lone hill and neighbourless.   *739*

*From nature
to culture*

Let us see then whether what I am maintaining here is
true and borne out by Nature. I say that there is hardly
a creature which, when young, can keep its body or tongue
still and is not perpetually trying to move and utter cries.
Thus, we see some springing and leaping, as if urged by
I know not what hidden delight to dance and frolic,
whilst others fill the air with a thousand and one different
cries. But no creature is sensible of the order or confusion
that movement is capable of and that we call measure
and harmony; whereas these same divinities who preside
over our festivities have given us, in addition to the sense
of pleasure, that of measure and harmony. Guided by
these gods, this sense governs our movements and teaches
us to form a kind of link between us, forged by our songs

Plato
429-347 B.C.
Laws

and dancing. Hence the word 'chorus', derived naturally
from the word meaning 'joy' (*charis*).   *740*

Our wish is that all men should be educated fully to full humanity; not only one individual, nor a few nor even many, but all men together and singly, young and old, rich and poor, of high and of lowly birth, men and women —in a word, all whose fate it is to be born human beings: so that at last the whole of the human race may become educated, men of all ages, all conditions, both sexes and all nations. . . .

Therefore we propose to recommend three things, repeating ourselves in order to be clearly understood: we must lead towards universal education (1) all men; (2) in all things, so that they become educated; (3) in all ways.

All men: that is to say, all peoples, conditions, families, persons, never omitting anybody; for all are human beings with the same future life before them and the same road leading to it, pointed out by God but beset with snares and divers obstacles. It will therefore be necessary to warn and instruct all men prudently about these things, in order to drive foolishness from out our midst, if that be possible, so that the lament of wise men that 'the world is full of fools' will be no longer called for.

In all things: that is to say, in all things that can make man wise and happy. But what are these things? They are the four wise things which Solomon commends in the four exceeding wise little creatures:

1. Provision for the future, which he praises in the ants....

2. Prudence in the present, to do nothing except by safe ways, which he observes in the conies. . . .

3. Inclination to concord, without coercive force, which he praises in the locusts. . . .

4. Finally, that whatever is done, however slight, should be harmonious, regular and systematic; as is the work of the spider, even if otherwise it is useless. . . .

In all ways: that is to say, towards truth, so that rightly formed by her each man will stand beyond the precipices of error and hazard, and walk in the paths of righteousness. For now few mortals rely on their own foundation or that of things; most of them follow blind instinct, or the opinions of others. These disagreeing diversely with each other and with things themselves, there is no end to hesitation,

J. A. Comenius
Czech writer
1592-1670
The Pampaedia

stumbling, lapsing and finally ruin. If an equal **remedy** is to be sought for this evil, it cannot be other **than to** follow not the guidance of blind habit or persuasion, **but** the adamantine rule of God and of things themselves.

741

Right to education

The ink of the savants and the blood of the martyrs will be weighed at the Day of Judgement.

Every Moslem man and every Moslem woman is under a duty to acquire knowledge.

Hadith
(Sayings
of the Prophet)

Allah imposes on a community the duty of instructing its neighbours, of explaining to them the law, of showing them the right path and of acquainting them with the [divine] commandments and moral imperatives, and it is the duty of these to receive instruction from their neighbours, to master the law and to profit from their lessons, otherwise they would draw upon themselves a swift punishment.

742

Koran
Al-Ghashiyah 21

Warn thou then; for thou art a warner only: thou hast no authority over them.

743

Romanian proverb

Though a learned man may not possess a foot of land, the whole world is his country.

744

Knowledge is power.

Russian proverbs

To be keen-eyed is to see, not the mountain, but what lies behind it.

745

今是の華城には、但だ一の大学のみ有りて
閻塾有ること無し。是の故に貧賤の子弟、津
を問ふに所無く、遠方の好事往還するに疲多
し。今此の一隅を建てて、普く童蒙を誘む。

空海 綜芸種智院式。八二八年

In our capital today, we only have a school reserved for the nobles and the rich, and none for the people, so that their children know not where they can go to learn, and students from afar, full of ardour and curiosity, grow weary of travelling endlessly to and fro. I found this Institute and will have all children taught. *746*

Kūkai
Rules of the
Shugei Shuchi. In
Institute
Founded in 828
at Kyoto, Japan

*Honours
and favours
for schools*

Above all else, this Inca [Pachacutec], embellished and greatly honoured and favoured the schools which the Inca King Roca founded in Cuzco; he increased the number of masters and teachers; and he commanded that all the feudal nobles, the captains and their families, and all Indians indiscriminately of whatever office, soldiers and those below them, should use the language of Cuzco, and that government, dignity or overlordship should go to none unless he knew it well. *747*

Blas Valera
Quoted by
Garcilaso de la Vega
Early 17th cent
Peru

*Answer to those
who are afraid
of education
for the people*

There are men (I know that such people exist) who will ask: What will happen, when all men have become wise? Will the erudite and erudition become commonplace, will there be a confusion of estates, will it be possible for anyone to set out at any time to teach others, or to judge religions and systems of government? This is my answer to them: The foundations of a State or a religion whose safety is dependent upon the ignorance and slavery of its subjects or followers must be—of necessity—shaky. Genuine religion and a true system of government (which we wish for the whole world) are shining realities and their certainty has its origins in the light, and not in obscurity. It ought to be made clear that we do not say that all people should become scholars (since this would not be compatible with the extent of their abilities, or with

J. A. Comenius
Czech writer
1592-1670
Via Lucis

their environment or status, nor is there any need for it). What we do say is that all should be able to attain in sufficient degree that wisdom which leads to salvation.   *748*

Let no one say: what is the use of giving learning to craftsmen, peasants, workmen, women and girls, how could they use it, to what purpose could they put it? My reply is this: when engaged in divers tasks, they will have pleasant thoughts; when resting, they will be able to read the Bible and other useful works (for they will be attracted by the beauty of the thought). They will, at all times, meditate on the works of God, and on all that is worthy pertaining to reasonable relations between men; they will find reason, everywhere and in all things, to praise God and will prepare themselves, joyfully, for the life hereafter. Will not life on this earth then be a paradise of delight?   *749*

J. A. Comenius
Czech writer
1592-1670
Didaktika

*In favour
of more equality
in education*

The kind of equality in education we may hope to attain, but which must be sufficient, is one that is devoid of any dependence, whether voluntary or otherwise. . . . By a careful choice both of the subjects themselves and of the right methods of teaching them, the great mass of people can be taught all that the average man needs to know in order to be able to run his home, manage his affairs, develop his industry and faculties to the full, identify his rights, defend and exercise them, fulfil them properly, and judge his actions and those of others according to his own lights. All that he needs to know, if he is not to be lacking in any of those lofty and delicate sentiments that do honour to human nature; if he is not to have to depend blindly on those to whom he is obliged to entrust the management of his affairs or the exercise of his rights; if he is to be in a position to choose them and keep an eye on them; to be no longer duped by those popular falsehoods which make life unbearable with superstitious fears and fanciful hopes; to be able to combat prejudices with the aid of reason alone, and, finally, not to be impressed by quackery, which is ever ready to make inroads on his personal fortune, his health, his freedom of expression and opinion, by assuring him that he is going to become rich, to be cured or to be saved.

Condorcet
Esquisse
d'un Tableau
Historique
des Progrès
de l'Esprit Humain
1798
France

If education is more equally distributed, then there will be more equality in industry also, and consequently in people's wealth, and equality of wealth will necessarily contribute to equality in education; whilst equality between nations and that enjoyed by each individual, necessarily exert a mutual influence on one another.   *750*

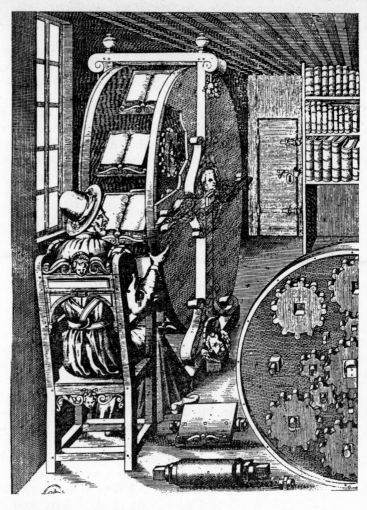

Proposed
machine for
reading several
books at a time
17th cent.
Italy

TRIBUTE TO GUTENBERG

When the night grows weary, the priests of chimeras
    disappear,
And the day no longer illumines a false knowledge;
. When the sword falls from the rough hands of violence
And murder no longer pollutes the sacred era of peace;
When here the devil, the rich oppressor,
And there the beast, the wretched peasant, at last become
    human;
When from West to East spreads the radiance
And the generous heart ennobles reason;
When, assembled in council, the peoples of the Earth
With one voice make the firmament ring with their cry
Of the one word 'Justice!' resounding above the din
And at last Heaven sends down this long-awaited
    ambassadress:
That will be a triumph worthy of thee, and the tribute
Of the praise thy name has deserved of the world. *751*

Mihály Vörösmarty
Hungarian
romantic poet
1800-55

*People should
at least know
how to read*

As it is impossible for everyone to succeed in understanding fully the knowledge contained in the books and languages which lead to knowledge, what I consider to be a prime necessity for everyone, and what I aim at with my advice, is that people should know how to read. If some people know this and no more, even if all they know is how to read in their own mother tongue, then already they will have profited themselves. . . . Thus, there are Christian nations where, thanks to the work of learned persons, many fine books are produced, chiefly in the language of the country; and the people themselves love and esteem books, the reading of which spreads wisdom, above all that wisdom which finds its stay in God. *752*

Miklós Tótfalusi-Kis
A scholarly printer
dedicated
to the education
of the people
1686
Hungary

Turkish proverb

God gives learning to him who desires it; fortune, to him whom He chooses. *753*

The Old Believers of the Vyg, a monastery founded at the end of the seventeenth century, open a school for all the local children.

Contemporary
Russian text

The people came there from various towns and places.... The children of both sexes were taught to read and write. *754*

*Education
for women*

Proclamation by the students of the Blanka Teleki School after the March revolution (1848).

Patriots! 'Liberty, Equality, Fraternity' is your watchword; in vindication of your word, we ask you for equal rights for women. We demand:
1. That women be admitted to the University;
2. That there be an end of sayings such as: 'everybody has the right to speak except women';
3. That there be schools throughout Hungary, even in the smallest village, and that all parents be able to send their children there;
4. That village teachers be paid a decent salary such as will make it possible for them to carry out their work successfully. *755*

Hungary

Teachers

Someone asked, 'How can good be promoted in the world?'
I said, 'Through teachers.'
'How is that?'
I said, 'In human nature there are only strength, weakness, good, evil, and the Mean.'

The questioner did not understand.

I explained, 'Righteousness, uprightness, strictness, and firmness of action are examples of strength that is good, and fierceness, narrow-mindedness, and violence are examples of strength that is evil. Kindness, mildness, and humility are examples of weakness that is good, and softness, indecision, and perverseness are examples of weakness that is evil. Only the Mean brings harmony. The Mean is the principle of regularity, the universally recognized law of morality, and that to which the sage is devoted. Therefore, the sage institutes education so as to enable people to transform their evil by themselves, to arrive at the Mean and to rest there. Therefore, those who are the first to be enlightened should instruct those who are slower in attaining enlightenment, and the ignorant should seek help from those who understand. Thus the way of the teachers is established. As the way of the teachers is established, there will be many good people.

Chou Tun-i
1017-73
Penetrating the
Book of Changes
China

756

Sorcerers, doctors, musicians, and the various craftsmen are not ashamed to study with teachers. And yet, among the families of scholar-officials if you speak of a teacher or a disciple everyone gathers around and begins to laugh. If you ask them why they laugh, they reply: 'These two men are practically the same age, and so they must understand the Way equally well.' Again if the teacher is lower in social status than the disciple it is considered shameful to study with him, while if he is a high official it is thought that one studies with him only to curry favour. Alas, it is obvious that in such circumstances the teaching of the Way can never be restored. Sorcerers, doctors, musicians, and craftsmen are not considered the equal of gentlemen, and yet gentlemen of these days cannot match them in knowledge. Is it not strange?

Han Yü
768-824
China

757

With no avidity for vast rice-fields and immense ponds, of all her suitors she favours only the scholar who can handle ink-slab and brush.

Viet-Namese
proverb

758

Certain of the wisest of the wise men of Israel were also hewers of wood and drawers of water, and yet they found time to study Torah day and night.

Moses receiving
the Tables of the Law
15th cent.
Germany

Maimonides
Mishneh Torah
12th cent.

It is forbidden to give oral instruction in Torah for payment. It was said [by Moses]: 'Take heed, for I have taught you statutes and judgements, even as the Lord commanded . . . I learnt them without payment, and so I teach them to you, and you shall do likewise for ever.'

759

Teaching should be based on love, not fear

I haue now wished, twise or thrise, this gentle nature, to be in a Scholemaster: And, that I haue done so, neither by chance, nor without some reason, I will now declare at large, why, in mine opinion, loue is fitter than feare, ientlenes better then beating, to bring vp a childe rightlie in learninge....

I do gladlie agree with all good Scholemasters in these pointes: to haue children brought to good perfitnes in learning: to all honestie in maners: to haue all fau[l]tes rightlie amended: to haue euerie vice seuerlie corrected: but for the order and waie that leadeth rightlie to these pointes we somewhat differ. For commonlie, many scholemasters, some, as I haue seen, moe, as I haue heard tell, be of so crooked a nature, as, when they meete with a hard witted scholer, they rather breake him, than bowe him, rather marre him, then mend him. For whan the scholemaster is angrie with some other matter, then will he sonest faul to beate his scholer: and though he him selfe should be punished for his folie, yet must he beate some scholer for his pleasure: though there be no cause for him to do so, nor yet fault in the scholer to deserue so. These ye will say, be fond scholemasters, and fewe they be, that be found to be soch. They be fond in deede, but surelie ouermany soch be found euerie where. But this will I say, that euen the wisest of your great beaters, do as oft punishe nature, as they do correcte faultes. Yea, many times, the better nature, is sorer punished: For, if one, by quicknes of witte, take his lesson readelie, an other, by hardnes of witte, taketh it not so speedelie: the first is alwaies commended, the other is commonlie punished: whan a wise scholemaster, should rather discretelie consider the right disposition of both their natures, and not so moch wey what either of them is able to do now, as what either of them is likelie to do hereafter. For this I know, not onelie by reading of bookes in my studie, but also by experience of life, abrode in the world, that those, which be commonlie the wisest, the best learned, and best men also, when they be olde, were neuer commonlie the quickest of witte, when they were yonge. *760*

Roger Ascham
A great
schoolmaster
16th cent.
The Scholemaster
England

Violence

One of them [of his wards] was wild, unruly, given to lying, and quarrelsome. On one occasion he broke out most violently. I was exasperated. I never punished my boys, but this time I was very angry. I tried to reason with him. But he was adamant and even tried to overreach me. At last I picked up a ruler lying at hand and delivered a blow on his arm. I trembled as I struck him. I dare say he noticed it. This was an entirely novel experience for them all. The boy cried out and begged to be forgiven. He cried not because the beating was painful to him; he could, if he had been so minded, have paid me back in the same coin, being a stoutly built youth of seventeen; but he realized my pain in being driven to this violent resource. Never again after this incident did he disobey me. But I still repent that violence. I am afraid I exhibited before him that day not the spirit, but the brute, in me. *761*

Mahatma Gandhi
1869-1948

SALARY AND ANNUAL PROVISION FOR THE SCHOOLMASTER, AND HIS DUTIES

The aforesaid Sages, seeing that the said revenue could not at any time or on any occasion be properly and legally used for the benefit of the Community or its members for such useful purposes as had been enacted, decided that the said Community, regardless of any other reasons or exceptions, should deduct annually from the said revenue from the forest of Gravelonne or from its other revenues, two hundred lire and eight pence for the purpose of appointing and remunerating a schoolmaster, and such other things as may be discussed by the Council and approved by their Most Excellent Lordships of Siena. The aforesaid Sages did so in order that good and beneficial public use should be made of the revenues and profits of this Community and, in particular, that the children of each and everyone should be well brought up and educated in the good virtues, in grammar, arithmetic and vernacular and Christian speech. The said schoolmaster should be worthy of his charge and diligent in teaching the said children, and should not leave the school on the days when he should be teaching. He is to teach for a year, and should he miss one day, he must compensate for it. And, apart from the said salary, he should be given a free house for the said period of teaching, furnished with tables and benches for the said children where they can sit down to write and keep their reading books and, similarly, he should not lack any commodities necessary for daily life, such as earthenware, glass, or wooden vessels. And let it always be thus when the schoolmaster is from outside; and if he is not a stranger and is already

Rural organization Community of Castello del Piano 1571 Italy

established, let him be given only the said salary or more, as the Council may see fit, and the free house suitable to teach in, and nothing other. And let there be no derogation. *762*

Learning, the best legacy

Naladyar 3rd or 4th cent. Sangam period Tamil tradition

It cannot be taken from its place of deposit; it does not perish anywhere by fire; if kings of surpassing grandeur are angry, they cannot take it away; [and therefore] what any man should provide for his children as a legacy is learning. Other things are not [real wealth]. *763*

Isocrates 436-338 B.C. Panegyricus Athens

The intellectual culture which has educated us for action and sweetened our relationships, which has distinguished between the misfortunes caused by ignorance and those arising from necessity, which has taught us to avoid the former and to bear the latter without repining, was brought forth by our city. *764*

Dictatorial tendencies hostile to progress

Sermon delivered on 25 March 1831 (anniversary of the Constitution) before the Emperor Pedro I, who abdicated the following year.

Clearly, the ideas of the old régime could no longer accommodate intellectual progress. The injurious monopoly of certain men, the still more noxious caste distinctions which reduced to the condition of abject pariahs the most useful elements of society, the revolting inequality of rights could no longer survive under the tremendous beam of light that was broadening the highways of culture. There was no alternative but to yield to this violent shock, which was to change the political centre of gravity and consolidate the civil institutions on a firmer basis by determining the boundaries of authority and the limits of obedience.

Francisco
de Monte Alverne
Brazil

765

Education is all

José Bonifacio
de Andrada
Notes for 'Civilization
of the Indian Savages
in the Empire
of Brazil'
1823

For primitive man is not by nature either good or bad: he is simply an automaton whose machinery can be set into motion by example, education and kindness. Had Cato been born among the satraps of Persia, he would have died unknown among the mass of base slaves. Had Newton been born among the Guarani Indians, he would just have been a biped born poor; but a Guarani brought up by Newton might perhaps have assumed his place. 766

*The inequality
of intelligence*

Condorcet
Vie de Turgot
1786
France

The inequality of intelligence and understanding among members of the human race cannot be destroyed; it derives from nature as it does from the state of society; it would be pernicious to halt the efforts of outstanding men: but (and this is the aim which society should pursue) it is possible to ensure that, all men being instructed in what they need to know, being saved from error by education and protected from all forms of imposture, superiority of knowledge or talent will be an advantage to those who possess it without at the same time affording a means of submitting others to their will or making them the victims of their cunning. This can best be achieved by making it easier to learn, by the simplicity and clarity of methods of teaching, by creating and strengthening the habit of clear thinking. Fairness of mind would then suffice to ensure that no men should have particular advantage over others in the ordinary business of life; for of all qualities fairness is that which most influences the details of conduct and that which nature has most universally and most equally bestowed. 767

*Education
against oppression*

After the abolition of the standing army and the police, the material instruments of compulsion of the former government, the Commune set out to break its spiritual means of oppression—the power of the priests; it disestablished the Church. . . . All educational establishments

Karl Marx
The Civil
War in France
1871

were made open to the people free of charge and, at the same time, freed from all interference by the Church and the State. Thus, not only was education rendered accessible to all, but learning itself was freed from the shackles laid upon it by class prejudice and governmental power.   *768*

*Training
for a variety
of labours*

Modern industry... imposes the necessity of recognizing... variation of work and consequently, the greatest possible development of (the labourer's) varied aptitudes as a fundamental law of modern production. . . . It becomes a question of life and death. . . . Modern industry, indeed, compels society, under penalty of death, to replace the detail-worker of today, crippled by life-long repetition of one and the same trivial operation, by the fully-developed individual, fit for a variety of labours, and to whom the different . . . functions he performs are but so many modes of giving free scope to his own natural and acquired powers.

The bourgeoisie which, in setting up technical and agricultural schools, etc., was merely following the basic trend of industrial progress, gave the proletariats no more than a fiction of technical instruction. Though the Factory Act, that first concession wrung from capital, was forced to combine elementary education, rudimentary as it was, with work in the factory, there can be no doubt that when the working class comes into power, as inevitably it must, technical instruction, both theoretical and practical, will take its proper place in the working-class schools. There is also no doubt that the final result of such revolutionary ferments will be the abolition of the old division of labour....

'*Ne sutor ultra crepidam!*' Shoe-maker, stick to thy shoes! This *nec plus ultra* of handicraft wisdom became sheer nonsense, from the moment the watchmaker Watt invented

Karl Marx
Das Kapital
1867

the steam-engine, the barber Arkwright, the throstle, and the working-jeweller Fulton, the steamship.   *769*

*Machinery
and humanity*

The Machine Age: to replace purpose by speed.   *770*

Karel Čapek
Czech writer
1890-1938

What I object to, is the 'craze' for machinery, not machinery as such. The craze is for what they call labour-saving machinery. Men go on 'saving labour' till thousands are without work and thrown on the open streets to die of starvation. I want to save time and labour, not for a fraction of mankind, but for all; I want the concentration of wealth, not in the hands of a few, but in the hands of all. Today machinery merely helps a few to ride on the back of millions. The impetus behind it all is not the philanthropy to save labour, but greed. It is against this constitution of things that I am fighting with all my might.

Mahātma Gandhi
1869-1948

771

Tzu-kung asked: 'If someone spread abroad his benefits among the people and was thus able to succour the multitude, what would you think of him? Could it be said that he possesses the virtue of humanity (*which consists in loving mankind*)?'

The Master replied: 'That man possesses not only the virtue of humanity, but holiness itself. Yao and Shun themselves found difficulty in attaining it.

'He who possesses the virtue of humanity wishes to strengthen himself and thereafter to strengthen other men; he wishes to understand himself and thereafter to make them understand themselves. To know how to start with what is near at hand (and then move further afield) that is the art needed for the virtue of humanity.'

Confucius
551-479? B.C.
Analects
China

772

Āpastamba-
Dharmasūtra
450-350 B.C.
Sanskrit

He [the teacher] gives birth to him [the child] from the point of view of learning. That is the best birth. The mother and the father give birth only to [the] body [of the child].

773

True nobility

He then went over to Gautama, son of Haridrumat, and said: 'I wish to live the life of a student of sacred knowledge under thee, the revered one; may I become a pupil of thine, the revered one.' He [Gautama] asked him: 'Now, of what family art thou, my dear?' He replied: 'I do not know this, sir, of what family I am. I asked my mother. She answered me: "When, in my youth, I used to go about a good deal serving as a maid, I obtained you [as son]. So I do not know this, of what family thou art. However, I am Jabālā by name and thou art Satyakāma by name." So I am Satyakāma Jabālā, sir.' He [Gautama] then said to him: 'No one but a [person who should be considered to be a true] Brāhmana could have spoken

Chāndogya-
Upanishad
8th to 6th cent. B.C.
Sanskrit

out this [truth so frankly]. Bring the fuel, my dear, I shall initiate thee as my pupil. Thou hast not departed from the truth.' 774

*False and true
superiority*

Since there are thus, among these four social orders, Vāsettha, both bad and good qualities, [respectively] despised and admired by the wise, when the Brāhmanas assent that: 'The social order of the Brāhmana as alone is the best social order, other social orders are low; only the social order of the Brāhmanas is fair, other social orders are dark; only the Brāhmanas are of pure breed; only the Brāhmanas are the legitimate sons of Brahman, born from his mouth, offspring of Brahman, created by Brahman, and heirs of Brahman'—that claim of theirs the wise do not admit. And this for what reason? Because, Vāsettha, whoever from these four social orders becomes a Bhiksu, an Arhant, one whose taints have worn away, who has lived the life, who has done whatsoever deserves to be done, who has borne the burden, who has attained his own salvation, in whose case the bond of rebirth has fallen off, and who has become liberated on account of his perfect knowledge—he is declared chief among them. 775

Dīghanikāya IV
3rd cent. B.C.
Pali

Condorcet
L'Atlantide
1794
France

I shall speak . . . of the bringing together of the learned from all over the world in a universal republic of the sciences—the only kind that can be of practical use and is not just a day-dream. 776

Knowledge and food; knowledge and medicine; joy, poetry, freedom

*'Development'
through schools*

Let the five *mu* of land surrounding the farmer's cottage be planted with mulberry trees, and persons over fifty may all be clothed in silk. Let poultry, dogs and swines be kept and bred in season, and those over seventy may all be provided with meat. Let the cultivation of the hundred-*mu* farm not be interfered with, and a family of eight mouths need not go hungry. Let attention be paid to teaching in schools and the people be taught the principles of filial piety and brotherly respect, and white-headed old men will not be seen carrying loads

Mencius
372?-289? B.C.
China

on the road. When the aged wear silk and eat meat and the common people are free from hunger and cold, never has the lord of such a people failed to become king. *777*

Huang Tsung-hsi
Ming-i tai-fang lu
17th cent.
China

Until the end of the Three Dynasties there was law. Since the Three Dynasties there has been no law. Why do I say so? Because the Two Emperors and Three Kings knew that mankind could not do without sustenance and therefore gave men fields to cultivate. They knew that men could not do without clothes and therefore gave them land on which to grow mulberry and hemp. They knew also that men could not go untaught, so they set up schools, established the marriage ceremony to guard against promiscuity, and instituted military service to guard against disorders. This constituted law until the end of the Three Dynasties. It was never laid down for the profit of one man alone. *778*

Kemal Pasha
Atatürk
1937

If lasting peace is desired, action must be taken to improve the lot of the masses. Throughout mankind, hunger and oppression must be replaced by prosperity. *779*

Kuan-tzu
4th to 3rd cent. B.C.
China

If you give a man a fish, he will have a meal.
If you teach him to fish, he will have a living.

If you are thinking a year ahead, sow seed.
If you are thinking ten years ahead, plant a tree.
If you are thinking one hundred years ahead, educate the people.
By sowing seed once, you will harvest once.
By planting a tree, you will harvest tenfold.
By educating the people, you will harvest one hundred-fold. *780*

OATH OF HIPPOCRATES |(460?-377? B.C.)

Compulsory in many countries, with some variations, for all those who enter the medical profession.

I swear by Apollo the physician, and Aesculapius, and Hygeia, and Panacea, and all the gods and goddesses, that, according to my ability and judgement, I will keep this Oath and this stipulation—to reckon him who taught me this Art equally dear to me as my parents, to share my substance with him, and relieve his necessities if

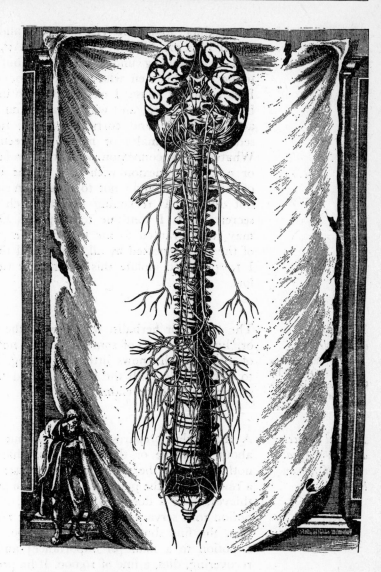

The anatomy lesson
1714
France

required; to look upon his offspring in the same footing
as my own brothers, and to teach them this Art, if they
shall wish to learn it, without fee or stipulation; and that
by precept, lecture, and every other mode of instruction,
I will impart a knowledge of the Art to my own sons,
and those of my teachers, and to disciples bound by a
stipulation and oath according to the law of medicine,
but to none others. I will follow that system of regimen
which, according to my ability and judgement, I consider
for the benefit of my patients, and abstain from whatever
is deleterious and mischievous. I will give no deadly
medicine to any one if asked, nor suggest any such counsel;
and in like manner I will not give to a woman a pessary

to produce abortion. With purity and with holiness I will pass my life and practise my Art. I will not cut persons labouring under the stone, but will leave this to be done by men who are practitioners of this work. Into whatever houses I enter, I will go into them for the benefit of the sick, and will abstain from every voluntary act of mischief and corruption; and, further from the seduction of females or males, of freemen and slaves. Whatever, in connexion with my professional practice or not, in connexion with it, I see or hear, in the life of men, which ought not to be spoken of abroad, I will not divulge, as reckoning that all such should be kept secret. While I continue to keep this Oath unviolated, may it be granted to me to enjoy life and the practice of the Art, respected by all men, in all times! But should I trespass and violate this Oath, may the reverse be my lot!   *781*

The duty of knowledge

Blas Valera
Quoted by
Garcilaso de la Vega
Early 17th cent.
Peru

The doctor or herbalist who ignores the virtues of herbs or, knowing those of some, attempts not to learn those of all, in truth knows little or nothing. Let him labour to discover all, both the beneficial and the noxious, and so earn the title he claims.   *782*

Medical offences and the unequal value of human lives

Kutāraçāstra code
14th cent.
Java

A man who prepares potions without knowing much about medicine or the practice of charms, who knows nothing about the symptoms of diseases and yet claims a reward from the patient, he should be put on a par with thieves; such a doctor is a liar. Now, if he prescribes a potion to a servant and this man, not recovering, finally dies, the fine should be fixed at 4,600. If he prescribes a potion to a man [of importance] and this man, not recovering, dies, a fine of 10,000. If he prescribes a potion to a brahmin, and the brahmin, not recovering, dies, a fine of 20,000, [collected] by the king. If the one who drinks the potion dies, the king is entitled to kill the man who prescribed the potion. This is the law as it always has been.   *783*

Medical and agricultural 'development'

Everywhere, two kinds of medical treatment have been established by king Priyadarsin, the beloved of the gods, namely, medical treatment for men and medical treatment for animals. Medicinal herbs useful for men and useful for animals have been imported and planted wherever they were not to be found. Similarly, roots

Asoka's Rock Edict II
3rd cent B.C.
Prakrit

and fruits have also been imported and planted wherever they were not to be found. On the roads trees have been planted and wells have been dug for the use of men and animals. *784*

Asoka's Pillar
Edict VII
3rd cent B.C.
Prakrit

On the roads, banyan trees have been planted by me so that they should give shade to men and animals. Mango-groves have been planted. At every half *krosa*, I have caused wells to be dug. Rest-houses for the night have been built. Many water points have been provided in various places for the use of men and animals. *785*

Work well done

The sage asked the Spirit of Wisdom thus: 'What is the business of the well-endeavouring, the artisans?'

The Spirit of Wisdom answered thus: 'The business of the artisans is this, that as to that work which they do not understand, they do not bring a hand to it; and that which they well understand, they perform well and with attention, and they demand wages lawfully. For as to him who persists in doing that work which he does

Dādistān ī Mēnōg
ī Xrad
Sassanian period
3rd to 7th cent.
Persia

not understand, it is he by whom that work is done that work is spoiled and becomes useless; and when, moreover, he is a man whose work makes him satisfied, it then becomes even an origin of sin for him.' *786*

Education

Dēnkart
9th cent.
Persia

One ought to treat one's wife and children well and not to leave them without education. For he is always afflicted and savours less the taste of food who does not treat his wife and children well or who leaves them uneducated. *787*

Prosperity

Avesta
Vendidad
1st cent. B.C.
to 1st cent. A.D.
Persia

Creator of the material world, possessor of Righteousness! Where, secondly, is it most joyful upon this earth? Then spoke Athura Mazdā: There indeed where a righteous man has built a house, endowed with fire, milk, a wife, a son and good herds. In that house there is abundance of cattle, abundant righteousness, abundant fodder, abundance of dogs, an abundant wife, abundance of children, abundant fire, abundance of all that pertains to good living. *788*

Great truth, formidable moral order, sacrificial initiation, penance, brahman, and sacrifice—these sustain the earth. May that earth, mistress of our past and our future, afford us ample space. May she, who is characterized by numerous heights and slopes and plains and who bears herbs of many qualities, spread freely and afford nourishment for us. May that earth, in whom are the sea and rivers and waters, in whom grow food and crops, in whom stirs whatever lives and breathes, grant unto us the first fruits of her provisions.   *789*

Atharvaveda XII
2200-1800 B.C.
Sanskrit

Immediate knowledge is gained through living

The principal character, Adam, transformed into Kepler, wakes from a dream in which he has seen the French Revolution.

ADAM:

The day will come, as I have already said,
When men will laugh at all that! The Statesman
Reputed great, the orthodox thinker
Whose infallibility was vaunted,
Will be regarded by posterity
As play-actors. Real greatness
Will then appertain to naturalness,
To simplicity, which keep straight on,
Which only take a leap if they have to clear
An unexpected obstacle, and which trace new paths
Only if the old ones are disappearing
Or if they must venture into the unknown.
On that day Science, so abtruse,

Teaching the birds
to sing
End of 15th cent.
Sweden

De docilitate quarundam Auium.

So inextricable as to drive mad
Those who try to fathom her—all men
Will understand her without the need to learn.

. . . .

Go throw these yellow parchments on the fire,
These mildewed folios
Which make us forget how to walk,
Nay, even how to think, and which spread wide
In our time the false beliefs and corruption
Of past ages. Into the fire with them,
And then go breathe the pure air, rather
Than seek in dusty writings
Between the cheerless walls of a room
What a song is, what a bird is like,
Or what makes a forest.
Is life so long, think'st thou,
That man can—and why not until the grave?—
Endlessly study the theory of it?
Farewell to school, for both of us.
Let thy youth in its flower, 'midst song
And sunshine, lead thee to joy!

Imre Madách
1823-64
The Tragedy of Man
Scene ix
Hungary

790

THE POET'S VOCATION

Address delivered on the occasion of the 84th anniversary of the death of Pushkin.

We are familiar from earliest childhood with the magic name of Pushkin, and these syllables cast their spell over many days of our lives. The names of kings and captains, inventors of instruments of assassination, torturers and martyrs ring heavy; but that of Pushkin strikes a joyous note.

Pushkin bore his creative gift so easily and gaily, though the fate of the poet is neither easy nor gay, but tragic. Pushkin was a consummate master of his art, working with breadth and confidence and freedom; yet our hearts often sink at the thought of Pushkin. The triumphal, joyous advance of the poet—who could not harm the world around him, for his concern was with the human soul— was all too often halted by the acts of base individuals more interested in goods and chattels than in God.

. . . .

What is a poet? A man who writes verse? Of course not. It is not because he writes in verse that he is called a poet; but he writes in verse, making harmony of words and sounds because he is a child of harmony, a poet.
What is harmony? Harmony is the accord of the forces

of the universe, the order in universal life. Order is Cosmos, as opposed to disorder, which is Chaos. Chaos, according to the teaching of the ancients, gives birth to Cosmos, or peace. Cosmos is related to Chaos, even as the leaping waves of the sea are related to the massive ocean swell. A son may resemble his father in nothing but one hidden trait; yet this it is that makes father and son alike.

Chaos is primeval, elemental anarchy; Cosmos—ordered harmony, culture; Cosmos is born of Chaos; the elemental harbours the seeds of culture; harmony is created out of anarchy.

Universal life consists of an unending succession of new forms, new species, cradled by primeval chaos, nurtured and selected by culture, and moulded by harmony into shapes which then dissolve anew into the primeval mists. The significance of this process is beyond our understanding, its essence obscure; we console ourselves with the thought that new species are better than the old; but the wind snuffs out this tiny candle with which we strive to illumine the cosmic night. The order of the world is disquieting, akin to disorder, and may not always coincide with what we consider good and evil.

. . . .

The poet is the child of harmony; and he is given a part to play in world culture. His mission is threefold; firstly, to free sounds from the original, primeval element wherein they are submerged; secondly, to imbue them with harmony and form; thirdly, to bring this harmony into the external world.

The sounds, reft from the elements and transformed into harmony, themselves begin to work their effect when introduced into the world. 'The poet's words are his deeds.'

. . . .

Down in the fathomless depths of the spirit, where man ceases to be man, depths beyond the reach of civilization's creations—State and Society—are waves of sound akin to the waves of ether in which the universe is bathed, and swaying rhythms the processes which engender the mountains, winds and ocean currents, the vegetable and the animal kingdoms.

The depths of the spirit are hidden by the forms of the external world. Pushkin declared that they are hidden from the poet even more, perhaps, than from other people: 'and of the idle children of the world the idlest of all, perhaps, is he'.

The first task imposed upon the poet by his calling is to cast aside 'the cares of the bustling world' in order that he may raise the outer veils and reveal the depths. This sets the poet apart from the 'idle children of this world'.

> *He flees, wild and austere,*
> *Filled with sounds and confusion,*
> *To the shores of deserted seas,*
> *Into vast, resounding forests.*

Wild, austere, filled with confusion, because to reveal the depths of the spirit is as difficult as giving birth to a child; 'towards the seas and the forests' because only there, in solitude, can he gather all his strength and commune with 'original chaos', the primeval element out of which the waves of sound are born.

The mysterious task is accomplished, the veil lifted, the depths uncovered, the sound received into the soul. The second demand of Apollo is that this sound, reft from the depths and alien to the external world, be incorporated in the palpable, solid form of the word, with sounds and words combining in a harmonious whole. This is the realm of craftsmanship and it calls, no less than communion with 'primeval chaos', for inspiration. Inspiration, Pushkin said, is a state of mind giving a heightened awareness of impressions, a deeper understanding of the significance of ideas and the ability to explain them. Hence the poet's first and second tasks are inseparable, indissolubly intertwined: as more and more veils are lifted, as communion with chaos becomes more intimate and the birth of sound more difficult, the forms it assumes become clearer, more lingering and more harmonious, and it pursues the human ear with ever greater persistence.

Then comes the poet's third task: to bring into the world the sounds perceived by his soul and ranged in harmony. It is here that the notorious clash between the poet and the rabble occurs.

The term 'rabble' can never have been applied to the common people, save by such as themselves deserved the name. Pushkin collected folk songs, wrote in popular language; his village nurse was very near to him. Thus none but the stupid or the wicked can ever imagine that Pushkin could use the term 'rabble' to describe the common people. This will be clear from any Pushkin lexicon —if Russian culture is reborn.

Pushkin meant by 'rabble' much the same as we do. He frequently coupled it with the epithet 'mundane' to form a collective noun describing the kind of hereditary courtiers who possessed nothing but their titles of nobility. But even in Pushkin's time, the aristocracy was fast being replaced by the bureaucracy. And it is precisely these officials who constitute our 'rabble', the 'rabble' of yesterday and today: neither nobles nor common people, neither beasts nor clods of earth, neither wisps of mist nor fragments of planets, neither devils nor angels—in short one thing only can be said of them—that they are people. This is not particularly flattering: people, smart dealers and rogues whose souls are hopelessly, firmly smothered by 'the cares of the bustling world'.

. . . .

The rabble, like all other categories of people, progress extremely slowly. Thus for instance, despite the fact that the human brain has developed monstrously in recent centuries, to the detriment of other organs, people have only contrived to detach one State organ—the censorship— to defend the order of the world, expressed in government structures. By this means they have only paralysed the poet's third task—that of bringing harmony into the world. They might have contrived to paralyse the first two as well; they might have sought ways of troubling the very sources of harmony. What prevents them from doing so? Lack of ingenuity? Timidity? Pangs of conscience? No one can tell. Or perhaps some means of doing this are already being sought?

. . . .

We have no wish, on this day consecrated to the memory of Pushkin, to dispute whether the distinction the poet drew between individual freedom and what we now call political freedom was correct or not. We know that he claimed 'another', 'mysterious' freedom. We would call this 'personal' freedom; but for the poet it is something more:

> *To account*
> *To none; to serve and please*
> *Oneself alone; to power and rank*
> *Neither one's conscience nor one's head to bow;*
> *To wander freely, as the spirit moves,*
> *Marvelling at the beauties of nature*
> *And the creations of art and inspiration—*
> *Silently to drown in tender ecstasy.*
> *Such is happiness, such man's right!*

These words were written shortly before his death. In his youth Pushkin said, on the same subject:

> *Love and a mysterious freedom*
> *Taught my heart a simple hymn.*

'This mysterious freedom', this whim, is not merely personal freedom, but something much more: it is intimately linked with the first two demands Apollo makes on the poet. Every element of Pushkin's verse is essential for the liberation of harmony. Whilst allowing himself to be impeded in the third of his tasks—testing human hearts through harmony—Pushkin could brook no interference with the first two: and these two are not personal.

. . . .

Pushkin is dead. But 'for children, Posa and his like will never die', as Schiller said. And Pushkin likewise was never killed by Dantès' bullet. He was killed by lack of air. And culture died with him.

The time has come, my friend! My heart seeks peace.

Such were Pushkin's dying words; the dying words, also of the culture of Pushkin's age.

There is no happiness on earth,
but peace and freedom there are.

Peace and freedom. Both are essential to the poet for the liberation of harmony. But they, too, can be suppressed: not outer peace, but the peace to create; not a child's freedom, but freedom to hold liberal views, creative freedom, the mysterious freedom. And the poet dies because there is no more air for him to breathe, because life for him has lost its meaning.

The worthy officials who prevented the poet from testing human hearts by harmony will bear for ever the name of 'rabble'. But they prevented the poet only in the third of his tasks. The testing of the human heart by Pushkin's poetry has been achieved without reference to them.

An epithet far worse may still, if they do not take care, be applied to those officials who are now endeavouring to force poetry into patterns of their own devising, encroaching on its inner freedom and preventing it from fulfilling its mysterious vocation.

Aleksandr Blok
11 February 1921
U.S.S.R.

791

Maimonides
A Doctor's Prayer
12th cent.

Let me, oh Lord, by my knowledge discover today what I did not know yesterday, because art has no end, and because the spirit of man always presses onwards.

792

Servitude and violence

*Man
and might*

Might is that which makes a thing of anybody who comes under its sway. When exercised to the full, it makes a thing of man in the most literal sense, for it makes him a corpse. There where someone stood a moment ago, stands no one. . . .

From the power to transform a man into a thing by killing him there proceeds another power, and much more prodigious, that which makes a thing of him while he still lives. He is living, he has a soul, yet he is a thing. A strange being is that thing which has a soul, and strange the state of that soul. Who knows how often during each instant it must torture and destroy itself in order to conform? The soul was not made to dwell in a thing; and when forced to it, there is no part of that soul but suffers violence. . . .

For violence so crushes whomever it touches that it appears at last external no less to him who dispenses it than to him who endures it. So the idea was born of a destiny beneath which the aggressors and their victims are equally innocent, the victors and the vanquished brothers in the same misfortune. The vanquished is a cause of misfortune for the victor as much as the victor is for the vanquished. . . .

Whoever has had to mortify, to mutilate in himself all aspiration to live, of him an effort of heart-breaking generosity is required before he can respect the life of another. . . . In default of such generosity the vanquished soldier is the scourge of nature; possessed by war, he, as much as the slave, although in quite a different way, is become a thing, and words have no more power over him than over inert matter. In contact with might, both the soldier and the slave suffer the inevitable effect, which is to become either deaf or mute. . . .

Such is the nature of might. Its power to transform man into a thing is double and it cuts both ways; it petrifies differently but equally the souls of those who suffer it, and of those who wield it. . . .

By whatever means, this poem (the *Iliad*) is a miraculous object. The bitterness of it is spent upon the only true cause of bitterness: the subordination of the humna soul to might, which is, be it finally said, to matter. That subordination is the same for all mortals, although there is a difference according to the soul's degree of virtue, according to the way in which each soul endures

it. No one in the *Iliad* is spared, just as no one on earth
escapes it. None of those who succumb to it is for that
reason despised. Whatever, in the secret soul and in
human relations, can escape the empire of might is
loved, but painfully loved because of the danger of destruction that continually hangs over it. Such is the spirit
of the only veritable epic of the western world. . . .

But nothing of all that the peoples of Europe have
produced is worth the first known poem to have appeared
among them. Perhaps they will rediscover that epic
genius when they learn how to accept the fact that
nothing is sheltered from fate, how never to admire
might, or hate the enemy, or to despise sufferers. It is
doubtful if this will happen soon. . . .

Whoever does not know just how far necessity and a
fickle fortune hold the human soul under their domination
cannot treat as his equals, nor love as himself, those
whom chance has separated from him by an abyss. The
diversity of the limitations to which men are subject
creates the illusion that there are different species among
them which cannot communicate with one another.
Only he who knows the empire of might and knows
how not to respect it is capable of love and justice. *793*

Simone Weil
The Iliad
Poem of Might
1939-40
France

Slavery
and the dignity
of man

This is prescribed by the order of nature: it is thus that
God has created man. For 'let them', He says, 'have
dominion over the fish of the sea, and over the fowl of
the air, and over every creeping thing which creepeth
on the earth' (Genesis 1: 26). He did not intend that His
rational creature, who was made in His image, should
have dominion over anything but the irrational creation—
not man over man, but man over the beasts. And hence
the righteous men in primitive times were made shepherds
of cattle rather than kings of men, God intending thus
to teach us what the relative position of the creatures is,
and what the desert of sin; for it is with justice, we believe,
that the condition of slavery is the result of sin. And this
is why we do not find the word 'slave' in any part of
Scripture until righteous Noah branded the sin of his
son with this name (Genesis 9: 25-26). It is a name,
therefore, introduced by sin and not by nature.

When will
'the duty of ruling'
cease?

Those who are true fathers of their households desire
and endeavour that all the members of their household,
equally with their own children, should worship and win
God, and should come to that heavenly home in which
the duty of ruling men is no longer necessary, because

St. Augustine
354-430
The City of God

the duty of caring for their everlasting happiness has also ceased; but, until they reach that home, masters ought to feel their position of authority a greater burden than servants their service. *794*

Letter of Isidore
of Pelusium
Egyptian monk
5th cent.

We should treat slaves as we treat our own kind. For they are men as we are. . . . And, in truth, we are all one by nature, by faith and by the judgement awaiting us. *795*

St. John Chrysostom
c. 354-407
Homilies

In general, slavery is only the result of sin. Only avarice, envy, and insatiability have produced it. *796*

'DIE ALTDEUTSCHE GENESIS'

Genesis
c. 1065
16th-cent.
manuscript
Old German

It is Ham's fault
that there were ever serfs.
Before were all men
equal, free and noble. *797*

When the Jews asked Samuel to appoint over them a king, he told them of what use a king could be:

Hebrew Bible
I Samuel 8

This will be the manner of the king that shall reign over you: he will take your sons and appoint them unto him for his chariots, and to be his horsemen; and they shall run before his chariots. And he shall appoint them unto him for captains of thousands, and captains of fifties; and to plow his ground, and to reap his harvest, and to make his instruments of war, and the instruments of his chariots. And he will take your daughters to be perfumers, and to be cooks, and to be bakers. And he will take your fields and your vineyards, and your oliveyards, even the best of them, and give them to his servants. And he will take the tenth of your seed, and of your vineyards, and give to his officers, and to his servants. And he will take your men-servants, and your maid-servants, and your goodliest young men and your asses, and put them to his work. He will take the tenth of your flocks; and you shall be his servants. *798*

*Slavery
is contrary
to Christianity*

It is absolutely outrageous, and must therefore be published forth throughout Christendom, this scandal of anyone daring, in the sight of the Lord, to say to another man 'You are mine'—to someone whom God has redeemed at a great cost and set free. It is heathen. God has freed us from all fetters, and no one should henceforth presume to coerce another. This the Lord himself confirmed. His disciples were some high-born, some humble, and some were arrogant in their hearts. Christ knew well all that was in their hearts and said: Let he who would be first among you be the servant of all. God wills that we should be equal. Whosoever has been baptized and believes shall be saved; none has more freedom in heaven than another. Let all therefore know in what manner to hold him who dares say 'You are mine': he is no Christian. But if he does not leave off and honour God, let him be stripped of his goods like a heathen (*or: let him be to you as the heathen*), for he stands against Christ, and God's commandments in him are vain.

Reform of the Emperor Sigismund 15th cent.

799

Manoel da Nobrega Letter from Bahia 1549

On the Indians: In many things they are superior to the Christians, because they are better-living morally and have a greater respect for the natural law.

800

Indians and Negroes are men like others

S. de Vasconcellos Chronicle of the Society of Jesus in the State of Brazil 1663

By pronouncement of the Supreme Pastor of the Church, who has rendered judgement, . . . they [the Indians] are truly of the human race and truly men as we are, worthy to receive the sacraments of Holy Church, free by nature, and masters of their goods and actions.

801

How can a country inhabited at all times by a mass of brutal and hostile slaves have a liberal and enduring Constitution?

If the negroes are men like us, if they do not form a race of brute beasts, if they feel and think as we do, what a picture of sorrow and misery do they not offer to the imagination of any sensitive and Christian man?

José Bonifacio de Andrada Address to the Constituent Assembly concerning the Abolition of Slavery 1823 Brazil

The apologists of slavery quote the Greeks and Romans, forgetting that among the Greeks and Romans the eternal principles of the natural law were still imperfectly known and established.

802

Limits of submission to the law

In the course of his travels the author meets an old friend, a judge, who tells him the following tale:

A man of humble origin having worked his way up to the rank of assessor, became the master of several hundred peasants whom he exploited and oppressed. One of his two sons arranged to carry off and rape a young peasant girl on the very day of her wedding. The peasants rose in revolt against the masters, and the father and his two sons were killed.

Despite pressure and threats from the gentlefolk, the narrator, who had to sit in judgement on the peasants as murderers, stated their case as follows:

'Every man is born into the world equal to all others. All have the same bodily parts, all have reason and will. Consequently, apart from his relation to society, man is a being that depends on no one in his actions. But he puts limits to his own freedom of action, he agrees not to follow only his own will in everything, he subjects himself to the commands of his equals; in a word, he becomes a citizen. For what reason does he control his passions? Why does he set up a governing authority over himself? Why, though free to seek fulfilment of his will, does he confine himself within the bounds of obedience? For his own advantage, reason will say; for his own advantage, inner feeling will say; for his own advantage, wise legislation will say. Consequently, wherever being a citizen is not to his advantage, he is not a citizen. Consequently, whoever seeks to rob him of the advantages of citizenship is his enemy. Against his enemy he seeks protection and satisfaction in the law. If the law is unable or unwilling to protect him, or if its power cannot furnish him immediate aid in the face of clear and present danger, then the citizen has recourse to the natural law of self-defence, self-preservation, and well-being. For the citizen, in becoming a citizen, does not cease to be a man, whose first obligation, arising from his very nature, is his own preservation, defence, and welfare. By his bestial cruelty the assessor who was murdered by the peasants had violated their rights as citizens. At the moment when he abetted the violence of his sons, when he added insult to the heartfelt injury of the bridal pair, when he, seeing their opposition to his devilish tyranny, moved to punish them, then the law that protects a citizen fell into abeyance and its efficacy disappeared; then the law of nature was reborn, and the power of the wronged citizen, which the positive law cannot take from him when he has been wronged, comes into operation, and the peasants who killed the beastly assessor are not guilty before the law. On rational grounds my heart finds them not guilty, and the death of the assessor, although violent, is just. Let no one presume to seek in reasons of state or in the maintenance of public peace grounds for condemning the murderers of the assessor, who expired in the midst of his wickedness. No matter in what estate heaven may have decreed a citizen's birth, he is and will always remain a man; and so long as he is a man, the law of nature, as an abundant wellspring of goodness, will never run dry in him, and whosoever dares wound him in his natural and inviolable right is a criminal. Woe to him, if the civil law does not punish him. He will be marked as a pariah by his fellow citizens, and may whosoever has sufficient power exact vengeance against him for his evildoing.

'I fell silent. The governor said not a word to me. Now and then he gave me lowering glances charged with the fury of impotence and the malice of vengeance. Everyone was silent, expecting that I, the profaner of all laws, would be put under arrest. Every now and then a murmur of disapproval could be heard on their servile lips. Everyone turned his eyes away from me. It looked as though terror had seized those who stood near me. Imperceptibly they withdrew from me, as from one infected with a deadly plague. Weary of the spectacle of this mixture of arrogance and basest servility, I left this assembly of flatterers.

'Unable to find any means to save the innocent homicides whom my heart acquitted, I did not want to be an accomplice in or a witness of their execution. I petitioned for my retirement and, having been granted it, I am now on my way home to bewail the lamentable fate of the peasant class, and to relieve my weariness in association with my friends.'

A. N. Radishchev
A Journey
from St. Petersburg
to Moscow
1789-90

As he said this, we took leave of one another, and each went his own way. *803*

Slavery and exploitation; master and slave

Hebrew Bible
Leviticus 25

God said:
For unto me the children of Israel are servants.

Talmud
Kiddushin 22

and the Talmud comments:
But not servants unto servants. *804*

*Limits
to slavery*

And if thy brother, a Hebrew man, or a Hebrew woman, be sold unto thee, and serve thee six years; then in the seventh year thou shalt let him go free from thee.

And when thou sendest him out free from thee, thou shalt not let him go away empty:

Thou shalt furnish him liberally out of thy flock, and out of thy floor, and out of thy winepress: of that wherewith the Lord thy God hath blessed thee thou shalt give unto him.

And thou shalt remember that thou wast a bondman in the land of Egypt, and the Lord thy God redeemed thee: therefore I command thee this thing today.   *805*

Hebrew Bible
Deuteronomy 15

And ye shall hallow the fiftieth year, and proclaim liberty throughout the land unto all the inhabitants thereof; it shall be a jubilee unto you; and ye shall return every man unto his possession, and ye shall return every man unto his family.   *806*

Hebrew Bible
Leviticus 25

Solon's reform included the remission of debts and the freeing of peasants enslaved by their creditors. He describes it as follows:

Of the ends for which I assembled the people, which of them did I leave unattained? She best could bear me witness in the court of time, the great Mother of the Olympian Gods, black earth, from whom I took away the landmarks, driven in on every side, and she, before, enslaved, now was free. And many men did I bring back to Athens, to their country founded of the Gods, men sold, some unjustly, others with justice, and some driven into exile by dire necessity, no more uttering the Attic tongue, wanderers in every place; and those, even here, that knew shameful slavery, trembling before the humours of their masters, I set free. These things I did by compulsion, joining together right with might, and that which I promised I performed in order. Laws I drew up for good and bad alike, fitting to each strict justice.

If another than I had taken up the goad, an evil-minded man and greedy of gain, he would not have controlled the people. Had I willed that which was then the pleasure of their enemies, or again, the avowed intent of the rest towards them, this city had been widowed of many men. Therefore I gave help on every side, turning about like a wolf amid a pack of hounds.   *807*

Solon
640-558 B.C.
Quoted by Aristotle
c. 384-322 B.C.
Constitution
of Athens

*Courage
wins
freedom*

'Antara was a famous warrior and poet of pre-Islamic times; he has been called 'the Arab Achilles'.

'Antara was already a grown man when his father recognized him as his son. His mother was a Negro slave called Zubaiba, and in the days before Islam, any Arab who had a son by a slave considered the child to be a slave as well. 'Antara, then, had brothers who, sons of the same mother, were all slaves.

It was in these circumstances that 'Antara's father

recognized him as his son: some Arab tribes raided the Banu Ags (the poet's tribe), killed a number of them and drove off their camels. The Absites chased them, caught up with them, and began to fight for their property. That day, 'Antara was with them. His father shouted to him: 'Charge! 'Antara!' but 'Antara replied: 'Slaves are not meant to fight, but to milk the she-camels and tie up their udders when they have been milked.' 'Charge!' repeated his father, 'and you shall be free!' And so he charged, reciting these lines:

انا العمين عنترة -كل امرئ لحمي حر - اسوده واحمره

والواردات مسفرة

I am 'Antara, he of mixed blood,
Each man defends what is his—
The red and the black—
When the hour of trial comes!

Abu-al Faraj al-Isfahani Book of Songs Pre-Islamic period 10th cent.

That day, he fought with great bravery; and afterwards, his father recognized him as his son, and counted him in his family. *808*

Ransom

Pope Gregory the Great 6th cent. Registrum Epistularum

The Pope instructs a bishop regarding the freeing of prisoners-of-war treated as slaves by the Lombards:

The obligation of seeing to the ransom of prisoners is made clearly evident by the sanction of both Canon and secular law. *809*

Omar ibn al-Khattāb to Amr ibn al-As

The Caliph writes to the Governor of Egypt (seventh century):

How couldst thou reduce human beings to servitude, knowing that they were born free on leaving their mother's womb? *810*

ABOLITION OF SERFDOM ACT

18 May 1525 Zürich

As for serfdom, the notion first came to our overlords that we are all the children of God and should live as brothers. Hence the decision that we free our serfs from slavery and absolve them from the duties resulting from that condition. *811*

The Franchises of Strasbourg, about 1130.

Following the example of other towns, Strasbourg is favoured by the law [of peace] so that every man, whether native-born or a foreigner, will find here at all times and on the part of all people [the blessings of] peace.

(The term 'peace' means here: public order and its guarantee by the authorities, the body of police measures, and the protection afforded by the laws.)   *812*

The 'peace' liberates serfs after a year and a day's residence as is stated in the German proverb:

Stadtluft macht frei nach Jahr und Tag.
     (The town air gives freedom after a year and a day.)   *813*

Whereas from the beginning nature created all men freely or free, and afterward the law of nations (*jus gentium*) subjected some of them to the yoke of servitude, we therefore judge that it would be a pious act and one to be deservedly rewarded by God to restore some of those, whose deserts require it, to their pristine liberty. *814*

Speech attributed to the leader of a peasant revolt.

They treat their serfs as one might treat one's cattle. And
     what do they care! All they think of is how to fill their
     pockets!
The spring flowers, the summer corn, the autumn fruits,
The mists of winter, the sand swept by the wind from the
     rocks,
The stars in the sky, ah! it would be easier to count them
     all
Than for me to count the sins of which they are no longer
     ashamed.
Meanwhile we remain fast bound in the chains of slavery,
Our only refuge is to grit our teeth under the same yoke.
But since fate today bands itself with our wrath,

Onwards against the tyrants! make haste! let us break
     our bonds!
Friends, give me power to carry through this combat. *815*

Talk of conquest, of bringing peoples under one's yoke, or of servitude—the Turk would not say more—is due to the ignorance and blindness of the members of the

Council, who did not remark that such words were not fitting for any Christian monarch and especially the King of Castile, failing to realize the difference between the abhorrent infidels, the enemies of our faith, who have usurped our lands, and the Indians who were living peacefully in their own land and who owed no duty to the Christians nor to the kings of Castile. These words were long used in the Council of the Indies, as long as such blindness continued and until after many years, the cleric Bartolomé de Las Casas made them recognize their error. *816*

Bartolomé
de Las Casas
Historia
de las Indias
1547

Because the Spaniards oppressed them, robbed them, killed them, they tried by every possible means to defend themselves. Was that so heinous a crime on their part? Do we not admit that even wild beasts have the right to defend their own existence?

. . . .

Verily, I say unto you, the Infidel has the right to hold all the positions, public offices, royal jurisdictions throughout his kingdoms and provinces: it is his right; it is a natural law, as much for him as for a Christian; there is no difference between the two. The proof of this lies in that both infidels and faithful, equally, are rational animals; they are naturally prone to live in a community and to have councils, kingdoms, villages and cities, and consequently to have kings and governors, choosing or electing them—all this constitutes a law and a natural right.

. . . .

The distribution of land and property which was imposed by the Spaniards on the Indians . . . is still in force among these gentle, humble, peaceful peoples, incapable of offending anyone; among these freedom-loving citizens; among these natives of powerful and numerous kingdoms, who were ruled and governed by their own kings and nobles. Those foreigners subdued them at the cost of bloody, vile and unjust wars, for they were stronger and better armed than the Indians who lacked horses, side-arms, artillery and other material to defend themselves. They dispersed them in all directions, regardless of social considerations—kings, subjects, vassals, all mixed up together, and reduced them to the direst slavery; night and day, until death releases them, they are made to toil; it is impossible for them to improve their minds, let alone practise the Christian faith. *817*

Bartolomé
de Las Casas
1474-1566

The Brothers of the Dominican Order, and their Vicar, Friar Pedro de Córdoba, sent their best preacher, Montesinos, to Hispaniola to censure the conduct of the conquistadores towards the Indians; Friar Bartolomé de Las Casas, who was present, reports his words as follows:

I rise to speak to you here, as the voice of Christ in the desert of this island, wherefore it behoves you to pay heed, not indifferently but with your whole heart and mind; that voice will proclaim the newest tidings you have ever heard, the harshest and most grievous message you ever thought to hear. . . . That voice proclaims that you are all in mortal sin, that you are living and dying in such sin by reason of your cruelty and tyrannical behaviour towards these innocent people. Say, by what right and with what justice do you keep those Indians in such cruel and horrible slavery? With what authority have you waged such hateful war on these people, who were living quietly and peacefully in their homes and on their lands? . . . How can you keep them so oppressed and weary, without giving them food or caring for them when they fall sick and die of their excessive labours—nay more, how can you kill them for the sake of amassing gold each day? And what do you care who teaches them? . . . Are they not men? Have they not reasoning minds? Are you not required to love them as yourselves? . . . Rest assured that in the state in which you are you cannot save yourselves any more than the Moors or Turks who lack and do not love the Christian faith.

Antón
de Montesinos
Sermon
1510 or 1511

818

Right to contract marriage freely

It is Our will that the Indians of both sexes may, as is right, have full liberty to contract marriage with whomsoever they wish, both with Indians and with natives of our Kingdoms or with Spaniards born in the Indies, and that in this no obstacle should be placed in their way. And We command that no order of Ours which may have been, or might be, issued by Us may or might prevent marriage between Indians of either sex with Spaniards of either sex.

Charter granted
by Ferdinand V
and Queen Juana
in 1514
and by Philip II
in 1556

819

BULL OF POPE PAUL III, 1537

To all the faithful in Christ who shall read these presents, Our greeting and Apostolic blessing.

We know that, when appointing the preachers of the Faith to their preachers' office, the Truth Itself, which can neither deceive nor be deceived, said unto them: *Go ye and teach all nations.* '*All*', It said, without any distinction, inasmuch as all are capable of instruction in the Faith. Seeing this and grudging it, the enemy of the human race, who ever opposeth human works that they may come to naught, devised a means, hitherto unheard of, whereby he might prevent the word of God from being preached to the nations for their salvation, and hath moved certain of his abettors, in their greed for gain, to oppress, like brute beasts existing to serve them, the Indians of the West and South and other peoples lately come unto Our notice, on the pretext that they are without the Catholic Faith. We, therefore, Who represent (albeit unworthily) Our said Lord on earth and Who use Our utmost endeavours to bring into His fold those sheep of the flock He hath entrusted to Us who are without it; considering that the said Indians, as true human beings, are not only capable of the Christian Faith but (as hath been reported to Us) hasten eagerly to embrace it; and wishing to provide fitting remedies in respect of these matters: decree and declare by these presents, upon Our Apostolic authority and notwithstanding earlier pronouncements or aught else whatever to the contrary, that the aforementioned Indians, and all other peoples that shall subsequently come to the notice of Christians, although they be without the Faith, neither have been nor may be deprived of their freedom and the ownership of their property, but may freely and lawfully use, hold and enjoy such freedom and ownership and must not be reduced to slavery; that whatever shall have been done otherwise shall be null and void; and that the aforementioned Indians and other peoples are to be encouraged to embrace the said Faith in Christ by the preaching of the word of God and the example of a virtuous life.

Given at Rome, this second day of June, 1537, in the third year of our Pontificate.   *820*

DECREES OF THE EMPEROR CHARLES V

In accordance with what is stipulated concerning the freedom of the Indians: It is Our Will and Command, that no governor of a province, governor, captain, mayor or other person of whatsoever estate, dignity, office or quality, in time or circumstances of peace or of war, be it just and ordered by Us or empowered by Us, dare capture Indians native to our Indies, Islands and Mainland of the Ocean Sea, discovered or to be discovered, or hold them as slaves, even though they be from the isles and lands against which We, or anyone who has or may have been empowered by Us, have declared that war may justly be waged; or kill, capture or imprison them, except in respect of cases and nations where it be allowed and established by the laws under this title; in so far as concerns all authorizations and declarations hitherto made which may not have been incorporated in these laws, and in so far as those which were given or made were not given or made by Us with specific mention of this law, We revoke and suspend them in whatever has reference to capturing and enslaving Indians in war, though it be a just war having given, or giving cause for so doing; and to ransoming those whom other Indians have captured on the occasion of wars between them. And We likewise order that no one, whether in war or not, may seize, apprehend, employ, sell or exchange as a slave any Indian, or hold him as such, on the plea that he was obtained in a just war, or by purchase, ransom, barter or exchange, or for any other reason or cause, even in the case of Indians whom the natives themselves regarded, regard or might regard among themselves as slaves, on penalty that if anyone be found who has imprisoned any Indian, or holds him as a slave, he shall be liable to confiscation of all his possessions, adjudged to Our Chamber and Treasury, and that the Indian or Indians shall be handed back and restored to their own land and kind, with full and natural freedom, at the expense of those who captured them or held them as slaves. And We order Our justices to be especially strict in investigating and punishing with the full rigour of this law, on penalty of removal from office and a fine of one hundred thousand maravedis imposed by Our Chamber against anyone acting to the contrary and in negligence of his duty. *821*

Decrees
promulgated
between 1526
and 1548

Free men

All Indians living in the so-called 'repartimientos' are free and *sui juris*, as much by natural right, *quod omnes homines facit liberos*, as by the Declaration of the Apostolic See made by Paul III in the year 1537, and by other Supreme Pontiffs who have declared all these Indians to be free men before receiving baptism and much more so after, and that they may not be deprived of their freedom but rather should enjoy it as do Spaniards and all free men among the nations of Christendom. And the same is said in the charters of their Catholic Majesties, from King Ferdinand and Queen Isabella of glorious

Juan Ramírez
On the Personal
Service and the
Allotment of Indians
16th cent.

memory, down to our Lord King Philip and the present Queen; who have all wished, and do wish, that the Indians be treated and governed as free vassals and not as slaves. *822*

*Prohibition of
cruel, inhuman
or degrading
treatment of
the indigenous
population*
19 December 1593

DECREE OF PHILIP II

We order and command that Spaniards who outrage, offend or ill-treat the Indians be punished with the utmost rigour as though these offences had been committed against Spaniards, and We declare these to be public crimes. *823*

The institution of perpetual serfdom, abolished in Hungary in the fifteenth century, was brought into force again after the 'peasant war' of 1514.

Peasants living in any part whatsoever of this country... lose their freedom of residence as a punishment for their disloyalty. As peasant serfs, they and their descendants are condemned to be life subjects of their lords, in order that future generations may realize the magnitude of the crime perpetrated by the subject who rebels against his lord. *824*

Hungarian laws
1514

Against serfdom

Matthew Baškin
Landed proprietor
condemned as a
heretic and
imprisoned for life
in Volokolamsk
in 1554
Russia

It is written in the Epistles: The whole law is contained in these words: thou shalt love thy neighbour as thyself.... Now, we in our country restrain servants of Christ. Christ calls all men brothers, but we have some who are serfs, some of them fugitives brought back, others so designated, others utterly enslaved by deed. For my part, I thank my God: all I possessed in deeds of serfdom I have torn up, and the men I keep it is of their own will. He who is content stays, the others go as they please. *825*

A sixteenth-century Russian publicist puts his own political ideas into the mouth of Sultan Mahomet II, conqueror of Constantinople, so that Ivan the Terrible may give heed:

Ivan Peresvetov
Tale of
Sultan Mahomet
c. 1547

Thus spake Sultan Mahomet: 'In a kingdom in which men are servile, they have no courage, or zeal to fight the enemy. For a man enslaved fears not shame and seeks not glory. Whether he be strong or not, he says to himself: "In any case, I am a slave and shall never know any other name." ' *826*

Passion for gold

They offered the Spaniards oriflammes of gold, of quetzal feathers, and necklets of gold. At the sight of these gifts the Spaniards' faces lit up, their joy was immense, they trod on air. Like monkeys, they filled both hands with the gold, and were overcome with delight. The blood coursed through their veins and fired their hearts. A thirst unquenchable possessed them. Greed inflamed their appetites. They hankered after this gold like a herd of famished swine. Thereupon, they snatched at the golden oriflammes ravenously and waved them up and down, examining first one side then the other. They behaved just like barbarians; their every utterance was savage. *827*

Sahagún
16th cent.
Mexico

*The invaders
bring calamity*

By the madness of the times, by the madness of the priests, sorrow came to us, 'Christianity' entered into us. Yes, the 'Most Christian' people arrived with their true God; then began the time of affliction for us, the time of 'alms-giving', origin of our secret hatred; the time of battles with firearms, of brawls, of plundering; the time of enslavement for debt, of the death penalty for debt; a time of incessant strife; the time of suffering.

*Before the white
man came*

They were given a little time in which to gaze upon the network of stars; up there the gods looked down on them from their starry prison. Then, any and every means was good, and they were slaughtered.

They had a wisdom of their own. They were unaware of sin. They were not filled with holiness. They enjoyed good health. They did not know what illness was; their limbs never ached; they were never attacked by fevers; smallpox was unknown to them, and so was pneumonia; they suffered no pain in the bowels, they were not consumptive. So their health was of the best.

*When the white
man came*

It was not the same when the white men came. These taught them fear and blighted their flowers. In order that their own flowers might flourish, they destroyed and trampled on the flowers of others.

Those representatives of the Gods who came to us did not possess great knowledge, nor any sacred language, nor divine learning. Castrated the sun—that is what those foreigners did! And now, scattered among this people, are the sons of their sons, who have tasted of the people's bitterness.

Chilām Balām
de Chumayel
Sacred book
of the Mayas
Central America

He comes to enslave the spoken word, to enslave the trees and the stones, to enslave men! *828*

I want the Indians in their villages to govern themselves, so that they may look after their own interests as we look after ours. In this way they will find happiness through the exercise of responsibility and emerge from that state of abasement into which they have been plunged by their misfortunes. We must remember that they possess certain elementary rights and that it would be disgraceful were we to go on excluding them, as we have done up till now, simply because they happen to be Indians.   *829*

José Artigas
Declaration of
3 May 1815
in Argentina

Slavery is the negation of all law. Any law which was to codify it would be a sacrilege. What justification can there be for maintaining it? Consider this crime in all its aspects: I do not think a single Bolivian will be found so depraved as to attempt to justify this greatest assault on the dignity of man. I ask you: a man owning another man! A man, an object! One in the image of God yoked like an animal! Where are the titles to property of these usurpers of man?—that is what we want to know!   *830*

Simón Bolívar
Speech
1826
Bolivia

Exploitation

As a result of its innumerable excesses, that accursed redistribution accompanied by a host of defects, as it is, has placed us in a lamentable situation: all that remains for us is to die. Here, to begin with, because goods and produce from Castile came to be in short supply in our regions and the profit made out of them was insufficient, His Majesty allowed the regional governors to lay in a stock of such goods—which was known as 'tariff'—on behalf of each provincial capital, of which the natives took advantage, being anxious to buy them because they were better finished and sold at local prices. Because there were certain differences, standard prices were adopted so as to make it impossible to cheat the Royal Excise. Prices have not risen up to the present, which is why we have a supply of cheap goods. But when articles from Castile have been transported over the mountains, we are forced to pay ten or twelve pesos for the most ordinary article which was only worth about two or three pesos. . . . With us who have a certain social standing they traffic in all manner of expensive articles—velvets, silk stockings, lace, belt buckles, cloth from Rouen (rather than from Olonnes or Cambrai)—as if we Indians were going to adopt those Spanish fashions to the tune of prices that are way beyond what we can afford. If only they had allowed us the time and opportunity to complete the redistribution, that load would have been bearable

José Gabriel
Tupac Amaru
Inca leader of a
Peruvian revolt
Letter addressed to
Inspector-General
Areche
1781

since, after redistribution, they were going to take charge of us—ourselves, our wives, our children and our flocks, depriving us of all freedom of action. However, acting as they are doing, they force us to abandon house, family, wife and children. *831*

*Exploitation
justified*
Dominge Muriel
Spanish Jesuit
Professor at the
University of Cordoba
del Tucumán
Argentina
1791

But this right [to property] is less developed among them than it has been in other countries. Hence, in order to deprive them of it, it is not necessary to find so many weighty reasons as it is in the case of other peoples. Indeed, they make no distinction between their own life and liberty and the lives and liberties of others: all that, to them, is a matter of little importance. *832*

AN ENCOUNTER IN SURINAM

As they drew near the town, they saw a negro stretched on the ground with only one-half of his habit, which was a kind of linen frock, for the poor man had lost his left leg and his right hand. 'Good God,' said Candide in Dutch; 'what dost thou here, friend, in this deplorable condition?' 'I am waiting for my master, Mynheer Van-derdendur, the famous trader,' answered the negro. 'Was it Mynheer Vanderdendur that used you in this cruel manner?' 'Yes, sir,' said the negro; 'it is the custom here. They give a linen garment twice a year, and that is all our covering. When we labour in the sugar-works, and the mill happens to snatch off a finger, they instantly chop off our hand; and when we attempt to run away, they cut off a leg. Both these cases happened to me; and it is at this expense that you eat sugar in Europe; and yet when my mother sold me for ten patacoons on the coast of Guinea, she said to me: "My dear child, bless our fetishes; adore them for ever; they will make thee live happy; thou hast the honour to be a slave to our lords the whites, by which thou wilt make the fortune of us thy parents." Alas! I know not whether I have made their fortunes; but they have not made mine. Dogs, monkeys, and parrots are a thousand times less wretched than I. The Dutch fetishes who converted me tell me every Sunday that the blacks and whites are all children of one father, whom they call Adam. As for me, I do not understand anything of genealogies; but if what these preachers say is true, we are all second cousins; and you must allow that it is impossible to be worse treated by our relations than we are.'

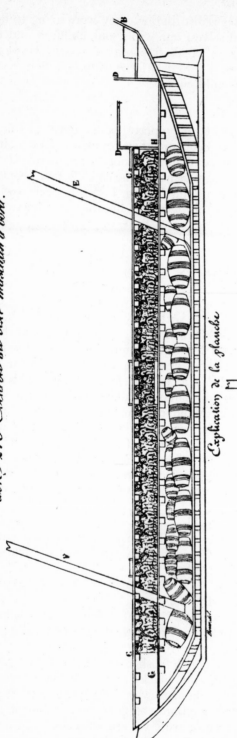

'O Pangloss!' cried out Candide, 'such horrid doings never entered thy imagination. Here is an end of the matter; I find myself, after all, obliged to renounce thy optimism.' 'Optimism,' said Cacambo, 'what is that?' 'Alas!' replied Candide, 'it is the obstinacy of maintaining that everything is best when it is worst'; and so saying, he turned his eyes towards the poor negro, and shed a flood of tears; and in this weeping mood he entered the town of Surinam.   *833*

Voltaire
Candide
1759

On slavery

The slave naturally is always guilty.

A slave who eats sheep, weeps.

If a slave behaves himself, his purchase-price is discharged.

A slave's wisdom is in his master's head.

If a slave is ill behaved it is due to his master.

Akan proverbs
Ghana

A slave is like farina, a little liquid and it is solvent.   *834*

Yombé proverb
Congo

Kill him, he is a savage (*or elsewhere*, a slave), he is kin to no one!   *835*

It is not Poland alone that commits injustice. Moscow, Bohemia, and certain French and Spanish provinces still subjugate the people with equal violence. The French islands and the British and Dutch colonies mete out even crueller treatment to the Negroes, those wretched Citizens of two continents whose produce, watered with tears, brings pleasure and comfort to refined Europeans. But can the violation of natural Rights be justified on the ground of the injustice inflicted by others and of age-old prejudice? Can remorse be stifled as long as human nature is suffering such obvious injustice?... Philosophers! You who denounce fanaticism, who castigate the many acts of cruelty caused by false or passing enthusiasms! Why do you not protest against the legal enslavement of men who are your peers? Why do you not rise up against this crying injustice inflicted by Man, with the aid of the law, on his fellow Man?... The white man or the black slave, oppressed by unjust law or weeping in his shackles, is a Man, no different from ourselves. Whether he be in Europe or on another continent, he is still a citizen of Earth and may still say to anyone, in the words of Terence: *Homo sum, humani nihil a me alienum puto*. Thou who wishest to reduce me to slavery,

431

behold me, and then behold thyself: did nature make me in a different mould? *Homo sum.* Thou who defendest freedom, compare my feelings with thine own, measure thyself and stir the shame in the depths of thy heart, for thou wouldst have me for a slave, thou who livest on this same earth, under this same government, thou who art constantly at pains to ensure freedom for thyself!   *836*

Hugo Kołłataj
Political Law
of the Polish Nation
1790

The slave trade

We, sir, have long since emerged from barbarism. We have almost forgotten that we were once barbarians. We are now raised to a situation which exhibits a striking contrast to every circumstance by which a Roman might have characterized us, and by which we now characterize Africa. There is, indeed, one thing wanting to complete the contrast, and to clear us altogether from the imputation of acting even to this hour as barbarians; for we continue to this hour a barbarous traffic in slaves; we continue it even yet, in spite of all our great and undeniable pretensions to civilization.

... We are living under a system of government which our own happy experience leads us to pronounce the best and wisest which has ever yet been framed; a system which has become the admiration of the world. From all these blessings we must for ever have been shut out, had there been any truth in those principles which some gentlemen have not hesitated to lay down as applicable to the case of Africa. Had those principles been true, we ourselves had languished to this hour in that miserable state of ignorance, brutality, and degradation, in which history proves our ancestry to have been immersed. Had other nations adopted these principles in their conduct towards us; had other nations applied to Great Britain the reasoning which some of the senators of this very island now apply to Africa; ages might have passed without our emerging from barbarism; and we, who are enjoying the blessings of British civilization, of British laws, and British liberty, might, at this hour, have been little superior, either in morals, in knowledge, or refinement, to the rude inhabitants of the coast of Guinea.

... I trust we shall no longer continue this commerce, to the destruction of every improvement on that wide continent; and shall not consider ourselves as conferring too great a boon, in restoring its inhabitants to the rank of human beings. I trust we shall not think ourselves too liberal, if, by abolishing the slave trade, we give them the same common chance of civilization with other parts of the world, and that we shall now allow to Africa the

1. « Anglais faisans part aux « Africains du Traité de « Paix . . . . ° The English making the African natives of the treaty of peace between
« Indostre et Commerce ° . . . « Répresentatibes du . « du 20 Avril 180 : « Inhibitive de la traite des Noirs . . . the allied powers of the 20th of April 180 : upon the abolition of the slave trade.

Abolition of the slave trade. Presentation of the treaty to the Africans   Early 19th cent., England

Rohandria ou Grand & sa
femme tous deux blancs.

Madagasar

Lohavohits ou Maistre de Village
Et sa femme tous deux Negres.

The first travellers to visit Madagascar found two races of inhabitants living there on a footing of equality   Late 17th cent.

William Pitt
Speech delivered
in the House
of Commons
2 April 1792
Great Britain

opportunity, the hope, the prospect of attaining to the same blessings which we ourselves, through the favourable dispensations of Divine Providence, have been permitted, at a much more early period, to enjoy. *837*

TESTAMENT, 5 MAY 1798

I, Thaddeus Kościuszko, being just in my departure from America, do hereby declare and direct that should I make no other testamentary disposition of my property in the United States, hereby authorize my friend Thomas Jefferson to employ the whole thereof in purchasing negroes from among his own as any others and giving them liberty in my name, in giving them an education in trades or otherwise, and in having them instructed for their new condition in the duties of morality which may make them good neighbours, good fathers or mothers, husbands or wives, and in their duties as citizens, teaching them to be defenders of their liberty and country and of the good order of Society and in whatsoever may make them happy and useful, and I make the said Thomas Jefferson my executor of this. *838*

T. Kosciuszko
(Written in English)
Poland

Motion calling for the abolition of slavery presented by the Rev. Dr. José Simeón Cañas y Villacorta to the Constituent Assembly of the United Provinces of Central America in 1823.

I have dragged myself here, and even if I had been dying I would have come here, to put before you a proposal for the benefit of defenceless human beings. With all the vigour that a Deputy must display in promoting matters of importance to the homeland, I demand that before anything else and at today's session those of our brothers who are slaves be declared free citizens, without prejudice to the right of ownership legally proved by the owners of those who have bought them, and that the creation of a fund for the compensation of the owners be a matter for immediate discussion.

This is a situation that in all justice must prevail. What I regard as a natural law—natural because it is right—requires that he who has been dispossessed should in the first place have his possessions restored to him; and, since there is no possession comparable to freedom, no property more personal than freedom, it is clear that justice requires still more its immediate and full restoration to those who have been deprived of it. We all know,

that our brothers have been violently robbed of the
priceless gift of their freedom, that they are groaning in
bondage, sighing for a kindly hand to release them from
their shackles. Nothing, then, could bring greater glory
to this august Assembly, more happiness to the Nation
or more benefit to our brothers than the speedy proclamation of their freedom, a proclamation so manifestly
just that it should be ordained without discussion and by
general acclamation. The entire nation has declared
itself free; the individuals who make up the nation should
therefore also be free. Such a decree will immortalize the
memory of the justness of the Assembly in the hearts
of these unfortunate people, succeeding generations of
whom will bless their liberators. Moreover, so that no
one may think that I am trying to wrong any owner, poor
and ragged though I be—since neither my income nor
my allowance are being paid—I gladly waive my right
to whatever may be owed to me by the State, to set on
foot the compensation fund I spoke of earlier.   *839*

*Letter to the Sultan Mulay Ismaïl from the famous scholar Abu
al-Fadl Jassus, about the army of the Abids (slaves) (17th cent.).*

We learn that the Commander of the Faithful (may
God guide him in the right path!) intends to retake the
Haratins [former slaves], and form them into bands to
reinforce his army, which is, it is true, the pillar of religion
and the safeguard of Islam.

We know well that you are in no way actuated by any
base desire to enslave men. Nevertheless, the action you
are taking seems to me to be in flagrant contradiction
with equity and counter to the provisions of the Sharia
[Moslem law]. For how can you venture to do such a
deed, when God has more than once expressed his will
that it be authorized only in accordance with certain
precise rules? It is to be noted that the strength of the
army does not necessarily depend on the adoption of a
policy of enslavement. It is in your Majesty's power to
increase the number of your armies without having recourse
to so-called slaves. . . .

It is the duty of every intelligent, thinking, man to
prevent grave acts consisting in the open and illegal
enslavement of free men, and to show how unlawful it
is to have recourse to such methods. In such circumstances,
to keep silent or to show any degree of tolerance would
expose those so failing in their duty to the wrath of God.

Sire! if this be so, let me be permitted (may God ensure
that his orders are carried out and that his will triumphs

over those who depart from the right way!) to remind you that acts of this kind are truly the works of slavers. Everyone knows that the persons who are at present claimed, to be made into slaves, are, like the rest of the Moslem community, entirely free men; their freedom is manifest and it cannot in any way be called in question. It should also be noted, hereanent, that any admission by these so-called slaves, or any testimony tending to establish that they are not free men, is most certainly the result of duress. Here it should be noted that, by refusing to submit themselves to this policy, many people have exposed themselves to vengeance, torture and fines which have resulted in their being despoiled of their property. If those responsible have behaved in this way, admission and testimony thereby lose all value. It must be remembered that the greatest jurists of Islam all agree in stating that admissions and testimony obtained under duress are devoid of any legal value: according to the Imam Malik [a great Moslem jurist], no one who is married or divorced under duress, or who in general acts against his own will, is legally bound to honour his commitments. Ibn Arafa [a follower of Malik] has made identical comments on this subject, noting also that an admission of being a slave, even supposing it is obtained without duress, has no legal value, since it is presumed to have been obtained by threats. Liberty is among the rights accorded by God alone; whence it results that no man has the right to part with his liberty.   *840*

First official document on the abolition of slavery in Ethiopia.
Her Majesty the Queen of the United Kingdom of Great Britain and Ireland, Empress of India, and His Majesty John, by the Grace of God Emperor of Ethiopia, with a view to preventing and abolishing the trade in slaves, have agreed to conclude for this purpose a treaty which shall be binding on them and on their successors.

• . . . .

Article I
His Majesty the Emperor agrees to prohibit and to take measures to end, throughout his territory, the buying and selling of slaves, and this by every means in his power.

Article II
His Majesty the Emperor agrees to prohibit and to take the most active measures to prevent slaves bought outside from being brought into his territory and the exit abroad of slaves sold in his country.

Article III

His Majesty the Emperor undertakes to employ every means at his disposal to protect freed slaves, and to ensure the severe punishment of all who may attempt to ill-treat them or reduce them again to slavery.

Article IV

Her Majesty the Queen of England, enjoying treaty rights which authorize the commanders of Her Majesty's ships to seize ships belonging to other countries which have embarked and are transporting slaves by sea, undertakes to order that the commanders of Her Majesty's ships, should they discover on ships so seized subjects of His Majesty the Emperor captured as slaves, shall set free and return the said subjects to the territory of His Majesty the Emperor. *841*

Treaty signed at Aduna between Queen Victoria and King John 3 June 1884

OF THE SLAVERY OF THE NEGROES

Were I to vindicate our right to make slaves of the negroes, these should be my arguments:

The Europeans, having extirpated the Americans, were obliged to make slaves of the Africans, for clearing such vast tracts of land.

Sugar would be too dear if the plants which produce it were cultivated by any other than slaves.

These creatures are all over black, and with such a flat nose that they can scarcely be pitied.

It is hardly to be believed that God, who is a wise Being, should place a soul, especially a good soul, in such a black ugly body.

It is so natural to look upon colour as the criterion of human nature, that the Asiatics, among whom eunuchs are employed, always deprive the blacks of their resemblance to us by a more opprobrious distinction.

The colour of the skin may be determined by that of the hair, which, among the Egyptians, the best philosophers in the world, was of such importance that they put to death all the red-haired men who fell into their hands.

The negroes prefer a glass necklace to that gold which polite nations so highly value. Can there be a greater proof of their wanting common sense?

It is impossible for us to suppose these creatures to be men, because, allowing them to be men, a suspicion would follow that we ourselves are not Christians.

Weak minds exaggerate too much the wrong done to the Africans. For were the case as they state it, would

Montesquieu
The Spirit of the Laws
1748, France

European powers, who make so many needless conventions among themselves, have failed to enter into a general one, on behalf of humanity and compassion?   *842*

Sale of slaves

In the name of the King, Law and Justice,

Be it known to all concerned that on Sunday 26th instant, in the market place of the town of Saint-Esprit, at the termination of the mass, the following will be sold at public auction:

The slave Suzanne, negress, aged about forty, with her six children of thirteen, eleven, eight, seven, six and three years.

Proceeding from a distress. Payable in cash.

Steward of the Crown lands: J. Chatenay

In the name of the King, etc.

On the same day, at the same place and time, various objects will be sold, such as chairs, tables, etc.

Proceeding from a distress. Payable in cash.

Notice quoted by
Victor Schoelcher
in Esclavage
et Colonisation

Steward of the Crown lands: J. Chatenay
Official gazette of Martinique
22 June 1840   *843*

J.-J. Rousseau
The Social Contract
1762

To renounce one's liberty is to renounce one's quality as a man, the rights and also the duties of humanity. For him who renounces everything there is no possible compensation. Such a renunciation is incompatible with man's nature, for to take away all freedom from his will is to take away all morality from his actions.   *844*

THE BLACK MAN:

It's said that God made
The first man my colour.
But when his white Arrogance
Summons me, he forgets
Even my name, and I—well,
I'm just the nigger.

White men call the devil black,
And Black men call him white.

José Hernández
La Vuelta
de Martín Fierro
1879
Argentina

Whether a face be fair or dark,
It's all the same to me . . .
God created men—that's sure:
He didn't create them in separate lots.   *845*

THE EMANCIPATION PROCLAMATION BY PRESIDENT ABRAHAM
LINCOLN OF THE UNITED STATES, 1 JANUARY 1863

And by virtue of the power and for the purpose aforesaid,
I do order and declare that all persons held as slaves
within said designated States and parts of States are,
and henceforward shall be, free; and that the Executive
Government of the United States, including the military
and naval authorities thereof, will recognize and maintain
the freedom of said persons.

And I hereby enjoin upon the people so declared to
be free to abstain from all violence, unless in necessary
self-defense; and I recommend to them that, in all cases
when allowed, they labor faithfully for reasonable wages.

And I further declare and make known that such
persons of suitable condition will be received into the
armed service of the United States to garrison forts,
positions, stations, and other places, and to man vessels
of all sorts in said service.

And upon this act sincerely believed to be an act of
justice, warranted by the Constitution upon military
necessity, I invoke the considerate judgment of mankind
and the gracious favor of Almighty God.   *846*

*Lincoln, re-elected President of the United States, speaks of the
Civil War, 4 March 1865:*

One-eighth of the whole population was colored slaves,
not distributed generally over the Union, but localized
in the southern part of it. These slaves constituted a
peculiar and powerful interest. All knew that this interest
was somehow the cause of the war. To strengthen,
perpetuate, and extend this interest was the object for
which the insurgents would rend the Union even by war,
while the Government claimed no right to do more than
to restrict the territorial enlargement of it. Neither party
expected for the war the magnitude or the duration which
it has already attained. Neither anticipated that the
cause of the conflict might cease with or even before the
conflict itself should cease. Each looked for an easier
triumph, and a result less fundamental and astounding.
Both read the same Bible and pray to the same God,
and each invokes His aid against the other. It may seem
strange that any men should dare to ask a just God's
assistance in wringing their bread from the sweat of other
men's faces, but let us judge not, that we be not judged. *847*

*Protection
of a fugitive slave*

Hebrew Bible
Deuteronomy 23

Thou shalt not deliver to his master a bondsman that is
escaped from his master unto thee. He shall dwell with
thee in the midst of thee, in the place which he shall
choose within one of thy gates, where it liketh him best;
thou shalt not wrong him.   *848*

Huckleberry Finn *was written in the 1870s and published
in 1885, but describes life along the Mississippi in the fifties.*

We slept most all day, and started out at night, a little
ways behind a monstrous long raft that was as long going
by as a procession. . . .

We went drifting down into a big bend, and the night
clouded up and got hot. . . . We talked about Cairo, and
wondered whether we would know it when we got to it. . . .

Jim said it made him all over trembly and feverish
to be so close to freedom. Well, I can tell you it made me
all over trembly and feverish, too, to hear him, because I
begun to get it through my head that he *was* most free—and
who was to blame for it? Why, *me.* I couldn't get that out
of my conscience, no how nor no way. It got to troubling
me so I couldn't rest; I couldn't stay still in one place.
It hadn't ever come home to me before, what this thing
was that I was doing. But now it did; and it stayed with
me, and scorched me more and more. I tried to make
out to myself that *I* warn't to blame, because *I* didn't
run Jim off from his rightful owner; but it warn't no use,
conscience up and says, every time, 'But you knowed he
was running for his freedom, and you could 'a' paddled
ashore and told somebody.' That was so—I couldn't get
around that no way. That was where it pinched. Conscience say to me, 'What had poor Miss Watson done to
you that you could see her nigger go off right under your
eyes and never say one single word? What did that poor
old woman do to you that you could treat her so mean?
Why, she tried to learn you your book, she tried to learn
you your manners, she tried to be good to you every way
she knowed how. *That's* what she done.'

I got to feeling so mean and so miserable I most wished
I was dead. I fidgeted up and down the raft, abusing
myself, and Jim was fidgeting up and down past me. . . .

Jim talked out loud all the time while I was talking
to myself. He was saying how the first thing he would
do when he got to a free state he would go to saving up
money and never spend a single cent, and when he got
enough he would buy his wife, which was owned on a
farm close to where Miss Watson lived; and then they

would both work to buy the two children, and if their master wouldn't sell them, they'd get an Ab'litionist to go and steal them.

It most froze me to hear such talk. . . . Here was this nigger, which I had as good as helped to run away, coming right out flat-footed and saying he would steal his children—children that belonged to a man I didn't even know; a man that hadn't ever done me no harm.

I was sorry to hear Jim say that, it was such a lowering of him. My conscience got to stirring me up hotter than ever, until at last I says to it, 'Let up on me—it ain't too late yet—I'll paddle ashore at the first light and tell.' I felt easy and happy and light as a feather right off. All my troubles was gone. I went to looking out sharp for a light, and sort of singing to myself. . . .

A light shows up. Huck takes the canoe, Jim will wait on the raft. As Huck shoves off, Jim tells once more his gratefulness to Huck, his best friend, the only one he's got now. Shaken, Huck muses:

I was paddling off, all in a sweat to tell on him; but when he says this, it seemed to kind of take the tuck all out of me. I went along slow then, and I warn't right down certain whether I was glad I started or whether I warn't. . . .

Right then along comes a skiff with two men in it with guns. They stop and Huck stops. Five negroes have run off tonight up yonder, they question Huck about the man he says he left on his raft: is he white or black?

Huck hesitates, then lies: it's his father, who is sick. Sensing his hesitation, the two men get suspicious. But Huck catches back his breath and succeeds in setting their minds on a different trail: 'Your pap's got the small pox, and you know it precious well. Why didn't you come out and say so? Do you want to spread it all over?' They speed away, without checking the raft, afraid of the contagion.

. . . [Huck]: I got aboard the raft, feeling bad and low, because I knowed very well I had done wrong, and I see it warn't no use for me to try to learn to do right; a body that don't get *started* right when he's little ain't got no show—when the pinch comes there ain't nothing to back him up and keep him to his work, and so he gets beat. Then I thought a minute, and says to myself, hold on; s'pose you'd 'a' done right and give Jim up, would you felt better than what you do now? No, says I, I'd feel bad—I'd feel just the same way I do now. Well, then, says I, what's the use you learning to do right when it's troublesome to do right and ain't no trouble to do wrong, and the wages is just the same? I was stuck. I couldn't answer that. So I reckoned I wouldn't bother no more about it, but after this always do whichever come handiest at the time.

Mark Twain
The Adventures
of Huckleberry Finn
United States
of America

849

Derision

The slave:
To obey, means to share in the power of one's master.

One of the emancipated:
What a wonderful feeling that I am also We.

Karel Čapek
1890-1938
Czech writer

A dictator:
I took their freedom but in return
I filled their bosoms with self-confidence.   *850*

*Manhood
against slavery*

Julius Grégr
Czech writer
1831-96

Better prison and fetters than the freedom of a slave.   *851*

*Slavery
against man*

Sakae Ōsugi
1885-1923
Japan

The slave is servile and the master proud. The former is,
as it were, ruining his life passively, and the latter actively,
They are both hindering the development, among men,
of a worthwhile life.   *852*

As there are hyena-men and panther-
men, so I will be
a Jew-man
a Kaffir-man
a Hindu-man-from-Calcutta
a Harlem-man-without-a-vote
a famine-ridden, insult-ridden man,
a tortured man—one you can any time
fall on and beat the daylight out of,
kill him—that's it, kill him, give him the
coup-de-grâce—with no account to render
to any one, no excuse to make to
any one

Aimé Césaire
Cahier d'un Retour
au Pays Natal
1947
Martinique

a Jew-man
a progrom-man
a little runt
a panhandler   *853*

Aimé Césaire
L'Abolition
de l'Esclavage
1948
Martinique

No solution to this problem is possible unless and until
priority is given to the native inhabitant—the victim of
the clash between two worlds which is what colonization
is; so long as people persist in refusing to attach a higher
value to him than they do to their sugar cane or coffee,
their ground nut oil or their rubber.   *854*

*The patience
of the oppressed*

The patience of the Indian is one of the rarest and most admirable of virtues for two main reasons: first, because it relates to extreme toil and poverty; and second, because it is so deep and forbearing without so much as a sigh, a moan or complaint. . . .

However great their wrongs, rarely indeed are they so angry and incensed as to seek revenge or satisfaction, or even complain to those in charge, unless they perhaps be influenced or encouraged by Spaniards, priests, friars or other strangers who, from pity for their sufferings, or moved and understanding or for Your Majesty's sake and their preservation, or, from their own interests and indignation, persuade them to go and complain.   *855*

Juan de Palafox
y Mendoza
1600-59
Bishop in New Spain
Libro de las Virtudes
del Indio

Inner liberation
Katha-Upanishad II
5th cent. B.C.
Sanskrit

When all desires which shelter in man's heart are cast aside, then the mortal becomes immortal and [even] here he attains to Brahman (*that is, to the state of liberation*).   *856*

Mahābhārata XII
2nd cent. B.C.
to 1st cent. A.D.
Sanskrit

Whatever is the pleasure derived in this world from sex and whatever is the great pleasure enjoyed in heaven— these two are not worth even a sixteenth part of the pleasure derived from the destruction of all desires.   *857*

Atharvaveda XIX
2200-1800 B.C.
Sanskrit

May the mid-region grant us freedom from fear; may both these, heaven and earth, [grant us] freedom from fear. May there be freedom from fear for us from the rear, from the front, from the above, and from the below. May there be no fear from friend and from foe, from the known one and from the one who is away. May there be no fear for us by night and also by day. May all the quarters be friends to me.   *858*

*All men desire the
state of liberation*
Vārttikāsāra II
c. 800
Sanskrit

Longing for the attainment of infinite happiness and the destruction of [all] sorrow, all men here desire liberation from all objects.   *859*

It is in our nature as human beings to want to eat good meals, wear fine clothes, live in a beautiful house, grow rich, enjoy everybody's respect, and live to a ripe old age.

Norinaga Motoori
1730-1801
A Bamboo Basket
(Collected thoughts)
Japan

Many people, however, thinking that this is wicked and that it is good to have no desires, pretend that they want nothing and ask for nothing. Such is the irritating hypocrisy of Confucianism. *860*

FREE OF CHARGE

We live free of charge—it doesn't cost us a penny:
There is no charge for the air, the clouds, the hills
    and dales;
No charge for the rain and mud; ·
The outside of cars,
The doors of cinemas,
The shop-windows are all free of charge;
Bread and cheese . . . well, perhaps not . . .
But there is no charge for brackish water;
The cost of freedom varies with the individual,
But there is no charge for slavery.

Orhan Veli
1948
Turkey

We really do live free of charge—it doesn't cost us
a penny. *861*

Necessity, at times,
of violence

Manusmriti VIII
2nd cent. B.C. to
1st cent. A.D.
Sanskrit

A person killing others in defence of himself, in a conflict for sacrificial fees, and in assisting women and Brāhmanas [against assault], does not become liable according to law. One should, without hesitation, kill a desperado seeking to attack one, irrespective of whether that desperado is one's teacher or whether he is a child or an aged person or a well-versed Brāhmana. *862*

Revolt

Turkish proverb
11th cent.
Eastern Turkestan

Deep down, the slave is his master's enemy, just as the dog behaves like a wolf when opportunity offers. *863*

Turkish proverb
15th cent.

The stone thrown by the people goes far. *864*

Law against force

And now I shall tell a tale to kings, wise though they may be. Thus spoke the falcon to the speckled-throated nightingale as he bore him aloft amidst the clouds, impaled on his cruel talons. The nightingale groaned piteously and the falcon said roughly: 'Wretched creature, why are you complaining? You have fallen to someone far stronger than yourself. You will go wherever it pleases me to take you, sweet songster though you be, and I shall choose to eat you or to set you free. He who resists one more powerful than himself is insane; he cannot win, and suffering is added to his shame.' Thus spoke the swift falcon, soaring proudly with his wings outstretched....

But you, Perses, hearken to Justice. Do not allow extravagant thoughts to grow within you. Immoderation is an evil thing for poor people; even the great find it hard to support and the burden of it crushes them on the day when they run into adversity. Far better is the road which goes the other way and leads to works of Justice.

For you, Perses, take this advice to heart; listen well to Justice and put violence aside for ever. Such is the law prescribed for men by the Son of Cronus: let fishes, beasts and birds devour each other, for among them Justice is non-existent: but upon men Zeus has bestowed the gift of Justice which is by far the greatest of benefits. To him whose pronouncements are consciously guided by Justice, all-seeing Zeus gives prosperity; but he who deliberately takes oath on false statements, committing thus the inexpiable crime of offending against Justice, will see his posterity eventually decline, while the posterity of the man faithful to his oath will increase in the future. *865*

Hesiod
8th cent. B.C.
Works and Days
Greece

The rule of law is according to nature

DIALOGUE BETWEEN THE SPARTIATE (CLEINIAS) AND THE ATHENIAN

ATHENIAN. And what are the received principles of rule and obedience in cities, whether great or small; and similarly in families? What are they, and how many in number? Is not one claim of authority which is always just, that of fathers and mothers and in general of progenitors over their offspring?

CLEINIAS. Certainly.

ATHENIAN. Next follows the principle that the noble

should rule over the ignoble; and, thirdly, that the elder
should rule and the younger obey?

CLEINIAS. To be sure.

ATHENIAN. And, fourthly, that slaves should be ruled, and
their masters rule?

CLEINIAS. Of course.

ATHENIAN. Fifthly, if I am not mistaken, comes the
principle that the stronger shall rule, and the weaker
be ruled?

CLEINIAS. That is a rule not to be disobeyed.

ATHENIAN. Yes, and a rule which prevails very widely
among all creatures, and is according to nature, as the
Theban poet Pindar once said; and the sixth principle,
and the greatest of all, is, that the wise should lead
and command, and the ignorant follow and obey;
and yet, O thou most wise Pindar, as I should reply
to him, it surely is not contrary to nature, but according
to nature, being the rule of law over willing subjects,
and not a rule of compulsion.   *866*

Plato
429-347 B.C.
Laws

Babylonian
inscription
c. 700 B.C.

Unto your enemy let justice be done.   *867*

The rule of force
is plain to see

What is it like to have government by force? The answer
is, logically, the great will attack the small, the strong will
plunder the weak, the majority will maltreat the minority,
the clever will deceive the simple, the patricians will
despise the plebeians, the rich will disdain the poor and
the young will rob the old.   *868*

Mo-tzu school
5th cent. B.C.
China

The rule
of the spirit
goes unseen

Two brothers quarrel; one of them repents and re-awakens
the love that was lying dormant in him; the two again
begin to live in peace; nobody takes note of this. But if
the two brothers, through the intervention of solicitors
or some other reason take up arms or go to law—which
is another form of the exhibition of brute force—their
doings would be immediately noticed in the press, they
would be the talk of their neighbours and would probably
go down in history. And what is true of families and
communities is true of nations. There is no reason to
believe that there is one law for families and another
for nations. History, then, is a record of an interruption
of the course of nature. Soul-force, being natural, is not
noted in history.   *869*

Mahatma Gandhi
1869-1948

Death the great leveller: the Pope being led away by Death   *18th cent., Switzerland*

Difference of scale: Pharaoh and his prisoners   *Ancient Egypt*

The central vein separates the two parts of the palm leaf, earthen embankments separate the fields, and justice stands between angry people to contain them.

Malagasy proverbs   Justice cannot wait, law cannot bend.   870

Force and law   It is the ineluctable fate of every man to be caught fast by the force-based relations on which his life depends. Such is the inevitable culpability of all, the culpability of human kind. An endeavour will be made to overcome it by striving for the advent of the force that establishes law and human rights. To neglect to contribute towards building the structures on which the force-based relations are founded, towards the establishment of force in the service of law, is to commit a serious political and also a moral crime. Political culpability becomes moral culpability when force suppresses the justification for force—the upholding of law and of the ethos and the integrity of the people. For when force imposes no limits on itself, violence and terror reign and, finally, both life and spirit are destroyed.

When men do not reach agreement among themselves, it is *force* that decides. Every constitutional system is designed to curb this force, but it continues to exist—internally, inasmuch as law is imposed by force, externally, in the form of war. These facts were virtually forgotten in peace-time. . . .

Recourse to violence engenders violence. It is the victor who decides the fate of the vanquished. It is a case of *vae victis*. The vanquished must choose between dying, on the one hand, and doing and enduring what the victor wills, on the other....

The law is the noble fruit of the minds of men who desire to build a foundation for their life; this foundation must, it is true, be guaranteed by force, but it should not be determined by force. When men become conscious of their quality as men, and recognize the human person as such, they realize the rights of man, and take their stand on a natural law which all may invoke, victors and vanquished alike.

When the idea of law emerges, it becomes possible to negotiate, with a view to discovering, by discussion and methodical procedure, what true law is.

In the case of total victory, the part of abstract law in the relations between the victor and the vanquished and in the rights of the latter has always, hitherto, been extremely limited, wherever the course of events has been determined by political decisions. In such cases, these

449

become the basis of a positive, *de facto* law; they themselves are no longer justified by abstract law. . . .

Even those who are punished or declared responsible can admit the validity of law. The criminal can regard punishment as an honour and a means of rehabilitation. The man guilty of a political offence may recognize that the responsibilities he must assume, as a condition of his future existence, are imposed on him by a decree of fate.

The act of *clemency* mitigates the effects of pure law and of destructive force. Man has a certain faculty which enables him to perceive a truth higher than can be found in the rigid logic of cause and effect, in regard to law as well as to force.

(a) Despite the law, pity gives access to the domain of a justice not legally codified. For all human laws prove, when applied, to be full of imperfections and injustices.

(b) Though he could use force, the victor uses clemency, either for reasons of expediency—because the vanquished may be of use to him—or through a complacent feeling of magnanimity—because sparing the vanquished increases his feeling of power and moderation; or else because he feels morally bound to respect the exigences of a natural law, valid for all men alike, which makes it impermissible for the vanquished (as for the criminal) to be deprived of all his rights. *871*

Karl Jaspers
Die Schuldfrage
1946
Germany

*Inequality
of endowments
but reciprocity
of rights*

There exist, it is true, great inequalities of endowments as between men. Nature makes them strong and weak, conferring on some an intelligence it refuses others. It follows that there will be between them inequality of work, inequality of output, inequality of consumption or enjoyment; but it does not follow that there may be inequality of rights.

Since the rights of all derive from the same source, it follows that whoever would encroach upon the right of another oversteps his own; it follows that the right of each should be respected by every other, and that this right and this duty cannot but be reciprocal. Thus the right of the weak over the strong is the same as that of the strong over the weak. The strong man who succeeds in oppressing the weak produces an effect without producing an obligation. Far from imposing a new duty on the weak, he provokes in him the natural and imperishable right to throw off oppression.

It is thus an eternal truth, and cannot be too often repeated to men, that the act of subjugation of the weak by the strong can never become a right; and that, on the contrary, the act by which the weak man eludes the oppression of the strong is always a right, is always a pressing obligation to himself.

... The social State does not create an unjust inequality of rights alongside the natural inequality of endowments; on the contrary, it protects the equality of rights against the natural, but pernicious influence of such inequality. The social law is certainly not made to weaken the weak and strengthen the strong; on the contrary, it is concerned to shelter the weak from the encroachments of the strong; and, extending its tutelary authority to all citizens, it guarantees to all the plenitude of their rights.　*872*

Abbé Sieyès
Préliminaire
à la Constitution
20 and 21 July 1789
France

*Moderation
and respect for
one's neighbour.
Against violence*

This world we come to, they never take enwe to bury adaka. (*Enwe and adaka are species of monkey.*)
　When monolinguals of different tongues meet, they don't kill each other.

If a bush forbids bag, it must not grow fungus.
　One who does not wish to be abused, does not abuse.　*873*

Ibo proverbs
Nigeria

I go, but where you stay,
Stand firm, mature,
Kill the lion, kill the leopard,
Prosper, grow and live.
The lion roars, the leopard has its spots,
But you others, restrain your hearts,
Let each respect his brother,
Let not wrath take hold on you;
If any yields to wrath
He brings misfortune down on his own head.
Where you live, moderate the dances,
Moderate the drums (ngoma).
It is not by money and lust for gain that man lives.
To threaten is forbidden,
The knife is forbidden,
Blows are forbidden.
But go into the forest,
Hunt game, and divide it.
Yet, without the passion that leads to quarrels.
May you prosper,
Increase and be happy.
The village has just been rebuilt,
I have come to pacify it,
I pacify the men, I pacify the women,
I pacify kinsmen by marriage,

May they live on, in prosperity and peace,
May they have children, that their ancestors live again!
This I want, I want, Oh, Oh, Oh!   *874*

Bakongo tradition
Congo

Another's rights
Akam proverb
Ghana

Trampling on another's right to seek your own ends in
disappointment.   *875*

Justice and
non-violence

Amharic proverb
Ethiopia

The poor man pleads, the judge listens.
   (*Do not be your own justiciar; all are entitled to justice.*)   *876*

No punishment
without trial

Romanian proverb

Try a man first, hang him later.   *877*

The Grand Duke of Kiev, Svyatopolk, having blinded his cousin
Vasilko (1097):

Vladimir (Monomakh) and David sent envoys to say
to Svyatopolk: 'Why have you done this evil deed, unheard-
of in the land of Russia? It is against us that you have
wielded the dagger. Why have you blinded your brother?
If you had any complaint against him you should have
accused him before us. Then, having confounded him,
you might have acted against him. Well, then, say now
what his fault was, and why you have so dealt with him.'
                                                          878

Russian annals

Against
massacre

When Ivan the Terrible came to Novgorod in 1570 to crush a revolt
with fire and sword, a holy man exalted in Christ came before him:

. . . and he held out to the Tsar a glass filled with blood
and a morsel of raw flesh, inviting him to drink of the
blood and eat the morsel of flesh. The Tsar drew back
with repugnance, wondering what was the holy man's
purpose. Then the man of God said to him: 'This is a glass
of the blood shed at your orders.' And he had him brought
back . . . to the light of day. . . . Then the Tsar made a
sign with his kerchief that his regiments should stop their
massacre of the people.   *879*

Russian manuscript
18th cent.

Another version of this story in an earlier English text.

On the 18th of February 1570, Ivan the Terrible entered
Pskov, threatening to deal with it as he had dealt with
Novgorod. Nevertheless, he had a present sent to a holy
man exalted in Christ called Nicholas, who thanked him
and, in turn, sent him a morsel of raw flesh. This happened

J. Fletcher
Of the Russe
Common Wealth
1591
England

in Lent. The Tsar expressed his surprise that a good Christian should offer him meat in Lent. 'Does Ivan imagine,' said the saint in answer, 'that it is sinful to eat a little animal flesh in Lent and no sin to swallow so much human flesh as he has already devoured?' Thus did the man exalted in Christ save the lives of a multitude of people.   *880*

Denunciation, defamation, imprisonment, torture, capital punishment, violence, vengeance

Secret denunciations

Secret denunciations are evidently abusive but are sanctioned and made necessary in many nations by the weakness of their constitutions. It is a practice which makes men false and dissembling. He who suspects another of informing sees in him an enemy. Thus he becomes accustomed to masking his own feelings and, by dint of hiding them from others, he ends up hiding them from himself. Woe to men who have reached this point; lost and adrift without firm or clear principles upon the vast sea of opinion, always in fear of the monsters which threaten them. They cannot enjoy the present, for it is always poisoned by uncertainty for the future. Deprived of the lasting pleasures of peace of mind and security, the few happy moments scattered here and there in their sad lives and used up in haste and confusion hardly console them for having lived....

Cesare Beccaria
Treatise on Crimes
and Punishments
1764
Italy

Who can defend himself against calumny when it is armed with the strongest shield of tyranny, secrecy? What sort of government can it be where he who governs sees an enemy in each of his subordinates and thinks himself obliged to take away the peace of mind of each one of his subjects in order to ensure the peace of mind of all?   *881*

Against defamation

Nothing does more harm to freedom than licence, and nothing is so prejudicial to the free discussion of public business as wanton attacks on personal integrity. Recently promoted, as we have been, to the enjoyment of the rights and guarantees of popular government, it is not surprising that we have gone astray in the application and exercise of this privilege, and that, being unable to draw the line between what is permitted by law and what is forbidden, we imagine that restrictions and hindrances are placed in its way when, in fact, it is its abuses which are curbed. But what are laws with respect to all matters except obstacles placed in the way of our most natural inclinations, our most undoubted rights, in order to channel them in such a way as to suit the general welfare? And is personal reputation to be considered as any less sacred a possession than are material goods? Or are the wounds produced by the blows inflicted on our good name any less painful to bear than others? It follows that the legislator must provide for the proper compensation of this type of injury with no less care than he does for other types, and he would no less fail in his duty were he to leave the good name and social respectability of citizens exposed to libellous and slanderous abuse, than were he to leave their lives and property at the mercy of thieves and murderers. For slander to exist, it is not necessary that a crime should be imputed. All that is needed is that a person should be accused of a deed or act of omission which though not in its nature criminal, tends to make that person hateful or unworthy of respect in the eyes of the public. There is always slander whenever the words, signs or representations used tend to arouse feelings of hatred, ridicule or contempt towards a particular individual in the public mind.

Naturally, there must be free discussion of all the activities of State officials in their ministerial capacity, a strict inquiry into their public conduct, criticism of their writings, and, in general, of literary publications of all kinds. But the facts alleged must be true, otherwise they amount to slander.

Andrés Bello
El Araucano
1833
Chile

882

'NEMINEM CAPTIVABIMUS'

We [the King] promise and swear never to incarcerate or cause to be incarcerated any noble; never to punish any noble in any manner, whatever the crime or misdemeanour he has committed, unless he has first been justly condemned by the courts of law and delivered into our hands by the judges of his own province—save for those who may commit a crime under the ordinary law, such as murder, rape or highway robbery.

Constitution of
King Wladislaw
Jagiello
1430
Poland

883

*Against torture
and imprisonment*

Torture and racking are dangerous inventions, and seem rather to be trials of patience than essays of truth. And both he that can, and he that cannot endure them, conceal the truth. For wherefor shall pain or smart rather compel me to confess that which is so indeed, than force me to tell that which is not? And contrariwise, if he who hath not done that whereof he is accused, is sufficiently patient to endure those torments, why shall not he be able to tolerate them who hath done it, and is guilty indeed, so dear and worthy a reward as life being proposed unto him? I am of opinion that the ground of his invention proceedeth from the consideration of the power and faculty of the conscience. For, to the guilty, it seemeth to give a kind of furtherance to the torture, to make him confess his faults and weakeneth and dismayeth him: and on the other part, it encourageth and strengtheneth the innocent against torture. To say truth, it is a means full of uncertainty and danger. What would not a man say, nay what not do, to avoid so grievous pains and shun such torments? . . . Whence it followeth that he whom the judge hath tortured, because he shall not die an innocent, he shall bring him to his death, both innocent and tortured. Many thousands have thereby charged their heads with false confessions. . . . But so it is, that (as men say) it is the least evil human weakness could invent; though, in my conceit, very inhumanely, and therewithal most unprofitably. Many nations less barbarous in that than the Grecian or the Roman, who term them so, judge it a horrible and cruel thing to rack and torment a man for a fault whereof you are yet in doubt. Is your ignorance long of him? What can he do withal? Are you not unjust, who because you will not put him to death without some cause, you do worse than kill him? And that it is so, consider but how often he rather chooseth to die guiltless, than pass by this information, much more painful than the punishment of torment; and who many times, by reason or the sharpness of it, preventeth, furthereth, yea, and executeth the punishment.

Montaigne
Essays
1580-88

884

THE PRISONER

Captive I languish in the dank and gloom.
The eaglet, prison-reared, who shares my room,
Perched listless near me in the window-seat
Rattles one wing, pecks at a hunk of meat,

Then drops his meal to stare into the blue:
My selfsame thought, perhaps, has struck him too.
He seems to summon me with look and cry,
As if he wished to say, 'Come on! Let's fly!

Pushkin
1799-1837
Russia

'Free birds are we: time, brother, time to go
There, where beyond the clouds the white hills show,
And in the distance gleams the deep blue sea
And none dare venture save the wind... and me!'   *885*

If a thief or a brigand is captured and denies what he is accused of, you hold that the judge should rain blows on his head and pierce his sides with points of iron until he tells the truth. Neither divine law, nor human law, consents to this: confessions must be not forced, but spontaneous; they must not be extorted, but obtained voluntarily. If it so happens that after inflicting these punishments, you discover absolutely none of the offences with which the prisoner is charged, do you not blush, at least then, and do you not recognize how impious your judgement was? Similarly, if the prisoner, unable to stand such tortures, confesses to crimes that he has not committed, who, may I ask, bears the responsibility for such impiety if not the man who forced him to make these untrue confessions? Moreover, if someone utters words which do not come from his heart, he speaks but he does not confess. So abandon these execrable practices, and renounce, from the bottom of your heart, what you have been mad enough to do in the past. What benefit have you derived from that for which you now blush?   *886*

Pope Nicholas I
to the Bulgarians
13 November 866

Harsh penalties and rules that are not uniform must be entirely abolished. We establish laws and statutes in advance [before inflicting punishment] in the desire that men may no longer harbour the intention of transgressing and that the country may have regular punishments, according to the principle of punishing without anger. We hope that the time is perhaps not far off when [punishments] are fixed but not inflicted. Let the ten thousand countries and the hundred lords take note of Our intentions. From the days of the preceding dynasties it had become the invariable practice of the authorities to employ extra-legal methods in the interrogation of accused persons. Sometimes they used instruments [of torture to extort confessions], such as great cudgels, the flogging of bound [prisoners], the wheel, the boot, ankle-crushing, and the bastinado with laths. Under these varied and atrocious punishments, many accused persons resigned themselves to making false [confessions]. Even if [those accused] were handed over to justice in accordance with the letter

Legal treatise
of Sui-shu
Annals of the Sui
590-617
China

[of the law] there were always manipulations [of the laws] and excesses, so that no man could justify himself. Nowadays all cruel methods have been entirely abolished.   *887*

Letter to the Archduke in defence of a serf accused of stealing copper and who has been put to torture.

As if it were just to force out the truth by torture, in the absence of witnesses or any kind of material proof or argument. For the nature of torture is such as to compel without difficulty even the most innocent of men to confess his guilt....

Bálint Balassa
1587
Hungary

To be prosecutor and judge in the same case is . . . contrary to the law.   *888*

It is a cruelty which has its sanction of custom in most nations to submit the accused to torture during his trial, to force him to confess a crime or because of the contradictions in his statements; to seek out his accomplices or on some metaphysical and incomprehensible ground that torture purges out infamy; or to discover other offences he may be guilty of though not accused of them.

A man cannot be declared guilty before sentence, and society cannot withdraw its protection from him until such time as it has been proved that he has violated the conditions upon which it accorded him that protection. What law, then, other than that of force, can give a judge the right to inflict punishment on a citizen whilst his guilt or innocence is still in doubt? The dilemma is not new: the guilt of the accused is either certain or it is not; if certain, only the penalty established by the law should be administered, and torture is useless, since the admission of guilt is no longer necessary; if it is not certain, then it is wrong to torture one who is innocent, for such, according to the law, is a man whose offences have not been proved. And I would add this: it is flying in the face of all logic to demand of a man at the same time to be both accuser and accused, and to make pain the crucible in which truth

Cesare Beccaria
Treatise on Crimes
and Punishments
1764
Italy

is tested, as if the criterion of truth lay in the muscles and fibres of the unfortunate victim. Torture is the surest way of acquitting the sturdy rogue and convicting the delicate innocent.   *889*

457

Flogging

I frequently questioned my companions about this in an attempt to discover with what kind of suffering it might be compared. It was no idle curiosity that urged me. I repeat, I was moved and frightened. But it was all in vain; I could get no satisfactory reply.

'It burns like fire!' was the general answer. They all said the same thing.

First I tried to question M-tski. 'It burns like fire! Like hell! It seems as if one's back were in a furnace.'

One day I reached an interesting conclusion which may or may not have been well founded, although the opinion of the convicts themselves confirms my view, namely, that the rods are the most terrible punishment in use among us.

At first it seems absurd, impossible, yet five hundred strokes of the rods, four hundred even, are enough to kill a man. Beyond five hundred death is almost certain. The most robust man will be unable to survive a thousand strokes, whereas five hundred with the stick are endured without much inconvenience, and without the least risk in the world of losing one's life. A man of ordinary build can take up to a thousand with the stick without danger, and even two thousand will not kill a man of ordinary strength and constitution. All the convicts declared that rods were worse than sticks or ramrods.

'Rods hurt more and for longer!' they said.

They must hurt more than sticks, that is quite certain, for they cause a far greater shock to the nervous system, which they excite beyond measure. I do not know whether such people exist today, but not long ago there were some who derived such pleasure from the whipping of a victim that they reminded one of the Marquis de Sade, of the Marchioness of Brinvilliers. I think such delight must consist in a kind of horror, and that these noble ladies and gentlemen must have experienced pain and pleasure at the same time.

There are people who, like tigers, are greedy for blood. Those who enjoy unlimited power over the flesh, blood, and soul of their fellow creatures, of the brethren in Christ; those, I say, who enjoy that power and can so utterly degrade another being made in the image of God, are incapable of resisting their desires and their thirst for excitement. Tyranny is a habit which may be developed until at last it becomes a disease. I declare that the noblest nature can become so hardened and bestial that nothing distinguishes it from that of a wild animal. Blood and power intoxicate; they help to develop callousness and debauchery. The mind then becomes capable of the most abnormal cruelty, which it regards as pleasure; the man and the citizen are swallowed up in the tyrant; and then a return to human dignity, repentance, moral resurrection, becomes almost impossible.

It cannot be denied that the possibility of such licence has a contagious effect on the whole of society. A society which looks upon such things with an indifferent eye is already infected to the marrow. In a word, the right granted to a man of inflicting corporal punishment on his fellows is one of the plague-spots of our nation. It is the means of annihilating all civic spirit; it contains in germ the elements of inevitable, imminent decomposition.

Dostoevsky
The House
of the Dead
1861

890

*The man under
the thief's skin*

The man-thief is [a] man. But if there are many thieves, it is not that there are many men. If there is no thief, it is not that there is no man.

How can one demonstrate that?

To detest the fact that there are many thieves is not to detest the fact that there are many men.

To wish there were no thieves is not to wish there were no men.

Our contemporaries all agree in approving the foregoing propositions.

If they are sound one may conclude thus:

Although the man-thief is [a] man, someone loves [a] thief. It is not that he loves [a] man. If he does not love [a] thief, it is not that he does not love [a] man. If he kills [a] thief, it is not that he kills [a] man.

Mo-tzu
5th cent. B.C.
China

891

*Against
capital punishment*
Mahābhārata XII
2nd cent. B.C.
to 1st cent. A.D.
Sanskrit

Satyavat says: The extermination of the root [of existence] (*namely, of man*) is not to be countenanced; that by no means constitutes the eternal *dharma*. Indeed, proper expiation [for guilt] can be made without killing. *892*

Tirukkural
1st cent. A.D.
Tamil
Mauritius

For a king to punish criminals with death is like pulling up the weeds in the green corn. *893*

Talmud
Makkoth 7

A sanhedrin (*court*) which puts someone to death once in seven years deserves to be called a murderer; rabbi Eleazar ben Azaryah says: once in seventy years; rabbi Tarphon and rabbi Akiva say: if we were in the sanhedrin no one would ever be sentenced to death. *894*

Cesare Beccaria
Treatise on Crimes
and Punishments
1764
Italy

What right, I ask, have men to cut the throats of their fellow-creatures? . . . the punishment of death is not authorized by any right. . . . It is . . . a war of a whole nation against a citizen, whose destruction they consider as necessary, or useful.

895

ENTRY ON 'MAN'

Voltaire
Philosophical
Dictionary
1764

It requires twenty years to raise man from the state of a plant, in which he abides in his mother's womb, and from the pure animal state, which is the lot of his earliest infancy, to that in which the maturity of reason begins to flower. It has taken thirty centuries to learn a little of his bodily structure. It would take eternity to learn something of his soul. It takes only an instant to kill him.

896

Catherine the Great
1766
Russia

Frequent recourse to the death penalty has never made men better.

897

Dungeons

In 1783 I went with two of my friends to see the prison at Vincennes. There were no longer any prisoners there. I visited all the cells, including the dark and horrible dungeon at the bottom of the tower, the recollection of which still makes me shudder as I write this. Among other stories recounted to us by the gaoler who showed us around this dreadful building, this one deserves to be known:

A man was locked up in one of the cells in the tower. Since he was impatient of his misfortune, shouting and cursing those who had had him imprisoned, it was thought good to discipline him by moving him to that dungeon. There he spent nearly two years. There he went mad. The court commanded that he be taken to Bicêtre; but since it was impossible to get near him, they devised the notion of loosing at him an enormous mastiff, which soon felled him and thus made it easy to seize him. The worthy man who told us this anecdote found it very laughable; he had a constant flow of witticisms and was particularly impressed by the idea of using the mastiff, seeming to call upon us to note how ingenious the device was. I have since found out that the only reason why the unfortunate wretch who lost his reason in that hole suffered such horrible treatment was that he had not followed the example of so many honest people by condon-

Réprésentation du Susmentionné Archi - Scélérat & Meurtrier , nommé Chrystian
André Kaysebier , comme il est enchaîné dans sa prison sur la Forteresse
de Custrin.

Prison
18th cent.
Russia

ing his wife's misconduct with a base fellow who was then
a minister.

. . . .

Fréret was sent to the Bastille for producing an
excellent pamphlet. The Garde des Sceaux came to
question him and, after giving his answers, he said: 'You
appear satisfied with my replies to your questions; may
I ask you one?'

'What is that?'

'Why am I here?'

'You are very inquisitive, Sir', the Garde des Sceaux
replied, turning his back on him.

Someone said to Monsieur de la Tour that it was very
harsh to send wise men who wrote the truth to the Bastille.
'Why, Madame,' he answered, 'what else is there to do
with them?'   *898*

André Chénier
1762-94
Apologie
France

461

OF DEATH

Come in, my friends, sit down,
Welcome, you bring me joy.
I know, you entered my cell by the window while I was
    asleep,
You did not overturn the bottle with its slender neck
Nor the red box of medicines.
The starlight on your faces,
You stand there, hand in hand, at my bedside.
Welcome, you bring me joy

Hashim, son of Osman,
Why are you eying me so strangely?
Hashim, son of Osman,
How odd it is.
Had you not already met your death, brother,
At Istanbul, in the harbour, loading coal on to a foreign
    cargo-boat?
You fell with your bucket to the bottom of the hold;
The cargo-boat's winch hauled you up,
And before you were laid to rest for good
Your blood, all red, washed your black head.
How you must have suffered!

Don't stand there. Sit down.
I thought you were dead.
You entered my cell by the window,
The starlight on your face;
Welcome, you bring me joy.

Yakup, from the village of Kayalar,
Greetings, dear old friend,
Were you not dead, too?
Had you not gone to the treeless cemetery
Bequeathing malaria and hunger to the children?
It was terribly hot that day.
Well then, were you not dead?

And you, Ahmet Jemil, the writer?
With my own eyes I saw
Your coffin being lowered into the ground.
And I even seem to remember
That your coffin was a little shorter than you had been.
Leave that alone, Ahmet Jemil,
(I see you still have the same old habit)
It's a bottle of medicine, not *raki*.
You used to drink it in such quantities
So as to pick up fifty piastres a day
And forget the world in your solitude.

I thought you were dead my friends;
You are at my bedside, hand in hand.
Sit down, my friends, sit down.
Welcome, you bring me joy.

Death is just, says a Persian poet,
It strikes with equal majesty the poor man and the Shah.
Hashim, why be surprised?
Had you never heard tell, brother of a Shah
Dead in a ship's hold clutching a bucket?
Death is just, says a Persian poet.

Yakup, how handsome you are when you laugh, dear
    friend,
I never saw you laugh like that
When you were alive . . .
But let me finish—
Death is just, says a Persian poet.

Leave that bottle alone, Ahmet Jemil.
Getting annoyed won't help, I know what you want to
    say:
For death to be just
Life must be just

A Persian poet . . .
Why, my friends, why are you leaving me alone?
Why this anger? Where are you going?

Nazím Hikmet
1946
Turkey

899

THE VERDICT

The word fell, heavy as a stone
Upon my living breast.
It matters not, it's no surprise,
And I'll survive, somehow.

I've much to do today.
Destroy my last remaining shreds of memory,
Harden my soul until it's like a stone,
And learn to live again.

I must, or else . . . From outside
The sounds of summer, warm and merry, reach my ears.
I long ago foresaw this sunlit day
And this deserted house.

Anna Akhmatova
U.S.S.R.

Summer 1939

900

*Law
versus violence*

If one person does violence to another with an axe or a
knife, and the person attacked is seriously wounded, the
attacker must pay him smart-money so that he can buy

medicine. He must continue to pay until final recovery. In addition, the attacker must pay a fine of 20,000 to the king. This also applies for all those who abetted him, by rendering service or inciting him to attack. The fine must be paid to the king.

Kutāraçāstra code
14th cent.
Java

901

Ransom

A culprit who is taken to the execution-place and desires to live must pay 8,000 for a ransom; this is called 'buying a piece of jungle'. If a slave runs away, but does no more than that, and if he is tracked down, but in the meanwhile has married a woman without debts or a noble woman in the place where he went—if, therefore, he has by mere chance grown rich by marrying [a well-to-do woman], such a slave is entitled to pay ransom for himself and his children, a reasonable sum of money, as an indemnification to the owner. He should not be badgered about the price, if the ransom for himself and his children is reasonable. *902*

Kutāraçāstra code
14th cent.
Java

Prisoners of war

Prisoners of war (meaning women captured during a campaign, since male prisoners were always killed), if they wish to pay, are free after paying 8,000. This is called 'buying one's life'. Such were the rules with respect to prisoners of war in the Dwāpara-period (Brazen Age, before the end of the 4th millenary B.C.). *903*

Kutāraçāstra code
14th cent.
Java

Against vengeance
and violence

Blood cannot wash out blood. *904*

Turkish proverb
11th cent.
Eastern Turkestan

Do not shed blood [to settle a dispute]; settle it in accordance with the law. *905*

Turkish proverb

Two dervishes can make do with a single mattress; two Padishahs cannot share the surface of the earth. *906*

Turkmenian
proverb

Talmudic interpretation of the Bible's condemnation of vindictiveness and spite.

What is vindictiveness and what is spite? One man said to another, 'Lend me your saw', and the other replied, 'No.' The next day, the second said to the first, 'Lend me your axe', and the other replied, 'I will lend you nothing, since you lent me nothing.' That is vindictiveness. And what is spite? One man said to the other, 'Lend me your axe', and he replied, 'No.' The next day, the latter said to the former, 'Lend me your saw', to which the other replied, 'Here, take it, I am not like you who never lend anything.' This is spite.

Talmud
Yoma 23

907

Righteous vengeance

సంప (దనర యంటి కమువు దనశవ (
భెక్ర నె న కడు స్ఇరురాదు
పార (ర మెలు వె ని పొగవు సుత పాలు
విశ్పహ ఖ రా ము వి సు ర ఖ ెదు !

Vemana
15th cent.
Satakamu
Telugu tradition

Even if an enemy fit to be killed is caught in your hands, do him no harm. Help him to the best of your ability and let him go. This is enough—for him it is death! *908*

Against war

That is the great remorse of [Priyadarsin] the beloved of the gods, the conqueror of Kalinga. For, that conquest can be regarded as having been really no conquest at all because it was characterized by killing, death, or captivity of the people. That is the profoundly painful and regretful feeling of the beloved of the gods.

... [In war] there befall [to pious and innocent persons] violence, death, or the deportation of beloved kindred. The friends, esteemed comrades, companions, and kinsmen, who still entertain undiminished affection for those affected by war, themselves suffer a calamity, and that calamity proves to be a personal violence to them. This is the lot of all men and is considered deplorable by the beloved of the gods.

Asoka's
Rock Edict XIII
3rd cent. B.C.
Prakrit

909

Restoration of peace

Also I said, It is not good that ye do: ought ye not to walk in the fear of our God because of the reproach of the heathen our enemies? I likewise, and my brethren, and my servants, have lent them money and corn: I pray you, let us release this debt. Restore, I pray you, to them, even this day, their lands, their vineyards, their oliveyards,

465

and their houses, also the hundredth part of the money, and of the corn, the wine, and the oil, that ye have lent them. Then they said, We will restore them, and will require nothing of them; so will we do as thou sayest. Then I called the priests, and took an oath of them, that they should do according to this promise.   *910*

Hebrew Bible
Nehemiah 5

Against pretexts
for war

A man blushes with shame when he recalls the scandalous and frivolous motives Christian princes invoke to persuade their peoples to take up arms. One proves, or affects to prove, he possesses some antiquated right, as if it mattered very much which particular prince governs a State, provided that its administration is in the public interest. Another takes as a pretext some item omitted in a treaty of a hundred chapters. This one bears a grudge against that one because of the rejection or abduction of some bride-to-be or of some over-bold piece of raillery. But those princes reach the height of infamy who, feeling their authority waning as the result of too prolonged a period of peace and the good relations existing between their subjects, enter, with devilish intent, into a secret understanding with other princes who, as soon as a pretext has been found, provoke war with the object of setting at one another's throats those who were living in close unity and of plundering the unfortunate people, thanks to that unbridled authority which accompanies war.   *911*

Erasmus
of Rotterdam
Querela Pacis
Undique Gentium
Ejectae
Profligataeque
1515
Holland

Killing?

Why kill me? Now come on! Don't you live on the other side of the water? If you lived on this side, my friend, I should be an assassin; it would be wrong to kill you in this fashion: but since you live on the other side, I'm a fine fellow and what I do is right.   *912*

Pascal
1623-62
Pensées
France

Condemnation
of war in all
circumstances

We utterly deny all outward wars and strife, and fightings with outward weapons, for any end, or under any pretence whatever: this is our testimony to the whole world.   *913*

The Quakers'
Declaration
to King Charles II
1660
England

Reform of worldly management

The ultimate purpose of society is general peace and safety, and the *well-being of the people ought to be the supreme law of any republic or any kingdom.* Therefore, everything should be removed that may in any way disquiet, involve or inconvenience human society, or break up the links of general and public security. In this respect the principal causes of the evil are *wars, for there is no salvation in war.* For this reason, and in order to remove all opportunity to revert to hostilities and wars, weapons shall be done away with, as was ordered by God [Isaiah 2: 4]. Similarly we should eliminate the bloody councils, which engender nothing but threats of fire, steel and undoing of States. However, the question arises: What will then become of the *rifles and the guns*? My answer is: The rifles should be used against beasts of prey, whereas from the metal of the guns bells ought to be cast whereby people can be summoned, or musical instruments, and all this should serve to glorify God. . . .

J. A. Comenius
Czech writer
1592-1670
De Rerum
Humanarum
Emendatione
Consultatio Catholica

Truth and justice must be administered by law, and not by weapons—that means neither by weapons of steel, or by the weapons of the tongue and the passions—and everything should remain in peace.   *914*

*Federation
for peace*

The idea of the law of nations, understood as implying the right to make war, is really inconceivable (since this would mean the right to decide what is just, not according to external laws, universally applicable and limiting the freedom of each individual, but by force and according to subjective maxims). It is inconceivable unless we take it to mean that men of such a turn of mind are fully entitled to destroy one another and find eternal peace in the vast grave-mound that is heaped over them with all the horrors of violence. To the reasonable mind, there is no other way in which States maintaining reciprocal relations can escape from lawlessness, the source of declared wars, than by renouncing, as individuals, their primitive (anarchical) freedom and adapting themselves to the public constraint of laws, and thus form a 'State of Nations' (*civitas gentium*) which, growing freely and steadily would finally be extended to embrace all peoples of the earth. But since, according to their own idea of the law of nations, this solution is anathema to them, and they reject *in hypothesi* what is right *in thesi*, in the absence of the positive notion of a 'world republic', all that is left (if everything is not to be lost) is the 'negative' substitute of a permanent 'alliance', ever broadening in scope, and able to ward off hostilities and resist the pressure of all these aggressive and anti-legal propensities; nevertheless, the danger of their breaking loose remains. (*Furor impius intus fremit horridus ore cruento. Virgil.*)   *915*

Kant
Eternal Peace
1795

War, we are told, is a civilizing agent, and it is true that it fills us with lofty thoughts and inspires us to do heroic deeds in the face of danger and death, to scorn earthly goods which may be pillaged at any moment, and to feel profound sympathy for everything human, to which we are drawn by a common peril or common sufferings. But I trust you will not interpret this in any way as praise of your warlike instincts and thirst for blood, or as some humble prayer addressed to you by suffering humanity that you will not cease from plunging it into further bloody trials and tribulations. Only those who were already stout-hearted are stirred by war to acts of heroism; all it inspires in grosser natures is the urge to despoil and oppress the weak and unarmed. War has produced its heroes and its robbers, but which of these in greater number?

Fichte
German philosopher
1793

916

In the Old World, certain eloquent philosophers, and notably Voltaire, have protested against the injustice and absurdity of war; but they have barely succeeded in doing more than moderate martial ardour in certain respects. That vast crowd of men whose ambitions to achieve glory and fortune can be satisfied only by massacre have poured contempt on their zeal, and in books, in camps, in court-yards, the word has gone round that patriotism and valour no longer exist ever since the birth of a detestable philosophy advocating the avoidance of bloodshed.

Condorcet
L'Atlantide
1794
France

917

PRAYER OF THE 'POLISH FLOWERS' (1943)

Open Poland to us, as you cleave the stormy sky by your thunder. Suffer us to cleanse our house, cleanse it of our ashes and sacred ruins as well as of our faults and our accursed sins, that, raised from the tomb, it may be poor, but pure. . . .

Arm the proud with humility, and fortify the humble with haughty wrath. Teach us that, under your skies, there can be 'neither Jew nor Greek'. . . .

Strike down the vainglorious who take up arms in the name of their own glory, and suffer no longer the infamous sword to keep the cross of your martyrdom. . . .

But, above all, restore to our words, distorted by liars, their unique and true meaning, so that law may signify law, and justice—justice.

Julian Tuwim
Poland

918

Mercy

Wolfram
von Eschenbach
Willehalm
13th cent.
Old German

Whate'er the infidel hath done,
Yet shall ye make it clearly shown
That God himself, in mortal day,
Forgave the men that did him slay.
If God grant victory as ye strive
Show mercy, then, to foes alive.   *919*

Laws of war

Fénelon
1651-1715
France

There are laws of war which must be observed no less religiously than those of peace. Even when at war, there is still a certain law of nations which is inherent to mankind, a sacred and inviolable bond among the peoples which no war can disrupt.   *920*

*The law
of nations*

As soon as man enters into a state of society he loses the sense of his weakness; equality ceases, and then commences the state of war.

Each particular society begins to feel its strength, whence arises a state of war between different nations. The individuals likewise of each society become sensible of their force; hence the principal advantages of this society they endeavour to convert to their own emolument, which constitutes a state of war between individuals.

These two different kinds of states give rise to human laws. Considered as inhabitants of so great a planet, which necessarily contains a variety of nations, they have laws relating to their mutual intercourse, which is what we call the law of nations. As members of a society that must be properly supported, they have laws relating to the governors and the governed, and this we distinguish by the name of politic law. They have also another sort of laws, as they stand in relation to each other; by which is understood the civil law.

The law of nations is naturally founded on this principle, that different nations ought in time of peace to do one another all the good they can, and in time of war as little injury as possible, without prejudicing their real interests.

The object of war is victory; that of victory is conquest; and that of conquest preservation. From this and the preceding principle all those rules are derived which constitute the law of nations.

Montesquieu
The Spirit
of the Laws
1748
France

All countries have a law of nations, not excepting the Iroquois themselves, though they devour their prisoners: for they send and receive ambassadors, and understand the rights of war and peace. The mischief is that their law of nations is not founded on true principles.   *921*

Foundation of the Red Cross

There is therefore an appeal to be made, an entreaty to be addressed to men of all countries and stations, to the mighty of this world as to the humblest artisan, for all, in one way or another, each according to his place and capacities, can do something to further this good cause. Such an appeal goes out as much to women as to men, to the princess on the steps of a throne as to the humble, devoted orphan servant or the poor widow, alone on earth, who hopes to use her remaining strength to help relieve the sufferings of others; it is addressed to the general or field-marshal as to the philanthropist and the writer whose talent, working away unobtrusively on his own, produces writings that can illuminate a subject that concerns all mankind and, more specifically every people, every country, indeed every family, since none can say he is safe from the hazards of war.

. . . It is all the more important that agreement should be reached and measures taken beforehand because, once fighting begins, the belligerents are already inimically disposed and can see nothing except from the point of view of their own nationals. . . .

With so much talk nowadays of progress and civilization, and since wars cannot always be avoided, surely we must urge the necessity of trying to obviate or at least mitigate its horrors, not only on the field of battle but perhaps even more so in hospitals during those weeks that are so long and so miserable for the unfortunate wounded.   *922*

Henri Dunant
Un Souvenir
de Solferino
1862
Switzerland

CONVENTION FOR THE AMELIORATION OF THE CONDITION
OF THE WOUNDED IN ARMIES IN THE FIELD

The Swiss Confederation; His Royal Highness the Grand Duke of Baden; His Majesty the King of the Belgians; His Majesty the King of Denmark; Her Majesty the Queen of Spain; His Majesty the Emperor of the French; His Royal Highness the Grand Duke of Hesse; His Majesty the King of Italy; His Majesty the King of the Netherlands; His Majesty the King of Portugal and Algarve; His Majesty the King of Prussia; His Majesty the King of Wurtemberg, in their common desire, as far as lies within their power to mitigate the evils inseparable from war, to eliminate unnecessary suffering and to ameliorate the condition of soldiers wounded in combat, have resolved to conclude a Convention to this effect. . . .

Article 1

Military ambulances and hospitals shall be recognized as neutral, and as such shall be protected and respected by the belligerents as long as they contain the sick or wounded.

Neutrality shall cease if such ambulances or hospitals are under the guard of a military force.

Article 2

Hospital and ambulance staff, including supply personnel, the health, administrative and transport services for the wounded, and chaplains, shall be treated as neutral when these services function, and as long as wounded remain to be collected or assisted.

Article 3

The persons referred to in the preceding Article may, even after enemy occupation, continue to discharge their duties in the hospital or ambulance with which they serve, or withdraw and join the corps to which they belong.

In such circumstances, when these persons cease duty, they shall be handed over to the enemy outposts by the occupying army.

Article 4

Since the material of military hospitals remains subject to the laws of war, persons attached to such hospitals may not, when they withdraw, take with them anything except their private property.

In such cases, however, ambulances shall retain their material.

Article 5

Local inhabitants who assist the wounded shall be respected and shall remain free. It shall be the duty of the generals of the belligerent powers to inform the inhabitants of the appeal to their humanity and of the resultant neutrality.

Any house in which a wounded person is sheltered and cared for shall be immune from attack. An inhabitant who takes in the wounded shall not be required to billet troops, and shall be exempt from part of any forced contributions that may be levied.

Article 6

Wounded or sick soldiers shall be collected and cared for regardless of their nationality.

Commanders-in-Chief shall be at liberty to hand over enemy soldiers wounded in combat immediately to the enemy outposts when circumstances permit and by agreement between the two parties.

Those who, after recovery, are recognized as unfit for service shall be repatriated.

The others may also be repatriated, provided that they do not take up arms again during the war.

Evacuations and the personnel in charge of them shall be accorded complete neutrality.

Article 7

A standard, distinctive flag shall be adopted for hospitals, ambulances and evacuations. It shall in all cases be accompanied by the national flag.

An armlet shall also be allowed for personnel given neutral status but its issue shall be at the discretion of the military authority.

The flag and the armlet shall bear a red cross on a white ground.

Article 8

The detailed execution of the present Convention shall be arranged between the Commanders-in-Chief of the belligerent armies in accordance with the instructions of their respective governments and in conformity with the general principles set out herein.

Article 9

The High Contracting Parties agree to communicate the present Convention to Governments which have been unable to send Plenipotentiaries to the International Conference at Geneva and to invite them to accede to it; to this end the Protocol has been left open.

Article 10

The present Convention shall be ratified, and the ratifications shall be exchanged at Berne within four months, or sooner if possible.

In Witness Whereof the respective Plenipotentiaries have affixed their signatures and seals.

Convention
instituting
the International
Red Cross

Done at Geneva this twenty-second day of August eighteen hundred and sixty-four. *923*

I shall have lived on this earth in an age
When man had sunk so low that, of his own accord,
He took life gladly, with no need for compulsion.
His beliefs were nothing but delusions and errors,
His life, a tissue of haunting fears.

I shall have lived on this earth in an age
When denouncement was held to be deserving,
Whose heroes were assassins, brigands, traitors.
He who perchance refrained from applauding
Was, like the plague-stricken, viewed with hate.
. . . .
I shall have lived on this earth in an age
When the child cursed its mother. When
The woman with child was glad to miscarry
And the living man was envious of the dead
While the poison seethed on his table.
. . . .
I shall have lived on this earth in an age
When, mute, the poet waited till thy voice
Should sound again to thunder forth the just
Anathema—which none but thou can'st do—
Oh Isaiah, master of the dreadful Word!

*Miklós Radnóti
Hungarian poet
1909-44
Deported to Serbia,
his body was
discovered in 1947
in a common grave.
Manuscript poems
were found
in his pocket*

924

LETTER TO A GERMAN FRIEND, 1943

I would like to tell you at once what kind of greatness it
is we are concerned with; and that means telling you the
kind of courage that we admire, but that is not your kind
of courage. For it takes very little courage to advance
under fire when you have been trained for it all your life,
and when action comes more naturally to you than
thought. It takes a lot, on the contrary to go towards
torture and death when you know for certain that hate
and violence are essentially useless. It takes a lot to fight
when you despise war, to agree to lose everything and
yet keep the taste for happiness, to rush to destruction
nurturing the idea of a higher civilization. . . .

We have had to overcome our liking for man, forget
our ideas of a peaceful destiny and our profound conviction
that no victory ever pays and that any mutilation of man
is irremediable. We have had to renounce at once our
science and our hope, our reasons for loving and our
hatred of all war. To use a word that I suppose you will
understand, coming from me, whose hand you once were
pleased to shake, we have had to silence our passion for
friendship.

*Albert Camus
France*

925

THE CITADEL OF KAO-YU

> Citadel of Kao-yu,
> How long is your rampart!
> On the rampart they have sown corn, at its foot
> they have planted mulberries.
> Once you were stronger than iron;
> You have become a field that is tilled and sown.
> My only wish is that for a thousand, nay ten thousand, years
> The broad horizon of the four seas may be our frontier!
> How shady are the mulberries,
> How vast the fields of corn . . .
> May there never again be rampart nor moat!

Chieh Hsi-szŭ
1274-1344
China

926

National identity
and independence

On their arrival in Sparta, an Assembly was called in which the most violent objections were opposed by the Corinthians and the Thebans, followed by many other Greeks. There should be no parleying with the Athenians, they said, they must be annihilated. But the Lacedaemonians refused to reduce to slavery a Greek state which had done such great and splendid deeds in the terrible dangers which once had threatened Greece, and they decided to make peace.

**Xenophon
The Hellenica
c. 384 B.C.**

927

The Scottish people assert their claim to political freedom.

It is impossible for any whose own experience hath not informed him to describe, or fully to understand, the injuries, blood and violence, the depredations and fire, the imprisonments of prelates, the burning, slaughter and robbery committed upon holy persons and religious houses, and a vast multitude of other barbarities, which that king executed on this people, without sparing of any sex or age, religion or order of men whatsoever.

But at length it pleased God, who only can heal after wounds, to restore us to liberty from these innumerable calamities, by our most serene prince, king and lord Robert, who, for the delivering of his people and his own rightful inheritance from the enemy's hand, did like another Joshua or Maccabeus, most cheerfully undergo all manner of toil, fatigue, hardship, and hazard. The Divine Providence, the right of succession by the laws and customs of the kingdom (which we will defend till death) and the due and lawfull consent and assent of all the people, made him our king and prince. To him we are obliged and resolved to adhere in all things, both upon the account of his right and his own merit, as being the person who hath restored the people's safety in defence of their liberties. But after all, if this prince shall leave these principles he hath so nobly pursued, and consent that we or our kingdom be subjected to the king or people of England, we will immediately endeavour to expel him, as our enemy and as the subverter both of his own and our rights, and will make another king, who will defend our liberties: For so long as there shall but one hundred of us remain alive we will never give consent to subject

Letter
to the Pope
1320
Scotland

our selves to the dominion of the English. For it is not glory, it is not riches, neither is it honour, but is liberty alone that we fight and contend for, which no honest man will lose but with his life.   *928*

Human dignity

All human beings are men: all possess will and understanding, the five exterior senses and the four interior senses, and are urged to satisfy them; all love the good, rejoice in what is upright and beautiful, reject and abhor evil.

Bartolomé
de Las Casas
Historia
de las Indias
1547

There is not nor can there be any nation, however savage and depraved but may be converted to all the political virtues and all the humane attributes of the home-loving, politically minded and rational man.   *929*

Turkish proverb
15th cent.

Each country is [for its own inhabitants] as sacred as every other.   *930*

Vauvenargues
Réflexions
et Maximes
1746
France

We surpass the peoples whom we call barbarians neither in our courage, nor in our humanity, nor in our health, nor in our pleasures; and being neither more virtuous nor more happy, we nevertheless persist in believing ourselves much wiser.

The enormous difference we notice between savages and ourselves consists only in our being a little less ignorant.   *931*

A universal
society

The National Assembly solemnly declares:

1. That it regards the universality of the human race as forming but one and the same society, whose aim is the peace and happiness of all and every one of its members;

2. That in this great universal society, nations and States considered individually enjoy the same natural rights and are subject to the same rules of justice as are individuals belonging to subordinate or secondary societies;

3. That, consequently, no nation has the right to invade the land of another nation, or deprive it of its freedom and natural advantages;

4. That all war undertaken from any other motive and for any other object than the defence of a sovereign right, is an act of oppression whose retribution is the concern of the whole of this great society, because the invasion of one State by another State jeopardizes the freedom and security of all;

For these reasons, the National Assembly has declared
and hereby decrees as an article of the French Constitution:
That the French Nation is resolved henceforth not to
undertake any war with the object of increasing its present
territory.   *932*

Volney
Moniteur IV
1790
France

*In the thirteenth century, the Swiss cantons revolted against
Austrian domination, represented by the bailiff Gessler.*

A retired part of the forest; brooks dashing in spray over the
rocks. Enter BERTHA in hunting dress. Immediately afterwards
RUDENZ.

BERTHA. But are you sure they will not follow us?
RUDENZ. See, yonder goes the chase. Now, then, or never!
    I must avail me of this precious moment—
    Must hear my doom decided by thy lips
    Though it should part me from thy side for ever.
    Oh, do not arm that gentle face of thine
    With looks so stern and harsh! Who, who am I
    That dare aspire so high, as unto thee?
    Fame hath not stamped me yet; nor may I take
    My place amid the courtly throng of knights,
    That, crowned with glory's lustre, woo thy smiles.
    Nothing have I to offer, but a heart
    That overflows with truth and love for thee.
BERTHA [*sternly and with severity*]. And dare you speak to me
        of love—of truth,
    You, that are faithless to your nearest ties!
[RUDENZ *recoils*]
    You, that are Austria's slave, bartered and sold
    To her—an alien, and your country's tyrant!
RUDENZ. How! This reproach from thee! Whom do I see
    On Austria's side, my own beloved, but thee?
BERTHA. Think you to find me in the traitor's ranks?
    Now, as I live, I'd rather give my hand
    To Gessler's self, all despot though he be,
    Than to the Switzer who forgets his birth
    And stoops to be the minion of a tyrant.
RUDENZ. Oh heaven, what must I hear!
BERTHA. Say! what can lie
    Nearer the good man's heart, than friends and kindred?
    What dearer duty to a noble soul
    Than to protect weak, suffering innocence,
    And vindicate the rights of the oppress'd?
    My very soul bleeds for your countrymen.
    I suffer with them, for I needs must love them;
    They are so gentle yet so full of power;

They draw my whole heart to them. Every day
I look upon them with increased esteem.
But you, whom nature and your knightly vow,
Have given them as their natural protector,
Yet who desert them and abet their foes
In forging shackles for your native land.
You—you it is, that deeply grieve and wound me.
I must constrain my heart or I shall hate you.
RUDENZ. Is not my country's welfare all my wish?
What seek I for her, but to purchase peace
'Neath Austria's potent sceptre?
BERTHA. Bondage, rather!
You would drive freedom from the last stronghold
That yet remains for her upon the earth.
The people know their own true int'rests better:
Their simple natures are not warp'd by show
But round your head a tangling net is wound.
RUDENZ. Bertha, you hate me—you despise me!
BERTHA. Nay!
And if I did, 't were better for my peace.
But to see him despised and despicable
The man whom one might love.

Schiller
Wilhelm Tell
Act III, Scene ii
1804
Trans. by T. Martin

933

*Grant
of franchises
in Ukraine*

We, great Sovereign and Majesty, the Tsar, to our subject
Bogdan Hmelnicki, hetman of the Zaporogian Army,
and to our entire Zaporogian Army, grant the following:
They will be under the direct rule of Our Majesty with
the same rights and privileges as were previously granted
them by the Kings of Poland and the Grand Dukes of
Lithuania, and we forbid these rights and privileges to
be in any way impaired, and it is our will that they be
judged by their elders in accordance with their previous
laws. . . . And if, by the will of God, death should strike
the hetman, it is our will that the Zaporogian Army should
itself elect one of its number as hetman in accordance
with its custom. . . . We also forbid that the property and
land of the Cossacks which they hold for their subsistence
be taken away from them, or from their widows or children
after them.

Charter granted
following
the Treaty
of Pereyaslavl
1654

934

Nationhood

Today it is obvious to any Romanian with a mind and a
heart that the freedom of the nations cannot come from
the imperial courts, nor from the mercy of oppressors and
despots, but only from the close union of all Romanians
and from a general uprising in solidarity with all oppressed
peoples.

Speech
by N. Balcescu
May 1851

935

It is like throwing an egg at a rock for a relatively small power to exert its apparent strength—which, in any case, is not a ten-thousandth part of that of its opponent—against a great power. This power boasts that it has a high degree of civilization. It is therefore unlikely that it should have no morality, which is the very essence of civilization. Surely then a small power such as ours should arm itself with morality, an invisible might of which the other power cannot avail itself, however much it may want to. If our army and fleet were liberty, our fortress equality and our sword and cannon fraternity, no country in the world could rival us.   *936*

Chômin Nakae
1847-1901
Conversation
between
three drunken men
about State policy
Japan

The Revolt of the Poles, which was to break out in 1863 into armed insurrection, was already rumbling underground in 1861. On 8 April there was a great patriotic demonstration in the streets of Warsaw, directed against the Russians, with large numbers of Jews taking part. When the Polish priest bearing a cross at the head of the procession was cut down by a Cossack, a 17-year-old Jewish schoolboy called Michal Landy picked up the cross and carried it onward.

POLISH JEWS (1861)

I

Thou art for Europe, Oh! earnest Jewish nation,
A monument, sheltered somewhere in the East,
Whose fragments, bearing each the eternal stamp,
Are scattered through the world!
The men of the North in their forests of pine,
Coming upon thee, can only guess at the splendid refulgence
Of thy land, bathed in the light of the heavens
Like Moses in the waters of the Nile.
And they say: great is he who was raised so high
And then fell; and, like you, said no word.

II

We, flaxen-haired sons of the North,
We, snowy clouds of a dawning history,
Without consulting the omens or depart from the Earth
See straight through to the sanctuaries of heaven.
Like the sons of Haga, by the land of their birth,
Like the sons of Sarah, by the grace of our fathers,
Before the others, and by different tokens,
We have discerned you; and not from despair.
When the noble shared his coat of arms
With you—the Cross was there—and it does not lie!

481

III

History appears to be naught but disorder
But is in fact great strength and harmony.
It is a contract,
Kept by an archangel on high.
And behold: in the streets of Warsaw steps the Jew,
Filled with the same spirit as the Pole
Though the wealthiest nations on Earth
Offered him crosses, not crosses to die for

C. K. Norwid
1821-83
Poland

But crosses of glory, he preferred,
Like David, to go unarmed.   937

Excerpt from President Wilson's 'Fourteen Points', 8 January 1918.

An evident principle runs through the whole program
I have outlined. It is the principle of justice to all peoples
and nationalities, and their right to live on equal terms of
liberty and safety with one another, whether they be strong
or weak. Unless this principle be made its foundation

United States
of America

no part of the structure of international justice can
stand.   938

---

*Traditions threatened or destroyed; the right to one's own language;
enslavement of the defeated; legitimate defence*

---

*Foundations
threatened*

Shall we, perhaps, have to discard the teachings and traditions of our ancestors?
    All that is in our hearts; with it we live, with it we are
born; it is that which sustains us from childhood, that

Nahuatl tradition
Mexico

which schools us. It is the weft of our judgement, the
foundation of our prayer.   939

Loss of identity

It is a crime against reason to destroy the gods one is
accustomed to worship; such a thing has never yet been
done by the faithful of their own free will. No one will

Bartolomé
de Las Casas
Historia
de Las Indias
1547

be found willing to abandon the God who has been
worshipped from time immemorial, or to cast aside the
beliefs which he has sucked in with his mother's milk and
that his ancestors have revered.   940

Viet-Namese
proverb

Village customs prevail over royal decrees.   941

The answer of the Aztec wise men to the twelve missionaries (1524).

And now, are we
To destroy
The ancient order of life?
Of the Chichimecs,
Of the Toltecs,
Of the Acolhuas,
Of the Tecpanecs?

We know
On Whom life is dependent;
On Whom the perpetuation of the people depends;
By Whom begetting is determined;
By Whom growth is made possible;
How it is that one must invoke,
How it is that one must pray.

Hear, oh Lords,
Do nothing
To our people
That will bring misfortune upon them,
That will cause them to perish. . . .

Calm and amiable,
Consider, oh Lords,
Whatever is best.
We cannot be tranquil,
And yet we certainly do not believe;
We do not accept your teachings as truth,
Even though this may offend you.

Here are
The Lords, those who rule,
Those who sustain, whose duty is to
The entire world.
Is it not enough that we have already lost,
That our way of life has been taken away,
Has been annihilated.

Were we to remain in this place,
We could be made prisoners.
Do with us
As you please.

This is all that we answer,
That we reply,
To your breath,
To your words,
Oh, our Lords!

Aztec tradition
Mexico
Trans. by
M. León-Portilla

942

The need
to keep alive
the memory
of the past

Will the sun shine, will it dawn?
How will the people move,
How will they stand?
For they have gone away, they have carried off
The black and red ink, the painted books.
How will the people exist?
How will the earth continue, the city?
How will there be stability?
Who is it that will govern us?
Who is it that will guide us?
Who is it that will show us the way?
What will be our standard?
What will be our measure?
What will be our pattern?
From where should we begin?
What will be our torch, our light?

Then they invented the count of the days,
The annals and the year-count,
The book of dreams;
They ordained it as it had been kept,
And as it has continued,

Epic poem
of Toltec origin
10th cent.
Mexico
Trans. by
M. León-Portilla

The time that endured the domain of the Toltecs,
The domain of the Tepanecs,
The domain of the Mexicans,
And all the Chichimec domains.

943

Respect owed
to different men
and nations
and their customs

See that you refuse categorically to plant in those countries
the seeds of any party whatsoever, be it Spanish, French,
Turkish, Persian, or any other. . . . Make no effort, advance
no arguments so as to convince these nations that they
should change their ceremonies, customs or habits, except
these be clearly contrary to religion and morality. It is
ridiculous to transport France, Spain, Italy or some other
European country to the Chinese. It is not our countries
that should be brought there, but the faith. . . . In men's
nature there is, as it were, an implicit propensity to love
their country and its traditions above all else in the world.
That is why there is no more powerful motive for estrange-
ment and hatred than the introduction of changes in the
particular customs of a nation. . . . What will happen when,
having put an end to them, you try to replace them by the
customs of your own country, introduced from outside?
Be careful, therefore, never to draw a parallel between the
customs of those nations and those of Europe. On the
contrary, make haste to adapt yourselves to them, admiring
and praising all that deserves praise.

Briefing intended
for apostolic vicars
about to leave
for the Chinese
kingdoms
of Tongking
and Cambodia
1659

944

*In defence of the
native language*

First Hungarian poem written in couplets, as a preface to the
translation of the New Testament into Hungarian.

Behold the book through which He now speaks to thee:
He invites each one to make a profession of faith; let none
  refuse.
He who formerly spoke in Hebrew, Greek and later in
  Latin
Speaks to thee here in Hungarian:

János Sylvester
1541

To each people he speaks in its own language, that all
May observe the law of the Lord and worship his name.

945

*A single language
uniting the peoples*

Amongst other things the Inca Kings invented to govern
their Empire well was to command all vassals to learn
the Court language, now become the common language,
for whose teaching privileged Inca teachers were
established in each province, and it should be known
that the Incas had another, special language, which they
spoke among themselves and the other Indians did not
understand, nor, as a divine language, might they learn
it. This, they write me from Peru, is lost completely, for,
the particular commonwealth of the Incas having perished,
their language perished with it. Those Kings commanded
that the common language be learned for two main
purposes. One was so as not to have before them the
great multitude of interpreters needed to understand and
respond to so great a variety of languages and peoples as
their Empire contained. The Incas desired their vassals
to speak to them face to face (or personally at least, and
not through intermediaries) and to hear from their own
lips how affairs were dealt with, deriving as they did so
much more satisfaction and comfort from the same words
spoken by the Prince rather than by the Minister. The
other and more important cause was that foreign nations—
who, as we saw above, for not understanding each other,
considered themselves enemies and fought cruel wars—
speaking and communicating their inmost thoughts, should
cherish each other as if of the same family and parentage,
losing the asperity that inhibited their understanding.
Through this device, the Incas brought under control and
united that huge variety of peoples differing and opposed
in worship and customs which they found and subjected
to their Empire, and through the language brought
them to such unity and friendship that they loved each
other as brothers, for which reason many provinces to
which the Empire of the Incas did not extend, desiring
and convinced of the like, have since learned the common

Garcilaso de la Vega
(El Inca)
Comentarios Reales
de los Incas
1608 or 1609
Peru

language of Cuzco, and now many nations of different tongues speak it and can communicate, and by this alone have become friends and allies where once they were extreme enemies.   *946*

Minorities

LAW VIII OF 1849 ON NATIONAL MINORITIES IN HUNGARY

Having regard to the existence of various languages and also of Greek churches in the country, the National Assembly, with a view to reassuring the citizens of Hungary whose language is not Hungarian, and pending the adoption of more detailed measures on this subject in accordance with the provisions of the Constitution to be voted, declares:

1. The following provisions are intended to ensure the free national development of all the national groups residing on Hungarian territory.
2. In view of the fact that Hungarian is used as the diplomatic language in legislation, public administration, the administration of justice, and in the army, the use of the other languages spoken in Hungary shall be governed as follows.
3. In the proceedings on communes, each speaker will be free to use either Hungarian or his mother tongue; the official record shall be drawn up in one of the languages spoken in the commune, as desired.
4. In the proceedings of municipalities, all those authorized to speak may express their views either in Hungarian or in their mother tongue.
    If in a particular municipality a national group exceeds half of the population, the official record shall also, if requested, be drawn up in the language of this national group. . . .
14. The appointment of a candidate to any kind of public office will be made in the light of his merit and ability, irrespective of his language or religion.   *947*

Existing sacrilege.
Hope of justice
to come

THE MYTH OF INKARRI
(As known to a people speaking Quechua only)

Inkarri created everything that exists in the world. He is the first god. The Wamanis (*mountains*) are the second gods.
    The Wamanis care for man and beast; from them issues the stream of water which makes life possible.

Inkarri was the offspring born of the sun and a woman of the wilds.

While he was making all things which exist, he fastened the sun to the top of the great Osqonta mountain so that he might have light, and shut the wind up in the crest of the little Osqonta.

When he had finished making what exists and creating man, he gave him laws so that he might live properly. The aukis, the priests of the Wamanis, sing in their hymns that he should have no anger in his heart and should cast out idleness.

To found the city in which he would reside, Inkarri threw a gold bar. Where the bar fell, there he would found the city. The bar fell in Cuzco. We do not know where.

The Spanish king captured Inkarri and tortured him so much, so much, so much. Then he cut off his head.

Inkarri's head did not die. It is buried in Cuzco. As the head is alive, Inkarri's body is being reformed, under the earth so that they do not discover it.

Meanwhile, as he no longer exists, his laws have been forgotten and are not observed.

But when Inkarri's body is complete, he will return to us and will hold the last judgement.

As proof of Inkarri's existence, the birds of the coast sing: Go to Cuzco! The king is in Cuzco!

Collected at Puquio
Peru
948

Conquest

The Maya bewail the results of the conquest.

The foreigners made it different
When they arrived here.
They brought shameful things
When they came here....
No fortunate days
Were granted to us then....
This was the cause of our sickness.
No more fortunate days for us,
No more just decisions.
And in the end we lost our sight,
It was our shame.
Everything shall be revealed!

Chilām
Balām de Chumayel
Sacred book
of the Mayas
Central America
949

'*Absent from the universe*'

A South American, after the outbreak of the struggle for independence, writes to a Jamaican:

We were vexed by conduct which, in addition to depriving us of our due rights, left us in a kind of permanent tutelage in the matter of public business. If we had at least managed our domestic affairs in our internal administration, we should know the trend and machinery of public business and we should also enjoy the personal consideration which imposes on the public a certain mechanical respect which it is so necessary to preserve in revolutions. That is why I said that we were deprived even of active tyranny, since we were not permitted to exercise its functions.

In the prevailing Spanish system, perhaps with greater force than ever, the Americans' status in society is that of slaves for labour, or at best, that of mere consumers; and even this role is hedged about with shocking restrictions, for instance, the various prohibitions on growing European crops, the royal monopolies of certain productions, the ban on factories which the peninsula does not possess, the exclusive privileges of trading even in articles of prime necessity, the barriers between the various American provinces, designed to prevent trade, agreements and business; in short, would you like to know what was destined for us? The fields for growing indigo, cochineal, coffee, sugar-cane, cacao and cotton, the lonely plains for raising livestock, the deserts for hunting wild beasts, the entrails of the earth for mining the gold which satisfy that greedy nation.

Our condition was so negative that I find no parallel in any other civilized group, however much I review the ages and politics of all nations. To claim that a country so fortunately constituted, large, rich and populous, should be purely passive, is that not an infringement, a violation of human rights?

We were, as I have just said, isolated and as it were absent from the universe as regards the science of government and administration. We were never viceroys or governors, except in very extraordinary cases; seldom archbishops and bishops; never diplomats; soldiers only in subordinate capacities; nobles without real privileges; lastly, we were not magistrates or financiers and almost never merchants; all these were in direct contravention of our institutions.

Simón Bolívar
1815

950

The arguments of Aristotle.

1. *Some are slaves by nature and others masters by nature;*
2. *But it is far from easy to see the difference;*
3. *Some also are slaves through superior power;*
4. *When slavery is based on superior power, no just relationship is possible.*

... But it is nature's intention also to erect a physical difference between the body of the freeman and that of the slave, giving the latter strength for the menial duties of life, but making the former upright in carriage and (though useless for physical labour) useful for the various purposes of civic life—a life which tends, as it develops, to be divided into military service and the occupations of peace. The contrary of nature's intention, however, often happens: there are some slaves who have the bodies of freemen—as there are others who have a freeman's soul. But if nature's intention were realized—if men differed from one another in bodily form as much as the statues of the gods [differ from the human figure]—it is obvious that we should all agree that the inferior class ought to be the slaves of the superior. And if this principle is true when the difference is one of the body, it may be affirmed with still greater justice when the difference is one of the soul; though it is not as easy to see the beauty of the soul as it is to see that of the body.

It is thus clear that, just as some are by nature free, so others are by nature slaves, and for these latter the condition of slavery is both beneficial and just.

But it is easy to see that those who hold an opposite view are also in a way correct. 'Slavery' and 'slave' are terms which are used in two different senses. [There is, as we have seen, a kind of slavery which exists by nature; but] there is also a kind of slave, and of slavery, which exists [only] by law or (to speak more exactly) convention. (The law in virtue of which those vanquished in war are held to belong to the victor is in effect a sort of convention.)

That slavery can be justified by such a convention is a principle against which a number of jurists bring what may be called an 'indictment of illegality'. [They think that the principle violates the nature of law; and] they regard it as a detestable notion that anyone who is subjugated by superior power should become the slave and subject of the person who has the power to subjugate him, and who is his superior [merely] in power. Some, however, support, if some oppose [the principle]; and even men of judgement differ. The cause of this divergence of view, and the reason why the opposing contentions overlap one another, is to be found in the following consideration. There is a sense in which goodness, when it is furnished with an equipment [of material resources], has the greatest power to subjugate; and [conversely] a victor is always pre-eminent in respect of some sort of good. This connexion of power with goodness or some sort of good leads to the idea that 'power goes with goodness'; and [as this idea is shared by both sides in the dispute about slavery] the dispute between the two sides thus comes to turn exclusively on the point of justice. On this point, one side holds that justice is a relation of mutual goodwill [and is therefore incompatible with slavery imposed by convention]; the other side holds that the rule of a superior is in itself, and by itself, justice [and is therefore a justification of such slavery. But the ambiguity of the idea which is common ground for both sides obscures the whole issue]. If the divergent views are pitted separately against one another (*i.e., deprived of their common ground*), neither view has any cogency, or even plausibility, against the view that the superior in goodness ought to rule over, and be the master of, his inferiors.

[The same general result—that superior goodness is really the ground of owning and controlling slaves—may be attained in another way.] There are some who, clinging, as they think, to a sort of justice (for law is a sort of justice), assume that slavery in war is always and everywhere just [because it is warranted by law]. Simultaneously, however, they contradict that assumption; for in the first place it is possible that the original cause of a war may not be just [in which case, in spite of the warrant of law, slavery so caused will not be just], and in the second place no one would ever say that a person who does not deserve to be in a condition of slavery is really a slave. If such a view were accepted, the result would be that men reputed to be of the highest rank would be turned into slaves or the children of slaves, if it happened to them or their parents to be captured and sold into slavery. This is the reason why Greeks [though ready to defend the enslavement of prisoners of war] do not like to call such persons slaves, but prefer to confine the term to barbarians. But by this use of terms [they contradict their own view, and] they are, in reality, only seeking to express that same idea of the natural slave which we began by mentioning. They are driven, in effect, to admit that there are some (*i.e., the barbarians*) who are everywhere and inherently slaves, and others (*i.e., the Greeks*) who are everywhere and inherently free. The same line of thought is followed in regard to nobility, as well as slavery. Greeks regard themselves as noble not only in their own country, but absolutely and in all places; but they regard barbarians as noble only in their own country—thus assuming that there is one sort of nobility and freedom which is absolute, and another which is only relative. We are reminded of what Helen says in the play of Theodectes:

Scion of Gods, by both descents alike,
Who would presume to call me serving-maid?

When they use such terms as these, men are using the one criterion of the presence, or absence, of goodness for the purpose of distinguishing between slave and freeman, or, again, between noble and lowborn. They are claiming that just as man is born of man, and animal of animal, so a good man is born of good men. It is often the case, however, that nature wishes but fails to achieve this result.

It is thus clear that there is some reason for the divergence of view which has been discussed, and that not all those who are actually slaves, or actually freemen, are natural slaves or natural freemen. It is also clear that there are cases where such a distinction [of the natural slave and the natural freeman] exists, and that here it is beneficial and just that the former should actually be a slave and the latter a master—the one being ruled, and the other exercising the kind of rule for which he is naturally intended and therefore acting as master. But a wrong exercise of his rule by a master is a thing which is disadvantageous for both master and slave. The part and the whole, like the body and the soul, have an identical interest; and the slave is a part of the master, in the sense of being a living but separate part of his body. There is thus a community of interest, and a relation of friendship, between master and slave, when both of them naturally merit the position in which they stand. But the reverse is true [and there is a conflict of interest and enmity], when matters are otherwise and slavery rests merely on legal sanction and superior power.

Aristotle
c. 384-322 B.C.
Politics

951

---

*Guile and
lawful defence*

THE CATS AND THE RATS

It is said that the Cat clan once had a meeting. The purpose of the meeting was to make a decisive attack against the Rat clan. The meeting was chaired by the King of the Cat clan. When the meeting was convened and everybody was present, the King spoke and said:

'O Cat clan, greetings. Today we are assembled here because, as you all know, the Rat clan has been having a prosperous year. The world has been good to them. Their number have multiplied and they have grown very fat. We, on the other hand have been suffering from famine. We are all thin and weak. Therefore, O clansmen, we must think of a way to catch all the Rats in order to fatten ourselves on their juicy flesh. How shall we go about it?'

An old wise Cat then took the floor. He said: 'Long live the King! I have a suggestion to make. I suggest that we trick the Rat clan into making a solemn pledge of peace with us. We should call for an inter-clan peace conference. The meeting should be on a treeless plain where the Rat clan would have no shelter; and then it would be quite easy for us to catch them all.'

The suggestion of the old, wise Cat was received with enthusiasm. The King of the Cats spoke again. He said: 'Old one, may your wisdom live long! You have offered a wise suggestion. I will now go and inform the King of the Rats about this offer of peace, and I will try to secure his approval. Await news from me.' All the Cats then cheered: 'Long live the King!' And the meeting broke up.

The King of the Cats then went to the King of the Rats. Since there was no love lost between the two clans, and since they could not trust each other at that time, they had to speak to each other from a distance.

The King of the Cats spoke: 'O King of the Rats; O symbol of freedom; O wisest of all sages; may you live long! Peace be with you. How are you?'

The King of the Rats then came out and said: 'O King of the Cats; O tree whose shade covers all: O judge of the world; O shelter from evil; may peace be with you. How are you?'

The King of the Cats, coming directly to the point, said: 'I bring peace. I come to make a proposal to you and your subjects on behalf of my subjects and myself. As you know, the Cat clan and the Rat clan have always been enemies. This hostility has harmed both you and us. Our continuous practice of killing you has reduced your number. We, on our part, have suffered from the hunt. We have chased you through bushes, and our eyes have been pierced by the thorns. So now we are all half blind. We have therefore agreed among ourselves that peace would be the best thing. We now officially call for a meeting between us on the Plain of Dirindiir. There we shall solemnly pledge peace, and we shall be true brothers.

We propose that the meeting should take place on the day after the full moon, at mid-morning.'

The King of the Rats then responded: 'Long live the King! We have officially received this proposal. We agree to the day you have picked for the meeting. Let us hope for a conference of peace.'

The King of the Cats then left. When His Majesty was out of sight, the King of the Rats called his subjects. He said: 'The King of the Cats came to me. He talked to me about peace, and he suggested that we enter into a pledge of peace with them. I have accepted this offer. The meeting is to be held on the treeless Plain of Dirindiir. I cannot break my word. You know it is not a noble thing to do so. Therefore, we have to go and meet them. However, we cannot trust the Cat clan. Experience teaches us so. What shall we do?'

Then an old sage among the Rats spoke: 'I suggest that every Rat should dig himself a deep hole at Dirindiir before the day of the meet. When the appointed day comes, we should all go there in the early morning, and every Rat should remove the soil from the hole to a far place so as to avoid suspicion. Then every Rat should sit at the edge of his hole. If the Cat clan comes in peace, it is well and good. But if, as we expect, they attack us, then every Rat should immediately retreat into his hole.'

This advice was accepted, and they all dispersed. Every Rat then went to the plain and dug himself a hole, disguised its mouth, and removed the soil.

The day of the meeting came. The Rat clan went early to the Plain of Dirindiir, and every one of them sat at the edge of his hole. At mid-morning the Cat clan, expecting a feast, presented themselves. When they were near enough to be heard, the King of the Cats surveyed his subjects and asked them to sit down, because he did not want the Rat clan to be suspicious. And then he called to the King of the Rats and said: 'Great King of the Rats, are all your subjects present?'

The King of the Rats replied: 'Yes, we are all here. Are all your subjects here too?'

Confirming this, the King of the Cats then said: 'O King, I shall now inform my subjects of the protocol of the meeting. Please wait.' Saying this, he turned and looked critically at his clan. Being satisfied with their state of readiness for the assault, he turned once more in the direction of the Rat clan. He saw how the Rats were all fat and had had a good year. He saw the King of the Rats showing every sign of the affluence of his race in his abundant flesh. He decided to attack him personally.

He then raised his voice in the battle cry of the Cats and called to his army: 'Catch them all. Let no one escape!'

When the King of the Rats saw them charging, he stood on his tiny hind legs and called to the members of his clan: 'Clansmen, into your holes—dive!' In a second they were all in, and there was no trace of them.

The Cat clan therefore not only had no succulent feast that day; but what is worse, they suffered the disgrace of breaking a solemn promise. The Cats forgot the Somali proverb that says 'Tab hayow lagaa tab hayee' (*O you, who think yourself clever, remember that there is always someone cleverer still*).

Somali tale

952

Arbitration and the law of nations

Peace by the institution of law

General San Martín, South American liberator, addresses the Viceroy of Lima:

Your Excellency,

The troops under my command having duly wiped out, on the fifth of this month, the powerful army which Your Excellency despatched for the conquest of Chile, and seeing that the resources of your capital are now totally inadequate to offer any successful resistance to the victorious soldiers of our country, it would seem wise to allow reason to take the place of passion, and let those who preside over the destinies of peoples confine their attention to promoting their welfare. By an incomprehensible fatality, all that the quarrels between the Spaniards and the Americans claiming their rights has led to has been the war which began on 25 May 1810; official ears have been closed to our cries for peace, and the means of reaching a reasonable agreement have been persistently set aside.

Your Excellency is well aware that war is a terrible scourge, that the stage it has reached in America threatens her with destruction, and that the fortunes of war have already tipped the scales in favour of the rightful claims of the southern portion of the new world. Your Excellency has, furthermore, been able to appreciate in the course of seven years that all that the United Provinces and Chile are seeking is a liberal constitution and a reasonable amount of freedom, and that the population of the vice-royalty of Lima, who have been made to shed their blood in fighting their brothers, should share in their political destiny, cast aside their colonial chains, and rise to the dignity of neighbouring countries.

None of these aspirations is, indeed, incompatible with friendship, protective concern and close ties with the Spanish motherland; none of them, in this present age, is anything but the faithful echo of an enlightened Europe. To try to prevent by the use of bayonets the avalanche of popular opinion in the Americas is like trying to imprison nature. Let Your Excellency consider impartially the result of the Spanish Government's efforts over the past years and setting aside the short-lived victories obtained by the King's forces, he will see how powerless it has been to combat the spirit of freedom.

. . . Summon this noble population to a conference; consider in all good faith the wishes expressed by the governments of Chile and the United Provinces; lend an ear to the public expression of their rights; let the people decide, with the approval of Your Excellency, the type of government which suits their interests; allow the other provinces, at present under duress, to voice their requests with the same freedom. Their free deliberations will furnish the supreme law to which any future operations of mine will have to be submitted, according to the instructions of my government.

. . . When Your Excellency calls to mind the means I possess whereby to accelerate this progressive movement, I think you will do justice to my good intentions; all I desire is the good of my fellow human beings; I want the war to end, and my requests as regards this sacred objective are as sincere as my resolve is firm, if they are not agreed to, to spare no sacrifice for the freedom, the security and the dignity of our country.

Letter dated 11 April 1818

953

Peace and international order

Peace is maintained by justice, which is a fruit of government, as government is from society and society from consent.

Now if the sovereign Princes of Europe, who represent that society, or independent state of men that was previous to the obligations of society, would, for the same reason that engaged men first into society, viz. love of peace and order, agree to meet by their stated deputies in a General Diet, Estates, or Parliament, and there establish rules of justice for sovereign princes to observe one to another . . . and thus to meet yearly, or once in two or three years at farthest, or as they shall see cause, and to be stiled the Sovereign or Imperial Diet, Parliament, or State of Europe....

The place of their first session should be central, as much as is possible, afterwards as they agree . . . before which sovereign assembly, should be brought all differences depending between one sovereign and another, that can not be made up by private embassies, before the sessions begin;... and that if any of the sovereignties, that constitute these Imperial States, shall refuse to submit their claim or pretensions to them, or to abide and perform the judgement thereof, and seek their remedy by arms, or delay their compliance beyond the time prefixed in their resolutions, all the other sovereignties, united as one strength, shall compel the submission and performance of the sentence, with damages to the suffering party and charges to the sovereignties that obliged their submission.

William Penn
Essay towards
the Present
and Future Peace
of Europe
1692
England

954

Need
for arbitration

If the numerous cities and princes, refusing to recognize any higher authorities in the world that should exercise justice over them according to local laws and customs, wish to start wars, before whom should they plead their cause? One can reply that the Council must decree that ecclesiastical arbitrators or others shall be appointed, circumspect men, skilled and true, who after taking the oath [would elect] three judges from among the prelates and three others for each of the parties, well-to-do men and of such a character that they are most unlikely to be corrupted, whether by love, hatred, fear, greed, or in any other way; these would meet in an appropriate place, and being duly sworn in the strictest fashion, and having received beforehand the summary and detailed pleadings of either party, would be handed—after all that was unnecessary or inept had been eliminated—the pieces of evidence and the instruments which they would examine conscientiously. . . . If one of the parties is not satisfied with the verdict, the judges themselves shall refer the whole proceedings, together with the verdicts, to the Apostolic See, to be changed or amended by the Sovereign Pontiff, if justice demands, otherwise they shall be confirmed and entered in the Church archives 'ad perpetuam memoriam'.

Pierre Dubois
De Recuperatione
Terrae Sanctae
1306
France

955

*Mutual assistance
and arbitration*

PACT OF 1 AUGUST 1291
(Origin of the Swiss Confederation)

In the name of the Lord, Amen. It is a just procedure and
of advantage to the public weal that treaties should be
consolidated in an atmosphere of peace and tranquillity.
Be it known to all, therefore, that the men of the Uri
valley, the commune of the Schwyts valley and the commune
of the lower valley of Unterwald, in view of the insecurity
of the times and in order to defend and support themselves
more efficiently, have in good faith agreed to assist each
other mutually with all the strength, relief measures and
good offices at their disposal, both within and without
the country, against whomsoever should try to do them
violence, disturb or molest them in their persons or their
goods. And, as a measure of precaution, each of the
aforesaid communities promises the other to come to its
aid in case of need, to defend it, at its own expense, against
attacks by its enemies, and to avenge its feud, taking an
oath therefor in perfect good faith, and renewing by this
instrument the ancient confederation; all this without
prejudice to the services which each one, according to his
condition, is bound to render his lord.

And we decree and ordain, with one voice, that in the
aforesaid valleys we will refuse to recognize any judge
who has bought his office with money or in any other
way, or who should not be a native or inhabitant of these
regions. Should a quarrel at any time arise between
confederates, the wisest amongst them shall intervene by

Oath of 1291
1548
Zürich

arbitration to allay the dispute, in such way as they may deem fit, and if one or other of the parties should disregard their verdict, the other confederates shall turn against that party. . . .

And if one of the confederates should interfere with the property of another by stealing or any other means, any property which the guilty party possesses in the valleys will serve, as is only right, to indemnify the injured party. . . . In the event of war or strife between confederates, if one of the parties refuses to accept arbitration or compromise, the confederates shall side with the other party.

And may all of the above enacted for the common benefit, with God's grace, endure *ad perpetuum.*   956

Arbitration

Before resorting to arms [princes should] . . . refer their differences to arbitration by Potentates and Sovereign Lords. In so doing they would win the friendship of their peers, on which they would be able to rely in opposing their enemies, should these refuse to submit to the judgement of a third party. Of course, if a prince were to receive a judge who wished to interfere arrogantly in the settling of differences, that would in truth lower his dignity; but to accept arbitrators voluntarily is something that has been done in the past and is still done by Monarchs. . . . And this would be admirably served by that general assembly of which we shall speak later. . . . How is it possible, someone will say, to get peoples so different in spirit and feeling as Turks and Persians, French and Spanish, Chinese and Tartars, Christians and Jews or Mohammedans to agree? I say that all such animosities are only political and cannot take away from that unity which exists—and must exist—between men. Neither distances between places nor family separations diminish the strength of the blood tie. In the same way, they cannot take away from that similarity of nature, which lies at the root of human friendship and society. Why should I, who am French, wish any harm to an Englishman, a Spaniard or an Indian? I cannot bring myself to do so when I consider that they are men like myself, that, like them, I am liable to error and sin, and that all nations are linked by a natural and therefore indissoluble bond. *957*

Emeric Crucé
The New Cineas
or State oration
representing
the occasions
and means
of establishing
a general peace
and freedom
of trade
everywhere
in the world
1623
France

On trial before Lacedaemonian judges, the Plataeans justify their conduct during the Peloponnesian War:

The Thebans have committed great injustices against us; and you know their last, cause of our present plight: they brutally seized our city in time of peace and, what is more, on a holiday.

We thus had every right to punish them, by that universal law which enshrines the right to repel an aggressor. *958*

Thucydides
The Peloponnesian War
5th cent. B.C.

They shall settle all disputes by absolutely impartial arbitration, in accordance with established customs. The other cities in the Peloponnese may accede to this treaty and alliance, remaining autonomous and obtaining full sovereignty over themselves and their territory, on condition that they settle all disputes by absolutely impartial arbitration, in accordance with established custom. *959*

Thucydides
The Peloponnesian War
5th cent. B.C.

Free choice of persons

The battle was about to begin when the Corinthians, who happened to be present, intervened and, accepted by both sides as arbitrators, made peace between them and delimited their territories, it being agreed that the Thebans *would not interfere in any way with Boeotians who no longer wanted to belong to Boeotia.* *960*

Herodotus
The History
5th cent. B.C.

The law of nations

All civilized nations are governed in part by laws common to all men and in part by a code of their own. For when a nation has produced its own laws, they constitute, taken together, the law of that nation; what is called Civil Law. But the law which the light of reason has established in the minds of men is everywhere equally observed and is known as international law, because it is binding on all the nations. *961*

Institutes of Gaius
150
Rome

Just as the Laws of each State pertain to its particular advantage, the consent of all States, or at least of the majority, has resulted in producing certain Laws which are common to them all. It seems that such Laws have indeed been established, designed to serve the interests not of this or that particular Community but of the vast assemblage of all the Communities. This is what is called the Law of Nations, when distinguishing it from Natural Law. Carneades had no knowledge of this kind of Law, since he reduced all that is called Law to Natural Law and the particular Law of each State. It was, however, his intention to discuss the Law that is common to several Peoples; for later he speaks of War and of Conquests; he surely did not intend, therefore, to omit the Law of Nations.

He was also mistaken in calling Justice folly. For as, by his own admission, a Citizen who complies with the Laws of his Country is not thereby committing a folly, though he must, in consideration of those Laws, refrain from certain acts which would be advantageous to him as an individual, similarly it cannot reasonably be argued that a People is foolish which is not so greatly enamoured of its own particular interest as to trample underfoot on that account the Laws common to States and Nations. The case is precisely the same. A Citizen who, for his immediate advantage, transgresses the Civil Law of his country thereby undermines the foundation of his lasting interest and, at the same time, that of his descendants. A People which transgresses the Law of Nature and of Nations thereby breaches the rampart of its peace for the future. But, even if no practical advantage could be expected from the observance of the Rules of the Laws, it would still be wisdom, and by no means folly, to adopt the course to which our nature inclines us. *962*

Hugo Grotius
De Jure Belli
et Pacis
1624
Holland

Karel Čapek
Czech writer
1890-1938

War of the ants:
Yes, of course, but our side fights in the name of all ants. *963*

Universality

*Men are citizens
of the world
and sons of God*

If what philosophers say of the kinship between God and men be true, what has any one to do but, like Socrates, when he is asked what countryman he is, never to say that he is a citizen of Athens, or of Corinth, but of the universe? For why, if you limit yourself to Athens, do you not farther limit yourself to that mere corner of Athens where your body was brought forth? Is it not, evidently, from some larger local tie, which comprehends, not only that corner and your whole house, but the whole country of your fathers, that you call yourself an Athenian, or a Corinthian? He, then, who understands the administration of the universe, and has learned that the principal and greatest and most comprehensive of all things is this vast system, *extending from men to God*; and that from Him the seeds of being are descended not only to one's father or grandfather, but to all things that are produced and born on earth; and especially to rational natures, since they alone are qualified to partake of a communication with the Deity, being connected with him by reason—why may not such a one call himself a citizen of the universe! Why not a son of God? And why shall he fear any thing that happens among men? Shall kinship to Caesar, or any other of the great at Rome, enable a man to live secure, above contempt, and void of all fear whatever; and shall not the having God for our maker, and father, and guardian, free us from griefs and alarms?

'But wherewithal shall I be fed? For I have nothing.'

To what do fugitive slaves trust when they run away from their masters? Is it to their estates, their servants, their plate? To nothing but themselves. Yet they do not fail to obtain the necessaries of life. And must a philosopher, think you, leave his own abode to rest and rely upon others, and not take care of himself? Must he be more helpless and anxious than the brute beasts—each of which is self-sufficient, and wants neither proper food nor any suitable and natural provision? *964*

Epictetus
Discourses
1st cent.

We respect and honour those of good family, but we neither respect nor honour those of lowly birth; in this we behave as barbarians to one another. For, in the nature of things, we are all and in every way born alike, Greeks and Barbarians; and it can safely be said that those

Antiphon
5th cent. B.C.
Greece

things which are a natural necessity are common to all men. . . . On entering the world, none of us was distinguishable as Barbarian or Greek: we all breathe air through our mouths and nostrils.   965

Tzu-Lu questioned the Master about the cultivated man.

The Master replied: 'A cultivated man perfects himself with respect.' (*One can perfect oneself only by respecting oneself and fighting an unremitting battle against one's passions.*)

'Nothing else?' asked Tzu-Lu.

'He perfects himself so that other men may be at peace,' said the Master.

'Nothing else?' asked Tzu-Lu.

Confucius
551-479? B.C.
Analects
China

'He perfects himself so that all the common people may be at peace. That is what Yao and Shun found difficulty in attaining,' concluded the Master.

(*Yao and Shun were the two holy kings of Chinese antiquity.*)
966

Unity of origin

Hebrew Bible
Genesis 2

Then the Lord God formed man of the dust of the ground, and breathed into his nostrils the breath of life; and man became a living soul.   967

Ambrose, Bishop of Milan, to the Emperor Theodosius, after the massacre at Thessalonica:

According to Bishop
Theodoret of Cyrrhus
Ecclesiastical
History
c. 450

'It is, no doubt, the imperial power that prevents thee from knowing thy fault, and thy sovereign power obscures thy reason. Yet shouldst thou reflect how frail and fleeting is human nature, and remember that we must all return to the dust from which we have come.'   968

St. Thomas Aquinas
1225-74
Summa Theologica

All men are as one in so far as all alike partake of the nature they have received from their first parents.   969

The Bible tells how Pharaoh pursued the Hebrews into the desert until they were stopped by the sea. God divided the waters, letting the Hebrews pass and drowning the Egyptians beneath the waves. Moses sang a hymn to God for the miraculous deliverance of His people. The Talmud adds:

Talmud
Sanhedrin 39

When Moses began to sing his hymn the angels also burst out singing but the Holy One—blessed be He—said to them: The works of my hand are drowning, and you sing a song?   970

Virgin of mercy
protecting mankind
against the
wrath of God
German drawing
15th cent.

St. Augustine
De Moribus
Ecclesiae Catholicae
4th cent.

Citizens, peoples, nay the whole of mankind, are united by Thee, by the belief in their common origin, so that not content with associating, men become as brothers. *971*

All men were in Jesus Christ. So His body, the instrument of the Word, fulfilled in Him the whole mystery of our redemption.

When speaking of the city, Jesus referred to the flesh He had taken upon Himself: as a city is made up of a multitude and variety of inhabitants, so in Him, through this body which He had taken on, was contained the whole of mankind. As all men meet in Him, He is like unto a city and we, united in His flesh, are its inhabitants. *972*

Bishop Hilaire
of Poitiers
Commentaire
sur l'Évangile
de Sain Matthieu
4th cent.

Talmud
Babli

Rabbi Meir said: 'The dust from which the first man was made was gathered in all the corners of the world.' *973*

Natural dignity of every man

The scriptural statement that 'God created man' is indefinite; it applies to all mankind. In this description of the creation, indeed, Adam is not named, as history named him subsequently: the man who was created was not given any particular name, he was universal man. Thus we may understand the universal designation of nature to mean something such as this: by foreknowledge and by the Divine power, the creation of man implies that of the whole of mankind.

For God, of necessity, nothing is undetermined in the creatures who have their origin in Him; each has his limits and his measure, set by the wisdom of his Maker. Just as every man in particular is delimited by the dimensions of his body, and his existence is precisely commensurate with the size of the surface of his body, so, I think, mankind as a whole is contained as in a single body, thanks to the 'foreseeing power' which God has over all things. That is what the Scriptures mean by the words: 'God created man in His own image, in the image of God created He him.'

It is not in one part of nature alone that the image is found, any more than beauty resides in one particular quality of a single being, but in the whole of the human race alike. That this is so is clear from the fact that the spirit resides in all alike, and all alike are able to exercise their thought, their power of decision and all other faculties partaking of the divine nature possessed by Him who was made in the image of God. There is no difference between the man who appeared when the world was first created and the man who will be born at the end of everything; all alike bear the divine image.

That is why one man was designated to stand for the whole of mankind; for the power of God, there is neither past nor future, but that which is to take place and that which has taken place are alike submitted to his activity, which is all-embracing. Thus the whole of nature, from the beginning right until the end, constitutes a single image of Him who is. The division of mankind into man and woman was, I think, for the reason I shall state, superimposed afterwards on the original pattern.   *974*

Bishop Gregory
of Nyssa
The Creation
of Man
4th cent.
Asia Minor

The just among the Gentiles are the priests of God. I call heaven and earth to witness that whether a person be Jew or Gentile, man or woman, manservant or maidservant, according to his acts does the Divine Spirit rest upon him.   *975*

Midrash
Yalkut

*All men are one
in Christ*

New Testament
St. Paul's Epistle
to the Galatians 3

For as many of you as have been baptized into Christ
have put on Christ.

There is neither Jew nor Greek, there is neither bond
nor free, there is neither male nor female: for ye are
all one in Christ Jesus.   *976*

*The Word
dwelt in us all
through one man*

But John rightly says that the Word dwelt among us in
order to reveal to us another profound mystery, that is,
that we were all in Christ and that through Him the
common person of mankind came back to life. For He
is called the last Adam because He endowed the community of nature with every felicity and glory—while
the first Adam endowed it with corruption and shame....

In Christ therefore the race in bondage is truly delivered, raised to mystic union with Him who took on the form
of a servant, and we are freed from bondage by imitation
of Him who is without peer, through our relationship
in the flesh.

For what other reason did He take on Him the seed of
Abraham, and not the nature of angels, if not to be
'made in all things like unto his brethren' and to be really
man?

Or is it not manifest that He took upon Himself the form
of a servant, not for any benefit to Himself, but in order
to sacrifice Himself for us, so that through His poverty

Cyril of Alexandria
Commentary
on John
5th cent.

we might be rich, raised to His own excellence by our
resemblance to Him, and might appear through faith
gods and children of God?   *977*

William of Occam
c. 1280-1349
England

All human beings form one body and one community.
                                                            978

*Unity
of mankind*

Mahābhārata
Hindi tradition

There is no difference among classes of people. All the
world is of divine origin.   *979*

Rigveda
Hindi tradition

May all share the common food and drink.   *980*

Subhāsita-
Ratnabhāndāgāra
Sanskrit

This one belongs to us or [that one] to others—such is
the consideration of the petty-minded. For the magnanimous, on the other hand, the whole earth, verily, is their
family.   *981*

Tradition of the Sangam period Tamil	All this is mine and all men are my brothers.	*982*
Pampa 9th cent. Kanarese India	There is only one caste—humanity.	*983*
Koran Al-Hajj 40	And if God had not repelled some men by others, cloisters, and churches, and oratories, and mosques, wherein the name of God is ever commemorated, would surely have been destroyed.	*984*
Hadith (Sayings of the Prophet)	Whoever does wrong to a non-Mohammedan, I will go to war with him.	*985*
Koran An-Nissa 1	O men! fear your Lord who hath created you of one man [soul].	*986*
Hadith (Sayings of the Prophet)	All men are equal like the teeth of a comb. No Arab can regard himself as superior to a foreigner [non-Arab], except by reason of his religious devotion. Anyone who preaches racial prejudice is not a true follower of ours.	*987*
Romanian proverb	All men are baked of the same dough.	*988*
Talmud Avot 4	Ben Azzai said: 'Do not despise any person and do not discard anything, for there is not a man in the world for whom the hour does not strike and there is not a thing in the world for which there is no place.'	*989*
Koran Al-Maidah 53	And if God had pleased He had surely made you all one people; but He would test you by what He hath given to each. Be emulous, then, in good deeds. To God shall ye all return, and He will tell you concerning the subjects of your disputes.	*990*
Man Mahābhārata XII 2nd cent. B.C. to 1st cent. A.D. Sanskrit	This secret doctrine do I here pronounce unto you: Nothing, indeed, is more excellent than humanity.	*991*

Manusmriti I
2nd cent. B.C.
to 1st cent. A.D.
Sanskrit

Among all beings, the living are the best; among the living, those who possess intelligence; and among those who possess intelligence, the humans.   *992*

Mahābhārata XII
2nd cent. B.C.
to 1st cent. A.D.
Sanskrit

All beings desire birth as man, always and everywhere.   *993*

Uttarādhyayana-
Sūtra X
3rd cent. B.C.
to 6th cent. A.D.
Prakrit

Difficult to obtain, indeed, is human life.   *994*

Within a man, indeed, does this one first become an embryo. That which is this semen is the vigour accumulated from all the limbs. In the self, indeed, does one [thus] bear the self. When he emits this into a woman, then he engenders it. That is its first birth. It becomes one with the woman, just like her own limb. Therefore it does her no harm. She nourishes this self of his which has entered into her. She, the nourisher, is entitled to be nourished. Him the woman bears as an embryo. He nourishes the child even from its birth onward. In that he nourishes the child from its birth onward, he thereby

Aitareya-
Upanishad II
7th to 6th cent B.C.
Sanskrit

[really] nourishes his own self for the sake of the continuity of these worlds. For, it is thus that these worlds are continued. This is its second birth.   *995*

By whom were the two heels of man fashioned? By whom was his flesh brought together? By whom the two ankles? By whom the well-moulded fingers? By whom the apertures? By whom the two ucchlankhas in the middle? Who [gave him] firm footing? From what, now, did they make man's two ankles below and two knee-joints above? Having bifurcated the two shanks, where, forsooth, did they put them in? [Who fixed] the two knee joints? Who, verily, understands this? The fourfold frame is joined, with ends welded together, above the two knees, [namely] the pliant trunk; the two buttocks and what the two thighs are—who, indeed, produced that—by means of which the trunk has become very firm? How many gods and which ones were they who piled up [the bones] of man's breast and neck? How many [gods] fixed separately the two teats? Who the two kaphodas? How many piled up [the bones of] shoulders, how many the ribs? Who brought together his two arms, so that he might perform [acts of] heroism? Which god, then, put his two shoulders upon the trunk? Who pierced the seven apertures in the head, namely, these two ears, the two nostrils, the two eyes, and the mouth, in the greatness of whose conquest the quadrupeds and bipeds go their way in many places? For, between the two jaws, he placed the ample tongue and then made the mighty speech to rest upon it. He rolls about among the worlds clothing himself in waters. Who, indeed, understands that? Which was the god who first produced his brain, forehead, hind head, and skull? Having piled up the collection [of bones] of man's two jaws he ascended to heaven. Which one is that god? Numerous things dear and not dear, sleep, oppression and wearinesses, delights and pleasures—through whom does the formidable man bear these? Who put into him severally the waters, flowing variously, flowing amply, created to course in streams, strong, ruddy, red, copper-coloured, smoke-coloured, and [flowing] upward, downward, and crosswise in man? Who set in him the form, and who the bulk and the name? Who bestowed on this man the gait, who the distinguishing mark, who the behaviours? Who wove in him the in-breath, who the out-breath, and [who] indeed, the diffused breath? Which god made the concentrated breath dwell in this man?

Atharvaveda X
2200-1800 B.C.
Sanskrit

996

[The life-breath] moves within the divinities (*i.e., sense-organs*) as an embryo. Having pervaded, having [once] come into being, he is, indeed, born again. He is what has been, what is going to be, and what will be. [He], the father, has entered the son with his powers. He who is lord of all things born and of all moving things—to thee, such as thou art, having a swift bow among the others, O life-breath, be homage.

Atharvaveda XI
2200-1800 B.C.
Sanskrit

997

Turkish proverb
15th cent.
One people does not differ from another, save in manners and customs.

998

Man is harder than iron, stronger than stone, and more fragile than a rose.

Animals [recognize one another] by sniffing, men [understand one another] by exchanging words.

Turkish proverbs

999

For those who love God-the-Truth with a real love, the inhabitants of the whole world are as real brothers.

My sin? It is this: I have said that the seventy-two different peoples together constitute a single truth.

He who savours [the fragrance] of love has no further need of religion or of nation. He who holds his own being to be of no account, can he distinguish between religions and sects?

I have found him whom I sought, manifest in the soul of man. He strives unceasingly to free himself, to escape from the body in which he is imprisoned.

It is he who knotted the talisman; he who speaks in all tongues; he whom neither heaven nor earth can contain, and he is come to lodge in the soul of man.

It is he who causes almshouses to be built for the poor, as well as villas and palaces; it is he who busies himself a black mask on his face, before the furnace of a public bath.

Yunus Emre
Folk-poet
13th cent.
Turkey

Yunus, thy words have a profound meaning for those who can interpret them; they shall survive thee: in time to come they will still be spoken. *1000*

Theodosius Kosoj
A serf who became
a monk and
was condemned
for heresy in 1554
Russia

All men are as one before God: Tatars and Germans and other peoples.... If a man be endowed like us with reason, he is spiritually our brother or child. *1001*

THE WISHES OF THE QUICHÉ FOREFATHERS

Oh You, Tzacol, Bitol, Creator, Former,
Look upon us, hear us!
Do not leave us, do not forsake us.
Oh God, Who art in heaven and on earth,
Heart of the Heavens, Heart of the Earth!
Give us our offspring,
Our issue.
May the sun move along and give light.
May it dawn, may the light come!
Give us many good roads,
Level roads.

Popol Vuh
(Sacred book of the
Quiché)
Guatemala
Trans. by
M. León-Portilla

May the people be at peace,
Enjoy a long peace;
And make them prosperous,
Give us a good life and useful existence. *1002*

Meaning
of life

Aztec admonishments to a young woman.

Here you are, my little girl, my necklace of precious stones, my plumage, my human creation, born of me. You are my blood, my colour, my image.

Now listen, understand: you are alive, you have been born; Our Lord, the Master of the Close and the Near, the maker of people, the inventor of men, has sent you to earth.

Now that you begin to look around you, be aware. Here it is like this: there is no happiness, no pleasure. There is heartache, worry, fatigue. Here springs up and grows suffering, and distress.

Here on earth is the place of much wailing, the place where our strength is worn out, where we are well acquainted with bitterness and discouragement. A wind blows, sharp as obsidian it slides over us.

They say truly that we are burned by the force of the sun and the wind. This is the place where one almost perishes of thirst and hunger. This is the way it is here on earth.

Listen well, my child, my little girl: there is no place of well-being on the earth, there is no happiness, no pleasure. They say that the earth is the place of painful pleasure, of grievous happiness.

The elders have always said: So that we should not go round always moaning, that we should not be filled with sadness, the Lord has given us laughter, sleep, food, our strength and fortitude, and finally the act by which men propagate.

All this sweetens life on earth so that we are not always moaning. But even though it be like this, even though it be true that there is only suffering, and this is the way things are on earth, even so, should we always be afraid? Should we always be fearful? Must we live weeping?

But see, there is life on the earth, there are the lords; there is authority, there is nobility; there are eagles and tigers, knights. And who is always saying that so it is on earth? Who goes about trying to put an end to his life? There is ambition, there is struggle, work. One looks for a wife, one looks for a husband!   *1003*

Aztec tradition
15th cent.
Mexico

I am come, oh my friends,
With necklaces I entwine you,
With feathers of the macaw I adorn you,
A precious bird, I dress with feathers,
I paint with gold,
I embrace mankind.
With trembling quetzal feathers,
With circlets of song,
I give myself to the community.
I will carry you with me to the palace

Aztec song
15th cent.
Mexico
Trans. by
M. León-Portilla

Where we all,
Someday,
All must betake ourselves,
To the region of the dead.
Our life has only been loaned to us!   1004

Let us have friends here!
It is the time to know our faces.
Only with flowers
Can our song enrapture.
We will have gone to His house,
But our word
Shall live here on earth.
We will go leaving behind
Our grief, our song.
For this will be known,
The song shall remain real.
We will have gone to His house,
But our word
Shall live here on earth.   1005

Aztec song
15th cent.
Mexico
Trans. by
M. León-Portilla

People come to admire the python, they come to admire
the leopard; whether python or leopard, neither is lacking
in majesty.

When a python is killed, men go to see, and when a
leopard is killed, they also go and admire, for both are
noble beasts. Likewise with man: whether a woman is
delivered of a daughter or gives birth to a son, it is the
same; both are human. Whether a man be rich or poor,
we should hold him in affection, for he is man.

Whether a wife is beautiful or ugly, she tends you, cooks
your food, and so on. . . .

The pots come from firing [say] 'it is the pigment that
chooses us'.

All the pots have been fired in the same way and in the
same kiln, yet they are different, for the pigment takes
better on some than on others, and buyers choose one
rather than another because the colour varies in beauty.

Likewise, children of the same parents are different
and successful to different degrees despite their common
origin, because of differences in their behaviour, in their
qualities and in their defects.   1006

Mongo proverbs
Congo

All man are the offspring of God, no one is the offspring of Earth.

**Akan proverbs
Ghana**

All men have one head, but heads differ. *1007*

**Djerma-Songhai
proverb
Africa**

You may chew your brother, but not swallow him.

(*Limits imposed on hostility between men, on the grounds that they are brothers.*) *1008*

*The world
is one great city*

All men are related one with another and are marvellously incorporated in the Universal Republic.

All kingdoms, empires, tyrannies or republics in the world are linked together by a bond which is none other than the supremacy of reason or the law of nations. Whence it arises that this world is like unto a big city and all men are, as it were, fashioned according to one and the same law, so that they may understand that they are all of one blood and under the protection of the same reason. But because this empire of reason is devoid of constraint, it would be impossible to assemble all existing nations in a single Republic. That is why princes have recourse to battles and treaties. *1009*

**Jean Bodin
La République
1576
France**

Although the human race is divided up into various peoples and kingdoms, it none the less possesses not only a specific but also, as it were, a political and moral unity. This unity is exemplified by the natural attitude of mutual love and compassion that is extended towards all, even strangers, whatever their condition may be. That is why every sovereign State, republic or kingdom, although self-contained and firmly established, is none the less at the same time in a certain sense a member of that universe, in so far as it concerns the human race. No State is ever so self-sufficient that it needs no support of any kind, no association or mutual relations with any other State, whether for its own well-being and from a utilitarian motive, or from some reason of necessity and of moral support, as we know from experience. It follows, therefore, that States need to have a law which controls and governs them in this type of community and society. No doubt natural reason is of considerable help in this respect, but it does not always suffice; that is why special laws have come to be adopted through custom among the nations themselves. For just as in a State or in a province, it is through custom that law comes into being, so it is through habits common to the whole human race that the law of nations has come into being. *1010*

**Francisco Suarez
Tractatus de Legibus
ac de Deo
Legislatore
Late 16th cent.
Spain**

Humanity a single body Kemal Pasha Atatürk 1937	We should think of humanity as a body and of a nation as one of its limbs. Pain in a finger-tip affects the whole system. If there is disorder anywhere in the world, we cannot shrug it off. We must deal with it as if it had made itself felt in our midst. However distant an event, we must never forget this principle. *1011*

The same life in all of us

Mahatma Gandhi
1869-1948

I want to realize brotherhood or identity not merely with the beings called human, but I want to realize identity with all life, even with such things as crawl upon earth. I want, if I don't give you a shock, to realize identity with even the crawling things upon earth, because we claim descent from the same God, and that being so, all life in whatever form it appears must be essentially one. *1012*

The whole world is in every man

Mahatma Gandhi
1869-1948

This *ahimsā* (*non-violence*) is the basis of the search for truth. I am realizing every day that the search is vain unless it is founded on *ahimsā* as the basis. It is quite proper to resist and attack a system, but to resist and attack its author is tantamount to resisting and attacking oneself. For we are all tarred with the same brush, and are children of one and the same Creator, and as such the divine powers within us are infinite. To slight a single human being is to slight those divine powers, and thus to harm not only that being but with him the whole world. *1013*

Brotherhood

Men are linked by ties even in the heat of battle

Diomedes, the Achaean, son of Tydeus, and Glaucus, the Lycian, son of Hippolochus, meet and recognize each other, acknowledging the bonds of hospitality which link their two families.

Glaucus' tale delighted Diomedes of the loud war-cry. He stuck his spear into the fruitful earth, and now addressed the Lycian prince in cordial terms. 'Surely', he said, 'your family and mine are linked by old-established ties. Oeneus, my noble grandfather, once entertained the peerless Bellerophon in his palace and kept him there for twenty days, after which they gave each other the splendid gifts that host and guest exchange. . . .

'But I have said enough to show that in me you will now have a good friend in the heart of Argos, and I shall have you in Lycia, if ever I visit that country. So let us avoid each other's spears, even in the mêlée, since there are plenty of the Trojans and their famous allies for me to kill, if I have the luck and speed to catch them, and plenty of Achaeans for you to slaughter, if you can. And let us exchange our armour, so that everyone may know that our grandfathers' friendship has made friends of us.'

With these words they leap from their chariots, grasp hands and pledge their faith. *1014*

Homer
The Iliad
9th cent. B.C.

Prayer of vanquished Priam to victorious Achilles for the return of the body of his son, Hector.

'Most worshipful Achilles,' he said, 'think of your own father, who is the same age as I, and so has nothing but miserable old age ahead of him. No doubt his neighbours are oppressing him and there is nobody to save him from their depredations. Yet he at least has one consolation. While he knows that you are still alive, he can look forward day by day to seeing his beloved son come back from Troy; whereas my fortunes are completely broken. I had the best sons in the whole of this broad realm, and now not one, not one I say, is left. There were fifty when the Achaean expedition came. Nineteen of them were borne by one mother and the rest by other ladies in my palace. Most of them have fallen in action, and Hector, the only one I still could count on, the bulwark of Troy and the Trojans, has now been killed by you, fighting for his native land. It is to get him back from you that I have come to the Achaean ships, bringing this princely ransom with me. Achilles, fear the gods, and be merciful to me, remembering your own father, though I am even more entitled to compassion, since I have brought myself to do a thing that no one else on earth has done—I have raised to my lips the hand of the man who killed my son.'

Priam had set Achilles thinking of his own father and brought him to the verge of tears. Taking the old man's hand, he gently put him from him; and overcome by their memories they both broke down. Priam, crouching at Achilles' feet, wept bitterly for man-slaying Hector, and Achilles wept for his father, and then again for Patroclus. The house was filled with the sounds of their lamentation. But presently, when he had had enough of tears and recovered his composure, the excellent Achilles leapt from his chair, and in compassion for the old man's grey head and grey beard, took him by the arm and raised him. Then he spoke to him from his heart:

'You are indeed a man of sorrows and have suffered much. How could you dare to come by yourself to the Achaean ships into the presence of a man who has killed so many of your gallant sons? You have a heart of iron. But pray be seated now, here on this chair, and let us leave our sorrows, bitter though they are, locked up in our own hearts.'

. . . .

Achilles orders that Hector's body be anointed and restituted. He then treats Priam as his guest and prepares his meal.

Automedon fetched some bread and set it out on the table in handsome baskets; Achilles divided the meat into portions; and they helped themselves to the good things spread before them.

Their thirst and hunger satisfied, Dardanian Priam let his eyes dwell on Achilles and saw with admiration how big and beautiful he was, the very image of a god. And Achilles noted with equal admiration the noble looks and utterance of Dardanian Priam. It gave them pleasure thus to look each other over. But presently the old king Priam made a move. *1015*

Homer
The Iliad
9th cent. B.C.

*Homage
to the enemy's
dead*

In the course of excavations on St. Mary's Island off Chatham were found the remains of many of the French prisoners who died during the Napoleonic Wars, while incarcerated on board the hulks in the Medway. A little cemetery, about 200 feet square, was formed, railed in, and laid out in flower-beds and gravelled pathways; and a monument was erected in the centre bearing the following inscription:

Here are gathered together
The remains of many brave soldiers and sailors,
Who, having once been the foes, and afterwards
captives of England,
Now find rest in her soil,
Remembering no more the animosities of war or
the sorrows of imprisonment.
They were deprived of the consolation of closing
their eyes
Among the countrymen they loved;
But they have been laid in an honoured grave
By a nation which knows how to respect valour,
And to sympathize with misfortune. *1016*

Inscription
1869
United Kingdom

God's creatures

Wolfram
von Eschenbach
Willehalm
13th cent.
Old German

To slay like beasts our fellow men
Who ne'er of baptism had ken,
Is this a sin? A great sin, yea,
Is't thus to do, truly I say,
For they God's creatures likewise are,
With two-and-seventy tongues for dower.   *1017*

*Receptive
to all influences*

Béla Bartók
Letter
to Octavian Beu
1931
Hungary

My real governing idea, the idea which has completely dominated me ever since I have been a composer, is that of the brotherhood of all peoples, their brotherhood in the face of, and against, all war or conflict of any kind. This is the idea which, to the utmost of my strength, I try to serve through my work. It is for this reason that I do not set my face against any influence, whether its source be Slovak, Romanian, Arab or any other. All that matters is that the source shall be pure, fresh and healthy!
1018

Fraternity

Principles and Rules
of the Society
of Fraternal
Democrats
1845
United Kingdom

We condemn the 'national' hatreds which have hitherto divided mankind, as both foolish and wicked; foolish, because no one can decide for himself the country he will be born in; and wicked, as proved by the feuds and bloody wars which have desolated the earth, in consequence of these national vanities. Convinced, too, that national prejudices have been, in all ages, taken advantage of by the people's oppressors, to set them tearing the throats of each other, when they should have been working together for their common good, this society [the Society of Fraternal Democrats] repudiates the term 'Foreigner', no matter by whom or to whom applied. Our moral creed is to receive our fellow men, without regard to country, as members of one family, the human race; and citizens of one great commonwealth—the world. Finally, we recognise that great moral law 'Do unto thy brother, as thou wouldest thy brother should do unto thee', as the greatest safeguard of public and private happiness.   *1019*

Solidarity

Emeric Crucé
The New Cineas
or State oration
representing the
occasions and means
of establishing
a general peace
and freedom of trade
everywhere
in the world
1623
France

It seems to me that when one beholds a neighbour's house burning or falling down, one is seized with fear as much as with pity, seeing that human society is one body, all of whose members are united by a bond of sympathy, so that if a man is sick his sickness must needs be communicated to his fellows.   *1020*

*Requirements
for peace*

We all know that, if peace is to be prepared in the thoughts of men and in the minds of the nations, it can only be done if those minds come to a profound conviction of principles such as the following: that a good policy is first and foremost a just policy; that every nation must endeavour to understand the psychology, development and traditions, the material and spiritual needs, the personal dignity and historic vocation of other peoples, because each nation must keep in mind not only its own interests, but the common good of the family of nations; that this awakening of mutual understanding and of the consciousness of the civilized community, though it requires a sort of spiritual revolution, in view, alas, of the age-old habits of human history, is a necessity for public welfare in a world which henceforth is one for life or death, though remaining tragically divided as regards political interests and passions; that to place national interests above all is the surest way of losing all; that a community of free men is inconceivable without the recognition by it that truth is the expression of what is right and just and not of what, at a given moment, is most advantageous to a group of men; that it is not possible to put an innocent man to death because he has become a useless and costly burden to the nation or because he obstructs the activities of a particular group; that a human being has a dignity on which the good of the community is founded and which, in its own interests, it must respect, and that as a human being, as a civic being, as a social or working being, he has fundamental rights and fundamental duties; that the common weal must take precedence over individual interests, that the working world is entitled to undergo the social changes demanded by the fact that it has come of age historically, and that the masses are entitled to their share of the benefits of culture and of the intellect; that freedom of conscience is inviolable; that men of different creeds and different spiritual associations must recognize mutually

*Jacques Maritain
Speech at the
General Conference
of Unesco at its
Second Session
1947
France*

their rights as fellow-citizens in the civilized community; that, for the common good, it is the duty of the State to respect religious liberty and freedom of research; that because of the essential equality of men, racial, class or caste prejudices and racial discrimination are an affront to human nature and to personal dignity and are a crucial threat to peace. *1021*

*The virtue
of humanity*

Tang, the prime minister of Shang, questioned Chuang-tzu about the virtue of humanity.

Chuang-tzu replied: 'Tigers and wolves, too, have the virtue of humanity.'

'How so?' asked the prime minister.

'If father and son love each other, how can one say that tigers and wolves do not also have the virtue of humanity?' replied Chuang-tzu.

'Permit me to ask you what is the virtue of supreme humanity?'

'The virtue of supreme humanity no longer has parents (in the mind).'

'I have heard the following words spoken: "Whosoever no longer has parents (in his mind) cannot love them and thus has no filial piety." Could one say that the virtue of supreme humanity does not involve filial piety?'

*Chuang-tzu
3rd cent? B.C.
China*

'I do not agree with you,' replied Chuang-tzu. 'The virtue of supreme humanity is a higher virtue of which filial piety is not an adequate definition.' *1022*

*Man is a sociable
animal*

*Giovanni Pontano
c. 1467
Italy*

As for me, I declare myself a man, for that I live in a Community, in the society of other men, and busy myself with a hundred and one things. *1023*

*Montaigne
Essays
1580-88*

There is a marvellous clearness, or as I may term it, an enlightening of man's judgement drawn from the commerce of men, and by frequenting abroad in the world; we are all so contrived and compact in ourselves, that our sight is made shorter by the length of our nose. When Socrates was asked whence he was, he answered, not of Athens, but of the world: for he, who had his imagination more full and farther stretching, embraced all the world for his native city, and extended his acquaintance, his society, and affections to all mankind: and not as we do, that look no further than our feet. *1024*

Not because Socrates hath said it, but because such is in truth my humour, and peradventure not without some excuse, I do esteem all men as my countrymen; and I as kindly embrace a Polonian as a Frenchman, postponing his natural bond to universal and common.... Nature hath placed us in the world free and unbound; we imprison ourselves into certain straits, as the kings of Persia, who bound themselves never to drink other water than of the river Choaspez, foolishly renouncing all lawful right of use in all other waters, and for their regard dried up all the rest of the world. . . . The Stoics say that there is so great an affinity and mutual relation between wise men that he who dineth in France feedeth his companion in Egypt; and if one of them do but hold up his finger, wherever it be, all the wise men dispersed upon the habitable land feel a kind of aid thereby. *1025*

Montaigne
Essays
1580-88

*Freedom
and tyranny,
unity
of human kind*

Freedom, which is at all times such a great good, and so agreeable to possess that, once it is lost, all misfortunes seem to come one after the other; and even such good things as remain afterward lose all their flavour and piquancy, under the corrupting influence of servitude. Men do not really desire freedom as such; for this very good reason (or so it seems to me) that were they really to desire it, they would have it: they seem to take no interest in acquiring such a marvellous gift because it is too easy.

O wretched and unhappy people, races of madmen, nations which persist in your evil condition and are blind to what is for your good, how is it you allow the greater part of your belongings to be carried off, your fields pillaged, and your houses despoiled and emptied of all their ancestral furniture? You live after such a fashion that you may well say nothing belongs to you. And all this waste, this misfortune, this ruin are brought about, not by your enemies, but by an enemy indeed—that redoubtable one you yourselves have fashioned, on whose behalf you go off so bravely to war, for whose greatness you are quite prepared to lay down your lives! He who dominates you so has only two eyes, one pair of hands, one single body and in fact no more to show than the most insignificant human being from among the multitudes that inhabit your cities; except that he has more than you all have, which is the advantage you give him over you, to destroy you. Whence did he get so many eyes with which to spy on you, unless you give them to him? How is it he has so many hands with which to strike you, unless he gets them from you? Those feet that trample upon your cities, how did he come to possess them, unless they are actually your own feet? How can he wield any power over you, otherwise than through you yourselves?

Resolve to be servile no longer, and you will be free. Not that I would have you push against him or try to shake him, but simply not support him; then you will behold him, like a great Colossus undermined, topple over by his own weight and break into smithereens.

Since, then, our good mother [Nature] has given us all the earth to inhabit, one and the same house to dwell in together; has made us all out of the same clay, so that each can see and, as it were, recognize himself in his neighbour; has given us all in common that wonderful gift of voice and speech so that we may get to know and make friends with each other the more readily, and by communicating our thoughts to one another thus be able to reach a communion of minds; and since she has tried by every possible means to draw tighter and tighter bonds knitting us together in one society; if she has shown in all things a desire to make us, not so much united, as one in mind and heart; there can be absolutely no doubt that we are all naturally free, since we are all fellows; and no man of sense, therefore, can possibly hold that Nature should have placed any of us in servitude, since she has made us all to belong together in company. *1026*

Étienne de La Boétie
De la Servitude
Volontaire
ou Contr'un
1548
France

---

*Unity
through equality* •

Euripides
The Phoenician
Maidens
c. 408 B.C., Greece

Rather, my child, honour equality, that links friend closely to friend, city to city, ally to ally; for equality is a natural law to men. *1027*

---

*Unity
through harmony*

Hsün-tzu
The Way of Kings
3rd cent. B.C.
China

What makes society possible? Individual rights. What makes individual rights tenable? Justice. Therefore when justice and rights are adjusted, there is harmony. Where there is harmony, there is unity. *1028*

Laws

Kuan-tzu
4th to 3rd cent. B.C.
China

All countries have laws, but there is no law to enforce laws. *1029*

*Unity
through justice*
Sefer Hassidim
12th cent.
Jewish tradition

If a Jew attempts to kill an innocent Gentile, every Jew must go out against the Jew in order to save the Gentile.

1030

*Unity
through humility*
Ibn Hishām
Sira
9th cent.
North Africa

Kuraishites, God has delivered you from the arrogance of Paganism, and the pagan custom of boastfulness concerning ancestors: all men are descended from Adam, and Adam was a creature of dust.

1031

*All men are
companions in work*
Dēnkart
9th cent.
Persia

The whole of this world is labour, all the creatures are companions in labour. Only that man can love people who maintains: 'If there is one man less of all those that are in this world, I shall not be able to carry on my labour.'

1032

Mahatma Gandhi
1869-1948

A man cannot become self-sufficient even in respect of all the various operations from the growing of cotton to the spinning of the yarn. He has at some stage or other to take the aid of the members of his family. And if one may take help from one's own family, why not from one's neighbours? Or otherwise what is the significance of the great saying, 'The world is my family'?

1033

*Culture
is for everyone*

It is also to be desired that even utterly barbarous peoples should be enlightened and liberated from the shades of their barbarity, for they are a part of the human race and the part should be like the whole; and further, the whole is not whole if any part is lacking. Finally, to prefer the part to the whole (in the possession of anything good) is dear proof of lack of right judgement or of good will. Whoever then does not wish to show something of foolishness or ill will, must wish good to all men, and not only to himself, a few of his own near ones, or his own nation. For it cannot even go well with the whole body if it does not go well with all its members together and singly; for they are so bound together that if any one of them, even the smallest, is affected, it is immediately felt by them all, and one sick limb easily affects another. Nor is it otherwise in human society; for one man is infected by another man, one city by another city, one nation by another nation: but if all were healthy they would enjoy their common weal together. He then who would seriously not wish well to the whole of the human race, injures the whole human race. Nor is he a true friend to his own person if he wishes the healthy to mix with the sick, the wise man with fools, the good man with evil men, the fortunate man with unfortunates; yet this cannot be avoided if he indeed wishes only himself, and not others, to be whole, wise, good and happy. *1034*

J. A. Comenius
Czech writer
1592-1670
The Pampaedia

Somali proverb Every man has hanging to his neck a precious book. *1035*

*The interests
of a State
are the interests
of Christendom*

Since any State forms but a part of the whole world and, still more, a Christian Province is but a part of the whole Republic, I consider that even if a war is of advantage to a province or a State but is on the other hand of disadvantage to the world and to Christendom, then that war is *ipso facto* unjust. For example, should a war between Spain and France be entered into from just motives, and should it, from other points of view, serve the purpose of the Spanish Kingdom, but nevertheless be carried on to the detriment of Christendom at large (if, in the meantime, for instance, Christian Provinces were to be occupied by the Turks), then such a war should be stopped immediately. *1036*

Francisco de Vitoria
Reflectiones
Theologicae
1526
Spain

*My private interest
is the interest
of everyone*

Montesquieu
1689-1755
Mes Pensées

If I knew of a thing useful to my nation but ruinous to another, I would not propose it to my prince, because I am a man before being French, (or again) because I am of necessity a man, and only French by chance. *1037*

The general good

Leibniz
Letter to Peter
the Great
16 January 1716
Germany

I am not one of those who are fanatically attached to their own country or yet to any nation in particular; what I would do is to serve mankind as a whole; for I consider Heaven as our Fatherland and all men of goodwill as fellow citizens of that Heaven; and I would rather do much good among the Russians than little among the Germans or other Europeans. . . . For my inclinations and tastes tend toward the General Good. *1038*

Prayer

I now turn from men to address my words to Thee, God of all beings, of all worlds and of all time: if it is permitted to feeble creatures lost in the vastness and imperceptible to the rest of the universe, to dare to ask anything of Thee, who hast given all and whose decrees are unchanging and eternal, condescend to look with pity on the errors inseparable from our nature; let not these errors be our undoing. Thou didst not give us hearts to hate and hands to cut each other's throats; grant that we may help each other to bear the burden of a painful and fleeting life; that the little difference between the clothes which cover our poor bodies, between all our different and inadequate forms of speech, between all our ridiculous customs and imperfect laws, between all our senseless opinions and our estates, so disproportionately different in our eyes and so alike to Thee; grant that all these little nuances that distinguish the atoms known as men from each other may not be signals for hatred and persecution; that those who light candles at midday to worship Thee may tolerate those who make do with the light of Thy sun; grant that those who put a white cloth over their robes to say that men should love Thee may not hate those who say the same thing wearing a coat of black wool; that it may be the same to worship Thee in the jargon of an ancient tongue or of a newer; that those whose clothes are dyed red or violet, who reign over a small plot heaped from the mud of this earth and own a few rounded fragments of a particular metal may enjoy without pride what they call grandeur and riches, and that others may see them without envy; for Thou knowest that there is in these trifles nothing for envy or for pride.

Let all men remember that they are brothers, let them hold in abomination the tyranny exercised over souls, no less than the brigandage which forcibly robs labour and peaceful industry of their fruits! If the horrors of war are inevitable, at least let us not hate each other, let us not torment each other in time of peace, and let us use our moment of existence to bless, in a thousand different tongues from Siam to California, Thy bounty which has accorded that moment to us.

Voltaire
Treatise on Tolerance
1763

1039

Proposed Declaration of Rights made at the Jacobin Club by Robespierre, 21 April 1793

I. Men of all countries are brothers, and the various nations must assist each other according to their resources, like citizens of the same State.

II. Anyone who oppresses a nation is the declared enemy of all nations.

III. Those who go to war against a people to bar the progress of liberty and abolish the rights of man must be pursued by all, not just as ordinary enemies, but as assassins and outlaws.

IV. Kings, aristocrats, tyrants, whoever they may be, are slaves in rebellion against the sovereign of the earth, that is the human race, and against the legislator of the universe, which is nature.   *1040*

Moniteur XVI
France

We are not free so long as there is a single moral obstacle barring our physical progress in a single corner of the globe. The Rights of Man apply to the whole of mankind. Any Corporation which regards itself as all-powerful deals humanity a grievous blow and is thoroughly antagonistic to common sense and general well-being; it obstructs the channels of universal prosperity, and its Constitution, for want of a sure basis, will be contradictory, haphazard and vacillating.   *1041*

Anacharis Cloots
Member
of the French
National Convention
Speech delivered
on 26 April 1793

SOCIALISM

Men, though marked with the stamp of different races,
And speaking divers tongues,
Proclaim: Bad we may be—but we are the elect,
We must choose between rejoicing and despair.
Yes, the ancient Python is down in the pit.
Money? We'll destroy it. Harmony? Material, yes.

The work of History is not yet complete,
'Tis a boulder pushed up-hill by our hands.
The moment we desist, its weight presses upon our breasts,
The moment we rest, it crushes our heads.
The work of History is not yet complete,
This globe has not yet been tempered in the fire of the
    Spirit.   *1042*

C. K. Norwid
1861
Poland

Sources and ends

*Humanity
in each one of us
should be an end*

Kant
Grundlegung zur
Metaphysik der Sitten
1785

The foundation of this principle is as follows: *rational nature exists as an end in itself. . . .* The practical imperative will therefore be as follows: *Act always in such a way as to treat humanity, whether in your own person or in that of anyone else, at the same time as an end, and never simply as a means.*   *1043*

*Measure
or absolute*

H. Bergson
The Two Sources
of Morality
and Religion
1932
France

But it is a far cry from this kind of equilibrium, achieved mechanically and invariably unstable, like that of the scales in the hands of Justice in ancient times, to justice such as ours, the justice of the 'rights of man' which no longer evokes the idea of inter-relation or measure, but on the contrary, that of the incommensurable and the absolute.   *1044*

*The prestige
of man*
Maxim Gorky
The Lower Depths
1902, Russia

A man! There's a word that rings proudly.   *1045*

Chandidās
c. 15th cent.
Bengali, India

There is no Truth higher than man.   *1046*

*Worse
than death*

Dādistān ī Mēnōg
ī Xrad
Sassanian period
3rd to 7th cent.
Persia

The sage asked the Spirit of Wisdom thus: 'Is living in fear and falsehood worse, or death?'

The Spirit of Wisdom answered thus: 'To live in fear and falsehood is worse than death, because everyone's life is for the enjoyment and pleasure of the worldly existence, and when the enjoyment and pleasure of the worldly existence are not his, and fear and even falsehood are with him, it is called worse than death.'   *1047*

Natural law

Again, it is held by the Stoics to be important to understand that nature creates in parents an affection for their children; and parental affection is the source to which we trace the origin of the association of the human race in communities. This cannot but be clear in the first place from the conformation of the body and its members, which by themselves are enough to show that nature's scheme included the procreation of offspring. Yet it could not be consistent that nature should at once intend offspring to be born and make no provision for that offspring when born to be loved and cherished. Even in the lower animals nature's operation can be clearly discerned; when we observe the labour that they spend on bearing and rearing their young, we seem to be listening to the actual voice of nature. Hence as it is manifest that it is natural for us to shrink from pain, so it is clear that we derive from nature herself the impulse to love those to whom we have given birth. From this impulse is developed the sense of mutual attraction which unites human beings as such; this also is bestowed by nature. The mere fact of their common humanity requires that one man should feel another man to be akin to him. For just as some of the parts of the body, such as the eyes and the ears, are created as it were for their own sakes, while others like the legs or the hands also subserve the utility of the rest of the members, so some very large animals are born for themselves alone; whereas the sea-pen, as it is called, in its roomy shell, and the creature named the 'pinoteres' because it keeps watch over the sea-pen, which swims out of the sea-pen's shell, then retires back into it and is shut up inside, thus appearing to have warned its host to be on its guard—these creatures, and also the ant, the bee, the stork, do certain actions for the sake of others besides themselves. With human beings this bond of mutual aid is far more intimate. It follows that we are by nature fitted to form unions, societies and states.

Again, they hold that the universe is governed by divine will; it is a city or state of which both men and gods are members, and each one of us is a part of this universe; from which it is a natural consequence that we should prefer the common advantage to our own. For just as the laws set the safety of all above the safety of individuals, so a good, wise and law-abiding man, conscious of his duty to the state, studies the advantage of all more than that of himself or of any single individual. The traitor to his country does not deserve greater reprobation than the man who betrays the common advantage or security for the sake of his own advantage or security. This explains why praise is owed to one who dies for the commonwealth, because it becomes us to love our country more than ourselves. *1048*

Cicero
Of Good and Evil
106-43 B.C.

This Sociability, which was described in rough outline above, this concern for preserving Society in a manner consonant with the light of Human Understanding, is the source of Natural Law as it is rightly called, which in general can be summed up as follows: *We must have a scrupulous regard for other people's property, and restore any part of it that may be in our possession, or else the profit derived from it; we are bound to keep our promises; we must make amends for any damage for which we are responsible; any breach of these Rules deserves punishment, even on the part of Men.*

This idea gave rise to another of wider scope, which was later associated with the concept of Law. The preeminence of Man over the rest of the Animal Kingdom consists not only in the feelings of Sociability mentioned above, but also in the fact that Man can rightly assess the value of agreeable or disagreeable things, both present and future, and discern what may be useful or harmful. It may thus be understood that it is no less in conformity with Human Nature to be guided, in such matters, by an upright and sound Judgement, as far as the weakness of our Intellect permits; not to allow oneself to be perturbed by the fear of future trouble, or to be lured by the bait of present pleasure, or to be carried away by blind passion. Accordingly, that which is entirely opposed to such a Judgement is considered to be also contrary to the Natural Law, i.e., the Laws of our Nature. . . .

All that we have just described would come to pass in some way, even if we were to agree, which we could not do without being guilty of a horrible crime, that there is no God, or that if there is a God, he takes no interest in human affairs. But the light of our Reason, and a lasting Tradition, widespread in the world, convince us from our childhood to the contrary, and we are confirmed in this belief by many proofs and miracles attested through the Centuries. From this it follows that we should obey this Sovereign Being unreservedly, as our Creator, to whom we owe what we are and all that we have; the more so that he has in various ways demonstrated his infinite Goodness and Power: from which we are entitled to conclude that he has power to give those who obey him very great, even eternal, rewards, since he himself is eternal; and we should believe that this is his will, above all if he has expressly promised it, of which we *Christians* are convinced by virtue of undeniable testimonies.

Here, then, is another source of the Law: to know the free will of God, to which we should submit ourselves, as our very Reason dictates in a manner which leaves us no doubt on the subject. But the Law of Nature which we have defined above—both that which consists in the preservation of Society and that which is so called in a broader sense—this Law, I say, though it is derived from the

531

principles inherent in Man, may nevertheless, and with reason, be attributed to God, because it is by his will that such principles are inherent in us. It is in this sense that Chrysippus and the other *Stoics* said that the origin of the Law was to be sought solely in *Jupiter* himself. It would also seem that the Latin word *jus*, meaning *law*, comes from the name *Jupiter*.

Add to this that God, by the Laws which he has made known, has made these principles clearer and more perceptible, bringing them within the reach even of those whose mind has little power of penetration. He has also forbidden us to give way to those impulses which, against our own interest, and even to the detriment of that of others, deter us from following the Rules of Reason and Nature: for, since they are extremely ardent, it is necessary to keep a tight hold over them, and to confine them within somewhat narrow limits.

Moreover, Holy Scripture, in addition to the precepts by which it enjoins us to adopt feelings of Sociability, contributes notably to inspiring such feelings in us through what it teaches us about Mankind's first Parents, from which all men are descended. For one may say in this respect what Florentine, the ancient jurisconsult, said in another connexion: *that Nature has established among us a kind of kinship; from which he infers that it is very ill of a Man to lay a trap for another Man.*

Among Men, a Father and a Mother are like Gods in relation to their Children: thus children owe them an obedience, which is not in truth limitless, but is as far-reaching as is required by this relationship, and as great as is compatible with the dependence of both parents and children on a common Superior.

It is in accordance with the Natural Law that each should scrupulously observe the promises or agreements he has made; for it was necessary that Men should have some ways of entering into commitments among themselves, and one can conceive of no other way more in conformity with Nature. It is this which subsequently produced the various kinds of Civil Law. Those who entered into a Community, and who submitted themselves to one or more persons, promised either expressly or by a tacit commitment, which the nature of the agreement subsumed, they promised, I say, to acquiesce in what might have been decided either by the majority of the Community, or by those in whose hands had been placed the power to command them.

Therefore, the saying of Carnéades, which others have repeated after him, *that Utility is as it were the Mother of*

Justice and Equity—this, I say, is not strictly true. For the Mother of Natural Law is Human Nature itself, which would incline us to seek relationships with our fellow men, even if we had need of nothing. And the Mother of Civil Law is the obligation Man has assumed by his own assent: an obligation which, drawing its strength from Natural Law, leads us to look on Nature as the great-grandmother, so to speak, of Civil Law. It all comes to this that Utility is a concomitant of Natural Law; for the Author of Nature has willed that each individual person should be weak by himself and lacking in many things that are necessary for comfortable living, so that we might all be more eagerly inclined to preserve Society.   *1049*

Hugo Grotius
De Jure Belli
et Pacis
1624
Holland

In Pope's world, self-love becomes the principle of social harmony and respect for others.

So drives Self-love, thro' just and thro' unjust,
To one Man's pow'r, ambition, lucre, lust:
The same Self-love, in all, becomes the cause
Of what restrains him, Government and Laws.
For, what one likes if others like as well,
What serves one will, when many wills rebel?
How shall he keep, what sleeping or awake,
A weaker may surprise, a stronger take?
His safety must his liberty restrain:
All join to guard what each desires to gain.
Forc'd into virtue thus by self-defence,
Ev'n Kings learn'd justice and benevolence:
Self-love forsook the path it first pursu'd,
And found the private in the public good.

'Twas then, the studious head or gen'rous mind,
Follow'r of God or friend of human-kind,
Poet or Patriot, rose but to restore
The Faith and Moral, Nature gave before;
Relum'd her ancient light, not kindled new;
If not God's image, yet his shadow drew:
Taught Pow'r's due use to People and to Kings,
Taught not to slack, nor strain its tender strings;
The less, or greater, set so justly true,
That touching one must strike the other too;
'Till jarring int'rests, of themselves create
Th' according music of a well-mix'd State.
Such is the World's great harmony, that springs
From order, union, full consent of things:
Where small and great, where weak and mighty, made

Communicating
by carrier-pigeons
in Syria
15th cent.
Germany

To serve, not suffer; strengthen, not invade;
More pow'rful each as needful to the rest,
And, in proportion as it blesses, blest;
Draw to one point, and to one centre bring
Beast, Man, or Angel, Servant, Lord, or King.
For forms of Government let fools contest;
Whate'er is best administer'd, is best:
For Modes of Faith let graceless zealots fight;
His can't be wrong whose life is in the right:
In Faith and Hope the world will disagree;
But all Mankind's concern is Charity:
All must be false that thwart this one great end;
And all of God, that bless Mankind, or mend.

Man, like the gen'rous vine supported lives;
The strength he gains is from th' embrace he gives.
On their own Axis as the Planets run,
Yet make at once their circle round the Sun;
So two consistent motions act the Soul;
And one regards itself, and one the Whole.

Alexander Pope
1688-1744
An Essay on Man
England

Thus God and Nature link'd the gen'ral frame,
And bade Self-love and Social be the same.   *1050*

*Fulfilment
of the self*

Man's true purpose—not that towards which changing
inclination would tend but eternally immutable reason—is
to achieve the fullest and most integrated development of
all his powers. For this, the first—and wholly indispen-

534

sable—prerequisite is freedom. But the development of man's powers requires something else besides, though it is closely bound up with freedom: diversity of situations. Even the freest and most independent man develops less when placed in unvarying situations. Although it is certainly true that such diversity is a consequence of freedom, there is, on the other hand, a form of oppression which, instead of restricting man, gives the things around him a diverse appearance, so that both forms of diversity are more or less one and the same thing. However, for the sake of clarity, it is advisable still to maintain a clear distinction between the two. A human being can bring only one faculty to bear at a time, or, to put it another way, his whole being at any one time is ready only for one activity. Consequently, limitation seems to be man's lot, for as soon as he addresses himself to more than one thing his energy flags. His only way out of this limitation is for him to try to unite his individual and often individually exercised faculties, to let the already almost extinguished spark, which in future will burn brightly, also exert its action throughout his life, and to multiply not the objects of his endeavour but the forces with which he operates.... What anyone who wants to influence his fellow men must never lose sight of is the originality of power and creation. Just as this originality is brought out through people's freedom of action and different characters, so it in turn brings forth both itself. Even lifeless nature, which maintains a constantly regular course in accordance with eternally immutable laws, appears to the self-created man more original. He projects himself into it as it were, and thus it is in the highest sense true that everyone perceives richness and beauty outside himself to the extent that he has both in his own heart.

Wilhelm von Humboldt 1767-1835 Germany

1051

Reference to God, to nature

Beyond all earthly justice is the secret foundation

The Tao is the secret foundation common to all beings,
The treasure of good men,
And the refuge of those who are not good.
With fine words, one can buy men;
By fine conduct, one can rise above others.
But why reject men who are not capable of it?
Thus, for instance, one crowns the son of heaven,
One installs the three dukes,

One presents them with jade and a four-horse chariot;
All that is not comparable
With the one who, without moving, offers the Tao.
Why did the ancients esteem the Tao so much?
Is it not thanks to it that
He who seeks finds
And that any guilty man redeems himself?
That is why it is in such high esteem throughout the world.

Lao-tzu
Tao-Te-Ching
6th cent. B.C.
China

1052

Man is made in
the image of God

Or Ganuz
Hidden light
Hassidic tale
18th cent.

Rabbi Solomon of Karlin asked: 'What is the evil inclination's worst deed?' And he himself answered: 'When a
man forgets that he is a King's son.'   *1053*

St. John Chrysostom
Patriarch
of Constantinople
Homilies
on the Hexameron
386

Man is a great and wonderful being, dearer to God than
all creation; for him the heavens, the earth, the sea and
all the rest of creation were made. God so desired man's
salvation that for his sake He spared not His only Son,
nor ceases to shower gifts and benefits upon him, until
He makes him sit down at His right hand. . . . [Man] was
the last being created, like the Emperor, whom all others
precede.   *1054*

St. Augustine
354-430
Treatise
on the Epistle
of St. John
to the Parthians

We read how man was made in the image and likeness
of God. And what does God say to man? That he shall
have dominion over all the fish of the sea, and over the
fowl of the air and over every living thing that moveth
upon the earth. Did God say: Let man have power over
man? He said: Let him have power, power in accordance
with his nature. Power over what? Over the fish of the
sea, the fowl of the air and every thing that creepeth
upon the earth. Why should man have this natural
dominion over the beasts? Because he was created in the
image of God. But in what respect was man created in
the image of God? In his intelligence, his spirit and his
inner being: in that he can comprehend the truth, judge
what is just and what unjust, in that he knows by whom
he was made, and is able to know and praise his creator.
                                                      1055

When God created man, in the beginning, He 'created
man in His own image'; this image He did not impress
on the outside, but within man. . . .
    It is this image of which the Father said to the Son:
'Let us make man in our image, after our likeness.' The

artist who gave form to this image is the Son of God.
He was such a great artist that the image He created may
be hidden by negligence, but never destroyed by malice.
God's image remains ever within you, even when you
superimpose on it the image of the 'earthy' man. *1056*

The story is told of Rabbi Eleazar ben Shimon who
happened to meet an ugly person. The man greeted the
rabbi but the rabbi offered no greeting but shouted: 'You
good for nothing! Are all the inhabitants of your town as
ugly as you are?' The person replied: 'I don't know, but
you should really tell the artisan who fashioned me: what
an ugly vessel you made.' The rabbi then realized his
terrible sin and asked the man's forgiveness. *1057*

Talmud
Ta'anit 20

*Divine protection
of the unhappy*

The spirit of the Lord God is upon me; because the Lord
hath anointed me to bring good tidings unto the humble;
he hath sent me to bind up the brokenhearted, to proclaim
liberty to the captives, and the opening of the eyes to
them that are bound. *1058*

Hebrew Bible
Isaiah 61

He lieth in wait in a secret place as a lion in his lair,
He lieth in wait to catch the poor;
He doth catch the poor, when he draweth him up in his net.
He croucheth, he boweth down,
And the helpless fall into his mighty claws.
He hath said in his heart: God hath forgotten;
He hideth His face; He will never see.
Arise, O Lord; O God, lift up Thy hand;
Forget not the humble.
Wherefore doth the wicked contemn God,
And say in his heart: Thou wilt not require?
Thou hast seen; for Thou beholdest trouble and vexation,
    to requite them with Thy hand;
Unto Thee the helpless committeth himself;
Thou hast been the helper of the fatherless.
Break Thou the arm of the wicked;
And as for the evil man, search out his wickedness, till
    none be found.
The Lord is King for ever and ever;
The nations are perished out of His land.
Lord, Thou hast heard the desire of the humble:
Thou wilt direct their heart, Thou wilt cause Thine ear to
    attend;
To right the fatherless and the oppressed,
That man who is of the earth may be terrible no more. *1059*

Hebrew Bible
Psalm 10

The justice
that is in God

Leibniz
Theodicy
1710
Germany

God's justice is not as human justice, for man is just only through observing the laws made by his superior. . . . Justice is not dependent on the arbitrary laws of superiors, but on those eternal rules of wisdom and goodness, which are in men as well as in God.   *1060*

Equality
in God's sight

Are you, then, better than we are, because you are a great lady? But God has marshalled the heavens above us as well, for us also the sun and the moon shine, and likewise by the will of the All Highest the earth and all the plants are not at your service any more than at mine.... The one thing needful is to be received as one of the great ladies of Heaven.

Do not think of the greatness of your rank as a noble lady, renounce that idea and trample it underfoot: we are all servants of the Tsar of Heaven.

Berate him thus: 'In vain are you a boyar, you must die, and even if you were whipped, it is not the blood of Christ which would flow, but a man's.'

The Tsar is the master of us all, but together with us all he is the slave of God.

Avvakum
Russian archpriest
17th cent.

There is only one heaven, one earth, the wheat belongs to all, and the water also.   *1061*

Beyond
all ceremonies

Wherewith shall I come before the Lord and bow myself before God on high? shall I come before Him with burnt offerings, with calves of a year old?

Will the Lord be pleased with thousands of rams, with ten thousands of rivers of oil? shall I give my first-born for my transgression, the fruit of my body for the sin of my soul?

Hebrew Bible
Micah 6

It hath been told thee, O man, what is good; and what the Lord doth require of thee; only to do justly and to love mercy and to walk humbly with thy God.   *1062*

Every man
is universal
and unique

Only one single man was created in the world, to teach that, if any man has caused a single soul to perish, Scripture imputes it to him as though he had caused a whole world to perish; and if any man saves alive a single soul, Scripture imputes it to him as though he had saved a whole world. Again, but a single man was created for the sake of peace among mankind, that none should say to his fellow, 'My father was greater than your father'; also that the heretics should not say, 'There are many ruling powers in heaven.' Again, but a single man was created to proclaim the greatness of God, for man stamps many coins with one die, and they are all like to one another; but God has stamped every man with the die of the first man, yet not one of them is like his fellow. Therefore every one must say, 'For my sake was the world created.'   *1063*

Talmud
Sanhedrin 4

*Religion
and right*

Religion consists in justice towards all men; what can be the religion of a man who refuses to acknowledge that another may be right?

Man, who is capable of leading great armies, is incapable of leading his own soul towards the Good.

Though a man may proclaim: 'God be praised', say his prayers, and walk seventy—not merely seven—times around the Ka'ba, this will not necessarily make him a truly religious man.

He who cannot control his appetites cannot know true religion.

Good does not lie in fasting which brings torment; Good does not lie in Prayer, or the wearing of coarse wool.

Rather, it lies in the rejection of Evil, in emptying the heart of all hatred and envy.

As long as the beasts of the desert and the cattle live in fear of his claws, the lion will never make a convincing ascetic.

Abu-al-Ala al-Maari
11th cent.
Syria

Worship God, rather than his creatures; Law enslaves, Reason liberates.   *1064*

St. Thomas Aquinas
Summa Theologica
13th cent.

Now the Divine law, which is the law of grace, does not do away with human law, which is the law of natural reason.   *1065*

*Every man
has links with
every other man*

All things which participate in anything which is common to them all, move towards that which is of the same kind with themselves. Everything which is earthy turns towards the earth, everything which is liquid flows together, and everything which is of an aerial kind does the same, so that they require something to keep them asunder, and the application of force. Fire indeed moves upwards on account of the elemental fire, but it is so ready to be kindled together with all the fire which is here, that even every substance which is somewhat dry is easily ignited, because there is less mingled with it of that which is a hindrance to ignition. Accordingly, then, everything also which participates in the common intelligent nature moves in like manner towards that which is of the same kind with itself, or moves even more. For so much as it is superior in comparison with all other things, in the same degree also is it more ready to mingle with and to be fused with that which is akin to it. Accordingly among animals devoid of reason we find swarms of bees, and herds of cattle, and the nurture of young birds, and in a manner, loves; for even in animals there are souls, and that power which brings them together is seen to exert itself in a superior degree, and in such a way as never has been observed in plants nor in stones nor in trees. But in rational animals there are political communities and friendships, and families and meetings of people; and in wars, treaties, and armistices. But in the things which are still superior, even though they are separated from one another, unity in a manner exists, as in the stars. Thus the ascent to the higher degree is able to produce a sympathy even in things which are separated. See, then, what now takes place; for only intelligent animals have now forgotten this mutual desire and inclination, and in them alone the property of flowing together is not seen. But still, though men strive to avoid [this union], they are caught and held by it, for their nature is too strong for them; and thou wilt see what I say, if thou only observest. Sooner, then, will one find anything earthy which comes in contact with no earthy thing, than a man altogether separated from other men. *1066*

Marcus Aurelius
121-80
Meditations
Rome

Viet-Namese
proverb
Among created things man is sacred. *1067*

Justice in the past; the golden age

Two kinds
of humanity

THE MYTH OF ADANEVA

There have been two kinds of humanity, the present and one more ancient.

Ancient humanity was created by the god Adaneva. The men of old were very strong. They rolled great stones, striking them with whips, and so built monuments of rock.

The god Adaneva took by force the Virgin of Grace and made her his wife. When she was pregnant, Adaneva abandoned her.

The Virgin of Grace gave birth to our present god, Téete Mañuco. Téete Mañuco destroyed ancient humanity with a rain of fire. The few men who were left alive he exterminated, hitting them with long bones. Then he made modern man.

Téete Mañuco divided mankind into two classes: the Indians and the Mistis (*the word Misti denotes not only the whites but all belonging to the ruling class*). The Mistis had and still have the right to make the Indians work, whipping them if necessary. The Mistis are not obliged to work.

The social division established by Téete Mañuco will be eternal because this god does not have to perish, as every year he dies on a Friday and rises again on the Saturday.

But Téete Mañuco also made heaven and hell.

Everyone goes to hell and then everyone goes to heaven. They go to hell because there is no human being free from sin. Then they go to heaven. Heaven is exactly the same as earth, but in heaven those who were Indians on earth are changed into Mistis and make their former masters work, whipping them if necessary. Téete Mañuco is seated between two trees and has a large mirror behind him.

Quechua tradition
Peru

1068

The golden age

Once Confucius was taking part in the winter sacrifice. After the ceremony was over, he went for a stroll along the top of the city gate and sighed mournfully. He sighed for the state of Lu.

His disciple Yen Yen, who was by his side, asked: 'Why would the gentleman sigh?'

Confucius replied: 'The practice of the Great Way, the illustrious men of the Three Dynasties—these I shall never know in person. And yet they inspire my ambition! When the Great Way was practised, the world was shared by all alike. The worthy and the able were promoted to office and men practised good faith and lived in affection. Therefore they did not regard as parents only their own parents, or as sons only their own sons. The aged found a fitting close to their lives, the robust their proper employment; the young were provided with an upbringing and the widow and widower, the orphan and the sick, with proper care. Men had their tasks and women their hearths. They hated to see goods lying about in waste, yet they did not hoard them for themselves and disliked the thought

541

that their energies were not fully used, yet they used them not for private ends. Therefore all evil plotting was prevented and thieves and rebels did not arise, so that the people could leave their outer gates unbolted. This was the age of Great Unity.'   *1069*

Li-chi
2nd cent. B.C.
China

*When time
was in its fullness*

For if, from the fall of our first parents, which was the turning point at which all our going astray began, we carry our thoughts over the distribution of the human race and the order of its times, we shall find that never but under the divine Augustus, who was sole ruler and under whom a perfect monarchy existed, was the world everywhere quiet. And that then the human race was happy in the tranquillity of universal peace, this is the witness of all writers of history; this is the witness of famous poets; this, too, he who wrote the story of the meekness and gentleness of Christ has thought fit to attest. And last of all, Paul has called that most blessed condition 'the fullness of time'. For then, indeed, time was full, and all the things of time; because no office belonging to our felicity wanted its minister. But how the world has fared since that seamless robe has suffered rending by the talons of ambition, we may read in books; would that we might not see it with our eyes. O race of men, what storms must toss thee, what losses must thou endure, what shipwrecks must buffet thee, as long as thou, a beast of many heads, strivest after contrary things! Thou art sick in both thy faculties of understanding; thou art sick in thine affections. Unanswerable reasons fail to heal thy higher understanding; the very sight of experience convinces not thy lower understanding; not even the sweetness of divine persuasion charms thy affections, when it breathes into thee through the music of the Holy Spirit: 'Behold, how good and how pleasant a thing it is, brethren, to dwell together in unity.'   *1070*

Dante
De Monarchia
1308

The proper work of the human race, taken as a whole, is to set in action the whole capacity of that understanding which is capable of development; first in the way of speculation, and then, by its extension, in the way of action. And seeing that what is true of a part is true also of the whole, and that it is by rest and quiet that the individual man becomes perfect in wisdom and prudence; so the human race, by living in the calm and tranquillity of peace, applies itself most freely and easily to its proper work—a work which, according to the saying 'Thou hast made him a little lower than the angels', is almost divine. Whence it is manifest that of all things that are ordered to secure blessings to men, the greatest is universal peace.

*Dante
De Monarchia
1308*

1071

Time was

And, from Jacob's flock, he [the Emperor Claudios] sought the injured sheep lost in the Arab desert; and when he had found it he would place it on his shoulders, rejoicing more because of it than of those which had not been lost; and the sheep that came to him from the Arab flock he did not send back or drive away but brought them all together, himself, in one sheepfold with one shepherd.

And any who approached him of those who had done evil he did not spurn as did the Moabites and the Ammonites who had contumeliously treated the children of Israel.

And in those days, God favoured the heavens, and the heavens favoured the earth and the earth favoured the grain and the vine, and the grain and the vine favoured men. And there was peace throughout the flock and among the people, and neither offender nor offended, or any quarrel, the young not seeking disputation with the old, or the noble with the commoner.

And among the sage are some who say that those days were the time spoken of in the story of the first Sabbath and it is said: 'In those days the Elect shall be seated upon his throne and the secrets of wisdom shall issue from his mind and from out of his mouth, for the God of Spirit will have conferred on him this privilege and by this favour glorified him. And in those days the mountains shall skip like young calves, and the hills like lambs that had their fill of milk. There shall be no more death, nor mourning, nor lamentation for the old order will have passed away. And in glades where nymphs and satyrs sported, children shall play; and at the city gates, the old men shall be many, with each his cane in hand.' *1072*

*Chronicles of the
Emperor Claudios
1540-59
Ethiopia*

*The golden age
of chivalry*

He was cordially welcomed by the goatherds, and Sancho, having as best he could put up Rosinante and the ass, drew towards the fragrance that came from some pieces of salted goat simmering in a pot on the fire; and though he would have liked at once to try if they were ready to be transferred from the pot to the stomach, he refrained from doing so as the goatherds removed them from the fire, and laying sheepskins on the ground, quickly spread their rude table, and with signs of hearty good-will invited them both to share what they had. Round the skins six of the men belonging to the fold seated themselves, having first with rough politeness pressed Don Quixote to take a seat upon a trough which they placed for him upside down. Don Quixote seated himself, and Sancho remained standing to serve the cup, which was made of horn. Seeing him standing, his master said to him, 'That thou mayest see, Sancho, the good that knight-errantry contains in itself, and how those who fill any office in it are on the high road to be speedily honoured and esteemed by the world, I desire that thou seat thyself here at my side and in the company of these worthy people, and that thou be one with me who am thy master and natural lord, and that thou eat from my plate and drink from whatever I drink from; for the same may be said of knight-errantry as of love, that it levels all.'

'Great thanks,' said Sancho, 'but I may tell your worship that provided I have enough to eat, I can eat it as well, or better, standing, and by myself, than seated alongside of an emperor. And indeed, if the truth is to be told, what I eat in my corner without form or fuss has much more relish for me, even though it be bread and onions, than the turkeys of those other tables where I am forced to chew slowly, drink little, wipe my mouth every minute, and cannot sneeze or cough if I want, or do other things that are the privileges of liberty and solitude. So, señor, as for these honours which your worship would put upon me as a servant and follower of knight-errantry (which I am, being your worship's squire), exchange them for other things which may be of more use and advantage to me; for these, though I fully acknowledge them as received, I renounce from this moment to the end of the world.'

'For all that,' said Don Quixote, 'thou must seat thyself, because him who humbleth himself God exalteth'; and seizing him by the arm he forced him to sit down beside himself.

The goatherds did not understand this jargon about squires and knights-errant, and all they did was to eat in silence and stare at their guests, who, with great elegance and appetite, were stowing away pieces as big as one's fist. The course of meat finished, they spread upon the sheepskins a great heap of parched acorns, and with them they put down a half cheese harder than if it had been made of mortar. All this while the horn was not idle, for it went round so constantly, now full, now empty, like the bucket of a water-wheel, that it soon drained one of the two wine-skins that were in sight. When Don Quixote had quite appeased his appetite, he took up a handful of the acorns, and contemplating them attentively delivered himself somewhat in this fashion:

'Happy the age, happy the time, to which the ancients gave the name of golden, not because in that fortunate age the gold so coveted in this our iron one was gained without toil, but because they that lived in it knew not the two words "mine" and "thine"! In that blessed age all things were in common; to win the daily food, no labour was required of any save to stretch forth his hand and gather it from the sturdy oaks that stood generously inviting him with their sweet ripe fruit. The clear streams and running brooks yielded their savoury limpid waters in noble abundance. The busy and sagacious bees fixed their republic in the clefts of the rocks and hollows of the trees, offering without usance the plenteous produce of their fragrant toil to every hand. The mighty cork trees, unenforced save of their own courtesy, shed the broad light bark that served at first to roof the houses supported by rude stakes, a protection against the inclemency of heaven alone. Then all was peace, all friendship, all concord; as yet the dull share of the crooked plough had not dared to rend and pierce the tender bowels of our first mother that without compulsion yielded from every portion of her broad fertile bosom all that could satisfy, sustain and delight the children that then possessed her. Then was it that the innocent and fair young shepherdesses roamed from vale to vale and hill to hill, with flowing locks, and no more garments than were needful modestly to cover what modesty seeks and ever sought to hide. Nor were their ornaments like those in use today, set off by Tyrian purple, and silk tortured in endless fashions, but the wreathed leaves of the green dock and ivy, wherewith they went as bravely and becomingly decked as our Court dames with all the rare and far-fetched artifices that idle curiosity has taught them. Then the love-thoughts of the heart clothed themselves simply and naturally as the heart conceived them, nor sought to commend themselves by forced and rambling verbiage. Fraud, deceit or malice had then not yet mingled with truth and sincerity. Justice held her ground, undisturbed and unassailed by the efforts of favour and of interest, that now so much impair, pervert and beset her. Arbitrary law had not yet established itself in the mind of the judge, for then there was no cause to judge, and no one to be judged. Maidens and modesty, as I have said, wandered at will alone and unattended, without fear of insult from lawlessness or libertine assault, and if they were undone it was of their own will and pleasure. But now, in this hateful age of ours, not one is safe, not though some new labyrinth like that of Crete conceal and surround her; even there the pestilence of gallantry will make its way to them through chinks or on the air by the zeal of its accursed importunity, and, despite of all seclusion, lead them to ruin. In defence of these, as time advanced and wickedness increased, the order of knights-errant was instituted, to defend maidens, to protect widows, and to succour the orphans and the needy. To this order I belong, brother goatherds, to whom I return thanks for the hospitality and kindly welcome ye offer me and my squire; for though by natural law all living are bound to show favour to knights-errant, yet, seeing that without knowing this obligation ye have welcomed and feasted me, it is right that with all the good-will in my power I should thank you for yours.'

All this long harangue (which might very well have been spared) our knight delivered because the acorns they gave him reminded him of the golden age; and the whim seized him to address all this unnecessary argument to the goatherds, who listened to him gaping in amazement without saying a word in reply. Sancho likewise held his peace and ate acorns, and paid repeated visits to the second wine-skin, which they had hung up on a cork tree to keep the wine cool.

Cervantes
Don Quixote
1615
Spain

1073

The promise of justice: in another world; in another life

THE SERMON ON THE MOUNT

And seeing the multitudes, he went up into a mountain: and when he was set, his disciples came unto him:

And he opened his mouth, and taught them, saying,

Blessed are the poor in spirit: for theirs is the kingdom of heaven.

Blessed are they that mourn: for they shall be comforted.

Blessed are the meek: for they shall inherit the earth.

Blessed are they which do hunger and thirst after righteousness: for they shall be filled.

Blessed are the merciful: for they shall obtain mercy.

Blessed are the pure in heart: for they shall see God.

Blessed are the peacemakers: for they shall be called the children of God.

Blessed are they which are persecuted for righteousness' sake: for theirs is the kingdom of heaven.

Blessed are ye, when men shall revile you, and persecute you, and shall say all manner of evil against you falsely, for my sake.

Rejoice, and be exceeding glad: for great is your reward in heaven: for so persecuted they the prophets which were before you.

New Testament
St. Matthew 5

1074

The law of conscience

New Testament
St. Paul's Epistle
to the Romans 2

For when the Gentiles, which have not the law, do by nature the things contained in the law, these, having not the law, are a law unto themselves:

Which shew the work of the law written in their hearts, their conscience also bearing witness, and their thoughts the mean while accusing or else excusing one another. *1075*

Charity

Though I speak with the tongues of men and of angels, and have not charity, I am become as sounding brass, or a tinkling cymbal.

And though I have the gift of prophecy, and understand all mysteries, and all knowledge; and though I have all faith, so that I could remove mountains, and have not charity, I am nothing.

And though I bestow all my goods to feed the poor, and though I give my body to be burned, and have not charity, it profiteth me nothing.

Charity suffereth long, and is kind; charity envieth not; charity vaunteth not itself, is not puffed up,

Doth not behave itself unseemly, seeketh not her own, is not easily provoked, thinketh no evil;

Rejoiceth not in iniquity, but rejoiceth in the truth;

Beareth all things, believeth all things, hopeth all things, endureth all things.

Charity never faileth: but whether there be prophecies, they shall fail; whether there be tongues, they shall cease; whether there be knowledge, it shall vanish away.

For we know in part, and we prophesy in part.

But when that which is perfect is come, then that which is in part shall be done away.

When I was a child, I spake as a child, I understood as a child, I thought as a child: but when I became a man, I put away childish things.

For now we see through a glass, darkly; but then face

547

New Testament
St. Paul's
First Epistle to the
Corinthians 13

to face: now I know in part; but then shall I know even as also I am known.

And now abideth faith, hope, charity, these three; but the greatest of these is charity. *1076*

The true
hierarchical order

Good Gotama, brahmans speak thus: 'Only brahmans form the best caste, all other castes are low; only brahmans form the fair caste, all other castes are dark; only brahmans are pure, not non-brahmans; only brahmans are own sons of Brahma, born of his mouth, born of Brahma, formed by Brahma, heirs to Brahma.' What does the good Gotama say about this?

But, Assalayana, brahman wives of brahmans are known to have their seasons and to conceive and to give birth and to give suck. Yet these brahmans, born of woman like everyone else, speak thus: 'Only brahmans form the best caste . . . are heirs to Brahma.'

. . . What do you think about this Assalayana? If a noble made onslaught on creatures, took what had not been given, wrongly enjoyed pleasures of the senses, were a liar, of slanderous speech, of harsh speech, a gossip, covetous, malevolent in mind, of wrong view—would only he at the breaking up of the body after dying arise in the sorrowful way, the bad bourn, the Downfall, Niraya Hell, and not a brahman? Nor yet a merchant? And would a worker if he made onslaught on creatures . . . were . . . of wrong view, would he at the breaking up of the body after dying, arise in the sorrowful way . . . Niraya Hell, and not a brahman?

This is not so, good Gotama. If a noble, good Gotama, made onslaught on creatures, took what had not been given . . . at the breaking up of the body after dying he would arise in . . . Niraya Hell. And so would a brahman, good Gotama, and so would a merchant, good Gotama, and so would a worker, good Gotama—so, good Gotama, if they made onslaught on creatures, took what had not been given . . . were . . . of wrong view, all the four castes at the breaking up of the body after dying would arise in the sorrowful way, the bad bourn, the Downfall, Niraya Hell.

In reference to this then, Assalayana, on what strength and authority do brahmans speak thus: 'Only brahmans form the best caste . . . are heirs of Brahma'?

Although the good Gotama speaks thus, yet brahmans still consider it thus: 'Only brahmans form the best caste . . . are heirs to Brahma.'

What do you think about this, Assalayana? If a brah-

man refrained from onslaught on creatures, from taking
what had not been given, from wrong enjoyment of the
sense-pleasures, from being a liar, from slanderous speech,
from harsh speech, from being a gossip, were not covetous,
were benevolent in mind and of right view—would only
he at the breaking up of the body after dying arise in a
good bourn, a heaven world, and not a noble, not a
merchant, nor a worker?

That is not so, good Gotama. If a noble refrained from
onslaught on creatures . . . were benevolent in mind and
of right view, at the breaking up of the body after dying
he would arise in a good bourn, a heaven world. And so
would a brahman, good Gotama, and so would a merchant,
good Gotama, and so would a worker, good Gotama—so,
good Gotama, if they refrained from onslaught on creatures,
from taking what had not been given . . . were benevolent
in mind and of right view, all the four castes at the
breaking up of the body after dying would arise in a good
bourn, a heaven world.

In reference to this then, Assalayana, on what strength
and authority do brahmans speak thus: 'Only brahmans
form the best caste . . . are heirs to Brahma'?

Although the good Gotama speaks thus, yet brahmans
still consider it thus: 'Only brahmans form the best caste . . .
are heirs to Brahma.' *1077*

Majjhima Nikaya II
Pali

Man's rank
when reborn

Even a Ksatriya, Vāsettha, who has lived a bad life in
body (*that is, action*), who has lived a bad life in word,
who has lived a bad life in thought, whose view [of life]
is false, will, as the result of his activities arising from
the false view [of life], be reborn, after the breaking up
of the body at death, to misfortune, perdition and ruin.
Even a Brāhmana. . . . Even a Vaisya. . . . Even a Sūdra. . . .
Even a Sramana. . . .

Even a Ksatriya, Vāsettha, who has lived a good life
in body, who has lived a good life in word, who has
lived a good life in thought, whose view [of life] is proper,
will, as the result of his activities, arising from the proper
view [of life], be reborn, after the breaking up of the body
at death, to a blessed, bright world. Even a Brāhmana. . . .
Even a Vaisya. . . . Even a Sūdra. . . . Even a Sramana. *1078*

Dīghanikāya IV
3rd cent. B.C.
Pali

Justice
after death

Parable of the rich man in the second story of Setne-Khamuas

Setne heard lamentations. [He] looked [. . . and saw that
there was a rich man] being borne to the necropolis. . . .

He looked [again] and saw [. . . a poor man being carried from Memphis to the cemetery . . .] and he was wrapped [in a simple sheet . . .] and [no one] walked [behind him]. Setne [said . . . how much better it must be to be the rich man in the other world . . . if comparison be made with the poor man carried [without pomp] to the necropolis.

[But Sa-Osiris (*his son*) answered: 'May it be done to thee in the other world] as will be done to this poor man in the other world. [May it not be done to thee as will be done to the rich man.']

[To explain his remark, Sa-Osiris leads Setne into the other world. After passing through four halls. . . .]

They entered the fifth hall and Setne beheld the noble souls [. . . and] those accused of violence, praying at the entrance, while the hinge of the door of the fifth hall was fixed in the right eye of a man who prayed and uttered loud cries. . . .

They entered the seventh hall and Setne perceived the silhouette of Osiris, the great god, seated on a throne of fine gold and crowned with the atef. . . .

And Setne perceived a tall man clad in byssus, standing near to Osiris. The place in which he stood was set very high.

Setne marvelled greatly at what he saw in the other world. Sa-Osiris went out before him, and said: 'Setne, my father, didst thou not see the tall man clad in byssus standing near to Osiris? The poor man whom thou sawest being carried from Memphis, when there was no one to walk behind him, was brought into the other world, and his bad deeds and his good deeds were weighed in the balance. . . . His good deeds were found to be more numerous than his bad deeds. . . . And order was given in the presence of Osiris that the funerary array of the rich man thou sawest being borne from Memphis, and for whom there was much weeping, should be given to the poor man who, as a man of God, has been set among the noble souls.

The man of rank whom thou sawest was brought into the other world, and his bad deeds and his good deeds were weighed in the balance, and his bad deeds were found to be more numerous than his good deeds. . . .

That is the man thou sawest in whose right eye was fixed the hinge of the door of the other world. It is opened and closed on his eye, and his mouth utters loud lamentations.

1079

Demotic tale
c. 500 B.C.
Ancient Egypt

Divine aid

GO DOWN, MOSES

When Israel was in Egypt land,
Let my people go,
Oppressed so hard they could not stand,
Let my people go.

Go down, Moses,
Way down in Egypt land,
Tell old Pharaoh
To let my people go.

Thus spoke the Lord, bold Moses said,
Let my people go,
If not, I'll smite your first-born dead,
Let my people go. (*Chorus*)

Your foes shall not before you stand,
Let my people go,
And you'll possess fair Canaan's land.
Let my people go. (*Chorus*)

You'll not get lost in the wilderness,
Let my people go,
With a lighted candle in your breast,
Let my people go. (*Chorus*)

Negro spiritual
United States
of America

1080

DIDN'T MY LORD DELIVER DANIEL?

He delivered Daniel from the lion's den,
And Jonah from the belly of the whale,
And the Hebrew children from the fiery furnace,
So why not every man?

Didn't my Lord deliver Da- nu- el,
Da- nu- el, Da- nu- el,
Didn't my Lord deliver Da- nu- el,
And why not every man?

The wind blows east, the wind blows west,
It blows like judgement day,
And every soul that never did pray,
Will be glad to pray that day. (*Chorus*)

The moon run down in a purple stream,
The sun refuse to shine,
And every star will disappear,
King Jesus will be mine. (*Chorus*)

Negro spiritual
United States
of America

1081

The other world,
or this one

New Testament
St. John 18

Jesus answered, My kingdom is not of this world.   *1082*

Hebrew Bible
Psalm 145

Thy kingdom is an everlasting kingdom, and thy dominion endureth throughout all generations.   *1083*

Acceptance
or revolt

Lieh-tzu
Taoist school
4th to 3rd cent. B.C.
China

One should allow everything to run its course without check or restriction. Let the ear hear what it likes, let the eye see what it likes; let the nose smell what it likes, let the mouth say what it likes; let the body enjoy what it likes and let the mind think what it likes.   *1084*

Sudanese proverb
Africa

A beard would become the bull, but God gave it to the goat.
   (*Revolt against Fate or Providence because of the unfair distribution of material goods or intellectual qualities. Moslem theologians forbid such thinking, which they regard as blasphemous.*)
   1085

Justice
will follow

Tirukkural
1st cent.
Tamil
Mauritius

As this world is not for those who are without wealth, so that world is not for those who are without kindness.

All that has been obtained with tears [to the victim] will depart with tears [to him who has obtained]; but what has been obtained by fair means, though with loss at first, will afterwards yield fruit.   *1086*

God and the
divine justice
and solicitude
are present
in this world

Since God does not like wickedness, he gave every creature a name.

It is God who pounds fufu for the one-armed man (*fufu is an Akan diet*).

If God gives you a cup of wine and an evil-minded person kicks it over, He fills it up again.

Akan proverbs
Ghana

If God gave the sparrow no other gift, He gave it at least agility.
   (*Every human being has a special talent.*)   *1087*

Remove not the old landmark; and enter not into the fields of the fatherless:

For their redeemer is mighty; he shall plead their cause with thee.   *1088*

Hebrew Bible
Proverbs 23

The sun and the moon, all creatures have an equal share in them.   *1089*

Kazakh proverb

No soul shall labour but for itself; and no burdened one shall bear another's burden. At last ye shall return to your Lord, and He will declare that to you about which you differ.

And it is He who hath made you the successors of others on the earth, and hath raised some of you above others by various grades, that he may prove you by his gifts. Verily thy Lord is swift to punish. But He is also Gracious, Merciful.   *1090*

Koran
Al-An'am 164-165

The only bond existing between God and a human creature is one of obedience [of the latter]. All men, be they mighty or feeble, are equal before God.   *1091*

Caliph Omar
ibn al-Khattāb
7th cent.

For the Lord your God is God of gods, and Lord of lords, a great God, a mighty, and a terrible, which regardeth not persons, nor taketh reward:

He doth execute the judgement of the fatherless and widow, and loveth the stranger, in giving him food and raiment.   *1092*

Hebrew Bible
Deuteronomy 10

Common reason

If our intellectual part is common, the reason also, in respect of which we are rational beings, is common: if this is so, common also is the reason which commands us what to do, and what not to do; if this is so, there is a common law also; if this is so, we are fellow-citizens; if this is so, we are members of some political community; if this is so, the world is in a manner a state. For of what other common political community will any one say that the whole human race are members? And from thence, from this common political community comes also our very intellectual faculty and reasoning faculty and our capacity for law; or whence do they come? For as my earthly part is a portion given to me from certain earth, and that which is watery from another

Marcus Aurelius
121-80
Meditations
Rome

element, and that which is hot and fiery from some peculiar source (for nothing comes out of that which is nothing, as nothing also returns to non-existence), so also the intellectual part comes from some source.

1093

*Equity
above the law*

We see in contracts and other dealings which daily pass between man and man, that, to the utter undoing of some, many things by strictness of law may be done, which equity and honest meaning forbiddeth. Not that the law is unjust, but unperfect; nor equity against, but above, the law, binding men's consciences in things which law cannot reach unto. Will any man say, that the virtue of private equity is opposite and repugnant to that law the silence whereof it supplieth in all such private dealing? No more is public equity against the law of public affairs, albeit the one permit unto some in special considerations, that which the other agreeably with general rules of justice doth in general sort forbid. For with all good laws are the voices of right reason, which is the instrument wherewith God will have the world guided; and impossible it is that right should withstand right: it must follow that principles and rules of justice, be they never so generally uttered, do no less effectually intend, than if they did plainly express, an exception of all particulars, wherein their literal practice might any way prejudice equity.

Richard Hooker
The Lawes
of Ecclesiasticall
Politie
1594
England

1094

*All men are born
to justice*

But of all the notions that occupy the learned, the most important certainly is that which makes us clearly see we are born to justice and that right is founded, not on a convention, but in nature. This will be evident if we consider the social ties that bind men. For no creatures, compared with one another, are as similar or equal as we. If unfamiliar customs and the vanity of opinions did not divert and bend our feeble, sheeplike natures, no man would more resemble himself than all would resemble all. Any hypothesis we can apply to man will apply to all— proof that there are no dissimilarities in mankind, otherwise the same definition would not embrace all. For the reason which alone raises us above the beasts, and enables us to interpret, reason, refute, discuss, conclude, is common to all men; science may differ, but all indifferently can learn. . . . Speech interprets the mind; words differ, their meaning remains unchanged. There is no man, whatever his nation, who has nature to guide him, who cannot attain virtue. . . . Sorrows, joys, desires, fears, are all

Cicero
De Legibus
c. 51 B.C.

feelings common to us; and however diverse opinions may be, it does not follow that the superstition of peoples who venerate dog and cat as gods differs in form from that of other peoples.   *1095*

I have done four good deeds within the gates of the horizon:

I have made the four winds so that every man may breathe throughout his life. This is the [first] deed.

I have made the floods so that the poor man may profit from them as much as the rich. This is the [second] deed.

Inscription
on an Egyptian
sarcophagus
XIth dynasty
End of
3rd millenary B.C.

I have made every man equal to his fellow. I have not ordained that men should commit injustice. It is their hearts that are unjust towards me. This is the [third] deed.

I have caused their hearts to cease to forget the West (*the beyond*) so that offerings may be made to the secret gods. This is the [fourth] deed.   *1096*

The old [prince] who wished to bring out the manifest virtue [of each] in the universe, first of all governed his State; wishing to govern his State, he first of all secured agreement in his family; wishing to secure agreement in his family, he first of all perfected himself; wishing to perfect himself, he first of all made his mind impartial; wishing to make his mind impartial, he first of all made his intentions sincere; wishing to make his intentions sincere, he first of all sought knowledge of himself. Possession of a knowledge of oneself is based on a knowledge of things.   *1097*

Confucian school
The Great Learning
5th cent. B.C.
China

Pope Gregory the Great (540?-604) reprimands a powerful personage who, being put in charge of an investigation into the accounts of the Byzantine administration in Sicily, indulges in preventive arrests and even torture.

But that which I know well and have ever known is that if he has committed some malversation at the expense of the public coffers, then it is his goods that should be seized, not his freedom.

. . . .

There is this difference between the barbarian kings and the emperor of the Romans, that the barbarian kings are in command of slaves, the Roman emperor of free men. That is why, in everything you do, you must first show regard for justice and then strict respect for freedom. . . . Thus the freedom of those entrusted to you for investigation you must tend specially as your own; and if you do not want your own chiefs to threaten your freedom, then protect and respect that of your subjects.

. . . .

For it would be shameful for me to defend something which I did not at once feel to be just; for I do not place justice after men, but love men because of justice. *1098*

Diversity and oneness

Types manifold of diverse living things in order'd sequence I must first unfold, O Vāsettha (said the Blessed One), to show how nature stamps them diverse breeds.

Regard the grass and trees, which ne'er proclaim, but prove, how nature stamps them diverse breeds.

Pass next to insects, pass from moths to ants; and see how nature stamps them diverse breeds.

Regard four-footed creatures, great and small; and see how nature stamps them diverse breeds.

Regard the snakes whose length on belly goes; and see how nature stamps them diverse breeds.

Pass now to fish that dwell in water's depths; and see how nature stamps them diverse breeds.

Then pass to birds that wing their airy way—all show how nature stamps them diverse breeds.

While these thus widely differ, men alone show not that nature stamps them diverse breeds.

They differ not in hair, head, ears, or eyes, in mouth or nostrils, not in eyebrows, lips, throat, shoulders, belly, buttock, backs, or chest, nor in the parts of shame, female or male, nor yet in hands or feet, in fingers, nails, in calves or thighs; in hue, or sound of voice—naught shows men stamped by nature diverse breeds; nature's diversities leave man untouched—except in names, no difference exists.

The man that lives by keeping herds of cows, know him as farmer, not as brahmin true.

The man that lives by divers handicrafts, know him as tradesman, not as brahmin true.

The man that lives by selling merchandise, know him as merchant, not as brahmin true.

The man that lives by service done for hire, know him as hireling, not as brahmin true.

The man that lives by taking things not his, know him as robber, not as brahmin true.

The man that lives by warlike sword and bow, know him as soldier, not as brahmin true.

The man that lives by sacrificial rites, know him as chaplain, not as brahmin true.

The man whom realms and broad domains support, know him as monarch, not as brahmin true.   *1099*

Sutta Nipāta
Pali
Southern India
and Ceylon

*The vision
of man
triumphant*

How does Lenin see the new world?

'Before me, a marvellous vision of the earth. . . . All men are reasonable, each feels personally responsible for all that is done by and around him. In the garden-cities majestic buildings rise; the forces of nature, tamed and marshalled by his intelligence, are everywhere working for man; and he himself—at last!—is really master of the elements. His physical energy is no longer spent on heavy, dirtying work but made over to the spirit, and entirely concentrated on life's great problems....

Technically bettered, socially enhanced, work is becoming his pleasure. Really free at last, his reason has become the most precious thing in the world—and truly fearless.'...

I do not believe I am attributing dreams to Lenin that are foreign to him, or that I am romanticizing this man—I cannot imagine him without this splendid dream of future happiness for all men, of happy, joyous life. The greater the man, the more audacious his dreams.

1100

V. I. Lenin
Quoted by
Maxim Gorky
1920

*Collectivity
and the human
soul*

PRELUDE TO A DECLARATION OF DUTIES TO THE HUMAN BEING

We owe a cornfield respect, not because of itself, but because it is food for mankind.

In the same way, we owe our respect to a collectivity, of whatever kind—country, family or any other—not for itself, but because it is food for a certain number of human souls.

Actually, this obligation makes different attitudes, actions necessary according to different situations. But, taken by itself, it is absolutely identical for everybody. More particularly is this so for all those outside such a collectivity.

The degree of respect owing to human collectivities is a very high one, for several reasons.

To start with, each is unique, and, if destroyed, cannot be replaced. One sack of corn can always be substituted for another sack of corn. The food which a collectivity supplies for the souls of those who form part of it has no equivalent in the entire universe.

Secondly, because of its continuity, a collectivity is

already moving forward into the future. It contains food, not only for the souls of the living, but also for the souls of beings yet unborn which are to come into the world during the immediately succeeding centuries.

Lastly, due to this same continuity, a collectivity has its roots in the past. It constitutes the sole agency for preserving the spiritual treasures accumulated by the dead, the sole transmitting agency by means of which the dead can speak to the living. And the sole earthly reality which is directly connected with the eternal destiny of Man is the irradiating light of those who have managed to become fully conscious of this destiny, transmitted from generation to generation.

Because of all this, it may happen that the obligation towards a collectivity which is in danger reaches the point of entailing a total sacrifice. But it does not follow from this that collectivities are superior to human beings. It sometimes happens, too, that the obligation to go to the help of a human being in distress makes a total sacrifice necessary, without that implying any superiority on the part of the individual so helped.

Simone Weil
The Need for Roots
1942-43
France

1101

*Man left
to himself alone*

A delicate business, walking as it were on tiptoe across a worm-eaten beam over a gulf, with nothing beneath your feet; composing, by the pressure of your feet, the beam on which you are going to walk; walking on nothing but your own reflexion, glimpsed below you in the water; keeping the world there with your feet, clenching your hands only when you raise them in the air to help you surmount that effort.

Kafka
1883-1924
Diaries
Czechoslovakia

1102

Kafka
Meditations
1913
Czechoslovakia

The Messiah will not come until he is no longer necessary, he will not come until a day after his advent, he will not come at the last day but at the last of all.

1103

Bibliography

The Unesco Secretariat has made every effort to obtain explicit authorization for the reproduction of any excerpts included in this collection which are not already out of copyright, and has been courteously granted permission in almost all cases. It apologises for any omissions, and for having included certain passages despite the fact that it has been unable to trace the authors or publishers of the works concerned.

The Secretariat gratefully acknowledges the help received from all the publishers and authors listed in this bibliography, which was prepared by Mrs. Dilek Desaive.

The bibliography comprises two parts :
I. Names of authors or, failing this, the titles of the works from which the excerpts are taken.
II. Categories of material for which no author or title can be given. These are arranged in alphabetical order according to category.

I

ARDASHĪR I *or* Artaxerxes (3rd cent., Persia, founder of Sassanid dynasty). Translated into English by I. Abbas. In: *Ahd Ardashīr*, p. 56, 60-1. Beirut, Dar Sader, 1967   *259, 207*

ARISTOTLE (*c.* 384-322 B.C., Greece). *Constitution d'Athènes*, ch. XII, XXIX, XLV, LV. Translated into French by G. Mathieu and B. Houssaullier. Paris, Les Belles Lettres, 1958   *807, 155, 358, 357*

——. *The politics of Aristotle*. Translated into English by E. Barker. Oxford, Clarendon Press, 1946 (By permission of the publishers.)   *951*

ARNOLD, E. (Czech writer, 1800-69). The interim law on the press (1849). In: [*Czech Radical Democrats*]. Prague, SNPL, 1953   *448*

ARTIGAS, J. (1764-1850, Uruguay). Declaration of 3 May 1815, in Corrientes (Argentina). In: *Ideario de Artigas*, p. 27. Montevideo, 1952   *829*

ASCHAM, R. (1515-68, England). *The Scholemaster* (1570), p. 31-2. Arber, 1870   *760*

ASEEV, N. N. (1889-1963, U.S.S.R.). [Mayakovsky begins] (1940). Translated into French by E. Triolet in *La poésie russe*, p. 298-9. Paris, Seghers, 1965   *470*

ASVAGHOSA, attributed to (*c.* 50 B.C. to 50 A.D., India). Sanskrit. *Vajrasūci*, 8-9   *520*

ATATÜRK, Kemal Pasha (1881-1938, Turkey). In: *Atatürk*, p. 164, 201, 202. Ankara, Turkish National Commission for Unesco, 1963   *121, 779, 1011*

Atharvaveda (2200-1800 B.C., India). Vedic Sanskrit. I. 31. 4; X. 2. 1-9, 11-13; X. 8. 25, 28; XI. 4. 20, 23; XII. 1. 1-3; XIX. 15. 5-6   *69, 996, 128, 997, 789, 858*

AUGUSTINE, Saint, Bishop of Hippo (354-430). In: *The city of God*, XIX, 15-16. Translated into English by Marcus Dods. Published by W. Benton, Chicago, London and Toronto, Encyclopaedia Britannica Inc.   *794*

——. Hymn to the Church. In: *De moribus ecclesiae catholicae*, L. I, c. 30, n. 63. In: *Patrologia Latina*, vol. XXXII, col. 1336. Paris, Migne, 1861   *971*

——. *Treatise on St. John's Epistle to the Parthians*, VIII, 6 and 8. In: *Patrologia latina*, vol. XXXV, cols. 2039, 2040. Paris, Migne, 1861   *1055, 735*

Avesta. Vendidad (1st cent. B.C. to 1st cent. A.D., Persia). III, 2-3; III, 11; III, 34   *788, 88, 576*

——. *Yasna.* Gāthās (of Zarathustra) (pre-6th cent. B.C., Persia). 44, 12-14; 46, 1-8. Translated into English by M. Henning (from the French translation by J. Duchesne-Guillemin). In: *The hymns of Zarathustra*, p. 70, 75. London, John Murray, 1952. (Wisdom of the East series)   *59, 646*

AVVAKUM (1621-82, Russia). [The life of the archpriest Avvakum, written by himself.] In: [*Russian historical library*], vol. 39, cols. 65, 154-5; 823. Leningrad, 1927   *495, 432*

——. [Works.] In: [*Russian historical library*], vol. 39, cols. 917 and 928, 402; 928 and 929, paras. 4 and 5. Moscow, 1939   *1061*

BABA, T. (1850-88, Japan). [*Autobiography of Kentarō Kaneko*]   *426*

Babad Tanah Jawi (Javanese historiography) (1626). Edited by W. L. Olthof. The Hague, Martinus Nijhoff; Leiden, Kroninklijk Instituut voor Taal-, Land- en Volkenkunde, 1941   *227*

BABEUF, G. (1760-97, France). Letter to his wife. In: *Pages choisies de Babeuf*. Paris, 1935   *694*

——. Analysis of the *Doctrine* of Babeuf by P.-S. Maréchal. Cited by M. Leroy in *Histoire des idées sociales*, vol. II, p. 74-5. Paris, Gallimard, 1950   *696*

BAKUNIN, M. (1814-76, Russia). Cited in H. Avron, *Bakounine*, Paris, Seghers, 1966; F. Munoz, *Bakounine, la liberté*, Paris, Pauvert, 1965   *622; 123, 721*

BALASSA, B. (1554-94, Hungary). Letter to the Archduke Ernest in defence of a serf accused of stealing copper, 25 January 1587   *888*

BALCESCU, N. (1819-52, Romania). Speech. *Junimea Română*, Paris, no. 2, June 1851   *935*

BARBOSA, R., known as the Eagle of La Haye (1849-1923, Brazil). Comments on the Republican Constitution of 1891   *273*

BARBOUR, J. (*c.* 1320-95, Scotland). *The Brus.* In: *The Oxford book of English verse,* p. 10-11   *293*

BARTÓK, B. (1881-1945, Hungary). Letter to Octavian Beu, (Bucharest, 1931). In: *Bartók, sa vie et son œuvre.* Budapest, Corvina, 1956   *1018*

BAŠKIN, M. (16th cent., Russia). Cited by Grekov in [*Les paysans en Russie*], vol. II, p. 28. Moscow, 1954   *825*

BEAUPLAN, Marquis of (17th cent., France). *Description d'Ukraine,* p. 54, 61. Rouen, 1660   *168, 111*

BECCARIA, C. (1738-94, Italy). *Treatise on crimes and punishments* (1764). Printed for F. Newbury. London, 1770   *375, 895*
Translated into French by Chevalier in *Des délits et des peines.* Edited by F. Venturi. Geneva, Droz, 1965   *374, 397, 881, 889*

BELLO, A. (1781-1865, Chile). *El Araucano.* Santiago (Chile), 1833   *882*

BENTHAM, J. (1748-1832, Great Britain). False methods of reasoning on the subject of legislation. In: *Principles of legislation* (1789), ch. XIII. Text written by Etienne Dumont based on the comments and notes of Bentham   *258*

Beowulf (8th cent., England). Epic poem   *206*

BERGSON, H. (1859-1941, France). In: *Les deux sources de la morale et de la religion.* Paris, Alcan-Presses Universitaires de France, 1932   *1044*

BESSENYEI, G. (1746-1811, Hungary). [*The commonalty*] (1804)   *314*

BÈZE, T. de (1519-1605, France). *Du droit des magistrats sur leurs sujets* (1581)   *269*

BEZRUČ, P. (1867-1958, Czechoslovakia). [*The collier*] (1920). Translated into English by J. Milner. In: *Silesian songs.* Prague, Artia, 1966   *657*

Bhāgavata-Purāna (9th to 10th cent., India). Sanskrit. IX, 21, 12   *29*

BIBLE, *see* Hebrew Bible *and* New Testament

BLANC, L. (1811-82, France). *Catéchisme des socialistes.* Paris, 1849   *702*

BLANQUI, A. (1798-1854, France). Letter to Maillard (6 June 1852)   *703*

———. *Procès des quinze* (12 January 1832)   *698*

BLOK, A. (1880-1921, U.S.S.R.). Address delivered at the celebration of the eighty-fourth anniversary of the death of Pushkin, 11 February [29 January] 1921. In : V. Orlov (ed.), [*Collected works of Alexander Blok*]. Moscow, Leningrad, State Publishing House for Literature, 1946. Translated into French by J. Gauvain in *Nova et vetera,* Geneva, May-August 1948   *791*

BLUM, L. (1872-1950, France). Notes d'Allemagne (1945). In: *L'œuvre de Léon Blum,* vol. I, p. 503-7. Paris, Albin Michel, 1955   *547*

BODIN, J. (1529-96, France). *De la République* (1576)   *1009*

BOISSY D'ANGLAS, F. A. (1756-1826, France). Cited by J. Laferrière in *Manuel de droit constitutionnel,* p. 107. 2nd ed. Paris, 1947   *701*

BOLINGBROKE, Henry St.-John, Viscount (1678-1751, Great Britain). Letter to Alexander Pope (1730)   *445*

BOLÍVAR, S. (1783-1830, South America). Discurso del Libertador al congreso constituyente de Bolivia (1826). In: *Obras completas,* vol. III, p. 762-3. Havana, 1950   *830*

———. Letter from a South American to a Jamaican (1815)   *950*

———. Speech delivered to the Assembly of Angostura (Ciudad Bolivar), Venezuela, 15 February 1819   *326*

BONALD, L. de (1754-1840, France). In: *Œuvres*, vols. IV and V. Paris, 1882   *699*

Book of wisdom (Ptolemaic period, 7th to 6th cent. B.C., Egypt). Demotic. Translated by A. Volten, Die moralischen Lehren des Demotischen. In: *Studi in memoria di Ippolito Rosselini*, vol. II, p. 271. Pisa, Università degli Studi di Pisa and Industrie Grafiche V. Lischi e Figli, 1955   *104*

BOSSUET, J. B. (1627-1704, France). Sermon sur l'éminente dignité des pauvres dans l'Église (1659)   *665*

BUBER, M. (1878-1965, Israel). In: M. Buber and F. Rosenzweig, *Die Schrift und ihre Verdeutschung [On Germanizing the Bibel]*, p. 28. Berlin, New York, Schocken Verlag, 1936 (With the authorization of Mr. Rafael Buber.)   *146*

BUENO, P., Marquis of São Vicente (1803-78, Brazil). Comments on the Imperial Constitution of 1824   *272*

BUKHARIN, N. (1888-1938, U.S.S.R.). Cited by B. Goriely in *Les poètes dans la révolution russe*. Paris, Gallimard, 1934   *467*

BURCKHARDT, J. (1818-97, Switzerland). Original in *Weltgeschichtliche Betrachtungen* (1905). Translated into French by S. Stelling-Michaud in *Considérations sur l'histoire universelle*. Geneva, Droz, 1965   *328*

BURKE, E. (1729-97, Great Britain). Reflections on the revolution in France, (1790). In: *Works*, II, p. 330-6   *320*

BURLAMAQUI, J.-J. (1694-1748, Switzerland). In: *Principes du droit naturel*, p. 64, 66, 67, 150, 172. Geneva, 1747   *302*

CABELLO BALBOA, M. (16th cent., Spain). In: Luis E. Valcarcel, *Miscelánea Antártica*, part 3, ch. 19, p. 349. Lima, University of San Marcos, 1951   *335*

CALVIN, J. (1509-64, France). *Institution de la religion chrétienne*. Latin (1536) and French (1541)   *250*

CAMUS, A. (1913-60, France). Reply to Gabriel Marcel. Actuelles I (*Combat*, 1948); Letter to a German friend (July 1943). In: *Essais*, p. 395-6; p. 222-3. Paris, Gallimard, 1965 (Coll. Pléiade)   *435, 925*

CAÑAS Y VILLACORTA, J. S. (19th cent., El Salvador). Motion calling for the abolition of slavery, presented to the Constituent Assembly of the United Provinces of Central America (1823)   *839*

CANKAR, I. (Slovene poet, 1876-1918). [*Jernej the servant and his rights*], vol. XI, ch. V, p. 181 et seq. Ljubljana (Yugoslavia), 1930   *661*

ČAPEK, K. (Czech writer, 1890-1938). [*Fables and little tales*], p. 187. Prague, Ceskoslovensky Spisovatel, 1963   *450, 770, 850, 963*

CARLEN, A. (Switzerland). Das Oberwalliser Theater im Mittelalter. In: *Archives suisses de traditions populaires*, vol. 42, p. 65 et seq. Basle, 1945   *284*

CASTELLANE, B. de (1844-1917, France). Speech. In: *Annales de l'Assemblée Nationale*, III, 701. Paris, 3 July 1871   *722*

CATHERINE II, the Great (1729-96, Russia). Instruction to the commission in charge of drawing up a new code, art. 210   *897*

CELESTINE I (pope, 422-32)   *158*

CERVANTES, M. de (1547-1616, Spain). *Don Quixote* (1615), part I, ch. 2 and 4. Translated into English by John Ormsby. Chicago, Encyclopaedia Britannica Inc., 1952 (Great books of Western world series)   *1073, 638*

CÉSAIRE, A. (Martinique). In: *Cahier d'un retour au pays natal*. Paris, Présence Africaine, 1947   *853*

——. Speech (1948). In: *Commémoration du centenaire de l'abolition de l'esclavage*, p. 28 et seq. Paris, Presses Universitaires de France, 1950.   *854*

CHANDIDĀS (Bengali poet, *c.* 15th cent., India) 1046

Chāndogya-Upanishad (8th to 6th cent. B.C., India). Vedic Sanskrit. IV, 4, 3-5 774

CHAO CHIH-HSIN (17th cent., China). [The repudiated wife.] Translated into French by P. Guillermaz in *La poésie chinoise,* p. 246. Paris, Seghers, 1957 664

CHARLES V, *see* Decrees, Bibliog. II

CHASTUSHKI, *see* Folk-poetry, Bibliog. II

CHEKHOV, A. (1860-1904, Russia). *The cherry orchard* (1904) 652

——. *Gooseberries* (1898) 686

CHELČICKÝ, P. (Czech writer, *c.* 1390-1460). *Of three estates (clergy, state and people), or: Of secular power.* In: [*Otto's Encyclopaedical Dictionary*], vol. XII. Prague, Otto, 1897 153

CHÉNIER, A. (1762-94, France). *Apologie* 898

CHIEH HSI-SZŬ (1274-1344, China). *La citadelle de Kao-yeou.* Translated into French by Siao Che-kiun in *Anthologie de la poésie chinoise classique,* p. 421. Paris, Gallimard, 1962 926

Chilām Balām de Chumayel, (Text recorded in 16th cent., Central America). Sacred book of the Maya. Spanish translation by A. Mediz Bolio in *Libro del Chilām Balām de Chumayel,* 2nd ed., p. 16-17, 25-6, 158. Mexico, Universidad Nacional, 1952 828

——. Folio 20, translated into English by M. León Portilla 949

CHOU TUN-I (1017-73, China). [Penetrating the Book of Changes.] Translated into English by Chan Wing-tsit in *A source book of Chinese philosophy,* p. 468. New York and London, Columbia University Press, 1963 756

CHUANG-TZU (3rd cent.? B.C., China). In: L. Wieger, *Les pères du système taoïste,* p. 264 and 318 et seq. Paris, Cathasia/Belles Lettres, 1913 172, 1022

CICERO (106-43 B.C., Rome). *De legibus,* (*c.* 51 B.C.), book I, arts. 10 and 11. Translated into French by C. Appuhn in *Cicéron. De la République. Des lois.* Paris, Garnier, 1954 1095

——. *De officiis,* I, 10, 33. Latin legal adage quoted by Cicero. VII, 23 and 24. Translated into English by W. Miller. Cambridge, Mass., Harvard University Press; London, Heinemann, 1961 (Loeb classical library) 241, 369

——. *Of good and evil,* XIX, 62. Translated into English by H. Rackham. Cambridge, Mass., Harvard University Press; London, Heinemann, 1914 (Loeb classical library) 1048

CIEZA DE LEÓN, P. (Spanish chronicler of Peru, 1518-66). In: *Del señorío de los Incas,* ch. XIII, p. 84; ch. XIX, p. 115. Buenos Aires, 1943 210, 592, 674

CLOOTS, ANACHARSIS, J. B. du Val-de-Grâce, Baron de (1755-94, France). Speech delivered on 26 April 1793 1041

COBO, B. (1572-1659, South America). In: *Historia del Nuevo Mundo* (1653), vol. III, book 12, ch. 26, p. 238, 241. Seville, 1892 221, 222, 379

COMENIUS, J. A. (Czech writer, 1592-1670). *De rerum humanarum emendatione consultatio catholica* [General consultation on the reform of human affairs] 447, 498, 593
914

——. *Didaktika* 749

——. *The Pampaedia,* ch. II, 10 1034
Quoted in: *J. A. Comenius. Selections.* Paris, Unesco, 1957 741

——. *Via lucis* [The path of light] 748

CONDORCET, A. Caritat, Marquis of (1743-94, France). *Esquisse d'un tableau historique des progrès de l'esprit humain* (1798)   *713, 750*

——. *Fragment sur l'Atlantide, ou efforts combinés de l'espèce humaine pour le progrès des sciences* (1794)   *776*

——. *Œuvres* (1794), VIII, p. 27   *917*

——. *Vie de Turgot* (1786), p. 284-7   *454, 767*

CONFUCIAN SCHOOL (5th cent. B.C., China). *The great learning*   *185, 305*
In: S. Couvreur, *Les quatre livres*, I: *La grande étude*, p. 3-4. Paris, Cathasia/Belles
Lettres, 1895   *1097*

CONFUCIUS (551-479? B.C., China). *Analects.* Translated into English by L. Giles in
The sayings of Confucius, p. 40-1, 45. London, John Murray, 1907 (Wisdom of
the East series)   *184*
Translated into English by Chan Wing-tsit in *A source book of Chinese philosophy*,
p. 39. New York and London, Columbia University Press, 1963   *2*
In: S. Couvreur, *Les quatre livres.* III: *Entretiens de Confucius et de ses disciples*,
p. 135-6, 236. Paris, Cathasia/Belles Lettres, 1895   *772, 966*

——. *Shu-ching* (attr.) Translated into French by E. Balazs in *Le traité juridique de
Souei-chou.* vol. IX, p. 223. Leiden, Brill, 1954   *203*

CORNELIUS, Saint (3rd cent.)   *157*

CRUCÉ, E. (1590-1648, France), *Le nouveau Cynée ou discours d'Estat représentant les
occasions et moyens d'établir une paix generalle et la liberté du commerce par tout le monde.
Aux Monarques et Princes souverains de ce temps* (1623)   *957, 1020*

CURRAN, J. P. (1750-1806, Ireland). Speech (29 January 1794) in defence of
A. H. Rowan, Secretary of the Society of United Irishmen in Dublin, indicted
for publishing a seditious libel   *455*

CYRIL, Saint, Patriarch of Alexandria (376-444). *Commentarius in Joannis Evangelium*
[Commentary on the Gospel according to St. John], I, 9. In: *Patrologia graeca*, vol.
LXXIII, cols. 161c-164a. Paris, Migne, 1861   *977*

Dādistān i Dēnig (9th cent., Persia). Pursišn 34, 62   *61, 481*

Dādistān i Mēnōg i Xrad (Sassanian period, 3rd to 7th cent., Persia). Chap. 2, 19, 29,
32, 33. Taken with modifications from the English translation by E. West in *Sacred
books of the East*, vol. 24, Pahlavi texts, part III, p. 9, 50, 66-7, 68-9. Delhi, Vara-
nasi and Patna, Motilal Banarsidass, 1965   *542, 1047, 60, 786, 209*

DANTE (1265-1321, Florence). *De monarchia* (1308). Translated into French by
B. Landry in *De la monarchie.* Paris, Alcan-Presses Universitaires de France,
1933.   *1070, 1071*

——. *The divine comedy.* Translated into English by Carlyle and Wicksteed. New
York, Random House Inc., 1932. Inferno XXVI, 118-20; Purgatorio I, 71-2;
Paradiso IV, 124-32   *731, 292, 732*

DAVIES, Sir John (1569-1626, England). Man. In: *The Oxford book of English verse*,
p. 212-13   *152*

DEMBOWSKI, E. (1822-46, Poland). The absolute freedom of the people (1843)   *623*

DEMOSTHENES (384-322 B.C., Greece). Oration on financial organization (*c.* 349
B.C.). Translated into French by M. Croiset in *Démosthène, Harangues*, vol. I.
Paris, Les Belles Lettres, 1946   *607*

Dēnkart (9th cent., Persia). Book VI   *32, 33, 482, 687, 787, 1032*

Dhammapada [Verses on the law] (India). Pali   *733*

DIDEROT, D. (1713-84, France). Entry on 'Persecution'; entry on 'Refugees'. In:
Encyclopédie, ou dictionnaire raisonné des sciences, des arts et des métiers (1751-72)   *502, 507*

Dighanikāya (3rd cent. B.C., India). Pali. IV, 2. 6; IV, 4. 26   775, *1078*

DISRAELI, B. (1804-81, England). *Sybil, or The two nations*, p. 121. Paris, Baudry's European Library, 1845   *589*

DONNE, J. (1572-1631, England). *Donne's devotions* (1624), XVII   *37*

DOSTOEVSKY, F. (1821-81, Russia). *The brothers Karamazov* (1880). Translated into English by C. Garnett. New York, Random House Inc.; London, Heinemann (The modern library)   *147*

——. *The house of the dead* (1861), p. 193-4. Translated into English by H. S. Edwards. London, Dent; New York, Dutton, 1962 (Everyman's library) (Reprinted by permission of the publishers.)   *890*

——. *Notes from underground* (1864), vol. I, ch. 8.   *143*

DUBOIS, P. (14th cent., France). *De recuperatione Terrae Sanctae* (1306). French translation cited by C. Lange in *Histoire de l'internationalisme*. Christiania (Oslo), Ascheloug & Co. (W. Nygaard), 1919   *955*

DUNANT, H. (1828-1910, Switzerland). *Un souvenir de Solferino* (1862)   *922*

DUPLESSIS-MORNAY, P. (1549-1623, France). *Vindiciae contra tyrannos* (1579)   *285*

DUPONT DE NEMOURS, P. S. (1739-1817, France). *Cahier du bailliage de Nemours* (1789)   *700*

ECHEVERRÍA, E. (1805-51, Argentina). Socialist creed of the May Association. In: *El Iniciador*, vol. II. Montevideo, 1838   *716*

EHRENBURG, I. (1891-1967, U.S.S.R.). [*The fantastic adventures of Julio Jurenito*] (1921). Moscow, 1923. Translated into French by D. Meunier in *Les aventures extraordinaires de Julio Jurenito*. Paris, Plon, 1964   *304*

EMRE, Y. (13th cent., Turkey). In: A. Gölpinarli, *Yunus Emre ve Tasavvuf*. Istanbul, Remzi, 1961   *20, 21, 85, 497, 628, 1000*

ENGELS, F. (1820-95, Germany). *Die Lage der Arbeiterklasse* [The situation of the working classes in England] (1845). In: *Marx-Engels Werke*, vol. II. Berlin, Dietz, 1959   *655*

——. *Zur Kritik der Sozialdemokratischen Programmentwurfs* [Criticism of the Gotha and Erfurt Programmes] (1891). In: *Marx-Engels Werke*, vol. XXII. Berlin, Dietz, 1963.   *511*

——. *Anti-Dühring* (1878). In: *Marx-Engels Werke*, vol. XX, Berlin, Dietz, 1963   *512, 621*

——. Letter to August Bebel, 18-28 March 1875. In: *Marx-Engels Werke*, vol. XXXIV. Berlin, Dietz, 1966   *424*

EPICTETUS (1st cent., Greece). *Discourses*. Translated into English by T. W. Higginson in *Works of Epictetus*. Boston, Little, Brown & Co., 1890   *136, 964*

ERASMUS, D., of Rotterdam (1469-1536). *Querela pacis undique gentium ejectae profligataeque* (1515). Translated into French by E. Constantinescu-Bagdat in *La 'Querela Pacis' d'Erasme*. Paris, 1924   *911*

ESCHENBACH, W. von (1170-1220?, Germany). *Willehalm* (Old German, *c.* 1212), p. 306, v. 18-19 and 25-30, p. 307, v. 1-30; p. 309, v. 1-6; p. 450, v. 15-20. In: K. Lachmann, *Wolfram von Eschenbach*, 6th ed., Berlin and Leipzig, de Gruyter, 1926; re-edited, Berlin, 1962   *491, 919, 1017*

EURIPIDES (480-405? B.C., Greece). *Electra*. Translated into English by R. Potter, American translation by J. Warrington. In: *Plays by Euripides*. New York, Dutton; London, Dent, 1906 (Everyman's library) (Reprinted by permission of the publishers.)   *541*

——. *The Phoenician maidens* (*c.* 408 B.C.). Translated into French by G. Duclos in *Euripide, Théâtre*, vol. III. Paris, Garnier, 1935   *1027*

——. *The suppliants*. Translated into English by M. Woodhull, American translation by J. Warrington. In: *Plays by Euripides*, New York, Dutton; London, Dent, 1906 (Everyman's library) (Reprinted by permission of the publishers.)   *310*

FÉNELON, F. de Salignac de la Mothe- (1651-1715, France). *Examen de conscience sur les devoirs de la royauté* (1711)   *920*

FICHTE, J. G. (1762-1814, Germany). *Beiträge zur Berichtigung der Urteile des Publikums über die französische Revolution* (1793). In: *Sämtliche Werke*, vol. VI. Berlin, Verlag von Veit und Comp., 1846   *916*

FLETCHER, G., *see Life of St. Basil*

FOURIER, C. (1772-1837, France). *Théorie des quatre mouvements et des destinées générales* (1808)   *597*

FREYRE, R. J. (1868-1933, Bolivia). *Justicia India*. In: *Antología de cuentistas hispano-americanos*—texts chosen by J. Sanz y Sanz. Madrid, 1961   *651*

FUKUZAWA, Y. (1834-1901, Japan). *Encouragement of learning*. Cf. *Autobiography of Y. Fukuzawa*. New York and London, Columbia University Press, 1966   *519*

FUZŪLĪ (Turkish poet, 16th cent.,). A poem in Persian addressed to Sultan Suleiman I, the Magnificent. Translated into English from a Turkish version of 1834   *211*

GANDHI, Mahatma (1869-1948, India). *All men are brothers. Life and thoughts of Mahatma Gandhi as told in his own words*. Paris, Unesco, 1958. By permission of the Navajivan Trust, Ahmedabad (India)   *14, 38, 39, 116, 117, 151, 278, 308, 446, 518, 635, 690, 691, 761, 771, 869, 1012, 1013, 1033*

GARCILASO DE LA VEGA (El Inca) (1539?-1617, Peru). *Comentarios reales de los Incas*. Lima, Buenos Aires, 1959   *380, 381, 564, 747, 782, 946*

Gāthās of Zarathustra, *see Avesta*

Genesis (*c*. 1065). Old German. Sixteenth-century Viennese manuscript. In: V. Dolmayr (ed.), *Die altdeutsche Genesis*. Halle (Germany), Max Niemeyer Verlag, 1932   *797*

GHALIB (1797-1869, India). Urdu. *Diwan* (1841)   *149*

GONZAGA, T. A. (1744-1810, Brazil). *Tratado de direito natural* [Treatise on natural law] (1768)   *148*

GORDIAN, *see Institutes of Justinian*, Bibliog. II

GORKY, M. (A. M. Peshkov) (1868-1936, U.S.S.R.). [*The lower depths*] (1902)   *1045*

——. *Mother*. Original edition, Berlin, 1906. Translated into French by Huntzbucler in *Collection œuvres complètes*. Paris, Éditeurs Français Réunis, 1946   *658*

——. *Vladimir Iliitch Lénine* (1920). Translated into French by A. Pierre in *Écrits de révolution de Maxime Gorki*. Paris, Stock, 1922   *1100*

GREGORY I, the Great (pope, 590-604). *Registrum epistularum*, IV, epistle XIII, 15. In: *Monumenta Germaniae historica*, vol. I, p. 250 and vol. II, p. 383   *809, 486*

——. Letter. In: *Patrologia latina*, vol. LXXVII, col. 1106. Paris, Migne, 1861   *1098*

GREGORY IX (pope, 1227-41). *Decretals* (1191-98), book I, tit. VI, ch. XIV   *159*

GREGORY, Saint, Bishop of Nyssa (*c*. 334-94, Asia Minor). *The creation of man*, ch. XVI. Translated into French by J. Laplace in *La création de l'homme*, p. 159-61, Paris, Éditions du Cerf, 1943 (Coll. Sources Chrétiennes, no. 6)   *974*

GRÉGR, J. (Czech writer, 1831-96)   *851*

GROTIUS, H. (1583-1645, Holland). In: *De jure belli et pacis* [The law of war and of peace] (1624)   *962, 1049*

GUILLAUME DE MANDAGOUT (cardinal, 13th cent.). *Libellum super electionibus* (1285)   *162*

GÜVAHI, *see* proverbs (Turkish), Bibliog. II

Habeas Corpus, see Cases: *Sommersett's case*, Bibliog. II

Hadith [Sayings of the Prophet Mohammed]　*8, 11, 44, 66, 67, 232, 282, 341, 342, 555,*
627, 632, 742, 985, 987

Hankampu, see Arai, Hakuseki

HAN YÜ (768-824, China). [Discourse on teachers.] In: W. Theodore de Bary (ed.),
Sources of Chinese tradition, p. 430. New York and London, Columbia University
Press, 1960　　*757*

HARLAN, Judge, *see* Cases: *Plessy* v. *Ferguson*, Bibliog. II

HASSAN AL-YUSSI (sheikh, 17th cent., North Africa). Letter to Sultan Mulay
Ismaïl　　*235*

Hebrew Bible.
Genesis 2: 7　　*967*
Exodus 22: 25-6　　*535*
Leviticus 19: 18 and 34; 25: 10 and 55　　　　　*3, 348; 806, 804* (para. 1)
Deuteronomy 5: 12-16; 10: 17-18; 15: 1 and 12-16; 23: 16-17 and 25-6; 24: 6,
　14-15 and 21-2; 27: 19　　　*598; 1092; 599, 805; 848, 689; 595, 575, 5; 105*
I Samuel 8: 11-17　　*798*
I Kings 12: 7　　*202*
Nehemiah 5: 9-12　　*910*
Job 31: 13-15　　*524*
Psalms 8: 5-7; 10: 9-18; 145: 13　　　　*140, 1059, 1083*
Proverbs 23: 10-11; 24: 17　　　　*1088, 6*
Isaiah 3: 14-15 and 5: 8; 61: 1　　　*553, 1058*
Amos 2: 6-8　　*517*
Micah 4: 1-6; 6: 6-8　　　*475, 1062*
Quoted in: L. Finkelstein (ed.), *The Jews, their history, culture and religion,*
vol. III, ch. 27. Philadelphia, Harper & Row Inc., 1949

HERACLITUS, of Ephesus (*c.* 540-480 B.C., Asia Minor). In: A. Jeannière, *La pensée*
d'Héraclite d'Ephèse, avec la traduction intégrale des fragments. Paris, Aubier-Montaigne,
1959　　*247*

HERDER, J. C. von (1744-1803, Germany). Letter of 1796. In: *Briefe zur Beförderung*
der Humanität (1793-97)　　*62*

HERNÁNDEZ, J. (1834-86, Argentina). *La vuelta de Martín Fierro* (1879)　　*650, 845*

HERODOTUS (*c.* 484-425 B.C., Greece). *Discourse by Otanes.* In: *History*, Book III, ch. 80.
Translated into English by G. Rawlinson. New York, Random House Inc., 1942　　*309*

———. *History*, Book VI, ch. 108. Translated into French by P. E. Legrand.
Histoires, Paris, Les Belles Lettres, 1948　　*960*

HERZEN, A. (1812-70, Russia). *De l'autre rive.* Lettre V: *Consolatio.* In: *Textes philo-*
sophiques choisis, p. 454-5. Moscow, Éditions en Langues Étrangères　　*439*

———. Letter of 1 June 1849. In: *Lettres de France et d'Italie* (1847-52). Geneva, 1871　　*329*

HESIOD (8th cent. B.C., Greece). *Works and days.* Translated into English by Sir
W. Morris in *Oxford book of Greek verse.* Oxford, Clarendon Press, 1938 (By
permission of the publishers.)　　*865*

HIDALGO, B., attributed to (1788-1823, Uruguay). 'Cielito' [Ballad from Casa-Flores]　　*641*

HIKMET, N. (1902-63, Turkey). [*Of death*] (1946). Translated into French by
H. Güreh in *Anthologie poétique.* Paris, Éditeurs Français Réunis, 1964　　*899*

HILAIRE, Saint, Bishop of Poitiers, (died in 367). *Commentaire sur l'évangile de St.*
Matthieu, II, 5 and IV, 12. In: *Patrologia latina*, vol. IX, cols. 927 and 935. Paris,
Migne, 1861　　*972*

HIPPOCRATES (*c.* 460-377 B.C., Greece). Oath. English translation in *Hippocratic*
writings. Chicago, London and Toronto, W. Benton, Encyclopaedia Britannica Inc.　　*781*

HOLT, *see* Cases: *Ashby* v. *White*, Bibliog. II.

HOMER (9th cent. B.C., Greece). *The Iliad*, VI and XXIV. Translated into English by E. V. Rieu. Harmondsworth, Middlesex, Penguin Books Ltd., 1950   *1014, 1015*

HOOKER, Rev. R., known as The Judicious Hooker (1533-1600, England). *The lawes of ecclesiasticall politie* (1594)   *35, 1094*

HSÜN-TZU (3rd cent. B.C., China). *Hsün-tzu*
The biography of Tung Chung-shu   *255*
The way of the Emperor   *254*
Enriching the country   *608*
The way of kings   *187, 1028*
Cf. English translation by B. Watson in: *Hsün-tzu, basic writings*. New York and London, Columbia University Press, 1963

HUANG TSUNG-HSI (1610-95, China). *Ming-i tai-fang lu*. In: W. Theodore de Bary (ed.), *Sources of Chinese tradition*, p. 590-1. New York and London, Columbia University Press, 1960   *220, 778*

HUGO, V. (1802-85, France). Address delivered at the Legislative Assembly meeting of 9 July 1850   *458*

——. *Napoléon le Petit* (1852). II.5 and VII.3   *452*

HUMBOLDT, W. von (1767-1835, Germany). Wie weit darf sich die Sorgfalt des Staats an das Wohl seiner Bürger erstrecken? In: *Gesammelte Schriften*, vol. I, p. 106-11   *1051*

HUS, J. (Czech writer, 1371-1415). Letter to the faithful Czechs, 10 June 1415. Prague, National Library (4° D² 19/14)   *56*

IBN-HISHĀM (died in 834, North Africa). *Sira* [Life of the Prophet]   *483, 1031*

IBSEN, H. (1828-1906, Norway). *A doll's house* (1879). Translated into English by W. Archer. (Lowell's series of foreign literature)   *115*

INNOCENT III (pope, 1198-1216)   *165*

INNOCENT IV (pope, 1243-54)   *161*

Ishavasy-Upanishads (India). Sanskrit, verse I   *24*

ISHIDA, B. (1685-1744, Japan). [*Town and country*]   *212*

ISIDORE OF PELUSIUM (Egyptian monk, died *c.* 435). Letter no. 471. In: *Patrologia graeca*, vol. LXXVIII, col. 440. Paris, Migne, 1861   *795*

ISOCRATES (436-338 B.C., Athens). *Panegyricus*. Translated into French by G. Mathieu and E. Bremond. *Panégyrique*, vol. I, no. 47. Paris, Les Belles Lettres, 1938   *764*

JACKSON, *see* Cases: *West Virginia* v. *Barnett*, Bibliog. II

JASPERS, K. (born 1883, Germany). *Die Schuldfrage* (1946). French translation in *La culpabilité allemande*. Paris, Éditions de Minuit, 1948   *276, 333, 871*

JASSUS, Abu al-Fadl (17th cent., North Africa). Letter to Sultan Mulay Ismaïl   *840*

The Jataka (recorded 1st cent. B.C., India, Ceylon). Pali. Translated into English by H. T. Francis. Vol. V, p. 61-3. London, Cambridge University Press, 1905   *174*

JEFFERSON, T. (1743-1826, United States of America). First inaugural address (4 March 1801)   *419*

JOHN CHRYSOSTOM, Saint, Patriarch of Constantinople (*c.* 354-407). Homilies on the Epistle to the Ephesians. Cited in C. Baur, *John Chrysostom and his time*. London, Sands & Co., 1959   *796*

——. Homilies on the Hexameron, II, 1, (386). In: *Patrologia graeca*, vol. LIV, col. 587. Paris, Migne, 1861   *1054*

JOSEPH, Nez Percé Indian chief (19th cent., North America). Cited by M. Curti in *Growth of American thought*. New York, 1943   *336*

JOSEPH II OF AUSTRIA, *see* Edict of toleration, Bibliog. II

JUSTINIAN, *see Institutes of Justinian*, Bibliog. II

KABIR (1089-1172, India). Sanskrit   *526*

KAFKA, F. (Czech writer, 1883-1924). *Journal intime*, p. 230, 298. Translated into French by P. Klossovski. Paris, Grasset, 1945   *1102, 1103*

KĀLIDĀSA (4th cent., India). Sanskrit. *Meghadūta* 53   *27*

——. *Raghuvamsa* IV, 86   *581*

KANT, E. (1724-1804, Germany). *Grundlegung zur Metaphysik der Sitten* [Foundation of the metaphysic of ethics] (1785). In: *Gesammelte Schriften*, vol. IV, p. 429. Akad. Berlin, 1911   *1043*

——. *Idee zu einer allgemeinen Geschichte in weltbürgerlicher Absicht* (1784). In: *Sämtliche Werke*, vol. 6, p. 10 et seq. Leipzig, 1913   *322*

——. *Sämtliche Kleine Schriften* (1790). Königsberg, 1797   *318*

——. *Uber den Gemeinspruch: das mag in der Theorie richtig sein, taugt aber nicht für die Praxis* [Concerning the saying: 'That may be right in theory, but it doesn't work in practice'] (1793). In: *Gesammelte Schriften*, vol. VIII, p. 291-2. Akad. Berlin, 1912   *323*

——. *Zum Ewigen Frieden* [Eternal peace]. Königsberg, 1795   *915*

Katha-Upanishad (5th cent. B.C., India). Sanskrit. II, 3.14   *856*

KATONA, J. (1791-1830, Hungary). *Bánk Bán* [The Palatine Bánk], act III. Translated into French by P. Chaulot in *Anthologie de la poésie hongroise*. Paris, Éditions du Seuil, 1962   *643*

KAUTILĪYA (4th cent. B.C., India). Sanskrit. *Kautilīya-Arthasāstra* I.6, 1 and I.7, 1; I.19, 26-8; I.19, 33; I.19, 34; II.1, 26   *189, 363, 190, 197, 175*

KAUTSKY, K. J. (1854-1938, Germany). [*The social revolution*] (1902). From the French translation, *La révolution sociale*. Paris, Marcel Rivière, 1912   *466, 726*

KHUSRAU I ANŌSHARVĀN, attributed to (Persian king, Sassanian period, 531-79). Arabic translation cited by A. Badawi in *Al-hikma al-khalida*, p. 56. Cairo, Misr, 1952   *208*

KIYOSAWA, K. (1890-1945, Japan). In: *Ankoku-Nikki* [Diary], 2 December 1944. Tokyo, Toyo Keizai Shinposha, 1954   *277*

KOŁŁATAJ, H. (1750-1813, Poland). [The political law of the Polish nation] (1790)   *300, 301, 836*

KOMENSKY, *see* Comenius

Koran
  Al-An'am: 164-5   *1090*
  Al-Baqara: 117, 256   *81, 484*
  Al-Ghashiyah: 21   *743*
  Al-Hajj: 39, 40   *281, 984*
  Al-Hujurat: 9   *65*
  Al-Maidah: 32, 53   *64, 990*
  An-Najm: 39   *554*
  An-Nissa: 1, 75, 135   *986, 10, 340*
  An-Nur: 27-8   *338*
  Yunus: 99   *485*
  Translated into English by J. M. Rodwell. London, Dent, 1861 (Everyman's library)

KOŚCIUSZKO, T. (1746-1817, Poland). Testament, 5 May 1798. Written in English. In: *The democratic heritage of Poland. Anthology*. London, 1945   *838*

Kosoj, T. (16th cent., Russia). In: [*Communications to the Society of History, University of Moscow*] 1880, II, p. XV — *1001*

Krasicki, I. (1735-1801, Poland). Fables (1779): Birds in a cage; The wine and the water. Translated into French by A. Lanoux in *Anthologie de la poésie polonaise.* Paris, Éditions du Seuil, 1965 — *296, 660*

Kropotkin, P. A. (1842-1921, Russia). *Memoirs of a revolutionist* (1899). English translation 1906. London, Swan Sonnenschein & Co. Ltd. — *540*

Kuan-tzu (died in 645 B.C., China). *Kuan-tzu.* — *249, 780, 1029*

Kūkai (774-835, Japan). The rules of the Shugei Shuchi [In Institute], 825 — *746*

Kuruntokai (Sangam period, 2nd cent. B.C. to 2nd cent. A.D., India). Tamil. Verse 49. Cf. English translation by A. K. Ramanujan in: *The interior landscape.* Bloomington, Ind. (U.S.A.) and London, Indiana University Press, 1967. — *17*

La Boétie, E. de (1530-63, France). *Discours sur la servitude volontaire* or *Contr'un* (1548) — *1026*

Lactantius (Christian apologist, *c.* 250-317). *Divinarum institutionum*, book V, 19. In: *Corpus scriptorum ecclesiaticorum latinorum*, XIX, p. 469-70 — *489*

Lao-tzu (*c.* second half of 6th cent. B.C., China). *Tao-Te Ching.* Translated into French by Liou Kia-Hway in *Lao-tseu, Tao-Tö King*, p. 38, 100. Paris, Gallimard, 1967 — *129, 192, 1052*

Las Casas, B. de, O.P. (Spanish prelate, 1474-1566). *Antiguas gentes del Perú*, p. 135 — *225*

——. Carta al maestro fray B. Carranza de Miranda. In: *Obras escogidas*, vol. V, p. 437. Madrid, Biblioteca de Autores Españoles, 1957-61 — *817* (para. 3)

——. *Historia de las Indias* (1547) — *816, 929*

——. Book III, ch. 19 and 117. In: *Obras escogidas*, vol. II, p. 54 and 456. Madrid, Biblioteca de Autores Españoles, 1957-61 — *817* (para. 1), *940*

——. Tratado comprobatorio del imperio soberano y principado universal. In: *Obras escogidas*, vol. V, p. 385. Madrid, Biblioteca de Autores Españoles, 1961 — *817* (para. 2)

Lazarevskaja, J., *see Life of Juliana Lazarevskaja*

Leibniz, G. W. (1646-1716, Germany). *Essais de théodicée.* Appendix: Réflexions sur l'ouvrage que M. Hobbes a publié en anglais, de la liberté, de la nécessité et du hasard (1710). Amsterdam, 1720 — *1060*

——. Letter to Peter I, the Great (16 January 1716). Cited by T. Ruyssen, *Les sources doctrinales de l'internationalisme.* Paris, Presses Universitaires de France, 1958 — *1038*

Lenin, V. I. Ulyanov (1870-1924, Russia). Cited by M. Gorky, *Vladimir Ilyitch Lenin* (1920), in [*Souvenirs, stories and notes*]. Berlin, Kniga, 1927 — *513*

——. Declaration of the rights of the workers and exploited people, preamble. *Pravda*, 17 January 1918. In: [*Works*], 4th ed., vol. 26. Moscow, 1935. Cf. G. Walter, *Lénine*, p. 404-5, Paris, Julliard, 1950 — *625*

——. Draft programme for the Russian Social Democratic Party (1895 or 1896). In: [*Works*], 4th ed., vol. 2. Moscow, 1935 — *330*

——. Letter to Comrade Myasnikov (5 August 1921). In: [*Works*], vol. 32. Moscow, 1935 — *465*

——. Speech on International Women Workers Day (4 March 1921). In: [*Works*], vol. 26. Moscow, 1935 — *120*

——. [*The state and revolution*] (1917). French translation in *L'État et la révolution.* Paris, Éditions Sociales, 1966 — *710, 725, 727*

——. [*What is to be done?*] (1902). French translation in *Que faire?* Paris, Éditions Sociales, 1965 — *427*

Leo I, Saint, the Great (pope, 440-61) — *156*

LESKOV, N. (1831-95, Russia). [A simpleton.] Translated into French by B. de Schloezer in *Lady Macbeth au village*, p. 194-7. Paris, Gallimard, 1939   *47*

LEVAI, Y., Rabbi (1512-1609, Prague)   *139*

LIBELT, K. (1807-75, Poland). On civil courage (1843). In: *The democratic heritage of Poland. Anthology*. London, 1945   *461*

LI-CHI [*Book of rites*] (2nd cent.? B.C., China). Section 9. In: W. Theodore de Bary (ed.), *Sources of Chinese tradition*, p. 191-2. New York and London, Columbia University Press, 1960   *1069*

LIEH-TZU (4th to 3rd cent. B.C., Taoist school, China)   *193, 1084*

Life of Juliana Lazarevskaja (died in 1604). Written by her son. In: N. Gudzy, [*Chrestomathy of the old-Russian literature*], p. 353-4. Moscow, 1952   *617*

Life of St. Basil. Eighteenth-century Russian manuscript. In: [*Memoirs of the Institute of Archaeology*], vol. VIII, p. 82. Moscow, 1910   *879*

——. Another version. In: G. Fletcher, *Of the Russe Common Wealth*. London, 1591   *880*

LINCOLN, A. (1809-65, United States of America). The emancipation proclamation, 1 January 1863   *846*

——. Second inaugural address (4 March 1865)   *847*

LOCKE, J. (1632-1704, England). *The second treatise of civil government* (1690)   *154, 295, 565, 566, 580*

LUTHER, M. (1483-1546, Germany). Address to the Diet of Worms (1521)   *268*

MACHIAVELLI, N. (1469-1527, Florence, Italy)   *294*

MADÁCH, I. (1823-64, Hungary). [*The tragedy of man*], scene IX. French adaptation by J. Rousselot, *La tragédie de l'homme*. Budapest, Corvina, 1967 (Reproduced with the permission of J. Rousselot.)   *790*

MADISON, J. (1751-1836, United States of America). *Memorial and remonstrance* (1784)   *508*

MAGTIMGULI (Turkmenian poet, 1730-80)   *236*

Mahābhārata (200 B.C. to 100 A.D., India). Sanskrit
II.5, 103   *583*
III.117, 27   *521*
XII.34, 20; XII.59, 108-11; XII.89, 4; XII.90, 23;   *368, 191, 585, 582*
XII.173, 8; XII.181, 7-8; XII.251, 19; XII.259, 12;   *993, 522, 25, 892*
XII.268; 6; XII.288, 20   *857, 991*
XIII.60, 20; XIII.337   *279, 177*

—— (11th to 13th cent., India-Mauritius). Telugu   *18, 431*

—— *Shānti-Parva*, 188.10 (India-Mauritius). Sanskrit. Hindi   *979*

MAHMUD OF KASHGAR, *see* Proverbs (Turkish), Bibliog. II

MAIMONIDES, M. (1135-1204, Cordova, Spain). A doctor's prayer. In: *Revue d'histoire de la médecine hébraïque*, 25 March 1955 and 31 May 1956   *792*

——. *Hilchot Teshuva*, 5, 1   *134*

——. In: *Mishneh Torah*   *736, 759*

Majjhima Nikaya II (recorded 1st cent., Buddhist school, India). Pali. Translated into English by I. B. Horner in *Middle length sayings*, vol. II, p. 276-8 and 341-7. London, Pali Text Society, 1957   *372, 530, 1077*

MALIK IBN ANAS. (*c.* 715-95, Medina Moslem jurist.)   *9*

MALRAUX, A. (France). In: *La condition humaine*. Paris, Gallimard, 1933 (Published in English under the title *Storm in Shanghai*)   *150*

MANSFIELD, Lord Chief Justice, *see* Cases: *Sommersett's case*, Bibliog. II

Manusmriti [The laws of Manu] (200 B.C. to 100 A.D., India). Sanskrit 97
I.96; VIII.307, 336, 349-50; IX.44; XII.91 *992, 196, 365, 862, 579, 30*

—— (India-Mauritius). Hindi. III.12, 36 *96*

Manyōshū (beginning of 9th cent. Japan), *see* Okura. Cf. English translation published
by Columbia University Press, New York and London, 1965

MARCUS AURELIUS (121-80, Emperor of Rome, 161-80). *Thoughts*, book IV,
para. 4, book IX, para. 9. Translated into English by G. Long. Philadelphia,
Henry Altemus *1093, 1066*

MARITAIN, J. (France). Address delivered at the inaugural meeting of the General
Conference of Unesco at its second session (6 November 1947) *1021*

MARSILIUS OF PADUA. *Defensor pacis* (1324) *166*

MARTÍ, J. (1853-95, Cuba). Discurso en el liceo cubano, Tampa (26 November 1891).
In: *Obras completas*, vol. IV, 1963, p. 270 *332*

——. *La edad de oro* [The golden age] (1889) *275*

MARX, K. (1818-83, Germany). [*The civil war in France*] (written 1871). French
translation, *La guerre civile en France*. Paris, Éditions Sociales, 1953 *245, 246, 719, 724, 768*

——. Debatten über Pressefreiheit und Publikation der landständischen Verhand-
lungen [Debates on the freedom of the press]. *Die Rheinische Zeitung* (1842). In:
Marx-Engels Werke, vol. I. Berlin. Dietz. 1961 *463, 468*

——. *Die Deutsche Ideologie* [The German ideology] (1845-46), p. 584-5. Reviewed
by Engels. Berlin, Dietz, 1953 *620*

——. [*The Jewish question*] (1844). Translated into French by H. Lefebvre and
N. Gutermann in *Morceaux choisis*, p. 214-17. Paris, Gallimard, 1934 *717*

——. *Das Kapital* (1867). Translated into English by S. Moore and E. Aveling.
Chicago, Charles H. Kerr & Co., 1906 *656, 769*

——. Letter to Ruge (1844). Cf. Ein Briefwechsel von 1843. In: *Marx-Engels Werke*,
vol. I. Berlin, Dietz, 1961 *425*

——. *Manifesto of the Communist Party* (1848). English translation by S. Moore (1888).
In: H. J. Laski, *Communist manifesto: socialist landmark*, p. 133-5. London, Allen
& Unwin, 1948 *654*

——. Notes on Bakunin's book, *State socialism and anarchy* (1874, posthumous). French
translation in *Contre l'anarchie*. Paris, Bureau d'Éditions, 1935 *720*

——. Remarks on the Prussian censorship regulations (1842). Translated into
French by J. Molitor in *Œuvres philosophiques*, vol. I. Paris, A. Costes, 1937 *464*

MASCALL, R. (Carmelite Bishop of Hereford, 1404-16, England) *814*

MASUHO, Z. (1655-1742, Japan). [*The path of the gods*] *118*

MAYAKOVSKY, V. (1894-1930, U.S.S.R.). [Hymn to a judge]. In: [*Works*]. Moscow,
1941 *729*

MENCIUS (Meng-tzu) (*c.* 4th cent. B.C., China). Book I, A: 7 and B: 8. In: W. Theodore de Bary (ed.), *Sources of Chinese tradition*, p. 107-11. New York and London,
Columbia University Press, 1960 *777, 280*

——. Books I and VII *186, 306*

MERIKARE, *see* Precepts for Merikare, Bibliog. II

MESÍA VENEGAS, Padre A. (17th cent., South America). Memorial sobre la cédula del
servició personal de los Indios del Perú [On the regulations concerning the
personal service required of the Peruvian Indians] (1603). Cited by R. Vargas
Ugarte in *Pareceres jurídicos en asuntos de Indias, 1601-1718*, p. 113. Lima, 1951 *640*

MICKIEWICZ, A. (1798-1855, Poland). Programme of the Polish Legion (1848) *327*

Midrash (6th to 12th cent.). Yalkut. Cited in: L. Finkelstein (ed.), *The Jews, their
history, culture and religion*, vol. III, ch. 27. Philadelphia, Harper & Row Inc., 1949 *975*

MILTON, J. (1608-74, England). *Areopagitica* (1644)   *444*

MODRZEWSKI, A. F. (1503-72, Poland). *De republica emendanda* (1551). Basle, 1554. French translation cited by P. Mesnard in *L'essor de la philosophie politique au XVIe siècle*. Paris, Boivin/Hatier, 1936   *251, 383*

MONTAIGNE, M. Eyquem de (1533-92, France). *Essays*, books I, II (1580) and III (1588). Translated into English by J. Florio (*c.* 1603), *The essayes of Michael Lord of Montaigne*. London, Routledge, 1885. Book I, 26 and 39; II, 5, 11 and 12; III, 9 and 13   *1024, 544; 884, 73, 545; 1025, 334*

MONTALVUS, T. (Capuchin friar, 18th cent.). In: *Glossa fundamentalis statutorum cismontanae familiae ordinis fratrum minorum*, vol. II, p. 426. Matriti, 1740   *408*

MONTE ALVERNE, F. de, O.F.M. (1784-1858, Brazil). Sermon delivered before the Emperor Pedro I on 25 March 1831   *765*

MONTESINOS, A. de, O.P. (16th cent., South America). Sermon for the fourth Sunday in Advent (*c.* 1510). In the version of B. de Las Casas   *818*

MONTESQUIEU, C. de Secondat, Baron de (1689-1755, France). *Mes pensées*, fragment 350. In: *Œuvres complètes*, vol. I, p. 980. Paris, Gallimard, 1964 (Coll. Pléiade)   *1037*

——. *The spirit of the laws* (1748). Translated into English by T. Nugent. New York, Hafner Publishing Co., 1959 (Hafner library of classic series).
I, 3; XI, 3 and XII, 2, 4; XII, 4; XV, 5;   *921, 315, 376, 842,*
XIX, 27; XXIII, 29; XXV, 13   *453, 596, 503*

MORE, Saint Thomas (1478-1535, England). *Utopia* (1516). Translation from Latin into English in *St. Thomas More, the complete works*. New Haven, Yale University Press, 1965   *560*
Translated from Latin into English by R. Robynson, *The Utopia of Sir Thomas More* (1551), p. 66-7   *612*

MORELOS, J. M. (1765-1815, Mexico). Cited by J. S. Herzog in *El agrarismo mexicano y la reforma agraria*, p. 41-2. Mexico, Cuadernos Americanos, 1959   *708*

MORENO, M. (19th cent., Argentina). Supresión de los honores del Presidente [Suppression of presidential honours]. *Gaceta de Buenos Aires*, 8 December 1810   *715*

——. Sobre la libertad de escribir [On liberty of authorship]. *Gaceta de Buenos Aires*, 21 June 1810   *457*

MOTOORI, N. (1730-1801, Japan). [*A bamboo basket.*]   *860*

MO-TZU (5th cent. B.C., China). *Mo-tzu*, ch. 14, First discourse on universal love; ch. 45, The man under the thief's skin. In: Souen Yi-jan, *Mo-Tseu Kien-kou*. Shanghai, Tchou-tseu, Tsi-tch'eng, 1954. Cf. English translation by B. Watson, *Mo-tzu, basic writings*. New York and London, Columbia University Press, 1963   *40, 891*

MO-TZU SCHOOL (5th cent. B.C., China)   *194, 868*

MULLER, J. de (1752-1809, Switzerland)   *433*

MURIEL, D., S.J. (1734-95, Spain). *Rudimenta juris naturae* (1791). Cited by S. Zabala in *La filosofia politica en la conquista de América*, p. 67-8. Mexico, 1947   *832*

Nāgarakrtāgama (1365, Java, Indonesia). H. Kern (ed.). The Hague, Nijhoff and Leiden, Koninklijk Instituut voor Taal-, Land- en Volkenkunde, 1906-14   *477, 610*

NAKAE, C. (1847-1901, Japan). Conversation between three drunken men about State policy   *936*

Naladyar (3rd or 4th cent., Sangam period, India-Mauritius). Tamil. Verse 134   *763*

NAMIK KEMĀL (1840-88, Turkey). Ode to liberty   *297*

NEGRI, C. and RUSSO, A., *see* The Moldavian revolutionary programme, Bibliog. II

New Testament. In authorized King James' version of the Bible
Matthew 5: 1-13; 25: 31-46   *1074, 626*
John 18: 36   *1082*

Romans 2: 14-16   1075
I Corinthians 13   1076
II Corinthians 8: 13-15   611
Galatians 3: 27-8   976
I John 2: 9-11 and 4: 20-1   13

NICHIREN (1222-82, Japan). *Senji Shō* (1275)   260

NICHOLAS I (pope, 858-67). Letter to the Bulgarians (13 November 866). In: *Monumenta Germaniae historica*, vol. VI, ch. 86, v. 595. Translated into French by P. de la Chapelle in *La déclaration des droits de l'homme et le catholicisme*, p. 452. Paris, Librairie Générale de Droit et de Jurisprudence, 1967   886

NICHOLAS OF CUSA (1401-64, Germany). *De pace seu concordantia fidei* (1454)   476

NIETZSCHE, F. (1844-1900, Germany). *Der Wanderer und sein Schatten* [The wanderer and his shadow] (1880). Cited by A. Camus as exergue to *Essais*. Paris, Gallimard, 1965 (Coll. Pléiade)   242

Nihongi [Chronicles of Japan] (8th cent.). Cited in W. Theodore de Bary (ed.), *Sources of Japanese tradition*, vol. I, p. 66-7. New York and London, Columbia University Press, 1958   205

NIKITIN, A. (15th cent., Russia). [*Travels beyond three seas*] (1466-72), p. 16, 28. Moscow, Academy of Sciences, 1948   637, 494

NINOMIYA, S. (1787-1856, Japan). [*Lessons from nature*]   574

NISHIKAWA, J. (1648-1724, Japan). [*Memoirs of a bourgeois*]   534

NOBREGA, M. da, S.J. (1517-70, South America). Letter from Bahia (1549)   800

NORWID, C. K. (1821-83, Poland). In: *Anthologie de la poésie polonaise*. Paris, Éditions du Seuil, 1965
[Polish Jews] (1861). Translated into French by Y. Bonnefoy   937
[Socialism] (1861). Translated into French by Y. Bonnefoy   1042
[Their strength] (1851). Translated into French by C. Jelenski   462

Odin's stanzas, see Folk-poems and poetry, Bibliog. II

OKAMURA, T. (1866-1922, Japan). *Hogahu-tsuron* [A short treatise on law]. Tokyo, Yūhikaku-shobō, 1899   252

OKURA, Y. (660-733, Japan). A dialogue on poverty. In: D. Keene (ed.), *Anthology of Japanese literature, earliest era to mid-nineteenth century*, p. 46-8. Tokyo, Charles E. Tuttle Co.   684
In: *Manyōshū*. Translated into English by Nippon Gaku-jutsu Shinkōkāi. Tokyo, Iwanami Shōten, 1940   125

OMAR IBN AL-KHATTĀB, Caliph (*c.* 581-644). Letter to Amr ibn al-As, Governor of Egypt   231, 810, 1091

ONISHI, H. (1864-1900, Japan). [*The spirit of criticism*]   460

ORIGEN (185-254, Alexandria). Homilies on Genesis, XIII. Translated into French by L. Doutreleau in *Homélies sur la Genèse*, p. 224. Paris, Éditions du Cerf, 1943 (Coll. Sources chrétiennes, no. 7)   1056

OSTROVSKY, A. N. (1823-86, Russia). [*The storm*] (1860), act III, scene iii. Translated into French by G. Cannac in *Théâtre*, vol. I, p. 64-5. Paris, Éditions de l'Arche, 1966   653

ŌSUGI, S. (1885-1923, Japan). In: [*Complete works*]. Tokyo, Gendai-Shicho-sha, 1963-65   852

OU-YANG HSIU (1007-72, China). On parties. In: W. Theodore de Bary (ed.), *Sources of Chinese tradition*, p. 446-8. New York and London, Columbia University Press, 1960.   402

PAINE, T. (1737-1809, Great Britain). *Rights of man*, part II (1791)   *416*

PALAFOX Y MENDOZA, J. de (1600-59, South America). *Libro de las virtudes del Indio.* Ch. IX: De la paciencia del Indio. Cf. *Colección de libros raros o curiosos que tratan de América*, vol. X, p. 52-3. Madrid, 1893   *855*

PAMPA, The Old (9th cent., India). Kanarese   *983*

PANORMITANUS (15th cent.)   *163*

Pararaton (16th cent., Java). In: J. Brandes, *Sèrat Pararaton.* Batavia (Jakarta), 1896   *738*

PARKER, T., known as The Great American Preacher (1810-60). Cited by H. S. Commager in Who is loyal to America. In: *Living ideas in America.* New York, 1947   *423*

PASCAL, B. (1623-62, France). *Pensées*   *912*

PASCOLI, G. (1855-1912, Italy)   *601*

PAUL, Saint, *see* New Testament

PAUL III (pope). *See* Bull *Veritas ipsa*, Bibliog. II

PENN, W. (1644-1718, England and Pennsylvania). *Essay towards the present and future peace of Europe* (1692).   *954*

PERESVETOV, I. (16th cent., Russia). [*Tale of Sultan Mohamet*] (*c.* 1547). In: [*Communications to the Society of History University of Moscow*], 1908 vol. I   *826*

PESTALOZZI, J. H. (1746-1827, Switzerland). In *La voix de Pestalozzi.* Texts chosen by O. Müller. Neuchâtel, Delachaux-Niestlé, 1946   *288*

PHILIP II, *see* Charters, Bibliog. II

PINDAR (*c.* 521-441 B.C., Greece). *Nemean*, X. Translated into English by C.J. Billson in *Oxford book of Greek verse.* Oxford, Clarendon Press, 1938 (By permission of the publishers.)   *7*

PITT, W. (1759-1806, Great Britain). Speech delivered in the House of Commons on 2 April 1792   *837*

PLATO (429-347 B.C., Greece). *Laws.* Translated into English by B. Jowett in *Dialogues of Plato*, vol. V. Oxford, Clarendon Press, 1875   *400, 866*
Translated into French by E. Saisset in *Les lois*, Book II, 653e et seq. Paris, Charpentier & Cie., 1885   *740*

——. *Phaidon.* Translated into French by L. Robin in *Phédon.* Paris, Les Belles Lettres, 1960   *730*

——. *The statesman.* Washington and London, Walter Dunne, 1901   *253*

PLEKHANOV, G. V. (1856-1918, Russia). Message to the All-Russian Peasant Assembly. In: *Edinstvo*, no. 50, 28 May 1917   *624*

PLUTARCH (*c.* 45-125, Greece). Life of Publicola. Translated into English by B. Perrin in *Plutarch's lives: Publicola*, p. 20-2. London, Heinemann, 1914 (Loeb classical library)   *693, 712*

——. Life of Solon. Translated into English by B. Perrin in *Plutarch's lives: Solon*, p. 17-19. London, Heinemann, 1914 (Loeb classical library)   *103, 311*

PO CHÜ-I (772-846, China). [Looking at the harvest.] French translation in: *Anthologie de la poésie chinoise classique,* p. 290. Paris, Gallimard, 1962   *636*

PONTANO, G. (1426-1503, Italy)   *1023*

POPE, A. (1688-1744, Great Britain). *An essay on man*, III, 269 et seq.   *1050*

Popol Vuh, sacred book of the Quiché (Southern Maya), Guatemala. Fol. 35r. Paris, National Library   *1002*

POSOŠKOV, I. (18th cent., Russia). [*Paternal testament*] (1712-18), p. 18, 57, 119, 122. St. Petersburg, Poezaev, 1893   *112, 142*

——. [*Treatise on poverty and wealth*] (1724). In: [*Works of Ivan Posoškov*], p. 42 and 49. Moscow, 1842   *392, 393*

PTAH-HOTEP (Vth dynasty, 3rd millenary B.C., Egypt). Transcription of the hieroglyphs by Devaud in *Les maximes de Ptahhotep*. Fribourg, 1916   *737*

Purananooru (Sangam period, 2nd cent. B.C. to 2nd cent. A.D., India). Tamil. 34.1-7, 55, 182   *23, 201, 16*

PUSHKIN, A. (1799-1837, Russia). [Freedom.] [The prisoner.] In: [*Complete works*]. Moscow, 1937   *256, 885*

RADISHCHEV, A. N. (1749-1802, Russia). In: R. P. Thaler (ed.), *A Journey from St. Petersburg to Moscow* (1789-90), p. 102-5. Translated into English by L. Wiener. Cambridge, (Mass.), Harvard University Press, 1958   *803*

——. Liberty. You ask who I am? Translated into French by A. Libérati in: Elsa Triolet (ed.), *La poésie russe*, p. 41, 43. Paris, Seghers, 1965   *436, 437*

RADNÓTI, M. (1909-44, Hungary). Fragment of a poem. Translated into French by R. Richard in *Anthologie de la poésie hongroise*. Paris, Éditions du Seuil, 1962   *924*

RAMESES II (XVIIIth dynasty, 2nd millenary B.C., Egypt). Speech. Translated by Hamada in *Annales du Service des Antiquités de l'Égypte*, vol. XXXVIII, p. 226. Cairo, 1948   *572*

RAMÍREZ, J., O.P. (16th cent., South America). Parecer sobre el servicio personal y repartimiento de los Indios. *Cuerpo de documentos del siglo XVI sobre los derechos de España en las Indias y las Filipinas*, p. 273. Mexico, Millarès, 1943   *822*

——. Advertencias sobre el servicio personal al cual son forzados y compelidos los Indios de la Nueva España por los virreyes que en nombre de Su Magestad la gobiernan [10 Octubre 1595]. *Cuerpo de documentos del siglo XVI sobre los derechos de España en las Indias y las Filipinas*, p. 285. Mexico, Millarès, 1943   *639*

Rigveda (2200-1800 B.C., India). Vedic Sanskrit. II. 27, 10; X. 117,1-6; X. 191, 2-4; other   *68; 670; 471; 473, 980*

ROBESPIERRE, M. de (1758-94, France). Proposed declaration of rights made at the Jacobin Club (21 April 1793). *Moniteur*, XVI, p. 214   *1040*

ROOSEVELT, F. D. (1882-1945, United States of America). Four freedoms speech, (6 January 1941)   *728*

ROUSSEAU, J.-J. (1712-78, Geneva). *Discours sur l'origine et le fondement de l'inégalité parmi les hommes* (1755)   *317*

——. A discourse on the origin and foundation of inequality among men. In: *Social contract and discourses*. Translated into English by G. D. H. Cole. New York, Dutton; London, Dent, 1913 (rev. ed. 1955) (Everyman's library) (Reprinted by permission of the publishers.)   *243, 377*

——. *Du contrat social* (1762), Book I, ch. I, VI   *287, 316*

——. *Emilius: or an essay on education* (1762), book IV. Translated into English by T. Nugent (1763)   *680*

——. *La nouvelle Héloïse* (1761), part I, LXII   *312*

——. *Lettre à M. d'Alembert* (1758)   *600*

——. *The social contract or principles of political right*, Book I, ch. IV, IX. Translated into English by H. J. Tozer. 3rd ed., London, Allen & Unwin, 1924   *844, 378*

SABINA, K. (Czech writer, 1813-77). [On freedom of the press]. [*Czech Radical Democrats*.] Prague, SNPL, 1953   *449*

Sahagún (16th cent., Mexico). Nahuatl. *Códice Florentino*, Book XII, ch. 13. Translated into Spanish by A. M. Garibay in: M. León Portilla, *Visión de los vencidos. Relaciones indígenas de la Conquista*, p. 53. Mexico, Universidad Nacional, 1961   *827*

SAINT-JUST, L. de (1767-94, France). *Institutions républicaines*   *695*

SAN MARTÍN, J. de (1778-1850, Argentina). Letter to Don Joaquín de la Pezuela, Viceroy of Lima (11 April 1818)   *953*

SANTA CRUZ PACHACUTI, J. de (16th to 17th cent., South America). Relación de antigüedades deste Reyno del Perú (*c.* 1600). Cited by J. de la Espada in *Tres relaciones de antigüedades peruanas,* p. 267. Madrid, 1879   *343*

SANTILLÁN, H. de (16th cent., South America). Relación ... del gobierno de los Incas (1563), § 52. Cited by J. de la Espada in *Tres relaciones de antigüe-dades peruanas,* p. 46. Madrid, 1879   *586*

Sārdūlakarnāvadāna (200-350, India). Sanskrit. 18, 50 and 52   *523*

SARMIENTO, D. F. (1811-88, Argentina). *Obras completas,* vol. X, p. 121, vol. XXIII, p. 14. Buenos Aires, 1887-1902   *114, 345*

SCHERER, J.-B. (18th cent., France). *Annales de la Petite-Russie ou Histoire des cosaques zaporogues et des cosaques de l'Ukraine,* vol. I, p. 106. Paris, 1788   *394*

SCHILLER, F. von (1759-1805, Germany). *Don Carlos* (1787), act III, scene x, vv. 3020-50   *456*

——. *Geschichte des dreissigjährigen Kriegs* [History of the thirty years' war] (1790). Leipzig, 1802   *324*

——. *Die Gesetzgebung des Lykurgus und Solon*   *274*

——. *Wilhelm Tell* [William Tell] (1804), act III, scene ii. Stuttgart and Tübingen, Cotta, 1823   *325*
English translation by T. Martin. London, George Bell & Sons, 1883   *933*

SCHOELCHER, V., *see* Notice for sale of slaves, Bibliog. II

SCHUBART, C. (1739-91, Germany). Chronik, Gott und Vaterland (1790). In: *Gesammelte Schriften,* VIII, p. 239-44   *319*

SCHWEITZER, A. (1875-1965, France). *A l'orée de la forêt vierge.* Paris, Payot, 1929   *734*

Sefer Hassidim (12th cent.). Jewish tradition   *1030*

SHAKESPEARE, W. (1564-1616, England). *King Henry V* (1599), act IV, scene i. In: C. J. Sisson (ed.), *William Shakespeare. The complete works,* p. 570. New York, Harper & Row; Feltham (Middlesex), Odhams, 1953   *137*

——. *Macbeth* (1606), act I, scene vii. In: C. J. Sisson (ed.), *William Shakespeare. The complete works,* p. 975. New York, Harper & Row; Feltham (Middlesex,) Odhams, 1953   *353*

Shu-ching, see Confucius

SIERRA, J. (1848-1912, Mexico). Cited by J. Silva Herzog in *El agrarismo mexicano y la reforma agraria,* p. 103. Mexico, Cuadernos Americanos, 1959   *709*

SIEYÈS, Abbé E. J. (1748-1836, France). Préliminaire à la Constitution (read on 20-21 July 1789)   *57, 303, 567, 872*

Sigālovāda Suttanta (recorded 1st cent., Buddhist school, India). Pali. Translated into English by C. A. F. Rhys Davids, *Dialogues of the Buddha,* vol. III. In: *Sacred Books of the Buddhists,* vol. IV, p. 92-4. London, Oxford University Press, 1921   *609*

SIMEON, Saint, The New Theologian, one the founders of Byzantine monasticism (949-1022, Byzantium). Practical and theological precepts. Translated into English by Kadloubovsky and Palmer in *Writings from the 'Philokalia' on prayer of the heart,* p. 127. London, Faber, 1954   *604*

SISMONDI, L. Simonde de (1773-1842, Switzerland). In: *Revue d'économie politique,* Paris, January 1835, p. 299   *697*

SOLON, *see* Aristotle and Plutarch

SOLÓRZANO PEREIRA, J. de (1575-1654, Spain). In: *Política indiana,* book II, ch. XXX, p. 38. Madrid   *286*

SOPHOCLES (c. 495-406 B.C., Greece). *Antigone*, verses 332-75 and 445-70. Translated into English by E. H. Plumptre. New York, P. F. Collier & Son, 1865 (Reprinted with the permission of the publishers.)   *130, 257*

SPINOZA, B. (1632-77, Holland). In a free republic everyone has full freedom of thought and speech. Translated into English by T. E. Jessop in *Tractatus theologico-politicus* (1670), ch. XX. Montreal, Mario Casalini Ltd., 1962   *271*

STASZIC, S. (1755-1826, Poland). [Mankind] (1780-1820)   *714*

STOIŃSKI, J. (1590-1654, Poland). Prayer   *559*

Stories of the saints (10th cent., Japan)   *531*

SUAREZ, F., S.J. (1548-1617, Spain). *Tractatus de legibus ac de Deo legislatore*, II, XIX, 9. Antwerp, 1614. In: C. Lange, *Histoire de l'internationalisme*. Christiania (Oslo), H. Ascheloug & Co. (W. Nygaard), 1919   *1010*

Subhāsita-Ratnabhāndāgāra (various periods, India). Sanskrit. 70/9, 172/830   *981, 28*

SUGITA, G. (1733-1817, Japan). In: [*An evening's anatomy*]   *539*

Sutta Nipāta (recorded in 1st cent., Southern India and Ceylon). School of Buddha. Pali. Translated into English by Lord Chalmers in *Buddha's teachings, being the Sutta-Nipata or Discourse-collection*, vol. 37, p. 149-51, Cambridge (Mass.), Harvard University Press, 1933 (By permission of the publishers.)   *543, 1099*

SWIFT, J. (1667-1745, Ireland). A modest proposal for preventing the children of poor people in Ireland from being a burden to their parents and for making them beneficial to the public (1729)   *679*

SYLVESTER, J. (c. 1504-51, Hungary). Poem written as a preface to the Hungarian translation of the New Testament (1541)   *945*

SZÉCHENYI, I. (1791-1860, Hungary). In: [*The credit*]   *109*

TACITUS (c. 55-120, Rome). *Germany* (98), ch. 19 and 20. Translated into English by T. Gordon in *Voyages and travels*. New York, Crowell Collier & Macmillan Inc., 1910 (The Harvard classics) (Reprinted with the permission of the publishers.)   *557*

Taittiriya-Upanishad (7th to 6th cent. B.C., India). Vedic Sanskrit. I. 11.2   *26*

Talmud
Avot 4   *270, 989*
Boba Mezia 58b   *634*
Kiddushin 22   *804* (para. 2)
Makkoth 7   *894*
Sabbath 31   *4*
Sanhedrin 4. In: L. Finkelstein (ed.), *The Jews, their history, culture and religion*, vol. III, ch. 7. Philadelphia, Harper & Row Inc., 1949   *1063*
Sanhedrin 39   *970*
Ta'anit 20b   *1057*
Yoma 23. In: L. Finkelstein (ed.), *The Jews, their history, culture and religion*, vol. III, ch. 7. Philadelphia, Harper & Row Inc., 1949   *261*
Yoma 23   *907*
Talmud Babli   *480, 973*

TÁNCSICS, M. (1790-1884, Hungary). Letter to Lajos Kossuth (article, 1847)   *421*
——. My political creed (article, 1848)   *509*
——. The workers' movement (article, 1869)   *422*

TAURINUS (15th to 16th cent., Hungary). *Stauromachia* (1519). Translated into French by P. Chaulot in *Anthologie de la poésie hongroise*. Paris, Éditions du Seuil, 1962   *815*

TERTULLIAN (Christian apologist, 155?-220?, Carthage). *Apologeticus*, I and II. Translated into French by Waltzing-Severyns, *Apologétique*, 1st ed., p. 2 and 4. Paris, Les Belles Lettres, 1939   *361*

——. *Ad scapulam*, 2. In: *Patrologia latina*, vol. I, col. 699. Paris, Migne, 1861 *488*

THEODORE II, *see* Chronicles, Bibliog. II

THEODORET, Bishop of Cyrrhus (Greek theologian, 393-460). [*Ecclesiastical history*] (*c.* 450), book V, ch. 17. In: *Patrologia graeca*, vol. LXXXII, col. 1232-33. Paris, Migne, 1861 *968*

THOMAS AQUINAS, Saint (1225-74). *Summa theologica* (1269-72), Ia, IIae, 81, 1; IIa, IIae, 10, 8c; IIa, IIae, 10, 12c; IIa, IIae, 10, 10 *969, 490, 487, 1065*

THOREAU, H. D. (1817-62, United States of America). *Civil disobedience* (1849) *291*

THUCYDIDES (*c.* 465-395 B.C., Greece). *Histoire de la guerre du Péloponnèse*, Book III, 56, 2; book V, 79. Translated into French by J. Voilquin. Vol. II., Paris, Garnier, 1936. *958, 959*

Tirukkural (1st cent., India-Mauritius). Tamil *22, 200, 893, 1086*

TIRUMALAYYA, P. (16th cent., India). Telugu. *Neeti Seesa Satakamu* *19*

TÓTFALUSI-KIS, M. (1650-1702, Hungary). Preface to the edition of the Psalms. Amsterdam, 1686 *752*

TUPAC AMARU, J. G. (Inca leader, 1740-82, Peru). Letter to Inspector General Areche (1781). Cited by B. Lewin in *La insurreccion de Tupac Amaru*, p. 12-13. Buenos Aires, 1961 *831*

TUWIM, J. (1894-1953, Poland). [Prayer of the 'Polish flowers'] (1943). In: *Wiersze Wybrane*, I, no. 184, p. 245-6. Wroclaw, Biblioteka Norodowa, 1964 *918*

TWAIN, M. (1835-1910, United States of America). *The adventures of Huckleberry Finn* (1885) *849*

UCHIDA, R. (1868-1929, Japan). In: *Shakai-Hyakumenso* [The broken hedge]. Tokyo, Iwanami Shōten, 1954 *459*

UCHIMURA, K. (1861-1930, Japan). [On independence.] In: [*Complete works*], vol. 2. Tokyo, Iwanami Shōten, 1933 *119*

UDDYOTANASŪRI (8th cent., India). Prakrit. *Kuvalayamālā* (779), p. 207 *479*

Uttarādhyayana-Sūtra (300 B.C.-526 A.D., India). Prakrit. X, 4 *994*

VALERA, B., *see* Garcilaso de la Vega

VARONA, E. J. (1849-1933, Cuba). El clericalismo en la universidad. Cited by F. Lizaso in *El pensamiento vivo de Varona*, p. 58. Buenos Aires, Losada, 1949 *510*

Vārttikāsara, attributed to Sures'vara (*c.* 800, India). Sanskrit. II, 41 *859*

VASCONCELLOS, S. de, S.J. (1597-1671, South America). Chronicle of the Society of Jesus in the State of Brazil (1663) *801*

Vasistha-Dharmasūtra (1st cent., India). Sanskrit. I, 42; XIX, 9; XIX, 35 *195, 367, 176*

VAUVENARGUES, L. de Clapiers de (1715-47, France). *Réflexions et maximes* (1746) *74, 501, 931*

VELI, O. (1914-50, Turkey). Free of charge (1948). In: *Bütün Siileri* [*Works*]. Istanbul, Varlik Yayinevi, 1957 *861*

VEMANA (15th cent., India). Telugu. *Vemana Satakamu* *630, 908*

VINET, A. (1797-1847, Switzerland). *Philosophie morale et sociale*. Cited in *Recueil du centenaire de la Constitution fédérale*. Zürich, Polygraphischer Verlag, A.G., 1948 *63*

VIŠENSKY, I. (18th cent., Ukraine). In: [*Works*], p. 42-3 and 68. Moscow, 1955 *618*

Visnusmriti (350-450, India). Sanskrit. III, 66-7 *364*

VITORIA, F. de (1480-1546, Spain). *Relectiones theologicae tredecim*, Venice (1526). Cited by C. Lange in *Histoire de l'internationalisme*. Christiania (Oslo), H. Ascheloug & Co. (W. Nygaard), 1919 *1036*

VLADIMIR MONOMAKH, Grand Duke of Kiev (1053-1125, Russia). Instruction to his sons. In: [*Laurentine chronicle*]. Cf. [*Complete collection of Russian annals*], vol. I, col. 245, 246 — *82, 84*

VOLNEY, C. de (1757-1820, France). In: *La loi naturelle.* (1793), ch. XI — *321*

——. To the National Assembly. In: *Moniteur* IV (1790), p. 403 — *932*

VOLTAIRE, F. M. Arouet de (1694-1778, France). *Candide* (1759), ch. XIX. English translation in 3rd ed. Glasgow and New York, Routledge & Sons, 1888 — *833*

——. *Dictionnaire philosophique* (1764, revised and enlarged 1771). Entry on 'Man' English translation 1901. Paris, London, New York, Chicago, E. R. Dumont. Entry on 'Equality' — *896*, *546*

——. *Traité sur la tolérance* (1763), ch. VI, XXII, XXIII — *505, 504, 1039*

VÖRÖSMARTY, M. (1800-55, Hungary). Tribute to Gutenberg — *751*

WASHINGTON, G. (1732-99, United States of America). Circular letter to the States (1783) — *414*

——. Farewell address, 17 September 1796 — *417*

WATANABE, K. (1793-1841, Japan). [In the event of famine] — *226*

WEIL, S. (1909-43, France). [*The Iliad, poem of might*] (1939-40). Translated into English by E. C. Geissbuhler in *Intimations of Christianity among the Ancient Greeks.* London, Routledge & Kegan Paul, 1957; New York, Humanities Press Inc. — *793*

——. *The need for roots, Prelude to a declaration of duties toward mankind* (1942-43). Translated into English by A. F. Wills. London, Routledge & Kegan Paul, 1952; New York, G. P. Putnam's Sons — *350, 434, 532, 659, 1101*

——. *The notebooks* (1942), II. Translated into English by A. F. Wills. London, Routledge & Kegan Paul, 1956; New York, G. P. Putnam's Sons — *349*

WENTWORTH, P. (16th cent., England). Speech delivered in the House of Commons (1576). In: G. R. Elton, *The Tudor constitution*, p. 263-4 — *443*

WILLIAM OF OCCAM, Franciscan friar (c. 1280-1349, England). *Super potestatem summi pontificis.* Preamble — *978*

WILSON, T. W. (1856-1924, United States of America). First inaugural address (4 March 1913) — *707*

——. The fourteen points (8 January 1918) — *938*

XENOPHON (c. 430-355 B.C., Greece). *Helléniques* (c. 384 B.C.), book II, 2. Translated into French by J. Hatzfeld. Vol. I, 5th ed. Paris, Les Belles Lettres, 1966 — *927*

Yājñavalkyasmriti (250-350, India). Sanskrit. I. 357-60; II. 2, 4 — *366, 362*

ZARATHUSTRA *or* Zoroaster, *see Avesta*

ZIMMERMANN, J.-I. (18th cent., Switzerland). *Wilhelm Tell, ein Trauerspiel.* Basle, 1777 — *289*

ZIYA PASHA, I. (1829-80, Turkey). Cited by S. Kurgan, *Ziya Paşa.* Istanbul, Varlik — *395*

II

Royal charter of 5 April 1530 (Spain). Cf. *Cedulario de las provincias de Santa Marta y Cartagena de Indias,* vol. I, p. 59-60. Madrid, 1913   *562*

CHRONICLES
Chronicle of the origin and of the government of the Incas (*c.* 1575). In: J. T. Medina, *La imprenta en Lima,* vol. I, p. 204, 214. Santiago (Chile), 1904   *223*
Chronicles of the Emperor Claudios (1540-59, Ethiopia). Gueze. Translated into French by W. E. Conzelman in *Chronique de Galâwdêwos.* Paris, 1895   *215, 217, 1072*
Chronicles of Theodore II (Ethiopia). Amharic. In: C. Mondon-Vidailhet, *Chronique de Theodoros II* (1855-68). Paris, 1905   *138*
First chronicle of Novgorod (Russia), late 14th-cent. manuscript   *283*

CODES
Code of Hammurabi (1730-1685 B.C., Babylon)   *351*
Kutāraçāstra code (14th cent., Java). In: J. C. G. Jonker, *Kutāramānawaçastra.* Leiden, Brill, 1885   *101, 126, 783, 901, 902, 903*
Legal code of Hermopolis (Ptolemaic period, Egypt). Translated into English by G. Mattha, A preliminary report on the legal code of Hermopolis West. In: *Bulletin de l'Institut d'Égypte,* XXIII, 1941, p. 297   *355*
National law code of Magnus Erikson (*c.* 1350, Sweden). Royal oath   *233*

Conditions for peace laid down by István Bocskay, Prince of Transylvania (July 1605)   *499*

CONSTITUTIONS
Constitution of Gordian, *see Institutes of Justinian*
Constitution 'Neminem captivabimus' of King Wladislaw Jagiello (1430, Poland)   *883*
Constitution 'Nihil novi' (1505, Poland)   *167*
Constitution of the Capuchin Friars Minor (1536), article 127   *173*
Constitution of the Carmelites Old Observance (1636-37), ch. XII, 1, p. 100   *265*
Constitution of the Society of Jesus (1556), part III, ch. I, 23   *267*
Epitome Instituti Societatis Jesu (1689), art. 785, 5 and 6; art. 22, 3/1; art. 471   *263, 409, 442*
The seventeen-article constitution of Prince Shōtoku (604, Japan). Art. V, VII, VIII, X and XVII. In: W. Theodore de Bary (ed.), *Sources of Japanese tradition,* vol. I, p. 47-51. New York and London, Columbia University Press, 1958   *371*

Convention for the amelioration of the condition of the wounded in armies in the field. (International Red Cross) (1864, Geneva)   *923*

Council of Nicaea (325)   *160*

DECLARATIONS
The declaration of independence of the American colonies (4 July 1776), drawn up by Thomas Jefferson   *413*
Declaration of the rights of man and of the citizens (5 October 1789, France). Translated into English by F. M. Anderson in *The constitution and other select documents illustrative of the history of France,* p. 58-60. Bronx (New York), H. W. Wilson & Co., 1904. Cited by Leo Gershoy in *The French Revolution and Napoleon,* p. 142-4. New York, F. S. Crofts & Co., 1946.   *415*
Declaration of Quakers to King Charles II (1660, England)   *913*
Royal Declaration (by Louis XV) concerning the privilege of the King (10 May 1728, France)   *451*
The Seneca Falls declaration of sentiments and resolutions (19 July 1848, United States of America). In: E. C. Stanton, S. B. Anthony and M. J. Gage, *The history of woman suffrage,* vol. I, p. 70 et seq.   *290*

DECREES
Decrees (1526-48) of the Emperor Charles V, Holy Roman emperor, King Charles I of Spain (1500-58). Cf. *Recopilación de leyes de los reinos de las Indias,* book 6, title 2, law I (1680). Madrid, Boix, 1841   *821*

Decree of Horemheb, fragment (XVIIIth dynasty, 2nd millenary B.C., Egypt).
Translated into French by B. Van der Walle, based on the text of Kurt Pflüger,
in *Chronique d'Égypte*, vol. XXII, p. 232-3. Brussels, Fondation Égyptologique
Reine Élizabeth, 1947   *602*
Decree of Philip II of Spain (19 December 1593). Cf. *Recopilación de leyes de los reinos
de las Indias* (1680), book 6, title 10, law 21. Madrid, Boix, 1841   *823*
Decree of 25 May 1753 (Russia). Cf. Legal Code, no. 10100   *113*

EDICTS
Edicts of Asoka (3rd cent. B.C., India). Prakrit   *474*
   Kalinga I   *198*
   Pillar IV, V, VII   *356, 370; 669; 785*
   Rock II, VI, XII, XIII   *784, 188, 478, 909*
Edicts of Augustus (7-6 B.C., Rome). First edict. In: F. De Visscher, *Les édits
d'Auguste découverts à Cyrène*. Paris, Les Belles Lettres, 1940   *360*
Edict of toleration of Joseph II (20 October 1781, Austria). Cf. G. Franz, *Das
Toleranzpatent Kaisers Joseph II*, urkundliche Geschichte seiner Entstehung
und seiner Folgen (1882). French translation by F. G. Dreyfus in: *Cahiers
pédagogiques*. Paris, Institut Pédagogique National, 1963. (Coll. Textes et
Documents, no. 16, p. 13.)   *506*
Epitome, *see* Constitutions

Fables from Burundi
   Big Club, the man who spoke the truth   *77*
   The pitcher that became a queen   *78*
FOLK-POEMS AND POETRY
   English. Anonymous 14th-century lyric   *515*
   Icelandic. Odin's stanzas (*c.* 800-1100). In: W. Kirkconnel, *The North American
   book of Icelandic verse*, p. 20-1. New York and Montreal, Louis Carrier &
   Alan Isles Inc., 1930   *36*
   Khmer poem, Cambodia   *633*
   Quechuan (South America). In: Jesus Lara, *Poesía popular quechua*. La Paz-
   Cochabamba, Canata, 1954   *347*
   Russian. Chastushki [popular quatrains]
     In: [*Popular Russian chastushkis*]. Moscow, Gosizdat, 1956   *100, 685* (1st)
     [*Rhymes of the Russian workers*]. Moscow Academy of Sciences, 1965   *662, 685* (2nd, 3rd)
     [*The songs of the Russian people*]. St. Petersburg, Imperial Geographic Society,
     1894   *663*
   Toltec (South America, 10th cent.). In: Codice Matritense, fol. 192 v. Library
   of the Royal Spanish Academy of History, Madrid. English translation by
   M. León Portilla   *943*
FOLK-SONGS
   Aztec (15th cent., Mexico.) Manuscripts. *Aztec songs*, (Latin American collection),
   fol. 2 r, fol. 27 v. Library of the University of Texas. English translation by
   M. León Portilla   *1004, 1005*
   Czech (14th cent.). A merry song of poor people. In: J. Vilikovský (ed.), [*Old
   Czech lyrics*], p. 82-5. Melantrich, 1940. English translation by K. Fink and
   E. Pavlátová   *676*
   Greek. The émigré; the death of the émigré. Translated into French by
   J. L. Leclanche in *Anthologie des chansons populaires grecques*, no. 110, 121. Paris,
   Gallimard, 1967 (Coll. Unesco)   *647, 648*
   Hungarian (mid-18th cent. and early 19th cent.)   *642, 644*
   Lithuanian 'daino' (folk-song). The wolf. Translated into English by U. Kat-
   zenelenbogen. Cited in: A. Landsbergis and C. Mills (eds.), *The green linden*.
   New York, Voyages Press, 1964   *1*

North American (United States of America). Negro spirituals. In: A. Lomax, *The Penguin book of American folk-songs*. Baltimore, Penguin Books, 1966
Go down Moses *1080*
Didn't my Lord deliver Daniel? *1081*
Peruvian (Andes) 'Mulizas'. Miner's lament; lament from the 'Cerro' *682, 683*
Quechuan (Peru). Shepherd song. In: *Folklore Americano*, no. 1, Lima, Museo Nacional de la Cultura peruana, 1953 *678*
Romanian *92*
Russian (mid-19th cent.). Dubinushka *588*
Turkish. Song of the ill-wed wife; Song of Baladíz *99, 677*
Valais (Switzerland) (1514). Cf. A. Carlen, *Archives suisses des traditions populaires*, vol. 42. Basle, 1945 *675*

FRANCHISES
Geneva (Switzerland) (1387), art. 2, 10, 19, 23, 55. In: A. J. P. Pictet de Sergy, *Genève, origine et développement de cette république*, p. 90-155. Geneva, 1847 *299*
Strasbourg (*c.* 1130) *812*

INSCRIPTIONS
Egypt
(Vth dynasty, 3rd millenary B.C.). Translated into English by S. Hassan in *Excavations at Gizah*, 1930-1931, pl. 61. Cairo, Government Press, Bulaq, 1936 *569*
(Vth dynasty, 3rd millenary B.C.). On a stele: litigation concerning the purchase of a house *571*
(VIth dynasty, 3rd millenary B.C.). Translated into English by W. M. F. Petrie in *Gizeh and Rifeh*, pl. VII A and p. 9, fig. 1-2. London, School of Archaeology in Egypt, 1907 *507*
(XIth dynasty, end of 3rd millenary B.C.). On a sarcophagus. Transcription in P. Lacan, *Sarcophages antérieurs au N.E.*, p. 220. Cairo, 1904 *1096*
(XIIth dynasty, early 2nd millenary B.C.). On the tomb of Amenemhat. Translated into English by P. E. Newberry and Beni Hasan in *Archaeological survey of Egypt*, vol. I, tomb no. 2. London, 1893 *171*
On a Babylonian tablet (*c.* 700 B.C.) *867*
Persia. On the tomb of Darius (522-486 B.C.) at Naksh-i-Rustam. Translated into English by R. G. Kent, *Old Persian grammar, texts, lexicon*, 2nd ed., p. 140. New Haven (Conn.), American Oriental Society, 1953 *31*
United Kingdom (1869). On the monument to the memory of French prisoners who died during the Napoleonic wars, while incarcerated on board the hulks in the Medway (St. Mary's Island, off Chatham) *1016*

Institutes of Gaius, *see Institutes of Justinian*

Institutes of Justinian (Byzantine empire, 482-565) (533). Translated into French by H. Hulot in *Les institutes de l'empereur Justinien*. Metz, Behmer-Lamort, 1806
Book II, title I. Of the distribution of things and their acquisition *549*
Constitution of Gordian (239, Rome). Reparation for wrongful occupation *550*
Law of the XII tables (450 B.C., Rome). Title VII. De judiciis *359*
Institutes of Gaius (150, Rome). De rebus; De jure naturali, gentium et civili *548, 961*

Instrument of government (1809, Sweden)
Duties of the King, in art. 16 *234*
Appointment of ombudsmen *398*

Inventory of the Henryków monastery (13th cent., Poland) *34*

Kentucky resolution of 1798 (United States of America) *418*

Land statutes of T'ang dynasty (618-907, China). In: D. C. Twitchett, *Financial administration under the T'ang dynasty*, p. 126. London, Cambridge University Press, 1963 *552*

LAWS

Canon law 1081, § 1, § 2; 1083, § 1, § 2, 1, 2; 1087, § 1, § 2; 2226, § 1, § 2, § 4; 2228, 2229, § 1, § 2, § 3, 1, 2, 3; 2213, § 1, § 2; 572, § 1, and para. 4, 214, § 1
106, 107, 108, 373, 496

Hungary

Law VI of 1945. On the abolition of large estates and the redistribution of land among those who cultivate it, art. I   *711*

Law VIII of 1849. On national minorities, 1, 2, 3, 4 and 14   *947*

Law XIV of 1514. Art. 3   *824*

Law for the kingdoms of the Indies (16th cent.). In: *Recopilación de leyes de los reinos de las Indias* (1680), book 6, title 4, law 2. Madrid, Boix, 1841   *590*

Law of the XII tables, *see Institutes of Justinian*

Laws of the Peruvians (1594). Cf. J. de la Espada, *Tres relaciones de antigüedades peruanas*, p. 204. Madrid, 1879   *224*

Legal treatise of the Sui-shu. [Annals of the Sui dynasty] (590-617, China). Translated into French by E. Balazs in *Le traité juridique du Souei-chou*, vol. IX, p. 77-8. Leiden, Brill, 1954   *887*

Letter from the Scottish people to the Pope (1320). In: Dickenson, Donaldson, Milme, *A source book of Scottish history*, i. 156-7   *928*

Lyric, *see* Folk-poems

Magna Carta, *see* Charters

Manifesto of the People's Society of Agneessens, founded in Brussels in De Klok tavern, in the Rue des Sablons (1844)   *718*

Manuscript (Russia), *see Life of St. Basil*, Bibliog. I.

Mayflower Compact (11 November 1620). In: *The federal and state constitutions*, part I, p. 931   *411*

Minimum programme of the Russian Social Democratic Workers' Party (1903-06). St. Petersburg, Priboi, 1906   *331*

Moldavian revolutionary programme of 1848, drawn up by C. Negri and A. Russo   *705*

Mulizas, *see* Folk-songs

Myth, *see* Traditions

Negro spirituals, *see* Folk-songs

NOTICES

Notice for sale of slaves (*Official Gazette of Martinique*, 22 June 1840). Quoted by Victor Schoelcher (1804-93) in *Esclavage et colonisation*, texts selected and annotated by E. Tersen, p. 43. Paris, 1948   *843*

Notice issued by the Board of Theologians and Jurists (1512, Burgos, Spain). Cited by B. de Las Casas in *Historia de las Indias* (1547), book 3, ch. 3 and 8. Mexico, Millares, 1951   *577, 561*

Nova collectio, see Statutes of the Carthusian Order

Oath of the Heliasts, as preserved in Demosthenes' oration in [*Against Timocrates*] (*c.* 353 B.C., Greece). French translation by N. d'Andria in *La démocratie athénienne. Son origine, son évolution et sa constitution définitive au siècle de Périclès.* Paris, Montchrestien, 1935   *248, 401*

Odin's stanzas, *see* Folk-poems

Official record (XXth dynasty, 2nd millenary B.C., Egypt). Account of a strike among the workers in a necropolis. Transcription of the hieroglyphs by A. Gardiner in *Ramesside administrative documents*, no. 13. Translated into English by W. F. Edgerton, The Thutmosid succession, *Journal of Near Eastern studies*, vol. X, July 1951. Chicago, University of Chicago Press   *688*

Ordinances

29th Ordinance (1311, England). In: Stephenson and Marcham (eds.), *Sources of English constitutional history*, p. 197   *406*

Ordinances to Corregidors issued by Don Melchor de Navarra y Rocafull, Duke of La Palata, Viceroy of Peru (1685). Ch. 18. Cited by G. Lohmann Villena in *El Corregidor de Indios en el Perú bajo los Austrias*, appendix VII, p. 573-94. Madrid, 1957   *382*

Ordinances to Corregidors issued by Lope García de Castro, Governor of Peru (1565). Ch. 11 and 43. Cited by G. Lohmann Villena in *El Corregidor de Indios en el Perú bajo los Austrias*, appendix I, p. 509-10. Madrid, 1957   *578, 591*

Ordinances of Alonso Vázquez de Cisneros concerning the Indians of Mérida in the New Kingdom of Granada (1605). Ch. 26 and 27. Cf. *Anuario de estudios americanos*, III, p. 1158 et seq. Seville, 1946   *587*

Pact of 1 August 1291 (Switzerland)   *956*

Pacta et consuetudines legum libertatumque exercitus zaporowiensis (1710, Ukraine). In: [*Communications to the Society of History, University of Moscow*], 1847   *420*

Precepts for King Merikare (Xth dynasty, end of 3rd millenary B.C., Egypt). Collection of hieratic papyri, no. 1115, 1116A, 1116B. The Imperial Hermitage of St. Petersburg, 1913   *603*

Principles and rules of the Society of Fraternal Democrats (1845, United Kingdom). Cited by G. D. H. Cole and A. W. Filson in *British working class movements; selected documents 1789-1875*. London, Macmillan, 1965   *1019*

Proclamation by the students of the Blanka Teleki School (Budapest) after the revolution of March 1848 (Hungary)   *755*

Proclamation of the programme of the Czech Radical Democrats (1848). Cf. [*Czech Radical Democrats*]. Prague, SNPL, 1953   *704*

Proverbs

Akan (Ghana)   *71* (para. 3, 4), *1087*

    In: J. B. Danquah, *The Akan doctrine of God. A fragment of Gold Coast ethics and religion*. London, Lutterworth Press, 1944   *71* (para. 1, 2, 5), *135, 182, 616, 834, 875, 1007*

    In: C. A. Akrofi, *Twi Mmebusem, Twi proverbs*. London, Macmillan, 1958   *71* (para. 6), *183, 337*

Amharic (Ethiopia)   *53, 54, 89, 219, 352, 429, 551, 556, 594, 629, 876*

Burundi   *75, 472, 528, 605*

Czech   *218*

Djerma-Songhai (Africa)   *388, 390, 1008*

Ewe (Togo). Translated into German by J. Spieth, *Die ewe Stämme*, p. 629. Berlin, D. Reimer, 1906   *58, 94, 133*

Fulani (Africa)   *50, 239*

German (*c.* 1130). Cf. Franchises of Strasbourg, no. *812*   *813*

Hausa (Africa)   *389*

Ibo (Nigeria). In: N. W. Thomas, *Anthropological report on the Ibo-speaking peoples of Nigeria*, part 6: Proverbs, stories, tones in Ibo, VIII, p. 114. London, Harrison, 1914   *873*

Jabo (Liberia). In: G. Herzog, C. G. Blooah, *Jabo proverbs from Liberia. Maxims in the life of a native tribe*, XIII. London, Oxford University Press, 1936   *72*

Kazakh (Kazakhstan)   *529, 1089*

Khmer (Cambodia)   *631*

Malagasy (Madagascar). Translated into French by P. de Veyrières, G. de Méritens in *Le livre de la sagesse malgache*. Paris, Éditions Maritimes et d'Outre-mer, 1967   *90, 870*

Mongo (Congo) In: G. Hulstaert, *Proverbes mongo*. Annales du Musée Royal de l'Afrique centrale, Série Sciences de l'homme, Linguistique, vol. 15. Tervuren (Belgium), 1958   *216, 346, 537, 615, 645, 1006*

Mongo (Tanzania). In: G. Hulstaert, *Proverbes mongo*. Annales du Musée Royal de l'Afrique centrale, Série Sciences de l'homme, Linguistique, vol. 15. Tervuren (Belgium), 1958   *229, 238*

Punjabi (India)   *527*

Romanian   *55, 744, 877, 988*

Russian   *46, 76, 95, 131, 144, 307, 438, 745*

Cf. [*Proverbs of Russian people*] (1853). Moscow, 1957   *83, 110, 493*

Somali. Collected by Musa Galaal   *240*

In: Shire Jaamac Axmed (ed.), *Light of education*, no. 5, February 1967, p. 4. Somalia   *52, 1035*

Songhai (Africa)   *51, 538*

Sudanese   *49, 1085*

Telugu (India-Mauritius)   *525*

Turkish

Quoted by Güvahî in *Pendnâma* [*Book of counsels*] (16th cent.). Manuscript in the Hamidiye Library, Lala Ismail Bequest no. 242, Istanbul   *132*

Quoted by Mahmud of Kashgar (11th cent., Eastern Turkistan). In: F. Birtek, *En eski türk savlari*. Ankara, Türk Dil Kurumu, 1964   *666, 863, 904*

Quoted in a 15th-century collection. In: V. Isbudak (ed.), *Atalarsözü*. Istanbul, Türk Dil Kurumu, 1936   *86, 102, 213, 667, 864, 930, 998*

Quoted in a 19th-century collection. In: M. N. Özön, *Türk Atasözleri*. Istanbul, Inkilâp, 1952   *214, 430, 668, 753, 905, 999*

Turkmenian. In: Berkeliev, *Nakillar ve atalarsözi*. Asgabat, Academy of Sciences of the Republic of Turkmenistan, 1961   *87, 673, 906*

Viet-Namese   *93, 98, 313, 516, 619, 758, 941, 1067*

Yombé (Congo). In: L. Bittremieux, *La société secrète de Bakhimba au Mayombe*, Brussels, Académie Royale des Sciences d'Outre-mer, 1935 (Memoirs, vol. 5, fasc. 3)   *835*

Provisions of Oxford (1258, England). In: Stephenson and Marcham, *Sources of English constitutional history*, p. 143-5   *405*

Recopilación de leyes de los reinos de las Indias, see Law for the kingdoms of the Indies

Reform of the Emperor Sigismond (1439, Germany). *Monumenta Germaniae historica*, Staatsschriften des Späteren Mittelalters, vol. 6, p. 86.6-88.9; p. 276.13-278.11. Edited by H. Koller. Stuttgart, A. Hiersemann, 1964   *492, 799*

Relación del origen e gobierno de los Incas, *see* Chronicle of the origin and of the government of the Incas

Report of a law-suit (XXth dynasty, 2nd millenary B.C., Egypt). In: T. E. Peet, *The great tomb robberies of the 20th Egyptian dynasty*. Oxford, Clarendon Press, 1930 (By permission of the publishers.)   *354*

Reports on the protection of persons by means of the Ombudsman (1848 and 1887, Sweden)   *399*

Resolution of the Bolshevik Party on literature (1924, U.S.S.R.)   *469*

Restitution made by Captain Diego de Agüero (23 March 1560, Lima). Cited by G. Lohmann Villena in *La restitución por conquistadores y encomenderos: un aspecto de la incidencia lascasiana en el Perú*, p. 59-60. Seville, Estudios Lascasianos, 1966   *563*

RULES

Rule of St. Benedict (529)   *410, 441*

Ch. II, translated into English by Abbot Gasquet, edited by I. Gollancz, p. 11-12. London, Chatto & Windus, 1909 (The King's classics collection)   *536*

Rule of St. Francis of Assisi (1223). Ch. X.   *264*

Rules of the Dominicans (1283). Art. 469, § III; 544   *262, 266*

Rural organization. Constitution of the Community of Castello del Piano (1571, Italy). Fondo Statuti Rurali. National Archives, Sienna, Italy

Preamble   *692*

Ch. II, 5th observation, p. 135   *762*

Speech by a peasant of the Molokan sect (end of 19th cent., Russia). In: [*Contemporary sects*], p. 69-70. Moscow, 1961 — 568

Statement adopted by the General Conference of the Methodist Episcopal Church (May 1908, United States of America). In: H. F. Ward, *A year book of the Church and social service in the United States* (1916), p. 197-8 — 706

Statutes of the Carthusian Order. *Nova collectio* (1582) — 164

Statutes of the Order of Premonstratensians (1503). Art. 7, para. 1 — 407

TALES

Demotic (*c.* 500 B.C., Egypt). Parable of the rich man in the second story of Setne-Khamuas. In: F. L. Griffith, *Stories of the high priests of Memphis*, p. 147-57. Oxford, 1900 — 1079

Egyptian (end of the 3rd millenary B.C.). The eloquent peasant. In: G. Lefebvre, *Romans et contes égyptiens*. Paris, Maisonneuve, 1949 — 440

Fang (Gabon). The three travellers and the ivory tusk — 387

Hassidic. Or Ganouz [Hidden light] (18th cent). In: M. Buber, *Tales of the Hassidim*, p. 282 et seq. New York, Schocken Books, 1947 — 1053

Khmer (Cambodia). The Lord and the lesser man — 649

Quechua, from Qatqa (Cuzco province, Peru). The dream of the Indian servant — 681

Somali. The cats and the rats — 952

Text (late 17th cent., Russia). Cited by Ljuborimov in [*The community of the Vyg*], p. 65, Moscow, 1924 — 754

TRADITIONS

Akan (Ghana). In: K. Antubam, *Ghana's heritage of culture*. Leipzig, Köhler & Amelang, 1963 — 70

Ashanti (Ghana)

In: R. S. Rattray, *Ashanti law and constitution*, ch. 19. London, Oxford University Press, and International African Institute, 1956 — 180

In: K. A. Busia, *The position of the chief in the modern political system in Ashanti*. London, Oxford University Press, 1951 — 179

Aztec (Mexico)

Admonishments to the young men. Human dignity (15th cent.). Collection of Huehuetlatolli. Fol. 116 r. Library of Congress, Washington, D.C. — 573

Admonishments to the young women. Meaning of life (15th cent.). Collection of Huehuetlatolli. Florentine Codex, book VI, fol. 74 v. Laurentian Library, Florence — 1003

Answers of the Aztec wise men to the twelve missionaries (1524). In: [*Book of the colloquies*]. Vatican Library — 942

Father's mission on earth (16th cent.). *Codice Matritense del Real Palacio*, VI, part 2, fol. 199. Madrid, Francisco del Paso y Troncoso, 1906 — 170

Ideals of Aztec education (15th cent.). Collection of Huehuetlatolli. Library of Congress, Washington, D.C. — 41

Qualities required to be elected high priest (15th cent.). Florentine Codex, book III, fol. 67 — 204

Bakongo (Congo)

The leper and the miserly woman. In: I. Struyf, *Les Bakongo dans leurs légendes*. Brussels, Académie Royale des Sciences d'Outre-mer, 1936 (Memoirs, vol. 7, fasc. 1) — 48

In: J. Van Wing, *Étude bakongo*, II. Brussels, Académie Royale des Sciences d'Outre-mer, 1938 (Memoirs, vol. 9, fasc. 1) — 874

Chagga (Tanzania). In: B. Gutmann, *Die Stammeslehren der Dschagga*. Munich, C. H. Beck, 1932-38 — 122, 127, 141, 228, 237, 613, 614

Ewe (Togo). In: S. J. Obianim, *Eve Konuwo, Sukugbalexexle*. London, Macmillan, 1956 — 606

Fulani (Africa). The odyssey of the valiant Goroo-Bâ-Dicko. Translated into French by M. Boubou Hama (collection in preparation), Niamey (Niger). (By kind permission of the author.) — 145

Guaraní (central part of South America). Translated into Spanish by
L. Cadogan in *Literatura de los Guaranies*, p. 107, 119. Mexico, Instituto
Indigenista Interamericano, 1965   *124*

Krobo (Ghana). In: H. Huber, *The Krobo. Traditional social and religious life of
a West African people*. St. Augustin near Bonn, Anthropos Institute, 1963
(Studia Instituti Anthropos, 16)   *181*

Nahuatl (Mexico). Translated into Spanish by A. M. Garibay in *Historia de
la literatura Nahuatl*, vol. I, p. 433, 446, 487, vol. II, p. 245. Mexico, Editorial
Porrua S.A., 1953   *671, 42, 672, 939*

Quechua (South America). The myth of Adaneva (Carhuaz, province Peru)   *1068*
The myth of Inkarri (Peru). In: J. R. Pineda and J. M. Arguedas, *Revista del
Museo nacional de la cultura peruana*, vol. XXV. Lima, 1954   *948*

Somali. Dheg-Dheer, the long-eared woman cannibal   *79*

Tamil (Sangam period, 2nd cent. B.C. to 2nd cent. A.D., India)   *982*

Treaty signed in Aduwa by Queen Victoria and King John of Ethiopia (3 June 1884)   *841*

Treaty of Zürich (1 May 1351, Switzerland). Translated into French by M. Bitchy
and B. Semperle in *Les chartes fédérales de Schwyz*, p. 43-7. Einsiedeln, Benziger, 1938   *298*

342.7

United Nations Educational, Scientific and Cultural Organization

Birthright of man; a selection of texts prepared under the direction of Jeanne Hersch. Paris, Unesco; New York, UNIPUB, 1969, 591 p., illus.
Bibliography: p. 559-591

Also published in French

I. Human rights   II. Quotations   III. Hersch, Jeanne (ed.)
IV. Title

69-4